African Politics
and Society

African Politics
and Society

A MOSAIC IN
TRANSFORMATION

PETER J. SCHRAEDER
Loyola University Chicago

Australia • Brazil • Japan • Korea • Mexico • Singapore • Spain • United Kingdom • United States

WADSWORTH
CENGAGE Learning™

**African Politics and Society
A Mosaic in Transformation**
Peter J. Schraeder

Publisher: Clark Baxter

Executive Editor: David Tatom

Assistant Editor:
    Heather Hogan

Editorial Assistant:
    Reena Thomas

Technology Project Manager:
    Melinda Newfarmer

Marketing Manager: Janise Fry

Marketing Assistant: Mary Ho

Advertising Project Manager:
    Stacey Purviance

Project Manager, Editorial
    Production: Ray Crawford

Print/Media Buyer: Karen Hunt

Permissions Editor: Kiely Sexton

Production Service:
    Publisher's Studio

Photo Researcher:
    Publisher's Studio

Copy Editor: Colleen Clifford

Cover Designer: Brian Salisbury

Cover Image: Photo illustration
    by Brian Salisbury

Compositor: Stratford
    Publishing Services, Inc.

For product information and
technology assistance, contact us at **Cengage Learning
Customer & Sales Support, 1-800-354-9706**

For permission to use material from this text or product,
submit all requests online at **www.cengage.com/permissions**
Further permissions questions can be emailed to
permissionrequest@cengage.com

Library of Congress Control Number: 2003102374

ISBN-13: 978-0-534-56769-9
ISBN-10: 0-534-56769-X

Wadsworth
10 Davis Drive
Belmont, CA 94002-3098
USA

Cengage Learning is a leading provider of customized learning solutions with office locations around the globe, including Singapore, the United Kingdom, Australia, Mexico, Brazil, and Japan. Locate your local office at:
www.cengage.com/global

Cengage Learning products are represented in Canada by Nelson Education, Ltd.

To learn more about Wadsworth, visit
www.cengage.com/wadsworth

Purchase any of our products at your local college store or at our preferred online store **www.ichapters.com**

Printed in Canada
6 7 8 9 13 12 11 10 09

TO

CATHERINE ANNE

You Still Complete Me

and

DAVID HARLOW RICE (1969–2001)

Your Spirit Lives On

About This Volume

A CRITICAL ELEMENT of this book's design is that *each chapter stands alone, allowing you to assign or read the chapters in any order you wish*. An emphasis has also been placed on making sense of general developments on the African continent as a whole while introducing the distinctive natures of Africa's fifty-three countries. Each chapter emphasizes the major trends associated with a topic, trends that are further explored through illustrative case studies that represent all regions of the African continent. Each chapter concludes with a list of readings for further exploration and research. Numerous maps, tables, figures, and boxed elements highlight fundamental issues of interest.

This book is divided into six major parts. Part I is composed of an introductory chapter that sets out the key themes of the book. This chapter also highlights several research tools devoted to Africa, including Internet sites, African studies journals from several academic disciplines, and a country-by-country list of introductory volumes, bibliographies, and historical dictionaries. These resources are especially designed to help students prepare class papers.

Part II is devoted to the historical context of African politics and society. Chapter 2 explores the rich mosaic of political and economic systems that existed during the precolonial independence era (before 1884). Chapter 3 outlines the political-military and socioeconomic impacts of the colonial era (1884–1951), including an extended discussion of the slave trade. Chapter 4 discusses the rise of African nationalist movements and the emergence of the contemporary independence era (1951–present). Together these three chapters provide the basis for assessing continuity and change in African politics and society from the precolonial era to the present.

The remainder of the book focuses on trends and developments during the contemporary independence era, with a special focus on the post–cold war era (1989–present). Part III focuses on the sociocultural contexts of African politics and society. This section begins (in Chapter 5) with an analysis of two competing concepts, ethnicity and class, that have served as the basis for often vitriolic debates among specialists of African studies. An important conclusion of this chapter is that, although each concept can explain one piece of the African puzzle, neither alone can explain African politics and society as a whole. Chapter 6 explains how three major ideologies—capitalism, socialism, and Marxism—have competed for influence in the development strategies of African leaders. An emphasis is placed on discerning whether different ideological pathways have led to greater or lesser development performance for their adherents. This section concludes (at Chapter 7) with a discussion of the evolving political themes of the African novel, a form of literature social scientists recognize as a unique means of gaining insight into African politics and society.

Part IV examines continuity and change in the politics of African governance. This section begins (at Chapter 8) with a discussion of the evolving relationship between the African state and civil society. An important theme of this chapter is that the state-society relationship serves as the foundation of any comprehensive understanding of African politics and society. Chapter 9 explores the nature and impacts of one state actor, the African military, through an analysis of coups d'etat and the rise and decline of military governance. Special attention is paid to understanding the prospects for demilitarization and transitions to civilian rule. Chapter 10 explores the African continent's highly diverse experiences in political transition, ranging from the creation of single-party regimes during the 1960s to the establishment of multiparty political systems as part of the spread of the "third wave" of democratization to the African continent at the end of the twentieth century.

Part V is devoted to the foreign relations of the African continent. Chapter 11 begins with an analysis of the various actors involved in formulating and implementing African foreign policies. The remainder of the chapter examines the development of the "pan-African ideal" of strengthening cooperation among Africa's diverse fifty-three countries, as witnessed most recently by the launching in 2002 of the African Union. Chapter 12 explores Africa's relationships with a host of international actors, most notably France, the United States, the International Monetary Fund, the World Bank, and the United Nations. An emphasis is placed on understanding the nature and evolution of great power competition, including an analysis of evolving U.S. foreign policy in the aftermath of the terrorist attacks of September 11, 2001.

The last section (Part VI), which is primarily targeted toward more advanced African studies classes, explores the evolution of two rival bodies of theoretical literature that have competed in their quest to explain African politics and society. Chapter 13 describes the evolution of the dominant "liberal school" of scholarship that ultimately envisions the development of free-market democracies on the African continent like those found in the northern industrialized democracies. Chapter 14 describes the evolution of a "critical school" of scholarship that has provided important critiques of the prevailing liberal model of development. In its most extreme form, this school emphasizes that true development will only occur in the aftermath of revolutionary struggle and the creation of socialist regimes throughout Africa. Both chapters conclude with analyses of emerging theoretical trends in the cold war's aftermath.

I wholeheartedly welcome your comments and criticisms (please send them to pschrae@luc.edu), regardless of whether you are an undergraduate student taking your first African studies class, a graduate student carrying out your dissertation research, a professor teaching this course for the first or the fiftieth time, or someone who picked up this book due to an interest in all things African.

Acknowledgments

A NY UNDERTAKING THAT attempts to take stock of an entire field of study must depend on the generosity and wisdom of others. The second edition of *African Politics and Society: A Mosaic in Transformation* is no different.

First and foremost, this edition has benefited greatly from my intellectual exchanges with my students and colleagues at Loyola University Chicago. Through the trial and error of teaching this course to hundreds of undergraduate and graduate students, I was able to set out the themes and arguments of the first edition and hone their presentation in the second. I am grateful to Patrick Boyle, a colleague and fellow Africanist in my department, who adopted this book for his courses and provided revision suggestions. I am also grateful to three graduate research assistants—Vassilios Damiras, Jonathan Riggs, and Adina Sigartau—who provided exceptional research assistance with both speed and good humor.

Over 100 Africanists too numerous to mention individually provided invaluable updates, factual corrections, critical commentary, and encouragement. Nonetheless, I would be remiss without at least mentioning Crawford Young and Richard Sklar, whose pictures grace the opening pages of Chapters 13 and 14, respectively, for the inspiration and advice they have provided over the years. I alone, however, take full responsibility for any remaining errors of fact or interpretation that are surely present in this edition and look forward to being corrected by all who share my fascination for Africa politics and society. (Please send all comments to pschrae@luc.edu).

Several foundations provided critical financial support. I am particularly grateful to those institutions, most notably the Council for International Exchange of Scholars (CIES), and the Educational and Cultural Affairs Bureau of the U.S. State Department, that facilitated my involvement as a Fulbright lecturer at Cheikh Anta Diop University in Senegal (1994–96) and at the University of Tunis in Tunisia (2002–03). Whereas the grant to Senegal allowed me to reflect on the changes in African politics and society associated with the cold war's end, the grant to Tunisia gave me insight into how the Arab world is responding to those changes. As I have often noted to Ellen Berelson, the brightest light in the U.S. policymaking establishment as concerns cultural exchange programs with the African continent, I cherish the Fulbright program as the most innovative and effective tool of U.S. foreign policy.

My family and friends have provided constant encouragement. As became apparent long before I was formally initiated to the concept of clan politics during my initial field experience in Somalia in 1985, one's extended family members are the key to success in any endeavor. In addition to my close high school friends—Mike Thomas, Tim and Ginny Ryan, and Mark "Spanks" Przybyla— I wish to thank Bill and Helen, Bill and Laura, Tom and Jorja, Jason and Tammy, Jerry, Paul, Philip, Tricia, Natasha, Brianne, and all other members of the extended Schraeder clan. And, of course, life simply would not be near as exciting without the wonderful distractions provided by the Scanlon (my wife's) clan, including Pat and Marianne, John and Julie, Sue and Mike, Beth and Scott, Margaret, Emmie, Jack, Patrick, Abbie, Katy, Meghan, and Connor.

My greatest sustenance, however, remains my wife, Catherine Anne. We met as a result of the Fulbright program, she leaving for Bangladesh and I for Senegal. When my Fulbright grant was renewed for a second year, Catherine Anne joined me in West Africa, and we were subsequently married on the Island of Zanzibar. We are currently introducing our children, Maximilian Edward and Marianne Susan, to our passion for international work and travel as we spend two academic years in Tunisia (2002–03) and Italy (2003–04). My favorite line of Max's to date, which clearly demonstrates that we are doing something right, is, "Daddy, every day is a beautiful day in Africa." Together Catherine Anne and I have witnessed and experienced many of the events recorded in this book. As a result, it is as much Catherine Anne's as it is mine.

Last, but not least, this second edition of *African Politics and Society: A Mosaic in Transformation* is codedicated to David Harlow Rice (1969–2001), who died in the tragic events of September 11, 2001. An interest in Africa led David to my class and blossomed into a graduating senior Fulbright to South Africa, including attendance at Nelson Mandela's swearing-in ceremony as president in 1994, which inspired him to undertake graduate work at the London School of Economics and a highly successful career in international investment. David's passion for everything in life, including Africa, lives on in all who had the great fortune to meet and know him.

Contents

About This Volume   vii

Acknowledgments   xi

Illustrations, Tables, and Boxes   xxi

About the Author   xxv

PART I   INTRODUCTION

1   UNDERSTANDING AFRICAN POLITICS AND SOCIETY   1

Africa Is a Rich Mosaic of Diversity   2
Necessity of a Continental Perspective   3
To Understand the Present, One Must Understand the Past   5
A Continent in Transformation   6
Influential Impact of the International System   8
Central Importance of the Domestic Dimension   11
Balancing Afro-Pessimism and Afro-Optimism   14
Undertaking Further Research   15
Key Terms   20
For Further Reading   21
Notes   22

PART II   HISTORICAL CONTEXT

2   POLITICS AND ECONOMICS OF THE PRECOLONIAL INDEPENDENCE ERA (BEFORE 1884)   23

Segmented Political Systems   24
    Band Organization   24
    Classical Segmented System   26
    Universalistic Segmented System   28
    Ritually Stratified Segmented System   28
    Autonomous Village System   29
Centralized Political Systems   29
    Pyramidal Monarchy   30
    Associational Monarchy   31
    Centralized Monarchy   32
Economic Systems and Trade   33
Diplomacy and Warfare   39
Women and Gender   42
Key Terms   45
For Further Reading   46
Notes   47

3   POLITICAL AND ECONOMIC IMPACTS OF COLONIALISM (1884–1951)   49

Early Contacts with Europe and the Arab World   50
Imposition of Direct Colonial Rule   57
Political–Military Impacts of Colonialism   62
    Application of the European Nation-State System to Africa   62
    Division of African Nations among Several States   62
    Incorporation of Several African Nations into One State   64
    Destruction of Traditional Checks-and-Balances   66
    Reinforcement of Patriarchal Forms of Governance   66
    Authoritarian Political Legacy   67
Socioeconomic Impacts of Colonialism   69
    Creation of Closed Economic Systems   69
    Creation of Export-Oriented Mono-Crop or Mono-Mineral Economies   70
    Promotion of Perverse Infrastructural Development   72
    Strengthening of Gender Bias in National Development   73
    Authoritarian Legacy of the State   74
Key Terms   75
For Further Reading   76
Notes   77

4 NATIONALISM AND THE EMERGENCE OF THE CONTEMPORARY INDEPENDENCE ERA (1951–PRESENT)   80

Trends in African Nationalism   81

Domestic Influences on the Rise of Nationalism   86

Creation of Administrative Centers and the Rise of Urbanization   86

Educational Training and Development   87

Formation and Spread of Voluntary Associations   88

International Influences on the Rise of Nationalism   89

Spread of Pan-Africanism   89

Involvement of African Soldiers in World War I and World War II   90

Demonstration Effect of Decolonization in Asia   91

Shifting Structure of the International System   93

Self-Determination and the Rise of Secessionist Movements   94

Key Terms   96

For Further Reading   96

Notes   97

PART III   SOCIOCULTURAL ENVIRONMENT

5 ETHNICITY AND CLASS   100

Ethnic Dimension of African Politics and Society   101

Ethnic Intermediaries and the Creation of Ethnic Compacts   103

Ethnic Violence and the Breakdown of Ethnic Compacts   106

Class Dimension of African Politics and Society   110

Class Divisions in African Society   112

Class Cooperation and Conflict   116

Competing Explanations of the Nigerian Civil War (1967–1970)   120

Perceiving Events through an Ethnic Lens   120

Perceiving Events through a Class Lens   122

Continuing Debate   123

Key Terms   124

For Further Reading   125

Notes   125

6 IDEOLOGY AND THE POLITICS OF DEVELOPMENT   130

Evolution of African Development Ideologies   131

Ideology and Development Choice   134

Primary Purpose of Development   135

Primary Engine of Development   136

Role of Agriculture in National Development   137

Perception of the Rural Peasantry   140
Role of Foreign Powers and Investment   141
Ideology and Development Performance   143
Economic Growth   143
Socioeconomic Equality   145
Autonomy from Foreign Control   145
Human Dignity   146
Political Participation   147
Toward a Capitalist-Socialist Hybrid?   149
Key Terms   151
For Further Reading   151
Notes   152

7 **POLITICS OF THE AFRICAN NOVEL   155**

Political Dilemmas Faced by the African Novelist   156
Political Themes of the African Novel during the Early Years   158
Re-Creation of Africa's Past   158
Colonial Intrusion   159
Colonial Injustice   159
Nationalism and Independence   159
Disenchantment with Elites   161
Freedom as Despair   162
Status of Women in African Society   162
Emergence of Politically Committed African Novelists   163
Neglected Popular Elements of Society   163
Destructive Nature of Societal Divisions   164
Promoting Gender Equality   164
Nuruddin Farah and the Politics of Commitment in Somalia   165
Early Years as Critic of Social Injustice   165
Qualified Optimism after the 1969 Military Coup d'État   166
Opposition to the Dictatorship of Siad Barre   167
Evolving African Identity   171
Politics of the African Novel in Perspective   172
Key Terms   172
For Further Reading   173
Notes   173

PART IV CONTINUITY AND CHANGE IN GOVERNANCE

8 STATE AND CIVIL SOCIETY 176

Concentration of State Power at the Expense of Civil Society 177
  Africanization of the State 178
  Bureaucratic Expansion and the Growth of Parastatals 179
  Dismantling of Institutional Checks-and-Balances 180
  Co-Optation and the Silencing of Civil Society 181
  Expansion of the Coercive Apparatus 182
  Creation of Personal Rule Networks 183
Crisis of the State and the Resurgence of Civil Society 186
  Deepening Economic Crisis 186
  Growing Inability to Provide Social Goods 188
  Resurgence of Civil Society 189
  Intensification of Domestic Violence and Conflict 191
In Search of a State-Society Balance 193
Key Terms 197
For Further Reading 197
Notes 198

9 MILITARY COUPS D'ÉTAT AND MILITARY GOVERNANCE 201

Trends in Military Coups d'État 202
Role of the Military in Political Governance 205
  Civilian Supremacy Model 205
  Watchdog Model 206
  Balance Wheel Model 206
  Direct Rule Model 208
  Social Transformation Model 208
Myths Concerning the Effectiveness of Military
    Governance 209
  Military Enjoys Greater Legitimacy 209
  Military Rule Is More Efficient 210
  Military Is Best Able to Maintain Stability 211
  Military Constitutes a Better Unifying Structure 212
  Military Is Best Prepared to Promote Development 214
Demilitarization and Transitions to Civilian Rule 215
Key Terms 218
For Further Reading 218
Notes 219

10 DEMOCRATIC EXPERIMENTS AND MULTIPARTY POLITICS   222

Establishment of Single-Party Political Systems   223
Political Transition and Experimentation with
      Multiparty Politics   226
  Change via Multiparty Elections   228
  Change via the National Conference   229
  Guided Democratization   230
  Co-Opted Transitions   231
  Authoritarian Reaction   233
  Civil War and Contested Sovereignty   234
Democratic Consolidation or Decay?   236
Key Terms   240
For Further Reading   240
Notes   241

PART V   FOREIGN RELATIONS

11 FOREIGN POLICY MAKING AND THE PURSUIT OF PAN-AFRICANISM   244

Understanding the Foreign Policy–Making Context   245
  President and Bureaucracies of the Executive Branch   246
  Role of National Legislatures in Foreign Policy   248
  Foreign Policy Impact of Nongovernmental Actors   249
Pan-Africanism and the Search for African Unity   253
Regional Economic Cooperation and Integration   261
Key Terms   266
For Further Reading   266
Notes   267

12 AFRICA IN WORLD POLITICS   271

Role of Foreign Powers   272
Great Powers and Africa during the Cold War (1947–1989)   274
  Complementary Interests among the Western Powers   274
  Africa as a Proxy Battlefield for East-West Conflict   276
  Contradictions in the Search for Allies   278
Cold War to Cold Peace (1989–Present)   278
  Evolving Foreign Policy Interests   279
  Economic Competition among the Great Powers   280
  Rhetoric versus Reality in Support for Democratization   282
Involvement in the United Nations   285

Influence of International Financial Institutions   288
Evolving Equation of Military Intervention   291
Key Terms   295
For Further Reading   295
Notes   296

PART VI   RIVAL THEORETICAL PERSPECTIVES

13   STUDY OF AFRICA IN THE LIBERAL TRADITION   301

Predominance of Modernization Theory (1950s–Early 1960s)   302
Rise of Modernization Revisionism (Late 1960s)   304
Concern with Stability and the Politics of Order
        (Late 1960s–Early 1970s)   308
Demands for Policy Relevance and Public Policy Research
        (Mid-1970s–1980s)   311
New Directions (1990s–Present)   313
Key Terms   318
For Further Reading   318
Notes   319

14   STUDY OF AFRICA IN THE CRITICAL TRADITION   322

Dependency Theory and the Development of Underdevelopment
        (Late 1960s–Early 1970s)   323
Circulationist Revisions of Dependency Theory (1970s)   325
Marxism's Impact on the Development of Critical Thought
        (Early 1970s)   327
Marxism and the Emergence of a Neo-Marxist School of Thought
        (Late 1970s–1980s)   330
New Directions (1990s–Present)   333
Key Terms   337
For Further Reading   337
Notes   338

Appendix 1 List of Acronyms   341

Appendix 2 Country Name Changes in Africa during the
        Contemporary Independence Era   347

Appendix 3 Political Leadership in Africa during the Contemporary
        Independence Era   349

Index   359

ILLUSTRATIONS, TABLES, AND BOXES

MAPS

Map 1.1   Contemporary Africa   3

Map 1.2   Africa's Primary Regions   4

Map 1.3   Women in National Parliaments (2002) (Percent of Lower or Single House Seats Held by Women)   7

Map 2.1   Trans-Saharan Trade Network (Eleventh to Sixteenth Centuries)   36

Map 2.2   Areas of Saharan Nomads in the Contemporary Era   37

Map 3.1   Portugal's Empire in the Sixteenth Century   51

Map 3.2   Colonial Partition on the Eve of World War I (with Contemporary Country Names)   60

Map 3.3   Territories Inhabited by the Somali People   63

Map 3.4   Nigerian Mosaic   65

Map 3.5   Railroads in Colonial West Africa (1930s)   72

Map 4.1   Waves of African Independence   82

Map 6.1   African Ideologies   132

Map 6.2   HIV/AIDS Infection Rate (2001) (Percent of Adults Aged 15–49)   139

Map 9.1   Successful Military Coups d'État   203
Map 10.1   Strength of Democracy (2002)   233
Map 11.1   Diplomatic Representation (Number of Embassies
                 Maintained Abroad in 2000)   247
Map 11.2   Select Regional Economic Organizations   262

FIGURES

Figure 2.1   Segmented Political Systems   25
Figure 2.2   Centralized Political Systems   30
Figure 5.1   Ethnic Intermediaries   104
Figure 5.2   Class Relationships   113
Figure 9.1   Spectrum of Civil-Military Relations   205
Figure 9.2   Incidence of Military Coups (Five-Year Averages,
                1950–2002)   217
Figure 10.1 Spectrum of Political Transition   228
Figure 10.2 Protection of Political Rights   237
Figure 10.3 Protection of Civil Liberties   238

TABLES

Table 2.1   Compensation for Permanent Injuries to Men   27
Table 2.2   Exchange Rates for Compensation (in Livestock)   27
Table 3.1   Estimates of the Global Slave Trade (Number of
              Africans)   53
Table 6.1   Policy Implications of African Ideologies   142
Table 6.2   Comparative Development Performance of African
              Ideologies   148
Table 7.1   Award Winners at the 2003 FESPACO Film Festival   161
Table 10.1   Legislative Election Results in Botswana (Parties
              Winning at Least One Seat)   238
Table 11.1   ANC Diplomatic Missions Maintained Abroad during
              the Anti-Apartheid Struggle   252
Table 12.1   United Nations Peacekeeping Missions in Africa
              (As of April 2003)   287
Table 13.1   Should Researchers Work with the U.S. Government?   310

BOXES (A CLOSER LOOK)

Researching Africa on the Internet   10
Researching Africa in Scholarly Journals   12
The Issa *Xeer:* Regulating Conflict in Segmentary Societies   26
Great Zimbawe   35
Island of Gorée and the Atlantic Slave Trade   56

Liberia: Sole American Colony?   68

Nelson Mandela's "Long Walk to Freedom"   84

Africa's Fifty-Fourth Country? Secession of the Somaliland
    Republic   95

Transcending Ethnicity and Class? Marabouts as Religious
    Intermediaries   108

Transcending Ethnicity and Class? Gender and the Debate
    over Female Circumcision   118

HIV/AIDS and National Development   138

Ivory Trade and the Politics of Conservation   144

Politics of African Cinema   160

Somali Alphabet Politics   168

The Exit Option: African Emigration to the United States   184

Rebuilding Trust: South Africa's Truth and Reconciliation
    Commission   194

Hidden Killers: Land Mines in Africa   207

Female Guerrillas after the Wars   212

Nonparty Systems? Uganda's "Movement Democracy"   226

Assessing the Spread of Democracy in Africa   232

Leon H. Sullivan (African/African-American) Summit   250

African Summitry   256

Franco-African Summits in the Pursuit of la Francophonie   276

Japanese Neomercantilism in Africa   284

African Studies Association   306

Should Researchers Work with the U.S. Government?   310

Association of Concerned Africa Scholars   326

Western Social Science as Imperialism?   331

About the Author

PETER J. SCHRAEDER received his doctorate in international studies from the University of South Carolina in 1990, after completing undergraduate work in French language and politics at the Sorbonne and international studies at Bradley University. He is a professor in the Department of Political Science at Loyola University Chicago, where he also teaches as part of the interdisciplinary Black World Studies and International Studies programs. A specialist of African politics and international relations, Schraeder has lived, worked, and traveled in more than half the fifty-three countries that compose the African continent. In addition to teaching at the University of Tunis in Tunisia (2002–2003) and at Cheikh Anta Diop University in Senegal (1994–1996) as part of the Fulbright scholar exchange program, he has held visiting appointments at Somali National University (1985), the African Studies Program at Northwestern University (1989–1990), the Harare (Zimbabwe) branch of the French Institute of African Research (1996), and the University of the Antilles in Guadeloupe (1999). Schraeder's research has been published in such diverse journals as *African Affairs, The Journal of Modern African Studies, The Journal of Politics, Middle East Journal, Politique Africaine,* and *World Politics.* He is the author of *United States Foreign Policy toward Africa: Incrementalism, Crisis, and Change* (1994) and the editor of *Exporting Democracy: Rhetoric vs. Reality* (2002) and *Intervention into the 1990s: U.S. Foreign Policy in the Third World* (1992). He is currently working on a book, *Beyond the "Big Man": Formulation and Implementation of African Foreign Policy in the Era of Democratization* (author). Schraeder's tenure (1998–1999) as president of the International Studies Association/Midwest (ISA/Midwest) is complemented by active involvement in a wide variety of professional organizations, most notably the African Studies Association (ASA), the American Political Science Association (APSA), and the International Studies Association (ISA). Fluent in English and French, Schraeder is also actively involved in a wide number of international research networks, most notably in France and francophone Africa.

1

Understanding African Politics and Society

Supporters of the Front for the Liberation of Mozambique (FRELIMO) rallying in the capital city, Maputo, in 1999.

THE DAWN of the twenty-first century serves as an exciting time of change for all those interested in the African continent and its peoples. Hundreds of African pro-democracy groups have sought to capitalize on a wave of democratization that seeks to replace authoritarian political systems with more inclusive forms of political governance. African activists have stressed the importance of creating multiethnic societies based on an ethic of tolerance, the protection of universal human rights, and the rule of law. African policymakers, technocrats, and private entrepreneurs are in the forefront of restructuring once-moribund African economies to unleash the African entrepreneurial spirit. A new generation of African reporters, writers, and scholars has contributed to the flourishing of newspapers, literature, and scholarship that opposes the vestiges of state-sponsored censorship, and in 2002 African leaders launched the African Union, a pan-African organization that is committed to the ideals of economic liberalization, regional integration, and democracy promotion. The primary purpose of this chapter is to set out some core introductory themes as we together attempt to make sense of these changes in African politics and society against the larger backdrops of African history and international relations. This chapter also highlights a wide variety of resources for conducting research on Africa, including compilations of some of the most noteworthy academic journals and Internet sites devoted to African politics and society and a country-by-country list of introductory volumes, bibliographies, and historical dictionaries that can be consulted for each African country.

AFRICA IS A RICH MOSAIC
OF DIVERSITY

First and foremost, the African continent is a rich mosaic of diverse countries and peoples. Encompassing a landmass three times larger than the continental United States, Africa is composed of fifty-three sovereign countries that range in size from the microstate of Djibouti (approximately the size of Massachusetts) to the continental giant of Sudan (approximately the size of Western Europe) (see Map 1.1). The populations of African countries are equally diverse in both size and ethnicity. Whereas the Seychelles have a population of less than 100,000 Seychellois of mixed African, South Asian, and European descent, Nigeria leads the continent with over 100 million citizens divided among nearly 250 ethnic groups. Economically, oil-rich Libya boasts a gross national product (GNP) per capita of over $7,600, whereas economically impoverished Mozambique struggles to recover from decades of civil war with a GNP per capita of less than $900. The political dimension of this African mosaic is also diverse. African leaders have employed capitalism, Marxism, socialism, and Islamic revivalism as the bases for creating a wide variety of political regimes, including monarchies, military dictatorships, Islamic republics, and liberal democracies.

MAP 1.1   Contemporary Africa

NECESSITY OF A
CONTINENTAL PERSPECTIVE

A second theme of this book is that a complete understanding of African politics and society requires a continental perspective inclusive of both North Africa (often called **Saharan Africa**) and the four regions (East Africa, Central Africa, West Africa, Southern Africa) typically called **Sub-Saharan Africa** (see Map 1.2). Classic studies often focus exclusively on Sub-Saharan Africa due to the belief that several dimensions of North African politics and society, most notably the influence of Arab culture and Islam, combine to make that region unique and therefore noncomparable to neighboring regions in the south. Although specific geographical regions, countries, and even regions within countries may embody varying degrees of uniqueness, this book nonetheless seeks to examine the continental trends that transcend individual regions and therefore provide us with a comprehensive understanding of

African politics and society. For example, one by necessity must focus on both Saharan and Sub-Saharan Africa to understand the rise and decline of the trans-Saharan trade network during the precolonial and colonial eras, as well as the subsequent impact of this trend on contemporary African politics and society. Similarly, any comprehensive understanding of the rise of African nationalism and the emergence of the contemporary independence era must necessarily begin with that region—North Africa—which witnessed the first wave of nationalism and independence during the 1950s. In short, a comprehensive understanding of African politics and society requires the bridging of the gap that historically has separated studies of Saharan and Sub-Saharan Africa.

MAP 1.2   Africa's Primary Regions

TO UNDERSTAND THE PRESENT,
ONE MUST UNDERSTAND THE PAST

A third theme of this book is that any comprehensive understanding of contemporary African politics and society must draw upon Africa's past. The evolution of African history can be divided into three broad historical periods:

- **Precolonial Independence Era (before 1884):** A rich and varied political history of the rise and fall of hundreds, if not thousands, of independent African political systems.

- **Colonial Era (1884–1951):** The period of direct European colonial rule in which the vast majority of previously independent African political systems were replaced by colonial states controlled by Belgium, Britain, France, Germany, Italy, Portugal, and Spain. The Berlin Conference of 1884, a gathering primarily attended by the European Great Powers that consecrated the creation of formal empires in Africa, marks the beginning of this period.

- **Contemporary Independence Era (1951–present):** A new era of political independence, marked by the end of colonialism and the emergence of the fifty-three countries that compose the African continent. This period began symbolically with Libya's independence in 1951 and continues to the present.

The **dependency–decolonization debate** over the degree to which the colonial era still influences contemporary African politics and society testifies to the significance of understanding the past. According to scholars belonging to the **dependency school of thought,** the granting of legal independence that began in the 1950s did little to alter the constraining web of economic, political, military, and cultural ties that continued to bind African countries to the former colonial powers (see Chapter 14).[1] This conceptualization of African politics—often called **neocolonialism**—is especially prominent in writings about the relationship between France and its former colonies, primarily due to policies designed to maintain what French policymakers refer to as their *chasse gardée* (exclusive hunting ground) in francophone Africa. Even in those former colonies where the European power was either too weak (e.g., Spain) or uninterested (e.g., Britain) to preserve privileged ties, the rise of the cold war and superpower intervention ensured the gradual replacement of European neocolonial relationships with a new set of ties dominated by Moscow and Washington. According to this perspective, direct colonial rule has been replaced by a series of neocolonial relationships that perpetuates external domination of African politics and society.

Scholars of the **decolonization school of thought** argue instead that legal independence was but the first step of an evolutionary process permitting African leaders to assume greater control over their respective political and social systems.[2] According to this perspective, although external influences were extremely powerful in the immediate postindependence era, layer upon layer of this foreign control is slowly being "peeled away" with the passage of time. While carefully underscoring that individual African countries can follow different pathways, proponents of the decolonization school argue that the most common pattern of political self-realization begins with legal independence, followed by efforts to assure national sovereignty in the military, economic, and cultural realms. "In this view, each layer of colonial influence is supported by the others, and as each is removed, it uncovers and exposes the next underlying one, rendering it vulnerable, untenable, and unnecessary," explains I. William Zartman, one of the most prominent proponents of the decolonization school. "Thus, there is a natural progression to the removal of colonial influence: Its speed can be varied by policy and effort, but the direction and evolution are inherent in the process and become extremely difficult to reverse."[3] Although the dependency–decolonization debate is far from being resolved, the year 2018 will mark a symbolic turning point as the contemporary independence era (1951–2018) will have then lasted as long as the colonial era (1884–1951).

A CONTINENT IN TRANSFORMATION

A fourth theme of this book is that the African continent is in the midst of socioeconomic and political-military transformations of historic proportions. The most dramatic example of this theme is the process of political transition toward greater levels of democracy that emerged full bloom in the 1990s. In sharp contrast to the end of the 1980s, when only five African countries (Botswana, Gambia, Mauritius, Senegal, and Zimbabwe) held competitive multiparty elections, the first 5 years of the 1990s witnessed multiparty contests in thirty-eight African countries, with twenty-nine of these constituting "founding elections" in which "the office of the head of government is openly contested following a period during which multiparty political competition was denied."[4] In the case of South Africa, for example, the inauguration of Nelson Mandela as that country's first democratically elected president after being imprisoned for nearly 28 years by apartheid-era dictatorial regimes symbolized the efforts of hundreds of African pro-democracy groups to instill democratic practices throughout the African continent.

Disagreements nonetheless have emerged over whether Africa's socioeconomic and political-military transformations are inherently for the better. At the beginning of the 1990s, those prone to underscore the positive side of these changes typically spoke of the emergence of an **African renaissance**—the "rebirth" of economic, social, and political freedoms that had been extinguished during the colonial era and subsequently denied to African peoples by dictatorial elites during the initial decades of the contemporary independence era.[5] An important point of departure of this position, at least as it concerns the process of political transition, is an optimistic belief in both the willingness and the ability of democratically elected leaders to correct deficiencies in governance and to ensure a better future for their peoples. Others who are more critical, however, are prone to adhere to the classic French maxim: "*Plus ça change, plus c'est la même chose*" ("The more things change, the more they remain the same"). According to Claude Ake, for example, Africa's initial experiments with multiparty elections at the beginning of the 1990s in many cases ensured the "democratization of disempowerment": a process whereby multiparty elections allow for the rotation of self-interested political elites of different parties, while the vast majority of the population remains disempowered from the political system.[6]

The competing nature of these two visions, and hence potentially conflicting images of continuity and change in African politics and society, is demonstrated by the evolving role of gender in African politics.[7] According to statistics compiled by the Inter-Parliamentary Union, the number of African women being elected to national parliaments more than doubled during the 1990s to an average of 13 percent in 2003 (see Map 1.3). To put this figure in perspective, argue proponents of an African renaissance, female representatives

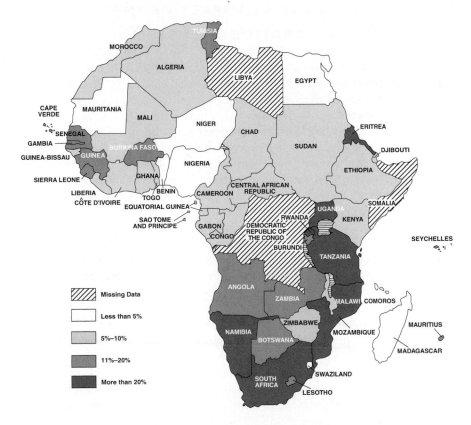

MAP 1.3   Women in National Parliaments (2002) (Percent of Lower or Single House Seats Held by Women)

Source: Inter-Parliamentary Union (IPU) Web Site (http://www.ipu.org/wmn-e/classif.htm).

in 2003 constituted 18 percent of the British House of Commons, 13 percent of the U.S. Senate, and 11 percent of the French Senate. Critics could nonetheless respond that extremely high averages for a select number of African countries (e.g., women constitute 30 percent of Mozambique's parliament) severely skew Africa's overall average; that even the 13 percent figure is not indicative of true social change in that seats are often reserved under a quota system on the basis of gender (e.g., 30 percent of all elected seats in Uganda's local councils are reserved for women); or that overall levels for the African continent still lag behind those for all other regions except the Middle East, where women constitute only 5 percent of elected representatives. I intend in this book to cite and explore the transformations taking place (in this case, the rising percentage of African female parliamentarians) while leaving normative questions, such as whether such transformations are ultimately for the better, to you.

INFLUENTIAL IMPACT OF THE
INTERNATIONAL SYSTEM

A fifth theme of the chapters that follow is that changes in the international system have significantly influenced African politics and society. From the middle of the fifteenth to the end of the nineteenth century, the international community's acceptance of slavery as a legitimate form of commerce had a devastating impact on the African continent. It has been estimated that the European and Arab slave trades together were responsible for the forced removal and enslavement of more than 30 million Africans (see Chapter 3). This international norm was finally rejected during the nineteenth century, only to be replaced by the legitimization of Europe's occupation of Africa and the creation and expansion of European empires.

Four international events significantly influenced the global balance of power and the evolution of African politics and society during the contemporary independence era. First, the extended conflict of World War II heralded the decline of Europe as the most powerful region of the world, as well as the rise of the United States and the former Soviet Union as the unparalleled superpowers of the twentieth century. Africa's direct involvement in the war began with fascist Italy's invasion and occupation of Ethiopia in 1935. The war weakened the European empires to such a degree that the first wave of decolonization began during the 1950s. Subsequent waves of decolonization ensured that, except in the case of Spain's continued control over several small coastal enclaves (most notably Ceuta and Melilla) in Morocco, African independence from direct colonial rule was largely complete by the end of the twentieth century (see Chapter 4).

A second turning point within the international system was the outbreak of the cold war (1947–89).[8] An important outcome of this ideological struggle was the emergence of the African continent as a battlefield for proxy wars between the United States and the former Soviet Union. During the 1960s, for example, the White House ordered a series of covert campaigns in the Democratic Republic of the Congo (Congo-Kinshasa, formerly Zaire) that not only led to the assassination of Prime Minister Patrice Lumumba (denounced in Washington as a "Castro or worse") but ensured the rise to power in 1965 of a pro–West military strongman, Mobutu Sese Seko.[9] The cold war also fostered the longevity of numerous African dictators who were courted by the superpowers with lavish offers of economic and military aid in exchange for loyalty. In the case of Congo-Kinshasa, the United States provided Mobutu's military dictatorship with approximately $1.5 billion in economic and military aid during a period of more than 25 years, as long as Mobutu was willing to support Washington's anticommunist agenda throughout Africa.

The cold war's end in 1989 served as a third turning point within the international system. The collapse of single-party regimes throughout Eastern Europe and the former Soviet Union powerfully influenced African prodemocracy activists and sparked a wave of democratic transitions in all regions of the African continent (see Chapter 10). Authoritarian leaders could no longer successfully ally themselves ideologically with one of the superpowers in exchange for protection against opposition movements. The Soviet Union had ceased to exist, and a new Russian regime preoccupied with domestic economic restructuring had largely withdrawn from African politics. Also, the United States began to downplay anticommunist political-military relationships in favor of promoting trade and economic investment. The Clinton administration's refusal in 1997 to prevent the pro–United States Mobutu from being overthrown by a popular guerrilla movement, led by Laurent-Désiré Kabila, exemplified this new international order (see Chapter 12). Although Mobutu's downfall was primarily determined by the emergence of organized domestic opposition to his increasingly corrupt regime, the inaction of the Clinton administration would have been unthinkable before the end of the cold war.

The most recent turning point within the international system, especially as concerns U.S. relations with the African continent, was the terrorist attacks of September 11, 2001 against the World Trade Center in New York and the Pentagon in Washington, D.C. The U.S. response to these attacks, most notably the Bush administration's pursuit of a global war on terrorism, indicated the continued importance of strategic imperatives in international affairs. One of the Bush administration's priorities is courting African allies in North and East Africa, due to their proximity to the Middle East and inclusion in the Islamic world. In North Africa, for example, the construction and opening in December 2002 of a new $42 million U.S. Embassy in Tunis demonstrated Tunisia's rising strategic importance as an Arab country that offers strong support for the war on terrorism. Tunis boasts a State Department office for assessing regional threats, a U.S. Defense Department regional training center for U.S. Special Forces destined for combat in the Arab world, and a Foreign Service Institute for teaching the Arabic language to numerous U.S. government personnel who are preparing to work in Arabic-speaking countries. The undemocratic nature

A Closer Look: RESEARCHING AFRICA ON THE INTERNET

Contemporary News Updates

AllAfrica News Wire
   http://allafrica.com/

Electronic News on Africa
   http://www.columbia.edu/cu/web/indiv/africa/ejournals.html

Washington Post
   http://www.washingtonpost.com/wp-srv/inatl/africa.htm

The New York Times
   http://www.nyt.com

United States–Based Resource Centers

Berkeley-Stanford Joint Center for African Studies
   http://www.stanford.edu/dept/AFR

Boston University
   http://www.bu.edu/afr/

Central Connecticut State University
   http://www.ccsu.edu/afstudy

Columbia University
   http://www.columbia.edu/cu/lweb/indiv/africa/

Harvard Africa Studies
   http://www.fas.harvard.edu/cafrica/

Howard University
   http://www.howard.edu/

Indiana University—Bloomington
   http://www.indiana.edu/~afrist/

Lincoln University
   http://www.lincoln.edu/politicalscience

Northwestern University
   http://www.nwu.edu/african-studies/

Michigan State University
   http://www2.h-net.msu.edu/~africa/

Ohio State University
   http://www.acs.ohio-state.edu/

Ohio University
   http://www.ohiou.edu/

Tuskegee University
   http://www.tusk.edu/

University of California—Los Angeles
   http://www.isop.ucla.edu/jscasc/

University of Florida—Gainesville
   http://www.clas.ufl.edu/africa

University of Illinois—Champaign/Urbana
   http://www.afrst.uiuc.edu/univ.html

University of Kansas
http://www.ukans.edu/~afs/

University of Pennsylvania with Bryn Mawr, Haverford, and Swarthmore Colleges
http://www.sas.upenn.edu/African_Studies/AS.html

University of Wisconsin-Madison
http://polyglot.lss.wisc.edu/afrst/asphome.html

Yale University
http://www.yale.edu/ycpo/ycps/A-D/afamstFM.html

Non-United States–Based Resource Centers

African Studies Centre (Afrika-StudienCentrum) (Leiden, The Netherlands)
http://asc.leidenuniv.nl

Center for African Area Studies, Kyoto University (Japan)
http://www.africa.kyoto-u.ac.jp/

Center for Afrikastudier (Copenhagen, Denmark)
http://www.teol.ku.dk/cas/default.htm

Centre d'Etude d'Afrique Noire (CEAN) (Bordeaux, France)
http://www.cean.u-bordeaux.fr/

International African Institute (IAI) (London, United Kingdom)
http://www.oneworld.org/iai/info.htm

Nordic Africa Institute (Uppsala, Sweden)
http://www.nai.uu.se/indexeng.html

Peacelink for Africa (Rome, Italy)
http://www.peacelink.it/afrinews.html

School of Oriental and African Studies (SOAS), University of London (United Kingdom)
http://www.soas.ac.uk/cas/

---

of Tunisia's political system, as well as those of other U.S. allies in the war on terrorism, nonetheless raises once again a potential dilemma reminiscent of the cold war: the degree to which security imperatives (in this case, the war on terrorism) should take precedence over other foreign policy objectives, such as the normative goal of strengthening democracy on the African continent.

CENTRAL IMPORTANCE OF THE DOMESTIC DIMENSION

A sixth theme of this book is the central importance of African domestic actors in any understanding of continuity and change in African politics and society. The international environment may provide the context within which decisions are made, but it is ultimately Africans who make and carry out the decisions. In the pages that follow, we will explore the crucial roles played by a wide array of Africans, including the leaders and citizens of the political systems of the precolonial independence era, the armed resistance movements of African kingdoms and ethnic groups that challenged the imposition of colonial rule, the nationalist movements that led their countries to independence beginning in the 1950s, the military officers who illegally took power in coups d'état and

---

A Closer Look: RESEARCHING AFRICA IN SCHOLARLY JOURNALS

The following list is designed to serve as a starting point for carrying out research. Dates in parentheses mark the first years of publication.

African Studies Association Journals (with Political Content)

African Studies Association (United States): *African Studies Review* (1957)

Canadian Association of African Studies: *Canadian Journal of African Studies/Revue Canadienne des Études Africaines* (1967)

Nordic Association of African Studies: *Nordic Journal of African Studies* (1992)

Royal African Society and the African Studies Association of the United Kingdom: *African Affairs* (1901)

Swiss Society of African Studies: *Genève-Afrique. Journal of the Geneva Institute of Development Studies and the Swiss Society of African Studies* (1962)

Other Journals on African Politics

Africa: Journal of the International African Institute/Revue de l'Institut Africain International (1928)

Africa Quarterly (1961)

Africa Today (1954)

African Issues (formerly *Issues: A Journal of Opinion*) (1970)

The African Review: A Journal of African Politics, Development, and International Affairs (1971)

Afrique et Développement/Africa Development (1976)

Asian and African Studies (1965)

Indian Journal of African Studies (1988)

Journal of African Policy Studies (1995)

Journal of Asian and African Studies (1966)

Journal of Contemporary African Studies (1981)

The Journal of Modern African Studies (1963)

Journal of Southern African Studies (1974)

The Maghreb Review (1976)

Northeast African Studies (1979)

Review of African Political Economy (1974)

TransAfrica Forum (1982)

Ufahamu: Journal of the African Activist Association (1970)

Journals of Related Disciplines

African Archaeological Review (1983)

African Economic History (1972)

African Journal of International and Comparative Law/Revue Africaine de Droit International et Comparé (1989)

African Literature Today (1968)

African Urban Quarterly (1986)

African Urban Studies (1978)

The International Journal of African Historical Studies (1968)

Journal of African Civilization (1968)

Journal of African Economies (1992)

The Journal of African History (1960)

Journal of African Languages and Linguistics (1979)

Journal of African Law (1957)

Journal of Religion in Africa (1967)

Research in African Literatures (1970)

Leading Non-English-Language Journals

Africa. Rivista Trimestrale di Studi e Documentazione dell'Istituto Italiano per l'Africa e l'Oriente (Italian: 1946)

Afrika Spectrum (German: 1966)

Afrique Contemporaine (French: 1962)

Estudios Africanos (Spanish: 1985)

Politique Africaine (French: 1980)

Revista Internacional de Estudos Africanos (Portuguese: 1985)

Current Events Summaries

Africa Analysis (1986)

Africa Confidential (1960)

Africa Research Bulletin: Political Series (1964)

Annuals and Yearbooks

Africa Contemporary Record: Annual Survey and Documents (1970)

Africa South of the Sahara (1971)

New African Yearbook (1982)

Journals for Bibliographical Searches

The African Book Publishing Record (1975)

A Current Bibliography on African Affairs (1963)

International African Bibliography (1971)

established military dictatorships, the civilian politicians who have led democratization movements intent upon replacing authoritarian regimes with democratic forms of governance, African writers and filmmakers who have spoken out against abuses of human rights, and presidents and other national leaders who manage the foreign relations of their countries. In short, a true understanding of African politics and society must emphasize the socioeconomic and political-military impacts of Africans themselves.

BALANCING AFRO-PESSIMISM
AND AFRO-OPTIMISM

A final theme is the necessity of seeking balance in our understanding of African politics and society. It is widely recognized, for example, that the vast majority of the U.S. public maintains what can be called a **National Geographic image of Africa.** The mention of Africa typically conjures stereotypical images of lush jungles and wild animals, poverty and famine, "tribal" warfare, and deadly diseases, such as ebola and HIV/AIDS.[10] These images are reinforced by the nature of media reporting, which usually concentrates on the negative aspects of the African continent. An analysis of Africa's coverage in *The New York Times* demonstrates, for example, that 73 percent of all articles published between 1955 and 1995 embodied negative images of African politics and society.[11] Not surprisingly, news editors interested in "what will sell" most often cover the sensational events, such as famine in Ethiopia, civil war in Somalia, and ethnic genocide in Rwanda, which neatly fit the preconceived images of their audiences.

The principal dilemma associated with this incomplete understanding of Africa is that it has contributed to the rise of **Afro-pessimism,** the belief that grinding poverty, outbreaks of devastating diseases, and intensifying conflicts will remain staples of the African landscape for the foreseeable future. Extreme adherents of this view suggest that Africans cannot reverse the continent's slide toward anarchy.[12] One need not err on the side of **Afro-optimism,** that is, the belief that all is well, to recognize the imperative of achieving a more balanced understanding of African politics and society. For every famine there exists an agricultural "success story" such as Botswana, where forward-thinking leadership has made that country a net exporter of foodstuffs. For every military coup d'état there exists a transition to civilian rule, such as in Benin, where 19 years of military dictatorship (1972–91) were replaced by democracy (1991–present). For every civil war there exists a case of conflict resolution, as in Mozambique, where a peace accord signed in 1992 ended nearly 30 years of guerrilla warfare. For every ethnic conflict there exists a well-meaning attempt to create multiethnic cooperation, such as South Africa's democratization under the leadership of president Nelson Mandela (1994–99) and his successor, President Thabo Mbeki (1999–present). These issues and others are examined in the chapters that follow.

UNDERTAKING FURTHER RESEARCH

Those interested in undertaking research related to the African continent should first consult the Internet sites and scholarly journals listed earlier in this chapter. The following books also constitute excellent starting points for conducting research on individual African countries. Three series are represented. The *World Bibliographical Series (WBS)*, published by Clio Press, offers annotated bibliographies of sources relevant to each country. Each volume also includes an introductory overview essay and an extensive index. The *African Historical Dictionaries (AHD)* series, published by Scarecrow Press, constitutes mini-encyclopedias of a country's historical figures, places, terms, and events. Each volume also includes an introductory overview essay and a comprehensive bibliography. Finally, the *Nations of the Modern World (NMW)* and the *Nations of Contemporary Africa (NCA)* series, published by Westview Press, offer descriptive overviews of the history, economics, politics, and international relations of individual African countries.

Algeria

Lawless, Richard I. (1995). *Algeria* (WBS).

Naylor, Phillip Chiviges, and Alf Andrew Heggoy (1994). *Historical Dictionary of Algeria (AHD,* 2nd ed.) (1st ed., 1981, by Heggoy).

Angola

Black, Richard (1992). *Angola (WBS,* vol. 151).

Broadhead, Susan H. (1992). *Historical Dictionary of Angola (AHD,* 2nd ed.) (1st ed., 1980, by Phyllis Martin).

Tvedten, Inge (1997). *Angola: Struggle for Peace and Reconstruction (NMW).*

Benin

Decalo, Samuel (1995). *Historical Dictionary of Benin (AHD,* 3rd ed.) (2nd ed., 1987; 1st ed., 1976, by Decalo).

Eades, J. S., and Chris Allen (1996). *Benin (WBS).*

Botswana

Morton, Fred, Barry Morton, and Jeff Ramsay (1996). *Historical Dictionary of Botswana (AHD,* 3rd ed.) (2nd ed., 1989, by Morton, Andrew Murray, and Ramsay; 1st ed., 1975, by Richard P. Stevens).

Parson, Jack (1984). *Botswana: Liberal Democracy and the Labor Reserve in Southern Africa (NCA).*

Wiseman, John A. (1992). *Botswana (WBS).*

Burkina Faso

Decalo, Samuel (1994). *Burkina Faso (WBS,* vol. 169).

Englebert, Pierre (1996). *Burkina Faso: Unsteady Statehood in West Africa (NCW).*

McFarland, Daniel Miles, and Lawrence Rupley (1998). *Historical Dictionary of Burkina Faso (former Upper Volta) (AHD,* 2nd ed.) (1st ed., 1978, by McFarland).

Burundi

Daniels, Morna (1992). *Burundi (WBS).*

Eggers, Ellen K. (1997). *Historical Dictionary of Burundi (AHD,* 2nd ed.) (1st ed., 1976, by Warren Weinstein).

Cameroon

DeLancey, Mark W. (1989). *Cameroon: Dependence and Independence (NCA).*

DeLancey, Mark W., and Mark Dike DeLancey (2000). *Historical Dictionary of Cameroon (AHD,* 3rd ed.) (2nd ed., 1990, by DeLancey and H. Mbella Mokeba; 1st ed., 1974, by Victor T. LeVine).

DeLancey, Mark W., and Peter J. Schraeder (1986). *Cameroon (WBS).*

Cape Verde

Lobban, Richard, and Marlene Lopes (1995). *Historical Dictionary of Republic of Cape Verde (AHD,* 3rd ed.) (2nd ed., 1988; 1st ed., 1979, by Lobban and Halter).

Lobban, Richard A., Jr. (1995). *Cape Verde: Crioulo Colony to Independent Nation (NMW).*

Shaw, Caroline S. (1991). *Cape Verde (WBS).*

Central African Republic

Kalck, Pierre (1993). *Central African Republic (WBS).*

Kalck, Pierre (translated by Thomas O'Toole) (1992). *Historical Dictionary of the Central African Republic (AHD,* 2nd ed.) (1st ed., 1980, by Kalck).

O'Toole, Thomas (1986). *Central African Republic: The Continent's Hidden Heart (NCW).*

Chad

Azevedo, Mario J., and Emmanuel U. Nnadozie (1997). *Chad: A Nation in Search of Its Future (NMW).*

Decalo, Samuel (1997). *Historical Dictionary of Chad (AHD).*

Joffé, Emile G. H., and Valerie Day-Viaud (1995). *Chad (WBS).*

Comoro Islands

Newitt, M. D. D. (1984). *The Comoro Islands: Struggle against Dependency in the Indian Ocean (NCA).*

Ottenheimer, Martin, and Harriet Ottenheimer (1994). *Historical Dictionary of Comoro Islands (AHD).*

Congo-Brazzaville

Decalo, Samuel, Virginia Thompson, and Richard Adloff (1996). *Historical Dictionary of Congo (AHD,* 3rd ed.) (2nd ed., 1984, by Thompson and Adloff; 1st ed., 1974, by Thompson and Adloff).

Fegley, Randall (1993). *Congo (WBS).*

Côte d'Ivoire

Daniels, Morna (1996). *Côte d'Ivoire (WBS).*

Mundt, Robert J. (1995). *Historical Dictionary of Côte d'Ivoire (The Ivory Coast) (AHD).*

Democratic Republic of the Congo (Congo-Kinshasa)

Bobb, F. Scott (1998). *Historical Dictionary of the Democratic Republic of Congo (Zaire) (AHD,* 2nd ed.) (1st ed., 1988, by Bobb).

Leslie, Winsome J. (1993). *Zaire: Continuity and Political Change in an Oppressive State (NCA).*

Williams, Dawn Bastian, Robert W. Lesh, and Andrea L. Stamm (1995). *Zaire (WBS).*

Djibouti

Alwah, Daoud A., and Yohanes Mibrathu (2000). *Historical Dictionary of Djibouti (AHD).*

Schraeder, Peter J. (1991). *Djibouti (WBS).*

Egypt

Goldschmidt Jr., Arthur (1994). *Historical Dictionary of Egypt (AHD,* 2nd ed.) (1st ed., 1984, by Joan Wucher King).

Makar, Ragai N. (1988). *Egypt (WBS).*

Equatorial Guinea

Liniger-Goumaz, Max (2000). *Historical Dictionary of Equatorial Guinea (AHD,* 3rd ed.) (2nd ed., 1988; 1st ed., 1979, by Max Liniger-Goumaz).

Sundiata, I. K. (1990). *Equatorial Guinea: Colonialism, State Terror, and the Search for Stability (NCA).*

Eritrea

Fegley, Randall (1995). *Eritrea (WBS).*

Killion, Tom (1998). *Historical Dictionary of Ethiopia and Eritrea (AHD,* 3rd ed.) (2nd ed., 1994; 1st ed., 1981, by Chris Prouty and Eugene Rosenfeld).

Ethiopia

Fegley, Randall (1995). *Eritrea (WBS).*

Killion, Tom (1998). *Historical Dictionary of Ethiopia and Eritrea (AHD,* 3rd ed.) (2nd ed., 1994; 1st ed., 1981, by Chris Prouty and Eugene Rosenfeld).

Wubneh, Mulatu, and Yohannis Abate (1987). *Ethiopia: Transition and Development in the Horn of Africa (NCA).*

Gabon

Barnes, James Franklin (1992). *Gabon: Beyond the Colonial Legacy (NCA).*

Gardinier, David E. (1992). *Gabon (WBS).*

Gardinier, David E. (1994). *Historical Dictionary of Gabon (AHD,* 2nd ed.) (1st ed., 1981, by Gardinier).

Gambia

Gamble, David P. (1988). *The Gambia (WBS).*

Hughes, Arnold, and Harry A. Gailey (1999). *Historical Dictionary of the Gambia (AHD,* 3rd ed.) (2nd ed., 1987; 1st ed., 1975, by Gailey).

Ghana

Myers, Robert A. (1991). *Ghana (WBS).*

Owusu-Ansah, David, and Daniel Miles McFarland (1995). *Historical Dictionary of Ghana (AHD,* 2nd ed.) (1st ed., 1985, by McFarland).

Pellow, Deborah, and Naomi H. Chazan (1986). *Ghana: Coping with Uncertainty (NCA).*

Guinea

Binns, Margaret (1996). *Guinea (WBS).*

O'Toole, Thomas, and Ibrahima Bah-Lalya (1995). *Historical Dictionary of Guinea (AHD,* 3rd ed.) (2nd ed., 1987; 1st ed., 1978, by O'Toole).

Guinea-Bissau

Forest, Joshua B. (1992). *Guinea-Bissau: Power, Conflict, and Renewal in a West African Nation (NCA).*

Galli, Rosemary E. (1990). *Guinea-Bissau (WBS).*

Lobban, Jr., Richard Andrew, and Peter Karibe Mendy (1996). *Historical Dictionary of the Republic of Guinea-Bissau (AHD,* 3rd ed.) (2nd ed., 1988, by Lobban and Joshua Forrest; 1st ed., 1979, by Lobban).

Kenya

Coger, Dalvan (1996). *Kenya* (WBS).

Maxon, Robert M., and Thomas P. Ofcansky (2000). *Historical Dictionary of Kenya (AHD)* (1st ed. 1981, by Bethwell A. Ogot).

Miller, Norman N. (1993). *Kenya: The Quest for Prosperity (NCA,* 2nd ed.) (1st ed., 1984, by Miller).

Lesotho

Bardhill, John E., and James H. Cobbe (1985). *Lesotho: Dilemmas of Dependence in Southern Africa (NCA).*

Haliburton, Gordon (1977). *Historical Dictionary of Lesotho (AHD).*

Johnston, Deborah (1996). *Lesotho (WBS).*

Liberia

Dunn, D. Elwood (1995). *Liberia (WBS)*.

Dunn, D. Elwood, Amos J. Beyan, and Carl Patrick Burrowes (2001). *Historical Dictionary of Liberia (AHD)* (2nd ed.) (1st ed., 1985, by Dunn and Svend E. Holsoe).

Libya

Lawless, Richard I. (1987). *Libya (WBS)*.

St. John, Ronald Bruce (1998). *Historical Dictionary of Libya (AHD)*.

Madagascar

Bradt, Hilary (with Mervyn Brown) (1993). *Madagascar (WBS)*.

Covell, Maureen (1995). *Historical Dictionary of Madagascar (AHD)*.

Malawi

Decalo, Samuel (1995). *Malawi (WBS)*.

Kalinga, Owen J. M., and Cynthia A. Crosby (2001). *Historical Dictionary of Malawi (AHD* 3rd ed.) (2nd ed., 1993; 1st ed., 1980, by Crosby).

Mali

Imperato, Pascal James (1996). *Historical Dictionary of Mali (AHD,* 3rd ed.) (2nd ed., 1986; 1st ed., 1977, by Imperato).

Imperato, Pascal James (1989). *Mali: A Search for Direction (NCA)*.

Mauritania

Calderini, Simonetta, Delia Cortese, and James L. A. Webb Jr. (1992). *Mauritania (WBS)*.

Pazzanita, Anthony G. (1996). *Historical Dictionary of Mauritania* (AHD, 2nd ed.) (1st ed., 1981, by Alfred G. Gerteiny).

Mauritius

Bennett, Pramila Ramgulam (1992). *Mauritius (WBS)*.

Bowman, Larry W. (1991). *Mauritius: Democracy and Development in the Indian Ocean (NCA)*.

Selvon, Sydney (1991). *Historical Dictionary of Mauritius (AHD,* 2nd ed.) (1st ed., 1982, by Lindsay Rivière).

Morocco

Findlay, Anne M., and Allan M. Findlay (1995). *Morocco (WBS)*.

Park, Thomas K. (1996). *Historical Dictionary of Morocco (AHD,* 2nd ed.) (1st ed., 1980, by William Spencer).

Mozambique

Azevedo, Mario (1991). *Historical Dictionary of Mozambique (AHD)*.

Darch, Colin (assisted by Calisto Pacheleke) (1987). *Mozambique (WBS)*.

Isaacman, Allen F. (1983). *Mozambique: From Colonialism to Revolution, 1900–1982 (NCA)*.

Namibia

Grotpeter, John J. (1994). *Historical Dictionary of Namibia (AHD)*.

Schoeman, Stanley, and Elna Schoeman (1997). *Namibia (WBS)*.

Sparks, Donald L., and December Green (1992). *Namibia: The Nation After Independence (NCA)*.

Niger

Charlick, Robert B. (1991). *Niger: Personal Rule and Survival in the Sahel (NCA)*.

Decalo, Samuel (1997). *Historical Dictionary of Niger (AHD,* 3rd ed.) (2nd ed., 1989; 1st ed., 1979, by Decalo).

Zamponi, Lynda F. (1994). *Niger (WBS)*.

Nigeria

Myers, Robert A. (1989). *Nigeria (WBS)*.

Oyewole, Anthony, and John Lucas (2000). *Historical Dictionary of Nigeria (AHS,* 2nd ed.) (1st ed., 1987, by Oyewole).

Wright, Stephen (1999). *Nigeria: Struggle for Stability and Status (NMW,* 2nd ed.) (1st ed., 1988, by Timothy M. Shaw and Julius O. Ihonvbere).

Rwanda

Dorsey, Learthen (1994). *Historical Dictionary of Rwanda (AHD)*.

Fegley, Randall (1993). *Rwanda (WBS)*.

Sao Tome and Principe

Hodges, Tony, and Malyn Newitt (1988). *Sao Tome and Principe: From Plantation Colony to Microstate (NCA)*.

Shaw, Caroline S. (1994). *Sao Tome and Principe (WBS)*.

Senegal

Clark, Andrew F., and Lucie Colvin Phillips (1994). *Historical Dictionary of Senegal (AHD,* 2nd ed.) (1st ed., 1981, by Colvin).

Dilley, Roy M., and Jerry S. Eades (1994). *Senegal (WBS)*.

Gellar, Sheldon (1995). *Senegal: An African Nation between Islam and the West (NMW,* 2nd ed.) (1st ed, 1982, by Gellar).

Seychelles

Bennett, George (with the collaboration of Pramila Ramgulam Bennett) (1993). *Seychelles (WBS)*.

Franda, Marcus F. (1982). *The Seychelles: Unquiet Islands (NCA)*.

Sierra Leone

Binns, Margaret, and Tony Binns (1992). *Sierra Leone (WBS)*.

Foray, Cyril Patrick (1977). *Historical Dictionary of Sierra Leone (AHD)*.

Somalia

DeLancey, Mark W., Sheila L. Elliott, December Green, Kenneth J. Menkhaus, Mohammad Haji Moqtar, and Peter J. Schraeder (1988). *Somalia (WBS)*.

Laitin, David D., and Said S. Samatar (1987). *Somalia: Nation in Search of a State (NCA)*.

Mukhtar, Mohamed Haji (2002). *Historical Dictionary of Somalia (AHD,* 2nd ed.) (1st ed., 1975, by Margaret F. Castagno).

South Africa

Davis, Geoffrey V. (1994). *South Africa (WBS)*.

Saul, John, and Patrick Bond (1998). *South Africa: Apartheid and After (NMW)*.

Saunders, Christopher, and Nicholas Southey (2000). *Historical Dictionary of South Africa (AHD,* 2nd ed.) (1st ed., 1983, by Saunders).

Sudan

Daly, M. W. (1992). *Sudan (WBS)*.

Lobban, Jr., Richard A., Robert A. Kramer, and Caroline Fluehr-Lobban (2002). *Historical Dictionary of the Sudan (AHD,* 3rd ed.) (2nd ed., 1992, by Fluehr-Lobban, Lobban, Jr., and John Voll; 1st ed., 1978, by Voll).

Swaziland

Booth, Alan R. (2000). *Historical Dictionary of Swaziland (AHD,* 2nd ed.) (1st ed., 1975, by John J. Grotpeter).

Booth, Alan R. (1983). *Swaziland: Tradition and Change in a Southern African Kingdom (NCA)*.

Nyeko, Balam (1994). *Swaziland (WBS)*.

Tanzania

Darch, Colin (1996). *Tanzania (WBS)*.

Ofcansky, Thomas P., and Rodger Yeager (1997). *Historical Dictionary of Tanzania (AHD,* 2nd ed.) (1st ed., 1978, by Laura S. Kurtz).

Yeager, Rodger (1991). *Tanzania: An African Experiment (NCA)* (1st ed., 1982, by Rodger Young).

Togo

Decalo, Samuel (1996). *Historical Dictionary of Togo (AHD,* 3rd ed.) (2nd ed., 1987; 1st ed., 1976, by Decalo).

Decalo, Samuel (1995). *Togo (WBS)*.

Tunisia

Lawless, Richard I., Allan M. Findlay, and Anne M. Findlay (1982). *Tunisia (WBS)*.

Perkins, Kenneth J. (1997). *Historical Dictionary of Tunisia (AHD,* 2nd ed.) (1st ed., 1989, by Perkins).

Uganda

Nyeko, Balam (1996). *Uganda (WBS,* 2nd ed.) (1st ed., 1981, by Robert L. Collison).

Ofcansky, Thomas P. (1995). *Uganda: Tarnished Pearl of Africa (NMW)*.

Pirouet, M. Louise (1995). *Historical Dictionary of Uganda (AHD)*.

Zambia

Bliss, Anne M., and J. A. Rigg (1984). *Zambia (WBS)*.

Burdette, Marcia M. (1988). *Zambia: Between Two Worlds (NCA)*.

Grotpeter, John J., Brian V. Siegel, and James R. Pletcher (1998). *Historical Dictionary of Zambia (AHD,* 2nd ed.) (1st ed., 1979, by Grotpeter).

Zimbabwe

Potts, Deborah (1993). *Zimbabwe (WBS)*.

Rubert, Steven L. and Kent R. Rasmussen (2001). *Historical Dictionary of Zimbabwe (AHD,* 3rd ed.) (2nd ed., 1990, by Rasmussen and Rubert; 1st ed., 1979, by Rasmussen).

Sylvester, Christine McNabb (1991). *Zimbabwe: The Terrain of Contradictory Development (NCA)*.

KEY TERMS

Saharan Africa
Sub-Saharan Africa
Precolonial Independence Era
   (before 1884)
Colonial Era (1884–1951)
Contemporary Independence Era
   (1951–present)
dependency–decolonization debate

dependency school of thought
neocolonialism
decolonization school of thought
African renaissance
National Geographic image of Africa
Afro-pessimism
Afro-optimism

FOR FURTHER READING

Alden, Patricia, David Lloyd, and Ahmed I. Samatar, eds. *African Studies and the Undergraduate Curriculum*. Boulder: Lynne Rienner, 1994.

Appiah, Kwame Anthony, and Henry Louis Gates, Jr., eds. *Africana: The Encyclopedia of the African and African American Experience*. New York: Basic Civitas Books/Perseus Books Group, 2000.

Aryeetey-Attoh, Samuel, ed. *Geography of Sub-Saharan Africa*. Upper Saddle River: Prentice-Hall, 1997.

Azevedo, Mario, ed. *Africana Studies: A Survey of Africa and the African Diaspora*. Durham: Carolina Academic, 1993.

Bastian, Misty L., and Jane L. Parpart, eds. *Great Ideas for Teaching about Africa*. Boulder: Lynne Rienner, 1999.

Bates, Robert H., V. Y. Mudimbe, and Jean O'Barr, eds. *Africa and the Disciplines: The Contributions of Research in Africa to the Social Sciences and Humanities*. Chicago: University of Chicago Press, 1993.

Cook, Chris, and David Killingray. *African Political Facts since 1945* (2nd ed.). New York: Facts on File, 1991.

Danaher, Kevin. *Beyond Safaris: A Guide to Building People-to-People Ties with Africa*. Trenton: Africa World Press, 1991.

DeLancey, Mark W., ed. *Handbook of Political Science Research on Sub-Saharan Africa: Trends from the 1960s to the 1990s*. Westport: Greenwood, 1992.

Gates, Jr., Henry Louis. *Wonders of the African World*. New York: Alfred A. Knopf, 1999.

Gordon, April A., and Donald L. Gordon, eds. *Understanding Contemporary Africa* (3rd ed.). Boulder: Lynne Rienner, 2001.

Guyer, Jane I. *African Studies in the United States: A Perspective*. Atlanta: African Studies Association, 1996.

Klein, Curtis A. *Mistaking Africa: Curiosities and Inventions of the American Mind*. Boulder: Westview Press, 1999.

Lohrentz, Kenneth P. "Africana at the Center for Research Libraries: A Survey of Collections and Access." *African Studies Review* 41, no. 2 (September 1998): 113–32.

Martin, William G., and Michael O. West, eds. *Out of One, Many Africas: Reconstructing the Study and Meaning of Africa*. Urbana: University of Illinois Press, 1999.

Neve, Herbert T., ed. *Homeward Journey: Readings in African Studies*. Trenton: Africa World, 1994.

Pfister, Roger. *Internet for Africanists and Others Interested in Africa: An Introduction to the Internet and a Comprehensive Compilation of Relevant Addresses*. Bern: Swiss Society of African Studies; Basel: Basier Afrika Bibliographien, 1996.

Schmidt, Nancy J. "Africana Resources for Undergraduates: A Bibliographic Essay." In Phyllis M. Martin and Patrick O'Meara, eds., *Africa* (3rd ed.). Bloomington: Indiana University Press, 1995.

Witherell, Julian W., ed. *Africana Resources and Collections: Three Decades of Development and Achievement; A Festschrift in Honor of Hans Panofsky*. Metuchen: Scarecrow, 1992.

Zell, Hans M., and Cecile Lomer, eds. *The African Studies Companion: A Resource Guide and Directory*. London: Hans Zell, 1997.

NOTES

1. For a discussion, see Timothy M. Shaw and Catherine M. Newbury, "Dependence or Interdependence: Africa in the Global Political Economy," in Mark W. DeLancey, ed., *Aspects of International Relations in Africa* (Bloomington: Indiana University Press, 1979), pp. 39–89.

2. For example, see I. William Zartman, "Europe and Africa: Decolonization or Dependency?" *Foreign Affairs* 54 (1976): 325–43.

3. Ibid., pp. 326–27.

4. Michael Bratton and Nicolas van de Walle, *Democratic Transitions in Africa: Regime Transitions in Comparative Perspective* (Cambridge: Cambridge University Press, 1997).

5. For a more detailed discussion of this term, see Peter Vale and Sipho Maseko, "South Africa and the African Renaissance," *International Affairs* 74, no. 2 (1998): 271–88.

6. Claude Ake, "The Democratization of Disempowerment." Paper presented at a conference on democratization sponsored by the Transnational Institute, Cologne, Germany, November 13, 1993.

7. This paragraph was inspired by and draws upon an extremely insightful article written by Aili Marie Tripp, "The New Political Activism in Africa," *Journal of Democracy* 12, no. 3 (2001): 141–55.

8. See Peter J. Schraeder, *United States Foreign Policy toward Africa: Incrementalism, Crisis, and Change* (Cambridge: Cambridge University Press, 1994).

9. Ibid., Chapter 3, esp. pp. 53–80.

10. For a comprehensive overview, see Curtis A. Klein, *Mistaking Africa: Curiosities and Inventions of the American Mind* (Boulder: Westview Press, 1999).

11. Peter J. Schraeder and Brian Endless, "The Media and Africa: The Portrayal of Africa in *The New York Times* (1955–1995)," *Issue: A Journal of Opinion* 26, no. 2 (1998): 32.

12. For an example of this extreme view, see Robert D. Kaplan, "The Coming Anarchy," *The Atlantic Monthly* 273, no. 2 (1994): 44–76. See also Goran Hyden, "African Studies in the Mid-1990s: Between Afro-Pessimism and Americo-Skepticism," *African Studies Review* 39, no. 2 (1996): 1–17.

2

♔♔♔

Politics and Economics of the Precolonial Independence Era (Before 1884)

Queen Sylvia Nagginda Luswata and King Ronald Muwenda Mutebi of Buganda, the largest of five kingdoms in present-day Uganda, on their wedding day, August 27, 1999. "King Ronnie" was crowned kabaka (king) in 1993, and Queen Luswata, having lived in the United States for 18 years, is a graduate of New York University.

THE AFRICAN CONTINENT is the **cradle of humankind.** Archaeological findings have confirmed the emergence of modern *Homo sapiens* along the East African coast as early as 150,000 to 100,000 years ago.[1] Yet Western missionaries, soldiers of fortune, entrepreneurs, and colonial administrators dismissed such a possibility as heresy as late as the 1950s. An important corollary to this Eurocentric view was the denunciation of African civilizations as "primitive," "backward," and therefore "inferior" to the "superior" civilizations of Western Europe.[2] Nothing, however, could be further from the truth. The history of the precolonial independence era, the period that officially ended with the imposition of direct colonial rule in 1884–85, is rich with examples of political and economic sophistication. Although some of these political systems degenerated into authoritarianism and economic stagnation, others embodied the blossoming of democratic practices and economic expansion. Most political systems fell between these two extremes. A clear understanding of Africa's multifaceted past is an essential building block in understanding the challenges confronted by African leaders at the beginning of the twenty-first century.

SEGMENTED POLITICAL SYSTEMS

A rich mosaic of political systems existed during the precolonial independence era. One of the most difficult forms of African political organization for Westerners to understand is what anthropologists call a **segmented political system.** The term "segmented" refers to a decentralized system marked by the diffusion of political power. Segmented political systems lacked a centralized state and a recognized political authority capable of enforcing a preferred set of policies throughout a territory. Though political authority was diffuse, many communities were still nations in that community members often shared the same language, customs, and cultural history. The nation simply lacked a central political authority to which the members of that society owed allegiance. In short, a segmented system constituted a nation without a state. According to the work of Christian P. Potholm, there are at least five types of segmented political systems (see Figure 2.1).[3]

Band Organization

The most decentralized type of segmented political system in precolonial Africa was the **band organization.**[4] Sharing the same language, customs, and cultural history, the population was divided into small **hunter-gatherer groups** that ranged in size from several dozen people during times of plenty, to ten to twelve individuals during periods of economic hardship. The hunter-gatherer groups were principally comprised of members of an extended family and did not have any form of centralized political authority. Even political authority at the level of the band was neither formally structured nor permanently embodied in one person. Decisions were the result of a face-to-face decision-making process in which all adult males took part.

Band Organization   **Classical Segmented System**

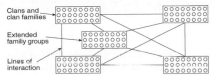

Universalistic Segmented System   **Ritually Stratified Segmented System**

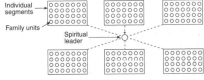

Autonomous Village System (City-State System)

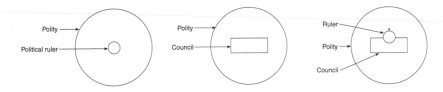

FIGURE 2.1 Segmented Political Systems

Source: Christian P. Potholm, *The Theory and Practice of African Politics* (Englewood Cliffs, NJ: Prentice-Hall, 1979), pp. 13–19.

The band organization was the dominant form of political organization approximately 30,000 years ago but is increasingly rare in Africa today. One of the most notable examples was the San people, who currently make up a very small portion of the populations of Namibia and Botswana.[5] This hunter-gatherer people is often derogatorily referred to in the West as the "Bushmen" of Southern Africa. The Tswana of Botswana also denigrate the San as *Basarwa:* "people from the sticks." The San became better known in the West as a result of their depiction in a popular movie, *The Gods Must Be Crazy,* and their unique use of a "click" language that is spoken through a series of clicks formed by moving the tongue against the teeth and palate. According to recent estimates, fewer than 1,000 San maintain their traditional hunter-gatherer lifestyles in the Kalahari Desert.

Classical Segmented System

The second type of decentralized political authority was the **classical segmented system.**[6] This system differed from the band organization principally in terms of the size and scope of the distinctive groups that composed the common nation. Individual groups based on kinship, often called "clans," could number in the tens or hundreds of thousands and could trace their common lineages back thousands of years to specific founding members. The size of the clan ensured that more formal forms of leadership, often a group of leaders or a committee of elders, emerged to manage clan affairs, although no central authority ever evolved. Classical segmented systems typically fostered competition and conflict between extended clan families, especially in nomadic environments when drought and famine diminished already scarce water and food resources.

The Somali ethnic group constituted an excellent example of the classical segmented system.[7] The approximately 6 million Somalis who inhabited the Horn of Africa spoke the same language (Somali), adhered to the same religion (Islam), and shared a common cultural past, but they were divided according to at least six major clan families: Daarood, Dir, Hawiye, Isaaq, Digil, and Rahanweyn. These clan families were subdivided into smaller units that assumed responsibility for organizing social, economic, and political activities. The smallest group, known as the *reer* (nomadic hamlet), ranged in size from five to fifty Somali families, and the largest, the clan, often included thousands or tens of thousands of members. The cornerstone of Somali political life was clan adherence to this maxim: "There are no permanent clan friends or enemies, only permanent clan self-interests." The precolonial history of Somali politics is therefore best described by the rise and fall of clan alliances in the absence of any central government, resulting in alternating periods of peaceful competition and clan warfare (see the accompanying box).

A Closer Look: THE ISSA *XEER*: REGULATING CONFLICT IN SEGMENTARY SOCIETIES

Many people mistakenly assume that the lack of a centralized state or political authority in segmented societies fostered unending and unresolvable conflicts during the precolonial independence era. Nothing could be further from the truth. Among the Somalis of the Horn of Africa, a complex system of conflict resolution was based on the payment of *dia* (literally, "blood payments"). The nomadic-pastoral tradition of the Somalis ensured that *dia* was normally paid in livestock. The amount paid to the injured party was based on tradition and decided by the elders of the parties to the conflict.

The Issa clan of the Somalis main-tained one of the strictest and most detailed forms of *dia,* known as the Issa *xeer*. According to a renowned Djiboutian scholar, Ali Moussa Iye, the *xeer* served as the base of Issa pastoral democracy and resembled Jean-Jacques Rousseau's notion of the "social contract." The *xeer* clearly outlined the exact compensations to be paid to victims and included specific livestock "exchange rates" depending on the type of animal to be used in payment (see Tables 2.1 and 2.2). The *xeer* not only played an important role in preventing conflict within and between clans, it served as an important peacemaking device once conflict broke out.

Table 2.1   Compensation for Permanent Injuries to Men

BODY PART	AFFECTED PORTION OF BODY PART	COMPENSATION (Number of Camels)
Right Leg	Entire	15.0
	Foot	5.0
Left Leg	Entire	16.0
	Foot	5.0
Right Ear	Entire	1.0
Left Ear	Entire	1.0
Teeth	One Upper Incisor	2.5
	One Lower Incisor	2.5
Back	Permanent Injury Not Affecting Procreation	50.0
	Spinal Cord Injury Affecting Procreation	100.0
Right Arm	Entire	15.0
Left Arm	Entire	16.0
	Hand	5.0
	Forearm	5.0
Right Eye	Injured Pupil	14.0
	Punctured Pupil	15.0
Left Eye	Injured Pupil	15.0
	Punctured Pupil	16.0

Table 2.2   Exchange Rates for Compensation (in Livestock)

TYPE OF LIVESTOCK	AGE	EQUIVALENT (in Lambs)
Large Livestock		
Male Camel	1 year	3.0
	2 years	6.0
	3 years	9.0
	4 years +	14.0
Female Camel	1 year	3.0
	2 years	6.0
	3 years	9.0
	4 years +	12.0
Cow	1–4 years	6.0
Bull	1–4 years	4.0
Small Livestock		
Goat	Adult	0.5
Sheep	1 year	1.0
	3 years +	2.0
Other Domesticated Animals		
Female Donkey	Adult	6.0
Male Donkey	Adult	4.0
Female Horse	Adult	30.0
Male Horse	Adult	72.0
Mule	Adult	4.0

Tables and discussion adapted from Ali Moussa Iye, *Le Verdict de l'Arbre: Le Xeer Issa; Étude d'une Démocratie Pastorale*, Dubai, p. 176.

Universalistic Segmented System

The **universalistic segmented system** constituted a slightly more centralized version of the classical segmented system.[8] Despite the continued lack of
any central authority, the members of various clan families were more closely
unified by the existence of **age-grade systems** in which the period within
which an individual was born was more important than and therefore transcended clan affiliation. Age-grade systems were composed of specific **age-sets,**
which differentiated groups of different ages. Age-set status applied regardless
of the clan into which one was born and allowed for a more systematic organization of the social, economic, and political affairs of the nation as a whole. In
an age-grade system based on 5-year blocks of time, for example, a new age-set
was created every 5 years. Everyone born during that period would constitute a
member of the group. These age-sets predetermined an individual's assumption
of various responsibilities within society, ranging from militarily defending the
nation through the attainment of warrior status to entering the ranks of senior
political leader or senior elder. The underlying assumption of the age-set system was that different groups of individuals are better suited for specific tasks at
different ages in their lives.

The Maasai ethnic group was one of the most renowned examples of a
universalistic segmented system.[9] Revered for their military and hunting
prowess and distinguished by their deep red garments and ocher-colored hair,
the Maasai today number approximately 300,000 and straddle the Kenyan-
Tanzanian border. The precolonial clans of the Maasai were joined by a complex age-set system for males that began when a young Maasai was circumcised
between ages 13 and 17. From that point forward, the age-set determined
when the newest elite group of *moran* (warrior-recruits) would become junior
warriors and subsequently graduate to the rank of senior warriors in the prestigious *eunoto* (graduation) ceremony. The *moran* period lasted approximately
7 years. This period of a young Maasai's life was rivaled in importance only by
his eventual assumption of senior elder status.

Ritually Stratified Segmented System

The **ritually stratified segmented system** constituted a variation of its classical counterpart in that otherwise independent clans were unified in the spiritual realm by a commonly revered spiritual or religious leader.[10] It is important
to note that such leaders served primarily as symbols of national unity, with
duties usually restricted to presiding over religious ceremonies. They wielded
very little, if any, political power, and were incapable of forcing recalcitrant
clans or subclans to adopt specific courses of action. The religious and spiritual
leaders often used their possession of sacred objects as the means of achieving
and maintaining their special status within society.

The Shilluk people of Sudan represented a ritually stratified segmented system.[11] The symbolic head of the Shilluk nation was the *reth* (divine king). The
reth served as the embodiment of the spirit of *Nyikang,* a mythical savior who
conquered a new homeland for his people that was subsequently divided

among the various Shilluk clans. The *reth* enjoyed no formal authority over the Shilluk clans. He was a ritual leader who, in the words of anthropologist E. E. Evans-Pritchard, "reigned but did not govern."[12] The *reth* was responsible for guarding the "sacred spears" of *Nyikang* and making animal sacrifices to seek rain during drought and to celebrate victories in wartime. Although the sacred nature of his position ensured that the *reth* enjoyed significant powers of persuasion, he nonetheless lacked the formal political power necessary to impose his will on highly independent clans.

Autonomous Village System

As demonstrated in the previous four examples, most segmented societies were largely nomadic or seminomadic; their peoples followed **transhumance** patterns in which the pursuit of food, water, and grazing lands for livestock were predetermined by seasonal changes in weather patterns. In the **autonomous village system,** however, urbanized groups sometimes ranging in the thousands and tens of thousands served as the cornerstones of local political organization.[13] Despite sharing the same language and culture, the populations of these highly autonomous villages were not unified by a central political authority or a centralized state. In some cases, these urban areas constituted virtual **city-states,** similar to the Italian city-state system of the Renaissance era. As opposed to its autonomous village counterpart, the population of the city-state was not always ethnically homogeneous. Most important, individual city-states enjoyed varying forms of centralized rule, ranging from despotic rulers to more democratic city councils. All these varied forms of the city-state system belong under the broad category of segmented political system, because the city-states as a whole were not controlled by a central authority.

A renowned example of an African city-state system existed along the Swahili coast of East Africa. At the beginning of the fifteenth century, a vast network of Swahili city-states dotted the coastline from Mogadishu, the capital of present-day Somalia, to the southern city of Kilwa Kisiwani in present-day Tanzania.[14] A flourishing Indian Ocean trade network in slaves, gold, and spices fueled the rise of these city-states and particularly favored the geographically well-situated islands of Zanzibar, Pemba, and the Lamu Archipelago. The golden age of this system, roughly the first half of the fifteenth century, witnessed rising economic and political competition between city-states that had never succumbed to centralized political rule. These city-states nonetheless shared an overarching Swahili culture that included a common religion (Islam) and language (Kiswahili), as well as a social system dominated by an elite of Arab and Persian descent.

CENTRALIZED POLITICAL SYSTEMS

The diversity of segmented political systems was complemented by an equally rich number of **centralized political systems.** This type of political system corresponds to what Westerners consider to be the "normal" form of political organization: a political authority controls a centralized state that can uniformly apply policies throughout a given territory, and the inhabitants of this political system owe their allegiance to the state. This broad category of political system encompasses what Westerners commonly call the **nation–state.** In its purest form, the nation–state consists of one central authority (the state) and one ethnic group (the nation). In practice, however, most centralized political systems of the precolonial independence era were multiethnic, although one ethnic group often dominated. Drawing upon Christian P. Potholm's work, one can distinguish three specific types of centralized political systems (see Figure 2.2).

Pyramidal Monarchy

A common form of centralized political system was the **pyramidal monarchy.**[15] Unlike its segmented counterparts, the pyramidal monarchy had a centralized authority in control of a centralized state and capable of enforcing its will throughout the nation. The system was nonetheless pyramidal in that the king, despite his position at the top of the political pyramid, did not wield absolute control over his kingdom. Instead, the political culture of the pyramidal monarchy dictated that nonroyal clans and other ethnic groups enjoyed var-

Pyramidal Monarchy

Associational Monarchy   **Centralized Monarchy**

FIGURE 2.2   Centralized Political Systems

Source: Christian P. Potholm, *The Theory and Practice of African Politics* (Englewood Cliffs, NJ: Prentice-Hall, 1979), pp. 20–22.

ious degrees of autonomy from central government control, most notably in terms of their ability to raise their own taxes. The pyramidal monarchy therefore embodied a federal form of government similar to that of the United States, in which federal power is counterbalanced by the existence of fifty autonomous states. Most important, the political powers of the kingdom's subgroups were usually formalized through the creation of some type of royal council, which included leaders from the nonroyal clans and other ethnic groups. The royal council often served as an important source of countervailing power, similar to the U.S. model of "checks-and-balances" between the executive and legislative branches of government.

The Oyo empire of the Yoruba people of present-day Nigeria reached its height during the eighteenth century and is one of the best-documented examples of a pyramidal monarchy.[16] The original Oyo kingdom and its spiritual city of Ile Ife served as the cornerstones of an empire that ruled over other Yoruba kingdoms, as well as various neighboring political systems controlled by non-Yoruba ethnic groups. The empire was headed by a sacred leader (the Alafin) drawn from the royal lineage of Yoruba kings *(obas)* and a royal council (the Oyo Mesi), also known as the Council of Seven Notables (a reference to the heads of the seven most important nonroyal lineages). An interesting set of checks-and-balances existed between these two bodies of government. The Alafin enjoyed several formal powers, such as the appointment of provincial governors and the ability to declare war, in addition to an equally important set of informal powers, such as public persuasion, which grew out of the sacred nature of his office. The Oyo Mesi likewise enjoyed numerous formal powers: the selection of the Alafin's successor from a list provided by the royal clan in the case of death or incapacitation; control over the process for choosing the *Bashorun,* the supreme Yoruba military leader who was drawn from the ranks of the royal council; and, most important, the ability to impeach the Alafin should he stray too far from the accepted norms of Yoruba culture. As a result, a "delicate balance of power" existed between the two branches of government that fostered the maintenance of a relatively democratic society.[17]

Associational Monarchy

The second type of centralized political system was the **associational monarchy.**[18] The associational monarchy was similar to its pyramidal counterpart in all respects, most notably in terms of maintaining a federal system in which nonroyal clans and other ethnic groups enjoyed a certain measure of autonomy from the central authority. The unique aspect of the associational monarchy was the existence of "associational" groups that transcended individual clan or ethnic attachments. These groups served as intermediaries between local villages and the central authorities and were often responsible for important duties, such as the collection of taxes within the political system. An important outcome of the existence of these associational groups was the further integration of the political system. Membership was highly prized as it provided opportunity to make contacts beyond one's own clan or ethnic group in the pursuit of economic or political gain.

The Mende people of Sierra Leone provides an interesting example of an associational monarchy.[19] A unique aspect of this political system was the widespread adherence to **secret societies,** known as the Poro society for men and the Sande society for women. Members were sworn to secrecy concerning the rites of passage. These societies transcended individual clan groups within Mende society and served both social and political functions. The most important social goal was the promotion of "socially acceptable behavior—womanly character and virtue, codes of male honor, or rules of public conduct on which there was common agreement as the ethical foundations for a healthy society."[20] Political functions of the secret societies ranged from wielding influence over central authorities on policy matters to grooming eventual leaders with strong ties to the Poro and Sande societies.

Centralized Monarchy

The **centralized monarchy** was potentially the most authoritarian of the centralized political systems.[21] The most influential figure of what is also called a **hierarchical political system** was a king to whom all within society were required to pledge their direct allegiance. The royal council, if one existed, was composed of representatives directly chosen by the king and was less likely to serve as a check on royal power than was the case in the pyramidal or associational monarchies. The political system was based on a very strong central authority that allowed little, if any, autonomy for nonroyal clans or other ethnic groups. These groups were unified by an age-set system that was completely loyal to the king. Other ethnic groups were readily absorbed into the political system when neighboring territories were conquered. The basis of citizenship was neither clan nor ethnic ties but an individual's willingness to swear complete loyalty to the king.

The Zulu empire under the leadership of Shaka Zulu at the beginning of the nineteenth century is one of the most famous centralized monarchies.[22] The reign of Shaka is widely renowned for his creation of a militaristic Zulu empire that expanded its authority by conquering neighboring peoples and absorbing their warriors into the national army. Warriors refusing to pledge direct allegiance to Shaka's rule were put to death on the battlefield. The national army was designed around a series of military-oriented age-sets and successfully used military innovations such as *assegais* (short spears) on the battlefield. A standing national army and a militaristic ethic fostered a sense of unity that was strongly tied to Shaka's personal rule. As a result, the royal council and the heads of nonroyal clans constituted mere figureheads in a system that revolved around the Zulu king. Shaka's roughly 10-year reign was cut short in 1928 when he was assassinated by his half-brother, Dingane. **Regicide,** the murder of the king, was a common form of succession in highly centralized and authoritarian political systems, such as the Zulu empire under Shaka.

ECONOMIC SYSTEMS AND TRADE

Three major types of economies existed during the precolonial independence era. The first and earliest form of economic practice involved the continual search for food and water in the hunter-gatherer societies, such as the afore-mentioned San people of Namibia and Botswana. The activities of these groups ranged from foraging for fruits and edible roots to hunting for wild animals. The success of these very mobile groups depended on a sophisticated understanding of the relationship between the environment and food sources. The hunter-gatherer had to understand how the changing seasons affected not only the migration patterns of hunted animals but the availability of specific types of fruits or edible roots in different regions. Once the dominant form of economic organization, the hunter-gatherer societies experienced a sharp decline by the middle of the nineteenth century as civilizations increasingly became based on the domestication of animals and/or the cultivation of crops.

A second form of economic system, **pastoral nomadism,** was based on the domestication and ownership of animals, most notably camels, cattle, sheep, and goats. The pastoral nomadic societies relied upon their herds as their primary sources of nutrition. Like hunter-gatherers, they were highly mobile out of necessity. The constant search for food and water to nourish their animals often led to a particular animal serving as the centerpiece of their social status and customs.

Western scholars historically perceived pastoral nomadism as a highly irrational way of living, in which the nomad contended with extremely harsh environmental conditions simply to achieve basic, subsistence-level needs. This stereotypical image of nomadic irrationality and obscurantism is clearly incorrect. As argued by I. M. Lewis, a noted observer of pastoral societies, the pastoral tradition in reality constituted a rational response to changing, and often deteriorating, environmental and economic conditions within marginal societies. The successful pastoralist required an "impressive knowledge of the faunal resources of his environment and his adjustment of herd movements to secure the best grazing and watering conditions which [were] accessible to him."[23]

An excellent example of a pastoral society was the Somalis of the Horn of Africa. Somali pastoralists shared a common nomadic tradition that placed great value on livestock, virtues of bravery and individualism, adherence to the Islamic faith, and an oral tradition that held singers and poets in high esteem. The camel was the mainstay of the economy, and a man's wealth was judged by the number of camels he owned.[24] The male camel was the primary means of transport, carrying the Somali *geer* (pastoral home) and goods for local and long-distance trade and was also sometimes used for riding purposes. The female camel was the source of milk, one of the primary sources of nutrition for Somali nomads, and especially honored for her reproductive capacity. Other animals, such as cattle and goats, were also raised as important sources of milk and meat.

The third and most prevalent form of economic practice during the precolonial independence era revolved around the cultivation of food crops.

Agriculturally based societies depended on sedentary farmers who tilled the land season after season within a specific region. Sometimes pastoralism and agricultural practices were combined within one economy known as **agro-pastoralism.** Under such an arrangement, some of the farmers who tended crops during the growing season would move with the society's herds during the dry season. By the nineteenth century, however, agriculturally based economies represented the dominant form of economic organization. Many farmers typically practiced the **slash-and-burn technique,** due to the generally poor quality of African soils and the wide availability of land.[25] According to this technique, a patch of land was cleared by burning and seeds were planted in the mounds of fertile ashes. When the soil became less productive after 2 or 3 years, a new area of land was cleared through fire and the process would begin again.

The degree to which a particular precolonial political system could depend on the cultivation of food crops by sedentary farmers significantly influenced a society's prospects for economic growth and political expansion. In the case of the Oyo empire, a strong agricultural base capable of yielding agricultural surpluses allowed for the creation of large armies, including highly trained cavalry units. Self-sufficiency in food also ensured that soldiers were not dependent on pillaging local communities to sustain themselves on the battlefield. Food was carried into the field, with some armies capable of sending their troops with up to 3 weeks of provisions. In the case of the Oyo empire, surpluses allowed Yoruba soldiers to carry a combination of "parched beans and a special kind of hard bread made of beans and maize flour."[26]

Surpluses were also critical to the development of regional trade. One broad type of trading pattern is best described as **subsistence-oriented trade.**[27] This form of trade primarily, though not exclusively, revolved around the exchange of foodstuffs and other agricultural products. An impressive example of a subsistence-oriented trade network was maintained by the Tonga people of present-day Zambia. In addition to trading foodstuffs among themselves, the Tonga exchanged at least thirty different goods with ten neighboring ethnic groups over distances up to 300 miles.[28] The cornerstone of this largely regional trade was the import of various iron implements, such as hoes and spear blades in exchange for Tonga salt, a valuable commodity for food preservation. Although the Tonga were familiar with the procedures for creating iron implements, iron ore deposits were nonexistent in Tonga territory and therefore hindered the rise of a local iron-making industry.[29] Aside from a reliance on imported iron implements, the Tonga trade system remained largely focused on the subsistence economy. This tendency was demonstrated by the seasonal nature of Tonga trade. Rather than promoting a permanent trading economy in which goods were constantly imported and traded, the Tonga system was highly seasonal in that it largely took place during the postharvest dry season.[30]

A second trading pattern that existed during the precolonial independence era was **market-oriented trade,** which differed from subsistence trade in that luxury goods were often traded over long distances.[31] Permanent marketplaces and professionals who both created and responded to local demands for various

---

A Closer Look: GREAT ZIMBABWE

The awe-inspiring complex of stone walls and buildings known as the Great Zimbabwe is one of the most magnificent archaeological sites in southern Africa. The centerpiece of this site is the "Great Enclosure," a circular area approximately 255 meters in circumference in which walls up to 5 meters thick rise to heights approaching 11 meters. The stone bricks were cut by hand and fit together without mortar to create one of Africa's oldest and most impressive stone structures, which dates back to the thirteenth century.

The term *Zimbabwe* is derivative of one of two words from the Shona language, *dzimba dza mabwe* (houses of stone) or *dzimba woye* (venerated houses), and serves as the proud name of the present-day country of Zimbabwe that emerged from white-minority rule in 1980. Even as late as 1980, former colonists and the white leadership of Rhodesia, the precursor to independent Zimbabwe, refused to recognize the possibility that an ancient African culture was responsible for building the stone structures at the Great Zimbabwe. Some even went to great pains to suggest that builders from non-African civilizations, such as the Phoenicians or the ancient Greeks, were responsible for the stone structures.

An increasingly rich array of archaeological and historical evidence clearly demonstrates that the Great Zimbabwe was the center of a thriving Shona empire that lasted over 200 years. The domestic economy was based on agriculture and cattle raising. A vigorous coastal trade in gold from mines in Leopard's Kopje, near the present-day Zimbabwean city of Bulawayo, was at the heart of the empire. The royal leadership of the Great Zimbabwe is thought to have controlled a vast territory where the ruins of approximately 150 smaller stone enclosures may be found. At its height, the Great Zimbabwe is believed to have housed approximately 11,000 people.

Historians still disagree as to what led to the decline of the Shona empire in the mid-fifteenth century and the subsequent abandonment of the Great Zimbabwe site. Some argue that the move was forced by the depletion of local resources by a rapidly increasing population. Others argue that the true culprit was the loss of control over the gold trade, which led to economic impoverishment. Regardless of the reasons for its ultimate decline, the Great Zimbabwe monument serves as a testament to the ingenuity and prosperity of political systems during the precolonial independence era.

Discussion drawn from Peter S. Garlake, *Great Zimbabwe* (London: Thames and Hudson, 1973). See also S. I. G. Mudenge, *A Political History of Munhumutapa c. 1400–1902* (Harare: Zimbabwe Publishing House, 1988).

---

types of goods and services were the cornerstones of this economic system. These trading practices at times tremendously affected the social and economic norms of a given society. As a result, market-oriented trade played an important role in the rise and decline of local political systems.

One of the largest and most sophisticated market-oriented trading systems was the **trans–Saharan trade network** (see Map 2.1).[32] As early as 1000 BCE, the diverse political systems of West Africa were trading with North African kingdoms that shipped goods to and from the Middle East and Europe. As its

MAP 2.1   Trans-Saharan Trade Network (Eleventh to Sixteenth Centuries)

Source: Map based on Michael Kwamena-Poh et al., *Africa History in Maps* (Essex: Longman, 1987), p. 11.

name suggests, this trading system extended throughout the Sahara desert, an expanse of 3,320,000 square miles. "If you traveled across the United States from Boston to San Diego, you still wouldn't have crossed the Sahara," explain Marq de Villiers and Sheila Hirtle in a captivating history of this region, "and if you started from Paris you'd be at the Urals, deep into Russia, long before you ran out of Sahara."[33]

The mention of the Sahara desert among Americans conjures preconceived notions of a vast, desolate, inhospitable, and unpenetrable barrier that separates North Africa from all other regions of Sub-Saharan Africa. Nothing could be further from the truth, especially for the nomadic peoples who live in the region (see Map 2.2). "This may seem like the end of the earth to you [Westerners], but it is not for us," explains Ibrahim Salam Bouseif, a guerrilla fighter within the region. "We can see forever. We can cast our eyes to the horizon, and all we

MAP 2.2   Areas of Saharan Nomads in the Contemporary Era

Source: Map based on Marq de Villiers and Sheila Hirtle, *Sahara: A Natural History* (New York: Walker & Company, 2002).

can see is sand and sky. In the desert our spirits can fly."[34] This view, which perceives the desert's "austerity" as "merely a framework within which to imagine a larger life,"[35] is not surprisingly imbued with Islamic overtones due to the pervasiveness of Islam in the region. "As the desert saying goes, 'Allah removed all surplus human and animal life from the desert so that there might be one place for him to walk in peace . . . and so the Great Sahara is called the Garden of Allah.'"[36]

Especially when the trans-Saharan trade network was at its height during the precolonial independence era, traders and inhabitants viewed the Sahara desert as an ocean that, like the seven seas, could be crossed relatively easily with the proper preparations and vessels. As a result, the trans-Saharan network included various "ports of call" that developed into flourishing cities and allowed caravans of camels and traders to replenish supplies. Trans-Saharan trade not only was flourishing by the middle of the nineteenth century, its financial value had exceeded estimates for all comparable periods before and including the so-called "golden age" of the network during the sixteenth century.

The types of goods capable of being transported along the trans-Saharan trade network were limited by two factors.[37] The journey across the Sahara desert usually lasted between 70 and 90 days, with the caravans averaging 30 to 45 kilometers per day. Perishable items, such as foodstuffs, were clearly unsuitable for such a long journey. A second limiting factor involved the weight of the products shipped. Although caravans of two thousand camels could carry upwards of 300 tons of goods, including supplies to be consumed during the trip, merchandise nonetheless needed to have a "high value/low weight" ratio.[38] Freight charges alone often inflated the final cost of goods by 100 to 150 percent. Prices were further inflated if goods were lost, stolen, or exchanged for other services. The most profitable caravans therefore carried highly precious cargoes that weighed very little.

One category of merchandise, **state necessities,** was often essential to the pursuit of political power.[39] The state necessities sent northward included gold and slaves. Gold served as an important currency in Europe and the Middle East, and slaves served as soldiers or a form of cheap labor (see Chapter 3). The state necessities sent southward included cowry shells and weapons, most notably guns and swords. The cowry shells served as an important form of currency in West Africa, and weapons were sought to enhance both the defensive and the offensive capabilities of political systems. The trans-Saharan network also specialized in the trade of **luxury goods.**[40] The northern-bound luxury goods included ivory, leather goods, and ostrich feathers, as well as easily preserved foodstuffs, such as pepper and kola nuts. The southern-bound goods included cloths, copper, glassware, and decorative beads.

The vast economic reach of the trans-Saharan network contributed to the rise of four types of trading centers (see Map 2.1).[41] A series of **southern terminals** existed at the southern fringes of the Sahara desert, where northern-bound goods were packed onto camel caravans and southern-bound goods were unpacked for distribution among the political systems of West Africa. A number of **desert oases** served as important rest areas for weary travelers where water and food supplies could be replenished. On the northern fringes of the desert were the **northern terminals.** These cities served as the unpacking areas for northern-bound goods and the packing areas for southern-bound goods. Guides, provisions, guards, and camels were generally hired at both the northern and the southern terminals. Finally, a series of **northern coastal cities** oversaw the shipping of goods to and from Europe and the Middle East. A typical caravan might have begun in the southern terminal of Timbuktu, followed by an extended stop in the desert oasis of Ghat before arriving in the northern terminal of Ghadames. After the goods were unloaded from the caravan, they would eventually make their way to the coastal city of Tripoli for transport across the Mediterranean to the Middle East.

The trans-Saharan network constituted but one example of flourishing African trade that gradually integrated various regional economies into highly sophisticated trading relationships. Political systems of both the segmented and centralized varieties played important roles in these trading networks. Although much regional variation obviously existed, the African continent by the middle of the nineteenth century was creating the basis for integrated, sustainable development. This development built on African political and economic strengths and provided the basis for international relationships spanning the globe.

DIPLOMACY AND WARFARE

Both the segmented and centralized political systems maintained impressive arrays of foreign relations within their respective regions. Although diplomatic practices tended to be more formal when conducted by centralized monarchies, decentralized political systems nonetheless faced the same challenges of maintaining peaceful relationships with neighboring ethnic groups. When such efforts failed, or were met with confrontation, wars often broke out and required a diplomatic response, regardless of whether handled by clan elders within a classical segmented system or the reigning monarch of a centralized monarchy.

The case study of West Africa clearly demonstrates the existence of sophisticated diplomatic practices during the precolonial independence era that in many respects are similar to those at the beginning of the twenty-first century.[42] First, the dispatch of diplomats to neighboring political systems was extremely common. Often called "messengers," "linguists," or "heralds," these individuals sometimes lived as resident diplomats in neighboring political systems. Unlike contemporary diplomats who work in elaborate embassies that may employ hundreds of workers, the resident diplomats usually served as the sole representatives of their peoples.

African diplomats also carried diplomatic credentials or "badges of office." Whereas all present-day diplomats carry special diplomatic passports, their precolonial African counterparts carried various culturally significant credentials that included canes, staffs, whistles, fans, batons, and swords. Representatives of the Asante kingdom of present-day Ghana carried a diplomatic staff. The staff was topped by the figure of a hand holding an egg. This image was designed to "convey the warning that neither the king nor his representative should press a matter too hard nor treat it too lightly."[43] Regardless of culture or the period in which they lived, few, if any, diplomats would question the diplomatic message portrayed by the Asante staff's image.

A third similarity with current diplomatic practices was the observance of diplomatic protocol and etiquette. For example, it was not uncommon for African diplomats to enjoy diplomatic immunity (freedom from political harassment or persecution by local authorities). This practice was also an extension of the traditional African custom of warmly welcoming strangers in their midst. Another example of diplomatic protocol and etiquette was the tendency of African kings "to converse only indirectly with their visitors and subjects."[44] What was often intended as a sign of respect and courtesy inevitably ensured a prominent role for diplomatic intermediaries, especially those who were knowledgeable about foreign languages and practices.

A final example of diplomacy that resonates with the contemporary era revolves around the "deliberate" and "tortuous" pace of diplomatic negotiations.[45] The extensive use of public flattery and gift giving, most notably intricately woven cloths, were integral aspects of such negotiations. One custom, still popular in West Africa, is the tradition of beginning or ending negotiations with the mutual breaking and eating of kola nuts. Available throughout West

Africa, the kola nut is a stimulant and allows discussants to stay awake during extended periods of negotiations that sometimes last throughout the night. The kola nut, a symbol of West African hospitality, is broken into an equivalent number of pieces and shared among the participants attending the meeting.

The diplomatic network established by the Oyo empire during the eighteenth century offers important insights into the diplomatic practices of the precolonial independence era. The core of the empire consisted of the spiritual center of Ile Ife and the original Oyo kingdom led by the Alafin and the Oyo Mesi. The remainder of the empire was established by the Alafin and other political leaders as a series of concentric circles, in which those closest to the center were most closely tied to and dependent on the political favor of the Alafin; conversely, the further one ventured from Oyo and Ile Ife, the greater the independence of the local political leaders.

Four concentric circles of power roughly captured the diplomatic relations of the Oyo empire. The first circle consisted of Yoruba kingdoms, which owed direct allegiance to the Alafin due to the sharing of direct blood ties. These kingdoms were usually directly administered by Oyo. The second circle also consisted of Yoruba kingdoms, whose leaders recognized the authority of the Alafin. The lack of direct blood ties, however, ensured that the leaders of these kingdoms enjoyed some degree of political autonomy from the center. A third circle was composed of **suzerain kingdoms** that, although not inhabited by the Yoruba people, recognized the authority of the Alafin as the most influential leader within the region. A final circle consisted of largely independent political systems, such as the Nupe in the northeast, over which the Alafin had little or no influence.

The empire's citizens were divided into two basic categories: free and unfree. Free citizens were individuals who, depending on their clan or ethnicity, were more or less influential in the affairs of the empire. The most influential free subjects were members of the royal clan, followed by individuals of Yoruba descent and, finally, non-Yoruba ethnic groups. Unfree subjects included individuals who voluntarily submitted themselves or another member of their family to *iwofa* status: a temporary form of indentured servitude similar to that practiced in the American colonies during the eighteenth century. Once the debt that required *iwofa* status was repaid, the individual became a free person. The Oyo empire also included large numbers of slaves, often taken from enemy kingdoms that were defeated during wartime, who were "usually employed as farm laborers or servants in households, as bodyguards to the chiefs, and as long-distance traders *(alajapa)*."[46]

The administration of the Oyo empire was based on indirect rule. The Alafin exercised his authority by accrediting resident officials known as *agele* (also called *asoju oba*—"the eyes of the king"), who in turn were supervised by royal messengers known as the *ilari*. These resident officials were responsible for overseeing the **tribute** or payments to be made by subordinate towns and kingdoms in recognition of their submission to the empire. For example, in 1748 the king of the Abomey kingdom agreed to pay a yearly tribute of "forty men, forty women, forty guns, and forty loads of cowries and corals" after the defeat of his kingdom's forces in a series of military engagements with the Oyo.[47] The Alafin also exchanged gifts with the leaders of friendly neighboring kingdoms who were not under the control of the Oyo empire. In these cases, the provision of tribute represented a relationship of mutual respect.

The successful expansion of the Oyo empire promoted a vigorous "guns-or-butter" debate: Should the empire's resources be devoted to military preparation for further expansion, or should leaders concentrate on the economic development of those territories already conquered? From 1754 to 1774, the Alafin emerged as a voice of moderation, advocating for economic consolidation. The Bashorun (Secretary of Defense), however, promoted further military expansionism.[48] This period was marked by an intense power struggle between the office of the Alafin and the Bashorun, which ultimately favored the rise to power of an authoritarian Bashorun at the expense of the traditionally powerful and prestigious Alafin. The upsetting of this delicate balance between the office of the Alafin and the Oyo Mesi (royal council) signified the beginning of the decline of the Oyo empire and its ultimate replacement by what became known as the Ibadan empire.

The evolution of the "guns–or–butter" debate within the Oyo empire has important implications for understanding the regional diplomatic practices of African empires. First, warfare served as an important dimension of foreign relations. Unlike current international norms that make wars exceptional events, the norms of the precolonial independence era ensured that warfare was more frequent and understood by African leaders as a legitimate tool of foreign policy. During the eighteenth century, for example, the leaders of the Oyo empire pursued war as an "annual or biannual exercise."[49] War was also undertaken to satisfy both political and economic goals. The classic political rationales for launching attacks against neighbors ranged from placing more territory under the direct administration of the empire to demonstrating the military capabilities of the empire to other kingdoms and outside powers. Economic factors also played an important role in military calculations. A successful military campaign increased control over external markets to which goods could be sold, raised the levels of tribute to be received from newly subjugated kingdoms, and ensured that greater numbers of slaves could be put to work within the empire and sold to outside powers.

At the heart of territorial expansion, however, was the maintenance of a dynamic political center that was capable of marshalling economic and military forces. In the case of the Oyo empire, the rules and regulations surrounding the selection of a new Alafin constituted an elaborate system of checks-and-balances that fostered political dynamism. When an Alafin died or was deposed, the elders of the royal lineage made up a list of potential replacements. The prospects had to be of royal lineage, born to a free woman and not a slave, and without physical blemish. The Oyo Mesi then chose the new Alafin from the royal list. The royal council had an obvious interest in curtailing the future Alafin's power by selecting a candidate who would best adhere to the constitutional conventions of the kingdom and who did not have too commanding of a personality and therefore would not usurp or overshadow the power of the

Oyo Mesi. The delicate balance maintained by this selection process had a tremendous impact on diplomacy within the empire. As previously mentioned, the disruption of this delicate balance in the mid-eighteenth century served as an important factor in the eventual decline of the Oyo empire.

WOMEN AND GENDER

No examination of African politics and society during the precolonial independence era would be complete without an analysis of the role of African women and gender relations.[50] In the social realm, African women were honored first and foremost for their reproductive capabilities.[51] According to April Gordon, a sociologist, African societies placed a high premium on children as a source of wealth, as a guarantee of security in old age, and as an assurance that one would be "venerated as an ancestor" after death and therefore never forgotten. "These vital roles," explains Gordon, "were normally translated into high status for women and more autonomy than was typical for women in most regions of the world."[52] The pivotal reproductive role of the woman explains why **bridewealth**—money or something of high monetary value, such as cattle—was typically paid by the groom's family to that of the bride as part of the marriage of the two families. Unlike in other societies, such as in India or the United States, where tradition calls on the bride's family to offer a dowry, whether in the form of a payment or in assuming the costs of the wedding, bridewealth in African societies was intended to compensate the bride's family for the loss of a daughter's potential labor, not to mention that of the children she would bear for the family.

One of the most widespread and misunderstood social practices during the precolonial independence era was **polygamy,** a situation in which one is married to several spouses simultaneously. In fact, polygamy takes on two specific forms: **polyandry,** in which the woman takes two or more husbands, and **polygyny,** in which the man takes two or more wives. Only the latter was standard throughout African societies. In African political systems that adopted Islam, for example, Islamic strictures allowed men to marry up to four wives. In many African societies, the number of allowable wives was even higher, especially for kings for whom the number of wives and children served as a symbol of power. It was not uncommon for African chiefs and kings to have several hundred and, in some cases, several thousand wives.[53] In sharp contrast to Western societies, however, polygyny was widely accepted among both African men and women during the precolonial independence era. "Often misunderstood by Europeans as a sign of low status, polygyny is more accurately indicative of the centrality of women to the well-being of the family," explains Gordon. "Additional wives helped each other with tasks, provided companionship (often lacking with husbands), and gave pregnant, nursing, or older women a needed respite from the sexual demands of their husbands."[54]

African women also played an important role in the economics of African societies during the precolonial independence era. They typically hauled water and wood, grew most of the family food, and prepared the family meals. They also fashioned tools, helped construct the family home, and played an influential role in local trade networks.[55] African women also enjoyed a certain degree of economic independence from their husbands, not least of all due to traditional customs that often called for the woman and the man to keep their own properties and to maintain separate financial accounts.[56] This was due in part to the demands of polygyny, which made each wife responsible for the financial well-being of her own children.

The African woman's roles as entrepreneur and trader were critical in various regions. The role of women during the nineteenth century in the production, transportation, and sale of palm nuts (a source of cooking oil) in the Abomey political system (present-day Benin) is well documented, as is the woman's role in the kola-nut trade of the Bete political system (an area that straddles present-day Côte d'Ivoire and Ghana) during the same century. Especially in the case of the kola-nut trade, Bete women created and maintained a sophisticated trading network that relied predominantly on young female family members and slaves who served as porters for what was essentially an extended family business. "Women today tell of the exploits of their grandmothers or great-grandmothers, themselves under the direction of their own mothers, crisscrossing the country at the end of the nineteenth century," notes Catherine Coquery-Vidrovitch, a historian. "Such a level of organization suggests significant profits, even if they were not monetary and depended largely on the interdependence of female relatives."[57]

A woman's control over her economic destiny, especially her ability to inherit and bequeath economic power, was also influenced by whether she lived in a matrilineal or a patrilineal society. A **patrilineal society,** which was widespread throughout the African continent, is one in which family descent is traced through men, with the wife and children often living in the husband's family village **(patrilocal).** Inheritance is typically passed from father to son. In a **matrilineal society,** which was less widespread, family descent is traced through women, with the groom and any resulting children from a marriage sometimes living in the wife's family village **(matrilocal).** Inheritance is typically passed from uncle to sister's son. As a result, wealth in matrilineal societies passed through the male children of a woman, who sometimes was privileged as "mother in chief."[58]

The "mother-in-chief" reference raises the important issue of political power, most notably the degree to which that power was shared and enjoyed by African women during the precolonial independence era. The first and most basic form of power exerted by African women was derivative of the tradition of many African societies to create parallel organizations for men and women, be they the earlier discussed age-grade system of the Maasai people or the secret societies of the Mende people. Among the Ewe people of present-day Ghana, there existed a council of senior women who elected a Queen Mother, who in turn served as the female representative to a parallel council of senior men. In the Dahomey political system of present-day Benin, the king appointed a female counterpart, the *kpojito* (literally, "mother"), for male officials. "Most generally, parallel authority structures allowed men and women to exercise authority over their own sex and activities," explains Gordon. "There was also recognition that men could best make decisions about men's affairs, as could women about their own conditions."[59]

African women also enjoyed a significant degree of indirect political influence, most notably in matrilineal societies in which political power, in addition to economic wealth, was often transmitted through the female line.[60] "Among the Tonga in Southern Zambia, for example, although a woman's wealth was often in her brothers' custody, she had her own fields and granary as well as control over grain production," explains Jane L. Parpart. "This control over land enabled women to command the labor and allegiance of sons and sons-in-law and facilitated access to political power."[61] In such societies, African women often played an influential role in determining which groups of men would emerge as the political leaders of society. Indeed, although the Queen Mother of the Asante empire could not aspire to assuming the throne, she played a crucial role as kingmaker within society.

A third, more direct form of political power existed when African women themselves enjoyed the mantle of political leadership. In several African societies, women served as hereditary chiefs (i.e., they were born into leadership), as in the case of the Mende people of present-day Sierra Leone. Women were also appointed to positions of power by male leaders. During a period lasting nearly 400 years (1506–1889), the king of the Edo people of present-day Nigeria presented his mother with the title *iyoba* (literally, "official mother"), thereby empowering her to take part in the royal executive council that provided political and military advice to the king.[62] African women also sometimes assumed power when a male family member, be he husband, son, or brother, became incapacitated or otherwise unable to perform his leadership duties. In the case of the Ethiopian empire, Empress Menetewab took power in the name of her son until he was old enough to rule after the death of her husband, the king, in 1730. After her son's death, Empress Menetewab returned to the throne in the name of her grandson until he, too, was old enough to rule, although she was ultimately ousted by a rival claimant to the throne.[63]

The political power of African women is best demonstrated by the emergence of several African women as renowned political leaders within their respective societies. As aptly demonstrated by Coquery-Vidrovitch, at least three African women can serve as the basis of a much longer list of "eminent" female leaders[64] of the precolonial independence era:

- Queen Amina (or Aminatu) of Zazzau (renamed Zaria after her sister) of the Hausa city-state system of present-day Nigeria, whose nation-building exploits during the sixteenth century are enshrined by a statue of her, spear in hand on a horse, in downtown Lagos, Nigeria

- Queen Nzinga Mbande (or Mbundu) of the Kongo Kingdom of present-day Angola, who fought against the imposition of Portuguese colonial rule at the beginning of the seventeenth century

■ Queen Mother Yaa Asantewa of the Asante empire of present-day Ghana, who led armies that sought to overthrow the British protectorate that was established over the kingdom at the end of the nineteenth century

African women also periodically played influential military roles during the precolonial independence era. Apart from being the actual leaders of military forces, in at least one case, the so-called "Amazons" of Dahomey, women served as the cornerstone of an African kingdom's armed forces. As aptly described in Robert B. Edgerton's *Warrior Women: The Amazons of Dahomey and the Nature of War,* "full-time professional women soldiers fought so ferociously and successfully for so many years that they eventually became the elite force of Dahomey's professional, highly successful standing army."[65] Experts in hand-to-hand combat, the Amazons were highly trained in the use of muskets, bows and poisoned arrows, and 18-inch-long razors that folded into wooden handles.[66] Although estimates vary, roughly 3,000 to 5,000 women served as uniformed warriors at any given point during the nineteenth century.[67] The nearly 200-year history of this elite female fighting force would only come to an end in 1892 when, confronted with the superior firepower of French colonial troops, the Amazons were decimated and French colonial rule over the Kingdom of Dahomey was consolidated. It is specifically to this and other impacts of colonial rule that we turn to in the next chapter.

KEY TERMS

cradle of humankind
segmented political system
band organization
hunter-gatherer groups
classical segmented system
universalistic segmented system
age-grade systems
age-set
ritually stratified segmented system
transhumance
autonomous village system
city-states
centralized political systems
nation-state
pyramidal monarchy
associational monarchy
secret societies
centralized monarchy
hierarchical political system
regicide
pastoral nomadism

agro-pastoralism
slash-and-burn technique
subsistence-oriented trade
market-oriented trade
trans-Saharan trade network
state necessities
luxury goods
southern terminals
desert oases
northern terminals
northern coastal cities
suzerain kingdoms
tribute
bridewealth
polygamy
polyandry
polygyny
patrilineal society
patrilocal
matrilineal society
matrilocal

FOR FURTHER READING

Adjaye, Joseph K. *Diplomacy and Diplomats in Nineteenth Century Asante*. Trenton: Africa World, 1996.

Austen, Ralph. *Africa in Economic History: Internal Development and External Dependency*. London: James Currey, 1987.

Cambridge History of Africa (8 vols.). Cambridge: Cambridge University Press, 1975–82.

Connah, Graham. *African Civilizations: Precolonial Cities and States in Tropical Africa: An Archaeological Perspective* (2nd ed.). Cambridge: Cambridge University Press, 2001.

Connah, Graham, ed. *Transformations in Africa: Essays in Africa's Later Past*. New York: Cassell and Continuum, 1998.

Coquery-Vidrovitch, Catherine. *African Women: A Modern History*. Boulder: Westview Press, 1997 (originally published in French in 1997 by Éditions Desjonquères as *Les Africaines: Histoire des femmes d'Afrique noire du XIX au XX siècle*).

Davidson, Basil. *Africa in History: Themes and Outlines* (rev. ed.). New York: Collier Books and Macmillan, 1991.

de Villiers, Marq, and Sheila Hirtle. *Sahara: A Natural History*. New York: Walker & Company, 2002.

Diop, Cheikh Anta. *Precolonial Black Africa: A Comparative Study of the Political and Social Systems of Europe and Black Africa, from Antiquity to the Formation of Modern States*. Trenton: Africa World, 1987.

Edgerton, Robert B. *Warrior Women: The Amazons of Dahomey and the Nature of War*. Boulder: Westview Press, 2000.

General History of Africa (8 vols.). Berkeley: University of California Press; Oxford: Heinemann; Paris: UNESCO, 1981–93.

July, Robert W. *A History of the African People* (4th ed.). Prospect Heights: Waveland, 1994.

Kwamena-Poh, Michael, et al. *African History in Maps*. Burnt Mill, Harlow. Essex: UK Longman, 1982.

Lipschutz, Mark R., and R. Kent Rasmussen. *Dictionary of African Historical Biography* (2nd ed.). Los Angeles: University of California Press, 1989.

Newman, James L. *The Peopling of Africa: A Geographical Interpretation*. New Haven: Yale University Press, 1995.

Oliver, Roland, and Anthony Atmore. *Medieval Africa, 1250–1800*. Cambridge: Cambridge University Press, 2001.

Shillington, Kevin. *History of Africa*. New York: St Martin's, 1989.

Smith, Robert S. *Warfare and Diplomacy in Precolonial West Africa* (2nd ed.). Madison: The University of Wisconsin Press, 1976.

Vogel, Joseph O., ed. *Encyclopedia of Precolonial Africa: Archaeology, History, Languages, Cultures, and Environments*. Walnut Creek, CA: Altamira Press, 1997.

Zeleza, Tiyambe. *A Modern Economic History of Africa. Volume 1. The Nineteenth Century*. Dakar, Senegal: CODESRIA, 1993.

NOTES

1. This interpretation is based on anthropological digs ranging from Klasies River Mouth and Border Cave in South Africa to Omo in Ethiopia. See James L. Newman, *The Peopling of Africa: A Geographic Interpretation* (New Haven: Yale University Press, 1995), pp. 11–21. See also Christopher Stringer and Robin McKie, *African Exodus: The Origins of Modern Humanity* (New York: John Macrae/Holt, 1997).

2. The continuing prevalence of this Eurocentric bias is clearly demonstrated in Samuel P. Huntington, *The Clash of Civilizations and the Remaking of World Order* (New York: Simon & Schuster, 1996).

3. Christian P. Potholm, *The Theory and Practice of African Politics* (Englewood Cliffs: Prentice-Hall, 1979), pp. 11–24.

4. Ibid., pp. 12–14.

5. For example, see Elizabeth Marshall Thomas, *The Harmless People* (Capetown: Africa South Paperbacks, David Phillip, 1988). See also Alan Barnard, *Hunters and Herders of Southern Africa: A Comparative Ethnography of the Khoisan Peoples* (Cambridge: Cambridge University Press, 1992).

6. See Potholm, *The Theory and Practice,* pp. 14–15.

7. For an introduction, see the classic analysis by I. M. Lewis, *A Pastoral Democracy* (London: Oxford University Press, 1961).

8. See Potholm, *The Theory and Practice,* pp. 15–17.

9. See Cheryl Bentsen, *Maasai Days* (Garden City: Doubleday, 1989). See also Thomas Spear and Richard Waller, *Being Maasai: Ethnicity and Identity in East Africa* (London: James Currey, 1993).

10. See Potholm, *The Theory and Practice,* p. 17.

11. See E. E. Evans-Pritchard, *Essays in Social Anthropology* (London: Faber and Faber, 1962), pp. 66–86. See also Evans-Pritchard, *The Divine Kingship of the Shilluk of the Nilotic Sudan* (Cambridge: Cambridge University Press, 1948).

12. Ibid., p. 74.

13. See Potholm, *The Theory and Practice,* pp. 18–19.

14. See John Middleton, *The World of the Swahili: An African Mercantile Civilization* (New Haven: Yale University Press, 1992).

15. See Potholm, *The Theory and Practice,* pp. 19–21.

16. See Robert Smith, *Kingdoms of the Yoruba* (3rd ed.). (Madison: University of Wisconsin Press, 1988).

17. Ibid., p. 92.

18. See Potholm, *The Theory and Practice,* pp. 21–22.

19. See Kenneth Little, *The Mende People of Sierra Leone: A West African People in Transition* (rev. ed.). (Oxford: Alden, 1967).

20. Robert W. July, *A History of the African People* (4th ed.). (Prospect Heights: Waveland, 1992), p. 98.

21. See Potholm, *The Theory and Practice,* pp. 22–24.

22. See E. A. Ritter, *Shaka Zulu: The Biography of the Founder of the Zulu Nation* (New York: Penguin, 1978).

23. I. M. Lewis, "The Dynamics of Nomadism: Prospects for Sedentarization and Social Change," in Theodore Monod, ed., *Pastoralism in Tropical Africa* (London: Oxford University Press, 1975), p. 429.

24. For an overview, see Axmed Cali Abokor, *The Camel in Somali Oral Traditions* (Uppsala: Scandinavian Institute of African Studies, 1987).

25. For a discussion of other farming techniques, see Tiyambe Zeleza, *A Modern Economic History of Africa. Volume 1: The Nineteenth Century* (Dakar: CODESRIA, 1993), pp. 86–92.

26. Robert S. Smith, *Warfare and Diplomacy in Precolonial West Africa* (2nd ed.). (Madison: University of Wisconsin Press, 1976), p. 59.

27. Richard Gray and David Birmingham, "Some Economic and Political Consequences of Trade in

Central and Eastern Africa in the Precolonial Period," in Gray and Birmingham, eds., *Precolonial African Trade: Essays on Trade in Central and Eastern Africa before 1900* (London: Oxford University Press, 1970), p. 3.

28. Ibid., p. 5.

29. Kenneth P. Vickery, *Black and White in Southern Zambia: The Tonga Plateau Economy and British Imperialism, 1890–1939* (Westport: Greenwood, 1986), p. 27.

30. Gray and Birmingham, "Some Economic and Political Consequences," p. 6.

31. Ibid., p. 3.

32. See Anthony G. Hopkins, *An Economic History of West Africa* (New York: Columbia University Press, 1973). The following account is drawn largely from this work.

33. Marq de Villiers and Sheila Hirtle, *Sahara: A Natural History* (New York: Walker & Company, 2002), p. 9.

34. Ibid., p. 5.

35. Ibid.

36. Ibid.

37. Ibid., p. 81.

38. See Ralph Austen, *Africa in Economic History: Internal Development and External Dependency* (London: James Currey, 1987), pp. 31–40, 273–74. It has been recorded that caravans carrying salt across "only a portion of the Sahara" could number between 6,000 and 12,000 camels.

39. Hopkins, *An Economic History of West Africa,* p. 81.

40. Ibid.

41. Ibid., p. 85.

42. The following analysis of diplomatic trends draws heavily upon Smith. *Warfare and Diplomacy,* pp. 7–27. See also Joseph K. Adjaye, *Diplomats and Diplomacy in 19th Century Asante* (Trenton: Africa World, 1996).

43. Ibid., p. 12.

44. Ibid., p. 14.

45. Ibid., p. 16.

46. Smith, *Kingdoms of the Yoruba,* p. 96.

47. Ibid., p. 36.

48. Ibid., p. 38.

49. For discussion, see J. F. Ade Ajayi and Robert Smith, *Yoruba Warfare in the Nineteenth Century* (2nd ed.). (Cambridge: Cambridge University Press, 1971).

50. Catherine Coquery-Vidrovitch, *African Women: A Modern History* (Boulder: Westview Press, 1997).

51. Ibid., p. 10.

52. April A. Gordon, "Women and Development," in April A. Gordon and Donald L. Gordon, eds., *Understanding Contemporary Africa* (3rd ed.). (Boulder: Lynne Rienner, 2001).

53. Coquery-Vidrovitch, *African Women: A Modern History,* p. 10.

54. Gordon, "Women and Development," p. 275.

55. Ibid.

56. Coquery-Vidrovitch, *African Women: A Modern History,* p. 30.

57. Ibid., p. 31.

58. Ibid., p. 10.

59. Gordon, "Women and Development," p. 273.

60. Coquery-Vidrovitch, *African Women: A Modern History,* p. 34.

61. Jane L. Parpart, "Women and the State in Africa," in Donald Rothchild and Naomi Chazan, eds., *The Precarious Balance: State and Society in Africa* (Boulder: Westview, 1988), p. 209.

62. Coquery-Vidrovitch, *African Women: A Modern History,* p. 38.

63. Ibid., p. 63.

64. Ibid., pp. 40–44.

65. Robert B. Edgerton, *Warrior Women: The Amazons of Dahomey and the Nature of War* (Boulder: Westview, 2000), p. 2. See also Stanley B. Alpern, *Amazons of Black Sparta: The Women Warriors of Dahomey* (London: Hurst and Company, 1998).

66. Edgerton, *Warrior Women: The Amazons of Dahomey and the Nature of War,* p. 30.

67. Ibid., p. 32.

3

Political and Economic Impacts of Colonialism (1884–1951)

Courtesy of Keith June/produced by Marianne Scanlon.

Silhouette of Keith June, an African American, standing in the Gate of Tears at the House of Slaves on Gorée Island (Senegal), the final departure point for thousands of Africans who were loaded onto waiting ships and ultimately transported to a life of slavery in the Western Hemisphere.

IN OCTOBER 1884, the European colonial powers were invited to a conference in Berlin by German Chancellor Otto von Bismarck. The United States
also attended as an observer nation, and its representative, John A. Kasson,
signed the Berlin Convention, which formally ended the Berlin Conference
in 1885. The Berlin Conference was designed to dampen escalating imperial
conflict in Africa by officially demarcating the boundaries between European
possessions. The conference also set in motion efforts to fully occupy those portions of the continent that remained independent, a process that was largely
completed by the beginning of World War I. What became known as the
scramble for Africa consecrated the creation of formal European empires and
spheres of interest throughout Africa. Except for the unique cases of Ethiopia
and Liberia, independent Africa ceased to exist, and African politics and society
were controlled from the capital cities of seven European powers: Belgium,
Britain, France, Germany, Italy, Portugal, and Spain. Disregarding the wishes of
African leaders and their peoples, the European powers and their northern allies
had transformed African politics and society. Indeed, a firm grasp of the impacts
of colonial rule is essential to understanding the challenges African leaders confront as they lead their countries at the beginning of the twenty-first century.

EARLY CONTACTS WITH EUROPE
AND THE ARAB WORLD

A broad historical understanding of direct European colonial influence on the
African continent dates back at least to the spread of the Roman Empire to
North Africa. In 146 B.C., the Carthaginian Empire, which served as the precursor of present-day Tunisia, was defeated and occupied by Roman forces.
The North African coastal city of Carthage, which once dominated Mediter-
ranean trade, was completely destroyed. It would not be until 100 years later
under the reign of Roman Emperor Julius Caesar that Carthage would be
resuscitated as a center of Roman socioeconomic and political-military power
in Africa, emerging as the capital of the North African Roman province of
Africa Proconsularis that stretched from the western region of present-day
Libya to the eastern region of present-day Algeria. Other Roman provinces in
Africa included Mauritania Caesarensis and Mauritania Tingitana, which carried the Empire westward across the northern portions of present-day Algeria
and Morocco. It was Africa Proconsularis, however, that served as the bread-
basket of the Roman Empire, producing foodstuffs such as wheat and highly
valued olive oil from massive olive tree groves that remain in evidence today.
Although Rome's decline during the fifth century A.D. ensured that its North
African holdings would be contested by both local and other foreign powers,
the significant impact of Roman rule is evidenced by the hundreds of well-
preserved Roman ruins that still dot the North African landscape, such as the
still-standing coliseum in the Tunisian city of El Jem that is rivaled only by its
counterpart in Rome, Italy.

The more contemporary era of European colonialism, that was consecrated by the Berlin Conference of 1884–85, was preceded by a gradual process of European expansion into Africa over roughly 450 years. Beginning in 1434, Portuguese explorers under the leadership of Prince Henry the Navigator began sailing the West African coastline. Prince Henry was followed by Vasco de Gama, whose famous voyage of 1497–99 extended Portugal's reach around the Cape of Good Hope into the Indian Ocean. The overriding economic purpose of Portuguese exploration was to circumvent Arab traders who controlled Portugal's overland access to the gold trade of West Africa and the silk and spice trades of Asia. Other goals included to spread Christianity and to enhance Portuguese political-military power (see Map 3.1).[1]

The steady advance of Portuguese explorers marked the beginning of what is commonly called in the West the **age of exploration:** the charting and mapping of lands previously unknown to European powers, before the ultimate imposition of colonial rule, including in Africa. The Portuguese were neither the sole nor the most powerful European empire to compete for global influence. From Prince Henry's initial voyages to the beginning of the Berlin Conference in 1884, the world witnessed the rise and decline of three **hegemonic powers:** Portugal (sixteenth century), the Netherlands (seventeenth century), and Great Britain (eighteenth and nineteenth centuries). A hegemonic power is a country whose global reach and overwhelming economic and military power allow the country's leaders to create and enforce the rules of the international system. During the twentieth century, for example, the United States emerged as the unparalleled hegemonic power.

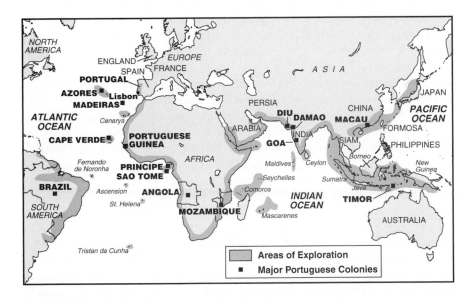

MAP 3.1   Portugal's Empire in the Sixteenth Century

Source: *The New York Times,* Sunday, November 7, 1999, p. A5.

The scramble for Africa was also preceded by the gradual expansion of Arab influence into Africa under the banner of Islam. After the death of the prophet, Muhammad, in 632 A.D., Muhammad's Arab followers embarked on a series of jihads (literally, "struggles," but often translated as "holy wars") that fanned out in all directions from the birthplace of Islam, the holy towns of Mecca and Medina in present-day Saudi Arabia. The conversion to Islam of Egypt, an important gateway to Africa from the Middle East, in 640 A.D., was followed by a series of jihads in North Africa that led to the region's Arabization and Islamization. The rapid and militant expansion of Islam and Arab culture into North Africa was followed by a more gradual and peaceful expansion led by Arab explorers and traders along the East African coast and into the Sub-Saharan region of West Africa. "They followed the established trade routes, many of which [such as the trans-Saharan trade network] had existed long before the rise of Islam," explains Ambrose Moyo.[2] In addition, "wherever they went, Muslims established commercial and religious centers near the capital cities" that served as the basis for the further Arabization and Islamization of their hosts.[3] Although jihads would become prominent in West Africa during the eighteenth and nineteenth centuries, Islam's peaceful adoption by the elites of this and other regions of Sub-Saharan Africa by the beginning of the fifteenth century was due to at least two factors: the advanced nature and cosmopolitanism of Arab-Muslim civilization and the compatibility of Islam with several traditional African practices, such as polygyny.[4]

One of the most devastating aspects of rising European and Arab influence in Africa at the end of the fifteenth century was a global perception of slavery as a legitimate and necessary tool of political-military and economic expansion. Four major slave networks specialized in the export of African slaves: (1) the **Atlantic slave trade,** which primarily shipped slaves to the Western Hemisphere (North and South America and the Caribbean); (2) the **trans-Saharan slave trade,** which principally sold slaves to the Mediterranean coastal regions; (3) the **Red Sea slave trade,** which sent slaves to the Middle East and South Asia; and (4) the **Swahili coast slave trade,** which focused on the Indian Ocean islands and South and Southeast Asia.

The Atlantic slave trade, also called the **European slave trade,** began during the fifteenth century and was dominated by the European powers. Slaves were sought as cheap labor to work the colonial plantations of the Western Hemisphere that produced a variety of products, such as sugar, tobacco, and cotton, for export to Europe.[5] The trans-Saharan, Red Sea, and Swahili coast trade networks are usually jointly called the **Islamic slave trade.** This network was dominated by the Islamic world, which began exporting slaves in significant quantities beginning in the ninth century.[6] Female slaves were sought to serve as concubines and servants, and males were inducted into imperial armies and worked on plantations.

One of the earliest recorded incidents of North American involvement in the Atlantic slave trade occurred in 1619, when a Dutch ship unloaded twenty African slaves in the British North American colonies. From this inauspicious beginning, the colonies became part of a worldwide slave-trading network, the legacy of which, nearly four centuries later, would be over 34 million African American citizens, roughly 12 percent of the U.S. population according to the 2000 U.S. Census. The colonies composing the future United States nonetheless constituted only a small portion (4.5 percent) of the Atlantic slave trade. The vast majority of the slaves were sent to work on plantations in South America (49 percent) and the Caribbean (42 percent), with relatively minor numbers sent to Central America (2 percent) and Europe (2 percent).[7]

The number and destinations of Africans sold into slavery have fostered a tremendous debate, what one scholar has called the "numbers game," with important implications for understanding the historical evolution of African politics and society.[8] Although precise numbers are impossible to obtain, and all estimates should be greeted with a certain degree of wariness, some tentative conclusions can be discerned from reliable estimates of the global slave trade of Africans (see Table 3.1).

Reputable estimates of the Atlantic slave trade suggest that between 11.7 and 15.4 million Africans were forcibly uprooted from Africa and shipped across the Atlantic Ocean, from the middle of the fifteenth century to the end of the nineteenth century.[9] The height of this trade occurred during the eighteenth century, when 6.1 to 8.8 million Africans were sold into slavery. Not all of the slaves arrived at their intended destinations. Analyses of often meticulously kept ship

TABLE 3.1 Estimates of the Global Slave Trade (Number of Africans)

TIME PERIOD	SLAVE NETWORK				
	Atlantic (Estimate I)	Atlantic (Estimate II)	Trans-Saharan	Swahili Coast	Red Sea
801–900	—	—	344,800	229,900	114,900
901–1100	—	—	2,000,000	459,800	229,900
1101–1450	—	—	2,143,700	804,600	402,300
Subtotal (800–1450)	—	—	4,488,500	1,494,300	747,100
1451–1600	367,000	442,400	879,300	344,800	172,400
1601–1700	1,868,000	2,158,100	816,100	229,900	114,900
1701–1800	6,133,000	8,792,600	821,800	229,900	229,900
1801–1900	3,330,000	4,000,600	1,385,100	862,100	1,063,200
Subtotal (1451–1900)	11,698,000	15,393,700	3,902,300	1,666,700	1,580,400
Total	11,698,000	15,393,700	8,390,800	3,161,000	2,327,500

Sources: Atlantic (Estimate I) figures are drawn from Paul E. Lovejoy, "The Volume of the Atlantic Slave Trade: A Synthesis," *Journal of African History* 23 (1982): 478. Atlantic (Estimate II) figures are derived from J. E. Inikori, "Africa in World History: The Export Slave Trade from Africa and the Emergence of the Atlantic Economic Order," in B. A. Ogot, ed., *General History of Africa. Volume 5. Africa from the Sixteenth to the Eighteenth Century* (Paris: UNESCO, 1992), p. 82. The Trans-Saharan, Swahili Coast, and Red Sea figures are derived from Ralph A. Austin, "The Trans-Saharan Slave Trade: A Tentative Census," in Henry A. Gemery and Jan S. Hogendorn, eds., *The Uncommon Market: Essays in the Economic History of the Atlantic Slave Trade* (New York: Academic Press, 1979), pp. 66, 68. All five sets of figures assume a 13 percent death rate.

logs suggest that at least 13 percent of the slaves did not survive the voyage across the Atlantic, most often due to severe dehydration and dysentery.[10] The implication of this figure is that between 1.5 and 2 million Africans died in transit.

The Islamic slave trade lasted at least 750 years longer than its European counterpart and was responsible for the forced displacement of nearly 14 million Africans.[11] The total number of slaves transported along the Atlantic slave network was either slightly higher (by 11 percent) or slightly lower (by 16 percent) than those traded within the combined Islamic network (based on the general range of estimates for the European slave trade contained in Table 3.1). If one also assumes that approximately 13 percent did not reach their destinations alive, especially for those slaves who were forced to march across the Sahara desert on foot, at least 1.8 million Africans perished in transit. Again, dehydration and dysentery were the primary culprits of slave deaths. The cumulative volume and death rate of the European and Islamic slave trades therefore were roughly similar.

The Atlantic slave trade nonetheless exceeded Islamic trade in terms of geographical scope and intensity. The Atlantic network was nearly worldwide and included a system of **triangular trade** that linked Europe and Africa with the Western Hemisphere. The triangle refers to the three major routes ships followed in the pursuit of economic profit (Europe–Africa, Africa–Western Hemisphere, and Western Hemisphere–Europe). Whereas ships bound for Africa from Europe usually carried a variety of manufactured products, and those bound for the Western Hemisphere from Africa carried slaves, the Europe-bound ships from the Western Hemisphere transported the output of colonial plantations, most notably rum, tobacco, sugar, and cotton.

The Atlantic slave trade also lasted a shorter period (roughly 450 years) but managed to transport much higher numbers of slaves. From 1451 to 1900, the number of slaves traded by the Atlantic network exceeded that of the Islamic network by 64 percent to 115 percent. Equally important, the yearly average of slaves traded within the Arab network (9,310) clearly exceeded that of the Atlantic (2,447–2,949) from 1451 to 1600, whereas the seventeenth century witnessed a dramatic reverse. Beginning in 1601, the yearly average of slaves traded within the Atlantic network had risen to between 18,680 and 21,581. The average for the Islamic slave trade during this same period had risen to only 11,609. The Atlantic slave trade therefore not only surpassed that of the Islamic world during the seventeenth century, it increasingly dominated the Islamic slave trade as the European powers expanded their political-military and economic control over Arab and African countries alike during the nineteenth century.

A notable turning point in rising European global influence was Great Britain's decision in 1807 to make the slave trade illegal. As the hegemonic power of the nineteenth century, Great Britain sought to enforce its antislavery vision throughout the international system. In the case of the United States, British actions led to diplomatic tensions despite the fact that the U.S. Congress had abolished the slave trade in 1808. Conflicts emerged over Washington's unwillingness to allow Great Britain to stop and board ships carrying the American flag, which were suspected of smuggling slaves. (It is estimated that at least 54,000 slaves were smuggled illegally into the United States between 1808 and 1861.)[12] Having successfully fought a war of independence against British colonialism, followed by the humiliating burning of Washington, D.C., by invading British troops during the War of 1812, neither the White House nor the U.S. Congress was willing to cooperate with Great Britain on the slavery issue. Active U.S. support for Britain's antislavery vision came about only after President Abraham Lincoln announced the Emancipation Proclamation in 1862 as part of the North's political-military strategy to win the Civil War against the South. By the end of the nineteenth century, most of the world's nations perceived the slave trade as illegitimate.

Great Britain's active opposition to the slave trade was not primarily driven by an enlightened vision of humankind that understood the West's domination of nonwhite peoples outside of Europe to be repugnant. The economic imperatives associated with the rise and spread of the **industrial revolution**— the introduction and widespread use of power-driven machinery throughout the economy—had simply made it more profitable for Great Britain and the other European powers to engage in legitimate trade with the African continent, as opposed to the illegitimate trade in human beings. The transformation that took place from the end of the eighteenth century to the end of the nineteenth century entailed the gradual replacement of the slave trade with the production in Africa of numerous primary products. For example, massive plantations were created to grow peanuts, a critical source of oil that lubricated the machines of Europe's industrial revolution and that served as the base of a variety of European-manufactured products, such as soap, candles, and butter. Cotton served as another important primary product whose production expanded in leaps and bounds to satisfy the textile mills of Europe. European manufacturers also ultimately perceived the African continent as the target for sales of manufactured goods. Simply put, the European industrialists thought, "Why destroy African markets by exporting slaves to plantations in the Western Hemisphere when we can better profit from trade with Africans who work their plantations closer to Europe?"

The shift to legitimate commerce throughout the nineteenth century was accompanied by the arrival of steadily rising numbers of official and nonofficial Europeans in Africa. The official Europeans were government civil servants who transformed early slave ports into administrative enclaves. In many cases, such as the Island of Gorée off the coast of Senegal, these enclaves changed hands as European powers rose and declined in influence (see the accompanying box). The enclaves primarily served as diplomatic outposts. The activities of local European officials ranged from the management of trade relations and coordination of naval visits to dealing with the unexpected problems confronted by their citizens. In most cases, the enclave was the centerpiece of an emerging **informal empire:** political-military and economic domination without the formal occupation and control usually associated with the establishment of a centralized government over a given territory.

Important pressures for further European expansion were found among the nonofficial Europeans. In the economic realm, private traders and entrepreneurs

A Closer Look: ISLAND OF GORÉE AND THE ATLANTIC SLAVE TRADE

One of the most moving experiences for visitors to Senegal is a visit to Gorée, a small island approximately 2 miles off the coast of the country's capital of Dakar that once served as a major slave depot in West Africa. The island's first contact with Europe occurred in 1444 with the arrival of the Portuguese explorer Dinis Dias. The Portuguese named the island Ilha de Palma (Isle of Palms) and constructed a chapel in 1481, but they never occupied the island permanently.

The island's strategic location made it one of the focal points of Great Power competition from the seventeenth to the nineteenth centuries. The Dutch seized the island in 1627, renamed it Goede Reede (Good Harbor), and established the first permanent settlement. French domination, beginning in 1677 and lasting until Senegal's independence in 1960, was punctuated by brief periods of British occupation of the island (1693, 1758–63, 1779–83, 1800–17).

A visit to the Maison des Esclaves (House of Slaves), originally built in 1776 and refurbished as a historical site in 1990, offers a stark reminder of the primary reason Europeans were interested in Gorée: the highly lucrative slave trade. The world-renowned curator, Joseph N'Diaye, leads daily visitors past the dark holding rooms and underground cells where thousands of slaves were held before being shipped to the Western Hemisphere. The slaves were kept in the most atrocious of conditions, perhaps exceeded only by the cruelty of being chained below decks in the long ocean voyage across the Atlantic.

Upon entering the courtyard, the visitor is struck first by a beautiful double-crescent staircase that surrounds both sides of a darkened central hallway. Immediately above the squalid slave quarters on the first floor were the living quarters of the Europeans who ran the slave house. It is difficult to imagine how human beings could bear to live above the tears and wails of other human beings separated from their families and held like animals.

The second vision the visitor encounters is the brilliance of sunlight and blue ocean that emerges from an open passage at the end of the darkened central hallway (see the photo at the beginning of this chapter). The visitor's sensibilities are once again shocked when told that this doorway is nicknamed the "Porte des Larmes" (the Gate of Tears), a reference to the fact that it served as the gate of departure for African slaves as they were loaded onto waiting ships. The Island of Gorée and the House of Slaves are currently recognized as internationally protected historical sites by the UN Educational, Scientific, and Cultural Organization (UNESCO).

Discussion based on an interview and a guided tour with curator Joseph N'Diaye. See also IFAN, *Gorée: The Island and the Historical Museum* (Dakar, Senegal: IFAN, 1993).

interested in gaining greater profits relentlessly pressed their home governments to extend the political–military reach of the enclaves into the interior. The European traders were especially interested in cutting out the African middlemen who controlled European access to the lucrative trade beyond the coastal regions. Demands for political–military expansion were also supported by numerous missionary societies, such as the London Missionary Society, which established themselves on the African continent. Renowned for establishing missionary outposts far beyond the political-military reach of their respective governments, missionaries demanding government protection during periods of civil unrest not surprisingly received a sympathetic hearing both at home and in the imperial enclaves.

One of the most written about groups of nonofficial Europeans was the explorers. Despite their preposterous claims to have "discovered" indigenous peoples, the explorers nonetheless charted territories that were previously unknown to European governments. They also captured the imaginations of their respective peoples by publishing detailed accounts of their travels and "discoveries." One such individual was Captain Sir Richard Francis Burton (1821–90), a British subject who spoke at least twenty-nine languages and who wrote over forty books about his travels. "Burton was the paradigm of the scholar-adventurer," explains one of his many biographers, "a man who towered above others physically and intellectually, a soldier, scientist, explorer, and writer who for much of his life also engaged in that most romantic of careers, undercover agent."[13]

European women constituted an important category of official and especially nonofficial Europeans often neglected in historical accounts of the colonial era. For example, when Samuel Baker achieved the dubious honor of "discovering" Lake Albert in 1861, the history books were completely silent about the fact that he was accompanied by his wife, Florence Baker (born Florence Ninian von Sass), who was an explorer in her own right.[14] The European writer typically known among American readers is Karen von Blixen, whose book, *Out of Africa,* written under the pseudonym Isak Dinesen, was turned into a popular movie of the same name.[15] The voices of several of these European women are brought to life in a book edited by Patricia W. Romero, *Women's Voices on Africa: A Century of Travel Writings.*[16] One of the most fascinating excerpts draws on a book, *African Apprenticeship: An Autobiographical Journey in Southern Africa in 1929,* written by Margary Perham, a British scholar whose field research and scholarly books on the Horn of Africa and Southern Africa inspired women seeking careers in the academic world, especially in the field of African studies.[17] "To these women, Perham was full of grit and determination," explains Romero. "She represented a bridge between the old [colonial-inspired] pseudoscientific racist notions of Africa inferiority and the more egalitarian attitudes prevalent today.[18]

IMPOSITION OF DIRECT COLONIAL RULE

Nineteenth century Europe embodied an **imperial mindset**[19] that accepted the necessity of promoting **direct colonial rule** throughout Africa. Racist and self-serving rationales, such as Britain's portrayal of its efforts as the "white man's burden" and France's pronouncement of its "mission civilisatrice" (civilizing mission), were offered to justify European domination over peoples deemed "backward," "ignorant," "uncivilized," "barbaric," "savage," and "godless heathens."

Two important turning points in this process were King Leopold II's declaration in 1884 that the Congo basin (present-day Democratic Republic of the Congo [Congo-Kinshasa]) constituted the private property of the Belgian crown and German Chancellor Bismarck's decision during that same year to declare protectorates over Togoland (Togo), Kamerun (Cameroon), and South-West Africa (Namibia). The decisions of these two leaders sparked the intensification of European efforts to occupy and declare ownership over those portions of Africa that remained independent. European leaders perceived themselves as locked in an imperial race to acquire territories to prevent the balance of power from tipping too heavily in favor of their perceived rivals, hence the characterization of this historical period as the "scramble for Africa."[20]

The "rules" of the scramble for Africa were simple and straightforward: To obtain ownership of a given territory that would be recognized as legally binding in the European nation-state system, the colonial power had to prove **effective occupation** by obtaining treaties signed by local African leaders. This pattern differed from that of an earlier age in which ownership was based on **discovery** (i.e., an explorer lands on a territory previously unknown to the European world and claims ownership for his country). The reason for the shift was that much of Africa was already charted and therefore "known" to the various European colonial powers.

The treaties signed with local leaders were dubious at best, in essence serving only to validate claims among the various European powers. Many Europeans filed treaties signed by local inhabitants who were not in positions of authority or who in any case were not allowed by local custom to sign away lands. Even when the proper local officials signed the treaties, the fact that they were written in a foreign language often meant that their true intent (i.e., European domination and ownership of local lands) was misunderstood or misrepresented. Often an African leader signed in good faith a paper described as representing a treaty of mutual respect and friendship, only to face the arrival of occupying forces determined to impose foreign rule.

The physical occupation of the African continent by the colonial powers was often met with political and even armed resistance from African kingdoms and ethnic groups. In the case of the Asante empire, Asante troops first clashed with the British colonial army in 1823. In fact, they fought a series of battles (1826, 1874, 1896) that ultimately delayed the final subjugation of the Asante to British colonial rule.[21] In battle, the Asante, driven by the desire to avoid foreign occupation, were empowered by a disciplined warrior tradition that had served the kingdom well before the arrival of the European colonial powers. The Asante military abided by the motto: *Fere ne owuo efenim owuo* (If it is a matter of choosing between disgrace and death, then I should choose death).[22] "Guided by this principle," explains F. K. Finn, a former member of the Ghanaian parliament, "an Asante military leader would normally commit suicide rather than fall into enemy hands."[23]

Even in the aftermath of British military victory and the establishment of a British protectorate over the Asante empire in 1897, sustained military resistance continued on the part of Asante forces. The most celebrated case involved Queen Mother Yaa Asantewa, who, beginning in 1900, led a series of military actions designed in part to force the British colonial authorities to allow for the return from exile of Prempeh I, heir to the Asante throne. In one battle alone, which involved a 2-month siege of the royal city of Kumasi, the Queen Mother was able to assemble a force of 40,000–50,000 Asante. "The British had to mobilize 1,400 men with the latest in weapons to break the siege, and it took 3 more months and 1,200 more men to capture the queen and the last of her loyalists," explains Catherine Coquery-Vidrovitch, a noted French historian. "She is said to have spit in the face of the British officer who arrested her."[24]

Several factors nonetheless ensured that armed resistance among the Asante and other ethnic groups opposed to European colonialism would ultimately fail.[25] First, the European colonial powers, regardless of their conflicts on the European continent, were united in their quest to occupy the African continent. Second, the European armies enjoyed technological superiority in the field of armaments. The Gatling gun, the precursor to present-day machine guns, was used to devastating effect against numerically superior African armies. Finally, the Europeans were able to exploit regional rivalries as part of a conscious policy of **divide-and-conquer.** In short, European subjugation of a particular African kingdom was often advanced by seeking the short-term aid of that kingdom's traditional African competitor in the region.

Except for the unique cases of Ethiopia and Liberia, the net result of the scramble for Africa was the imposition of foreign colonial rule and the end of the precolonial independence era. By the beginning of World War I, the African continent found itself divided into a series of colonial empires varying in size, shape, and geographical distribution (see Map 3.2). France and Britain maintained the most extensive colonial empires, with France dividing its territories into four major administrative regions: Afrique Occidentale Française (AOF—French West Africa), Afrique Equatoriale Française (AEF—French Equatorial Africa), the maghreb (Algeria, Morocco, and Tunisia), and Départements d'Outre Mer-Territoires d'Outre-Mer (DOM-TOM—Overseas Departments and Territories), including Mayotte and Réunion. The British empire was constructed along a north-south axis as part of an unrealized British dream to construct a Cape-Cairo railroad linking South Africa with Egypt and included significant holdings in West Africa, most notably Nigeria and Ghana.

Belgium and Portugal led the **second-tier empires** that were much less extensive than their French and British counterparts. Belgium and Portugal were largely restricted to two neighboring regions: Central Africa for Belgium and Southern Africa for Portugal, although Portugal also ruled Guinea–Bissau in West Africa and the island territories of Cape Verde and Sao Tome and Principe. Germany was stripped of its geographically widespread colonies following defeat in World War I.[26] In an experiment by the League of Nations

MAP 3.2   Colonial Partition on the Eve of World War I (with Contemporary Country Names)

(the forerunner to the United Nations), each German colony was temporarily transferred to another colonial power as a **mandate territory** pending transition to self-rule.[27] In the case of Italy, defeat in World War II ensured the loss of colonial holdings in Libya and Eritrea. The previously fascist Italian government was nonetheless "rewarded" for its final role in contributing to an Allied victory in World War II with permission to oversee a UN-mandated **trusteeship** of Italian Somaliland during the 1950s.[28] Spain maintained the smallest of the European empires, including control over the Moroccan coastal territories of Ceuta and Melilla.[29]

Each of the four major colonial empires that survived the ravages of World War II offered variations of colonial governance. British colonialism took on two specific forms. In territories like Rhodesia (Zimbabwe), in which a significant white population had permanently settled and was administering the domestic affairs of the colony, British policymakers envisioned granting some form of independent status in the British Commonwealth of Nations, following the models of Australia and New Zealand. Throughout the rest of Africa, British colonialism was based on the concept of **indirect rule.** This concept was popularized by Lord Lugard, the most renowned of British colonial administrators, who conceived of British colonialism as leading to independence under black majority-ruled governments.[30] Building on the assumption that it was neither possible nor desirable to transform Africans into English citizens, British colonial administrators sought to rule indirectly through existing traditional leaders. As a result, British colonial administrators not only kept in place, they in many cases strengthened, a myriad of traditional forms of leadership in their colonies.[31]

French colonialism was based on a highly centralized form of **direct rule** in which each colony was divided according to administrative subdivisions. French officials administered the highest levels directly; Africans considered loyal to France were appointed to administer the lower levels. The French model of colonialism was the most far-reaching in that it was based on a policy of **assimilation.**[32] According to this concept, all African subjects could theoretically achieve the status of full-fledged French citizens if they fully embraced French culture and in so doing fulfilled a variety of requirements, including achieving fluency in the French language, converting to Christianity, obtaining a high school education, and becoming a property owner. Several Africans, such as Léopold Sédar Senghor, the first President of Senegal, fully embraced this policy to achieve the status of *évolué* (literally, an evolved or a civilized person) and to lead prestigious political careers both before and after the independence of their countries from colonial rule (see Chapter 4). In reality, the policy of assimilation was at best limited to a very small portion of the African elite who often found themselves caught between two worlds, one African and one French, in which their French compatriots would never truly accept them as equal citizens.

The Belgian and Portuguese colonial models were similar to the French in their desire to create a class of *évolués* (*assimilados* in Portuguese) that had adopted the major cultural traditions of Belgium and Portugal, respectively. Unlike their French counterparts, neither the Belgian *évolués* nor the Portuguese *assimilados* were ever envisioned to wield political power, whether in the form of political inclusion (as in an expanded French Republic) or ultimate independence (as envisioned under the British model). The Belgians deemed their approach "scientific colonialism" in an effort to put the best public face on what in reality was an extremely despotic form of governance designed to promote Belgian economic interests.[33] The Portuguese were less concerned with such rationales, particularly after the 1928 emergence of a military dictatorship headed by Antonio de Oliveira Salazar. Like the British, the Salazar dictatorship supported the migration of Portuguese settler communities able to administer the colonies.[34]

POLITICAL-MILITARY
IMPACTS OF COLONIALISM

Although in terms of world history the period of direct colonial rule was relatively short (1884–1951), for the vast majority of African countries it nonetheless transformed the domestic and international politics of the African continent. Despite the varied nature of Europe's experiments in colonial rule, it is possible to distinguish several cross-national political trends that apply to the African continent as a whole.

Application of the European
Nation-State System to Africa

The most far-reaching political-military impact of colonialism was the imposition of the European nation-state system onto the extremely rich and varied African political systems that existed during the precolonial independence era. The origins of the nation-state system lie in the 1648 Treaty of Westphalia, which ended the Thirty Years' War (1618–48) in Europe. The treaty marked the beginning of the nation-state system, in which sovereign political entities independent of any outside authorities exercised control over peoples residing in separate territories with officially marked boundaries. When this system was grafted onto Africa, sovereignty remained in the hands of the occupying colonial powers. The application of this system to Africa therefore entailed the subdivision of the entire continent into separate colonies with clearly defined boundaries and centralized political authorities. With few exceptions, the boundaries of these colonial political units became the basis for the contemporary political map of Africa (see Chapter 4).

The imposition of the European nation-state system created a series of artificial states that, unlike their counterparts in Europe, did not evolve gradually according to the wishes of local African peoples. They instead were constructed by European authorities with little concern for local socioeconomic or political-military conditions. Indeed, a favorite account of Africanists is the image of two European leaders resolving a colonial territorial dispute by standing over a map and drawing a new line with a ruler. As a result, the artificially created colonial territories bore little resemblance to the classic definition of a nation-state: one people or ethnic group (the nation) ruled by a legitimate centralized authority (the state).

Division of African Nations among Several States

A second political-military impact of colonialism was the division of African ethnic groups among numerous colonial states. The Somali people of the Horn of Africa is a notable example. Previously united by a common culture but lacking a centralized authority, this classically segmented political system (see Chapter 2) was subjugated and divided among four imperial powers: Britain,

France, Italy, and an independent Ethiopia (see Map 3.3). The northwestern portion of the Somali nation became part of a French colony, Le Territoire Français des Afars et des Issas (French Territory of the Afars and the Issas), which achieved independence in 1977 as the Republic of Djibouti. The western Ogaden region was annexed by the Ethiopian empire and remains a province of present-day Ethiopia. The southwestern portion of the Somali nation be-came part of the British colony (and subsequent independent country) of Kenya. Two final portions, the British Somaliland Protectorate and Italian Somaliland, became part of the British and Italian colonial empires. These two portions achieved independence and formed a federation in 1961 that became known as the Republic of Somalia.

The primary long-term problem associated with the division of one people among many states is the potential emergence of **irredentism:** the political desire of nationalists to reunite their separated peoples in one unified nation-state.[35] In the case of Somalia, irredentism emerged as the cornerstone of a Somali nationalist movement during the 1950s, which called for a redrawing of

MAP 3.3   Territories Inhabited by the Somali People

inherited colonial boundaries in the Horn of Africa. Symbolized by the five-pointed star emblazoned on the national flag of the Republic of Somalia, this irredentist quest envisioned the reunification of all five Somali territories within one pan-Somali state. The Republic of Somalia already included two of these territories (British Somaliland and Italian Somaliland) and therefore sought the "return" of Ethiopia's Ogaden region, the Somali portion of Djibouti, and the Northern Frontier District of Kenya.[36]

Somali leaders of the irredentist movement opted to seek reunification by force of arms. As a result, Somali leaders funded guerrilla insurgencies in Djibouti, Ethiopia, and Kenya during the 1960s, which led to the further deterioration of relations between the Republic of Somalia and its neighbors. The Republic of Somalia and Ethiopia also fought a war (1977–78) over the Ogaden region, which became internationalized due to the superpower involvement of the United States and the former Soviet Union, as well as their respective allies (most notably Saudi Arabia and Cuba).[37] Regardless of whether one is sympathetic to past Somali demands to redraw the inherited colonial boundaries of the Horn of Africa, or accepts the extreme methods of military force employed, there is no question that the roots of these conflicts are at least partially the result of illogically drawn European colonial boundaries.

Incorporation of Several
African Nations into One State

A third political-military impact of European colonialism was the incorporation of previously separate and highly diverse African peoples in one colonial state. Britain's creation of Nigeria illustrates this colonial practice and its consequences (see Map 3.4). Nigeria is composed of over 250 different ethnic groups. Three major ethnic groups comprise roughly 66 percent of the total population and primarily reside in three geographical regions: the Igbo in the southeast, the Yoruba in the southwest, and the Hausa/Fulani in the north.[38]

A number of practical challenges are associated with the creation and maintenance of such a territory. For example, how does one communicate effectively? The British imposed English as the national language of administration, but only a minority of the population was fluent in the language at the time of independence. As a result, after independence a series of Nigerian governments included Igbo, Yoruba, and Hausa as official languages of administration and recognized the importance of adopting less widely spoken languages in local education. Indeed, thirteen additional "state" languages are each spoken by more than 500,000 people, and another fifty-four "local" languages are each spoken by at least 100,000 people.[39] The practical challenges and financial costs associated with such a multilingual effort are enormous: Should all government documents be published in the four major languages or expanded to include the thirteen state languages or the fifty-four local languages? Which language should be used for political debate in the National Assembly? Must television and radio broadcasting be transmitted in different languages? What should be the language of the

MAP 3.4   Nigerian Mosaic

nation's armed forces? Are some languages favored, providing a particular linguistic group an unfair advantage?

In the case of Nigeria, religious diversity also posed a problem for the sociopolitical unity of the territory. Although numerous Nigerian ethnic groups adhered to a variety of traditional religions, the Hausa/Fulani had converted to Islam and the Yoruba had converted to Christianity. During colonial rule, social and political identity became fragmented by the imposition of "Nigeria," a concept that initially meant nothing to the diverse ethnic members of the new colonial state. How would individuals describe themselves over time? Am I British? Am I Nigerian? Am I Igbo? Or am I some combination of all or some of these identities?

The most notable challenge associated with the creation of these artificial colonial states was the potential clash between highly diverse political cultures. In the case of Nigeria, the hierarchical political culture of the Hausa/Fulani clashed with the egalitarian political culture of the Igbo. The Hausa/Fulani political culture demanded complete deference of its subjects to the proclamations of the emir (king), whereas the Igbo political culture considered it the citizen's duty to publicly challenge and criticize the errors of his leaders. A Hausa/Fulani subject was expected to bow face down, his nose touching the ground, as a sign of his deference. An Igbo would never bow. The political ramifications of these differences, especially when one multiplies them by the over 250 ethnic groups that compose Nigeria, were enormous even under the best of circumstances. The worst-case scenario emerged on May 30, 1967, when the Igbo formally seceded from Nigeria and declared an independent Igbo country known as Biafra. A brutal 3-year civil war followed (1967–70), in which an ultimately victorious Nigerian military government, led by Lieutenant Colonel Yakabu Gowon, undertook a devastating policy of starvation designed to bring the secessionist Igbos to their knees (see Chapter 5).

Destruction of Traditional Checks-and-Balances

A fourth political–military impact of colonialism was the dismantling of the traditional **checks-and-balances** that regulated political systems during the precolonial independence era. Whereas traditional leaders answered to the political norms and customs of their individual societies during the precolonial independence era, the creation of the colonial state meant that the ultimate source of power became the European colonial administrator. In most cases, the European administrators would appoint only those Africans who pledged unswerving allegiance to the colonial power. Even under the British model of indirect rule, highly popular traditional rulers who were kept in power by British colonial administrators often saw their traditional power base deteriorate. Tensions frequently arose when the demands of British colonialism ran counter to the interests of the local population and the local ruler had to choose between siding with his people and risking removal from office or siding with the colonial authorities and maintaining favor with the Europeans. In many cases, even authoritarian African leaders could count on remaining in power as long as they served the interests of the European colonial power.

Reinforcement of Patriarchal Forms of Governance

A fifth political–military impact of colonialism was the reinforcement of patriarchal (male-dominated) forms of political governance at the expense of African women. As discussed in Chapter 2, although African men, like those of other regions of the world, generally dominated political affairs during the precolonial independence era, African women, especially those from matrilineal societies, played a number of informal and formal roles, including serving as the political leaders of several African societies. With the advent of European colonialism and the imposition of the Victorian ideal of politics as the sole preserve of men, African women increasingly found themselves politically marginalized in their respective political systems. "Colonial officials accepted Western gender stereotypes, which assigned women to the domestic realm, leaving economic and political matters to men," explains Jane L. Parpart. "As a result, although many African men suffered under colonialism, new opportunities eventually appeared for them, while African women's economic and political rights often diminished."[40]

The reinforcement of patriarchal forms of governance at the expense of women's political rights took on several forms. Again, as discussed in Chapter 2, the first and most basic form of political power exerted by African women derived from the tradition of many African societies to create parallel political organizations for men and women. The female side of these parallel structures was either ignored or undermined by colonial officials, who typically were only willing to deal with male African leaders.[41] It is precisely for this reason that the Ewe tradition of maintaining parallel councils for men and women gradually declined during the period of British colonialism in Ghana. The colonial era especially negatively impacted matrilineal societies, in which tradition allowed for senior African women to exert a significant degree of political influence. As a direct result of British pressure, for example, the year 1889 marked the abandonment of a nearly 400-year-old Edo tradition of making the king's mother one of five appointed members of a royal executive council that provided political and military advice to the king.[42] Most important, the patriarchal biases of colonial administrators ensured that the sporadic emergence of African women as national political leaders during the precolonial independence era would virtually become an impossibility during the period of colonial rule.

Authoritarian Political Legacy

A final political-military impact of colonialism, closely associated with the destruction of traditional checks-and-balances, was an authoritarian legacy that permeated all aspects of political life. In a normally functioning democracy, the legitimacy of the state is based on the consent of the governed. The primary objective of the colonial state, however, was to achieve and maintain European domination. This authoritarian model of state-society relations became known as **Bula Matari** ("he who breaks all rocks"). As Crawford Young explains, this title was bestowed on the famous explorer, Henry Stanley, after he successfully forced a caravan of African porters to dismantle and hand-carry several steamships up the Congo river. In the context of state-society relations, Bula Matari embodied the vision of a state "which crushes all resistance."[43]

A coercive apparatus of police and military forces was created in every colony with the intention of ensuring local compliance with colonial rules and regulations. Success was achieved through a conscious policy of **divide-and-rule.** Drawing on the multiethnic and sometimes multiracial nature of their empires, the European powers would station troops from other ethnic or racial groups in a given colony. In the case of the famous French colonial force, Les Tirailleurs Sénégalais (The Senegalese Soldiers), colonial administrators sought to avoid the stationing of troops in their colonies of origin and certainly avoided stationing those troops among their ethnic groups of birth.[44] The British were renowned for stationing troops from South Asia in their African colonies. The

A Closer Look: LIBERIA: SOLE AMERICAN COLONY?

The closest the United States ever came to becoming a colonial power in Africa revolved around its historically close special relationship with Liberia, a country founded in 1822 by freed American slaves who in 1847 declared their independence as a sovereign nation-state. The capital, Monrovia, was named after James Monroe, the fifth U.S. president. Thanks to its American patronage, Liberia, like Ethiopia, avoided occupation during the so-called scramble for Africa and was one of the founding members of the League of Nations and the United Nations.

The degree to which Liberia constituted a U.S. colony is open to interpretation. Unlike the European colonies, Liberia was neither the creation of, nor ultimately governed by, U.S. government officials. Liberia was instead founded by a private interest, the American Colonization Society, and the U.S. government consistently sidestepped international pressures to declare formal responsibility for the colony, which became independent 25 years after its founding and 61 years before the Conference of Berlin (1884–85). Liberia's independence was not even officially recognized by the U.S. government until 1862, the year in which President Abraham Lincoln signed the Emancipation Proclamation freeing U.S. slaves in the Confederate states, as part of Northern military strategy in the U.S. Civil War.

A case can also be made for the existence of a de facto (as opposed to a de jure) American colony. According to this interpretation, the U.S. government wielded a significant degree of influence over Liberian leaders, ultimately serving as the guarantor of Liberia's independence when confronted with European aggression. In what served as the first and perhaps most notable event in a series of displays of "gunboat diplomacy," a U.S. naval officer, Lieutenant Robert F. Stockton, acquired the rights to the first lands permanently settled by freed American slaves by threatening local chiefs at gunpoint. Stockton's successors not only provided military support to local efforts to expand the colony but served notice that threats to Liberia's sovereignty would not be tolerated. J. Gus Liebenow, a specialist of Liberian politics, notes that the mere presence of an American commission of inquiry in 1909 "prevented both England and France from taking over the country as a protectorate as a result of Liberia's defaulting on the repayment of a series of European loans."

All observers nonetheless agree that the United States was inextricably tied to the creation of Liberia, due to the simple reality that the country was principally founded by former slaves and a variety of other individuals of African descent, most notably slaves liberated from antislaving U.S. warships plying the West Africa coast. Although numbering less than 25,000, these resettled slaves evolved into a cohesive elite group, the so-called Americo-Liberians, that perceived themselves as both different from and superior to the local African populations. The Americo-Liberian elite, composing approximately 5 percent of Liberia's population, established an authoritarian form of government in which 95 percent of the population enjoyed few if any political rights. The "political paradox" of what became an Americo-Liberian dynasty lasting 133 years, explains Liebenow, was the "systematic denial of liberty" to the local population by "those who— on the basis of skin color alone— had been denied the rights and privileges of full participation in American society." In short, the oppressed became the oppressors with the tacit acceptance of the U.S. government.

The Americo-Liberian dynasty ended in 1980 when Master Sergeant Samuel K. Doe took power in a military coup d'état. Although many Liberians rejoiced at the overthrow of the hated Americo-Liberian elite, with many claiming that 1980 was truly the year of independence for the Liberian people, the Doe regime was uninterested in promoting democracy and created an authoritarian regime. President Doe was himself executed by opposition guerrilla forces in 1990, an event that heralded the collapse of the Liberian state and the unleashing of a brutal civil war. On July 19, 1997, Charles Taylor, the guerrilla leader whose forces executed Doe and bore the brunt of the fighting during the Liberian civil war, was elected president.

Discussion drawn from J. Gus Liebenow, *Liberia: The Quest for Democracy* (Bloomington: Indiana University Press, 1987).

cornerstone of this practice was the expectation that troops with little or no ethnic attachment to the subjugated population would have few reservations about taking military action against that population. The same divide-and-rule logic was employed when creating local police forces.

The coercive nature of colonial police and military forces contributed to the creation of an authoritarian environment that carried over into the contemporary independence era. As discussed in Chapter 8, the first generation of African elites, who were trained in this colonial system and who led their countries to independence, tended to create single-party political systems that banned political dissent. As further discussed in Chapter 9, this authoritarian trend was matched by an explosion of military coups d'état in the 1960s that replaced civilian regimes with various military forms of governance.

SOCIOECONOMIC IMPACTS
OF COLONIALISM

The period of direct colonial rule also transformed the socioeconomic fabric of the African continent. Once again drawing on the varied nature of Europe's colonial experiments, it is possible to distinguish several socioeconomic trends that apply to the African continent as a whole.

Creation of Closed Economic Systems

Leaders historically have sought to strengthen their economic power and to increase the diversity of products available to their peoples by trading with their neighbors. Neighboring peoples often share similar cultural and historical characteristics that facilitate economic interaction, as well as geographical proximity, which makes them logical partners for economic cooperation. It is precisely for these reasons that regional trading blocs, such as the European Union (EU), the North American Free Trade Association (NAFTA), and the Southern Africa Development Community (SADC), have proliferated in specific geographical regions of the world (see Chapter 11). As already discussed in Chapter 2, the same economic logic fueled burgeoning regional trade and economic cooperation throughout Africa during the precolonial independence era, as witnessed by the growth of the trans-Saharan trade network.

In the aftermath of the imposition of direct colonial rule, colonial administrators oversaw the destruction of regional economic ties through the transformation of individual colonies into **closed economic systems.** Colonial administrators sought to ensure that all economic interaction within a given empire took place exclusively between the European colonial power and its colonies. In the case of the German colony of Togoland, German colonial administrators strove to eliminate cross-border trade with the neighboring British colony of the Gold Coast (Ghana) and the neighboring French colonies of Dahomey (Benin) and Upper Volta (Burkina Faso) and instead fostered strong exclusive economic ties with Germany.

The defining element of the closed economic model was the government's granting of trade monopolies to **chartered companies** that often assumed complete responsibility for overseeing the socioeconomic and political-military transformation of the colony, at least until a "proper" state structure could be developed by colonial administrators. In Germany's East African colony of Tanganyika, the German government granted complete sovereignty to the Deutsch-Ostafrikanische Gesellschaft (German East Africa Company) headed by Carl Peters, one of the most fervent proponents of German colonialism.[45]

The most important impact of these closed trading systems was that all regional trade, except that which took place in individual empires, was virtually destroyed—as illustrated by the decline of the trans-Saharan trade network. Regional trade that once crisscrossed the Sahara desert was gradually replaced by the shipping of products from the interior to the coastal regions of individual colonies, for eventual transshipment to Europe and other outposts of the global European empires. As a result, the once vibrant outposts of the Sahara desert, such as the fabled city of Timbuktu, which were built on regional trade and economic development, entered a period of socioeconomic decline as their function as trade posts gradually disappeared. Indeed, one could associate emerging notions of the Sahara desert as a barrier to regional trade and investment with the gradual destruction of the trans-Saharan trade network at the end of the nineteenth century.[46]

Creation of Export-Oriented Mono-Crop
or Mono-Mineral Economies

A second socioeconomic impact of colonialism was the transformation of individual colonies into export-oriented economies that, in the extreme, produced one primary product desired by the European colonial power. These so-called **mono-crop economies** or **mono-mineral economies** were designed to serve as convenient and cheap sources of raw materials for European industry.

Once developed, the colonies were also expected to serve as markets for the sale of manufactured goods produced in Europe and other regions of the widely scattered European empires.

One example involved French efforts during the nineteenth century to expand the cultivation of peanuts in Senegal. Peanuts, the oil of which was used for a variety of cooking and industrial purposes in Africa and Europe, historically had been grown on a limited scale in Senegal before the imposition of direct colonial rule. The dramatic surge in peanut production that took place under the auspices of the colonial state resulted from an alliance between French colonial administrators and local Muslim religious leaders (marabouts), both of whom jointly recognized the financial profits to be gained from making Senegal a center for peanut production in the French colonial empire. The willingness of local marabouts to promote peanut production through the mobilization of their disciples (taalibe) achieved remarkable results. From 1885 to the eve of World War I, annual peanut production increased sevenfold, from 45,000 to 300,000 metric tons.[47] On the eve of independence from colonial rule in 1960, roughly two-thirds of Senegal's rural population was involved in peanut production, and the peanut crop accounted for at least two-thirds of the total value of all Senegalese exports.[48] As aptly noted by Sheldon Gellar, the prosperity of Senegal's colonial economy became "inextricably linked" to peanut production.[49]

The promotion of mono-crop or mono-mineral colonial economies entailed serious costs for the local African populations and hindered the long-term economic development of the African continent. Two trends in particular demonstrate that the peanut economy nurtured under French colonialism constituted at best a mixed blessing for Senegal's socioeconomic development. First, an economy geared toward the production of a primary product is vulnerable to the unreliability of international prices for that product. The economic history of the second half of the twentieth century clearly demonstrates that the prices for primary products fluctuate dramatically and in general have gradually declined relative to the costs of manufactured products. As a result, something as simple as estimating government revenues from taxes to ensure a variety of government services becomes extremely difficult, if not impossible. How can a government dependent on revenues from one product maintain its domestic and international financial commitments if a significant portion of the crop is decimated by poor weather? Moreover, how does the government respond when, as in the case of Senegal, the peanut production that formed the basis for its colonial economy suffers a sharp decrease in international demand due to its replacement by a cheaper and more effective substitute, in this case petroleum oil from the Middle East?

A second important point revolves around the negative relationship between the promotion of primary products and food production. Specifically, the creation of mono-crop and mono-mineral colonial economies was directly associated with a decline in the production of traditional foodstuffs. This agricultural shortcoming carried over into the contemporary independence era as levels of food production declined relative to the needs of growing populations, contributing to malnutrition and chronic famine conditions in various regions. One consequence of this trend is that Africa was the only region of the world that suffered from a per capita decline in food production from the 1960s to the 1980s.

Promotion of Perverse Infrastructural Development

A third socioeconomic impact of colonialism was the perverse development of the infrastructure, such as railroads and telecommunications, critical to economic development. An analysis of the railroad sector offers some telling insights (see Map 3.5). The colonial railroads were designed to haul primary products to the coast for eventual export to Europe and other geographical regions of the European empires. For example, the construction of the French colonial railroad linking Bamako, Mali, with Dakar, Senegal, the subject of a famous novel written by the Senegalese novelist Sembène Ousmane, was designed specifically to transport peanuts.[50]

The export-oriented nature of these railroads is significant for two reasons. First, the design of these transportation systems inevitably hindered regional development. If the primary purpose of the colonial railroads had been to promote regional development, one could envision a different configuration in West Africa that would have crisscrossed the Sahara desert or at minimum would have followed east-west trajectories across the northern and southern edges of the desert. In the case of the United States, one of the most notable achievements of the nineteenth century was the linking of the east and west coasts by one railway line that subsequently served as the basis for internal eco-

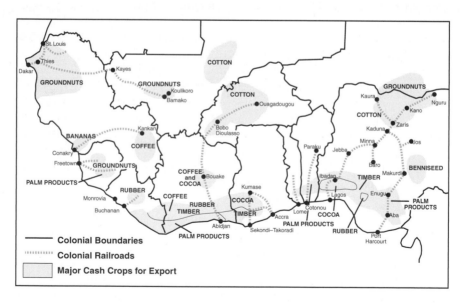

MAP 3.5   Railroads in Colonial West Africa (1930s)

Source: Map based on Michael Kwamena-Poh et al., *Africa History in Maps* (Essex: Longman, 1987), p. 61.

nomic growth and development. In the case of West Africa, however, a series of railroads designed with little consideration of the system's impact on regional development simply links the interior with the coastal regions. Dreams of linking these railroads, even if the financial resources were available, are unlikely to be realized in the near future because the railway lines were often built using different rail gauges.

The export-oriented railroad systems also fostered the growth of other perverse forms of infrastructural development. For example, the primary reason Bamako became the capital of Mali was its strategic location at the end of the Dakar-Bamako railway line. Indeed, the importance of the railroad as one of the cornerstones of the colonial economy ensured that roads, telephone lines, and small towns would eventually be built along the main railway line.

Inappropriately designed infrastructure contributed to the uneven development of the African colonies, prompting some colonial observers to speak of the creation of **dual economies,** the first revolving around a European-induced cash economy and the second revolving around African subsistence farming. In the case of Senegal, Gellar suggests that the colonial economy could be divided into at least three sectors: (1) a "modern," essentially European, sector principally based in the capital, Dakar, and other major urban areas where European colonial administrators and an emerging African elite would manage the major import-export houses and colonial banks; (2) a cash-crop sector principally located in the peanut-producing plantations and associated areas, such as mining towns along the railway line, where African farmers and workers could obtain cash employment; and (3) a predominantly subsistence sector where foodstuffs would be grown for local consumption.[51] The inherent inequality between these various sectors significantly challenged leaders of the contemporary independence era who were intent on promoting broadly shared economic development.

Strengthening of Gender Bias
in National Development

A fourth socioeconomic impact of colonialism was the strengthening of gender bias in national development. As discussed in Chapter 2, African women played an important role in economic affairs during the precolonial independence era. In many African societies, women could achieve a certain degree of economic autonomy from their husbands due to traditional customs that called for women and men to keep their own properties and to maintain separate financial accounts; the evolution, especially within matrilineal societies, of protected inheritance rights; and the important role of women in local trade networks. However, the same Victorian values of European colonialism that fostered the political marginalization of African women also contributed to their economic marginalization.

The strengthening of gender inequality in the economic realm took several forms during the colonial era. First, colonial economic policies presumed African men were the heads of households and economic breadwinners. As a result, men were typically favored to work in the export-oriented cash sectors of the colonial economy, such as the mining industry, large-scale plantations, and urban-based administrative offices, at the expense of women who were often relegated to subsistence farming in rural areas. Inheritance laws were also altered to favor men, diminishing the ability of women, especially in matrilineal societies, to ensure the transmission of wealth through their family lines. One of the most damaging policies introduced private land ownership.[52] Throughout the French colonies, for example, the Napoleonic Code conferred legal ownership of all duly registered private property to husbands as heads of families.[53] In addition, when colonial authorities deemed it necessary to provide technical training and education, usually African men, not African women, were selected. "Whatever their prior status," concludes Coquery-Vidrovitch, the fate of African women "worsened" under colonial rule, which "upset the fragile balance" that had existed between the sexes.[54] Indeed, "although both men and women were exploited within the colonial economy," concludes April Gordon, men nonetheless gained access to "important resources such as money, skills, land, and education less available to women."[55]

Authoritarian Legacy of the State

A final socioeconomic impact of colonialism was an authoritarian legacy that permeated all aspects of economic life. The most nefarious side of this legacy was the institution of forced labor to ensure that sufficient numbers of farmers and workers were available to meet the needs of the colonial economy, such as tending plantation crops, working at the mines, and constructing roads and railroads. In the case of the British colony of Ghana, the meticulously kept records of the Transport Department document that it was not uncommon at the beginning of the twentieth century for Africans to be forced to work as "carriers" of boxes or bundles in areas where other forms of transport were either impracticable due to the tsetse fly or simply unavailable. One report documents that these carriers were forced to work during a 12-month period in which they averaged approximately 400 miles a month. As a result, many carriers became incapacitated when their uncovered feet became "almost completely worn through."[56] The most shocking element of this report, explains Claude Ake, a Nigerian scholar, was how the British colonial authorities resolved this "technical" problem: Henceforth the feet of the carriers were to be tarred![57]

Britain abolished forced labor in its colonies in 1923 but retained another less intrusive—yet nonetheless authoritarian—element of the colonial economy: **marketing boards.** This colonial economic institution, adopted in varying forms by all colonial powers, maintained monopolistic control over the buying and selling of primary products in each colony. Each year the board would determine a set price to be paid to farmers for a specific amount of a product. Lacking alternatives, the farmers had no choice but to sell their goods through the colonial marketing board. The most egregious injustice of this economic relationship was the marketing board practice of purchasing products at prices well below that of the international market. In turn, the marketing board would then sell the product at a handsome profit for the colonial authority.[58]

In the British colony of Nigeria, four marketing boards maintained monopoly rights over the production and marketing of four primary export crops: the Nigerian Cocoa Marketing Board, the Nigerian Palm Produce Marketing Board, the Nigerian Groundnut Marketing Board, and the Nigerian Cotton Marketing Board. These four marketing boards were "so profitable" to the colonial state that they were transformed into four regional marketing boards with responsibility for all primary products produced in their respective zones.[59] The importance of these boards to the financial success of the colonial state, at the expense of African producers, is illuminated by the enormous profits obtained. The British colonial state in Nigeria made a 733 percent profit on peanuts and a 559 percent profit on palm oil, of which little was passed to the African producers.

Although the most coercive elements of the colonial economy, such as forced labor, were eventually abolished, the coercive role of the state in the economic arena carried over into the contemporary independence era. During the first three decades of this era, most African policymakers oversaw the strengthening of state involvement in the economy. As will be discussed more extensively in Chapter 8, an important element of state economic involvement was the creation and rapid expansion of government-owned or government-controlled corporations (known as "parastatals") in all sectors of the economy, especially telecommunications, energy, and transportation. The often corrupt and inefficient nature of these corporations contributed in the 1980s to what is now commonly called the "crisis of the African state": the increasing inability of the independent successor of the colonial state to respond to the day-to-day needs of African populations. The scope and impact of the political and economic legacies of the colonial state remain paramount issues at the beginning of the twenty-first century.[60]

KEY TERMS

scramble for Africa
age of exploration
hegemonic powers
Atlantic slave trade
trans-Saharan slave trade
Red Sea slave trade
Swahili coast slave trade
European slave trade
Islamic slave trade
triangular trade
industrial revolution
informal empire
imperial mindset
direct colonial rule
effective occupation
discovery
divide-and-conquer

second-tier empires
mandate territory
trusteeship
indirect rule
direct rule
assimilation
irredentism
checks-and-balances
Bula Matari
divide-and-rule
closed economic systems
chartered companies
mono-crop economies
mono-mineral economies
dual economies
marketing boards

FOR FURTHER READING

Allman, Jean, Susan Geiger, and Nakanyike Musisi, eds. *Women in African Colonial Histories*. Bloomington: Indiana University Press, 2002.

Boahen, A. Adu. *African Perspectives on Colonialism*. Baltimore: Johns Hopkins University Press, 1987.

Boahen, A. Adu, ed. *General History of Africa* (vol. 7), *Africa under Colonial Domination 1880–1935*. Berkeley: University of California Press; Oxford: Heinemann; Paris: UNESCO, 1985.

Echenberg, Myron. *Colonial Conscripts: The Tirailleurs Sénégalais in French West Africa, 1857–1960*. Portsmouth: Heinemann, 1991.

Farwell, Bryon. *The Great War in Africa 1914–1918*. New York: W. W. Norton, 1986.

Freund, Bill. *The Making of Contemporary Africa: Development of African Society since 1800* (2nd ed.). Boulder: Lynne Rienner, 1998.

Inikori, Joseph E., and Stanley L. Engerman, eds. *The Atlantic Slave Trade: Effects on Economies, Societies, and Peoples in Africa, the Americas, and Europe*. Durham: Duke University Press, 1992.

Mamdani, Mahmood. *Citizen and Subject: Contemporary Africa and the Legacy of Late Colonialism*. Princeton: Princeton University Press, 1996.

Mudimbe, V. Y. *The Idea of Africa*. Bloomington: Indiana University Press, 1994.

Oliver, Roland, and Anthony Atmore. *Africa since 1800* (4th ed.). Cambridge: Cambridge University Press, 1994.

Packenham, Thomas. *The Scramble for Africa: The White Man's Conquest of the Dark Continent from 1876 to 1912*. New York: Random House, 1991.

Perham, Margery. *African Apprenticeship: An Autobiographical Journey in Southern Africa in 1929*. New York: Africana Publishers, 1974.

Rice, Edward. *Captain Sir Francis Richard Burton: The Secret Agent Who Made the Pilgrimage to Mecca, Discovered the Kama Sutra, and Brought the Arabian Nights to the West*. New York: HarperPerennial, 1990.

Roberts, Andrew, ed. *The Colonial Moment in Africa: Essays on the Movement of Minds and Materials, 1900–1940*. Cambridge: Cambridge University Press, 1990.

Robinson, Ronald, and John Gallagher (with Alice Denny). *Africa and the Victorians: The Climax of Imperialism*. Garden City: Anchor, 1968.

Romero, Patricia W., ed. *Women's Voices on Africa: A Century of Travel Writings*. Princeton, NJ: Marcus Wiener Publishing, 1992.

Segal, Ronald. *Islam's Black Slaves: The Other Black Diaspora*. New York: Farrar, Straus & Giroux, 2001.

Thomas, Hugh. *The Slave Trade: The Story of the Atlantic Slave Trade: 1440–1870*. New York: Simon & Schuster, 1997.

Wesseling, H. L. *Divide and Rule: The Partition of Africa, 1880–1914*. Westport: Praeger, 1996.

Young, Crawford. *The African Colonial State in Comparative Perspective*. New Haven: Yale University Press, 1994.

NOTES

1. See M. Kwamena-Poh et al., *African History in Maps* (London: Longman, 1987), pp. 12–13.

2. Ambrose Moyo, "Religion in Africa," in April A. Gordon and Donald L. Gordon, eds., *Understanding Contemporary Africa* (3rd ed.) (Boulder: Lynne Rienner, 2001), p. 320.

3. Ibid.

4. Ibid.

5. See Joseph E. Inikori and Stanley L. Engerman, eds., *The Atlantic Slave Trade: Effects on Economies, Societies, and Peoples in Africa, the Americas, and Europe* (Durham: Duke University Press, 1992).

6. J. E. Inikori, "Africa in World History: The Export Slave Trade from Africa and the Emergence of the Atlantic Economic Order," in B. A. Ogot, ed., *General History of Africa. Volume 5. Africa from the Sixteenth to the Eighteenth Century* (Paris: UNESCO, 1992), p. 74. See also Ronald Segal, *Islam's Black Slaves: The Other Black Diaspora* (New York: Farrar, Straus & Giroux, 2001).

7. See Philip D. Curtin, *The Atlantic Slave Trade: A Census* (Madison: University of Wisconsin Press, 1969), pp. 88–89.

8. Curtin, *The Atlantic Slave Trade,* p. 3. See also David Henige, "Measuring the Immeasurable: The Atlantic Slave Trade, West African Population and the Pyrrhonian Critic," *Journal of African History* 27 (1986): 295–313.

9. See Paul E. Lovejoy, "The Volume of the Atlantic Slave Trade: Synthesis," *Journal of African History* 23 (1982): 478, and Inikori, "Africa in World History."

10. See Kenneth F. Kiple and Brian T. Higgins, "Mortality Caused by Dehydration during the Middle Passage," in Inikori and Engerman, eds., *The Atlantic Slave Trade,* pp. 321–38.

11. See Ralph A. Austin, "The Trans-Saharan Slave Trade: A Tentative Census," in Henry A. Gemery and Jan S. Hogendorn, eds., *The Uncommon Market: Essays in the Economic History of the Atlantic Slave Trade* (New York: Academic, 1979), pp. 23–76.

12. See Peter Duignan and L. H. Gann, *The United States and Africa: A History* (Cambridge: Cambridge University Press, 1984).

13. Edward Rice, *Captain Sir Richard Francis Burton: The Secret Agent Who Made the Pilgrimage to Mecca, Discovered the Kama Sutra, and Brought the Arabian Nights to the West* (New York: HarperPerennial, 1990), p. 1.

14. Patricia W. Romero, ed., *Women's Voices on Africa: A Century of Travel Writings* (Princeton, NJ: Marcus Wiener Publishing, 1992), p. 13.

15. Isak Dineson, *Out of Africa* (London: Putnam, 1937).

16. Romero, *Women's Voices.*

17. Margery Perham, *African Apprenticeship: An Autobiographical Journey in Southern Africa in 1928* (New York: Africana Publishers, 1974).

18. Romero, *Women's Voices,* p. 209.

19. See Andrew Roberts, "The Imperial Mind," in Andrew Roberts, ed., *The Colonial Moment in Africa: Essays on the Movement of Minds and Materials, 1900–1940* (Cambridge: Cambridge University Press, 1990), pp. 24–76. See also Ronald Robinson and John Gallagher (with Alice Denny), *Africa and the Victorians: The Climax of Imperialism* (New York: St. Martin's, 1961).

20. See Thomas Packenham, *The Scramble for Africa: The White Man's Conquest of the Dark Continent from 1876 to 1912* (New York: Random House, 1991).

21. See J. K. Fynn, "Ghana-Asante (Ashanti)," in Michael Crowder, ed., *West African Resistance: The Military Response to Colonial Occupation* (New York: Africana, 1971), pp. 19–52. See also Robert B. Edgerton, *The Fall of the Asante Empire: The Hundred-Year War for Africa's Gold Coast* (New York: The Free Press, 1995).

22. Ibid., p. 27.

23. Ibid.

24. Catherine Coquery-Vidrovitch, *African Women: A Modern History* (Boulder: Westview, 1997), p. 43.

25. See Michael Crowder, ed., *West African Resistance: The Military Response to Colonial Occupation* (New York: Africana, 1971), pp. 1–18.

26. See Prosser Gifford and Wm. Roger Louis, eds., *Britain and Germany in Africa* (New Haven: Yale University Press, 1967). See also Woodruff D. Smith, *The German Colonial Empire* (Chapel Hill: University of North Carolina Press, 1979).

27. The mandates were as follows: Burundi and Rwanda (Belgium), Togoland (France), Kamerun (France and Britain), Tanganyika (Britain), South-West Africa (South Africa).

28. For an overview, see Robert L. Hess, *Italian Colonialism in Somalia* (Chicago: University of Chicago, 1966).

29. For example, see Ibrahim Sundiata, *Equatorial Guinea* (Boulder: Westview, 1989).

30. See Sir F. D. Lugard, *The Dual Mandate in British Tropical Africa* (Edinburgh: Blackwood, 1922).

31. See Prosser Gifford and Wm. Roger Louis, eds., *France and Britain in Africa: Imperial Rivalry and Colonial Rule* (New Haven: Yale University Press, 1971).

32. For an overview, see Jean Suret-Canale, *Afrique Noire: L'Ere Coloniale, 1900–1945* (Paris: Editions Sociales, 1964).

33. For an overview, see Crawford Young, *Politics in the Congo: Decolonization and Independence* (Princeton: Princeton University Press, 1965).

34. For an overview of Portuguese colonial policies, see Norrie MacQueen, *The Decolonization of Portuguese Africa: Metropolitan Revolution and the Dissolution of Empire* (London: Longman, 1997). See also Gerald J. Bendor, *Angola under the Portuguese: The Myth and the Reality* (London: Heinemann, 1978).

35. See "The Sources of the Status Quo and Irredentist Policies," in Carl G. Widstrand, ed., *African Boundary Problems* (Uppsala: Scandinavian Institute of African Studies, 1969), pp. 101–18. See also Naomi Chazan, ed., *Irredentism and International Politics* (Boulder: Lynne Rienner, 1991).

36. For a discussion of this theme, see Saadia Touval, *Somali Nationalism: International Politics and the Drive for Unity in the Horn* (Cambridge: Harvard University Press, 1963), pp. 49–50. See also David D. Laitin and Said S. Samatar, *Somalia: Nation in Search of a State* (Boulder: Westview, 1987).

37. See I. William Zartman, *Ripe for Resolution: Conflict and Intervention in Africa* (New York: Oxford University Press, 1985).

38. The breakdown by population is estimated as follows: Hausa-Fulani (29 percent), Yoruba (20 percent), and Igbo (17 percent). See Chris Cook and David Killingray, *African Political Facts since 1945,* 2nd ed. (New York: Facts on File, 1991), p. 235.

39. See Conrad Max Benedict Brann, "Democratization of Language Use in Public Domains in Nigeria," *The Journal of Modern African Studies* 31, no. 4 (1993): 644–45.

40. Jane L. Parpart, "Women and the State in Africa," in Donald Rothchild and Naomi Chazan, eds., *The Precarious Balance: State and Society in Africa* (Boulder: Westview, 1988), p. 210.

41. April A. Gordon, "Women and Development," in Gordon and Gordon, eds., *Understanding Contemporary Africa,* p. 276.

42. Coquery-Vidrovitch, *African Women,* p. 38.

43. See Crawford Young, *The African Colonial State in Comparative Perspective* (New Haven: Yale University Press, 1994), p. 1.

44. See Myron Echenberg, *Colonial Conscripts: The Tirailleurs Sénégalais in French West Africa, 1857–1960* (Portsmouth: Heinemann, 1991).

45. Smith, *The German Colonial Empire,* pp. 97–99.

46. For an interesting discussion of this metaphor, see I. William Zartman, "The Sahara—Bridge or Barrier," *International Conciliation* 541 (1963): 1–62.

47. See Sheldon Gellar, *Senegal: An African Nation between Islam and the West,* 2nd ed. (Boulder: Westview, 1995), pp. 12–13.

48. Ibid., pp. 13, 60.

49. Ibid., p. 12.

50. See Sembène Ousmane, *God's Bits of Wood* (Harare: Zimbabwe Publishing House, 1984).

51. Gellar, *Senegal: An African Nation between Islam and the West,* p. 12.

52. Gordon, "Women and Development," p. 277.

53. Coquery-Vidrovitch, *African Women,* p. 65.

54. Ibid., p. 59.

55. Gordon, "Women and Development," p. 276.

56. See Claude Ake, *A Political Economy of Africa* (New York: Longman, 1981), p. 68.

57. Ibid.

58. Ibid., p. 64.

59. Ibid., p. 64.

60. See, for example, the seminal work of Crawford Young, *The African Colonial State in Comparative Perspective* (New Haven: Yale University Press, 1994).

4

♚

Nationalism and the Emergence of the Contemporary Independence Era (1951–Present)

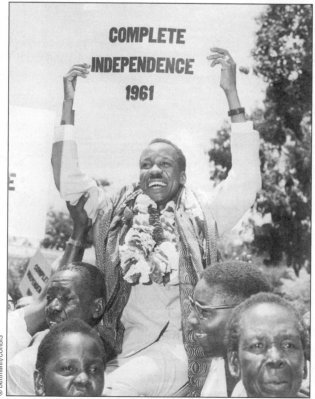

Julius K. Nyerere, former head of state of Tanzania (1961–85), whom his people affectionately called the mwalimu (teacher), celebrating his country's achievement of independence.

THE INDEPENDENCE OF LIBYA in 1951 marked the beginning of the end of European colonialism in Africa. Fewer than 66 years after European diplomats sealed the fate of the precolonial independence era at the Conference of Berlin (1884–85), a new generation of African political leaders and popular movements witnessed the first fruits of a **decolonization process** that gradually encompassed the African continent and ushered in the contemporary independence era. Decolonization was for the most part peacefully accepted by European leaders, who ultimately recognized the impossibility of maintaining permanent control. Intransigence on the part of Portugal and the minority white-ruled regimes in Southern Africa nonetheless prompted the rise of revolutionary movements intent on achieving independence by military force. Regardless of whether achieved peacefully or by force, decolonization resulted from the emergence of African nationalist movements that demanded independence and equality for their respective peoples. This process was largely completed in 1994, when democratic elections in South Africa ushered in a multiparty and multiracial government under the leadership of President Nelson Mandela. The remainder of this chapter is devoted to exploring the factors behind the rise of nationalism and the emergence of the contemporary independence era.

TRENDS IN AFRICAN NATIONALISM

The concept of **nationalism** is defined as a sense of collective identity in which a people perceives itself as different than (and often superior to) other peoples.[1] Nationalism also implies the existence of a variety of shared characteristics, most notably a common language and culture, but also race and religion, as shown by the rise of Islamic revivalist movements in North Africa and other regions of the world with sizable Muslim populations. In the case of the United States, scholars traditionally described American society as a "melting pot" in which the varied languages and cultures of immigrants were gradually replaced by a common American language and American culture. Even more recent multicultural conceptions that portray American society as a "mixed salad" in which each group maintains its uniqueness nonetheless recognize an overarching American culture and language.

The emergence of African nationalism and African demands for **national self-determination** (independence) of individual colonies followed a different pattern than its classic European counterparts of earlier centuries.[2] The emergence of European "nations" (i.e., cohesive group identities) generally preceded and contributed to the creation of European "states" (the structures of governance). The net result was the creation of viable nation-states that enjoyed the legitimacy of their peoples. This process was reversed in Africa. In most cases, the colonial state was created before any sense of nation existed. As a result, the creation and strengthening of a nationalist attachment to what in essence constituted artificially created African states became one of the supreme challenges of colonial administrators and the African leaders who replaced them during the contemporary independence era.

A second unique aspect of African nationalism was its inherently anticolonial character. African nationalist movements were sharply divided on political agendas, ideological orientation, and economic programs. Regardless of their differences, however, the leaders of these movements did agree on one point: the necessity and desirability of independence from foreign control. Anticolonial sentiment served as the rallying point of African nationalist movements to such a degree that African nationalism was equivalent to African anticolonialism.

The process of decolonization unfolded gradually in a series of waves, beginning in the 1950s with groups of countries becoming independent during specific historical periods (see Map 4.1).[3] Three countries, however, differed in this regard. Ethiopia was never colonized despite being occupied by fascist Italy from 1936 to 1941 during World War II. Liberia constituted at best a "quasi-American colony" that never fell under the direct authority of the U.S. government (see the box in Chapter 3). Instead, the country, principally founded in 1822 by freed American slaves, declared independence in 1847 and successfully avoided European colonization. Egypt, too, held a unique position in African history. Despite being subjected to British colonial rule, Egypt achieved its independence in 1922.

MAP 4.1   Waves of African Independence

The **first wave of independence** took place during the 1950s and was led by the heavily Arab-influenced North African countries of Libya (1951), Morocco (1956), and Tunisia (1956).[4] Three countries outside North Africa also obtained independence during this period: the former British colonies of the Sudan in 1956 and the Gold Coast (Ghana) in 1957, followed by the former French colony of Guinea in 1958. The latter case was especially noteworthy in that Guinea was the only French colony to cast a negative vote against a 1958 referendum concerning the creation of a revised French "community of states." A "yes" vote would have confirmed continued French sovereignty while at the same time granting some degree of political autonomy to Guinea and the other French colonies. The response of the French government was to order the immediate withdrawal of all French aid and advisors from Guinea. One infamous anecdote of the period suggested that departing French colonial administrators even went so far as to remove lightbulbs from their sockets. Despite the acrimony involved in this latter case, the first wave of independence was marked by a relatively peaceful transfer of power to African authorities.

The **second wave of independence** took place during the 1960s, when more than thirty African countries achieved independence.[5] Most of these countries were former British and French colonies in East, Central, and West Africa. All three Belgian colonies (Burundi, Rwanda, and the Democratic Republic of the Congo [Congo-Kinshasa]) also acquired independence during this period and were joined by the Republic of Somalia, which represented a federation of the former British and Italian Somaliland territories. Aside from some noteworthy exceptions, most notably France's unsuccessful attempt to defeat a pro-independence guerrilla insurgency in Algeria and the emergence of the Mau Mau guerrilla insurgency in Kenya, the decolonization process of the 1960s was also largely peaceful. The departing colonial powers had already accepted the inevitability of decolonization. Questions simply remained as to when and under what conditions.

The **third wave of independence** began in 1974. A military coup d'état in Portugal, led by junior military officers, resulted in a declaration that the Portuguese government intended to grant immediate independence to the colonies in Africa.[6] Coup plotters sought to end what they perceived as a series of African military quagmires that pitted poorly trained and unmotivated Portuguese military forces against highly motivated and increasingly adept African guerrilla insurgencies: the Frente de Libertação de Moçambique (FRELIMO, Front for the Liberation of Mozambique) in Mozambique, the Partido Africano da Indepêndencia da Guiné e Cabo Verde (PAIGC, Independence African Party of Guinea and Cape Verde) in Guinea Bissau and Cape Verde, and three guerrilla groups in Angola—the Frente Nacional de Libertação de Angola (FNLA, National Front for the Liberation of Angola), the União Nacional para a Indepêndencia Total de Angola (UNITA, National Union for the Total Independence of Angola), and the Movimento Popular de Libertação de Angola (MPLA, Popular Movement for the Liberation of Angola). The violent path to independence in the former Portuguese colonies was further complicated in 1975, when Angolan guerrilla groups clashed in what would become an extended civil war over who would lead an independent Angola. The former French colonies of Comoros (1975), Seychelles (1976), and Djibouti (1977), however, achieved independence under largely peaceful terms.

The **fourth wave of independence** emerged during the 1980s. Except for the unique case of Eritrea, which gained independence from Ethiopia in 1993 (and which is discussed at the end of this chapter), this wave was directed against the minority white-ruled regimes in Southern Africa.[7] Since 1948, South Africa was controlled by the descendants of white settlers known as Afrikaners. This minority elite established a highly racist system known as apartheid (apartness) in which blacks and other minorities (roughly 85 percent of the population) were denied political rights. The apartheid system was eventually exported to the former German colony of Namibia after it became a South African mandate territory in the aftermath of World War I. White settlers in Southern Rhodesia (Zimbabwe) led by Ian Smith in 1965 instituted a regional variation of apartheid after they announced their Unilateral Declaration of Independence (UDI) from British colonial rule.

The minority white-ruled regimes of Southern Africa were confronted by guerrilla organizations that enjoyed regional and international support: the African National Congress (ANC) and the Pan-African Congress (PAC) in South Africa, the South-West Africa People's Organization (SWAPO) in Namibia, and the Zimbabwe African Nationalist Union (ZANU) and the Zimbabwe African People's Union (ZAPU) in Zimbabwe.[8] In all three cases, military struggles were suspended after the white minority regimes agreed to negotiate transitions to black majority rule. Zimbabwe's transition to black majority rule in 1980 was followed by the creation of multiparty and multiracial democracies in Namibia in 1990 and South Africa in 1994. Except for some small coastal enclaves in Morocco (most notably Ceuta and Melilla) that remain under Spanish sovereignty, Nelson Mandela's emergence in 1994 as the first democratically elected leader of South Africa signaled the end of the decolonization process and the transition to the contemporary independence era (see the accompanying box).

A Closer Look: NELSON MANDELA'S "LONG WALK TO FREEDOM"

On May 10, 1994, Nelson Mandela was inaugurated as South Africa's first democratically elected leader. His inauguration in many respects represented the culmination of his "long walk to freedom," to quote the title of his internationally acclaimed autobiography. Mandela spent nearly three decades (1962–91) as a political prisoner due to his conviction that all means, including

guerrilla struggle, were to be employed to destroy the racist system of apartheid that existed in South Africa from 1948 to 1994. "I cannot pinpoint a moment when I became politicized, when I knew that I would spend my life in the liberation struggle," explains Mandela in his autobiography. "To be an African in South Africa means that one is politicized from the moment of one's birth, whether one acknowledges it or not."

A turning point in Mandela's political life occurred at age 36, when he became a formal member of the African National Congress (ANC), the oldest South African political party (established in 1912) and principal opponent of white minority rule. In its early years, the ANC was committed to the nonviolent transformation of South Africa's political system. However, the nonviolent approach of the ANC changed in the aftermath of the Sharpeville massacre of March 21, 1960. Without provocation, the South African police opened fire on marchers demonstrating against the "pass laws," legislation that controlled the movement of Africans throughout the country. Sixty-nine were killed and hundreds more were wounded. As demonstrations began to break out in other parts of the country, the South African government declared a state of emergency and outlawed all political organizations. The ANC was ultimately forced into exile.

Under the leadership of Mandela, the ANC moved away from its nonviolent approach and in 1961 formed a military wing, Umkhonto we Sizwe (Spear of the Nation), that could carry out acts of sabotage against the South African government. "This was a fateful step," explains Mandela. "We were embarking on a new and more dangerous path, a path of organized violence, the results of which we did not and could not know." From an organizational standpoint, this event marked the transformation of the ANC into a military organization capable of carrying out a sustained guerrilla struggle against the apartheid system. Concerning Mandela's personal life, however, this decision eventually earned him a life sentence in prison after he was captured by the South African police in 1962.

A significant portion of Mandela's sentence (nearly two decades) was spent at an isolated prison on Robben Island. Off the coast of Capetown, Mandela describes this small island, which now serves as a tourist attraction, as once constituting the "harshest, most iron-fisted outpost in the South African penal system." At the beginning of his sentence, Mandela was classified as a "Group D" political prisoner who threatened the national security. This classification allowed Mandela to receive only one visitor and to write and receive only one letter every 6 months. "I found this to be one of the most inhumane restrictions of the prison system," explains Mandela. "Communication with one's family is a human right; it should not be restricted by the artificial gradations of a prison system. But it was one of the facts of prison life."

Mandela's incarceration ended on February 11, 1991, in full view of the international media. At age 73, his unrelenting opposition to the apartheid system, which had cost him nearly three decades of freedom, had transformed him into one of the most celebrated and admired political figures in the world. He became the symbol of a domestic and international antiapartheid movement that culminated in South Africa's first multiracial, multiparty democratic elections in 1994. Rather than seeking to punish his former jailers once he and the ANC emerged victorious in those elections, Mandela magnanimously extended the olive branch of cooperation to all ethnic and racial factions in South Africa. It is this determination—to extend the hands of cooperation to all those interested in creating a South Africa devoid of racial and ethnic injustice—that has ensured Mandela's place as one of the greatest leaders of the twentieth century.

Quotations drawn from Nelson Mandela, *Long Walk to Freedom: The Autobiography of Nelson Mandela* (Boston: Little, Brown, 1994).

DOMESTIC INFLUENCES ON
THE RISE OF NATIONALISM

The socioeconomic and political military systems of the precolonial independence era underwent immense social change due to the imposition of colonial
rule. Although the principal duty of colonial administrators was to ensure
European domination in the colonies, social changes unleashed by colonial rule
unwittingly sowed the seeds for colonial demise. Three patterns of social
change in particular contributed to the rise of African nationalism and African
demands for decolonization.

Creation of Administrative Centers
and the Rise of Urbanization

The creation of the colony itself, most notably the designation of regional
administrative centers and a capital city, played an important initial role in providing the basis for the emergence of nationalism.[9] The urban areas served as mag-
nets for Africans seeking employment and education, contributing to a process of
urbanization in which Africans moved in increasing numbers from the countryside to the capital cities and towns. The "lure of the town," notes Kenneth Little,
was due to the role of the urban areas as centers of politics, economics, and education.[10] In short, those who desired political and economic success in the colonial states were invariably drawn to emerging administrative centers.

Newly created towns dramatically expanded in terms of population. Abidjan, the former capital of Côte d'Ivoire, initially was a fishing village inhabited
by approximately 700 people at the beginning of the twentieth century. The
growing need for French colonial administrators fueled population growth,
which exceeded 10,000 people by 1931. The 1951 completion of a canal linking Abidjan's lagoon with the Atlantic Ocean further hastened urbanization.
On the eve of independence in 1961, Abidjan's population exceeded 180,000;
the figure exceeded 2.5 million at the beginning of the twenty-first century.[11]

The new towns served as the focal points of emerging national identities. In
contrast to the relatively homogeneous nature of life in the villages, the colonial
towns served as meeting grounds for the numerous ethnic groups that inhabited
individual colonies. The towns served as "melting pots" in the sense that diverse
ethnic cultures were gradually overshadowed by a sense of belonging to a larger
political unit. It is important to note, however, that the promotion of nationalist
sentiment did not necessarily mean a weakening of ethnic identity, nor the
breaking of socioeconomic and political ties between the urbanized migrants
and their villages of birth. It is precisely for this reason that the multicultural
metaphor of a "mixed salad" is as relevant for most of Africa as it is for the
United States at the beginning of the twenty-first century. Simply put, the colonial towns fostered the emergence of an overarching national culture and language while individuals maintained their specific cultural attachments, just as
the separate ingredients of a mixed salad maintain their distinct flavors.

Educational Training and Development

The promotion of educational training for select groups of Africans served as a second pattern of social change that contributed to the rise of nationalism. The practical problem colonial administrators confronted was that the small number of Europeans posted in each colony could not manage all aspects of the colonial economic and political systems. To ensure effective rule, colonial administrators oversaw a series of educational programs designed to train the local peoples in the language and philosophy of the colonial power; create an auxiliary technical staff capable of performing a variety of technical tasks, such as accounting, plumbing, and electrical work; and train an elite to collaborate with the colonial powers.[12] Each colony therefore went beyond the traditional literacy programs of missionaries by creating grade schools, high schools, and technical training institutes.

Colonial education served as one of the seeds of nationalism that contributed to colonialism's ultimate demise. Small numbers of secondary schools for the most part located in the capital city meant that students selected by colonial administrators would arrive from all regions of the colony. As a result, students who had most likely never traveled outside their villages and who had rarely if ever met students their own ages from other ethnic groups suddenly found themselves in new surroundings with students from all over the colony. As time went by, friendships were created that transcended ethnic lines. Students began seeing themselves as part of a larger entity (the colony) that was multiethnic. In the British colony of Nigeria, for example, the vast majority of colonial civil servants were trained in the capital city at King's College, the standard name for such institutions throughout the British colonies. The formative years spent at this institution prompted students from various ethnic backgrounds, such as Yoruba, Igbo, and Hausa-Fulani, to think of themselves as belonging to a greater Nigerian nation that, in turn, formed part of the greater British Empire.

The sense of belonging to something larger than a particular ethnic group developed further when students were sent to study at regional colonial schools. Before World War II began, the only postsecondary school throughout Afrique Occidentale Française (AOF—French West Africa) was the École Normale William Ponty in Dakar, Senegal. The school was renowned as the "most important center" for elite training in francophone West Africa.[13] For the first time in their lives, students could interact with their counterparts from other colonies, realizing that they often shared much more with each other as colonized peoples than they did with their colonial educators, who in any case rarely accepted them as either political or intellectual equals. Furthermore, these institutions served as the training centers for individuals who often emerged as the Founding Fathers of the newly independent African countries. One of the most influential leaders to graduate from the École Normale William Ponty was Félix Houphouët-Boigny, one of the Founding Fathers of Côte d'Ivoire, who served as president from 1960 to 1993.

African students sent to Paris, London, and the capitals of other colonizing powers to pursue advanced education and training perhaps impacted nationalist demands for independence most. The sharing of ideas and the nurturing of lifelong friendships became possible, not only with students from colonies in other regions of the world, but with citizens from the host country. The extremely close personal relationship between Léopold Sédar Senghor, the first president of Senegal (1960–80), and Georges Pompidou, president of France from 1969 to 1974, was made possible by the fact that they were classmates during the same era at Lycée Louis-le-Grand, a prestigious secondary school in Paris.[14]

Africans studying abroad were also directly exposed to the inherent contradictions between the colonizer's democratic heritage and traditions and the reality of authoritarian rule at home in the colonies. As any student who has studied in Paris can attest, the French curriculum has always underscored the importance of French democracy, with special emphasis on the universal democratic ideals of the French revolution: "Liberté, Égalité, Fraternité" ("Liberty, Equality, Fraternity"). However, even the most enamored African student of French civilization and French culture was hard pressed to rationalize the realities of dictatorial rule throughout the French colonies. Indeed, regardless of whether they studied in Paris, Brussels, London, Lisbon, Madrid, or Rome, African students were inevitably confronted by the chasm that existed between the practice of democracy in Europe and the undemocratic realities of day-to-day life in the colonies. African students, once trained to serve as the colonial administrators of their respective colonies, more often than not returned home intent on doing everything in their power to achieve independence for their peoples.

Formation and Spread of Voluntary Associations

The emergence of **voluntary associations** also contributed to the rise of nationalist demands for independence. The initial rise of voluntary associations was based on the willingness of individuals to join groups and cooperate to achieve a certain goal. The proliferation of such groups was especially tied to the urbanization process. Individuals uprooted from the familiar setting of the village or simply interested in meeting people with shared interests joined a wide variety of organizations in rapidly expanding urban areas.

The vast numbers of voluntary associations could be divided into two major types, the first of which was based on ethnicity.[15] One common example of the **ethnic voluntary associations** that remain influential today is a **mutual aid society.** A mutual aid society essentially served as a social welcome wagon and social welfare system for individuals who arrived in town from the village. Newcomers could count on the mutual aid society to provide essential information, such as where to go to acquire housing and meals with members of the same ethnic group. The mutual aid society also served as a social network in the sense that it sponsored dances and dinners. The accruement of monthly financial contributions of members allowed the mutual aid society to provide periodic financial assistance, including loans to start a business.

Membership in the second type of voluntary association was based on an individual's specific functional interest. **Functional voluntary associations** transcended ethnic divisions by bringing together individuals who shared a profession, such as nurses, or a social interest, such as playing soccer.[16] Some of these societies were even based on an individual's perceived social standing in the colony. In the Belgian Congo, for example, the Association des Évolués du Stanleyville (Association of Évolués of Stanleyville) served as an exclusive club for Congolese who had "evolved" into "civilized" members of the Belgian colony by embracing Belgian culture.[17]

The spread of voluntary associations during the colonial era played three roles in the rise of nationalist sentiment and African demands for independence from colonial rule. First, the voluntary associations served as meeting grounds where issues related to colonialism and independence could be discussed. Created in London in the 1920s, the West African Students' Union for at least two decades served as the "main political and social meeting place" of Nigerian students studying in England.[18] Voluntary associations also provided the organizational and leadership training for those individuals who led their countries to independence.[19] "Most of the early nationalist leaders were people who had benefited from the educational programs of the urban associations," explains Claude Ake, a Nigerian social scientist. "Many of them had their first experience of politics and organization through their involvement in these secondary organizations."[20] Nnamdi Azikiwe, who served as president of Nigeria from 1963 to 1966, was one of the principal founders in 1923 of the Young Man's Literary Association, which in 1940 joined with ten similar organizations to create the Federation of Nigerian Literary Societies and increasingly became involved in political issues.[21]

Most important, voluntary associations served as ready-made organizational structures for nationalist movements.[22] A group of associations, each created for very different reasons, often became the organizational nucleus of a political movement seeking independence. One of the Nigerian colony's first truly nationalist political organizations, the National Council of Nigeria and the Cameroons (NCNC), constituted a federation of a vast array of voluntary associations, including local Nigerian chapters of the West African Student Union and the Nigerian Union of Students.[23]

INTERNATIONAL INFLUENCES
ON THE RISE OF NATIONALISM

The process of social change taking place in each of the colonies was also influenced by developments in the international environment. Four sets of international influences in particular contributed to the rise of African nationalism and African demands for independence from colonial rule.

Spread of Pan-Africanism

The first trend revolved around the emergence of pan-African linkages and organizations.[24] Inspired by the anticolonial and antiracist activities of peoples of African descent living in North America, the West Indies, and Europe during the nineteenth and twentieth centuries, African leaders sought to promote a unified African front against colonial rule.

Fascist Italy's 1935 invasion of Ethiopia (also known as Abyssinia) and defeat of Emperor Haile Selassie's 250,000-strong Ethiopian army marked a turning point in the emergence of pan-African sentiment. Ali A. Mazrui, the Kenyan historian, notes that foreign occupation of a country that served as a "proud symbol of African independence and black achievement" had a "resounding impact" on Africans and members of the African diaspora.[25] A noted example is found in the autobiography of Kwame Nkrumah, the first president of Ghana. At the time of the invasion, Nkrumah had just arrived in London to pursue his university studies. Nkrumah relates the moral outrage he felt when he first learned of the invasion while walking down a London street:

> At that moment it was if the whole of London had declared war on me personally. For the next few minutes I could do nothing but glare at each impassive face wondering if those people could possibly realize the wickedness of colonialism, and praying that the day might come when I could play my part in bringing about the downfall of such a system. My nationalism surged to the fore; I was ready and willing to go through hell itself, if need be, in order to achieve my object.[26]

What subsequently became known as the "pan-African ideal" (see Chapter 11) was forcefully enunciated for the first time at the 1945 meeting of the Pan-African Congress held in Manchester, England. Participants adopted a resolution, "Declaration to the Colonial Peoples," that affirmed the rights of all colonized peoples to be "free from foreign imperialist control" and to "elect their own governments, without restrictions from foreign powers."[27] In a separate resolution, "Declaration to the Colonial Powers," participants underscored that if the colonial powers were "still determined to rule mankind by force, then Africans, as a last resort, may have to appeal to force in the effort to achieve freedom."[28]

Involvement of African Soldiers
in World War I and World War II

The outbreak of two world wars in Europe served as a second international influence that contributed to the rise of African demands for independence from colonial rule. Each of the colonial powers maintained standing armies composed primarily of African recruits, several of which clashed during skirmishes on the African continent during World War I.[29] During World War II, African conscripts played an increasingly important combat role in the European theater, especially in the case of France. By the beginning of 1939, seven African divisions of the Tirailleurs Sénégalais, a fighting force composed of African recruits from francophone West Africa, constituted 7 percent of all

French military forces stationed in Europe, with 20,000–25,000 soldiers dying during World War II.[30]

The most decisive impact of African soldiers fighting in Europe was the shattering of colonially inspired images of whites as invincible and all powerful. The rank-and-file of the Tirailleurs Sénégalais were direct participants in numerous battles in which French military forces were overrun by other "white" (Nazi Germany) and "nonwhite" (Imperial Japan) military forces. The pace of Japanese victories was especially significant because Africans saw that European militaries could in fact be defeated by non-European armies. Indeed, many African soldiers concluded that Africans were militarily superior to Europeans in terms of both courage and valor. Laqui Condé, a Tirailleur Sénégalais recruited from Côte d'Ivoire, summarized a common belief among African soldiers:

> We were stronger than the whites. That bullet that hit my tooth would have killed a white. When the shooting came, the whites ran. They knew the area and we did not, so we stayed. Our officers? They were behind us.[31]

For many soldiers, a turning point in the development of nationalist sentiment occurred upon demobilization. Unlike their white French counterparts who were usually quickly demobilized, given "tumultuous welcomes," and provided back pay and demobilization premiums, the African soldiers, many of whom spent several years in prisoner-of-war (POW) camps, "languished" in demobilization centers in southern France and West Africa.[32] African soldiers, especially disenchanted when French authorities sought to deny them the same financial benefits accorded white soldiers, caused a series of protests and uprisings, the most notable of which occurred at a military camp in Thiaroye, Senegal. A heavy-handed French military response in Thiaroye resulted in at least thirty-five deaths and hundreds of casualties among the Tirailleurs Sénégalais and further inflamed the sense of betrayal felt by soldiers who perceived themselves as having sacrificed for France.[33]

Soldiers responded to the events of Thiaroye and other shortcomings of demobilization, such as the lack of jobs, by forming and joining veterans associations. Collectively, veterans asserted that equal sacrifices required equal benefits for both European and African soldiers.[34] The veterans associations not only fought for equal treatment for African veterans, they also played an integral role in the nationalist movements seeking independence.

Demonstration Effect
of Decolonization in Asia

The decolonization of Asia constituted a third international trend with implications for the rise of African nationalism.[35] Numerous Asian countries became independent during the 1940s, providing an important "demonstration effect" for African nationalist movements. For those seeking independence by peaceful means, the experience of India under the leadership of Mohandas K. Gandhi (1869–1948) served as a tremendous inspiration. From 1893 to 1915 Gandhi had lived in British-ruled South Africa, where he led a series of protests denouncing discrimination against Indian immigrants. It was during this period that Gandhi developed and tested his nonviolent approach to challenging unjust colonial rules and regulations. The cornerstone of his approach was the pursuit of a form of civil disobedience known as satyagraha (holding to the truth). After returning to India in 1915, Gandhi's vision of nonviolent civil disobedience became the hallmark of a nationalist movement that forced Great Britain to cede independence to India in 1947.

African nationalist leaders particularly drew inspiration from Gandhi's experiences for several reasons.[36] First, he had achieved a special level of legitimacy due to his personal involvement in the struggle for human dignity on the African continent. Second, the Christian faith shared by many African nationalist leaders, primarily in Sub-Saharan Africa, made them particularly receptive to nonviolent approaches; one of the hallmarks of Christianity is the denunciation of war and conflict. Most important, civil disobedience had achieved a stunning success in India, leading to independence relatively devoid of bloodshed and violence. If it could succeed in what at the time was considered to be the cornerstone of the British Empire, some African nationalists thought, then it surely could succeed in Africa.

The ultimate success of the nonviolent approach depended on the willingness of the colonial power to peacefully accede to nationalist demands for independence. For those nationalist leaders who believed that armed struggle was the only recourse to the intransigence of the colonial powers, inspiration was drawn from the success of Asian liberation movements. African nationalist movements were particularly affected by the dramatic 1954 defeat of French military forces at Dien Bien Phu: a geographical name that became synonymous with the beginning of French withdrawal from Indochina and eventual independence for the former French colonies of Vietnam, Cambodia, and Laos. Indeed, Ben Bella, a leader of the guerrilla insurgency that forced France to grant independence to Algeria in 1962, witnessed firsthand the promise of guerrilla insurgency while serving as a sergeant in the French army stationed in Indochina.[37]

The Asian nations themselves provided concrete support to African nationalist organizations by creating a series of mechanisms designed to enhance African-Asian solidarity. The 1955 Bandung Conference held in Bandung, Indonesia, was one of the earliest manifestations of Asian support. Five Asian countries—Burma, Ceylon (Sri Lanka), India, Indonesia, and Pakistan—hosted representatives from twenty-four other countries, including the independent African countries of Egypt, Ethiopia, and Liberia, and representatives from the soon-to-be-independent states of Ghana and Sudan. The common denominator of all present was a principled opposition to colonial rule, and the conference resulted in a final communiqué underscoring the obligation of member states to promote the independence of those countries still suffering under colonial rule.

Shifting Structure
of the International System

A final international trend with important implications for the emergence of African demands for independence was the shift in the structure of the international system. The end of World War II left European colonial powers economically, politically, and militarily devastated. Their power had been eclipsed by the rise of the United States and the former Soviet Union as the unparalleled superpowers of the post–World War II era. As a result, the center of gravity for African nationalists intent on seeking independence for their respective colonies gradually shifted toward Moscow and Washington.[38]

The Soviet Union in many respects enjoyed several advantages over the United States and the European colonial powers during the initial stages of the cold war.[39] First, neither the Soviet Union nor its communist allies had ever been colonial powers in Africa. The history of the Soviet Union, at least from the vantage point of the 1950s and the 1960s, suggested that following the Soviet economic model could lead to rapid industrialization and socioeconomic development. Most important, the Soviet Union actively provided economic and military aid to liberation movements, most notably those opposed to white minority rule in Southern Africa. This latter activity in particular earned high marks among African leaders who, regardless of ideology, shared the goal of eradicating all remaining forms of colonialism and apartheid on the African continent.

African nationalists were also drawn to the United States due to the vocal anticolonial rhetoric of American policymakers. The United States especially captured the imagination of African nationalists in 1941, when President Franklin D. Roosevelt enunciated the principles associated with the **Atlantic Charter,** the most important of which underscored strong U.S. support for the self-determination of African peoples from colonial rule. With the intensification of the cold war, however, the United States was increasingly perceived by African nationalists as too closely tied to the interests of the colonial powers. Indeed, when African demands for decolonization clashed with policies considered crucial to U.S. security interests in Europe, U.S. policymakers often sided with Europe at the expense of Africa.[40]

A commitment to the principles of **nonalignment** often served as one of the rallying points of African nationalists. According to this view, African and other developing countries could pursue a third path of development, independent of the liberal form of capitalism promoted by the United States and other Western powers, but also independent of the more critical form of Marxism promoted by the Soviet Union and its communist bloc allies. In practice, however, African nationalists often aligned themselves with one of the two major ideological blocs and sometimes even prompted virtual bidding wars between the United States and the Soviet Union as each superpower sought to curry favor with particular nationalist movements. As succinctly noted in 1957 by Senator (and future president) John F. Kennedy, the perceived stakes of the cold war contest were tied to whether the emerging leaders of Africa would "look West or East—to Moscow or to Washington—for sympathy, help, and guidance in their effort to recapitulate, in a few decades, the entire history of modern Europe and America."[41]

SELF-DETERMINATION AND THE RISE
OF SECESSIONIST MOVEMENTS

The four waves of African independence that culminated in South Africa's transition to democracy in 1994 involved the self-determination of individual colonial states. In the aftermath of the end of the cold war and the largely successful transition to the contemporary independence era, a series of nationalist movements has emerged that seeks the **self-determination of peoples** in individual nation-states.[42] The leaders of what may evolve into a **fifth wave of independence** often underscore the historic mistreatment of their peoples as part of their pursuit of two overriding objectives: the secession of their territories from existing African countries and international recognition of their territories as independent countries in the international system.

The emergence of secessionist movements is neither unique to Africa nor only a product of the post–cold war era. The end of the cold war has indeed fostered the reemergence of ethnically based nationalism on a global scale. The most notable outcome of this trend was the fragmentation of the former Soviet Union into numerous independent republics. As demonstrated by the efforts of Nigeria's Igbo people to create an independent Republic of Biafra at the end of the 1960s, however, secessionist movements have existed in Africa since the beginning of the decolonization process (see Chapter 5).[43] The post–cold war era is nonetheless unique in that the demands for the self-determination of individual peoples appear to have risen in both scope and intensity.

Eritrea serves as the only successful case of secession and independence during the contemporary independence era (see the accompanying box).[44] On May 24, 1993, an internationally monitored popular referendum resulted in a vote overwhelmingly in favor of independence. Out of 1,100,260 eligible voters, 99.8 percent voted in favor of independence.[45] The referendum officially marked the end of a 30-year guerrilla struggle against Ethiopian sovereignty, which began in 1961 against the United States–supported regime of Emperor Haile Selassie and ended in 1991 with the downfall of the Soviet-supported Marxist regime of Mengistu Haile Mariam. The guerrilla insurgency was initially led by the Eritrean Liberation Front (ELF), which was succeeded by the more powerful Eritrean People's Liberation Front (EPLF). It is estimated that nearly 65,000 guerrilla fighters and tens of thousands of civilians lost their lives during Eritrea's struggle for independence.

The strength and long-term viability of any secessionist movement depends on a variety of factors, most notably the responses of individual African countries and the wider international community. As discussed in Chapter 11, one of

A Closer Look: AFRICA'S FIFTY-FOURTH COUNTRY? SECESSION OF THE SOMALILAND REPUBLIC

Five days after achieving independence from colonial rule in 1960, the former British colony of northern Somalia voluntarily federated with the former Italian colony of southern Somalia to create the Republic of Somalia. In the eyes of northern leaders, however, the north-south compact that served as the foundation for one of Africa's newest democracies was violated in 1969 when a southerner, Mohammed Siad Barre, seized power in a military coup d'état and created a southern-dominated military dictatorship. Barre scrapped the constitution and destroyed the fragile political basis that had tenuously kept the democratic union together, most notably by carrying out a policy of genocide against the north during the 1980s as part of a widening civil war. Even after Barre was overthrown in 1991 by a coalition of guerrilla armies, northern expectations of a government of national unity were dashed when southern guerrilla movements reneged on an earlier agreement and unilaterally named a southerner president. On May 17, 1991, northern leaders responded to over 20 years of perceived victimization by declaring the Somali union null and void and reasserting their country's sovereign independence as the Somaliland Republic.

Despite enjoying de facto control over its domestic and international affairs more than a decade after its unilateral declaration of independence, the Somaliland Republic has yet to be recognized by any other country or international body in the international system. Those in favor of the Somaliland Republic's recognition as the fifty-fourth independent African country criticize international inaction, especially in light of the strides northern Somali leaders have made in fostering a functioning political and economic system that stands in sharp contrast to continued instability and conflict in southern Somalia. One measure of popular support for secession was included in a referendum that was held in the Somaliland Republic in 2001. Although ostensibly held to assess public support for a new constitution, the vote essentially constituted a referendum on independence, because the constitution contains an article on territorial independence. The referendum passed by an overwhelming margin of 97 percent in favor, clearly suggesting widespread popular support for independence.

"The Somaliland Republic has earned the right to have its wishes taken seriously by the international community," explains Ahmed Jirreh, a northern Somali living in the United States, who favors independence for his land of birth. "We northern Somalis are not asking for international charity, nor are we asking foreigners to assume responsibility for what we ourselves are capable of accomplishing," explains Jirreh. "We simply seek international recognition of our sovereign right to withdraw from a union we once voluntarily joined."

Quotations are from a personal interview with Ahmed Jirreh in Chicago, Illinois. See also Anonymous, "Government Recognition in Somalia and Regional Political Stability in the Horn of Africa," *The Journal of Modern African Studies* 40, no. 2 (2002): 247–72.

the hallmarks of African international relations during the contemporary independence era has been the acceptance of the inviolability of frontiers inherited from the colonial era, and therefore widespread opposition to secessionist movements. Due to the multiethnic nature of most African countries, African leaders remain fearful that changing even one boundary will open a Pandora's box of ethnically based secessionist movements and lead to the further **Balkanization** of the African continent into smaller and economically inviable political units.

KEY TERMS

decolonization process
nationalism
national self-determination
first wave of independence
second wave of independence
third wave of independence
fourth wave of independence
voluntary associations

ethnic voluntary associations
mutual aid society
functional voluntary associations
Atlantic Charter
nonalignment
self-determination of peoples
fifth wave of independence
Balkanization

FOR FURTHER READING

Afigbo, A. E., et al. *The Making of Modern Africa* (vol. 2): *The Twentieth Century*. London: Longman, 1986.

Carter, Gwendolen M., and Patrick O'Meara, eds. *African Independence: The First Twenty-Five Years*. Bloomington: Indiana University Press, 1985.

Chafer, Tony. *The End of Empire in French West Africa: France's Successful Decolonization?* Oxford: Berg, 2002.

Davidson, Basil. *The Black Man's Burden: Africa and the Curse of the Nation-State.* New York: Times Books, 1992.

Freund, Bill. *The Making of Contemporary Africa: The Development of African Society since 1800* (2nd ed.). Boulder: Lynne Rienner, 1998.

Geiger, Susan. *TANU Women: Gender and Culture in the Making of Tanganyikan Nationalism. 1955–1965.* Portsmouth: Heinemann, 1997.

Gifford, Prosser, and Wm. Roger Louis, eds. *The Transfer of Power in Africa: Decolonization, 1940–1960.* New Haven: Yale University Press, 1982.

Grimal, Henri (translated by Stephen DeVos). *Decolonization: The British, French, Dutch, and Belgian Empires, 1919–1963.* Boulder: Westview, 1978.

Hargreaves, John D. *Decolonization in Africa* (2nd ed.). London: Longman, 1996.

Hodgkin, Thomas. *Nationalism in Colonial Africa.* New York: New York University Press, 1957.

Iyob, Ruth. *The Eritrean Struggle for Independence: Domination, Resistance, Nationalism 1941–1993.* Cambridge: Cambridge University Press, 1995.

Little, Kenneth. *West African Urbanization: A Study of Voluntary Associations in Social Change.* Cambridge: Cambridge University Press, 1970.

Lloyd, Peter C. *Africa in Social Change: Changing Traditional Societies in the Modern World.* Middlesex: Penguin, 1971.

MacQueen, Norrie. *The Decolonization of Portuguese Africa: Metropolitan Revolution and the Dissolution of Empire.* London: Longman, 1997.

Mazrui, Ali A., and Michael Tidy. *Nationalism and New States in Africa from about 1935 to the Present.* London: Heinemann, 1984.

Neuberger, Benyamin. *National Self-Determination in Post-Colonial Africa.* Boulder: Lynne Rienner, 1986.

Rimmer, Douglas, et al. *Africa Thirty Years On: The Record and the Outlook after Thirty Years of Independence Examined for the Royal African Society.* London: James Currey, 1991.

Tostensen, Arne, Inge Tvedten, and Mariken Vaa, eds. *Associational Life in African Cities: Popular Responses to the Urban Crisis.* Uppsala: The Nordic Africa Institute, 2001.

Wilson, Henry S. *African Decolonization.* London: Edward Arnold, 1994.

Young, Crawford. *Politics in the Congo: Decolonization and Independence.* Princeton: Princeton University Press, 1965.

NOTES

1. For an overview, see Hans Kohn, *The Idea of Nationalism* (New York: Macmillan, 1943); Ernest Gellner, *Nations and Nationalism* (Ithaca: Cornell University Press, 1983); and Eric Hobsbawm, *Nations and Nationalism since 1780: Programme, Myth, Reality* (Cambridge: Cambridge University Press, 1990).

2. For an overview of the various meanings of this term, see Benyamin Neuberger, *National Self-Determination in Postcolonial Africa* (Boulder: Lynne Rienner, 1986).

3. For an overview, see Basil Davidson, *Modern Africa: A Social and Political History,* 3rd ed. (London: Longman, 1994).

4. See Henry S. Wilson, *African Decolonization* (London: Edward Arnold, 1994), pp. 112–33.

5. See John D. Hargreaves, *Decolonization in Africa,* 2nd ed. (London: Longman, 1996).

6. For an overview, see Norrie MacQueen, *The Decolonization of Portuguese Africa: Metropolitan Revolution and the Dissolution of Empire* (London: Longman, 1997).

7. For an overview, see William Minter, *King Solomon's Mines Revisited: Western Interests and the Burdened History of Southern Africa* (New York: Basic, 1986).

8. For an early overview, see Richard Gibson, *African Liberation Movements: Contemporary Struggles against White Minority Rule* (London: Oxford University Press, 1972). See also Sheridan Johns and R. Hunt Davis Jr., eds., *Mandela, Tambo, and the African National Congress: The Struggle against Apartheid, 1948–1990: A Documentary Survey* (New York: Oxford University Press, 1991).

9. See Thomas Hodgkin, *Nationalism in Colonial Africa* (New York: New York University Press, 1957), pp. 63–83.

10. Kenneth Little, *West African Urbanization: A Study of Voluntary Associations in Social Change* (Cambridge: Cambridge University Press, 1970), pp. 7–23.

11. See Peter C. Lloyd, *Africa in Social Change: Changing Traditional Societies in the Modern World* (Middlesex: Penguin, 1971), pp. 109–24.

12. See Claude Ake, *A Political Economy of Africa* (London: Longman, 1981), pp. 72–73.

13. J. F. Ade Ajayi, Lameck K. H. Goma, and G. Ampah Johnson, *The African Experience with Higher Education* (Accra: Association of African Universities, 1996), p. 39.

14. See Janet G. Vaillant, *Black, French, and African: A Life of Léopold Sédar Senghor* (Cambridge: Harvard University Press, 1990), pp. 64–86.

15. See Little, *West African Urbanization,* 1970, pp. 24–65.

16. Ibid., pp. 66–84.

17. Ibid., pp. 74–75.

18. Ibid., p. 77.

19. Ake, *A Political Economy of Africa,* 1981, p. 79.

20. Ibid., p. 79.

21. Little, *West African Urbanization,* 1970, pp. 107–8.

22. Ake, *A Political Economy of Africa,* 1981, p. 79.

23. Little, *West African Urbanization,* 1970, p. 147.

24. See P. Olisanwuche Esedebe, *Pan-Africanism: The Idea and the Movement 1776–1963* (Washington, DC: Howard University Press, 1982).

25. Ali A. Mazrui and Michael Tidy, *Nationalism and New States in Africa from about 1935 to the Present* (London: Heinemann, 1984), p. 7. For the reaction of African Americans, see William R. Scott, *The Sons of Sheba's Race: African Americans and the Italo-Ethiopian War, 1935–1941* (Bloomington: Indiana University Press, 1993).

26. Kwame Nkrumah, *Ghana: The Autobiography of Kwame Nkrumah* (London: Thomas Nelson and Sons, 1957), p. 27.

27. Adekunle Ajala, "Background to the Establishment, Nature, and Structure of the Organization of African Unity," *Nigerian Journal of International Affairs* 14, no. 1 (1988): 36.

28. Ibid., p. 39.

29. See Byron Farwell, *The Great War in Africa (1914–1918)* (New York: W. W. Norton, 1986).

30. For an overview, see Myron Echenberg, *Colonial Conscripts: The Tirailleurs Sénégalais in French West Africa, 1857–1960* (Portsmouth: Heinemann, 1991).

31. Quoted in ibid., p. 92.

32. Ibid., p. 98.

33. Ibid., pp. 96–104. The events of Thiaroye were depicted in a 1988 film, *Le Camp de Thiaroye* (The Thiaroye Military Camp), by the celebrated Senegalese novelist and filmmaker, Sembène Ousmane.

34. Ibid., p. 104.

35. For a comparison, see Elie Kedourie, ed., *Nationalism in Asia and Africa* (New York: World, 1970). See also D. A. Low, "The Asian Mirror to Tropical Africa's Independence," in Prosser Gifford and Wm. Roger Louis, eds., *The Transfer of Power in Africa: Decolonization, 1940–1960* (New Haven: Yale University Press, 1982).

36. Mazrui and Tidy, *Nationalism and New States in Africa,* 1984, pp. 17–18.

37. Ibid., 1984, p. 16.

38. For an overview, see Zaki Laïdi, *The Superpowers and Africa: The Constraints of a Rivalry 1960–1990* (Chicago: The University of Chicago Press, 1990).

39. See Colin Legum, "African Outlooks toward the USSR," in David E. Albright, ed., *Africa and International Communism* (Bloomington: Indiana University Press, 1980), pp. 7–34. See also Jeffrey A. Lefebvre, "Moscow's Cold War and Post–Cold War Policies in Africa," in Edmond J. Keller and Donald Rothchild, eds., *Africa in the New International Order: Rethinking State Sovereignty and Regional Security* (Boulder: Lynne Rienner, 1996), pp. 206–26.

40. See Steven Metz, "American Attitudes toward Decolonization in Africa," *Political Science Quarterly* 99, 3 (1984): 515–33. See also Peter J. Schraeder, *United States Foreign Policy toward Africa: Incrementalism, Crisis, and Change* (London: Cambridge University Press, 1994).

41. John F. Kennedy, "The New Nations of Africa," in Theodore C. Sorenson, ed., *"Let the Word Go Forth": The Speeches,*

Statements, and Writings of John F. Kennedy (New York: Delacorte, 1988), pp. 365, 368.

42. For an early analysis, see Benyamin Neuberger, *National Self-Determination in Postcolonial Africa* (Boulder: Lynne Rienner, 1986).

43. For a discussion of this and other cases, see Crawford Young, "Comparative Claims to Political Sovereignty: Biafra, Katanga, and Eritrea," in Donald Rothchild and Victor Olorunsola, eds., *State versus Ethnic Claims: African Policy Dilemmas* (Boulder: Westview, 1983), pp. 199–232.

44. See Ruth Iyob, *The Eritrean Struggle for Independence: Domination, Resistance, Nationalism* 1941–1993 (Cambridge: Cambridge University Press, 1995).

45. Ibid., fn. 27, p. 178.

5

ᴧᴧᴧ

Ethnicity and Class

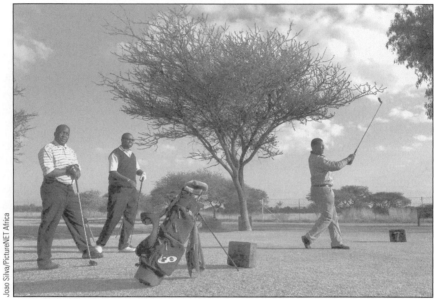

Three members of South Africa's new black business elite playing golf at the Pietersburg Golf Club, a former "whites-only" club that served as a bastion of white prestige during the apartheid era.

Joao Silva/PictureNET Africa

THE CONCEPTS OF ETHNICITY and class are analytical tools that identify the roles and interests influencing the choices of groups and individuals. Each concept has served as the basis of often-competing interpretations of African politics and society. Scholars typically emphasize the importance of one or the other, despite a recognition that both have influenced the socioeconomic and political-military evolution of the African continent during the contemporary independence era. Western scholars enamored with the unifying force of African nationalism during the 1950s initially overlooked the importance of ethnic and class differences. However, events of later decades, most notably the outbreak of ethnic tensions and the emergence of authoritarian ruling classes, clearly demonstrated the usefulness of ethnicity and class-based scholarship. Whereas interpretations based on ethnicity became especially prominent during the 1960s, class analysis emerged as a rich field of inquiry beginning in the 1970s. The intensification of ethnic competition and conflict that accompanied the end of the cold war prompted a renewal of interest among scholars in understanding the ethnic dimensions of African politics and society. Other events associated with the cold war's end, particularly the emergence of new classes at the head of pro-democracy movements, also fostered a reevaluation of class-based analyses. This chapter examines the evolving and often competing roles of ethnicity and class in African politics and society during the contemporary independence era.

ETHNIC DIMENSION OF AFRICAN POLITICS AND SOCIETY

Ethnicity defines a sense of collective identity in which a people (the ethnic group) perceives itself as sharing a historical past and a variety of social norms and customs, including the roles of elders and other age groups in society, relationships between males and females, rites and practices of marriage and divorce, legitimate forms of governance, and the proper means of resolving conflict. The African continent is composed of thousands of ethnic groups. One authoritative source, the *Encyclopedia of Africa South of the Sahara,* provides separate entries for nearly 200 of the largest and most influential African ethnic groups, with an appendix offering short descriptions for more than 1,000 others.[1] Although the total number of African ethnic groups differs depending on the source and the system of classification, all studies recognize the rich ethnic and cultural diversity of the African continent.

Many ethnic groups are divided into subgroup identities and loyalties. Individual subgroups based on kinship, often called **clans,** can trace their common lineage back hundreds of years to a specific founding member or ruling family dynasty. For example, the Somali ethnic group of the Horn of Africa is divided among ten major clans, each of which has a genealogy of clan leaders that can be traced to the mythical founding member. Other ethnic groups are divided according to **age-sets,** divisions based on the year or period in which one was born, that determine when an individual assumes various responsibilities in the ethnic group, such as entering the ranks of senior political leader or senior elder. Among the Maasai ethnic group of Kenya, for example, a series of age-sets determines when young boys enter the ranks of the moran (warrior recruits).

The Tswana ethnic group, which includes 1 million members composing more than two-thirds of the total population of Botswana, illustrates the polit-ical ramifications of complexity in an ethnic group. Though the Tswana speak the same language (Setswana), share a common historical past, and share social norms and customs, including participation in public kgotla meetings in which community issues are freely debated, the Tswana are divided among eight major clan groups: Bamangwato, Bakwena, Bangwaketse, Bakgatla, Barolong, Batlokwa, Bamalete, and Batawana. Each of these clans inhabits a specific geo-graphical region of Botswana and is headed by a traditional king who repre-sents his people in the House of Chiefs, an advisory legislative chamber that functions alongside the popularly elected National Assembly. The political impact of clan differences among the Tswana is evident in the national election results from 1969 to 1994.[2] During this period, the ruling Botswana Demo-cratic Party (BDP) averaged 68 percent of the popular vote. This was at least partially because many of the BDP leaders are members of the Bamangwato clan family, the largest of the Tswana clan families, which constitutes more than 35 percent of Botswana's total population.[3]

The concept of ethnicity was largely ignored by foreign observers during the first decade of the contemporary independence period. One reason for this neglect was the strong belief, especially among American researchers and policymakers, that ethnic divisions would fade away as modernizing African societies set aside ethnic identities in favor of Western cultural practices. Mod-ernization theory, the intellectual blueprint of development that was popular among American scholars and policymakers in the 1950s and 1960s, proposed that the march of modern industrial and economic progress would eclipse the importance of "primitive" ethnic loyalties (see Chapter 13).

The concept of ethnicity was also ignored due to the shared belief of African leaders and Western observers that the future success of newly inde-pendent African countries depended on their ability to promote a unifying nationalism that transcended ethnic differences. Those who suggested that eth-nic differences would endure and were a subject worthy of research ran the risk of being denounced by African leaders and Western observers alike as subvert-ing the African continent's struggle for independence and dignity. "If national-ism was a progressive and worthy topic, ethnicity was a retrogressive and shameful one," explains Crawford Young, a leading scholar on ethnicity. "To dwell unduly upon [ethnicity] was to summon forth from the societal depths demons who might subvert nationalism at its hour of triumph."[4]

Several political developments nonetheless ensured that the study of ethnic-ity would emerge in the 1960s as one of the most important fields of inquiry in African studies.[5] The creation of single-party regimes and the outbreak of military coups d'état were associated with the emergence of authoritarian political systems often dominated by one ethnic group (see Chapters 9 and 10). More often than not, ethnic majorities made their power felt at the ballot box, then resisted relinquishing their power and privileges. Of even greater importance was the outbreak of ethnically inspired violence that threatened to unravel the gains of independence and lead to the breakup of multiethnic nation-states. "Only when it became apparent that, bidden or not, the demons of disunity were at hand," concludes Young in a retrospective essay on his experiences during the 1960s, "did ethnicity begin to receive systematic examination."[6] The resurgence of ethnically based African conflicts in the aftermath of the cold war has once again prompted scholars to focus their attention on the importance of ethnicity in understanding African politics and society.

ETHNIC INTERMEDIARIES AND THE CREATION OF ETHNIC COMPACTS

A philosophical underpinning of Africa's multiethnic nation-states is that an **ethnic compact** can be achieved between the central government and ethnic leaders, that is minimally acceptable to all ethnic groups in society. This compact is based on the assumption that ethnic groups can compete peacefully in the established political framework for their share of national resources, such as federal budget allocations for local education, health care, and infrastructural development; salaried positions in the various bureaucracies of the executive branch; and representation in the political system itself, including political appointments, party representation, and election to local and national offices. The ethnic compact also assumes that African governments can treat these ethnic groups equitably regardless of whether they represent the largest or the smallest portion of the overall population. In other words, the government is seen as able to resolve conflicts between majorities and minorities and to protect individual rights.

An important contributor to the success or failure of the ethnic compact is the **ethnic intermediary:** an ethnic leader or "go-between" who represents and channels the demands of the ethnic group to the national political leadership and who also transmits the demands and expectations of that leadership to the ethnic constituents (see Figure 5.1).[7] Ethnic intermediaries employ various tactics to promote the interests of their ethnic groups in the national political arena. They may issue private appeals to politicians, public statements of support for sympathetic politicians, or public threats of noncompliance and noncooperation to those unwilling to listen.[8] The level of success is influenced by the ethnic intermediary's diplomatic and political skills; ethnic intermediaries not only must seek agreement among potentially competing factions in their own ethnic groups, they must also be able to negotiate and seek agreement with counterparts from other ethnic groups and regions when pressing their groups' demands in the national political arena.

FIGURE 5.1   Ethnic Intermediaries

The ethnic intermediary operates in all types of political systems: democratic or authoritarian, capitalist or socialist, civilian or military, secular or religious.[9] In the case of Ghana, ethnic intermediaries have continuously engaged in promoting their ethnic groups' interests, despite numerous shifts in government since independence in 1957. During four periods (1957–60, 1969–72, 1979–81, and 1992–present) in which multiparty politics have dominated the Ghanaian political system, ethnic intermediaries have made "extensive use" of forums in the national legislature to focus the attention of national leaders on the need for regional development.[10] With the rise of the single-party state from 1960 to 1966, as well as the emergence of a succession of military regimes during 1966–69, 1972–79, and 1981–92, ethnic intermediaries needed to shift tactics in favor of quieter, more concealed approaches, such as "face-to-face contacts" with individual leaders.[11] "What proved constant through all these switches was the critical roles played by the ethnic intermediary," explains one collaborative analysis of African politics and society, "even if the means used to advance the interests of rural constituents at the political center changed noticeably with each shift in authority system."[12]

African leaders committed to pursuing an ethnic compact often seek to promote an **ethnic balance** in governance through the **proportionality principle:** the provision of state resources, such as government jobs, federal budget allocations, and even political representation, according to an ethnic group's percentage of the total population.[13] As shown by Donald Rothchild, a specialist of conflict resolution in Africa, African leaders committed to maintaining some level of ethnic balance can employ varied policies, several of which have appeared with some regularity during the contemporary independence era:

- the inclusion of major ethnoregional representatives in the cabinet and/or party national executive committee

- the maintenance of an ethnic balance by replacing retiring ministers and high party officials with others from the same subregion

- the preservation, when succession occurs, of a geographical balance in appointments to the president and prime minister as well as in the cabinet and party

- special measures to include minority ethnic interests in the decision-making process

- an understanding not to discuss highly emotional, ethnicity-related issues outside the political coalition[14]

The concept of proportionality is in some ways similar to a patronage-style democracy in which diverse groups are kept happy with the provision of their expected portion of economic resources and power. However, even the most authoritarian of African leaders, who fashioned political systems largely dominated by their own ethnic groups, realized the importance of maintaining at least some semblance of ethnic balance in government. Indeed, the proportionality principle, like the efforts of the ethnic intermediary, can successfully operate regardless of whether the country is led by a democratically elected president, an authoritarian military dictator, a hereditary monarch, a revolutionary Marxist, or an Islamic revivalist. The cornerstone of the proportionality principle is the assumption that inclusiveness of diverse ethnic interests will provide for greater regime stability. "The benefits accruing from this exchange may well go to some groups disproportionately," explains Rothchild, "but if all partners gain some share, they may come to view continued participation in the process as serving their interests."[15]

The evolution of ethnic politics in Djibouti, a ministate in the Horn of Africa with a population of less than 500,000, shows how ethnic balancing has played a role in an authoritarian, single-party system.[16] Two ethnic groups, the Issa and the Afar, have competed for political power in Djibouti. The Issa, a clan of the Somali people, is Djibouti's largest ethnic group (33 percent of the population) and inhabits the southern one-third of the country. The Afar is the second largest ethnic group (20 percent) and inhabits the northern two-thirds of the country. The remainder of the population is divided among five major immigrant groups largely living in the capital, Djibouti City: Gadaboursi (15 percent) and Isaak (13 percent), also clans of the Somali people that migrated from northern Somalia during the twentieth century; Arabs, particularly Yemenis (6 percent), who work primarily in the commercial sector; French nationals and other Europeans (4 percent) working at all levels of the Djiboutian government, including troops of the French Foreign Legion; and illegal economic migrants and refugees from neighboring countries, who together constitute 10 to 15 percent of the country's population.

Hassan Gouled Aptidon, an Issa politician and leader of a nationalist movement, the Ligue Populaire Africaine pour l'Indépendance (LPAI, African Popular League for Independence), emerged as Djibouti's first president in 1977, and Ahmed Dini, an Afar and secretary-general of the LPAI, became prime minister. Like other African leaders during the initial decades of the contemporary independence era, Gouled strengthened the single-party system by bringing the party and the government increasingly under his personal control and restricting popular debate. According to the National Mobilization Law passed by the National Assembly in October 1981, for example, Djibouti was transformed into a single-party political system in which the only legal party before 1992 was the state-endorsed Rassemblement Populaire pour le Progrès (RPP, Popular Assembly for Progress), the party that succeeded the LPAI. Only those politicians approved by Gouled and the RPP were allowed to run on a single-party slate during election periods.

Despite his far-reaching powers, Gouled initially crafted a ruling coalition inclusive of all ethnic groups but that ensured control by his Issa ethnic group. An unwritten power-sharing agreement made before independence ensured that the office of the president would be occupied by an Issa and the office of the prime minister would be occupied by an Afar. Another unwritten agreement provided for the apportionment along ethnic lines of the sixty-five-seat National Assembly. Whereas Issas and others of Somali origin, such as the Gadaboursis and Isaaks, were guaranteed a total of thirty-three seats, Afars were apportioned the slightly smaller number of thirty seats, and Arabs were guaranteed two seats. Gouled also put together an initial cabinet of advisors that included seven Afars and six Issas, as well as one representative each from the Isaak, Gadaboursi, and Arab groups. Gouled's successful ethnic balancing earned Djibouti the label "eye of the hurricane" for its ethnic stability in the troubled region of the Horn of Africa.[17]

ETHNIC VIOLENCE AND THE BREAKDOWN OF ETHNIC COMPACTS

The breakdown of ethnic compacts has led to three sets of outcomes, each of which is characterized by ethnic violence. The first outcome involves the emergence of ethnically inspired opposition movements and guerrilla insurgencies.[18] In the case of Djibouti, Afar leaders increasingly became disenchanted with their second–class role in a political system essentially dominated by the Issa ethnic group, ultimately fueling Afar support for a variety of dissident movements.[19] In 1979, the Afar leaders of two Ethiopian-supported guerrilla movements, the Mouvement Populaire de Libération (MPL, Popular Movement of Liberation) and the Union Nationale de l'Indépendance (UNI, National Union for Independence), created a joint military organization, the Front Démocratique pour la Libération de Djibouti (FDLD, Democratic Front for the Liberation of Djibouti) and planned to overthrow the Gouled regime by force. In the political realm, former Prime Minister Ahmed Dini attempted to break the monopoly of the ruling RPP in 1981 by forming the Parti Populaire Djiboutien (PPD, Djiboutian Popular Party), an opposition political party that was quickly outlawed by the Gouled regime. Afar opposition to Gouled created an escalating cycle of violence as the government responded to Afar guerrilla attacks, particularly in the northern Afar-inhabited territories.

Rising frustrations in the Afar community reached a critical point in November 1991. At that time, the Front pour la Restauration de la Démocratie (FRUD, Front for the Restoration of Democracy), a military force of approximately 3,000 guerrilla fighters primarily from the Afar ethnic group, launched a sustained military offensive that eventually captured all major areas in the north except for the towns of Tadjoura and Obock. The military operation amounted to a "reform" insurgency as the leaders intended to maintain Djibouti's territorial integrity while reordering the ethnic compact in favor of greater political power for the Afar ethnic group (see Chapter 11). The Gouled regime sought to defuse this Afar-based military offensive, in part by holding multiparty legislative and presidential elections in December 1992 and May 1993. These elections were significantly marred, however, by massive electoral fraud by supporters of the Gouled regime and a FRUD-inspired boycott heeded by approximately 50 percent of the voting age population (primarily in the Afar ethnic group). As expected by most foreign observers, Gouled and the ruling RPP declared victory in these elections and subsequently launched a military offensive in July 1993 that defeated the FRUD guerrilla insurgency.

Despite ongoing pressures for democratization, principally from the Afar ethnic group, all organs of government remain firmly under the control of the Issa-dominated government. In 1999, Ismael Omar Guelleh, another Issa politician with close ties to Gouled, succeeded Gouled as president, ensuring continued Issa domination of the country. Although the Issa regime's manipulation of multiparty elections appears to have ensured political stability in the short term, it has done little to resolve the long-term grievances of the political opposition. Indeed, events of the 1990s have prompted foreign observers to use a new metaphor; they now refer to Djibouti as the "boiling cauldron" for its potential for ethnic violence.[20]

The launching of separatist movements by aggrieved ethnic groups is a second, more drastic response to the failure of ethnic compacts during the contemporary independence era (see Chapter 11). In these cases, aggrieved ethnic leaders and their constituents believe that an ethnic compact is no longer viable, either under existing circumstances or in the future. Instead, they believe that the only remaining option for their ethnic group is to secede and to seek recognition of their territory as an independent nation-state in the international system. All secessionist attempts in Africa have resulted in a military response from the centralized government; therefore, leaders of the secessionist movement prepare for and expect to be engaged in a protracted civil war.[21]

The declaration of independence by the Somaliland Republic on May 17, 1991, offers an interesting case due to its origins in a reformist guerrilla insurgency that was transformed into a separatist movement (see Chapter 4). The cornerstone of this conflict is the division of the Somali ethnic group into ten major clan families, the relations of which historically have alternated between peaceful competition and military conflict.[22] The Isaak clan represents approximately 70 percent of Somaliland's population, and the remainder is largely divided among four other clan groups: the Issa, Gadaboursi, Dulbahante, and Warsangeli.

The Isaak clan entered into an ethnic compact with the other Somali clans when they agreed in 1960 to voluntarily federate their territory (a former British colony) with the Italian colony of southern Somalia to create the Republic of Somalia.[23] The beginning of the end of this compact began in 1969, however, when Major-General Mohammed Siad Barre seized power in a military coup d'état and created a military dictatorship that revolved around the

---

A Closer Look: TRANSCENDING ETHNICITY AND CLASS? MARABOUTS AS RELIGIOUS INTERMEDIARIES

Religion plays an important role in African politics and society, most notably due to the ability of Christian, Muslim, and animist leaders to tap into religious beliefs that transcend ethnicity and class differences. In the case of Senegal, elected politicians historically have contended with the often competing interests of **marabouts,** the leaders of religious organizations known as Islamic brotherhoods, who represent the religious values of the country's heavily Muslim (94 percent) population.

   Three Islamic brotherhoods, the Qadiriyya, the Tijaniyya, and the Mouridiyya, claim the allegiance of more than two-thirds of Senegalese Muslims, thereby making their marabouts particularly powerful in Senegalese politics and society. A marabout can mobilize the Muslim faithful through an intricate network of patron-client ties in which thousands of lesser marabouts declare their allegiance to more senior leaders. The Mouridiyya, whose spiritual center is the holy city of Touba, are the most influential of the Senegalese marabouts. Their founder, Khalif General Amadou Bamba, is revered in Senegalese history as a charismatic leader who fought against French colonialism.

   The power of Senegalese marabouts derives from the population's belief in the spiritual and often magical powers of their personal religious guides. The senior marabouts serve as spiritual leaders for the brotherhood as a whole and enjoy a great deal of political power and prestige. During the 1960s, the term "marabout-cadillac" was coined to indicate the prestigious societal rank and financial success of these senior marabouts. Another type of marabout, the "marabout-teacher," is responsible for the religious instruction of his taalibe (disciples) in a variety of settings, most notably the koranic (Islamic) schools for young children. Finally, the "marabout-magician" is revered for his magical powers, such as an ability to predict and even alter the future. The "gris-gris" or talisman worn by many Senegalese for protection against evil is a visible manifestation of the disciples' faith in the magical powers of their respective marabout. All three types of marabouts enjoy financial independence thanks to a complex system of alms collection by their disciples who, depending on the charisma and power of the marabout in question, can channel enormous amounts of money to a designated cause.

Popular support has fostered the marabout's rise as an influential **religious intermediary** between the Senegalese government and the general population. Politicians actively court marabout support because of the religious leaders' ability to both facilitate and stymie government policies. During the colonial era, the French government's decision to allow Khalif General Bamba to return home from exile in 1902 marked the beginning of marabout financial participation in political campaigns.

In 1914, the Mouridiyya brotherhood, grateful for the return of their leader, offered political and financial support to Blaise Diagne, helping him to become the first African deputy in the French National Assembly in Paris. The Mouridiyya marabouts in return received important material advantages, most notably the deeds to large tracts of land for farming purposes.

A contemporary example of the political influence wielded by marabouts occurred in 1994, when Senegalese President Abdou Diouf was "rebuffed" by the religious leaders of the Mouridiyya and the Tijaniyya brotherhoods. Before this date, Diouf and his predecessor, Léopold Sédar Senghor, felt politically compelled to make internal "state visits" to the holy cities of these two brotherhoods, at least once every 2 months to personally consult with senior marabouts. In what amounted to a major political scandal, the marabouts unilaterally announced that such visits were no longer practical nor desirable. Simply put, senior marabouts had taken the extraordinary step of distancing themselves from the Diouf administration due to growing concerns over President Diouf's ability to govern effectively.

For further reading, see Leonardo A. Villalón, *Islamic Society and State Power in Senegal: Disciples and Citizens in Fatick* (Cambridge: Cambridge University Press, 1995).

clans of his father (Marehan), mother (Ogadeni), and wife (Dulbahante), the so-called MOD alliance. In 1981, political opposition was transformed into military opposition with the creation of an Isaak guerrilla insurgency known as the Somali National Movement (SNM), which ultimately contributed to Barre's overthrow in 1991.

The Isaak–inhabited areas of the north paid a tremendous price for the SNM's guerrilla victory; Barre's forces engaged in a "systematic pattern" of attacks against unarmed Isaak villages throughout the 1980s that, in the eyes of Isaak clan leaders, bordered on genocide. The two major northern cities of Berbera and Hargeisa were virtually destroyed.[24] To make matters worse, a southern-based guerrilla army of the Hawiye clan, the United Somali Congress (USC), reneged on an earlier agreement to create a military government of national unity and took advantage of its control of the former capital of Mogadishu to name a Hawiye clan member president. This proved the final straw for Isaak leaders weary of 22 years of civil war and dictatorship. In 1991, Isaak clan leaders officially declared the ethnic compact of 1969 to be null and void. From this point forward, Somaliland would "go it alone."[25]

The fact that the Somaliland Republic remains unrecognized by any other country underscores some of the obstacles associated with the pursuit of ethnically based secession in Africa.[26] First and foremost, regional and international norms are stacked against the legitimacy of ethnically based secession and strongly favor existing nation-states. One of the cardinal principles of African international relations is the inviolability of inherited frontiers from the colonial era. Only Eritrea successfully seceded during the contemporary independence era. Second, the African territories seeking to secede, including the Somaliland Republic, are never ethnically homogeneous, prompting critics to question whether secession is fair to potentially unwilling minorities in the proposed new country. Even if one could measure public opinion accurately, at what point does secession become both acceptable and desirable: a simple majority (51 percent), a clear majority (67 percent), or overwhelming support (90 percent or above)? In short, the lack of clear-cut precedents and prevailing regional and international norms make it unlikely that any of Africa's separatist insurgencies will result in international recognition.

The most extreme outcome associated with the failure of ethnic compacts is the outbreak of **genocide:** the systematic killing or extermination of an entire ethnic group. Most often associated with Nazi Germany's execution of millions of Jews throughout Europe during World War II, the label of genocide in the African context has become synonymous with the killings that took place in Rwanda in 1994.[27] In the aftermath of Rwandan President Juvenal Habyarimana's death in a mysterious plane crash on April 6, 1994, extremists among the majority Hutu ethnic group unleashed a reign of terror against the Tutsi minority as well as against Hutu deemed sympathetic to the plight of the Tutsi. At least half a million unarmed civilians were executed. The carnage was only stopped when a Tutsi guerrilla force, the Front Patriotique Rwandais (FPR, Rwandan Patriotic Front), invaded from Uganda and captured the capital of Kigali, subsequently establishing a Tutsi-dominated regime. As is the case with all regions of the world, genocide has rarely occurred in the African context.

CLASS DIMENSION OF AFRICAN POLITICS AND SOCIETY

The concept of **class** defines a group of individuals who share a common status in society based on cultural, political, or economic distinctions. For example, culturally based class distinctions served as the cornerstone of French colonial policies that distinguished between évolués ("evolved" or "civilized" Africans) and their "nonevolved" and "uncivilized" counterparts. French administrators granted évolué status to those Africans who had embraced French culture, including achieving fluency in the French language, converting to Christianity, obtaining at least a high school education, and becoming a property owner. The attainment of this status ensured access to a variety of privileges, such as protection under the French legal system and the right to pursue French citizenship, unavailable to most Africans in the colonies.

Some African societies, such as the African monarchies of both the precolonial and contemporary independence eras, are also stratified according to politically inspired class distinctions. In the case of the Oyo empire, which reached its zenith during the eighteenth century, only a member of the royal family could become the nation's supreme ruler, the Alafin, as well as the numerous obas (kings) who composed the royal lineage (see Chapter 2). The Alafin's formal powers included the appointment of provincial governors and the ability to declare war. His informal powers, most notably the art of public persuasion, grew out of the sacred nature of his office. The Alafin represented the pinnacle of a ruling political class in which power was hereditary.

The classic understanding of class draws on the works of Karl Marx and focuses on an individual's economic position in society (see Chapter 14). According to Marxian thought, all capitalist societies at the very least can be divided into a property-owning class that dominates society and an exploited, propertyless working class that is forced to accept poor jobs and unsafe working conditions or starve. Numerous classes exist between these two extremes. The working class is trapped in a system in which its labor provides the only means for its own survival while serving to create more wealth for the property-owning class. According to Marx, the exploitative nature of capitalist society can only be changed through class revolution.

Sembène Ousmane, a renowned Senegalese novelist and filmmaker, captures the economic dimension of class distinctions in his novel, *Les Bouts de Bois de Dieu* (published in English as *God's Bits of Wood*).[28] The novel documents the historic 6-month strike during 1947–48 on the railroad line that links Dakar, Senegal, with Bamako, Mali. The strike pitted African workers from Senegal and Mali against the French administrators of the colonial railroad. The primary demand of the African workers was higher wages and benefits commensurate with those provided the smaller group of European workers on the railroad. The strike constituted a classic encounter between the French owners who controlled the means of production (the railroad line) and an exploited, propertyless working class unrewarded for the efforts of their labor. "We are being robbed," explains Mamadou Keita, an elder in the novel who claims to have witnessed the epidemics, the famines, and the seizure of African lands associated with the railroad's advance. "Our wages are so low that there is no longer any difference between ourselves and animals."[29]

The scholarly community largely ignored the importance of class during the first two decades of the contemporary independence era.[30] African leaders and Western observers optimistically believed that the unifying forces of nationalism and modernization would erase any class differences that might exist, just as they predicted with regard to ethnicity. The cold war competition between the United

States and the Soviet Union reinforced this neglect. Western, particularly American, policymakers denigrated class analysis as an intellectual propaganda tool of the communist bloc, with little if any relevance to the African continent.[31] African leaders and scholars trained within the Western, liberal tradition largely shared these beliefs despite a well-established Marxist tradition in Western Europe, particularly in France.[32] Even Soviet-inspired Marxism, itself "tainted and twisted" by Stalinist orthodoxy, had "little impact" on interpretations of African politics and society during the 1950s and the early 1960s.[33]

Several political developments contributed to the proliferation of class-based scholarship from the late 1960s to the present.[34] Critics who sought explanations for the widespread emergence of Western-supported authoritarian regimes were naturally drawn to critical perspectives, such as Marxian-inspired class analysis, that underscored the extent to which self-interested ruling classes can impede development. Rising domestic protests against America's involvement in the Vietnam War fostered disillusionment with the liberal model of development, prompting African scholars and policymakers to seek alternative models of development. African leaders increasingly adopted variants of socialism and Marxism as official models of development, subsequently seeking close ties with the Soviet Union, the People's Republic of China, and other members of the socialist bloc (see Chapter 6). This trend reached its height in 1975, when Portugal's withdrawal from its colonies in Africa led to the establishment of self-proclaimed Marxist regimes in Angola, Cape Verde, Guinea-Bissau, Mozambique, and Sao Tome and Principe. Although the decline of communism in the former Soviet Union and Eastern Europe reinforced the rejection of Marxist and socialist models of development by the beginning of the 1990s, class analysis remains a vital and important tool for understanding African politics and society.

CLASS DIVISIONS IN AFRICAN SOCIETY

Debates over the origins and development of African classes have spawned a rich diversity of terms and categorizations for individual classes and **class factions** (divisions in classes).[35] Although scholars may disagree over specific titles, they agree on four general class categories (see Figure 5.2).

The first class, the **foreign bourgeoisie,** is usually divided into two class factions. The most important class faction, the **metropolitan bourgeoisie,** includes the political and business leaders of the Great Powers, most notably the former colonial powers, which have cultivated economic ties with individual African countries. The metropolitan bourgeoisie is especially discussed in writings about the relationship between France and its former colonies.[36] For example, Jacques Foccart, the architect of French foreign policy toward Africa under the administrations of Charles de Gaulle and Georges Pompidou, is recognized by both admirers and critics alike as having created an intricate web of ties that still closely links France to its francophone colonies.[37] Foccart and

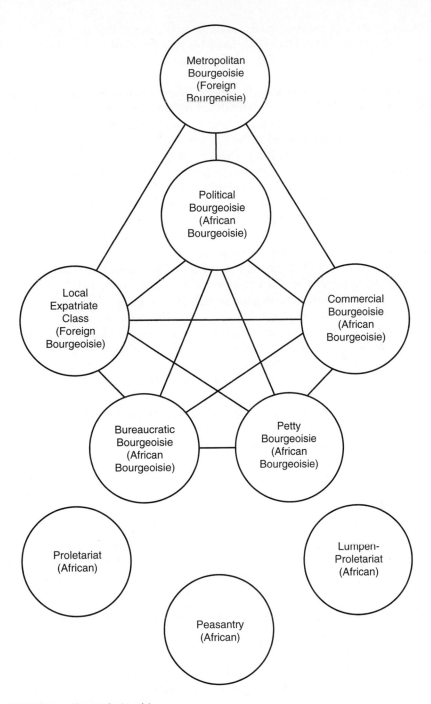

FIGURE 5.2 Class Relationships

other members of the metropolitan bourgeoisie ensured that the end of direct colonial rule (1884–1951) was replaced by a series of neocolonial economic ties that permitted continued external domination.

A second faction of the foreign bourgeoisie, the **local expatriate class,** lives and works in individual African countries. The expatriate class ranges in number from less than a hundred to several thousand and plays the vital role of serving as a daily reminder of the metropolitan power's economic reach and influence. As of this writing, several thousand French nationals were living in Senegal, which received its independence in 1960. These French citizens work at all levels of the Senegalese government and economy as special advisors to Senegalese President Abdoulaye Wade, administrators of the French Cultural Center and other local offices of the French government, military advisors, and troops stationed in the country as part of a bilateral French–Senegalese military agreement and as directors and personnel of French companies, most notably those in the lucrative petroleum, telecommunications, and automobile industries.[38]

A second major class group, the **African bourgeoisie,** constitutes the dominant class in most African countries, and is often subdivided into four class factions.[39] The **political bourgeoisie,** which encompasses the political elite, including the head-of-state and his senior advisors, holds the reins of political power in all African countries. The political bourgeoisie includes civilian and military leaders and spans the ideological spectrum from proponents of capitalism to self-proclaimed socialists and Marxists. The political bourgeoisie plays a critical role in the appointment of the **bureaucratic bourgeoisie,** the upper division of the civil service and other senior employees who staff government bureaucracies. A nongovernmental faction, the **commercial bourgeoisie,** includes private businesspersons, most notably the senior executives of major local businesses. Finally, a **petty bourgeoisie,** often called the lower middle class, includes small traders and shopkeepers, artisans, teachers, soldiers, and the lower ranks of government bureaucracies. The small size of the private sector has made the political and bureaucratic factions of the African bourgeoisie particularly important.

Kenya is often cited as one of the best examples of a well-developed and well-entrenched African bourgeoisie.[40] The country's founding father, President Jomo Kenyatta, served as the symbolic head of a political bourgeoisie that sought to maintain close ties with the major northern capitalist powers, most notably Great Britain, the former colonial power. As was the case in most African countries at the beginning of the contemporary independence era, Kenyatta's administration oversaw massive increases in public sector jobs, which established an extensive bureaucratic bourgeoisie. Kenyatta also supported national legislation, such as the Trade Licensing Act of 1967, that reserved significant portions of the Kenyan economy for Kenyan businesspersons and therefore fostered the rise of a commercial bourgeoisie. That this commercial bourgeoisie engaged in corrupt practices to ensure its economic monopoly was of little concern to the Kenyatta regime, as long as kickbacks and other forms of financial support were funneled to the political bourgeoisie. Even the Kenyan petty bourgeoisie was able to flourish, particularly in terms of trade, construction, and road transport, despite its general inability to achieve the scale of riches enjoyed by the other factions of the Kenyan bourgeoisie.

The **African proletariat** is a third major class category of African workers.[41] The proletariat is generally found in urban settings and earns a set wage that may range from an hourly to a monthly basis. The case of Zambia is illuminating. Although the proletariat on average constitutes less than 20 percent of the wage-earning population in most African countries, their numbers exceed more than 50 percent of wage earners in Zambia. These large numbers are due to the substantial industrial demands surrounding the sale of copper, Zambia's largest export. Thousands of workers were needed to create and maintain a massive mining industry and a railroad line to transport the copper to ports for export. Often called the "copperbelt," the broad territory following the railroad line from the copper fields to points of export is heavily urbanized. The urbanization of Zambian society and the development of a substantial proletariat has contributed to very powerful labor unions and movements.

An unemployed or underemployed urban working class, known as the **lumpenproletariat,** is an important class faction of the proletariat. In Senegal, high unemployment rates among a growing urban population sometimes drive violent confrontations between government forces and heavily politicized student groups and workers unions.[42] As depicted in the film, *La Génération Sacrifiée?* (The Sacrificed Generation?), coproduced in 1995 by a Senegalese and an American filmmaker, rising numbers of educated, yet discouraged, Senegalese youth were entering a job market that, in their eyes, offered them nothing but positions as street vendors, maids, and cooks. The concept of a "sacrificed generation" became especially poignant in the aftermath of France's 1994 decision to unilaterally impose a 50 percent devaluation on the common currency (CFA franc) shared by Senegal and thirteen other francophone members of the CFA Franc Zone. As a result, the francophone countries experienced a 50 percent decline in the purchasing power of an already economically marginalized population.

Finally, the **African peasantry** is usually the largest class category in most African countries.[43] The peasant is a rural dweller who grows food and raises livestock, either for personal consumption or for export to the urban areas and the wider international market. The most prosperous peasants, often called **kulaks,** hire other peasants to work larger land holdings and often participate in regional trade. The peasantry historically has been the most exploited class of African societies.[44] During the initial decades of the contemporary independence era, state-controlled marketing boards often fixed the price of agricultural goods well below market value to ensure the availability of cheap foodstuffs for the urban areas. The peasantry's response to these price controls, most notably selling crops illegally in the informal economy or simply deciding to only grow crops for personal consumption, demonstrated the "uncaptured" nature of the peasant class.[45] Members could opt out of the formal market economy and concentrate on their local interests and needs, or what has been called the **economy of affection.**[46] This dynamic was at least partially responsible for the decline of food production throughout Africa from the 1950s to the 1980s.

Tanzania offers one of the most widely examined cases of the role of the African peasantry.[47] Approximately 77 percent of the population lives in the rural areas and is involved in agricultural production.[48] Under the leadership of Julius Nyerere, Tanzania's first president, the government launched a socialist development strategy known as ujamaa (the Kiswahili word for brotherhood), which sought to regroup the peasant population in new communal villages. One of the goals of ujamaa was to create new educational, health care, and agricultural extension services in the modern centralized villages, to better serve the peasant class.[49] However, the gradual withdrawal of the peasantry from the formal economy and the subsequent decline in national food production ultimately ensured the failure of the economic dimension of the ujamaa strategy. Although this strategy was ultimately discarded by Nyerere's successor, President Ali Hassan Mwinyi, in the late 1980s, it nonetheless recognized the centrality of the African peasant in the pursuit of development (see Chapter 6).

CLASS COOPERATION AND CONFLICT

According to Marxist theorists, the "relations of production" that determine who owns and controls the means of economic production, such as property, factories, and investment capital, are crucial to understanding the evolving nature of class relationships in capitalist societies. They further argue that the exploitative nature of the relations of production in capitalist societies leads to class conflict and ultimately revolution (see Chapter 14). Marxist theorists who apply this model to Africa generally conclude that only class-based, national liberation struggles will be able to promote true change throughout the African continent.[50]

In a pathbreaking article that altered thinking in Africanist intellectual circles, Richard L. Sklar argues for the need to "liberate" class analysis from the economic preconceptions of Marxism and to focus instead on the *political* basis of class relations.[51] Sklar notes that the Marxist belief in the inevitable class conflict and revolution must be tempered in favor of a more nuanced understanding that recognizes the possibility of class cooperation in the pursuit of national development. "Class relations, at bottom," explains Sklar, "are determined by relations of power, not production."[52] In short, politics, not economics, is the defining aspect of class relations throughout Africa.

Four possible combinations of class cooperation and conflict deserve special mention. First, it is important to underscore the possibility of **interclass cooperation** in the peaceful pursuit of national development. In the case of Ghana, an interclass alliance between the political bourgeoisie and the peasantry turned Ghana into one of the most widely touted development success stories of the 1980s.[53] Under the leadership of Flt. Lt. Jerry Rawlings, a strong-willed, and at times, iron-fisted, charismatic leader with his "hand on the popular pulse," the political bourgeoisie implemented a series of structural adjustment economic reforms largely designed by the International Monetary Fund (IMF) and the World Bank.[54] Ghana succeeded where many other African countries had failed. This is in part because the political bourgeoisie overcame the protests of two urban-based classes that would be negatively affected by the economic reforms: the commercial bourgeoisie and the proletariat. The successful strategy was based on Rawlings' cultivation of an interclass alliance with the rural peasantry, which in 1985 constituted approximately 78 percent of the general population.[55] Indeed, voting in the 1988–89 district assembly elections clearly demonstrated strong peasant support for the Rawlings regime in all regions except that of "Greater Accra," the primary urban area inhabited by the commercial bourgeoisie and the proletariat, which suffered under reform policies.[56]

A second, more common class dynamic during the contemporary independence era is **transnational class cooperation** between the political bourgeoisie and the international bourgeoisie. In many cases, a threatened political bourgeoisie turns to its class allies in the international system to maintain its power. French intervention in the Democratic Republic of the Congo (Congo-Kinshasa) in 1977 is a striking example of transnational class cooperation.[57] On March 8, 1977, 2,500 guerrillas associated with the Front for the National Liberation of the Congo (FLNC) invaded Congo-Kinshasa from Angola with the intent of capturing Shaba province, the source of nearly 75 percent of Congo-Kinshasa's export earnings. The combined appeals of President Mobutu Sese Seko, the head of the Congolese political bourgeoisie, and the local European expatriate class, most notably French and Belgian nationals working in Shaba's mining industry, prompted French President Giscard d'Estaing to authorize French military intervention with Morocco. This and later French interventions would maintain Mobutu in power until 1997, despite the emergence of overwhelming rural and urban support for his removal from power. In short, the FLNC insurgency, which voiced popular discontent with the failed policies of the corrupt Mobutu regime, was defeated due to the interclass alliance between the Congolese political bourgeoisie, the local European expatriate class, and the French metropolitan bourgeoisie.

A third class dynamic explains how **intraclass conflict** in the African bourgeoisie can undermine democratic transitions by preserving politics as usual. Critics of the democratization process that swept the African continent during the first half of the 1990s are particularly wary of the false appearance of change associated with the holding of multiparty elections. According to Claude Ake, what one is witnessing in even the most widely heralded success stories of democratic elections can be characterized as the "democratization of disempowerment": a process whereby newly established multiparty political systems merely allow rotating and competing class factions of the African bourgeoisie to exploit the proletariat and the peasantry who remain disempowered from the political process (see Chapter 14).[58] In the case of Zambia, the initial optimism associated with President Frederick Chiluba's victory in that country's first multiparty elections in 1991 was sobered by growing concerns with the new administration's drift toward authoritarianism. Despite the fact that he was a distinguished union activist whose father was a mineworker, Chiluba increasingly was denounced as more interested in protecting his newfound status as a member of the ruling political bourgeoisie than in promoting the needs and interests of those who voted him into office: the peasantry and the proletariat. Indeed, he engineered several highly questionable political tactics to ensure victory in the 1996 presidential elections (see Chapter 10).

A final class dynamic is revolutionary **interclass conflict** and the reordering of class relations. Under such a scenario, rising popular dissatisfaction in the proletariat and the bourgeoisie prompts disenfranchised classes to seek to overthrow a weakened political bourgeoisie. The downfall of the Ethiopian regime of Emperor Haile Selassie offers one of the best-documented cases of revolution in an African context. As explained by Edmond J. Keller, a noted observer of the Ethiopian revolution, widespread drought and famine at the beginning of the 1970s ensured the "relentless worsening" of the peasant condition and the rising militancy of a small, urbanized proletariat.[59] Although the combined dissatisfaction of the peasantry and the proletariat was insufficient to ensure a revolutionary outcome, by 1974 the Selassie regime found itself abandoned by significant factions of the bourgeoisie, most notably the petty bourgeoisie.[60] Even U.S. policymakers, the most important faction of the international bourgeoisie that maintained close ties with Ethiopia, at best ignored the unfolding of the revolutionary situation and in any case were unwilling to provide the support necessary to maintain Emperor Selassie in power.[61]

The intensification of a revolutionary situation prompted a military coup d'état and the replacement of the Selassie regime with a Provisional Military Administrative Council (PMAC), a group of approximately 120 junior-grade and noncommissioned officers of the Ethiopian military who became known as the Dergue. As is the case in the aftermath of most revolutions, bloody infighting led to the emergence of a group of self-proclaimed Marxists under the leadership of Colonel Mengistu Haile Mariam, which assumed control over the political reins of government. Rather than overseeing the transformation of the

---

A Closer Look: TRANSCENDING ETHNICITY AND CLASS? GENDER AND THE DEBATE OVER FEMALE CIRCUMCISION

In May 1996, Fauziya Kasinga, a 19-year-old African woman from the country of Togo, was involved in a precedent-setting case for the U.S. Immigration and Naturalization Service. Kasinga argued that her family would force her to undergo **female circumcision** if she were deported. She fled Togo at age 15 to avoid being circumcised as part of a marriage that had been arranged for her after the death of her father. The U.S. Justice Department's Board of Immigration Appeals ruled favorably on Kasinga's case, thereby adding the gender-based fear of female circumcision to the list of factors constituting a "well-founded fear of persecution," the legal basis for seeking political asylum in the United States. Previously, political asylum was only granted to individuals who demonstrated a well-founded fear of persecution due to their race, religion, nationality, political opinions, or membership in a social group.

Female circumcision, also called **female genital mutilation,** is practiced throughout Africa, Asia, and the Middle East. The mildest form, **clitoridectomy,** involves the partial or total removal of the clitoris. A more severe type, **excision,** involves the removal of the clitoris and some or all of the labia minora (inner lips) and the labia majora (outer lips). The most severe form, **infibulation,** concludes the process of excision with the suturing of the raw tissue such that a scar tissue forms across the vaginal opening. A small opening is left to allow for urination and menstruation.

Female circumcision is not limited to a particular religious, ethnic, or class group on the African continent. It is common throughout West, North, and East Africa, with its most severe forms practiced in the countries of Djibouti, Eritrea, Mali, Somalia, and Sudan. The practice is often associated with a rite of passage. "In some areas, such as for the Gikuyu and Maasai [ethnic groups] of Kenya, excision is performed to mark a girl's transition to womanhood: by the Maasai just weeks prior to marriage and by the Gikuyu prior to the first menstruation," explains Ellen Gruenbaum, a specialist of circumcision and infibulation. "In many societies, however, the age at which the circumcisions are performed is so young [sometimes as early as the age of 3] that it is clearly not intended to mark the onset of womanhood," Gruenbaum continues. "The reasons for this in some cultures are explicitly related to the goal of attenuating sexual desire in preadolescent girls and women, and, in the case of infibulation, preventing illicit intercourse by constructing a barrier of scar tissue."

The publicity surrounding Kasinga's asylum case was indicative of growing international condemnation of female circumcision. African feminists, such as Raqiya Haji Dualeh Abdalla, a Somali woman who wrote *Sisters in Affliction: Circumcision and Infibulation of Women in Africa* (1982), have joined with a variety of international organizations in their quest to outlaw female circumcision throughout Africa and other regions of the world. Health concerns are usually at the forefront of anticircumcision efforts. Circumcised women are often afflicted with chronic urinary tract infections, menstrual problems, and difficult childbirth, not to mention the deaths that occur due to shock and hemorrhaging during the circumcision process itself. Other concerns involve the circumcised woman's ability to experience sexual pleasure and the psychological scarring that accompanies the circumcision. Although such activist measures as educational drives and the promotion of national legislation have led to the steady decline of female circumcision, it continues to be performed annually on approximately 2 million African girls, primarily between the ages of 4 and 12.

Quotations are from Ellen Gruenbaum, "Clitoridectomy and Infibulation," in John Middleton, ed., *Encyclopedia of Africa South of the Sahara,* vol. 2 (New York: Charles Scribner's Sons, 1997), pp. 382–83. See also Ellen Gruenbaum, *The Female Circumcision Controversy: An Anthropological Perspective* (Philadelphia: University of Pennsylvania Press, 2000).

relations of production in favor of proletarian and peasant interests, Mengistu and the other members of his junta unleashed a reign of terror against their former class allies, as well as against the remnants of the former ruling bourgeoisie. Mengistu's class faction ultimately transformed itself into a political bourgeoisie intent on maintaining power at all costs, only to be overthrown in 1991 by the combined forces of several guerrilla armies. Revolutions are extremely rare in Africa, and successful revolutions that reflect the interests of the peasant and proletariat classes are rarer still.[62]

COMPETING EXPLANATIONS OF THE NIGERIAN CIVIL WAR (1967–1970)

As artfully described by Richard L. Sklar and C. S. Whitaker, Nigeria was the "brightest star in the galaxy of new African states" when it achieved independence in 1960.[63] A democratically elected government took power in Africa's most populous and richly endowed country. Nigerians and outside observers alike thought that Nigeria was destined to play a leadership role on the African continent.

A brutal 3-year civil war (1967–70) tainted Nigeria's image as a potential role model for the continent. The civil war began with the May 1967 decision of Nigeria's Eastern Province to secede from the Nigerian federation and declare itself the independent Republic of Biafra, an act that had been preceded by two military coups d'état in January and July 1966. Although the secessionist province was militarily defeated in January 1970, the civil war and associated coups served as harbingers of several decades of military rule and authoritarianism.[64]

The Nigerian civil war is therefore an important turning point in both Nigerian and African history. As such, it offers a unique opportunity to understand how the concepts of ethnicity and class have contributed to different interpretations of African politics and society. Although most analyses of the Nigerian civil war include references to both ethnicity and class, they often emphasize the importance of one approach at the expense of another.[65] The following two narratives of the Nigerian civil war, one from the perspective of ethnicity and the other from the perspective of class, demonstrate the implications of ethnicity- and class-based interpretations of African politics and society. Each narrative portrays three crucial elements of the Nigerian civil war: historical origins before Nigeria's independence in 1960, mounting social tensions during Nigeria's First Republic (1960–66), and the unfolding of events associated with the military coups that preceded the outbreak of military hostilities in 1967.

Perceiving Events through an Ethnic Lens

One way to understand the historical origins of the Nigerian civil war is to begin with the multiethnic country created by Great Britain during the colonial era.[66] The colony was composed of over 250 ethnic groups, three of which constituted 66 percent of the total population and primarily resided in three geographical areas: the Igbo in the southeast, the Yoruba in the southwest, and the Hausa/Fulani in the north (refer back to Map 3.4 in Chapter 3). Upon independence in 1960, Nigerian leaders faced the challenge of creating an ethnic compact that balanced the interests, needs, and diverse political cultures of this ethnic mosaic inherited from the colonial era. For example, the Hausa/Fulani practiced a centralized political culture that demanded the complete deference of its subjects to the proclamations of traditional kings known as emirs. By contrast, in the egalitarian political culture of the Igbo it is considered the citizen's duty to publicly challenge and criticize the errors of political leaders. When multiplied by 250 ethnic groups, the differences in Hausa/Fulani and Igbo political cultures suggested that the possibility for ethnic competition and conflict was significant, even under the best of circumstances.

The Nigerian ethnic compact eroded and social tensions mounted in the 6 years (1960–66) preceding the outbreak of civil war. This was due to rising perceptions among ethnic intermediaries and their constituents that some ethnic groups were gaining more than their rightful share of national resources. The southern ethnic groups, most notably the Igbo, embraced British religious practices and colonial educational opportunities, prompting their preferential placement at all levels of colonial administration well beyond their respective share of the Nigerian population. This practice carried over into the contemporary independence era, as the more Westernized Igbo and other southern ethnic groups were positioned to take advantage of expanding government positions and economic opportunities in the private sector. The more numerous Hausa/ Fulani, who had resisted Westernization more than the southerners, increasingly feared that the Igbo and other southern ethnic groups would turn their educational advantages into long-term control of the civil service and the political system.[67]

Disputes over the 1962 national census, the first of its kind during the contemporary independence era, aptly demonstrated the political impact of Hausa/ Fulani fears. Fully aware that the census would serve as the primary vehicle for determining each ethnic group's future share of national resources, ethnic intermediaries fraudulently inflated the numbers of their respective ethnic groups. "Controversy flared when the initial results revealed much larger population increases in the South—sufficient to end the North's population majority— and demographic tests showed some of the Eastern Region's figures to have been 'grossly inflated,'" explains Larry Diamond, a specialist of Nigerian politics and society. "When the North then claimed to have discovered 8 million more people in a 'verification check' (thus preserving its population majority), the ensuing crisis forced Prime Minister Tafawa Balewa to cancel the census and order a new one for 1963."[68] The entire process had become tainted. "The result was a still greater fiasco," explains Diamond, "an 'altogether incredible' national increase of 83 percent in 10 years and a continued Northern population majority."[69]

Rising ethnic tensions, particularly among Nigeria's three major ethnic groups, culminated in the military coups of January and June 1966, which in turn triggered the Nigerian civil war. In the case of the January coup, there was an "undeniable ethnic selectivity" in terms of both leaders and victims: "Six of the seven majors involved were Igbo; of the seven senior officers killed who outranked the majors, only one was Igbo," explains Young. "The two regional governors who were murdered were not Igbo; the two who survived were."[70] What was increasingly perceived among the general population as a power grab on the part of the Igbo ethnic group was followed by a series of anti-Igbo riots that culminated in a countercoup led by Hausa-Fulani military officers. "This time," explains Young, "twenty-seven of the thirty-nine officers (including General Ironsi), and most of the 191 of other ranks who were murdered, were Igbo."[71] Confronted with spiraling ethnic violence and a northern-based military government unwilling to compromise, Colonel Chukwuemeka Ojukwu, the Igbo governor and military commander of the Eastern Region, announced his region's decision to secede and to establish the independent Republic of Biafra.

Perceiving Events through a Class Lens

A second way to understand the historical origins of the Nigerian civil war begins with the role played by the British metropolitan bourgeoisie during the colonial era.[72] At the end of the colonial era, the British encouraged the development of a Nigerian bourgeoisie that would accept a peaceful transfer of power and protect British financial interests after independence. The strategy worked, in that the anti-British rhetoric of Nigerian nationalist movements masked the emergence of a political bourgeoisie that shared Britain's belief in the strength of liberal capitalism. The Nigerian bourgeoisie was far from unified, however, with individual factions competing for power within the newly independent country. Different factions were part of the Nigerian bourgeoisie for different reasons: the northern emirs played a part, due to their role in traditional society during the precolonial and colonial eras; other factions, such as a rising economic bourgeoisie in southeastern Nigeria, owed their status to the regional structures created during the colonial era and maintained during the early independence years. Political and economic bourgeoisies emerged in each of Nigeria's three major regions, setting the stage for intraclass conflict in the Nigerian bourgeoisie as a whole.[73]

Intraclass competition, within the Nigerian bourgeoisie, over control of the means of production caused mounting tensions during the 6 years (1960–66) preceding the civil war. In the case of Eastern Nigeria, an emerging regional economic bourgeoisie was in competition with other factions of the national bourgeoisie over control of a booming industrial zone that included at least twenty-four major industries.[74] The most lucrative industry exploited the region's massive oil reserves. A quadrupling of oil prices, engineered by the Organization of Petroleum Exporting Countries (OPEC) in 1973–74, ensured that oil rights would be severely contested. Even as early as 1966, the economic and political bourgeoisies of the Eastern Region were locked in a struggle with other regional bourgeoisies over the exploitation of the region's oil resources. "Some of the members of the bourgeoisie [of the Eastern Region] began to dream dreams," explains Ikenna Nzimiro, a participant in the Nigerian civil war and a proponent of the class approach.[75] "Foremost in their minds was that control over the economic resource of oil would allow them to emerge as the dominant class in the economic and the political bourgeoisie."[76]

The workers' strike of June 1964 crippled the national economy for 13 days and was a turning point in mounting social tensions during the First Republic.[77] The strike pitted the urban proletariat against the political bourgeoisie. Although it originated in workers' demands for higher pay and greater benefits, it captured popular "disgust" with the corrupt and extravagant lifestyles of the Nigerian political bourgeoisie.[78] The net effect of the strike, which received widespread public support, especially in the urban areas, was to "further weaken" the already threatened legitimacy of the Nigerian political bourgeoisie "and to expose the weakness of its authority."[79]

Rising intraclass conflict in the Nigerian bourgeoisie, particularly between the petty bourgeoisie and the political bourgeoisie, culminated in the military coups of January and June 1966. The progressive faction of the petty bourgeoisie was made up of the young army majors and captains who led the January coup to end the corrupt practices of the dominant political bourgeoisie. Despite the fact that they were primarily Igbo, these officers were motivated by a higher commitment to create a more progressive Nigerian regime that served all ethnic groups. However, the progressive coup plotters failed to achieve all their military objectives, most notably the execution of J. T. U. Aguiyi Ironsi, an Igbo general who rallied federal troops in the defense of a unified Nigeria and who ultimately emerged as Nigeria's military leader in the aftermath of the failed coup.

General Ironsi's assumption of power, and subsequent execution in the countercoup of July 1966, signaled the intensification of intraclass struggle in the political bourgeoisie over control of national economic resources. Although successful in bringing down Nigeria's First Republic and destroying its ethnic base, the January coup nonetheless failed to win power for the progressive military officers.[80] "The top echelon of the officer corps, many of whom already identified, in terms of class interests, with the ousted politicians, grabbed power," explains Nzimiro.[81] In this regard, the decision of Colonel Ojukwu to declare Biafra's independence and to lead a protracted military campaign against the Nigerian central government was motivated less by his allegiance to the Igbo nation than by his desire to protect the class interests of an emerging regional political bourgeoisie, of which he was a member.[82]

CONTINUING DEBATE

The two preceding narratives of the Nigerian civil war demonstrate how the concepts of ethnicity and class have contributed to extremely rich and provocative yet different interpretations of African politics and society. Despite general agreement over most of the facts associated with the Nigerian civil war, specific interpretations of those facts have varied, depending on whether one focuses on the role of class or ethnicity as the defining characteristic. The interpretations vary by picking out different significant events and assigning different intentions and identities to the principal actors. Indeed, our understanding of the relationship between class and ethnicity has been hindered by the scholarly community's tendency to divide these concepts into two separate and highly divided fields of analysis. "An invisible wall has separated ethnicity and class analysis, which has only infrequently been scaled," explains Young. "On both sides of the wall, analysts tend to concede that the other exists, then proceed to ignore or trivialize it."[83]

The ideological cold war between the Western and Eastern blocs played a prominent role in strengthening this invisible wall. Many Western, and particularly American, scholars dismissed class as a tainted concept of Soviet-led Marxism, with little if any relevance to African politics and society. Although scholars in the 1960s optimistically believed that ethnic attachments would eventually fade as part of the modernization process, ethnicity was an important concept of the Western intellectual tradition and therefore remained an acceptable topic of research. Most important, the cold war reinforced the ideological divide separating ethnicity and class analyses; the concept of ethnicity was associated with an acceptable, mainstream liberal tradition, whereas the concept of class was associated with a critical tradition of scholarship considered on the fringe of intellectual debates (see Chapters 13 and 14).

The cold war's end removed the ideological foundations of the invisible wall and thereby set the stage for reinterpretations of African politics and society that allow for a creative synthesis of the concepts of class and ethnicity. At a minimum, such an analysis would recognize the important interplay between ethnicity and class, underscoring the importance of both concepts. "Although a creative synthesis of the concepts of class and ethnicity that is capable of explaining social stratification and politics in African states and societies has yet to appear," explains Patrick M. Boyle, "the time has never been more ripe for such an analysis as we attempt to explain the evolution of pro-democracy movements, shifting relationships between state and society, ideological debates, and altered international relationships at the beginning of the twenty-first century."[84] Although each concept can explain one piece of the African puzzle, neither can explain the puzzle as a whole. Future generations of ethnicity scholars will need to explain how systematic domination by particular ethnic groups differentiates them from a ruling class, while those scholars who emphasize class analysis will have to explain the persistence of ethnic divisions in societies seemingly divided into conflicting classes. Both concepts are necessary and relevant to a contemporary understanding of African politics and society.

KEY TERMS

ethnicity
clans
age-sets
ethnic compact
ethnic intermediary
ethnic balance
proportionality principle
marabouts
religious intermediary
genocide
class
class factions
foreign bourgeoisie
metropolitan bourgeoisie
local expatriate class
African bourgeoisie
political bourgeoisie

bureaucratic bourgeoisie
commercial bourgeoisie
petty bourgeoisie
African proletariat
lumpenproletariat
African peasantry
kulaks
economy of affection
interclass cooperation
transnational class cooperation
intraclass conflict
interclass conflict
female circumcision
female genital mutilation
clitoridectomy
excision
infibulation

FOR FURTHER READING

Badru, Pade. *Imperialism and Ethnic Politics in Nigeria, 1960–96*. Trenton, NJ: Africa World Press, 1998.

Boyle, Patrick M. *Class Formation and Civil Society: The Politics of Education in Africa*. Aldershot: Ashgate, 1999.

Ellis, Stephen. *The Mask of Anarchy: The Destruction of Liberia and the Religious Dimension of an African Civil War*. Washington Square: New York University Press, 1999.

Freund, Bill. *The African Worker*. Cambridge: Cambridge University Press, 1988.

Horowitz, Donald. *Ethnic Groups in Conflict*. Berkeley: University of California Press, 1985.

Huntington, Samuel P. *The Clash of Civilizations and the Remaking of World Order*. New York: Simon & Schuster, 1996.

Kasfir, Nelson, ed. *State and Class in Africa*. London: Frank Cass, 1984.

Laitin, David D. *Hegemony and Culture: Politics and Religious Change among the Yoruba*. Chicago: University of Chicago Press, 1986.

Lloyd, Peter C. *The New Elites of Tropical Africa*. London: Oxford University Press for International African Institute, 1966.

Lubeck, Paul M., ed. *The African Bourgeoisie: Capitalist Development in Nigeria, Kenya, and the Ivory Coast*. Boulder: Lynne Rienner, 1987.

Mamdani, Mahmood. *When Victims Become Killers: Colonialism, Nativism, and the Genocide in Rwanda*. Princeton: Princeton University Press, 2001.

Markovitz, Irving Leonard. *Power and Class in Africa*. Englewood Cliffs: Prentice-Hall, 1977.

Markovitz, Irving Leonard, ed. *Studies in Power and Class in Africa*. New York: Oxford University Press, 1987.

Robertson, Claire, and Iris Berger, eds. *Women and Class in Africa*. New York: Africana, 1986.

Rothchild, Donald. *Managing Ethnic Conflict in Africa: Pressures and Incentives for Cooperation*. Washington: Brookings Institution, 1997.

Rothchild, Donald, and Victor Olorunsola, eds. *State versus Ethnic Claims: African Policy Dilemmas*. Boulder: Westview, 1983.

Sklar, Richard. "The Nature of Class Domination in Africa." *The Journal of Modern African Studies* 17, no. 4 (1979): 531–52.

Suberu, Rotimi T. *Federalism and Ethnic Conflict in Nigeria*. Washington, DC: United States Institute of Peace Press, 2001.

Young, Crawford. *The Politics of Cultural Pluralism*. Madison: University of Wisconsin Press, 1977.

Young, Crawford. *The Rising Tide of Cultural Pluralism: The Nation-State at Bay?* Madison: University of Wisconsin Press, 1993.

NOTES

1. John Middleton, ed., *Encyclopedia of Africa South of the Sahara* (4 vols.), (New York: Charles Scribner's Sons, 1997).

2. See Andreas Danevad, "Responsiveness in Botswana Politics: Do Elections Matter?" *The Journal of Modern African Studies* 33, no. 3 (1995): 381–402.

3. The leading opposition party, the Botswana National Front (BNF), increasingly has made inroads in national politics (winning 37 percent of the popular vote in 1994), at least partially due to the fact that its leaders are from the Bangwaketse clan family, the second largest of the Tswana clan groupings.

4. Crawford Young, "Nationalism, Ethnicity, and Class in Africa: A Retrospective," *Cahiers d'Etudes Africaines* 26, no. 6 (1986): 443.

5. For an introduction to this vast literature, see Crawford Young, *The Politics of Cultural Pluralism* (Madison: University of Wisconsin Press, 1975). See also Crawford Young, "Evolving Modes of Consciousness and Ideology: Nationalism and Ethnicity," in David E. Apter and Carl G. Rosberg, eds., *Political Development and the New Realism in Sub-Saharan Africa* (Charlottesville: University Press of Virginia, 1994), pp. 61–86.

6. Young, "Nationalism, Ethnicity, and Class in Africa," p. 443.

7. See Naomi Chazan, Robert Mortimer, John Ravenhill, and Donald Rothchild, *Politics and Society in Contemporary Africa* (Boulder: Lynne Rienner, 1992), pp. 110–16.

8. Ibid., p. 114.

9. Ibid., p. 112.

10. Ibid., pp. 114–15.

11. Ibid.

12. Ibid., p. 115.

13. See Donald Rothchild, "State-Ethnic Relations in Middle Africa," in Gwendolen M. Carter and Patrick O'Meara, eds., *African Independence: The First Twenty-Five Years* (Bloomington: Indiana University Press, 1985), p. 83. See also Donald Rothchild, *Managing Ethnic Conflict in Africa: Pressures and Incentives for Cooperation* (Washington, DC: Brookings Institution, 1997).

14. Rothchild, "State-Ethnic Relations," p. 82.

15. Ibid., p. 82.

16. For an overview, see Peter J. Schraeder, "Ethnic Politics in Djibouti: From 'Eye of the Hurricane' to 'Boiling Cauldron,'" *African Affairs* 92, no. 367 (1993): 203–23. See also Absieh Omar Warsame and Maurice Botbol, *Djibouti: Les institutions politiques et militaires* (Paris: Banque d'Information et de Documentation de l'Océan Indien, 1986).

17. See Schraeder, "Ethnic Politics in Djibouti."

18. For an excellent overview, see Donald Rothchild and Victor A. Olorunsola, eds., *State versus Ethnic Claims: African Policy Dilemmas* (Boulder: Westview, 1983).

19. For an overview, see Kassim Shehim and James Searing, "Djibouti and the Question of Afar Nationalism," *African Affairs* 19, no. 315 (1980): 209–26.

20. See the English-language translation of an article written by Catherine Simon for *Le Monde:* "Influx of Refugees Heightens Vulnerability," FBIS, *Daily Report Sub-Saharan Africa* (July 28, 1991): 6.

21. For discussion of the major attempts at secession during the contemporary independence era, see Rothchild and Olorunsola, *State versus Ethnic Claims.*

22. The classic statement on the Somali clan system is I. M. Lewis, *Somalia: A Pastoral Democracy* (London: Oxford University Press, 1960).

23. For an overview of this history, see David Laitin and Said Samatar, *Somalia: Nation in Search of a State* (Boulder: Westview, 1987).

24. See Robert Gersony, *Why Somalis Flee: Synthesis of Accounts of Conflict Experience in Northern Somalia by Somali Refugees, Displaced Persons, and Others* (Washington, DC: Bureau for Refugee Programs, Department of State, August 1989), and Africa Watch, *Somalia: A Government at War with Its Own People; Testimonies about the Killings and the Conflict in the North* (London: Africa Watch, 1990).

25. See Gérard Prunier, "Somaliland Goes It Alone," *Current History* 97, no. 619 (1998): 225–28.

26. For a more extended analysis, see Crawford Young, "Comparative Claims to Political Sovereignty: Biafra, Katanga, Eritrea," in Rothchild and Olorunsola, *State versus Ethnic Claims,* pp. 199–232.

27. For example, see Alain Destexhe (translated from the French by Alison Marschner), *Rwanda and Genocide in the Twentieth Century* (New York: New York University Press, 1995).

28. Sembène Ousmane, *God's Bits of Wood* (London: Heinemann, 1970).

29. Quoted in ibid., p. 8.

30. See Young, "Nationalism, Ethnicity, and Class in Africa," p. 423.

31. See Martin Staniland, *American Intellectuals and African Nationalists, 1955–1970* (New Haven: Yale University Press, 1991).

32. The recognized leading light in the French tradition is J. Suret-Canale, *Afrique Noire, Occidentale et Centrale* (vol. 2): *L'Ère Coloniale 1900–1945* (Paris: Editions Sociales, 1964). Cited in Young, "Nationalism, Ethnicity, and Class," p. 422.

33. Young, "Nationalism, Ethnicity, and Class," p. 422.

34. Ibid., p. 423.

35. For an introduction to this literature, see Irving Leonard Markovitz, ed., *Studies in Power and Class in Africa* (New York: Oxford University Press, 1987).

36. See Stephen Smith and Antoine Glaser, *Ces Messieurs Afrique: Le Paris-Village du Continent Noir* (Paris: Calmann-Lévy, 1992). See also Guy Martin, "Francophone Africa in the Context of Franco-African Relations," in John W. Harbeson and Donald Rothchild, eds., *Africa in World Politics: Post-Cold War Challenges* (Boulder: Westview, 1995), pp. 163–88.

37. For example, see Pierre Péan, *L'Homme de l'Ombre: Eléments d'Enquête Autour de Jacques Foccart, l'Homme le Plus Mystérieux et le Plus Puissant de la Ve République* (Paris: Fayard, 1990).

38. For an early analysis of the evolving French presence in Senegal, see Rita Cruise O'Brien, *White Society in Black Africa: The French of Africa* (London: Faber & Faber, 1972).

39. For a general discussion of the African bourgeoisie, see Paul M. Lubeck, ed., *The African Bourgeoisie: Capitalist Development in Nigeria, Kenya, and the Ivory Coast* (Boulder: Lynne Rienner, 1987). See also Richard L. Sklar, "Social Class and Political Action in Africa: The Bourgeoisie and the Proletariat," in David E. Apter and Carl G. Rosberg, eds., *Political Development and the New Realism in Sub-Saharan Africa* (Charlottesville:

University Press of Virginia, 1994), esp. pp. 121–27.

40. For example, see Colin Leys, *Underdevelopment in Kenya: The Political Economy of Neocolonialism 1964–1971* (Berkeley: University of California Press, 1975). See also Gavin Kitching, *Class and Economic Change in Kenya: The Making of an African Petite Bourgeoisie, 1905–1970* (New Haven: Yale University Press, 1980), and Leys, "Learning from the Kenya Debate," in Apter and Rosberg, eds., *Political Development,* pp. 220–46.

41. For a general overview, see Bill Freund, *The African Worker* (Cambridge: Cambridge University Press, 1988). See also Sklar, "Social Class and Political Action in Africa," esp. pp. 127–34.

42. See Momar Coumba Diop and Mamadou Diouf, *Le Sénégal sous Abdou Diouf: Etat et Société* (Paris: Editions Karthala, 1990), especially Chs. 5, 9, and 12.

43. For an introduction, see John S. Saul and Roger Woods, "African Peasantries," in Teodor Shanin, ed., *Peasants and Peasant Societies* (Harmondsworth: Penguin, 1971), pp. 80–88.

44. See Jonathan Barker, *Rural Communities under Stress: Peasant Farmers and the State in Africa* (Cambridge: Cambridge University Press, 1989).

45. See Goran Hyden, *Beyond Ujamaa in Tanzania: Underdevelopment and an Uncaptured Peasantry* (Berkeley: University of California Press, 1980).

46. See James C. Scott, *The Moral Economy of the Peasant: Rebellion and Subsistence in Southeast Asia* (New Haven: Yale University Press, 1976).

47. For example, see Hyden, *Beyond Ujamaa in Tanzania.*

48. United Nations Development Program (UNDP) and the World Bank, *African Development Indicators* (Washington, DC: UNDP and the World Bank, 1992), p. 317.

49. For a sympathetic overview, see Issa G. Shivji, *Class Struggles in Tanzania* (London: Heinemann, 1976).

50. For example, see Georges Nzongola-Ntalaja, *Class Struggles and National*

Liberation in Africa (Roxbury: Omenana, 1982).

51. Richard L. Sklar, "The Nature of Class Domination in Africa," *The Journal of Modern African Studies* 17, no. 4 (1979): 531–52. For an update and application of Sklar's view, see Larry Diamond, "Class Formation in the Swollen African State," *Journal of Modern African Studies* 25, no. 4 (1989): 567–96.

52. Ibid., p. 537.

53. For an overview, see Jeffrey Herbst, *The Politics of Reform in Ghana, 1982–1991* (Berkeley: University of California Press, 1993).

54. Ibid., p. 33.

55. UNDP and World Bank, *African Development Indicators,* p. 317.

56. See ibid. for election results.

57. See Alain Rouvez (with the assistance of Michael Coco and Jean-Paul Paddack), *Disconsolate Empires: French, British, and Belgian Military Involvement in Postcolonial Sub-Saharan Africa* (Lanham: University Press of America, 1994), pp. 169–71.

58. Claude Ake, *Democracy and Development in Africa* (Washington, DC: Brookings Institution, 1996).

59. See Edmond J. Keller, *Revolutionary Ethiopia: From Empire to People's Republic* (Bloomington: Indiana University Press, 1988), pp. 142, 149.

60. See Robert D. Grey, "The Petite Bourgeoisie in the Ethiopian Revolution," in Markovitz, *Studies in Power and Class in Africa,* pp. 118–30. See also John Markakis and Nega Ayele, *Class and Revolution in Ethiopia* (Lawrenceville: Red Sea, 1986).

61. For a historical overview, see Jeffrey A. Lefebvre, *Arms for the Horn: U.S. Security Policy in Ethiopia and Somalia 1953–1991* (Pittsburgh: University of Pittsburgh Press, 1991).

62. For discussion, see Nzongola-Ntalaja, *Revolution and Counterrevolution in Africa: Essays in Contemporary Politics* (London: Zed, 1987).

63. Richard L. Sklar and C. S. Whitaker, "Nigeria: Rivers of Oil, Trails of Blood, Prospects for Unity and Democracy,"

CSIS Africa Notes no. 179 (December 1995): 1.

64. For a good overview, see Paul A. Beckett and Crawford Young, eds., *Dilemmas of Democracy in Nigeria* (Rochester: University of Rochester Press, 1997).

65. One of the most noteworthy attempts at achieving a balance between ethnicity and class-based analyses is Richard A. Joseph, *Democracy and Prebendal Politics in Nigeria: The Rise and Fall of the Second Republic* (Cambridge: Cambridge University Press, 1987).

66. The ethnic interpretation primarily draws on Crawford Young, "Comparative Claims to Political Sovereignty: Biafra, Katanga, Eritrea," in Donald Rothchild and Victor A. Olorunsola, eds., *State versus Ethnic Claims: African Policy Dilemmas* (Boulder: Westview, 1983), pp. 199–232. See also Robert Melson and Howard Wolpe, eds., *Nigeria: Modernization and the Politics of Communalism* (East Lansing: University of Michigan Press, 1971), and Rotimi T. Suberu, *Federalism and Ethnic Conflict in Nigeria* (Washington, DC: The United States Institute of Peace Press, 2001).

67. See David Abernethy, *The Political Dilemma of Popular Education: An African Case* (Stanford: University of California Press, 1969).

68. Larry Diamond, "Nigeria: The Uncivic Society and the Descent into Praetorianism," in Larry Diamond et al., eds., *Politics in Developing Countries: Comparing Experiences with Democracy,* 2nd ed. (Boulder: Lynne Rienner, 1995), p. 425.

69. Ibid., pp. 425–26.

70. Young, "Comparative Claims to Political Sovereignty," pp. 206–7.

71. Ibid., p. 207.

72. The class interpretation primarily draws on Ikenna Nzimiro, *The Nigerian Civil War: A Study in Class Conflict* (Lagos: Frontline, 1982). See also Sakah Saidu Mahmud, *State, Class, and Underdevelopment in Nigeria and Early Meiji Japan* (New York: St. Martin's, 1996), and Pade Badru, *Imperialism and Ethnic Politics in Nigeria,*

1960–96 (Trenton, NJ: Africa World Press, 1998).

73. Larry Diamond, *Class, Ethnicity, and Democracy in Nigeria: The Failure of the First Republic* (Syracuse, NY: Syracuse University Press, 1988), pp. 31–32.

74. Nzimiro, *The Nigerian Civil War,* pp. 109–12.

75. Ibid., p. 112.

76. Ibid.

77. Diamond, "Nigeria: The Uncivic Society," p. 426.

78. Ibid., p. 426.

79. Ibid., p. 426.

80. Nzimiro, *The Nigerian Civil War,* p. 88.

81. Ibid., p. 88.

82. See Nzimiro, *The Nigerian Civil War,* esp. pp. 109–27.

83. Young, "Nationalism, Ethnicity, and Class in Africa," p. 471.

84. Personal correspondence. For an overview of such attempts, see Young, "Nationalism, Ethnicity, and Class," pp. 470–74. For a specific formulation applied to the case of Nigeria, see Joseph, *Democracy and Prebendal Politics in Nigeria.*

6

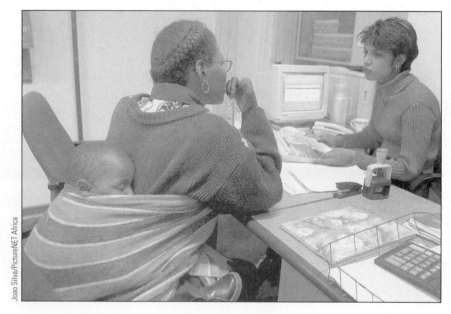

Ideology and the
Politics of Development

A South African taxpayer working out her tax bill with a representative of the South African Revenue Service in Pretoria, South Africa, in 2002.

Joao Silva/PictureNET Africa

D URING THE 1960s, the leaders of Kenya and Tanzania engaged in an acrimonious ideological debate over the proper path to development. Tanzanian President Julius Nyerere sharply criticized Kenyan capitalism as an inherently flawed "man-eat-man" system in which only a few would prosper at the expense of society as a whole. Kenyan President Jomo Kenyatta responded by denouncing Tanzanian socialism as a "man-eat-nothing" system in which the lack of production incentives would stall the economy and impoverish everyone. This ideological debate widened in East Africa after the Ethiopian revolution of 1974 and the emergence of a Marxist regime under the leadership of Mengistu Haile Mariam. Together these regimes exemplified the three major ideologies—capitalism, socialism, and Marxism—that have competed for influence in the development strategies of African leaders during the contemporary independence era.[1] Though capitalism was the legacy of the departing colonial powers, socialist and Marxist alternatives began appearing in the 1950s and the 1960s and together represented nearly 30 percent of all African regimes during the 1970s. By the mid-1990s, both socialism and Marxism had fallen into disrepute and most African leaders adopted some variation of a capitalist path to development. This chapter examines the evolution and impact of ideology on the development of the African continent.

EVOLUTION OF AFRICAN
DEVELOPMENT IDEOLOGIES

Ideology refers to the principles that guide a country's political and economic policies. In Africa, ideology has particularly guided national development strategies. It can also serve as the basis for cooperation among like-minded elites or as a source of competition and conflict. Especially during the cold war, ideology tended to intensify existing regional rivalries, such as that between Kenya and Tanzania, sometimes transforming them into ideological flashpoints between the United States and the Soviet Union.

African leaders who took power at the beginning of the 1950s inherited economic systems largely based on capitalist principles of development, the most important of which is a belief in the benefits of a free-market economy (see Map 6.1).[2] In the aftermath of World War II, the European colonial powers shared a belief in the universality of a **capitalist model of development** and had implanted its basic elements in their African colonies. The willingness of most of Africa's new leaders to embrace capitalist economic policies suggested that this model would dominate African development thinking throughout the remainder of the twentieth century. After independence, former colonies approached capitalist development strategies differently. Some countries, such as Côte d'Ivoire under the leadership of Félix Houphouët-Boigny, pursued a brand of capitalism that relied on close links with the former colonial power (in this case, France). Others, such as Nigeria, pursued a more nationalist brand of

MAP 6.1   African Ideologies

capitalism that sought to reduce the influence of the other major capitalist powers, most notably the United States and Great Britain.

A **socialist model of development** emerged in the early 1950s as the first ideological challenge to the capitalist orthodoxy of African development thinking.[3] This socialist alternative, often called **populist socialism,** is philosophically grounded in African populism and advocates state control over the national economy. Its initial adherents, Gamal Abdel Nasser of Egypt and Ahmed Sékou Touré of Guinea, displayed a strident anti-West populism that, in the case of Egypt, also included a pan-Arabist populism. In other cases, such as Algeria and Guinea-Bissau, popular support for socialist alternatives stemmed directly from extended guerrilla insurgencies against the former colonial powers. It is important to note, however, that anti-West populism is not a necessary ingredient of socialism. In Zambia, for example, President Kenneth Kaunda promoted a unique brand of "humanist" socialism, while maintaining close ties with a variety of Western powers. Indeed, some of Africa's most eloquent proponents of socialism, such as Léopold Sédar Senghor, the first president of Senegal, not only maintained close ties with the West but oversaw a national development strategy that largely drew from capitalist principles.

A second challenge to capitalist development orthodoxy, the **Marxist model of development,** emerged in the late 1960s and was inspired by the works of Karl Marx and the communist regimes of the Soviet Union and Eastern Europe.[4] The Marxist alternative, also called **scientific socialism,** is based on the belief that revolutionary struggle will eventually lead to the development of communism throughout the world. The first African–Marxist regime emerged in Congo-Brazzaville in 1969 as a result of a military coup led by a self-proclaimed Marxist leader, Marien Ngouabi. His assumption of power, which overthrew a populist-socialist regime, underscored Marxist disdain for capitalist and populist-socialist regimes alike. It also marked the beginning of a trend in which military rulers in Somalia (1970), Benin (1974), Madagascar (1975), and Ethiopia (1976) also announced the creation of Marxist regimes. A second wave of Marxist regimes emerged in Angola, Cape Verde, Sao Tome and Principe, and Mozambique in the latter half of the 1970s, after extended guerrilla insurgencies and a military coup d'état in Lisbon prompted Portuguese authorities to grant independence to their colonies in Africa. To the great concern of Western, particularly American, policymakers, Marxism was becoming increasingly popular among African leaders.[5]

A series of political and economic developments in the 1980s gradually spurred the ideological transformation of socialist and Marxist regimes. Economic decline and the emergence of pro-democracy movements throughout the African continent forced African leaders of all ideological persuasions to reassess the economic and political dimensions of their national development strategies (see Chapter 10). These reassessments were strongly influenced by the end of the cold war and the decline of communism in the former Soviet Union and Eastern Europe. "If communism could not succeed in its birthplace," explained Bathie Mbodj, a Senegalese student, "why should we continue to debate its relevance to the African experience?"[6] More important, the International Monetary Fund (IMF) and the World Bank became influential in the restructuring of African development strategies and economies. To obtain access to desperately needed international financial capital, socialist and Marxist regimes were forced to implement structural adjustment programs (SAPs) designed to restructure African economies and political systems according to free-market principles (see Chapter 12).

The 1990s witnessed the resurgence of capitalist ideology in African development thinking. All of Africa's Marxist regimes renounced their Marxist ideologies, and Libya (under the leadership of Muammar Qaddafi) remained the only African country officially committed to a version of populist socialism, albeit one largely informed by pan-Arabism.[7] The case of South Africa is particularly illuminating. During the guerrilla struggle against the former apartheid regime, the leaders of the African National Congress (ANC) underscored the usefulness of populist-socialist, and especially Marxist, ideological models of development in the future transformation of South Africa into a nonracist society. "Marxism's call to revolutionary action was music to the ears of a freedom fighter," explains Nelson Mandela in his autobiography. "In my reading of Marxist works, I found a great deal of information that bore on the type of problems that face a practical politician."[8] Upon entering office in 1994, how-ever, Nelson Mandela and the ruling ANC embarked on a development pro-gram strongly influenced by capitalist ideology. We will return to this point in the concluding section.

IDEOLOGY AND DEVELOPMENT CHOICE

Except for Crawford Young's thought-provoking book, *Ideology and Development in Africa,* published in 1982, the field of African studies lacks comprehensive, comparative analyses of the degree to which different ideologies influence the development choices of individual African regimes.[9] A careful reading of Young's book suggests that the potentially different policy implications of Africa's three major ideologies—capitalism, socialism, and Marxism—are aptly demonstrated by how their African proponents respond to five questions:

- What is the primary purpose of development?

- What is the primary engine of development?

- What is the role of agriculture in development?

- What is the role of the peasantry in development?

- What is the role of foreign powers and investment in development?

The answers to each of these questions can be obtained by focusing on one model case for each of our three broad ideological categories. The ideological choices associated with African capitalism are represented by the Kenyan regime of President Jomo Kenyatta (1963–78).[10] Kenyatta led his country to inde-pendence in 1963 and was an ardent defender of capitalist values. He was also a popular leader who was respectfully referred to by Kenyans as the mzee (the wise old man). Kenyatta's successors, presidents Danial arap Moi (1978–2002) and Mwai Kibaki (2002–present), have maintained Kenya's adherence to the capitalist model of development.

African socialism is represented by the Tanzanian regime of President Julius Nyerere (1962–85).[11] Nyerere led his country to independence in 1962, and subsequently emerged as Africa's most ardent proponent of socialism. Affection-ately referred to by Tanzanians as the mwalimu (teacher), Nyerere is best known for his launching of Tanzania's socialist experiment in development known as ujamaa (brotherhood). Nyerere voluntarily stepped down from power in 1985, and his successors have gradually dismantled the major components of Tanzania's experiment in socialism.

Finally, African Marxism is represented by the Ethiopian regime of Mengistu Haile Mariam (1976–91).[12] Mengistu initiated a Marxist "revolution from above" 2 years after he and several other members of the Ethiopian mili-tary took power in a military coup d'état in 1974. Mengistu never achieved a wide degree of popular support beyond his core Amhara ethnic group. As a result, his regime was plagued by popular unrest that ultimately developed into a series of regime-threatening guerrilla insurgencies. Ethiopia's experiment in Marxism ended in 1991, when the Tigrean People's Liberation Front (TPLF), one of several guerrilla armies opposed to Mengistu's rule, captured the capital city of Addis Ababa. Mengistu lives in exile in Harare, Zimbabwe. Together these three cases—Kenyan capitalism, Tanzanian socialism, and Ethiopian Marxism—offer important insights as to how ideological beliefs affect development choices.

Primary Purpose of Development

Different ideologies manifest different purposes of development. African capitalists seek evolutionary change in the confines of their socioeconomic systems. They share an overriding concern with ensuring the industrialization of their societies, particularly as measured by the growth rate of the gross national product (GNP). As a result, African capitalists are wary of state-promoted measures designed to ensure economic equality at the expense of economic growth. For advocates of capitalist economic strategies, the socioeconomic benefits of a rising GNP will eventually "trickle down" to all levels of society. The growth-oriented nature of African capitalists is captured in the Kenyan government's blueprint for economic development, *African Socialism and Its Application to Kenya,* which, despite its misleading title, firmly placed Kenya in the capitalist sphere of development.[13] "The most important [policy] is to provide a firm basis for rapid economic growth," explains the report. "Other immediate problems, such as Africanization of the economy, education, unemployment and welfare services, and provincial policies, must be handled in ways that do not jeopardize growth. . . . Growth then is the first concern of planning in Kenya."[14]

African socialists perceive the primary purpose of development as an attempt to gradually return to a socialist past—the indigenous communal economies that existed before the colonial era. They argue that African development historically was based on a "communitarian ethos" in which successes and failures were shared by the community as a whole.[15] Both then and now, development was and remains correctly targeted toward satisfying the basic human needs of every member of the overall community. It is precisely for this reason that Nyerere chose ujamaa—the Kiswahili term for brotherhood—as the symbolic title of Tanzania's experiment in socialism. "Both the 'rich' and the 'poor' were completely secure in [precolonial] African society," explains Nyerere in his treatise on Tanzanian socialism, *Ujamaa: Essays on Socialism,* which was originally published in 1962. "Nobody starved, either of food or of human dignity, because he lacked personal wealth; he could depend on the wealth possessed by the community of which he was a member. That was socialism. That is socialism."[16]

African Marxists seek a revolutionary break with both present and past forms of African development. They argue that the primary goal of development is the revolutionary transformation of class relationships to create a classless society. African Marxists often cite the Ethiopian revolution (1974–77) that brought the Mengistu regime into power as a unique example of revolutionary transformation of an African society. During that 4-year period, an aging and unresponsive monarchy under the leadership of Emperor Haile Selassie was overthrown and replaced by the Provisional Military Administrative Council (PMAC), a group of approximately 120 progressive officers of the Ethiopian military who became known as the Dergue. Despite initial policy pronouncements that emphasized the importance of hebrettesebawinet (Ethiopian socialism) and Ethiopia Tikdem (Ethiopian unity), the Dergue in 1977 announced its firm ideological commitment to the transformation of Ethiopian society according to the Marxist principles of scientific socialism.[17] The Marxist faction under Mengistu's leadership assured its ascendancy by unleashing a wave of "revolutionary red terror" that resulted in the execution of 10,000 members of the civilian opposition in 1977 alone. To deter future anti-Marxist opposition, the regime terrorized citizens by "leaving [the] bodies of their assassinated victims in the streets with signs marking them as 'counterrevolutionaries' attached to their clothes."[18]

Primary Engine of Development

Different ideologies also lead to different policy choices as to what should constitute the primary engine of development. African capitalists share an unabiding faith in the free-market economy as the most important engine of development. An emphasis is placed on the private ownership of capital and the entrepreneurship of private businesspersons. As a result, the role of the African state theoretically should be limited to that of regulating an essentially free-market economy. Kenyan capitalism nonetheless demonstrates the highly interventionist role of the state even in African capitalist systems. Often called **nurture capitalism,** this particular brand of African capitalism assumes that the state must actively promote the emergence and protection of private businesses that can successfully compete with foreign enterprises.[19] It is precisely for this reason that the Kenyan state promoted such national legislation as the Trade Licensing Act of 1967, which was designed to reserve significant portions of the Kenyan economy for Kenyan businesspersons. The Kenyan state also authorized the transfer of ownership of 1.5 million acres of land from white settler families (approximately 21 percent of their total holdings) to nearly 500,000 Kenyan farmers and their families.[20] The authorized transfer of land served as a powerful symbol of the role of the state under nurture capitalism. "Africans had cracked the hitherto impenetrable sanctuary of the white highlands," explains Young, "while domestic and external private sector interests were reassured by the market-centered principles that had guided the operation."[21]

African socialists are suspicious of private ownership because of its proclivity toward an unequal distribution of wealth. For socialists, the public sector is the primary engine of development. At the local level, African socialists usually favor the creation of communally owned lands and enterprises under the guidance of local leaders. A cornerstone of Tanzania's ujamaa strategy, for example, was the resettlement of all Tanzanian peasants to new communally owned villages known as ujamaa vijijini (Kiswahili for "village socialism" or "rural socialism"). At the national level, African socialists favor state control over the **commanding heights of the economy,** including all major financial and commercial enterprises. In Tanzania, banking was the first industry to be nationalized under an aggressive nationalization campaign, which by the mid–1970s had assumed control over 80 percent of all large-scale economic activity.[22] Tanzania's two-tiered approach to public sector involvement in the economy demonstrates that the socialist state usually serves as the coordinator of national development, setting forth the major principles of national socialism while allowing communally owned villages a great deal of latitude in local economic affairs.

African Marxists are strongly opposed to private sector involvement in the economy. African Marxists agree with their socialist counterparts that the public sector should serve as the primary engine of development. However, African Marxists advocate highly centralized economies in which the state achieves total control over the process of development. Immediately after the Ethiopian revolution, the Marxist regime brought all aspects of the economy under state rule. In early 1975, the Derg nationalized the financial and banking industries and completely abolished private ownership over land.[23] To enforce these efforts in the countryside, the Mengistu regime dispatched over 50,000 students who were to educate and guide the rural peasantry. During that same year, all urban land and housing was placed under the control of radical urban associations known as kebeles. These associations served as the primary tools— and battlegrounds—of the red terror of 1977–78 that ensured Mengistu's rise as the unparalleled leader of Ethiopia.

Role of Agriculture in National Development

The policy implications of different ideologies are particularly relevant to the role of agriculture in national development.[24] African capitalists traditionally have formulated national development strategies that favor urban-based industrialization at the expense of rural-based agriculture. However, they encourage private ownership of agricultural production and limited state involvement, typically in the form of agricultural extension services that disseminate agricultural innovations, such as new fertilizers and high-yield seeds. Kenya was exemplary among the African capitalist countries due to the Kenyatta regime's strong support of agricultural development. Kenyatta wholeheartedly embraced a colonial development strategy, *A Plan to Intensify the Development of African Agriculture in Kenya,* that proposed the registration and provision of private land titles.[25] The privatization of Kenyan lands was designed to strengthen agricultural production by making individual owners responsible for their own profits. The program was in progress in all provinces in 1965 and accounted for more than 15 percent of government expenditures on agricultural development during the first half of the 1970s.[26]

African socialists typically focus more attention on agricultural development than either their capitalist or Marxist counterparts. In Tanzania during the experiment with ujamaa socialism, the leadership treated the communal ownership of land as the cornerstone of agricultural development. Indeed, ujamaa was the most far-reaching attempt at promoting agrarian socialism on the African conti- nent. From 1967 to 1976, more than 90 percent of Tanzania's rural population was resettled into communal villages.[27] These villages were responsible for coor- dinating agricultural development, in addition to providing health care and edu- cation. Although land was communally owned, farmers were given plots of land that could be passed on from generation to generation. Farmers were allowed to keep the profits generated by their cultivation of agricultural products but were

---

A Closer Look: HIV/AIDS AND NATIONAL DEVELOPMENT

One of the greatest development challenges the African continent confronts at the beginning of the twenty-first century is how best to respond to a spreading HIV/AIDS epidemic. According to a United Nations report that was issued just before the start of the 14th Inter- national AIDS Conference in Barcelona, Spain, in 2002, Africa is the continent that has been most severely affected by the HIV/AIDS virus. As of 2003, 28.5 million Africans were infected, and 11 million African children had lost at least one parent to the virus. The average infection rate for the African continent as a whole is 9 percent, although important regional variations exist (see Map 6.2). At one extreme is North Africa, where national HIV/AIDS infection rates are well below 1 percent. At the other extreme is Southern Africa, in which national infection rates typically exceed 10 percent. Indeed, the infection rates in four countries— Lesotho (31 percent), Swaziland (33 percent), Zimbabwe (34 percent), and Botswana (39 percent)—are particularly high, affecting nearly one-third of the national populations.

The development challenge of the HIV/AIDS epidemic is enormous. HIV/AIDS drug "cocktails" developed by international pharmaceutical companies are available to treat those who are infected, but their prohibitive cost has contributed to a situation in which fewer than 30,000 of the 28.5 million infected Africans were taking them. In addition to treating those infected, an aggressive policy of prevention is needed to stem, and ultimately reverse, the spread of the disease. Such preventive actions require a commitment of often scarce administrative and financial resources that could entail the diversion of funds from equally critical programs, such as those for a variety of other widespread diseases, most notably malaria and tuberculosis. Yoweri Museveni, the president of Uganda, has been a continental leader in launching aggressive policies to combat HIV/AIDS in his country, which has a 5 percent infection rate, and, according to Dr. Peter Piot, director of the United Nations HIV/AIDS program, Zambia is poised to become the second African country after Uganda to reverse the spread of HIV/AIDS. Recent statistics demonstrate that infection rates among young women have dropped from 28 percent in 1966 to 24 percent in 1999. The massive costs associated with the HIV/AIDS epidemic have prompted the international community to create a Global Trust Fund that provides financial support for programs designed to combat HIV/AIDS and other diseases.

Data from Lawrence K. Altman, "U.N. Forecasts Big Increase in AIDS Death Toll," *The New York Times,* Wednesday, July 3, 2002, p. A1. Map adapted from Joint United Nations Programme on HIV/AIDS (UNAIDS), *Report on the Global HIV/AIDS Epidemic* (Geneva: UNAIDS, 2002).

MAP 6.2 HIV/AIDS Infection Rate (2001) (Percent of Adults Aged 15–49)

Source: Joint United Nations Programme on HIV/AIDS (UNAIDS), *Report on the Global HIV/AIDS Epidemic* (Geneva: UNAIDS, 2002).

not allowed access to lands beyond that which they could till by themselves. Limiting access to land precluded farmers from hiring other peasants, which, socialists argued, provides the basis for exploitation and runs counter to the egalitarian goal of African socialism. Although initially voluntary, the villagization program ultimately became coercive, especially from 1974 to 1976, when an "astonishing" 70 percent of peasants were coerced into taking part.[28]

African Marxists agree with African socialists that the private ownership of agricultural lands and production contradicts socialist and Marxist ideals. They nonetheless espouse a more centralized approach to agriculture that goes beyond socialist communalism. Inspired by the collective farms of the Soviet Union and the peasant communes of the People's Republic of China (PRC), African Marxists claim all agricultural lands for the state and set production standards for individual collectives.[29] Ethiopia is recognized as the African Marxist country that most closely mirrored the Soviet Union's approach to collectivization.[30] Less than 1 year after taking power, the Derg in 1975 issued decrees that nationalized all land and called for the creation of voluntary peasant associations. Four years later, the Derg issued another decree calling for the voluntary creation of peasant collectives and began investing heavily in the creation of large-scale, mechanized

collectives patterned after the Soviet model. Unhappy with the rate of collectivization—only 7 percent of all peasants had joined peasant collectives or the
larger state-controlled collectives—the Derg in 1985 issued yet another decree
that essentially sought the forced collectivization of all peasants.[31]

Perception of the Rural Peasantry

Though most African regimes share an urban bias and perceive the rural peasantry as both backward and resistant to change, there are important distinctions
between the three ideologies' treatment of the peasantry.[32] African capitalists
are the most likely of the three ideological groups to ignore the importance of
the peasant in national development. The urban, industrially biased capitalist
development programs place the peasantry near the bottom of national development concerns. Even the Kenyatta regime of Kenya, known for its support
of rural agriculture, focused its agricultural policies on the **progressive farmer,**
not the peasantry in general. The progressive farmer typically is a wealthy, land-
owning individual who hires other peasants to work the land and who is perceived by the government as more open to innovative ideas and therefore more
capable of expanding national agricultural production. It is precisely due to the
progressive farmers' perceived openness to innovation that they are targeted for
help with extensive agricultural extension services.

African socialists are the most likely of the three ideological groups to focus
on the role of the peasantry in development and even to "exalt" that group as
"the carrier of the moral values of society."[33] Nyerere's speeches and writings
glorify the peasant as the cornerstone of ujamaa socialism. However, the
rhetorical glorification of the peasantry did not deter senior Tanzanian policymakers from implementing the forced villagization of unwilling Tanzanian
peasants. Even as representatives of socialist values, the peasants were manipulated by the architects of socialist policy. Whereas the progressive farmer was
exalted under African capitalist systems, he was derisively called a kulak by
Tanzania and its socialist counterparts throughout Africa. A Russian term popular during the Soviet era, kulak refers to peasants who opposed collectivization in the Soviet Union. As was the case in the Soviet Union, the Tanzanian
kulak represented the portion of the peasantry that needed to be crushed to
advance the egalitarian goals of Tanzanian socialism.

African Marxists perceive the entire peasantry, but particularly the kulak,
as an inherently conservative portion of society, likely to oppose the radical
changes associated with the movement toward scientific socialism. As a result,
the African Marxists at best view the peasantry with suspicion and at worst perceive them as a potential threat to the consolidation of communist rule. In
Ethiopia, the vast majority of the peasantry, particularly in southern Ethiopia,
strongly welcomed the Derg's nationalization decree of 1975. This support was
not due to the peasantry's support for Marxism–Leninism but to the fact that
the decree essentially removed hated rural landlords who had systematically
exploited the rural population for centuries.[34] When the Derg issued decrees in
1979 and 1985 that sought the collectivization of the new peasant holdings, the
peasantry fought back to maintain its newfound independence.

Role of Foreign Powers and Investment

A final point of comparison is the impact of ideology on African foreign relations, especially concerning a regime's openness to foreign investment.[35] African capitalists traditionally have maintained their closest relations with the world's major capitalist countries. Whereas African capitalists heavily courted the former colonial powers, particularly France, and the United States during the cold war, Japan and Germany have become increasingly prominent in African capitalist foreign relations since the end of the cold war (see Chapter 12). In the case of Kenya, the Kenyatta regime maintained close financial ties with Great Britain (the former colonial power) while successfully diversifying its economic links with other major capitalist powers, most notably the United States. The inherently open nature of capitalist free-market economies ensures that African capitalists are also the least likely of the three ideological types to impose significant restrictions on foreign investment. However, when national leaders do implement investment restrictions, they do so to protect or ensure the entry of national capitalists into a specific industry or area of economic competition. In the case of Kenya, national investment policies ensured the entry of Kenyan businesspersons, particularly those closely allied with the Kenyatta regime, into the tea and coffee plantation industries. During the colonial era, these highly lucrative industries were exclusively reserved for white plantation owners.

African socialists publicly profess their aversion to free-market enterprise and therefore highly regulate or prohibit multinational corporations (MNCs). As a result, African socialist countries provide a relatively inhospitable economic environment to foreign investment. Tanzania under Nyerere was particularly restrictive of foreign investment to boost "self-reliance," one of the guiding principles of ujamaa socialism. Nyerere argued that "true" development, free from external domination and exploitation, could only be achieved if Tanzanians relied on their own labor and national resources. However, Nyerere's aversion to foreign investment did not preclude the acceptance of foreign aid, especially when it was provided in the form of grants. In 1977, an astonishing 59 percent of Tanzania's development budget was underwritten by foreign assistance, making that country the largest African foreign aid recipient on a per capita basis.[36] A significant portion of these funds was provided by countries that shared Nyerere's socialist ideals, such as Sweden and other Scandinavian countries, as well as the People's Republic of China (PRC), which provided one of the models for Tanzania's agrarian socialism. Tanzania also received lucrative foreign aid packages from the United States and Japan, effectively demonstrating that adherence to socialism did not preclude fruitful economic relationships with the international proponents of other ideologies.

African Marxists have often sought close ties with the former Soviet Union and other members of the Eastern Bloc.[37] However, some Marxist countries established important relationships with noncommunist states. Especially in the case of francophone West Africa, self-proclaimed African Marxists usually maintained their privileged economic, political, and even military relationships with France. Despite a shared aversion to capitalism, African Marxists are more open to foreign investment than their socialist counterparts. However, the Marxist policy to seize the commanding heights of the economy, which invariably involves the nationalization of foreign-owned industries, creates an environment of distrust that makes meaningful levels of foreign investment highly unlikely. In the aftermath of the Ethiopian revolution, the Derg nationalized twenty U.S.–owned industries, the largest of which was the Ethiopian subsidiary of the Michigan-based Kalamazoo Spice Extraction Company (valued at roughly $11 million). This action not only made U.S. investors wary of future investments but triggered congressionally mandated financial sanctions that prohibited any further U.S. foreign aid (except for disaster relief) to the Mengistu regime.

The preceding discussion of Kenyan capitalism, Tanzanian socialism, and Ethiopian Marxism illustrates how an African regime's commitment to a specific ideology significantly influences development choices (see Table 6.1 for an overview). African leaders can choose from a wide array of policy alternatives, but historically choices concerning development are largely determined by regime ideology. In short, different ideologies lead to different development choices.

Table 6.1   Policy Implications of African Ideologies

	AFRICAN CAPITALISTS	AFRICAN SOCIALISTS	AFRICAN MARXISTS
Primary Purpose of Development	Promote economic growth; evolutionary change	Promote basic human needs; return to African past	Promote classless society; revolutionary change
Primary Engine of Development	Individual entrepreneurs in free market economy; state as regulator	Public sector, especially communal villages; state as coordinator	State in highly centralized economy; state has total control
Role of Agriculture	Private ownership of land; state-provided extension services	Communal ownership of land; communal villages manage agricultural production	State ownership of land; ideally creation of large-scale, state-managed, mechanized collectives
Perception of Rural Peasantry	Ignored in favor of urban, industrial bias; preference for "progressive farmers"	Exalted as carrier of moral values; cornerstone of development efforts; opposition to kulaks	Suspiciously viewed as inherently conservative and opposed to change; opposition to kulaks
Role of Foreign Powers and Investment	Close ties with the major capitalist powers, especially the United States; very favorable toward MNCs and foreign investment	Close ties with the Nordic countries and the PRC; adverse to MNCs and foreign investment; strategy of self-reliance	Close ties with the major communist countries, especially the former Soviet Union; open to MNCs and foreign investment

IDEOLOGY AND
DEVELOPMENT PERFORMANCE

Ideology's impact on development choice raises the much-debated issue of ideology's impact on **development performance.** Does the selection of different ideological pathways lead to varied development performance, or have all African ideologies performed equally well during the contemporary independence era? This question has led to much debate largely because development is defined differently by different people. Whereas an economist might focus on the economic dimensions of development and a political scientist might focus on its political dimensions, a sociologist might reject both views and instead focus on the social aspects of development. Any realistic assessment of ideology's impact on development performance ultimately depends on how one actually defines development.

Young argues in *Ideology and Development in Africa* that one can evaluate Africa's experience with capitalism, socialism, and Marxism according to five different dimensions of development performance: economic growth, socio-economic equality, autonomy from foreign control, human dignity, and political participation.[38] It is important to note that a wide variety of statistics could be employed to characterize each dimension of development performance. The following analysis focuses on the one or two most widely used or representative indicators for each performance dimension. In so doing, the analysis seeks to highlight general trends. Each ideological pathway is once again represented by the three model cases: Kenyan capitalism under the Kenyatta regime (1963–78), Tanzanian socialism under the Nyerere regime (1962–85), and Ethiopian Marxism under the Mengistu regime (1976–91).

Economic Growth

Economic growth, typically measured in terms of the per capita growth rate in a country's GNP, serves as a starting point for understanding the varied development histories of the African continent's three ideological pathways.[39] This statistic offers a crude, yet widely recognized, indicator of the overall health of an African country's economy. "Certainly no African leader would dismiss it," explains Young. "Indeed, without growth none of the other goals [of development] can be achieved."[40] Statistics compiled by the World Bank suggest that the African capitalist countries have usually outperformed their socialist and Marxist counterparts in terms of GNP per capita.[41] The Kenyatta regime oversaw a capitalist economy that witnessed a 3.4 percent annual increase in GNP per capita from 1963 to 1978. In contrast, socialist Tanzania averaged a negative growth rate of 5.5 percent during the Nyerere administration, and Marxist Ethiopia averaged a negative growth rate of 2.75 percent during the Mengistu administration. If each of these countries truly serves as the model of its ideology, African capitalism emerges as the most able to promote economic growth.

A Closer Look: IVORY TRADE AND THE POLITICS OF CONSERVATION

African policymakers, regardless of ideology, not surprisingly have looked upon their countries' natural resources, whether oil, gold, or ivory, as important tools in the quest for national development. Interestingly, whereas few would question the sale of oil or gold in the pursuit of this goal, the sale of ivory has contributed to one of the most vociferous debates in the field of African development.

The trade of African ivory is a time-honored tradition. "The earliest records of ivory trade in Africa date to the Sixth Dynasty of ancient Egypt (2420–2258 B.C.E.) and later records, including royal burials, make it clear that ivory was among the most prized possessions of its rulers," explains Edward A. Alpers. "Following the collapse of the Roman Empire, India and China emerged as the main markets for ivory from northeastern and eastern Africa by the tenth century." By the beginning of the twenty-first century, Japan had earned the distinction of being the world's largest market for ivory, typically using the material to manufacture chopsticks, signature seals for letters and documents, and ornamental decorations.

On June 19, 1997, the Convention on International Trade in Endangered Species (CITES) ratified an exception to the international ban on trading ivory that had been put in place in 1989. According to the exception, Botswana, Namibia, and Zimbabwe were permitted to sell to Japan nearly 50 tons of stockpiled ivory that had been culled from overpopulated elephant herds. This exception, sought again in 2003, unleashed a firestorm of international debate that pitted international conservation groups against African conservation groups, and African governments against each other, in the process illuminating the **politics of conservation** on the African continent.

Opponents of the exception argue that even the smallest opening in the worldwide ban will encourage the resurgence of illegal poaching that previously led to an alarming decline in Africa's elephant population from approximately 1.3 million in 1979 to 500,000 in 1989. They also question the ability and the resolve of international monitors to ensure that illegal ivory will not be mixed with legal ivory stocks and that the emergence of parallel illegal markets will be aggressively contained. African opponents to any easing of the ban note that their conservation services will be hard-pressed to effectively stem the expected rise in illegal poaching. In the case of Kenya, for example, which depends on tourism for nearly 40 percent of its foreign exchange earnings, the Kenya Wildlife Services managed to stem the rising tide of poachers in the country's national parks only beginning in the mid-1990s. Kenyan leaders are opposed to any renewal of the ivory trade that will potentially embolden Kenyan poachers.

Proponents of relaxing the ban, most notably Botswana, Namibia, South Africa, Zambia, and Zimbabwe, argue that they should not be penalized for successfully protecting their elephant herds. Indeed, the wildlife services in each of these countries are forced to cull an annual percentage of their elephant herds to prevent the overpopulation of national wildlife parks. In their eyes, why should they not be allowed to reap the profits of culled ivory, especially when it is primarily destined to further enhance national wildlife programs?

Quotations are from Edward A. Alpers, "Ivory Trade," in John Middleton, ed., *Encyclopedia of Africa South of the Sahara*, vol. 2 (New York: Charles Scribner's Sons, 1997), pp. 403–4. See also Doran Ross, ed., *Elephant: The Animal and Its Ivory in African Culture* (Los Angeles: University of California Press, 1992).

Socioeconomic Equality

The promotion of socioeconomic equality, most notably meeting the **basic human needs** (BHNs) of a given population, is a second dimension of development performance.[42] BHN encompasses a wide variety of specific socioeconomic indicators of development, such as life expectancy, access to health care, and literacy rates. The African socialist countries have typically outperformed their capitalist and Marxist counterparts in this dimension of development performance due to a strong commitment to social equality. The socialist ujamaa policies of the Nyerere regime ensured that 53 percent of Tanzania's population, including 46 percent in the rural areas, were guaranteed access to safe water by the mid-1980s.[43] In contrast, only 28 percent (21 percent in the rural areas) had access to clean water in capitalist Kenya and a meager 18 percent (11 percent in the rural areas) in Marxist Ethiopia during the same period.[44] Tanzania's ujamaa policies were equally effective in the realm of health care, with nearly 85 percent of children under 1 year of age immunized against tuberculosis, diphtheria, polio, and measles by the beginning of the 1980s.[45] Kenya approached this total with a 72 percent average, followed distantly by Ethiopia with only 14 percent.[46] In short, Tanzania managed to fulfill the socialist commitment to provide for basic human needs.

Autonomy from Foreign Control

A third measure of development performance, autonomy from foreign control, is the African leadership's ability to pursue a path of development that is not heavily dependent on external involvement and resources, most notably foreign aid.[47] This dimension of development performance is based on the assumption that countries heavily dependent on external sources of financing are more likely to pursue development programs that serve foreign interests, as opposed to the true development needs of their own peoples. For example, Nyerere's brand of ujamaa socialism was heavily dependent on foreign aid despite the call for self-reliance. During the second half of the 1970s, foreign aid accounted for 10.5 percent of Tanzania's gross domestic product (GDP), compared with only 4.5 percent for both capitalist Kenya and Marxist Ethiopia.[48] The legacy of socialist Tanzania's dependence on foreign economic resources is particularly striking when examined in terms of its debt-GDP ratio (the country's foreign indebtedness as a percentage of GDP). By the end of the 1980s, Tanzania's average debt-GDP ratio was a staggering 85 percent, followed by 34 percent for capitalist Kenya and 25 percent for Marxist Ethiopia.[49] If we assume that foreign aid and indebtedness are valid indicators of dependency, African socialism clearly emerges as the least capable of promoting autonomy from foreign control, with Kenyan capitalism and Ethiopian Marxism faring about the same.

A focus on the military dimension of the dependency equation suggests that Kenyan capitalism is more autonomous than Ethiopian Marxism. Similar to the experience of other Marxist countries in Africa, the Mengistu regime was heavily dependent on communist-bloc military aid to stem domestic dissent and the spread of regime-threatening guerrilla insurgencies. From 1977 to its demise in 1991, the Mengistu regime reportedly received more than $5 billion in

communist-bloc military aid.[50] Indeed, Soviet and Cuban military aid was decisive in preventing the fragmentation of Ethiopia during the 1977–78 Ogaden
war between Ethiopia and Somalia. With northern secessionists on the verge of
military victory and Somali military forces in control of the eastern provinces,
the Soviet Union began a massive airlift of 15,000 Cuban troops from bases in
Cuba, Angola, and Congo-Brazzaville. Accompanied by Soviet tactical commanders and nearly $2 billion in Soviet military weaponry, the Cuban troops
spearheaded a series of Ethiopian counteroffensives in spring 1978 that forced
Somali troops to flee across the border and ensured a military stalemate in the
north. Marxist Ethiopia was so dependent on communist-bloc military aid that
the Mengistu regime was overthrown not long after the end of the cold war and
the Soviet Union's disengagement from the Horn of Africa.[51]

Human Dignity

The promotion of human dignity, often conceived in terms of the protection
of civil liberties and human rights, is the fourth dimension of development
performance.[52] In 1972, Freedom House, a think tank in Washington, D.C.,
began annually rating the protection of civil liberties in individual countries.
The checklist of questions, which subsequently forms the basis of the civil liberties assessment, includes the following:

- Are there free and independent media, literature, and other cultural
  expressions?

- Is there open public discussion and free private discussion?

- Is there freedom of assembly and demonstration?

- Is there freedom of political or quasi-political organization?

- Are citizens equal under the law, with access to an independent,
  nondiscriminatory judiciary, and are they respected by the security
  forces?

- Is there protection from political terror and from unjustified imprisonment, exile, or torture, whether by groups that support or oppose the
  system, and freedom from war or insurgency situations?

- Are there free trade unions and peasant organizations or equivalents, and is
  there effective collective bargaining?

- Are there free professional and other private organizations?

- Are there free businesses or cooperatives?

- Are there personal social freedoms, which include such aspects as gender
  equality, property rights, freedom of movement, choice of residence, and
  choice of marriage and size of family?

- Is there equality of opportunity, which includes freedom from exploitation
  by or dependency on landlords, employers, union leaders, bureaucrats, or

any other type of denigrating obstacle to a share of legitimate economic gains?

■ Is there freedom from extreme government indifference and corruption?[53]

The Freedom House ratings suggest that African countries across the ideological spectrum fared poorly in the protection of civil liberties during the initial decades of the contemporary independence era. In many African countries, ruling regimes put constraints on the freedom of speech of individuals, organizations, and the media. Capitalist countries nonetheless fared better on average than their socialist or communist counterparts. On a scale of 1 to 7 ("1" being the best score and "7" being the worst), the Kenyatta regime consistently received a score of "5," whereas Marxist Ethiopia under the Mengistu regime consistently received the worst possible score of "7." Socialist Tanzania under Nyerere found itself consistently between these two extremes with an average score of "6."[54] Whereas Ethiopia's poor score was primarily due to state-sponsored political terror against its own population, Tanzania's low score was primarily due to the lack of freedom of organization for independent trade unions, peasant organizations, and private businesses.

Political Participation

The quality of political participation is the final measure of development performance.[55] Freedom House also annually rates the protection of political rights in individual countries. The checklist of questions, which subsequently forms the basis of the political rights assessment, includes the following:

■ Is the head of state and/or head of government or other chief authority elected through free and fair elections?

■ Are the legislative representatives elected through free and fair elections?

■ Are there fair electoral laws, equal campaigning activities, fair polling, and honest tabulation of ballots?

■ Are the voters able to endow their freely elected representatives with real power?

■ Do the people have the right to organize in different political parties or other competitive political groupings of their choice, and is the system open to the rise and fall of these competing parties and groupings?

■ Is there a significant opposition vote, de facto opposition power, and a realistic possibility for the opposition to increase its support or gain power through elections?

■ Are the people free from domination from the military, foreign powers, totalitarian parties, religious hierarchies, economic oligarchies, or any other powerful group?

- Do cultural, ethnic, religious, and other minority groups have reasonable self-determination, self-government, autonomy, or participation through informal consensus in the decision-making process?[56]

The Freedom House survey shows that African countries across the ideological spectrum fared poorly in the promotion of political participation during the initial decades of the contemporary independence era. During this time, many African leaders established single-party regimes that prohibited true political competition (see Chapter 10). In each of our three model cases of African ideology, for example, opposition parties were intimidated or completely banned in favor of a single state-sponsored party: Kenya African National Union (KANU) in Kenya, Chama Cha Mapinduzi (CCM) in Tanzania, and the Workers Party of Ethiopia (WPE). Capitalist countries nonetheless fared better on average than their socialist or communist counterparts. On a scale of 1 to 7, the Kenyatta regime consistently received a score of "4" or "5," whereas Marxist Ethiopia under the Mengistu regime consistently received a "7." Socialist Tanzania under Nyerere once again found itself consistently between these two extremes with an average score of "6."[57] Whereas Kenya scored the best due to the Kenyatta regime's willingness to permit a limited degree of opposition party activity, Tanzania's single-party system was recognized for its ability to allow for genuine electoral competition in the party ranks. Ethiopia's highly centralized single-party system scored the worst due to its unwillingness to allow for any internal political dissent.

The preceding discussion of Kenyan capitalism, Tanzanian socialism, and Ethiopian Marxism clearly suggests that an African regime's commitment to a specific ideological pathway leads to varied development performance (see Table 6.2 for a summary overview). African capitalism outperformed its socialist and Marxist counterparts in four out of five categories, with socialism performing best in one and Marxism performing best in none. Perhaps for this reason neither socialist nor Marxist regimes, except for the unique case of Libya, exist at the beginning of the twenty-first century.

These results nonetheless must be treated with a great deal of caution. The results could change with the selection of different statistical indicators, the inclusion of new dimensions of development performance, or an examination of different case studies of capitalism, socialism, and Marxism. Indeed, the field of African studies is still awaiting a comprehensive statistical comparison of the development performance of competing ideologies during the contemporary independence era.

Table 6.2 Comparative Development Performance of African Ideologies (× = Best Performer)

	AFRICAN CAPITALISTS	AFRICAN SOCIALISTS	AFRICAN MARXISTS
Economic Growth	×		
Socioeconomic Equality		×	
Autonomy from Foreign Control	×		
Human Dignity (Human Rights)	×		
Political Participation	×		

TOWARD A CAPITALIST-
SOCIALIST HYBRID?

The one undeniable result of ideological competition between capitalism, socialism, and Marxism during the contemporary independence era is that capitalism emerged in the 1990s as the ideology of African development. African leaders and foreign observers alike agree that some form of private enterprise is the key to the future development success of the African continent.[58] Richard Sklar, a noted observer of African ideology, refers to this phenomenon as a **capitalist movement,** the turning point of which was marked by the attendance of African ministers and civil servants at the Conference on the Enabling Environment for Private Sector Contributions to Development, held in Nairobi, Kenya, in October 1986.[59] According to Sklar, this conference signaled the "confluence of various currents of African capitalist thought," setting the stage for its widespread resurgence in the post–cold war era.[60]

The emergence of capitalism as the predominant African ideology is partially due to the widespread perception among African policymakers and foreign observers that socialism and Marxism lack convincing incentives for individual producers to expand production.[61] In both Nyerere's Tanzania and Mengistu's Ethiopia, for example, coercion was ultimately used to force recalcitrant peasants to take part in villagization or collectivization programs. "In this century," concludes Sklar, "revolutionary socialists from [Leon] Trotsky and [Josef] Stalin to Mao Zedong, [Fidel] Castro, and Sékou Touré have tried to compensate for the weakness of socialist incentives for both workers and managers by resorting to combinations of moral suasion and coercion—poor substitutes for personal motivation."[62]

Africa's growing embrace of capitalist ideology does not mean that African policymakers are blind to its negative outcomes nor necessarily willing to forsake all elements of African socialism or Marxism.[63] African policymakers recognize that African capitalism has failed to deliver in the one area that African socialism has registered at least some short-term success: the promotion of social equality and justice. The dilemma, of course, is how best to balance the perceived trade-offs between growth and equality. Whereas the capitalist regimes typically have fostered economic growth at the expense of equality, their socialist counterparts have pursued equality at the expense of economic growth. A focus on one at the expense of another is a recipe for disaster. In Tanzania, the lack of economic growth ultimately wiped out many of the short-term gains of ujamaa socialism in the realm of equality. In Kenya, unbalanced support of economic growth strengthened socioeconomic inequalities that have contributed to growing societal strains in contemporary Kenya.[64]

South Africa's experiment in development, since the transition to a multiracial democracy under the leadership of President Nelson Mandela in 1994, is indicative of a new hybrid form of African capitalism with some important socialist elements that may prove able to simultaneously promote growth and equality. "Any South African leader is bound to be preoccupied with the economy, which must generate enough employment to ease chronic black impoverishment," explains Michael Bratton, a specialist of democratic transition. "As the government's own targets reflect, economic growth must reach 6 percent per year to keep up with population growth and at the same time lift the poor."[65] However, the ANC gained power under the leadership of President Mandela with the mandate of aggressively redistributing the wealth of the South African economy, to make up for the injustices of the apartheid era. Indeed, the administration's two major sources of support beyond the ANC—the Confederation of South African Trade Unions (COSATU) and the South African Communist Party (SACP)—were particularly vocal in terms of the need for redistributional justice.

The hybrid solution of the Mandela administration was the formulation of a development strategy known as Growth, Employment, and Redistribution (GEAR) that simultaneously pursues the economic objectives of promoting economic growth, reducing unemployment, and ensuring the redistribution of national resources. Economic growth is the most important development objective, without which the other two objectives would be impossible. GEAR is nonetheless unique in that its third objective—the socialist-inspired goal of redistribution—has served as a development priority of both President Mandela (1994–99) and his successor, Thabo Mbeki, who was elected president in 1999.

Optimists note that the South African economy has experienced important overall economic growth, while at the same time economically empowering black South Africans who were marginalized during the apartheid era. According to one analysis, black South Africans in 1996 accounted for 13 percent of the income received by the wealthiest one-fifth of the population, a figure that had increased to 23 percent in 2000.[66] President Mbeki has hailed the emergence of this "black capitalist class" as proof of his administration's ability to simultaneously pursue economic growth and economic redistribution.[67] "But in many ways," explains Rachel L. Swarns, "the success of this upwardly mobile class only magnifies the enormity of the struggles of those left behind."[68] Indeed, more sanguine observers counter that the Mbeki administration faces at best an "uphill challenge"[69] as his administration attempts to resolve the extraordinary development challenges inherited from the apartheid era, including a 35-percent unemployment rate among the black majority population (which constitutes 75 percent of a total population of approximately 43 million people) and the impoverished condition of the historically neglected black townships, in which 7.5 million citizens still lack access to running water and 3 million citizens lack adequate housing. To these apartheid-era remnants one can add the more recent but related challenge of an HIV/AIDS pandemic that in 2001 afflicted approximately 11 percent of the South African population. In short, if the Mbeki administration and its successors are successful in responding to these socioeconomic challenges while at the same time ensuring economic growth, South Africa's hybrid form of capitalism could serve as a model of development for the rest of the African continent.

KEY TERMS

ideology
capitalist model of development
socialist model of development
populist socialism
Marxist model of development
scientific socialism
nurture capitalism

commanding heights of the
economy
progressive farmer
development performance
politics of conservation
basic human needs
capitalist movement

FOR FURTHER READING

Apter, David E., and Carl G. Rosberg, eds. *Political Development and the New Realism in Sub-Saharan Africa.* Charlottesville: University Press of Virginia, 1994.

Babu, Abdul Rahman Mohamed. *African Socialism or Socialist Africa?* Harare: Zimbabwe Publishing House, 1981.

Berman, Bruce J., and Colin T. Leys, eds. *African Capitalists in African Development.* Boulder: Lynne Rienner, 1993.

Cohen, Robin, and Harry Goulbourne, eds. *Democracy and Socialism in Africa.* Boulder: Westview, 1991.

Coplin, William D., and Michael K. O'Leary, eds. *Political Risk Services: The Handbook of Country and Political Risk Analysis.* East Syracuse, NY: Political Risk Analysis, 1994.

Englebert, Pierre. *State Legitimacy and Development in Africa.* Boulder: Lynne Rienner, 2000.

Friedland, William H., and Carl G. Rosberg, eds. *African Socialism.* Stanford: Stanford University Press, 1964.

Gordon, April A. *Transforming Capitalism and Patriarchy: Gender and Development in Africa.* Boulder: Lynne Rienner, 1996.

Hodges, Tony. *Angola: From Afro-Stalinism to Petro-Diamond Capitalism.* Oxford: James Currey, 2001.

Hughes, Arnold, ed. *Marxism's Retreat from Africa.* London: Cass, 1992.

Keller, Edmond J., and Donald Rothchild, eds. *Afromarxist Regimes: Ideology and Public Policy.* Boulder: Lynne Rienner, 1987.

Kennedy, Paul. *African Capitalism: The Struggle for Ascendancy.* Cambridge: Cambridge University Press, 1988.

Lubeck, Paul M., ed. *The African Bourgeoisie: Capitalist Development in Nigeria, Kenya, and the Ivory Coast.* Boulder: Lynne Rienner, 1987.

Ottaway, Marina, and David Ottaway. *Afrocommunism* (2nd ed.). New York: Africana, 1986.

Rosberg, Carl G., and Thomas M. Callaghy, eds. *Socialism in Sub-Saharan Africa: A New Assessment.* Berkeley: University of California Institute of International Studies, 1979.

Seidman, Ann, and Frederick Anang, eds. *Twenty-First Century Africa: Toward a New Vision of Self-Sustainable Development.* Trenton: Africa World, 1997.

Sender, John, and Sheila Smith. *The Development of Capitalism in Africa.* London: Methuen, 1986.

van de Walle, Nicolas. *African Economies and the Politics of Permanent Crisis, 1979–1999.* Cambridge: Cambridge University Press, 2001.

Young, Crawford. *Ideology and Development in Africa.* New Haven: Yale University Press, 1982.

World Bank. *African Development Indicators.* Washington, DC: World Bank, published annually.

NOTES

1. Michael Chege, "Swapping Development Strategies: Kenya and Tanzania after Their Founding Presidents," in David E. Apter and Carl G. Rosberg, eds., *Political Development and the New Realism in Sub-Saharan Africa* (Charlottesville: University Press of Virginia, 1994), p. 248.

2. For an introduction, see John Sender and Sheila Smith, *The Development of Capitalism in Africa* (London: Methuen, 1986). See also Paul Kennedy, *African Capitalism: The Struggle for Ascendancy* (Cambridge: Cambridge University Press, 1988).

3. For an introduction, see William H. Friedland and Carl G. Rosberg, eds., *African Socialism* (Stanford: Stanford University Press, 1964). See also Abdul Rahman Mohamed Babu, *African Socialism or Socialist Africa?* (Harare: Zimbabwe Publishing House, 1981).

4. For an introduction, see Marina Ottaway and David Ottaway, eds., *Afrocommunism,* 2nd ed. (New York: Africana, 1986).

5. For an overview, see Peter J. Schraeder, *United States Foreign Policy toward Africa: Incrementalism, Crisis, and Change* (Cambridge: Cambridge University Press, 1994).

6. Personal correspondence, Dakar, Senegal, May 1996.

7. For an overview, see Edmond J. Keller, "Whither Afromarxist Regimes? A Comparative Preliminary Analysis," *Journal of Third World Studies* 9, no. 2 (1992): 285–312. See also Arnold Hughes, ed., *Marxism's Retreat from Africa* (London: Frank Cass, 1992).

8. Nelson Mandela, *Long Walk to Freedom: The Autobiography of Nelson Mandela* (Boston: Little, Brown, 1994), pp. 120–21.

9. Crawford Young, *Ideology and Development in Africa* (New Haven: Yale University Press, 1982). Other studies typically have focused on one ideology. For example, see Edmond J. Keller and Donald Rothchild, eds., *Afro-Marxist Regimes: Ideology and Public Policy* (Boulder: Lynne Rienner, 1987); Carl G. Rosberg and Thomas M. Callaghy, eds., *Socialism in Sub-Saharan Africa: A New Assessment* (Berkeley: Institute of International Studies, 1979); and Bruce J. Berman and Colin T. Leys, eds., *African Capitalists in African Development* (Boulder: Lynne Rienner, 1993).

10. For a general introduction, see Norman N. Miller, *Kenya: The Quest for Prosperity* (Boulder: Westview, 1993).

11. For a general introduction, see Rodger Yeager, *Tanzania: An African Experiment* (Boulder: Westview, 1991).

12. For a general introduction, see Mulatu Wubneh, *Ethiopia: Transition and Development in the Horn of Africa* (Boulder: Westview, 1987).

13. Republic of Kenya, *African Socialism and Its Application to Planning in Kenya* (Nairobi: Government Printer, 1965), as cited in Chege, "Swapping Development Strategies," p. 248.

14. Ibid.

15. Young, *Ideology and Development,* p. 98.

16. Julius Nyerere, *Ujamaa: Essays in Socialism* (London: Oxford University Press, 1966), pp. 3–4, as quoted in Young, *Ideology and Development,* p. 98.

17. Ottaway, *Afrocommunism,* p. 130.

18. Ibid., pp. 152–54.

19. For an overview, see John Iliffe, *The Emergence of African Capitalism* (London: Macmillan, 1983). See also Young, *Ideology and Development,* p. 189.

20. Young, *Ideology and Development,* p. 209.

21. Ibid., p. 210.

22. Ibid., p. 106.

23. Ibid., pp. 74–75.

24. For a general introduction, see Robert H. Bates, *Markets and States in Tropical Africa: The Political Basis of Agricultural Policies* (Berkeley: University of California Press, 1981).

25. R. J. M. Swynnerton, *A Plan to Intensify the Development of African Agriculture in Kenya* (Nairobi: Government

Printer, 1955), as discussed in Colin Leys, *Underdevelopment in Kenya: The Political Economy of Neocolonialism 1964–1971* (Berkeley: University of California Press, 1975), pp. 52–53, 69.

26. Leys, *Underdevelopment in Kenya,* p. 69.

27. Young, *Ideology and Development,* p. 114.

28. Jackson and Rosberg, *Personal Rule in Black Africa,* p. 225.

29. Marina and David Ottaway, *Afrocommunism,* pp. 138–46.

30. Ibid.

31. See Marina Ottaway, *Africa's New Leaders: Democracy or State Consolidation?* (Washington, DC: Carnegie Endowment for International Peace, 1999), p. 53.

32. See Peter J. Schraeder, "Involuntary Migration in Somalia: The Politics of Resettlement," *The Journal of Modern African Studies* 24, no. 4 (1986): 641–62.

33. Young, *Ideology and Development,* pp. 102–3.

34. Ottaway, *Afrocommunism,* p. 139.

35. For an overview, see Young, *Ideology and Development,* pp. 253–97.

36. Jackson and Rosberg, *Personal Rule,* p. 229.

37. For an early analysis, see David E. Albright, ed., *Africa and International Communism* (Bloomington: Indiana University Press, 1980).

38. Young, *Ideology and Development,* Ch. 6. Young also adopts a sixth measure, "expansion of societal capacity," which essentially refers to the "ability of the state to respond to new challenges and demands and to adapt to changing needs" (p. 19). I discuss the role of the state in Chapter 8.

39. Young, *Ideology and Development,* pp. 15–16, 298–301.

40. Ibid., p. 298.

41. Data are from *World*Data 1995: World Bank Indicators on CD-ROM.*

42. Young, *Ideology and Development,* pp. 16, 302–8.

43. World Bank, *African Development Indicators 1996* (Washington, DC: World Bank, 1996), p. 339.

44. Ibid.

45. Ibid., p. 336.

46. Ibid., p. 336.

47. Young, *Ideology and Development,* pp. 16–17, 308–13.

48. United Nations Development Program and World Bank, *African Development Indicators* (Washington, DC: World Bank, 1992), p. 298.

49. Ibid., p. 163.

50. See Robert G. Patman, *The Soviet Union in the Horn of Africa: The Diplomacy of Intervention and Disengagement* (Cambridge: Cambridge University Press, 1990).

51. Ibid.

52. Young, *Ideology and Development,* pp. 17–18, 313–19.

53. Freedom House, *Freedom in the World: The Annual Survey of Political Rights and Civil Liberties, 1996–1997* (New Brunswick: Transaction, 1997), pp. 573–74.

54. Ibid., various years.

55. Young, *Ideology and Development,* pp. 18–19, 319–20.

56. Freedom House, *Freedom in the World, 1996–1997,* p. 573.

57. Ibid., various years.

58. For an early view, see Bruce R. Bartlett, "Capitalism in Africa: A Survey," *The Journal of Developing Areas* 24 (1990): 327–50. See also the review essay of E. Wayne Nafziger, "African Capitalism, State Power, and Economic Development," *The Journal of Modern African Studies* 28, no. 1 (1990): 141–50.

59. Richard L. Sklar, "Beyond Capitalism and Socialism in Africa," *The Journal of Modern African Studies,* 26, no. 1 (1988): 12.

60. Ibid.

61. See Richard L. Sklar, "The Future of Socialism in Africa: The Failure of Economic Statism," *Dissent* (1992): 399–407.

62. Ibid., p. 15.

63. See Robin Cohen and Harry Goulbourne, eds., *Democracy and Socialism in Africa* (Boulder: Westview, 1991).

64. For a comparison of Kenyan and Tanzanian development efforts in the post-Kenyatta and post-Nyerere era, see Chege, "Swapping Development Strategies."

65. Michael Bratton, "After Mandela's Miracle in South Africa," *Current History* 97, no. 619 (May 1998): 215.

66. An analysis conducted by DRI-WEFA, an economic research group, as reported in Rachel L. Swarns, "Rich, But Not Comfortable, in South Africa's Black Elite," *The New York Times,* Friday. August 2, 2002, pp. A1.

67. Ibid., p. A6.

68. Ibid.

69. Leonard Thompson, "Mbeki's Uphill Challenge," *Foreign Affairs* 78 (November–December 1999): 83–94.

7

♛

Politics of the African Novel

Lori Waselchuk

Yvonne Vera, acclaimed novelist from Zimbabwe.

S OCIAL SCIENTISTS HAVE typically sought to understand African politics and society by focusing on the structure and development of African political institutions, such as national legislatures and political parties, or the historical evolution of political events on the African continent, such as the rise in military coups d'état during the 1960s. These classic building blocks of knowledge can be enriched by examining the political and historical content of African arts and literature, including filmmaking, oral and written poetry, novels and short stories, and theater.[1] One form of African literature, the African novel, is increasingly recognized by social scientists as a unique means of gaining insight into the evolution of African politics and society.[2] In essence constituting a Western form of literature that African writers gradually adopted during the colonial era, the African novel has flourished throughout the contemporary independence era. The African novel is particularly suited to the teaching goals of social scientists interested in African politics. In addition to raising a variety of politically inspired themes, from critiques of colonialism to the trials and tribulations of the contemporary independence era, African writers in the extreme have used their novels as platforms to call for the overthrow of authoritarian regimes in their respective countries. The primary purpose of this chapter is to introduce these politically inspired novelists, most notably in terms of the evolving political content of their works.[3]

POLITICAL DILEMMAS FACED
BY THE AFRICAN NOVELIST

A much-debated dilemma facing African novelists is the **politics of language choice.** Should they write in the indigenous languages of the African continent, such as Kiswahili in Eastern and Central Africa, Hausa in northern Nigeria, and Arabic in North Africa, or should they employ the imported languages of the colonial era, most notably French, English, and Portuguese? One of the most famous African proponents of writing in indigenous languages is Kenyan writer Ngugi wa Thiong'o, whose book, *Decolonising the Mind: The Politics of Language in African Literature,* has fostered a lively debate in African academic circles.[4]

Ngugi's basic argument is that, because the majority of the populations in most African countries do not speak the inherited European languages, the African novelist adopting this medium speaks only to a very small national elite and foreign audiences, which reinforces an intellectual dependency on the former colonial powers. According to Ngugi, true independence means writing in African languages. As underscored by the image contained in the title of another of his works, *Barrel of a Pen: Resistance to Repression in Neocolonial Kenya,*[5] African writers must be political activists, meaning that their words must be employed to transform African politics and society according to socialist principles. To match words with deeds, Ngugi decided in 1977 to stop writing novels in English in favor of the indigenous languages of Kenya, resulting in the publication in 1980 of his first novel in the Kikuyu language, *Caitaani*

Mutharaba-ini, which subsequently was translated into English for publication in 1980 as *Devil on the Cross.*

The proponents of writing in the inherited colonial languages advance equally compelling arguments. As explained by the famed Nigerian novelist, Chinua Achebe, if the goal of the writer is to reach the widest audience possible, writing in an ethnic language accessible to only a small group simply will not do.[6] Even in countries with national indigenous languages (such as Kiswahili in Kenya), illiteracy, especially in the countryside, prevents active readership by a significant portion of the population. The most important argument for writing in the European languages is the potential for linguistically unifying numerous ethnic groups, leading to the national integration of the country.[7] In short, a literature in a national language, even if it did not originate on the African continent, provides a basis for creating a national identity in countries such as Nigeria, where three major ethnic groups (Igbo, Yoruba, and Hausa/Fulani) and over 250 minor ethnic groups speak dozens of languages (see Chapter 5).

A second dilemma facing the African writer is **official censorship** by African governments that often denounce their critics in the literary world as instigators of "antigovernment propaganda."[8] Topics historically considered taboo in government circles included the ethnic makeup of the ruling regime, the moral character of the president, the nature of political rule (especially "attacks" on military regimes and civilian-based single-party systems), or the ideology and foreign relations of the country. Although official censorship is on the decline in countries transitioning to more democratic forms of governance (see Chapter 10), in more cases than not, African writers still do not share the same liberty of expression enjoyed by their counterparts in the northern industrialized democracies. Under these constraints, African writers are forced to decide whether to make politics an issue of their novels. This choice can result not only in the banning of a book but the jailing of the author. As a result, dozens of African authors have been forced to flee their countries as they continue to write from exile.[9]

Books by the noted Cameroonian novelist, Alexandre Biyidi, who has written under the pseudonyms Eza Boto and Mongo Beti, have been banned for political reasons.[10] Born in Cameroon and educated in France, Biyidi wrote four novels criticizing French colonial rule that were banned in Cameroon before independence in 1960.[11] A Marxist, Biyidi also found himself at odds with the French colonial authorities due to his support for the Union des Populations du Cameroun (UPC, Union of the Populations of Cameroon), a political-turned-military nationalist organization that was banned by the French. Rather than being embraced by the Cameroonian leaders who assumed power in the aftermath of French colonial rule, Biyidi's novels were banned as the works of a radical who threatened stability. In his novels, Biyidi had criticized Cameroon's first independence regime, led by President Ahmadou Ahidjo, as a "neocolonial" puppet of the French government. He also supported the UPC, which was seeking to gain power by promoting guerrilla warfare in the countryside.[12]

African writers must also confront the dilemma of which **publishing out-let** to use for their works, a choice that affects both content and style.[13] Because most African publishing companies historically were owned by governments unfavorable to political critiques, a decision to publish in the writer's home country usually meant that works had to be apolitical, or, if it were political, reflect the political orientation of the regime in power. It is for precisely this reason that numerous African authors have sought foreign publication of their works, most notably with the London-based African Writers Series of Heinemann Press.

It is important to recognize, however, that publication by foreign publishing houses is not cost free in terms of intellectual freedom of expression. Such a decision not only virtually guarantees that the work must be written in the language of the foreign press, it favors a publishing process often more sensitive to foreign, as opposed to African, editorial concerns. For example, Western presses during the cold war era often refused to consider "radical" works, leading several African writers in the critical tradition to publish their novels with Eastern bloc publishing houses, such as Seven Seas Press in the former Eastern Germany.

Even when a foreign press decides to publish a book, political concerns may still intrude on the process. The French government successfully banned the sale upon publication of one of Biyidi's books, *Main Basse sur le Cameroun: Autopsie d'une Décolonisation* (1972; *Heavy Hand on Cameroon: Autopsy of Decolonization*), despite the fact that he maintained a French passport and the book was published by a French publishing house. The primary reason for the ban, which lasted 5 years, was a desire on the part of the French government to stifle a critique of Cameroon's "neocolonial" relationship with France.

POLITICAL THEMES OF THE AFRICAN NOVEL DURING THE EARLY YEARS

The African novel has undergone several thematic revolutions during the contemporary independence era. Though these thematic changes are presented chronologically, it is important to remember that all themes are employed by contemporary African novelists.

Re-Creation of Africa's Past

The earliest African novelists sought to re-create the political heritage of the precolonial independence era, to emphasize that Africa had a noble past before the arrival of the colonial powers. Writing in the Sesotho language in 1908, Thomas Mofolo's *Chaka* provided a historical romance set against the rule of the renowned Zulu leader, Shaka. Although publication was initially delayed by Mofolo's missionary patrons, due to what they perceived as anti-Christian, "pagan" elements in the text, the novel was eventually published in 1925.[14]

Colonial Intrusion

During the 1950s, African novelists continued to glorify the African past and added a new twist: the intrusion of colonial cultures on traditional African cultures. The classic work of this type is Chinua Achebe, *Things Fall Apart* (1958), which seeks to re-create the dignity and integrity of Igbo culture in what constitutes present-day Nigeria.[15] The protagonist is Okonkwo, a great wrestler of the village of Umuofia, who achieves a level of success unparalleled by his contemporaries but who falls from grace and is exiled from the village due to acts of sacrilege committed against his "chi" (personal god) and the "earth goddess" of the land. When Okonkwo seeks to follow traditional customs and to return to the village triumphantly, he is ignored by a culture that is "falling apart," and he commits suicide. British colonialism during the nineteenth century negatively impacted Igbo culture, causing turmoil in the village and fragmentation of Igbo culture. According to Achebe, the combination of British administration, trading practices, and missionary influence undermined traditional Igbo values to such a degree that the harmony of the past was lost forever.

Colonial Injustice

A third genre of the African novel that also emerged in the 1950s focused on the cruelty and injustice of colonial rule, especially the inherent contradiction between European rhetorical promotion of democracy in Africa and the authoritarian reality of colonial regimes. One of the most noted writers in this genre is the Cameroonian author, Ferdinand Oyono, whose French-language works have been translated into English. In one of his most well-known books, *Une Vie de Boy* (appearing in English in 1956 as *Boy!*), Oyono criticizes the French policy of assimilation, by which Africans could theoretically achieve total acceptance as French citizens. The main character of the book is Toundi, a young boy who runs away from home to work as a houseboy, first for a local French missionary, then later for the local French commandant. A variety of actions taken by local French administrators, such as the savage beating, whipping, and chaining of two Africans simply because they are accused of stealing (a charge never proven and, indeed, false), slowly make Toundi question and ultimately flee the inhumanity of the culture he previously sought to emulate.

Nationalism and Independence

The 1950s also witnessed the emergence of novels that portrayed African nationalist leaders as saviors fighting to end colonial rule and to lead their nations to independence. One of the most celebrated writers of this theme is Peter Abrahams, a South African writer who lived in London just before the initial wave of African independence and who had the opportunity to interact with several future African leaders, including Kwame Nkrumah of Ghana. In *A Wreath for Udomo* (1956), Abrahams describes the life of a fervent nationalist

(Udomo) who returns home from London to lead a fictitious African country (Panafrica) to independence. Abrahams paints an idyllic view of the commitment and integrity of the African nationalist leaders of the 1950s and the 1960s; his story is based on the independence experience of Ghana and the nationalist fervor of its first leader, Kwame Nkrumah.

A Closer Look: POLITICS OF AFRICAN CINEMA

African filmmakers are renowned among foreign film critics as especially politically engaged in terms of the films they produce. One reason for this reputation is the very powerful political messages that African filmmakers transmit to audiences, such as the destructive impact of colonialism, the emergence of corrupt elites more interested in acquiring wealth than promoting broadly shared development, the horrors of racially based authoritarian rule under the apartheid regime of South Africa, and the destruction of traditional values and ways of living due to urbanization, modernization, and globalization. In this regard, many African filmmakers firmly believe that their art should serve a political function in the sense of promoting an "African struggle" for dignity and equality in the international system. As Gaston Kaboré, a Burkinabé filmmaker and former secretary general of the Fédération Panafricaine des Cinéastes (FEPACI, Pan-African Film-Makers Federation), noted, the primary goal of African films is to "develop African cinema as an art, industry, and mass media that can aid the African people in their full social, cultural, and political liberation."

The most prestigious international showcase for African filmmakers is the Festival Panafricain du Cinéma et de la Télévision de Ouagadougou (FESPACO, Pan-African Film and Television Festival). FESPACO is held every two years in Ouagadougou, the capital of Burkina Faso, alternating with the Journées Cinématographiques de Carthage (JCC, Film Days of Carthage), that is held in a suburb of Tunis, Tunisia. Whereas the first FESPACO held in 1969 offered a small selection of films from 5 African countries, its 18th edition, held February 22–March 1, 2003, included the showing of more than 200 films and videos from the African continent and the larger African diaspora in Europe and the Western Hemisphere.

Despite FESPACO's prominent place in international film circles, however, politically engaged African filmmakers cite several problems with Africa's film industry. First, African movie theaters have progressively closed throughout the African continent as television has grown in importance in the last two decades. Second, even in those countries where movie theaters have managed to retain a foothold, imported films from India, Europe, and the United States—what Patrick Ilboudo, another Burkinabe film critic, refers to as "cultural toxic waste"— tend to dominate African commercial markets. Third, and perhaps most important, cash-starved African filmmakers often find themselves heavily dependent on foreign financing, either from the governments of the former colonial powers or international development agencies, and therefore potentially subject to limitations imposed by those sources. One exception to this trend is the South African government's strong financial commitment to ensuring a vibrant indigenous South African film industry.

Table 7.1   Award Winners at the 2003 FESPACO Film Festival

FEATURE FILM PRIZES

STALLION OF YENNEGA (Top Prize): *Heremakono* by Abderrahmane Sissako (Mauritania)

SPECIAL PRIZE OF THE JURY: *Kabala* by Assane Kouyate (Mali)

OUMAROU GANDA PRIZE: *L'Afrance* by Alain Gomis (Senegal)

BEST FEMALE ACTOR: Awatef Jendoubi in *Fatma* by Khaled Ghorbal (Tunisia)

BEST MALE ACTOR: Cheick Doukouré in *Paris Selon Moussa* by Cheick Doukouré (Guinea)

BEST SCREENPLAY: *Kabala* by Assane Kouyate (Mali)

BEST PICTURE: Abraham Hailé Biru for *Abouna* by Mahamat Saleh Haroun (Chad)

BEST SOUND: Hachim Joulak for *Fatma* by Khaled Ghorbal (Tunisia)

BEST MUSIC: Wasis Diop for *Le Prix du Pardon* by Mansour Sora Wade (Senegal)

BEST SET: Joseph Kpobly for *Heremakono* by Abderrahmane Sissako (Mauritania)

BEST EDITING: Ronelle Loots for *Promised Land* by Jason Xenopoulos (South Africa)

SHORT FILM PRIZES

BEST SHORT FILM: *Source d'Histoire* by Adama Roamba (Burkina Faso)

SPECIAL PRIZE OF THE JURY: *A Drink in a Passage* by Zola Masseko (South Africa)

TELEVISION-VIDEO COMPETITION

BEST WORK: *Tanger le Rêve des Bruleurs* by Leila Kilani (Morocco)

BEST SERIES OR SITCOM: *Houria* by Rachida Krim (Algeria)

SPECIAL PRIZE OF THE JURY: *Sanoudje* by Boubacar Sidibe (Mali)

Quotations are from Marco Werman, "African Cinema: A Market in the U.S.?," *Africa Report* 34, no. 3 (1989): 69, and David Turcamo, "Culture: A Celebration of Cinema," *Africa Report* 38, no. 3 (1993): 69. See also Manthia Diawara, *African Cinema* (Bloomington: Indiana University Press, 1992); and N. F. Ukadike, *Black African Cinema* (Berkeley: University of California Press, 1993). See also the FESPACO Web site www.fespaco.bf

Disenchantment with Elites

After the initial honeymoon period African leaders enjoyed in the first decades of independence, a variety of negative trends—socioeconomic decline, the rise of single-party rule, the increase in military rule, and the general authoritarianism inherent in numerous African states—led African novelists of the 1960s to begin articulating themes of disenchantment with national elites and disillusionment with previously held ideas of progress.[16] The Malawian writer, David Rubadiri, in his novel, *No Bride Price* (1967), portrays African elites as unscrupulous, immoral, and corrupt individuals whose primary concern is maintaining themselves in power at any cost. The despicable nature of African elites is underscored by Rubadiri's portrayal of government ministers who force lower-grade civil servants to set them up with Indian and European prostitutes and who fire those workers who refuse or fail to deliver. Ironically, Rubadiri implies that only the military can restore order and end corruption.

In the novel, the people rejoice when the military overthrows the inept government that has wielded power since independence. This image of the military changed as it soon became clear that military coups d'état often led to new forms of military-led authoritarianism as bad as, if not worse than, its civilian counterparts.

Freedom as Despair

Disillusionment with African leaders became so prevalent during the 1960s that several novelists, such as the Ghanaian author, Ayi Kwei Armah, in *The Beautyful Ones Are Not Yet Born* (1962), emphasized a theme of despair in which the amelioration of dismal living conditions in Africa was portrayed as a near impossibility. "So wicked, so dirty, and so corrupt is humanity that there is no point in the individual's trying to change it," as one reviewer explains Armah's main theme. "The individual has got to learn to live in the midst of the filth and must try to secure his own private salvation."[17] Indeed, the "senses of the reader are assaulted to the point of being numbed" by such images as a child's nose overflowing with mucus while a mother sucks it, women disfigured by creases of prematurely dried skin, littered streets overflowing with trash, and lavatory walls streaked with excrement. The title confirms that "the beautyful ones are not yet born" and that those that are living are "corrupt, greedy, selfish, and dishonest."[18]

Status of Women in African Society

The early years of the contemporary independence era also witnessed the growing voice of female African novelists who focused on the status of women in African society. Flora Nwapa, a Nigerian novelist, served as a leader in this regard. The publication of her first novel, *Efuru* (1966), signaled the formal emergence and critical acceptance of an entire generation of world-renowned female African novelists, including Buchi Emecheta of Nigeria, Ama Ata Aidoo of Ghana, Aminta Sow Fall of Senegal, and Bessie Head of South Africa.[19]

Although their writings reflect many of the same socioeconomic and political themes raised by their male African counterparts, female African novelists are particularly vocal about how male-dominated, authoritarian African regimes have paid insufficient attention to a variety of gender-related challenges of the contemporary independence era. Female African novelists raise many issues, including the lower literacy rates and higher mortality rates for African women compared to African men; the rise of prostitution and rape as African societies become urbanized; the underrepresentation of African women in wage labor; the injustices involved in polygamous marriages; and culturally inspired constraints, which range from the veiling of women in Muslim societies to the physical mutilation of women as part of the practices of circumcision and infibulation (see the relevant box in Chapter 5).

One of the most celebrated female African novelists is Mariama Bâ, a Senegalese author who wrote *Une si Longue Lettre* (1979; published in English in 1981 as *So Long a Letter*). This novel is written in the form of a letter from

Ramatoulaye, a widowed Senegalese woman living in Dakar, to her childhood friend, Aîssatou, who has emigrated to the United States. Ramatoulaye's letter represents a journey in self-discovery as she explains her feelings of sorrow and betrayal over her late husband's decision to take a second wife after nearly 20 years of marriage, as permitted by Islamic law. Unlike her friend, Aîssatou, who divorced her husband when he did the same thing, Ramatoulaye remained with her husband, only to be left neglected, penniless, and responsible for the care of twelve children after his death. This tragic and moving tale became a best-seller in Senegal due to its insightful exploration of the nature and impacts of polygyny. "Ramatoulaye's life story resonated with many women, which explains the novel's extraordinary reception in Senegal and the fact that it is now a classic of African letters," explains one reviewer of the novel. "But the great appeal of the text resides not in its reflection of the life drama lived by so many but in the vitality of Ramatoulaye, a woman among many who became a heroine and a role model in spite of herself."[20]

EMERGENCE OF POLITICALLY COMMITTED AFRICAN NOVELISTS

The 1970s and the 1980s witnessed the coalescence of a group of **politically committed novelists** who, perceiving highly unjust forms of governance in their respective countries, called for the overthrow of those governments. Unlike the previous period of despair, these authors believe in the ability of people to change their history and to unite in a struggle toward a particular social ideal. Many of these authors have written novels that at some point were banned in their countries of birth and have been jailed and/or forced to write from exile. Whereas African governments have attempted to explain away such acts of official censorship by claiming that novelists have wrongfully and maliciously misrepresented the intentions and contributions of their regimes, their opponents, most notably the novelists themselves, have responded that such novels have been banned because they represent the authoritarian and degenerative nature of domestic politics all too well. In addition to incorporating several of the themes already noted, the politically committed African novelist often focuses on at least one of three topics often neglected by other writers.

Neglected Popular Elements of Society

Many politically committed novelists exalt the values and ideals of neglected popular elements of society—the rural peasantry, urban workers, and popular guerrilla movements—all of which are perceived as being oppressed by authoritarian elites more interested in acquiring personal power and wealth rather than promoting the well-being of most of the population. One of the most notable writers in this regard is Ngugi wa Thiong'o, who, in addition to publishing several novels, created a rural-based theater company that sought to actively involve the Kenyan peasantry in theater productions focusing on sensitive social and political topics. In 1977, the publication of *Petals of Blood,* a novel critical of the Kenyan ruling elite, as well as the production in Kikuyu of an equally critical play, *Ngaahika Ndeenda* ("I Will Marry When I Want"), led to his imprisonment for nearly 1 year, after which he left the country and continued to write from exile.[21]

Destructive Nature of Societal Divisions

A second theme explored by politically committed African novelists is the destructive nature of racial, ethnic, and class divisions in African societies and how these are manipulated by the "divide-and-rule" policies of authoritarian African regimes. One of the most celebrated writers on this theme is Alex La Guma, a South African novelist who portrayed the racist apartheid system of South Africa as one that promoted frustration, aggression, and violence. As demonstrated in one of his most noted novels, *In the Fog of the Season's End* (1972), La Guma celebrated the activities of such organizations as the African National Congress (ANC), which before 1992 sought to overthrow the apartheid system by force of arms. The novel also denounces the police-state mentality that led to the imprisonment, torture, and death of numerous antiapartheid activists, including Steven Biko, the founder and leader of the Black Consciousness Movement. As demonstrated by the writings of Zimbabwean novelist, Yvonne Vera, however, the transition to majority rule in South Africa and the other formerly white minority-ruled countries of Southern Africa, most notably Zimbabwe, has not been free of violence. Indeed, as explored in her novel, *Stone Virgins* (2002), Zimbabwe's transition to black majority rule in 1980 was followed by government-sponsored suppression of the Ndebele ethnic group, at least partially due to its support for a rival guerrilla group during the independence struggle.

Promoting Gender Equality

A final theme of many politically committed African novelists is the need to promote gender equality in African societies. These authors argue that African women are underprivileged and unequal members of African societies who need to be more fully included in their respective political systems. One of the most insightful African proponents of greater equality for African women is Sembène Ousmane, the famous Senegalese novelist and filmmaker. In one of his most acclaimed novels, *Xala* (1973), which he turned into a film (1974) by the same name, Ousmane criticizes the custom of polygyny by weaving a tale of a rich African businessman who is struck by xala (the Wolof term for sexual impotence) upon the taking of a third wife. His most famous novel, however, *Les Bouts de Bois de Dieu* (1960; appearing in English as *God's Bits of Wood*), describes the events surrounding the historic 1947–48 workers' strike against the colonial railroad system that links Dakar, Senegal, and Bamako, Mali. Describing this book as Ousmane's "novelistic masterpiece," one reviewer perceptively notes that it is "an eloquent account of the strength, courage, and foresight of women—not educated or aristocratic, but ordinary, illiterate womenfolk of modest origin and rank in society, including a prostitute and a common blind woman beggar" who became involved in the railroad strike.[22]

NURUDDIN FARAH AND THE POLITICS OF COMMITMENT IN SOMALIA

An in-depth analysis of the evolving political themes of Somali novelist Nuruddin Farah, one of the most provocative writers in the tradition of the politically committed African novelist, offers insight into the invaluable role of African novels in any understanding of African politics and society. Somali politics, particularly the dictatorial practices of the Siad Barre regime, which seized power in a military coup d'état in 1969 and ruled until its overthrow in 1991, are at the center of a series of novels that Farah has written since the late 1960s.[23] Fluent in several languages, Farah decided to write his novels in English rather than in his native language of Somali. Although a desire to reach the broadest international audience contributed to this decision, the Siad regime left him with little choice when it banned the publication and distribution of any of his works, thereby denying him access to the most significant potential market for literature written in Somali.[24] Most important, Farah's commitment to writing about social and political injustice in Somalia, coupled with government threats that his "subversive" writings could lead to imprisonment, led him to begin writing from voluntary exile beginning in 1974.[25] The political content of Farah's novels can be analyzed according to several phases, in which an early commitment to exploring social issues is gradually replaced by acute political engagement with perceived injustice in Somalia.[26]

Early Years as Critic of Social Injustice

Farah's first novel, *From a Crooked Rib* (1970), focuses on the unequal status of women in Somali society[27] and was written in 1968 while he was a student of literature and philosophy at the Punjab University of Chandigarh, India. During this period, Somalia enjoyed a functioning multiparty political system in which national elections in 1967 led to a peaceful change in government, from the administration of President Aden Abdulla Osman to that of President Abdirashid Ali Shermarke. Both regimes were generally pro-Western and sought to maintain strong links with Britain and Italy (the former colonial powers), as well as with the United States.[28]

The main character of the novel is Ebla, a rural woman from the Somali-inhabited Ogaden region of Ethiopia who desires emancipation from her subservient status in Somali society. Ebla first runs away from her family to the city of Belet Wene because she refuses to accept her arranged marriage with Giumaleh, "an old man of 48 fit to be her father." Once established at the house of her cousin Gheddi, however, Ebla learns that, to pay off some debts, he had secretly offered her hand in marriage to a "broker" friend. Ebla thus flees a second time by eloping to Mogadishu, the capital of Somalia, with a civil servant named Awill, only to become infuriated when she learns that he is cheating on her. Ebla gains revenge by secretly marrying Tiffo, a wealthy man of the city with whom she trades sexual favors for money. Ebla has learned to manipulate men through a brand of prostitution in which she realizes that her body is "my treasure, my only treasure, my bank, my money, my existence."

This first novel established Farah's credentials as an outspoken critic of the unequal status of women in African society: "From experience [Ebla] knew that girls were materials, just like objects, of items on the shelf of a shop. They were sold and bought as shepherds sold their goats at marketplaces, or shopowners sold their goods to customers. To a shopkeeper what was the difference between a girl and his goods? Nothing, absolutely nothing." Farah is particularly vocal in terms of his opposition to the circumcision and infibulation of young Somali girls, a traditional ritual he describes as "barbaric"[29] and that often leads to severe health problems ranging from urinary tract diseases to complications during childbirth (see the relevant box in Chapter 5).

Qualified Optimism after the 1969 Military Coup d'État

Farah's second novel, *A Naked Needle* (1976), was written in Mogadishu in 1972, 3 years after the 1969 military coup d'état that ushered in Siad's dictatorship.[30] Announcing the creation of a revolutionary, single-party socialist state under the stewardship of the Somali Revolutionary Council, Siad rationalized his seizure of power as necessary to overcome the corrupt excesses of the civilian era—a perception generally shared by the Somali people who initially rallied around the military government. Siad was particularly vocal in the early years about the need to create a national political identity able to transcend clan divisions in Somali society and expected the educated class of Somalia to aid him in this quest.[31] Although Farah was initially sympathetic to the general goals of the revolution, his decision to criticize political corruption and clan-based patronage practices via his second novel placed him in conflict with the Siad regime.

The main character of the novel is Koschin, a university professor and fervent revolutionary committed to the advancement of socialism and the welfare of the masses. Koschin is nervously awaiting the arrival of Nancy, a woman he had met in London and had agreed to marry if within 2 years neither had found someone else. Koschin wonders how Nancy, a white non-Muslim who has never been to his country, will fit into Somali society. The rekindling of their relationship is set against those of Koschin's Somali friends (Barre, Warsan, and Mohamed) who have married foreign white women.

A fascinating twist of the novel is that these Somali marriages with foreign women are used by Farah to explore and critique Somalia's evolving relationships with foreign powers under the Siad regime.[32] Barre's relationship with his American wife is fraught with problems and is symbolic of the Siad regime's growing tensions with the United States as that regime increasingly adopted socialist rhetoric. Warsan's Soviet wife irritates Koschin with her overbearing manner, indicative of Somali perceptions of Soviet racism and paternalism toward African countries, even those of a socialist orientation. Representing Somalia's love-hate relationship with the former colonial powers, the relatively successful relationship of Mohamed and his British wife nonetheless disgusts Koschin due to their reactionary statements concerning the Somali revolution. Koschin thinks only British-born Barbara, perhaps of the lower class and of socialist sympathies (her former fiancé and her father were both revolutionaries), understands the true principles of the Somali revolution.

Several other aspects of the initial years of the Siad regime are probed in Farah's second novel. For example, Koschin is disturbed by the corrupt "tribalistic" practices of his superior and the revelation that the top echelons of the government, despite socialist rhetoric to the contrary, are hesitant "to take any steps to bring this ill practice and what it entails to an end." "I do not owe any loyalty to any tribe," emphatically proclaims Koschin. "I owe loyalty to the nation, the government in power." In fact, a dialogue between Koschin and his friend Mohamed indicates Farah's own journey in self-awareness as concerns the political aftermath of the 1969 military coup d'état. Koschin states that "Somalia very badly needed a revolution," and Mohamed replies: "Was Somalia in need of terror and horror from dawn to dusk?" Koschin responds by noting that revolution "is a pill that tastes bitter, the benefits of which are felt only when one has gone through the preliminary pain and pestilence." The reader has the impression that although there are questionable aspects of the revolution, a "wait-and-see" attitude was appropriate to judge whether it would remain true to its goals. Indeed, Farah shows initial approval as Koschin proclaims, "Why Somali is a written language! Bless the revolution!" indicating that Siad's successful introduction in 1972 of a written script for the Somali language was an important and constructive outcome of the 1969 revolution (see the accompanying box).

Opposition to the Dictatorship of Siad Barre

The qualified optimism of the second novel is firmly rejected in a subsequent trilogy of works that Farah entitled "Variations on the Theme of an African Dictatorship."[33] This trilogy represents the most politically committed phase of Farah's literary career, as he comes out adamantly opposed to the Siad regime (called "the General") and begins writing his novels from exile in England and Italy. The growing authoritarianism of the Siad regime, as well as its gradual movement away from the socialist ideals of the early years of the revolution, served as pivotal factors in this stage of Farah's writing.[34] Farah was particularly troubled by the fact that a variety of state-sponsored instruments of repression, such as the National Security Service, the National Security Court, the Somali Revolutionary Council, and the Gulwadhayal (Victory Pioneers), were being used to silence anyone deemed "antisocialist," "antirevolutionary," or "anti-Siad" by the military regime.[35] This authoritarian trend intensified in the aftermath of

Somalia's defeat in the 1977–78 Ogaden War with Ethiopia, an event that led to the influx of thousands of refugees, the devastation of the economy, and a rupturing of ties with the former Soviet Union (which supported Ethiopia).[36]

The first part of the trilogy, *Sweet and Sour Milk* (1979), begins with the mysterious death of Soyaan, an economic adviser answerable only to the General and a leading member of a clandestine opposition movement composed of Somali intellectuals and professionals. Soyaan's twin brother, Loyaan, is drawn into a personal investigation of the mysterious circumstances surrounding his brother's death, eventually learning his brother was "silenced" by the regime because he secretly wrote and distributed antigovernment pamphlets. To discredit the clandestine opposition movement, the government proclaims Soyaan a "hero of the revolution" whose last words were, "Labor is honor and there is no General but our General." Loyaan's efforts to keep the government from making a mockery of his deceased brother's true political beliefs bring him into direct opposition with the regime. The novel ends with Loyaan facing exile overseas or imprisonment if he refuses to leave.

The central themes of this novel are the authoritarian practices of the Siad regime and its links with the Soviet Union. Farah's opinion of the ruling elite is summarized in a secret memo penned by Soyaan: "Clowns. Cowards. And (tribal) upstarts: These are who I work with. The top civil service in this country is composed of them. Men and women whose pride has been broken by the General's security; men and women who have succumbed and accepted to be humiliated." Special ridicule is directed toward Siad. In Soyaan's words: "Listen to these ludicrous eulogies of the General. The father of the nation. The carrier of wisdom.

A Closer Look: SOMALI ALPHABET POLITICS

On October 21, 1972, the military dictatorship of Siad Barre ushered in a linguistic milestone in Somali history by announcing that it had chosen a slightly modified version of the Latin script as the official alphabet for the Somali language. Before this date, the lack of an official script contributed to a less than ideal linguistic mosaic in which the Somali language, spoken by the vast majority of Somalia's population, served as the primary means for oral communication, but all written forms of communication, such as newspapers, government documents, and literature, depended on the uneven usage of three nonindigenous languages: English, Italian, and, to a lesser degree, Arabic. The most curious aspect of this event was not that it

took place but that its arrival took as long as it did in a society that has a deep respect and love for its language and bestows great honors on those who can skillfully use its rich poetic heritage in oral discourse.

The political infighting that took place before Siad's 1972 decision provides fascinating insights into the politics of language choice. Powerful wadaads (men of religion) argued for the adoption of the Arabic script for the Somali language due to Somalia's status as an Islamic country (over 99 percent of the population is Muslim) situated at the crossroads of the Middle East, as well as the fact that almost all Somali children learn the Arabic script to study the *Qur'an* (the Muslim holy book). These arguments were countered by Somali nationalists who sought to establish their uniqueness as a people free of any external control, including the Arabs, whom Somalis have traditionally mistrusted. According to this group, adoption of the Arabic script would weaken the Somali identity and make it more susceptible to Arab influence.

The Latin script constituted the second alternative for a written Somali language, and proponents included the former colonial powers and Somali administrators trained in English or Italian. These groups argued that adoption of the Latin script not only would place Somalia securely in the camp of the "modern" world but would facilitate the use of existing technologies (such as typewriters and printing presses) in the dissemination of written materials. Such arguments were dismissed by Somali nationalists who associated the Latin script with Somalia's subjugation by the former colonial powers. As explained by one Somali intellectual, Ibraahiim Xaashi, "Somalia came in contact with the Latin script as a result of colonialism. We were compelled to learn it. Now that we are free, we must get rid of all colonial roots—and Latin would just remind us of the dark deeds of the colonialists." The wadaads reinforced these arguments by portraying the Latin script as a tool of foreign "infidels" (nonbelievers) seeking to replace Islam with Christianity and developed a religious slogan that become common during the debates: "Laatiin waa laa Diin" ("Latin is without God").

A third and final major competitor in Somali alphabet politics, the Cismaaniya script, was invented by a Somali scholar, Cismaan Yuusuf Keenadiid. From a nationalist point of view, the script was attractive in that it did not rely on the "foreign" scripts of Arabic or Latin and represented a Somali creation underscoring the uniqueness of the Somali people and language. However, in addition to being opposed by the wadaads and Somali administrators, Cismaaniya was criticized as an attempt by its creator's clan grouping (the Majertein) to achieve an unwarranted level of political influence in an independent Somalia. Critics also noted that adoption of Cismaaniya would impose undesired educational costs by requiring Somalis to learn at least three separate scripts: Cismaaniya (for Somali), Arabic (for religious training), and Latin (for contact with the Western world).

In short, competing political interests, each of which was strong enough to block the adoption of another script but not strong enough to impose its will, postponed the adoption of written language in Somalia until the seizure of power by the Siad regime. Indeed, the adoption of an official alphabet for the Somali language is perhaps the only political decision made by the Siad regime (1969–91) that will be remembered favorably in Somali history books.

Quotations are from David D. Laitin, *Politics, Language, and Thought: The Somali Experience* (Chicago: University of Chicago Press, 1977). See also B. W. Andrzejewski, "Language Reform in Somalia and the Modernization of the Somali Vocabulary," *Northeast African Studies* 1, no. 3 (1979–80): 59–71.

The provider of comforts. A demi-god. I see him as a Grand Warden of a Gulag." Even more disturbing to Farah is the degree of control and influence the Soviets maintained with the Siad regime. This is portrayed in the novel by Loyaan's anger when told that an accomplice of Soyaan was arrested for anti-Soviet activities. Loyaan proclaims: "But we are not in the Soviet Union. We are in the Somali Democratic Republic, a sovereign African state. Not in the Soviet Union. We are *not*."

Sardines (1981), the second part of Farah's antigovernment trilogy, breaks new ground by exploring the role of women in opposing the Siad regime. The story revolves around Medina, an avowed feminist and sole female member of an antigovernment clandestine movement composed of members of Somalia's educated upper class. Medina has been banned from writing and fears that Ubax, her daughter, will be forced to undergo the traditional circumcision and infibulation performed on the vast majority of young women in Somalia. Medina also guides the intellectual development of her friend's daughter, Sagal, a nationally recognized swimming star who may be taking part in a sporting event sponsored by the communist bloc in Budapest, Hungary. Medina's husband, Samatar, has been blackmailed by the regime into accepting a cabinet position—from which he ultimately resigns—and is eventually jailed.

This fourth novel is unique in that the opposition movement to the Siad regime is led by women. Medina typifies the educated, cosmopolitan woman who seeks a better life for her daughter. She is concerned about intellectual freedom and is disgusted with traditional customs that harm women. Farah seems to speak through his protagonist when, in an impassioned speech, Medina asserts, "I want to spare my daughter these and many other pains. She will not be circumcised. Over my dead body."

Female students also play an important role in this novel. Sagal, who has always dreamed of "painting the dawn" with antigovernment slogans, is jealous when her two closest competitors are arrested for committing this act. The girls had painted the slogan, "Down with the one-man, one-tribe dictatorship! Down with the General's regime." Farah nonetheless warns through Samatar that most of the educated class is corrupt and self-serving: "We the intellectuals are the betrayers; we the so-called intellectuals are the entrance the foreign powers use so as to dominate, designate, name and label; we the intellectuals are the ones who tell our people lies."

Close Sesame (1984) is the final and most politically engaged novel of Farah's antigovernment trilogy, in which he appears to call for Siad's assassination and seeks to rationalize such a call. The plot of the novel revolves around Deeriye, a principled Somali nationalist who had been a "Sayyidist" all his life, a reference to Sayyid Mohamed Abdulle Hassan, revered nationalist in Somali history who fought against British colonialism.[37] Deeriye had paid for his nationalist activities by spending 8 years in colonial prisons. A respected man in Somali society in the 1980s, Deeriye confronts a personal dilemma when he learns that his son Mursal, with three other accomplices, is plotting the General's assassination. Originally stating he would never use "violent means to overthrow a tyrannical regime," Derriye changes political opinions when the General seeks to discredit his public image. Upon learning that his son has been killed by the regime, Deeriye is driven to assassinate the General, "not to avenge his son but to vindicate justice." Deeriye dies in an unsuccessful attempt.

This novel is especially powerful in that it equates the authoritarianism of the Siad regime with that of the colonial era. Drawing parallels with the colonial past, the plot suggests that the Siad regime's political harassment of Deeriye constituted the moral equivalent of the Italian colonialists' imprisonment of

Deeriye in 1934. Just as the colonial authorities had wanted Deeriye to hand over a suspected assassin and disassociate himself from the individual's actions, so Siad is portrayed as attempting the same thing. "The only difference, *if there is a difference*," explains Farah, "is that in 1934 the enemy and the famine-creating power was colonial and foreign; and now it is neocolonial and local."

Evolving African Identity

The completion of Farah's trilogy of novels on the authoritarian abuses of the Siad regime marked a turning point in his career as a politically committed novelist. Although still set in Somalia, a new "Blood in the Sun" trilogy of novels—*Maps* (1986), *Gifts* (1992), and *Secrets* (1998)—represents Farah's desire to move beyond the specific abuses of the Siad regime and to return to the political dilemmas all African countries confront. One of the most fascinating themes of this new trilogy, which is best captured in *Maps* (1986), is the potentially destructive forces of an **evolving African identity** that must simultaneously balance the competing political demands of ethnicity, race, and gender.

Maps takes place in the historical context of the 1977–78 Ogaden War between Ethiopia and Somalia. The primary character of the story is Askar, an orphaned Somali boy who was born in the Ogaden region of Ethiopia and is adopted by Misra, an Amharic-speaking Oromo woman from the highlands of Ethiopia. Askar and Misra are separated when the young boy is sent to Mogadishu to live with his Uncle Hilaal and Aunt Salaado and are only reunited after Misra arrives in Mogadishu as a refugee from the fighting in the Ogaden. The relationship between Askar and Misra at first is extremely strained due to accusations that Misra, a non-Somali, had betrayed the positions of the Western Somali Liberation Front (WSLF), a guerrilla force fighting for the Ogaden's independence from Ethiopian rule, an act that in turn contributed to the massacre of over 600 Somali freedom fighters at the hands of Ethiopian forces. The story ends with Askar being interrogated concerning his involvement in the death of Misra, who was brutally murdered by the WSLF despite her vehement disavowal of any complicity in the massacre.

The cornerstone of the novel is the shifting "maps" of Africa, both in terms of geographical realities and individual emotional attachments to ethnic and national identities. In a geographical sense, one of the primary origins of the Ogaden War dates back to the colonial era, when the Somali-inhabited territories of the Horn of Africa were arbitrarily divided among four European and African powers into five separate territories, including the Somali-inhabited Ogaden region controlled by Ethiopia (see Chapter 3). As symbolized by the five-pointed star emblazoned on the Somali flag—one point for each of the five "lost" portions of the Somali nation—Somali nationalists from the 1950s through the 1970s pursued an "irredentist" policy seeking to unite all the Somali peoples in the Horn of Africa in one country.[38] This policy reached its height in 1977, when Somalia militarily invaded and managed to capture most of the Ogaden. However, a Soviet-managed airlift to Ethiopia of nearly $2 billion in military weaponry and 15,000 Cuban troops preceded a military counteroffensive that quickly overwhelmed the outnumbered and internationally isolated Somali troops in a matter of weeks, ultimately destroying the short-lived Somali dream of a "Greater Somalia."[39] As concluded by Askar's Uncle Hilaal, "There is truth in maps. The Ogaden, as Somali, is truth. To the Ethiopian mapmaker, the Ogaden as Somali, is untruth."

The most devastating map of this novel, however, is the ethnic one that inhabitants of the Horn of Africa carry in their psyches. Although Misra, an Oromo woman, raised and loved an orphaned Somali boy, learned the Somali language and adopted a local Somali village in the Ogaden as her own, she is scapegoated and ultimately killed by ethnic Somalis consumed by their hate for Ethiopians who, for their part, have also committed acts of hatred during war. Indeed, socially reinforced ethnic divisions, which historically have been intensified by colonialism and self-interested African elites, lie at the center of this tragic tale in which a young boy is forced to choose between his love for his adopted mother and his love for his people.

POLITICS OF THE AFRICAN NOVEL
IN PERSPECTIVE

The novels of Nuruddin Farah, like those of other African writers who have consciously decided to integrate political ideals into their writings, offer unique insights into the evolution of African politics and society. One of the primary roles of the African novelist, explains Farah, is to touch the raw political nerve of the reader and in so doing promote political reflection, discussion, and even action.[40] It is important to remember, however, that African novelists do not deliver mere **documentary realism** (i.e., exact portayals) of political events in their respective countries. They instead strive to capture the essence of a particular political situation or historical period, which is then presented in story form to the public, who may judge it on its own merits. African novelists therefore should not be regarded as simple recorders of events but rather as interpreters acting on their perceptions of events. In the end, it is up to the reader to determine how well the African novelist captures the political realities of the African country in question.

KEY TERMS

politics of language choice
official censorship
publishing outlet

politically committed novelists
evolving African identity
documentary realism

FOR FURTHER READING

Awoonor, Kofi. *The Breast of the Earth: A Survey of the History, Culture, and Literature of Africa South of the Sahara.* New York: Nok Publishers International, 1975.

Bruner, Charlotte, ed. *The Heinemann Book of African Women's Writing.* Portsmouth: Heinemann, 1993.

Egejuru, Phanuel A. *Toward African Literary Independence: A Dialogue with Contemporary African Writers.* Westport: Greenwood, 1980.

Farah, Nuruddin. *Yesterday, Tomorrow: Voices from the Somali Diaspora.* London: Cassell, 2000.

Gakwandi, Shatto Arthur. *The Novel and Contemporary Experience in Africa.* London: Heinemann, 1977.

Harrow, Kenneth W., ed. *Faces of Islam in African Literature.* Portsmouth: Heinemann, 1991.

Harrow, Kenneth W. *Thresholds of Change in African Literature: The Emergence of a Tradition.* Portsmouth: Heinemann, 1997.

Hay, Jean, ed. *African Novels in the Classroom.* Boulder: Lynne Rienner, 1999.

Irele, Abiola. *The African Experience in Literature and Ideology.* Bloomington: Indiana University Press, 1990.

James, Adeoloa, *In Their Own Voices: African Women Writers Talk.* London: James Currey, 1990.

Lindfors, Bernth. *Long Drums and Canons: Teaching and Researching African Literatures.* Trenton: Africa World, 1995.

Maja-Pearce, Adewale. *Who's Afraid of Wole Soyinka? Essays on Censorship.* Portsmouth: Heinemann, 1991.

Makuchi, Juliana, and Nfah-Abbenyi. *Gender in African Women's Writing: Identity, Sexuality, and Difference.* Bloomington: Indiana University Press, 1997.

Mortimer, Mildred, ed. *Journeys through the French African Novel.* Portsmouth: Heinemann, 1990.

Ngara, Emmanuel. *Art and Ideology in the African Novel: A Study of the Influence of Marxism on African Writing.* London: Heinemann, 1985.

Ngugi wa Thiong'o. *Barrel of a Pen: Resistance to Repression in Neocolonial Kenya.* Trenton: Africa World, 1982.

Ngugi wa Thiong'o. *Decolonizing the Mind: The Politics of Language in African Literature.* London: James Currey, 1981.

Owomoyela, Oyekan, ed. *A History of Twentieth-Century African Literatures.* Lincoln: University of Nebraska Press, 1993.

Snipe, Tracy D. *Arts and Politics in Senegal: 1960–1996.* Trenton: Africa World, 1998.

Wilkinson, Jane, ed. *Talking with African Writers: Interviews with African Poets, Playwrights, and Novelists.* Portsmouth: Heinemann, 1992.

NOTES

1. For a general overview, see Kofi Awoonor, *The Breast of the Earth: A Survey of the History, Culture, and Literature of Africa South of the Sahara* (New York: Nok Publishers International, 1975). See also Jane Wilkinson, ed., *Talking with African Writers: Interviews with African Poets, Playwrights, and Novelists* (Portsmouth: Heinemann, 1992).

2. For a brief discussion of this trend, see Mark W. DeLancey, December Green, and Kenneth Menkhaus, "African Politics at American Colleges and Universities: Topics, Approaches, and Readings," *The Political Science Teacher* 2, no. 2 (1989): 3.

3. For some general overviews of the African novel, see Simon Gikandi,

Reading the African Novel (London: James Currey, 1987); Emmanuel Ngara, *Art and Ideology in the African Novel: A Study of the Influence of Marxism on African Writing* (London: Heinemann, 1985); and Shatto Arthur Gakwandi, *The Novel and Contemporary Experience in Africa* (London: Heineman, 1977).

4. Ngugi wa Thiong'o, *Decolonizing the Mind: The Politics of Language in African Literature* (London: James Currey, 1986). See also Feroza Jussawalla, "The Language of Struggle: Ngugi wa Thiong'o on the Prisonhouse of Language," *Transition* 54 (1991): 142–54.

5. Ngugi wa Thiong'o, *Barrel of a Pen: Resistance to Repression in Neocolonial Kenya* (Trenton: Africa World, 1982). See also Ngugi's *Moving the Center: The Struggle for Cultural Freedom* (Portsmouth: Heinemann, 1993).

6. See, for example, Chinua Achebe, *Hopes and Impediments: Selected Essays 1965–1987* (Oxford: Heinemann, 1988).

7. For a discussion of this theme, see David D. Laitin, "Can Language Be Planned?" *Transition* 54 (1991): 130–41.

8. For a general overview, see Adewale Maja-Pearce, *Who's Afraid of Wole Soyinka? Essays on Censorship* (Portsmouth: Heinemann, 1991).

9. For a general overview, see Roger G. Thomas, "Exile, Dictatorship, and the Creative Writer in Africa: A Select Annotated Bibliography," *Third World Quarterly* 9, no. 1 (1987): 271–96.

10. This summary is drawn from ibid., pp. 276–77.

11. Under the pseudonym Eza Boto, see *Ville Cruelle* (1954). Under the pseudonym Mongo Beti, see *Le Pauvre Christ de Bomba* (1956; published in English in 1971 as *The Poor Christ of Bomba*), *Mission Terminée* (1957; published in English in 1958 as *Mission Accomplished*), and *Le Roi Miraculé: Chronique des Essazam* (1958; published in English in 1960 as *King Lazarus*).

12. See, for example, *Remember Ruben* (1974; published in English in 1980 under the same title), and *Perpétue et l'Habitude du Malheur* (1974; appeared in English in

1974 as *Perpetua and the Habit of Unhappiness*).

13. See, for example, Philip G. Altbach, Amadio A. Arboleda, and S. Gopinathan, eds., *Publishing in the Third World: Knowledge and Development* (Portsmouth: Heinemann, 1985).

14. See Gakwandi, *The Novel and Contemporary Experience in Africa,* p. 3.

15. For an overview of Achebe's works, see Simon Gikandi, *Reading Chinua Achebe: Language of Ideology in Fiction* (London: James Currey, 1991). For an analysis of the scholarship that Achebe's works have inspired, see Anna Rutherford and Kirsten Holst Petersen, eds., *Chinua Achebe: A Celebration* (Portsmouth: Heinemann, 1991).

16. See, for example, Bernth Lindfors, "The African Politician's Changing Image in African Literature in English, *The Journal of Developing Areas* 4 (1969): 13–28.

17. Gakwandi, *The Novel and Contemporary Experience in Africa,* p. 97.

18. Ibid., p. 98.

19. See Sonia Lee, "Women Writers," in John Middleton, ed., *Encyclopedia of Africa South of the Sahara,* vol. 3 (New York: Charles Scribner's Sons, 1997), p. 42. For a discussion of these and other female African novelists, see Adeoloa James, ed., *In Their Own Voices: African Women Writers Talk* (London: James Currey, 1990). For a selection of novels and short stories written by African women, see two volumes edited by Charlotte Bruner: *Unwinding Threads* (Portsmouth: Heinemann, 1983) and *The Heinemann Book of African Women's Writing* (Portsmouth: Heinemann, 1993).

20. Lee, "Women Writers," p. 47.

21. For a more extensive analysis of the evolution of Ngugi's career, see G. D. Killam, *An Introduction to the Writings of Ngugi* (London: Heinemann, 1980), esp. pp. 1–19.

22. See Edris Makward, "Women, Tradition, and Religion in Sembène Ousmane's Work," in Kenneth W. Harrow, ed., *Faces of Islam in African*

Literature (Portsmouth: Heinemann, 1991), p. 195.

23. Farah also has written several short stories and plays, including *Why Dead So Soon?* (1966); *A Dagger in Vacuum* (1969), *The Offering* (1976), and *Yussuf and His Brothers* (1982). For an overview of his works, see Derek Wright, *The Novels of Nuruddin Farah* (Bayreuth, Germany: Eckhard Breitinger, 1994).

24. See Nuruddin Farah, "A Combining of Gifts: An Interview," *Third World Quarterly* 11, no. 3 (1989): 173–74.

25. See Nuruddin Farah, "Why I Write," *Third World Quarterly* 10, no. 4 (1988): 1591–99.

26. Parts of this portion of the chapter were drawn from Peter J. Schraeder, "The Novels of Nuruddin Farah: The Sociopolitical Evolution of a Somali Writer," *Northeast African Studies* 10, no. 2–3 (1988): 15–26.

27. For a discussion of this theme in this and other of Farah's novels, see Juliet I. Okonkwo, "Nuruddin Farah and the Changing Roles of Women," *World Literature Today* 58, no. 2 (1984): 215–21.

28. For a discussion of this era, see David D. Laitin and Said S. Samatar, *Somalia: Nation in Search of a State* (Boulder: Westview, 1985).

29. Farah, "A Combining of Gifts," p. 179.

30. For discussion, see I. M. Lewis, "The Politics of the 1969 Coup," *The Journal of Modern African Studies* 10, no. 3 (1972): 383–408.

31. For examples of his speeches, see Somali Ministry of Information and National Guidance, *My People and My Country: Selected Speeches of Jaalle Major General Mohammad Siad Barre* (Mogadishu: State Printing Agency, 1979).

32. For an overview of these relationships, see Jeffrey A. Lefebvre, *Arms for the Horn: U.S. Security Policy in Ethiopia and Somalia, 1953–1991* (Pittsburgh: University of Pittsburgh Press, 1991);

Robert G. Patman, *The Soviet Union and the Horn of Africa: The Diplomacy of Intervention and Disengagement* (Cambridge: Cambridge University Press, 1990); and Harold G. Marcus, *Ethiopia, Great Britain, and the United States, 1941–1974: The Politics of Empire* (Berkeley: University of California Press, 1983).

33. For a discussion of this theme, see Barbara Turfan, "Opposing Dictatorship: A Comment on Nuruddin Farah's 'Variations on the Theme of an African Dictatorship,'" *Journal of Commonwealth Literature* 24, no. 1 (1989): 193–206. See also Jacqueline Bardolph, "L'Evolution de l'Écriture dans la Trilogie de Nourredine Farah: Variations sur le Thème d'une Dictature Africaine," *Nouvelles du Sud* 6 (1986–87): 79–92.

34. For discussion, see David D. Laitin, "The Political Economy of Military Rule in Somalia," *The Journal of Modern African Studies* 14, no. 3 (1976): 449–68.

35. Mohamed Hassan, "Status of Human Rights in Somalia," *Horn of Africa* 3, no. 2 (1980): 4.

36. For discussion, see Harry Ododa, "Somalia's Domestic Politics and Foreign Relations since the Ogaden War of 1977–78," *Middle Eastern Studies* 21, no. 3 (1985): 285–97.

37. See Said S. Samatar, *Oral Poetry and Somali Nationalism: The Case of Sayyid Mahammad Abdille Hasan* (Cambridge: Cambridge University Press, 1982).

38. For a discussion of this theme, see Saadia Touval, *Somali Nationalism: International Politics and the Drive for Unity in the Horn* (Cambridge: Harvard University Press, 1963), and I. M. Lewis, *A Modern History of Somalia: Nation and State in the Horn of Africa* (Boulder: Westview, 1988).

39. For discussion, see Tom J. Farer, *War Clouds on the Horn of Africa: The Widening Storm* (New York: Carnegie Endowment for International Peace, 1979).

40. Quoted in "Close Sesame: The End of a Trilogy," *Africa Now* 32 (1983): 82.

8

⋀⋀⋀

State and Civil Society

Hundreds of demonstrators from around the world protesting against the lack of attention to the global poor and the environment at the United Nations Forum on Development held in Johannesburg, South Africa, in 2002.

AFP/CORBIS

THE RELATIONSHIP BETWEEN the state and civil society is an important foundation of African politics and society. Whereas the **African state** encompasses the formal institutions of power in African political systems, including but not limited to the presidency, judiciary, government bureaucracies, national legislature, and military forces, **African civil society** incorporates the vast array of voluntary associations throughout society, such as women's groups, labor unions, student organizations, and religious groups that seek access to that power. From the 1950s to the 1970s, the **state-society relationship** was marked by the creation of authoritarian and centralized states seeking to co-opt or silence those very elements of civil society that had contributed to the independence struggles. However, the expansion of state power was challenged during the 1970s and the 1980s by the reemergence of civil societies intent on seeking greater political and economic rights. Hobbled by decades of corruption and economic mismanagement, authoritarian states were increasingly incapable of maintaining control over their respective territories. The net result of what became known as the **crisis of the African state** was the emergence, during the 1990s, of efforts to restructure state-society relations in light of the legitimate interests and needs of both states and civil societies. The primary purpose of this chapter is to assess three broad trends in the evolution of state-society relations in Africa: (1) the concentration of state power at the expense of civil society from the 1950s to the 1970s, (2) the crisis of the state and the resurgence of civil society during the 1970s and the 1980s, and (3) the emergence of new efforts to restructure state-society relationships during the 1990s and the beginning of the twenty-first century.

CONCENTRATION OF STATE POWER
AT THE EXPENSE OF CIVIL SOCIETY

The first generation of African leaders, who took office at the beginning of the 1950s, was immediately challenged by what can be termed the **great expectations-minimal capabilities paradox.** The newly elected leaders had to contend with popular expectations that the fruits of independence, most notably higher wages and better living conditions, would be quickly and widely shared after the departure of the former colonial powers. In almost every case, however, the newly independent African states simply did not have the capabilities to satisfy public demands. In addition to being heavily dependent on the former colonial power for trade, investment, and even personnel to staff key governmental ministries, African leaders were often constrained by export-oriented mono-crop and mono-mineral economies, low levels of education among the general population, and perverse infrastructural development favoring the maintenance of external links at the expense of national development and regional cooperation (see Chapter 3).

The vast majority of African leaders resolved this paradox of independence by promoting the concentration of state power at the expense of civil society.

Even the most democratic of African leaders agreed that the numerous challenges of the contemporary independence era, such as the need for rapid socio-economic development, the creation of a sense of "nation" among numerous ethnic groups, and the maintenance of political-military order, required the creation of powerful, centralized states. This process continued the authoritarian colonial model of state-society relations known as "Bula Matari" ("he who breaks all rocks," see Chapter 3). In the context of state-society relations, Bula Matari embodied the vision of a state that "crushes all resistance."[1]

Six distinct patterns illustrate the ways in which the concentration of state power generally unfolded throughout the African continent from the 1950s to the mid-1970s. Each of these patterns is highlighted by the details and events surrounding the evolution of state-society relations in the Democratic Republic of the Congo (Congo-Kinshasa).[2] Congo-Kinshasa is an excellent case study because Congolese citizens and foreign observers alike shared high expectations that the country would emerge as one of the leaders of the African continent, and therefore serve as a model for other African countries. Indeed, the concentration of state power that unfolded in Congo-Kinshasa represented similar processes throughout Africa.

Africanization of the State

The first and most immediately visible form of state concentration of power involved the **Africanization of state institutions:** the replacement of departing colonial administrators with African politicians and civil servants. In the case of Congo-Kinshasa, a process of almost "instantaneous"[3] Africanization of the civil service that accompanied independence in 1960 took on several interesting dimensions after Joseph Désiré Mobutu assumed power in a military coup d'état in 1965. In 1971, Mobutu announced a broad policy of "authenticity" that sought to replace the remaining cultural vestiges of Belgian colonialism with more "authentic" forms of African consciousness. Similar to an earlier edict that renamed the country "Zaire" (a designation that ended after the fall of the Second Republic in 1997), all citizens were to drop their Christian forenames in favor of African names. To set the example for the rest of the nation, Mobutu renounced the Christian portion of his name (Joseph Désiré) and assumed the new name of Mobutu Sese Seko. The policy of authenticity also changed the ways in which Congolese spoke and dressed. The formal French titles of *Monsieur* and *Madame* were replaced by *Citoyen* for men and *Citoyenne* for women, terms derivative of the French Revolution that literally mean "Citizen." European suits were replaced by the abacost, a collarless suit worn without a shirt or a tie.[4] (The term abacost is actually shorthand for the chant, "A Bas le Costume" ["Down with Suits"], associated with the anti-West policy of authenticity.)

A second dimension of Africanization, the "Zairianization" campaign of 1973, was targeted toward immigrants of Asian or Mediterranean origins.[5] As was the case in many African countries at the beginning of the contemporary independence era, Congo-Kinshasa's commercial sector was dominated by immigrant groups, most notably Greeks, Jews, Italians, and Portuguese, who had migrated to the territory and who had been treated preferentially during the colonial era. These individuals, especially the owners of local shops that sold traditional food staples, were often viewed derisively by the local population as "foreigners" who charged unfair prices and monopolized the market. They therefore became tempting targets for newly formed governments seeking to curry the favor of public opinion. On November 30, 1973, Mobutu announced that all small and medium foreign-owned commercial businesses were to be handed over to the state authorities for redistribution to "true" Congolese nationals. In less than 3 months, the vast majority of such businesses had been turned over to Congolese, who became known as acquéreurs (acquirers), with little if any compensation to their original owners, many of whom fled the country in fear.

Bureaucratic Expansion and the Growth of Parastatals

African leaders also sought to strengthen state power by expanding the number of civil servants working in the various bureaucracies of the executive branch. According to one study, African civil services grew at such a rapid rate during the 1960s—an annual average of 6 percent—that by 1970 approximately 60 percent of all African wage earners were employed by their respective governments.[6] In the case of Congo-Kinshasa, the number of civil servants had grown to approximately 400,000 by 1973, more than double the number employed at the time of independence. Such positions were highly coveted due to the popular perception of the state as the most lucrative source of wage employment and privileges, including government-provided cars, chauffeurs, and housing. From the state's perspective, the doling out of ever-increasing numbers of jobs was an important form of political patronage intended to win public approval.

The creation and expansion of state-owned or state-controlled corporations known as **parastatals** illustrates the process of bureaucratic expansion. In some cases, the parastatals existed during the colonial era and were responsible for providing a public service, such as electricity. In Congo-Kinshasa, the state-owned electric company, Société Nationale de l'Electricité (National Electric Company), not only expanded in size and in number of civil servant slots, but supported several massive public works projects designed to enhance the country's energy infrastructure. One of the most ambitious undertakings was the Inga-Shaba project, an 1,800-kilometer power transmission line between the massive hydroelectric dam at Inga that cost $140 million to construct, and an electricity grid centered in Kolwezi, the capital of the Shaba Province, to supply energy for Congo-Kinshasa's mining industry. Almost all African states continued this "public" direction of services and industry and neither encouraged nor facilitated the expansion of the private sector.

The process of bureaucratic expansion was further fueled by the **nationalization** of foreign corporations, a process whereby the state names its own agents to the boards of directors of companies formerly owned and governed privately. The state, when in this mode, attempts to bring under its control all economic activity, especially economic decision making. The purpose, generally speaking, is obtaining power, but equally important is the economic gain one derives from the *revenues* of all these activities. In 1966, for example, the Mobutu regime nationalized the Belgian mining conglomerate, Union Minière, which generated more than 50 percent of government revenues during the colonial era. This event served as the precursor of a later, more widespread nationalization campaign. On December 30, 1974, after spending a month with Chinese leader Mao Zedong in the People's Republic of China (PRC), Mobutu announced the beginning of a ten-point "radicalization campaign" that included the nationalization of large-scale industries in a variety of sectors, including construction, manufacturing, publishing, food processing, and transportation.[7]

One of the most common forms of parastatals was the **marketing board:** a state agency that set the prices and maintained monopolistic control over the buying and selling of primary products. Originally derivative of the colonial era, this particular form of parastatal expanded to include almost all forms of primary products, including both natural resources (such as mineral wealth) and agricultural products (such as cotton). In Congo-Kinshasa, nearly all mineral production, including copper, cobalt, and diamonds, was marketed by the Société Zairoise pour la Commercialisation des Minérais (SOZACOM, Zairian Company for the Commercialization of Minerals). Fourteen agricultural enterprises personally acquired by the Mobutu family were similarly grouped under the conglomerate Cultures et Elevages du Zaire (CELZA, Farms and Ranches of Zaire). In each case, the process of nationalization and the creation of parastatals served the dual function of creating state-oriented revenue streams and adding to the growing number of state-provided jobs for the local population.

Dismantling of Institutional Checks-and-Balances

Many African leaders also concentrated state power by undertaking presidential actions designed to limit, and in some cases completely destroy, the ability of other state actors to challenge the decision-making supremacy of the presidential mansion. Presidential actions essentially dismantled the ill-conceived systems of checks-and-balances that were hastily constructed by the departing colonial powers. In short, African leaders sought to create highly centralized states in which the executive mansion reigned supreme.

The case of Congo-Kinshasa demonstrates that the dismantling of institutional checks-and-balances usually followed three patterns. First and foremost, leaders sought to underscore the unitary nature of the state by dismissing any federalist arrangements that allowed for the political autonomy of groups or regions based on ethnic, linguistic, or religious claims. After assuming power in 1965, Mobutu effectively ended the unitary-federalist debate that dominated the politics of the First Republic (1960–65) in favor of a highly unitary state.[8] The number of administrative regions, which in the past had increased to take into account regional and especially ethnic differences, was reduced from twenty-one to nine.[9] The founding constitution of 1960 was replaced by a new constitution that gave the office of the president sweeping powers. This new constitutional framework, supported by "spectacular margins of approval" in a national referendum held in 1967, underscored the belief of both the Congolese population and the Mobutu regime that federalist arrangements were at least partially responsible for the ethnic and regional political instability of the First Republic.[10]

Institutional checks-and-balances were also dismantled via the marginalization, and sometimes even the disbanding, of independent parliaments and judiciaries. On November 30, 1965, less than 1 week after assuming power, Mobutu announced that all the constitutionally mandated powers attributed to the national legislature, such as the authority to pass legislation, henceforth were vested in the head-of-state. Although the legislature continued to meet and hold debates, generating nearly 1,400 pages of proceedings during 1966 alone, Mobutu's edict had "rendered it powerless."[11] The charade of powerless legislators publicly debating national priorities was ended on March 23, 1967, when Mobutu announced the formal dissolution of the national legislature. Although a new legislative body was created in 1970, it constituted at best a rubber stamp institution that merely endorsed Mobutu's legislative initiatives.

The dismantling of institutional checks-and-balances usually culminated in the outlawing of all opposition political parties and the creation of a single-party system subservient to the presidential mansion (see Chapter 10). Mobutu had suspended all activities by political parties on November 24, 1965. He subsequently established his own political party, the Mouvement Populaire de la Révolution (MPR, Popular Movement of the Revolution). Although the constitution of 1967 provided for a two-party system, the MPR was the only political party officially allowed to exist. The MPR's single-party status was formalized in 1970 by a constitutional amendment that recognized the party as the "supreme institution" of the land.[12]

Co-Optation and the Silencing of Civil Society

The desire of African leaders to concentrate state power around the presidential mansion invariably conflicted with the increasingly vocal demands of civil society, the vast array of voluntary associations throughout African societies that seeks access to state power.[13] Numerous components of African civil society, including but not limited to women's groups, labor unions, student organizations, and religious groups, had played important roles in the ultimate downfall of colonialism and the transition to independence during the 1950s. After independence these groups expected to wield equal or greater levels of influence in their newly independent countries (see Chapter 4). These expectations proved ill founded, however, as African leaders consistently employed two sets of policies—co-optation and repression—to silence the legitimate demands of civil society.

Mobutu's handling of opposition political figures demonstrated the tactics African leaders typically used to co-opt and silence civil society. Potential opponents were wooed with the offer of important and lucrative administrative positions. For example, Kamanda wa Kamanda, one of the "most articulate" leaders of an influential student umbrella group, the Union Générale des Etudiants Congolais (UGEC, General Union of Congolese Students), was given the powerful post of general secretary to the presidency.[14] As demonstrated by Mobutu's response to the so-called Pentecost Plot of 1966, however, political opponents who became real or perceived threats to the regime were dealt with harshly. On May 30, 1966, Mobutu ordered the arrest of four politicians—Prime Minister–designate Evariste Kimba, Defense Minister Jérôme Anany, Finance Minister Emmanuel Banda, and Minister of Mines and Energy Alexander Mahamba—on the charge of plotting a military coup against the government. Three days later they were publicly executed before a crowd of 50,000 spectators. This swift, public act had a "tremendous psychological effect" on politicians and civil society in general: "Opposition, it was now clear, carried mortal perils."[15]

Co-optation and repression were also employed with success against other elements of Congolese civil society. In June 1967, all labor unions were forced to join one government-approved umbrella union, the Union Nationale des Travailleurs Congolais (UNTC, National Union of Congolese Workers). In June 1969, all student organizations were banned in favor of the Jeunesse du Mouvement Populaire de la Révolution (JMPR, Youth of the Popular Movement of the Revolution), the youth wing of the sole ruling party. As part of this process, all institutions of higher learning were nationalized by the government and placed under the authority of the Université Nationale du Zaire (UNAZA, National University of Zaire). Even the Catholic Church, which represented 40 percent of the Congolese population, was forced to succumb to the centralizing tendencies of the state, especially after an August 1969 conference of Congolese bishops noted the "dictatorial tendencies" of the Mobutu regime.[16] Beginning in 1972, the Mobutu regime banned all religious broadcasts and dissolved church-sponsored youth networks, subsequently nationalizing religious schools.[17] All Protestant denominations were similarly reorganized under one state-imposed umbrella group, Les Eglises du Christ au Zaire (Churches of Christ in Zaire).

Expansion of the Coercive Apparatus

Leaders intent on dismantling institutional checks-and-balances and silencing outspoken elements of civil society depended on loyal military troops and police forces that were both willing and able to enforce presidential directives. As a result, the creation and rapid expansion of a **coercive apparatus** that included various security forces served as a critical component of the concentration of state power. According to one study, military spending as a percentage of gross national product (GNP) nearly doubled throughout the African continent during the 1960s, from 1.8 percent in 1963 to 3.4 percent in 1971.[18]

Mobutu oversaw a vast coercive apparatus that operated at three major levels in Congo-Kinshasa. As the military leader of the 1965 military coup that brought his regime into power, Mobutu first and foremost relied on the Armée Nationale Congolaise (ANC, Congolese National Army), which was subsequently renamed the Forces Armées Zairoises (FAZ, Zairian Armed Forces). The number of troops was increased from 23,100 in 1960 to 63,200 in 1970 and included the creation of elite paracommando battalions, such as the Division Spéciale Présidentielle (DSP, Special Presidential Division), which was staffed with soldiers from Mobutu's Equateur province.[19] A national police force known as the Garde Civile (Civil Guard) served as the second general level of the coercive apparatus. A presidential decree authorized the expansion of the police force from 9,000 in 1960 to 25,000 in 1966.[20] By 1974, this force was buttressed by approximately 29,000 local police. The secret police were the third and most feared level of Mobutu's coercive apparatus. Originally known as the Sûreté de l'Etat (State Security) and renamed the Centre National de Documentation (CND, National Documentation Center), this secretive organization was responsible for the arrest, interrogation, and torture of anyone considered to be a threat to the Mobutu regime.

Mobutu's coercive apparatus was further enhanced by extensive reliance on foreign security advisors and military forces, especially those from Belgium, France, and the United States. During fall 1963, for example, the U.S. Central Intelligence Agency (CIA) contracted with Cuban exiles who had taken part in the ill-fated Bay of Pigs invasion of Cuba in 1961 to pilot T-6 planes against a guerrilla insurgency in Congo-Kinshasa's Kwilu province. In spring 1964, when the insurgency had spread to other eastern provinces, the CIA hired additional Cuban paramilitary fighters to pilot six T-28 fighters delivered by the U.S. Department of Defense. Maintenance for the fighters was carried out by European mechanics associated with the Western International Ground Maintenance Organization (WIGMO), a CIA front organization based in Liechtenstein. CIA efforts were buttressed by the Pentagon's establishment of a U.S. military mission in Congo-Kinshasa in the fall of 1963, as well as the arrival, in spring 1964, of three mobile training teams (MTTs) and approximately seventy technicians to offer guidance in counterinsurgency tactics against the guerrillas. This case indicated the beginning of a pattern in which the United States and the other northern industrialized democracies, most notably Belgium and France, periodically came to Mobutu's aid to thwart a series of regime-threatening guerrilla insurgencies and external invasions.[21]

Creation of Personal Rule Networks

A final trend associated with the concentration of state power was the creation of **personal rule networks,** often referred to by the Weberian concept of **neopatrimonialism:** a system of governance in which power is ultimately vested in an individual leader as opposed to legally based institutions.[22] The system is based on a series of concentric circles of **patron–client relationships**

in which the leader at the center of the system personally selects senior government appointees, who in turn select their appointees, and so on. The leader is
exalted in this system and seeks to instill loyalty through the provision of economic and political patronage. The inherently personal nature of patron–client
systems ensures that they often do not survive the death of the leader. However,
as long as the leader can maintain the political and economic resources provided

---

**A Closer Look: THE EXIT OPTION: AFRICAN EMIGRATION TO THE
UNITED STATES**

Emigration to other African countries
and continents historically has served
as an important **exit option** for Africans
seeking to better their lives and those
of their families. This took on new
meaning in the 1970s as the emerging
"crisis of the African state" contributed
to rising levels of political persecution,
civil conflict, and socioeconomic hardship throughout the African continent.
For many Africans, emigration literally
meant the difference between freedom and prison and even life and
death.

The largest numbers of Africans
historically have chosen Europe as
their destination of choice due to the
impact of European colonialism and
the continuation of privileged ties
during the contemporary independence era. Beginning in the 1970s, however, increasing numbers of Africans
have sought to emigrate to the United
States. According to a study carried
out by April A. Gordon, the number
of visas the U.S. Immigration and
Naturalization Service annually grants
to African citizens increased from less
than 10,000 in 1975 to more than
40,000 presently. Statistics compiled
by the U.S. Census Bureau confirm
this upward trend. The 2000 census
documents that the foreign-born
portion of the U.S. population that is
from Africa is 881,300 individuals, with
56.6 percent of that total (498,927
immigrants) having arrived from
1990 to 2000.

Three types of African immigrants
are favored by immigration legislation
passed by the U.S. Congress in 1965
and 1990. First, preference is given to
the immediate family members, most
notably spouse and children, of a U.S.
permanent resident or naturalized
citizen. This **family reunification program** became increasingly important
during the 1980s, as larger numbers of
African immigrants decided to make
the United States their permanent
home. Preference is also given to
African immigrants with special
employment skills, favoring educated professionals. Forty-three
percent of African immigrants who
are 15 years old or older have at least
some college education; many hold
advanced degrees. (The average for
the U.S. population as a whole is only
20 percent.) The final category
includes political refugees who
demonstrate a "well-founded fear
of persecution" based on ethnic
background, political beliefs, or
religious affiliation should they be
forced to return to their country of
birth. A precedent-setting case in
1996 expanded this definition to
include a woman's fear of being
forced to submit to the traditional
practice of female genital mutilation known as circumcision (see
Chapter 5).

The African continent nonetheless
has constituted the smallest source of
immigrants relative to all other regions

of the world, accounting for less than 5 percent of the U.S. total throughout the 1990s. In response to growing criticism that this low number reflected a racial bias in U.S. immigration policy toward Africa and other regions of the developing south, the U.S. Immigration and Naturalization Service launched a **diversity visa program lottery** in 1995 that grants 50,000 additional visas through a random lottery drawing to people who come from countries with low rates of immigration to the United States. The lottery has not only increased the number of Africans entering the United States as legal immigrants, it has emerged as one of the most popular and reported U.S. programs throughout the African continent. For many African families, the "winning" of the visa lottery by one of their members ignites dreams of a better life in America by establishing a foothold they hope will become the basis for other family members to follow.

Statistics are drawn from April Gordon, "The New Diaspora: African Immigration to the United States," *Journal of Third World Studies* 15, no. 1 (1998): 79–103. See also Joel Millman, *The Other Americans: How Immigrants Renew Our Country, Our Economy, and Our Values* (New York: Viking, 1997).

through the patronage network, he can at least ensure his continued domination of the political system.

Mobutu distinguished himself as a master tactician of personal rule.[23] He fostered a virtual "cult of the personality" in which he was popularly called Founding President, Father of the Nation, Guide of the Revolution, and Helmsman of the Nation. He even went so far as to declare "Mobutuism" the official ideology of the state. As exemplified in a public declaration by Interior Minister Baanga Engulu, Mobutu was even successful in making his rule synonymous with a virtual "third coming of Christ":

> In our religion, we have our own theologians. In all religions, and at all times, there are prophets. Why not today? God has sent us a great prophet, our prestigious Guide Mobutu—This prophet is our liberator, our Messiah. Our church is the MPR. Its chief is Mobutu, we respect him like one respects a Pope. Our gospel is Mobutuism. This is why the crucifixes must be replaced by the image of our Messiah.[24]

The cornerstone of Mobutu's neopatrimonial system was the judicious use of political-economic rewards and sanctions. Supporters were rewarded with high-paying government positions and easily augmented their salaries through state-approved corruption and state-obtained private businesses.[25] Mobutu also kept administrators and cabinet members on the move from post to post so that none of them could establish a firm power base capable of challenging presidential power. Indeed, potential claimants to the presidency and opponents in general were dealt with harshly. This combination of reward and punishment ensured that, by 1974, the year marking the height of Mobutu's political and financial success, "there was literally no one in the state domain who held a position other than through presidential grace."[26]

CRISIS OF THE STATE AND THE
RESURGENCE OF CIVIL SOCIETY

The rise of centralized, authoritarian African states at the expense of civil society was challenged during the 1970s and the 1980s by a series of economic, political, and military developments often called the crisis of the African state.[27] African leaders found their hold on power simultaneously threatened by the economic demands of faltering national economies, the resurgence of civil society, and, in some cases, the emergence of civil unrest and conflict. Hobbled by decades of corruption and economic mismanagement, the **predatory states** (i.e., those that stalked and intimidated their own citizens)[28] of the earlier independence era increasingly proved incapable of maintaining control over their respective territories and became known as **lame Leviathans** (i.e., relatively impotent states) and **shadow states** (i.e., those in which large areas of the national territory were no longer effectively governed by central authorities).[29] In the extreme, the breakdown of effective central authority fosters the emergence of **warlord states** in which vast stretches of the hinterland are actually controlled by regional military leaders opposed to the state.[30]

Four patterns in particular exemplify the process of state decline that generally occurred throughout the African continent from the mid-1970s to the beginning of the 1990s. Each of these patterns is once again illustrated by the evolution of state–society relations in Congo-Kinshasa.

Deepening Economic Crisis

A continent-wide economic crisis during the 1980s severely threatened the economic foundations of the African state. The first symptom of this crisis, which appeared during the second half of the 1970s as extremely weak economic growth, was followed by sharp economic decline during the 1980s. A simple yet telling indicator, per capita income, captured the economic dilemma confronted by African policymakers. From 1975 to 1979, per capita income for the African continent registered less than 1 percent annual growth rate. During the decade of the 1980s, this meager growth rate turned into a 2.2 percent annual *decline* in per capita income.[31] African leaders had expanded the scope of state power without also increasing the state's capacity to use that power to create wealth. As a result, African leaders were increasingly incapable of mustering the resources to maintain the African state's unparalleled control of the economic and political systems. The indebtedness of the African continent further compounded the problem. From 1980 to 1989, Africa's debt burden nearly tripled in size, from $55 billion to $160 billion.[32] Nearly every economic indicator compiled by the World Bank and the International Monetary Fund suggested an emerging economic crisis of epic proportions.

The economic turning point in Congo-Kinshasa occurred when the international price of copper declined 62 percent, from an all-time high of $1.40 a pound in 1974 to $0.53 a pound 1 year later.[33] Because copper was the mainstay of the economy, the price decline ensured a loss of nearly $600 million in purchasing power for the state in 1975, causing a short-term financial crisis of confidence in the Mobutu regime.[34] This short-term crisis coincided with the dramatic oil price increases adopted by the Organization of Petroleum Exporting Countries (OPEC), diminishing the ability of developing countries like Congo-Kinshasa to maintain their balances of payments. From this point forward, Congo-Kinshasa confronted hyperinflation that averaged 60 to 80 percent annually throughout the 1980s.[35]

The most important outcome of the copper and oil "shocks" of 1974–75 was that they revealed the Mobutu regime's ill-fated policies of economic development and the sheer economic mismanagement associated with the drive to concentrate power around the presidential mansion. The Zairianization and radicalization campaigns of 1973 and 1974 proved utter failures, with most of the new owners either stripping the stores of stocks for short-term gain or financially mismanaging their businesses into bankruptcy. As was the case throughout Africa, the expanding parastatal sector did equally poorly, leading to massive financial losses. The marketing boards in particular hampered the Congolese agricultural economy for the simple reason that rural farmers were paid below-market prices to ensure a steady flow of cash into the state's coffers. For example, the government-index price paid for manioc, a food staple for rural dwellers, actually decreased by more than 70 percent from 1960 to 1974.[36] The net result of such pricing policies was a decline in food production and thus the growing inability of Congo-Kinshasa to feed itself.

Pervasive and widespread corruption at all levels of government, often called "le mal Zairois" (the Zairian sickness), served as both the cement that held together Mobutu's neopatrimonial system and the primary impediment to economic growth and development. Although **petty corruption,** such as police officers seeking bribes from defenseless motorists, has always existed in Africa and other regions of the world, the Mobutu regime fostered an extreme form of corruption best described as a **kleptocracy,** a political system in which the state's wealth is systematically plundered by the ruling elite. The politically and economically ambitious looked upon all forms of state employment, including that with the civil service, parastatals, marketing boards, or the ruling party, as the principal path to getting rich. For example, as the manager of a marketing board, one drew a regular salary, skimmed a portion of the profits from the products regulated by that board, and pocketed bribes from buyers and sellers seeking "special" consideration. "A regional economic affairs inspector confided [in me] that his superiors had showed him the way to making $2,000 monthly in illegal bribes (although his official salary was $120), on condition, however, that he offer substantial kickbacks to them," explains David J. Gould, a specialist of corruption in Africa. "At a higher level, a regional commissioner in 1974–75 had so misused the 'Zairianized' property entrusted to him by the state that he let the former owners manage it in return for a $100,000 kickback (fifty times his salary)."[37] Mobutu himself set the standard for this system by amassing a personal fortune that reportedly exceeded $5 billion and included luxurious châteaux in Belgium, France, Italy, and Switzerland. His only "warning" to state employees was made in a oft-cited public speech on May 20, 1976: "Yibana mayele" (steal cleverly) so as to avoid inflaming public opinion.[38]

Growing Inability to Provide Social Goods

The crisis of the African state was also demonstrated by the growing inability of the state to provide a variety of **social goods,** expected by civil society and normally taken for granted in the northern industrialized democracies, including effective transportation and telecommunications networks, access to electricity and clean water, and a well-functioning public school system. Decline in public services was often due to cuts in government social spending devoted to these sectors, in favor of increases in government military spending for the police and other portions of the coercive apparatus.

The combination of corruption and economic mismanagement in Congo-Kinshasa fostered a severe decline in social services by the beginning of the 1990s. As explained by John F. Clark, who carried out field research in Congo-Kinshasa during 1994, an expansive and effective road network that had crisscrossed the country in the early 1960s had deteriorated to such a degree as to become virtually nonexistent.[39] Something seemingly as simple as traveling 60 miles by car between the capital of Kinshasa and a neighboring town had become a "grueling, 4-hour journey" due to the extremely poor condition of the road system.[40] The telephone system had also deteriorated to the point that the only effective means of telephone communication was through a variety of cell-phone systems offered by private companies. To make matters worse, power and water service outages became so frequent as to constitute the norm, and most public hospitals had declined to the point that local residents found "little use in going to them."[41]

An analysis of Congo-Kinshasa's federal budget demonstrates the conscious trade-off that was taking place between the security focus of the presidential mansion and the social demands of civil society. The portion of the federal budget devoted to the presidency and national defense rose from 23 percent in 1982 to 58 percent in 1988.[42] According to one figure, the presidency alone was consuming 95 percent of all government expenditures as of 1992.[43] By contrast, federal expenditures for education had declined from 23 percent in 1982 to 10 percent in 1988.[44] By the beginning of the 1990s, federal support for education had all but vanished, with the public education system in a state of near total collapse. Those with the financial means placed their children in foreign schools or in one of the hundreds of private schools that emerged in Congo-Kinshasa at the beginning of the 1990s.[45] The vast majority of the nation's schoolchildren, especially those at the primary school level, would receive no education. These children, like others throughout Africa, have literally become a **génération sacrifiée (sacrificed generation),** often discouraged by the fact that a poor job market offers them nothing but positions as street vendors, maids, and cooks.

The state's inability to provide social goods was compounded by its declining control over the country except for a few urban areas, control that, according to Jeffrey Herbst, was at best sporadic and incomplete, even at the height of state power during the early independence era.[46] Despite devoting ever-increasing amounts of the federal budget to the security apparatus, Congo-Kinshasa had become a shadow state in which large areas of the national territory were no longer effectively governed by the central authorities.[47] Several regions, such as the southeastern Shaba province, achieved a large degree of autonomy, with local leaders controlling the local economy and pursuing foreign relations independent of, and sometimes contrary to, the wishes of the enfeebled central government in Kinshasa.[48]

The intrusiveness of state-sponsored corruption further impairs the effectiveness of state control while strengthening the spread of **informal economies,** webs of economic activities that are "unmeasured, unrecorded, and, in varying degrees, illegal."[49] Vast amounts of unrecorded smuggling along Congo-Kinshasa's southern, northeastern, and western borders linked those regions more closely with neighboring countries than with their own capital of Kinshasa or other national provinces during the 1980s.[50] The illegal trade in coffee, an important primary product, offers insight. From 1975 to 1979, 30 to 60 percent of the national coffee crop was illegally smuggled out of the country, costing the Congolese state nearly $350 million in lost revenues.[51] During the 1985–86 planting season, the Lubero coffee zone of northeastern Congo-Kinshasa "officially" exported 32 percent (41,117,000 kilograms) of a total estimated harvest of 129,000,000 kilograms; hence, nearly 68 percent of that harvest was smuggled illegally through the informal market.[52] When this one harvest is multiplied by dozens of regions and dozens of other primary products, the negative impact on the national economy is staggering.

A final trend that accompanied the declining socioeconomic reach of the African state was the rising influence of international financial institutions, such as the International Monetary Fund (IMF) and the World Bank, in the restructuring of African economies and political systems in the image of the northern industrialized democracies (see Chapter 12). During the 1980s, African leaders were forced to accept externally imposed reform measures called "structural adjustment programs" (SAPs), to obtain IMF and World Bank loans. However, in Congo-Kinshasa and other African countries, the maneuvering between African leaders and the international financial institutions often turned into what Thomas Callaghy aptly called the "ritual dance of the debt game." No sooner had loans been granted did the Mobutu regime renege on its promised reform package, subsequently promising 1 year later to abide by a new set of reforms, only to be followed once again by a rejection of those reforms after funds had been disbursed, and, 1 year later, an entirely new set of promised reforms.[53]

Resurgence of Civil Society

The crisis of the African state was paralleled by the resurgence of vocal civil societies intent on opening up the political space in their respective countries.[54] Student organizations and trade unions that played a role in the independence struggle reemerged as vocal opponents of existing regimes, in response to the often severe deterioration of national educational systems, the lack of professional jobs for university graduates, and insufficient and often declining wages for workers in general. Student organizations became particularly politicized in Congo-Kinshasa, leading to violent clashes with security forces. On May 11, 1990, twelve (some estimates go as high as 150) students at Lubumbashi University were killed when members of Mobutu's Special Presidential Division attacked the dormitories of students who had led a series of antigovernment protests. In response to this and other acts of government repression, students formed an umbrella organization, the Union Progressiste des Etudiants Zairois (UPEZA, Progressive Union of Zairian Students), that, with a variety of independent union groups, regularly launched public demonstrations and 1-day strikes known as villes mortes (dead cities).

Religious groups and organizations also emerged as vocal elements of civil society.[55] In Congo-Kinshasa, the Catholic Church and its local bishops took the lead in advocating for the transformation of the Congolese state.[56] In April 1990, a letter addressed to Mobutu and signed by twelve Congolese Catholic bishops was made public. In this letter, the bishops denounced the Mobutu regime as the "principal cause" of paralysis in governance and the intensifying crisis of the Congolese state. The letter marked a shift in the Catholic Church's historic position of remaining removed from politics to one in which church leaders spoke out against injustices within the political system.[57] Several religious figures, most notably Archbishop Monsengwo Pasyina, sought to position themselves as "honest-brokers" in negotiations between the Mobutu regime and other portions of civil society seeking to transform the Congolese state.[58]

An important component of the resurgence of civil society was the formation and expansion of opposition political parties, particularly after single-party regimes had become discredited by their decline in Eastern Europe and the former Soviet Union at the end of the 1980s (see Chapter 10). In the case of Congo-Kinshasa, the leading opposition party, the Union pour la Démocratie et le Progrès Social (UDPS, Union for Democracy and Social Progress), was formed in 1981 by thirteen members of the National Assembly and headed by Etienne Tshisekedi. Although the party was banned and its members jailed or co-opted into the ruling MPR, it re-emerged in 1990 under the leadership of Tshisekedi after Mobutu bowed to political pressure and allowed for the creation of opposition political parties. Dozens of new parties appeared literally overnight. One year later, Tshisekedi oversaw the creation of an opposition coalition, the Union Sacrée de l'Opposition Radicale (USOR, Sacred Union of Radical Opposition), composed of the UDPS and the vast majority of new political parties opposed to the Mobutu regime.

Opposition politicians sought to force the Mobutu regime into taking part in a "national conference," an extended national gathering of leaders from the state and civil society that debates the outlines of a new democratic order (see Chapter 10). Although such a conference was sporadically convened between August 1991 and December 1992, it largely failed in its overall objective, due primarily to Mobutu's successful co-optation of significant portions of its membership. The national conference nonetheless succeeded in further expanding

Congo-Kinshasa's political space and cemented Tshisekedi's role as the leader of that portion of the political opposition seeking peaceful change in Congo-Kinshasa.

Intensification of Domestic Violence and Conflict

A final dimension of the crisis of the African state was the state's inability to contain the intensification of domestic violence and conflict. In the case of Congo-Kinshasa, the almost routine manner in which the military and other portions of the coercive apparatus preyed on civil society had created an atmosphere of fear and distrust, even among foreign diplomats who are normally exempt from these types of practices. As explained by Helen Winternitz, who visited Congo-Kinshasa during the 1980s, a common form of harassment involved the creation of roadblocks to extort money from motorists, under the pretense of checking the validity of driver's licenses and vehicle paperwork:

> Better not to be grabbed at all, which is the strategy the American Embassy recommends to its staff. It issues a manual to arriving Americans that tells them never to roll down the windows of their cars when they are stopped by police officials and never to hand over their driver's licenses or travel documents. They are to show their papers through a rolled up window and from behind a locked door. The gendarmes are known for robbing with impunity not only on the city streets but also at fraudulent roadblocks, where passage is granted for money or an impromptu gift, like a pack of cigarettes or a wristwatch.[59]

Despite Mobutu's periodic promises to rein in corruption and to punish those who went beyond the realm of acceptability, by the beginning of the 1990s his regime was increasingly incapable of asserting its authority in this realm, particularly because it could not adequately train, feed, or control its own military.

A second dimension of domestic violence and conflict included the periodic outbreak of spontaneous protests, riots, and uprisings. In September 1991, nearly 3,000 mutinous troops protesting the lack of pay touched off several days of violent riots and looting in Congo-Kinshasa's capital, which quickly spread to regional capitals and cities, most notably in Shaba province, leaving thirty dead and more than 1,250 injured. The mutinous soldiers are said to have "systematically plundered" the most affluent areas of town.[60] "Expatriate observers described scenes of drunken soldiers driving around in cars stolen from dealerships, firing their weapons into the air indiscriminately," explains Winsome Leslie, a specialist of Congo-Kinshasa. "Ordinary citizens suffering economic hardship soon followed the soldiers, taking whatever they had left behind."[61] Fearful that the mobs were going to turn on Western nationals living in the country, approximately 1,750 French and Belgian troops intervened on September 24 (with the blessing of Mobutu) to ensure the evacuation of nearly 8,000 foreigners, including over 700 U.S. citizens.

Similar to the sporadic outbursts of civil unrest and conflict that have occurred throughout Africa during the independence era, the 1991 riots in Congo-Kinshasa were directed at neither explicit political goals nor the issue of regime change.[62] They were instead triggered by one disgruntled portion of the state—the Congolese military—over a specific economic concern: the lack of pay. These riots nonetheless constituted a turning point in Congolese political history in that they represented the beginning of a spiral of lawlessness and civil conflict. In 1993, renewed rioting led to pitched battles in several cities between loyalist and dissident portions of the Congolese military. These battles resulted in the deaths of more than 300 citizens, including the French ambassador, who was killed by a stray bullet.

An especially threatening form of domestic conflict, from the perspective of the state, was the rise and spread of guerrilla insurgencies intent on reordering state-society relations by force. The contemporary independence era has witnessed four types of insurgencies.[63] First and foremost, **liberation insurgencies** were directed against colonial empires unwilling to cede power peacefully, as well as against white minority regimes in Southern Africa (see Chapter 4). Other guerrilla groups sought greater rights for specific regions of already independent countries. In the extreme, such **separatist insurgencies** sought the secession and ultimate recognition of their territories as independent countries in the international system. Although another group of **reform insurgencies** sought to maintain the territorial integrity of existing countries, their leaders were nonetheless committed to overthrowing existing regimes and reordering state-society relations. A fourth group, best called **warlord insurgencies,** lacked a coherent vision of the future beyond the more immediate goal of overthrowing the regime in power. Such insurgencies were usually unable to reestablish centralized states after achieving victory, often leading to the continuation of conflict among competing warlords and their respective armies.

Beginning in 1996, a reform insurgency led by Laurent-Désiré Kabila, a guerrilla fighter who had taken part in a series of insurgencies during the 1960s, threatened the Mobutu regime. Kabila's guerrilla forces, the Alliance des Forces Démocratiques pour la Libération (AFDL, Alliance of Democratic Forces for Liberation), originated in eastern Congo-Kinshasa and received the strong backing of neighboring countries, including weapons and troops from the Ugandan regime of Yoweri Museveni and the Rwandan regime of Paul Kagame. The AFDL was able to capitalize on widespread public dissatisfaction with the Mobutu regime and the decay of the Congolese state, particularly the highly corrupt and incapable coercive apparatus. The Congolese Armed Forces had neither the financial resources nor the organizational capacity to mount a defense against either domestic or foreign foes. The AFDL was therefore able to advance westward across Congo-Kinshasa with almost lightning speed. Confronted with an impending guerrilla victory, Mobutu and his family fled to Côte d'Ivoire on May 15, 1997. Two days later, Kabila's forces entered Kinshasa and in so doing ended nearly 27 years of dictatorship under the Mobutu regime.

IN SEARCH OF A
STATE-SOCIETY BALANCE

The most important outcome associated with the crisis of the African state was the emergence of efforts to restructure state-society relationships during the 1990s. The crisis of the African state had demonstrated that authoritarian and centralized states were ineffective managers of Africa's economic, political, and social systems. It also highlighted the rising importance of African civil societies. As was the case just before their marginalization in the immediate post-independence era, African civil societies had played limited, but important, roles in the downfall of authoritarian African states during the 1990s and expected to wield equal or greater levels of influence in their newly restructured societies. The international dimension had also changed with the cold war's end. African leaders could no longer count on the diplomatic, financial, or military support of foreign powers to compensate for the African state's increased inability to manage its economic, political, and military affairs.

Whether a new generation of African leadership will be successful in refashioning state-society relationships that will both foster and reinforce an economic and political renaissance on the African continent has emerged as a topic of considerable debate.[64] Skeptics note that Kabila's actions in the aftermath of overthrowing the Mobutu regime in 1997 did not bode well for the future of creating more equitable state-society relations.[65] Rather than establishing democratic practices and setting a timetable for national elections, Kabila's victory ushered in a new dictatorship that failed to resolve the crisis of the Congolese state. In a series of moves that harkened back to the rise of authoritarianism under the Mobutu regime, the Kabila regime banned all opposition party activity, arrested several leading opposition political figures, including sending Tshisekedi into internal exile, banned leading human rights organizations, and arrested journalists who criticized the new regime.[66] Less than 2 years after assuming power, the Kabila regime found itself confronting a guerrilla insurgency in the Eastern provinces funded by its former military benefactors of Uganda and Rwanda, with Kabila himself being assassinated at the beginning of 2001. In short, the primary failing of the Kabila regime was its transparent desire to re-create, rather than reformulate, the state-society relationships that had existed under Mobutu.

There are, however, other situations where new conceptualizations of state-society relations are making a difference. One form of restructuring has been implemented by a group of victorious guerrilla leaders, once called the **new bloc of African leaders,** who succeeded in overthrowing discredited states through their leadership of strong, disciplined, and battle-tested guerrilla armies.[67] This group typically includes Isaias Afwerki of Eritrea, Meles Zenawi of Ethiopia, Yoweri Museveni of Uganda, and Paul Kagame of Rwanda, each of whom has underscored the necessity of creating "responsible and accountable" state-society relationships that are, at least in principle, based on their common commitment to the free-market economy, the reduction of corruption at all levels of governance, observance of the rule of law, and the creation of a disciplined security apparatus. However, these former guerrilla leaders have tended to view the creation of multiparty democracy as a "luxury" that must take a back seat to the promotion of political-military stability and socioeconomic development. In the case of Uganda, for example, Museveni's regime has instituted a "no-party" system that prohibits political candidates from campaigning under the banner of opposition parties. As a result, Museveni and the other former guerrilla leaders in this group increasingly have been criticized by dissident elements of civil society and international observers who question the long-term wisdom of stifling political dissent.

A second form of state-society restructuring that has fostered significant debate revolves around Ethiopia's ethnically based federal system.[68] In 1991, after nearly 30 years of civil war, the Ethiopian People's Revolutionary Democratic Front (EPRDF) overthrew a highly authoritarian and centralized state that had been ruled by the U.S.-supported monarchy of Emperor Haile Selassie (1930–74) and the Soviet-supported Marxist regime of Mengistu Haile Mariam (1974–91). The EPRDF leadership believed that the centralized, authoritarian state of both the Selassie and Mengistu years was the principal contributor to the rise and intensification of ethnic hatreds and polarizing tendencies. A crucial outcome of this overthrow was the determination of Eritrean leaders to field a

---

A Closer Look: REBUILDING TRUST: SOUTH AFRICA'S TRUTH AND RECONCILIATION COMMISSION

Numerous countries have grappled with the dilemma of how best to heal the psychological, emotional, and political wounds left behind by state-sponsored atrocities against their own peoples and in the process rebuild trust between the state and civil society. In the aftermath of World War II, the victorious Allies held the Nuremberg trials to prosecute Nazi war criminals who had committed crimes against humanity. Other forms of reckoning with the past have included the purging of discredited elites, the granting of blanket amnesties, offering compensation to victims and their families, and the construction of national monuments.

In the case of South Africa, a political consensus supported the creation of a **Truth and Reconciliation Commission** as the best vehicle for overcoming 46 years of violence between the apartheid state of South Africa (1948–94) and a variety of liberation movements led by the African National Congress (ANC). Headed by Archbishop Desmond Tutu, a Nobel Peace Prize laureate, the commission was given a triple mandate: (1) uncover the truth concerning human rights abuses prior to the inauguration of Nelson Mandela as president of South Africa on May 10, 1994; (2) bestow amnesty on those owning up to and asking forgiveness for their politically motivated crimes; and (3) assess and provide reparations to the victims of those human rights abuses. The actual process was relatively simple and straightforward. Those requesting amnesty provided sworn testimony in a public hearing, including responses to questions by members of the commission and victims and their families. The commission used the power of subpoena to pursue additional corroborating evidence.

The testimony of victims and perpetrators alike produced tearful, shocking, and gruesome revelations. Extensive documentation has now become public as to how state security officers routinely extracted confessions through a variety of grisly techniques, such as administering the "black bag," the use of a tightly wrapped cloth to repeatedly bring a prisoner to the brink of asphyxiation. Former opponents of the apartheid state have similarly confessed to their involvement in the execution of informants, most notably by the use of "necklacing," in which an automobile tire doused in gasoline is wedged around the informant's body and set on fire.

The commission was not without controversy. The family of Steve Biko, a famous antiapartheid activist who founded the Black Consciousness Movement and whose life is documented in the celebrated movie, "Cry Freedom," successfully challenged the applications of five officers whose actions led to Biko's death while in police custody in 1977. The Biko family and others whose family members were murdered by agents of the apartheid state understandably desired those petitioning for an official pardon to be tried for murder and sentenced accordingly in a criminal court. In short, they do not recognize the right of the commission to pardon those responsible for murder.

Defenders of the commission's work countered that the issue of amnesty, however flawed, constituted a necessary political compromise that allowed for a peaceful transition to democracy in South Africa. "We could have chosen the revolution and overthrow route, but we chose the negotiations route," notes Dullah Omar, an ANC member of the South African parliament, "and that means having to live and work with and rebuild the country together with people who have treated us very badly in the past and against whom we have very strong feelings." Defenders also noted that the public chronicling of past abuses represented an important first step in healing a nation still seriously divided by racial and ethnic differences. "It is important that victims be allowed to tell their stories; survivors often feel misunderstood and ignored, their sacrifice unacknowledged, their pain unrecognized, and their identity destroyed," explains Lyn S. Graybill. "Reconciliation requires that there be some general agreement between both sides as to the wrongs committed."

Quotations are drawn from Lyn S. Graybill, "South Africa's Truth and Reconciliation Commission: Ethical and Theological Perspectives," *Ethics and International Affairs* 12 (1998): 43–62. See also Truth and Reconciliation Commission, *Truth and Reconciliation Commission of South Africa Report* (5 vols.), (New York: Grove, 1999), and the Truth and Reconciliation Commission's homepage: http://www.truth.org.za/back/bill.htm

guerrilla army that not only contributed to the ultimate defeat of the Mengistu regime but ensured the eventual independence of the Eritrean province. In a referendum in May 1993, 99.8 percent of all Eritreans voted in favor of independence (see Chapter 4). The EPRDF leadership believed that the only way to "save" the remaining portions of the multiethnic Ethiopian state was to create a federal system composed of nine ethnically based local states and two autonomous cities (Addis Ababa and Dire Dawa). Although critics have argued that such an arrangement has further polarized ethnic politics as ethnic leaders compete for federal resources, proponents have countered that further separatist tendencies have been quelled. This experiment in ethnically based federalism nonetheless has been marred by the authoritarian practices of the Tigrean People's Liberation Front (TPLF), the political-military core of the EPRDF that controls both the presidency and the vast majority of the seats in the Council of People's Representatives, the national legislature.

The most comprehensive example of state-society restructuring is the continued transformation of South Africa's former apartheid system into a multiracial and multiethnic democratic political system.[69] The historic turning point in this process was Nelson Mandela's victory in 1994 as the first president of South Africa elected by a majority vote. Before 1994, South Africa had been ruled by a white minority regime that instituted racial segregation. As part of the democratization process, South Africans were challenged to confront their collective past and to create a democratic culture of forgiveness through involvement in the public hearings of the Truth and Reconciliation Commission (see the accompanying box). Subsequent negotiations and debates among all the major political parties resulted in the adoption of a new constitutional framework in February 1997, which enshrined the separation of powers between the executive, legislative, and judicial branches of the federal government; the creation of a three-tiered structure of governance in which specific powers are outlined for local municipalities, nine provincial governments, and the federal government; and a bill of rights detailing an extensive array of political, economic, and social rights for the individual and civil society. Although the constitution recognizes the importance of protecting the "cultural" rights of individual racial and ethnic groups, the federal system is nonetheless "unitary" in that representation is not based on race or ethnicity.

South Africa's carefully crafted state-society balance is nonetheless threatened by high crime levels and the continued poverty of a large portion of the nation's population. Constitutional guarantees of political freedoms may mean very little to working parents who cannot safely walk about their townships or earn enough money to move their families out of poverty. Indeed, the suggestion that the new constitution will eventually evolve into a living testament to the multiracial and multiethnic ideals of the African National Congress (ANC) misses the crucial point associated with political transition and the restructuring of state-society relations through constitutional means: The vast majority of South Africa's population *expects* and *demands* immediate rewards and benefits to make up for the past injustices of the apartheid system.[70] "However it evolves, it seems safe to conclude that the [South African] constitution nonetheless provides a solid basis for representative, transparent, and accountable governance, with meaningful protection and promotion of fundamental rights," explained a report of Carnegie Foundation's Commission on Preventing Deadly Conflict. "As such, it does hold promise as an inspiration for other countries in transition, particularly those that are attempting to build viable state-society coalitions under conditions of diverse cultures, deep economic disparities, and limited political authority and financial resources."[71]

KEY TERMS

African state
African civil society
state-society relationship
crisis of the African state
great expectations–minimal capabilities
   paradox
Africanization of state institutions
parastatals
nationalization
marketing board
coercive apparatus
personal rule networks
neopatrimonalism
patron-client relationships
family reunification program
diversity visa program lottery
exit option

predatory states
lame Leviathans
shadow states
warlord states
petty corruption
kleptocracy
social goods
génération sacrifiée (sacrificed
   generation)
informal economies
liberation insurgencies
separatist insurgencies
reform insurgencies
warlord insurgencies
new bloc of African leaders
Truth and Reconciliation
   Commission

FOR FURTHER READING

Bayart, Jean-François. *The State in Africa: The Politics of the Belly*. London: Longman, 1993.

Bayart, Jean-François, Stephen Ellis, and Béatrice Hibou. *The Criminalization of the State in Africa*. Oxford: James Currey, 1999.

Chabal, Patrick, and Jean-Pascol Daloz. *Africa Works: Disorder as Political Instrument*. London: James Currey, 1999.

Clapham, Christopher, ed. *African Guerrillas*. Oxford: James Currey, 1998.

Comaroff, John L., and Jean Comaroff, eds. *Civil Society and the Political Imagination in Africa: Critical Perspectives*. Chicago: University of Chicago Press, 1999.

Fatton, Robert. *Predatory Rule: State and Civil Society in Africa*. Boulder: Lynne Rienner, 1992.

Harbeson, John W., Donald Rothchild, and Naomi Chazan, eds. *Civil Society and the State in Africa*. Boulder: Lynne Rienner, 1994.

Herbst, Jeffrey. *States and Power in Africa: Comparative Lessons in Authority and Control*. Princeton: Princeton University Press, 2000.

Hyden, Goran, Dele Olowu, and H. W. O. Okoth Ogendo, eds. *African Perspectives on Governance*. Trenton: Africa World, 2000.

Jackson, Robert H., and Carl G. Rosberg. *Personal Rule in Black Africa: Prince, Autocrat, Prophet, Tyrant*. Berkeley: University of California Press, 1982.

Joseph, Richard, ed. *State, Conflict, and Democracy in Africa*. Boulder: Lynne Rienner, 1998.

Kasfir, Nelson, ed. *Civil Society and Democracy in Africa: Critical Perspectives*. London: Frank Cass, 1998

Olukoshi, Adebayo O., and Liisa Laakso, eds. *Challenges to the Nation-State in Africa*. Helsinki: Institute of Development Studies, 1996.

Osaghae, Eghosa, ed. *Between State and Civil Society in Africa: Perspectives on Development*. Dakar: CODESRIA, 1994.

Parpart, Jane L., and Kathleen A. Staudt, eds. *Women and the State in Africa*. Boulder: Lynne Rienner, 1990.

Reno, William. *Warlord Politics and African States.* Boulder: Lynne Rienner, 1998.

Rothchild, Donald, and Naomi Chazan, eds. *The Precarious Balance: State and Society in Africa.* Boulder: Westview, 1988.

Schatzberg, Michael G. *Political Legitimacy in Middle Africa: Father, Family, Food.*

Bloomington: Indiana University Press, 2001.

Villalón, Leonardo, and Phillip Huxtable, eds. *The African State at a Critical Juncture: Between Disintegration and Reconfiguration.* Boulder: Lynne Rienner, 1998.

Young, Crawford. *The African Colonial State in Comparative Perspective.* New Haven: Yale University Press, 1994.

NOTES

1. See Crawford Young, *The African Colonial State in Comparative Perspective* (New Haven: Yale University Press, 1994), p. 1.

2. The discussion of Congo-Kinshasa primarily draws on Crawford Young and Thomas Turner, *The Rise and Decline of the Zairian State* (Madison: University of Wisconsin Press, 1985). See also Winsome J. Leslie, *Zaire: Continuity and Political Change in an Oppressive State* (Boulder: Westview, 1993); Thomas M. Callaghy, *The State-Society Struggle: Zaire in Comparative Perspective* (New York: Columbia University Press, 1984); Michael G. Schatzberg, *The Dialectics of Oppression in Zaire* (Bloomington: Indiana University Press, 1988); and Georges Nzongola-Ntalaja, *The Congo from Leopold to Kabila: A People's History* (London: Zed Books, 2002).

3. Patrick Boyle, "A View from Zaire," *World Politics* 60, no. 2 (1988): 270.

4. See Young and Turner, *Rise and Decline,* pp. 43, 65, 68, 117.

5. Ibid., pp. 326–50.

6. See Irving Leonard Markovitz, "Bureaucratic Development and Economic Growth," *Journal of Modern African Studies* 14, no. 2 (1970): 183–200, as cited in Naomi Chazan et al., *Politics and Society in Contemporary Africa* (Boulder: Lynne Rienner, 1992), p. 55.

7. Young and Turner, *Rise and Decline,* pp. 350–62.

8. Ibid., pp. 40–42.

9. Ibid., p. 55.

10. Ibid., p. 59.

11. Ibid., pp. 54–55.

12. Ibid., p. 192.

13. See Donald Rothchild and Naomi Chazan, eds., *The Precarious Balance: State and Society in Africa* (Boulder: Westview, 1988).

14. Young and Turner, *Rise and Decline,* p. 56.

15. Ibid., p. 57.

16. Ibid., p. 67.

17. Ibid., p. 68.

18. U.S. Arms Control and Disarmament Agency, *World Military Expenditures and Arms Trade 1963–1973* (Washington, DC: U.S. Government Printing Office, 1975), p. 16, as quoted in Chazan et al., *Politics and Society,* p. 58.

19. Young and Turner, *Rise and Decline,* p. 267.

20. Ibid., p. 273.

21. See Peter J. Schraeder, *United States Foreign Policy toward Africa: Incrementalism, Crisis, and Change* (Cambridge: Cambridge University Press, 1994), Ch. 3. See also Michael G. Schatzberg, *Mobutu or Chaos? The United States and Zaire, 1960–1990* (Lanham: University Press of America, 1991).

22. See Robert H. Jackson and Carl G. Rosberg, *Personal Rule in Black Africa: Prince, Autocrat, Prophet, Tyrant* (Berkeley: University of California Press, 1984). See also Nicolas van de Walle, *African Economies and the*

Politics of Permanent Crisis, 1979–1999 (Cambridge: Cambridge University Press, 2001).

23. See J. C. Williame, *Patrimonialism and Political Change in the Congo* (Stanford: Stanford University Press, 1972). See also Jackson and Rosberg, *Personal Rule in Black Africa,* pp. 167–81, and Young and Turner, *Rise and Decline,* Ch. 6.

24. Quoted in Young and Turner, *Rise and Decline,* p. 169.

25. Ibid., p. 166.

26. Ibid., p. 165.

27. See Leonardo Villalón and Phillip Huxtable, eds., *The African State at a Critical Juncture* (Boulder: Lynne Rienner, 1998).

28. Robert Fatton, *Predatory Rule: State and Civil Society in Africa* (Boulder: Lynne Rienner, 1992).

29. See Thomas Callaghy, "The State as Lame Leviathan: The Patrimonial Administrative State in Africa," in Zaki Ergas, ed., *The African State in Transition* (Basingstoke: Macmillan, 1987), pp. 87–116, and William Reno, *Corruption and State Politics in Sierra Leone* (Cambridge: Cambridge University Press, 1995).

30. See William Reno, *Warlord Politics and African States* (Boulder: Lynne Rienner, 1998).

31. John Ravenhill, "A Second Decade of Adjustment: Greater Complexity, Greater Uncertainty," in Thomas M. Callaghy and John Ravenhill, eds., *Hemmed In: Responses to Africa's Economic Decline* (New York: Columbia University Press, 1993), p. 18.

32. Ibid.

33. Young and Turner, *Rise and Decline,* p. 307.

34. Ibid., p. 307.

35. Ibid., p. 71.

36. Ibid., p. 94.

37. David J. Gould, *Bureaucratic Corruption and Underdevelopment in the Third World: The Case of Zaire* (New York: Pergamon, 1980), p. xiv.

38. Ibid., p. xiii.

39. John F. Clark, "Zaire: The Bankruptcy of the Extractive State," in Villalón and Huxtable, eds., *The African State at a Critical Juncture,* pp. 109–25.

40. Ibid., p. 116.

41. Ibid.

42. Leslie, *Zaire,* p. 116.

43. William Reno, "Sovereignty and Personal Rule in Zaire," *African Studies Quarterly* 1, no. 3 (1997): 5.

44. Leslie, *Zaire,* p. 116.

45. See Patrick M. Boyle, *Class Formation and Civil Society: The Politics of Education in Sub-Saharan Africa* (Aldershot: Ashgate, 1999).

46. See Jeffrey Herbst, *States and Power in Africa: Comparative Lessons in Authority and Control* (Princeton: Princeton University Press, 2000). See also Crawford Young, "Zaire: The Shattered Illusion of the Integral State," *The Journal of Modern African Studies* 32, no. 2 (1994): 247–63.

47. See William Reno, *Warlord Politics and African States* (Boulder: Lynne Rienner, 1998).

48. See Christopher Clapham, *Africa and the International System: The Politics of State Survival* (Cambridge: Cambridge University Press, 1996).

49. Janet MacGaffey, *The Real Economy of Zaire: The Contribution of Smuggling and Other Unofficial Activities to National Wealth* (Philadelphia: University of Pennsylvania Press, 1991), p. 12.

50. Ibid., p. 23.

51. Ibid., p. 19.

52. Ibid., pp. 49–50.

53. Thomas M. Callaghy, "The Ritual Dance of the Debt Game," *Africa Report* (September–October 1984): 22–26.

54. See John W. Harbeson, Donald Rothchild, and Naomi Chazan, eds., *Civil Society and the State in Africa* (Boulder: Lynne Rienner, 1994).

55. For example, see Jeff Haynes, *Religion and Politics in Africa* (London: Zed, 1996).

56. Patrick M. Boyle, "Beyond Self-Protection to Prophecy: The Catholic

Church and Political Change in Zaire," *Africa Today* (1992): 49–66. See also Boyle, "School Wars: Church, State, and the Death of the Congo," *The Journal of Modern African Studies* 33, no. 3 (1995): 451–68.

57. Patrick M. Boyle, "Bishops as Brokers: Ecclesiastics, Political Reform, and Regime Transitions in Sub-Saharan Africa," unpublished paper.

58. Ibid.

59. Helen Winternitz, *East along the Equator* (New York: Atlantic Monthly, 1987), p. 19, quoted in Leslie, *Zaire,* pp. 44–45.

60. Ibid., p. 45.

61. Ibid.

62. For a discussion, see Michael Bratton and Nicolas van de Walle, *Democratic Experiments in Africa: Regime Transitions in Comparative Perspective* (Cambridge: Cambridge University Press, 1997), pp. 101–3.

63. See Clapham, *Africa and the International System,* pp. 208–44.

64. For example, see Jeffrey Herbst, "Responding to State Failure in Africa," *International Security* 21, no. 3 (Winter 1996–97): 120–44, Richard Joseph and Jeffrey Herbst, "Correspondence: Responding to State Failure in Africa," *International Security* 22, no. 2 (Fall 1997): 175–84.

65. For example, see Michael G. Schatzberg, "Beyond Mobutu: Kabila and the Congo," *Journal of Democracy* 8, no. 4 (1997): 70–84.

66. See Peter Rosenblum, "Kabila's Congo," *Current History* 97, no. 619 (1998): 193–99.

67. See Don Connell and Frank Smyth, "Africa's New Bloc," *Foreign Affairs* 77, no. 2 (March–April 1998): 80–94.

68. See Kidane Mengisteab, "New Approaches to State Building in Africa: The Case of Ethiopia's Ethnic-Based Federalism," *African Studies Review* 40, 3 (1997): 111–32; John Young, "Ethnicity and Power in Ethiopia," *Review of African Political Economy* 70 (1996): 531–42; and Walle Engedayehu, "Ethiopia: Democracy and the Politics of Ethnicity," *Africa Today* 40, no. 2 (1993): 29–52.

69. John Stremlau (with the cooperation of Helen Zille), *A House No Longer Divided: Progress and Prospects for Democratic Peace in South Africa* (Washington, DC: Carnegie Corporation of New York, 1997).

70. See Michael Bratton, "After Mandela's Miracle in South Africa," *Current History* 97, no. 619 (1998): 214–19.

71. Ibid., p. 17.

9

Military Coups d'Etat and Military Governance

Agence France-Presse

A rally in 2000 at the national stadium in Freetown, Sierra Leone, in support of former soldiers led by Lt. Col. Johnny Paul Koromah, who was chief of a military junta that ruled briefly in 1997.

A FRICAN MILITARIES EMERGED from the shadows of obscurity during the 1950s to become one of the most important institutional actors in African politics and society. The primary means for African military personnel to achieve power and influence over their respective political systems was the **military coup d'état:** the sudden and illegal overthrow of an existing government by a portion of the state's armed forces. By the end of the 1960s, military leaders had launched over twenty-five successful coups, ushering in a period of militarization that soon left more than 50 percent of all African countries governed by military regimes. Even in cases where they led their troops back to the barracks after turning over power to elected civilian regimes, military leaders maintained—and often enhanced—their newfound levels of political influence. Once having enjoyed the fruits of power, military leaders, often called the **men on horseback** or **leaders in khaki,** were prone to return to presidential mansions in later coups, leading foreign observers to characterize African militaries as the primary forces for change throughout the African continent. By the beginning of the 1990s, however, the emergence of pro-democracy movements and several successful transitions to democracy led to a rebirth of civilian regimes intent on permanently returning African militaries to their barracks. The primary purpose of this chapter is to examine the nature and evolution of military intervention in African politics and society.

TRENDS IN MILITARY COUPS D'ETAT

Scholars overlooked the role of the military in African politics and society during the initial decade (the 1950s) of the contemporary independence era. The militaries inherited by newly elected African leaders were usually small and lacked sophisticated weapons, such as armored vehicles, combat aircraft, and guided missile systems.[1] African militaries were therefore more symbols of sovereignty and independence than independent actors capable of influencing their political systems. Moreover, most African militaries played little if any role in the largely peaceful decolonization process of the 1950s. Even after military leaders overthrew five civilian governments from 1958 to 1965, scholars still perceived military coups d'état as mere aberrations from the expected consolidation of multiparty democracies.[2]

An early inkling that the so-called aberrations were becoming the norm of African politics occurred in 1966, when military coups overthrew eight civilian regimes, ranging from the monarchy of King Ntare V of Burundi to the multiparty democracy of Prime Minister Abubakar Tafawa Balewa of Nigeria. From this point forward, scholars and analysts took serious note of the explosion of military involvement. According to a series of statistical studies conducted by Patrick J. McGowan and Thomas H. Johnson, the period 1956–2001 witnessed 188 attempted military coups, of which 80 (43 percent) were successful. If one also includes reported **military plots** in which coup leaders were arrested before they were able to launch any sort of military action, the total number of attempted coups during this same period rises to 372, and the success/failure ratio changes to 24 percent and 76 percent.[3]

The prevalence of military coups is graphically demonstrated in Map 9.1. Most African countries have experienced at least one successful military coup, and several have experienced two or more. The record for the greatest number of successful military coups (six) is jointly held by Benin, Burkina Faso, and Nigeria. The pervasiveness of military leaders as the principal agents of regime change is demonstrated by the unfolding of eighty-six successful military coups from 1951 to 2002. Only six African countries—Botswana, Cape Verde, Eritrea, Mauritius Namibia, and South Africa—have never faced armed challenges (successful or unsuccessful) from their military personnel.

Most coups share several characteristics. First, military leaders have been able to intervene successfully in their political systems due to the weak nature of the African state in the immediate postindependence era (see Chapter 8). Weak state power was often exacerbated by the rise to power of illegitimate leaders,

MAP 9.1 Successful Military Coups d'État

whose corrupt and authoritarian practices led to widening gaps between the self-interested policies of incumbent regimes and the needs and demands of their respective populations. Indeed, regardless of regime type (e.g., monarchical, democratic, or authoritarian) or ideology (capitalist, socialist, or Marxist), African states increasingly incapable of responding to their citizens fell prey to military leaders professing a special ability to undertake political-military reforms and socioeconomic development.

African coups are also similar in the sense that they are usually carried out by members of African armies, as opposed to other branches of the armed services, such as the air force or the navy. The primary reason for this similarity is that African navies and air forces are usually the smallest and most poorly equipped branches of African militaries, therefore lacking both the capability and the prestige to carry out a coup that can garner the support of officers within the army. The only exceptions to this general rule are the successful coups in Ghana in 1979 and 1981 that were led by Air Force Flight Lieutenant Jerry Rawlings and the unsuccessful military bid for power in Kenya in 1982 that was led by the Air Force. No African country has ever experienced a coup led by naval personnel.

A third similarity involves what can be termed **coups of descending order.** The first coup that occurs in a country is usually led by the most senior members of the military establishment, most notably generals, who command the respect of lower-ranking military officers. Once they assume control of the political system, however, their refusal to relinquish the perks of their new-found political power can lead to grumbling in the lower ranks. The lower-ranking officers often regard their commanders as pursuing a lifestyle as bad as, if not worse than, their deposed civilian counterparts. The response is a **palace coup** in which the senior commanders are overthrown by junior officers who, after assuming power, can fall prey to yet another coup by even lower-ranking officers. In the case of Burkina Faso, President Maurice Yaméogo was overthrown in 1966 by Lieutenant Colonel Sangoulé Lamizana, who was in turn overthrown by Colonel Sayé Zerbo in 1980. Zerbo was overthrown by non-commissioned officers in 1982, followed by three further coups led by Major General Jean Baptiste Ouedraogo (1983), Captain Thomas Sankara (1983), and Captain Blaise Compaoré (1987). In each of these cases, senior officers were overthrown by other officers of lower or equal rank.

The **contagion effect** constitutes a fourth common characteristic of military coups.[4] The underlying principle of this phenomenon is that once a coup occurs in one country, there exists a greater possibility of a coup taking place in a neighboring country. As in the case of a contagious illness, military leaders are affected by the activities of their neighbors and perhaps become emboldened by the thought: "If *they* can do it, so can we!" This trend also holds true in terms of successive coups in a single country. Once the military intervenes against civilian leaders, military leaders become much more confident and willing to pursue similar actions in the future.

ROLE OF THE MILITARY
IN POLITICAL GOVERNANCE

The range of military involvement in African politics and society is best characterized as a **spectrum of civil-military relations,** ranging from little if any military involvement in the civilian realm at one extreme end of the spectrum to complete military domination of the civilian realm at the other end of the spectrum. Drawing on the work of J. Gus Liebenow, one can distinguish between five specific models of civil-military relations (see Figure 9.1).[5]

Civilian Supremacy Model

At one extreme is the **civilian supremacy model,** in which the military is firmly under the control of civilian politicians. "Essentially," explains Liebenow, "the civilian supremacy model requires that civilians, rather than the military, control decision making with respect to the issue of war and peace, the determination of the size and general shape of the military establishment, the basic methods of recruiting both officers and enlisted personnel, the allocation of major privileges and rewards within the service, and, most important, the allocation of government revenues for the funding of all military and paramilitary activities."[6] This is the model adhered to and promoted by the northern industrialized democracies.

Botswana offers the most clear-cut example of the civilian supremacy model.[7] Often called Africa's "oldest democracy," Botswana did not create a national army, the Botswana Defence Force (BDF), until 1976, 10 years after independence. Botswana's president is recognized by the constitution as commander in chief of the armed forces. He is responsible for appointing members to a civilian-dominated Defence Council, which includes the BDF Commander as an ex-officio member. The Defence Council oversees all matters related to the military. The BDF constitutes a highly professional corps of officers and soldiers that has never intervened militarily in Botswana's domestic political system.

FIGURE 9.1 Spectrum of Civil-Military Relations

Source: Derived from J. Gus Liebenow, *African Politics: Crises and Challenges* (Bloomington: Indiana University Press, 1986), pp. 250–54.

Watchdog Model

A second type of civil–military relations, known as the **watchdog model,** represents a greater degree of military intervention in the domestic political system.[8] Like the civilian supremacy model, the cornerstone of the watchdog model is the military's strong support for the supremacy of civilian rule. However, the officer corps perceives the military as the ultimate guarantor of democracy. As a result, military intervention in the domestic political arena, including the launching of a military coup, is considered acceptable if the country's democratic principles are threatened (e.g., a defeated incumbent refuses to step down after losing a democratically held election). The hallmark of this model is a short-term military intervention with a very specific objective in mind (e.g., ensuring that the victor in democratically held elections assumes office). According to this model, the restoration of democratic principles is followed by the military's swift return to the barracks.

A military coup in Mali in 1991 reflected the watchdog model.[9] A group of military officers headed by Lieutenant Colonel Amadou Toumani Touré (nicknamed "A.T.T.") took power after President Moussa Traoré's brutal suppression of a pro-democracy movement led to over 100 deaths and 700 wounded. Touré's forces arrested President Traoré, formed a National Reconciliation Council, and pledged a return to democracy within 1 year. During the next 12 months, the military government convened a national conference that debated the outlines of a new democratic political system, conducted a national referendum on a new constitution, and oversaw the holding of legislative and presidential elections. After President Alpha Oumar Konaré assumed office on June 6, 1992, the Malian army returned to the barracks and Lieutenant Colonel Touré retired. Ten years later, Touré's continued popularity contributed to his return to politics, only this time as victor in the presidential elections of 2002.

Balance Wheel Model

The military plays a stronger role in the **balance wheel model,** which constitutes a civil–military coalition.[10] Unlike the short-term and limited nature of military involvement under the watchdog model, military leaders under the balance wheel model proclaim that full decision-making authority is vested in the military. However, the military leaders have neither the interest nor the ability to staff individual ministries and government offices with military bureaucrats. As a result, the actual running of government ministries is left in the hands of civilian bureaucrats.

The military government of Liberia, led by Master Sergeant Samuel K. Doe from 1980 to 1986, is an example of the balance wheel model.[11] After seizing power through a military coup, Doe created a People's Redemption Council (PRC), which underscored the supreme authority of the new military government. As explained by Liebenow, who also is a specialist of Liberian politics, Doe's PRC had "no intentions of immediately returning to the barracks" in the aftermath of the 1980 coup.[12] "On the other hand, they recognized that they lacked the talents to perform the broad spectrum of duties which the Liberians

A Closer Look: HIDDEN KILLERS: LANDMINES IN AFRICA

Sometimes called the "hidden killer" or the "maiming machine," the land-mine remains one of the greatest scourges of African wars and civil conflicts. The International Campaign to Ban Landmines, corecipient of the 1997 Nobel Peace Prize with its direc-tor, Jody Williams, estimates that the African continent is afflicted by 30 million landmines. The devastating impact of these weapons has been most strongly felt in Angola, where nearly one in every four hundred people has been maimed. Angola has earned the sad distinction of being the "amputee capital of the world."

The use of landmines is extremely popular among guerrillas seeking to overthrow existing governments. In addition to being relatively inexpen-sive ($3–$7), the landmine is a potent weapon that greatly restricts the free-dom of movement of government troops. The sowing of landmines around villages and in crop-growing regions also exacts a heavy toll on the national economy. Farmers scared to plant or harvest their crops become the unwilling allies of guerrilla warfare.

The greatest scourge of landmines is that they remain hidden and lethal long after the combatants have settled their differences. In Mozambique, a country roughly twice the size of California, the 1992 peace accord ending three decades of civil war left 1 to 2 million landmines, which every month continue to maim and kill fifty innocent civilians, one-third of whom are women and children. The govern-ment of President Joaquim Alberto Chissano has collaborated with the international donor community and the Mozambique Association for the Handicapped to launch several de-mining programs, including the creation of a school to train local specialists in the systematic clearing of minefields. Despite the best of intentions, such efforts are ham-pered by extraordinary costs (it is estimated that each mine costs $1,000 to remove), donor fatigue in the post–cold war era, and the limited capacities of Mozambique's impoverished national economy. "The magnitude of the problem is staggering and provides just one illustration why a return to normalcy in a landmined territory takes years if not decades," explains Isebill V. Gruhn. "Meanwhile, vehicles drive over unsafe tracks and people walk along mined pathways and fields, compounding the death toll and loss of limbs and making villagers fearful of returning to their homes and farms."

Growing international pressures to eliminate the landmine threat prompted the ratification in Decem-ber 1997 of an international treaty on landmines, the Convention on the Prohibition of the Use, Stock-piling, Production, and Transfer of Antipersonnel Mines and on Their Destruction. Accepted by 143 coun-tries as of 2002, the treaty calls for a complete ban on the manufacture and sale of landmines, as well as the destruction of stockpiles. The treaty's effectiveness is hampered by the lack of support among important regional and global powers, such as China, India, Iran, and the United States, several of which are also major arms exporters. Only five African countries (Central African Republic, Egypt, Libya, Morocco, and Somalia) have not signed the treaty.

Discussion draws on Andrew Meldrum, "The Maiming Machines," *Africa Report* 40, no. 3 (May–June 1995): 18–21, and Isebill V. Gruhn, "Land Mines: An African Tragedy," *The Journal of Modern African Studies* 34, no. 4 (1996): 687–99. See also the Landmine Monitor Website: www.icbl.org/lm/

had come to associate with the government," explains Liebenow. "This was signaled early by the co-optation of a number of prominent Liberian civilians to undertake many of the responsibilities with respect to economic development, foreign affairs, health delivery, and other governmental functions."[13]

Direct Rule Model

The military officers who adhere to the **direct rule model** of civil-military relations assume that the overthrown civilian leaders, including the heads of individual bureaucracies, are "creatures of their own pasts" and therefore incapable of providing adequate leadership for the country.[14] As a result, the new military leadership announces the establishment of direct rule, in which military officers assume responsibility for the day-to-day functioning of the central government, including individual bureaucracies and government agencies.

The military government established in Nigeria in July 1966 by Lieutenant Colonel Yakabu Gowon offers an interesting example of this model.[15] Gowon favored portrayals of himself as the Abraham Lincoln of Nigeria, due to his successful management of the 1967–70 Nigerian civil war that preserved the federal union. At the end of the war, however, the vast majority of important administrative posts remained headed by military officers. The dramatic rise in state-controlled corruption, which resulted from the lucrative oil boom at the beginning of the 1970s, reinforced the desires of military officers to maintain control over the reins of power. Despite early assurances to swiftly return Nigeria to democratic rule, the transition process was repeatedly delayed and finally indefinitely postponed in a major address to the nation on October 1, 1974. Gowon's military regime remained in power for a total of 9 years, only to be overthrown by yet another military coup, led by Brigadier General Murtala Mohammed on July 29, 1975.

Social Transformation Model

A final form of civil-military relations, known as the **social transformation model,** is similar to that of direct rule in that military officers take charge of individual bureaucracies and government agencies.[16] However, this model represents an even greater level of military involvement due to the explicit intentions of the new military leaders to seek the complete transformation of their country's socioeconomic and political systems. The military leaders who adopt this model are often driven by an ideology that differs from that of the displaced civilian elite. As a result, the military coup becomes the vehicle for the radical transformation of society, according to the military's understanding of the new ideology.

The emergence of a Marxist-inspired military regime in Ethiopia from 1974 to 1977 constitutes a clear-cut example of the social transformation model.[17] A series of mutinies in the Ethiopian Armed Forces over demands for higher pay and better living conditions led to the overthrow of Emperor Haile Selassie and his replacement by the Provisional Military Administrative Council (PMAC), a group of approximately 120 junior-grade and noncommissioned officers of the Ethiopian military who became known as the Derg. Factional infighting favored the emergence of Colonel Mengistu Haile Mariam, a self-proclaimed Marxist officer, as the unparalleled leader of Ethiopia. Among the radical steps undertaken by the Mengistu-led Derg in the months that followed were the execution of fifty-seven officials of the deposed monarchy, the creation of a single-party communist state, the nationalization of all financial institutions and major companies, and the initiation of a full-scale military offensive to end a guerrilla insurgency in the northern province of Eritrea. In short, the military coup of 1974 served as the basis for a full-scale **revolution from above** in which ideologically driven military leaders sought the transformation of Ethiopian society.

MYTHS CONCERNING THE EFFECTIVENESS OF MILITARY GOVERNANCE

Not surprisingly, African military leaders seek to justify their seizure of power and the institution of military rule. Most often these rationales are at best a misinterpretation of political and social realities and at worst a thinly disguised attempt at obtaining and maintaining control over the reins of power. Indeed, the common assumption of African military leaders—that they as opposed to their civilian counterparts have more effectively governed during the contemporary independence era—is based on a variety of myths that are strongly challenged by four decades of military governance. Drawing once again on the work of Liebenow, one can distinguish five sets of myths.[18]

Military Enjoys Greater Legitimacy

The first myth of military governance is that military leaders enjoy greater levels of legitimacy than their civilian counterparts.[19] The primary reason for this claim is the outpouring of public support that usually follows the military's assumption of power. It is important to note, however, that public support is usually not due to public preferences for military rule, nor the perception of military leaders as more effective rulers. To the contrary, the public often greets military intervention as a blessing due to strong disenchantment with the perceived shortcomings of civilian leadership. As a result, the public is willing to grant military leaders a brief "honeymoon period" in which to correct any deficiencies in the socioeconomic and political systems. The longer the military remains in power, however, the greater the likelihood that the honeymoon period will dissipate amidst popular demands for a return to civilian government.

In Somalia, public opinion overwhelmingly favored Major General Mohammed Siad Barre's seizure of power through a military coup on October 21, 1969.[20] In the days that followed, Siad created a Supreme Revolutionary Council (SRC) composed of twenty-four military officers, replaced civilian leaders at

the regional and local levels with military governors and district commissioners, and named senior military personnel to head Somalia's diplomatic missions
abroad. Overwhelming popular support for the essentially **bloodless coup** was
fostered by widespread dissatisfaction with the corrupt practices of the governments of the civilian era (1960–69). The civilian politicians, especially legislators of the National Assembly, were perceived as primarily driven by the
self-interest of financial gain, while the nation's business and the national economy stagnated. Popular support for the military coup subsided, however, as it
became clear that the Siad regime had no intention of ever ceding political
power to a new generation of civilian politicians. Rising disenchantment
throughout the mid-1970s ultimately coalesced in the form of a 10-year guerrilla insurgency that succeeded in overthrowing the Siad regime in 1991.

Military Rule Is More Efficient

A second myth posited by military leaders is that the very nature of military
organization makes military rule more efficient than that of its civilian counterparts.[21] The core of this argument is that military personnel are members of
a hierarchical chain of command and trained in discipline. Lower-ranking military personnel are expected to follow orders without question. This hierarchical structure theoretically allows military leaders to avoid the "inefficient
compromises" of civilian governance. Even if one accepts the basic premise of
the argument that military rule is efficient rule, most African militaries are
incapable of staffing all civilian positions with adequately trained personnel. As
a result, civil-military coalitions become the norm, and the presumably "inefficient" civilian politicians remain at various levels of governance. Even the most
extreme form of military involvement in the political system requires some
level of civilian participation.

The most serious contradiction associated with the "efficiency" argument
is that the military's direct entry into the political system via military coup
invariably politicizes that organization and makes it subject to the same political
demands and shortcomings confronted by civilian politicians. In the simplest
sense, the newfound access to the privileges associated with leadership, such
as luxury housing and access to state wealth, almost invariably "creates a gulf
between senior and junior grade officers as well as between officers and the
rank and file."[22] It is precisely for this reason that one witnesses coups of
descending order as more junior members of the military chain of command
seek access to the privileges enjoyed by their superiors.

The corruption associated with the long series of coups and military
regimes in Nigeria is but one counterpoint to military claims of greater efficiency.[23] In the aftermath of Major General Ibrahim Babangida's seizure of
power in August 1985, official promises of prosecuting the corrupt civilian officials of the Second Republic "quietly evaporated" as military-dominated patterns of corruption steadily emerged.[24] According to Larry Diamond, a noted
specialist in Nigerian politics and society, Babangida acquired the status of the

"most massively corrupt ruler" in Nigerian political history.[25] "Numerous recipients and one-time insiders confirmed the pattern of largesse, and one former top-ranking officer and longtime associate of Babangida's claimed he entered the presidency with a net worth in the tens of millions of dollars from previous corruption in weapons purchases and other transactions," explains Diamond. "As in the Second Republic, foreign business leaders privately estimated the personal wealth of top [military] officials in the hundreds of millions, and objective evidence pointed to annual leakages of revenue in the billions of dollars, approximating 10 percent of the country's total annual output of goods and services!"[26] As is the case in both civilian and military regimes alike, the extreme corruption of Babangida's regime was a double-edged sword. "It oiled the wheels of a constantly whirring political machine, buying support, compliance, and alliances within and outside the military," explains Diamond, "but it also greatly intensified public alienation and revulsion toward the regime, the sense of acute injustice, the readiness to protest, and the need for [government] repression to suppress that protest (as well as any concrete exposure of what was happening)."[27]

Military Is Best Able to Maintain Stability

A third myth associated with military regimes is that they are better able than their civilian counterparts to maintain stability.[28] Militaries control and are trained in the use of the instruments of violence in society and are theoretically capable of ensuring stability by force. Even if one assumes that militaries are well-positioned in the short term to take power and provide some semblance of stability, over time the military finds itself discredited and prone to the same types of attacks experienced by its civilian predecessors. The inherent problem associated with military rule is that long-term stability is not based on the military officer's natural tendency to ensure compliance through the use of force but on the civilian politician's ability to create political compacts through the use of political bargaining. Political understandings imposed and maintained by the barrel of the gun are destined to fail.

The Ethiopian military regime (1974–91) headed by Mengistu offers important insights into the inability of military-based regimes to maintain stability over the long term.[29] The primary pillar of Mengistu's dictatorship was one of the African continent's largest and best-equipped standing armies. By the end of the 1980s, over 500,000 troops maintained an impressive and extremely lethal military arsenal that included sophisticated fighter aircraft and thousands of tanks and other armored personnel carriers. However, the regime's reliance on force to promote its narrow political vision fostered the emergence and growing strength of antigovernment guerrilla insurgencies. A northern secessionist insurgency was led by the Eritrean People's Liberation Front (EPLF). Other, more ethnically dominated guerrilla groups included the Tigrean People's Liberation Front (TPLF) and the Oromo Liberation Front (OLF). Together, these and other guerrilla groups formed a loose coalition of opposition forces, the Ethiopian People's Revolutionary Democratic Front (EPRDF), that succeeded in overthrowing the Mengistu regime on May 25, 1991. Ultimately, the largest military organization on the African continent was incapable of maintaining stability over the long term.

Military Constitutes a Better Unifying Structure

A fourth myth promoted by military leaders is that the military is more capable than its civilian counterparts of forging a national identity.[30] This argument is based on the assumption that the military constitutes one of the few (if not the only) national organizations inherited from the colonial era that socializes new recruits into serving the state regardless of their race or ethnicity. A sense of national identity supposedly is forged due to the camaraderie associated with a common training experience, as well as the unifying mission of protecting the integrity of the state rather than serving an individual administration. In practice, however, African militaries historically have reflected the ethnic and racial divisions and conflicts of their larger societies. This shortcoming is primarily due to the tendency of the first generation of African leaders to employ recruits and officers from their personal ethnic or racial groups. The consequence of

---

A Closer Look: FEMALE GUERRILLAS AFTER THE WARS

African women have served in combat roles in several successful guerrilla insurgencies during the contemporary era. One of the earliest examples of this phenomenon was the active involvement of female guerrillas in Algeria's nationalist war for independence against France at the end of the 1950s. Several years later in 1967, the military leaders of the Front for the Liberation of Mozambique (FRELIMO) created a female combat unit that served as the precursor of widespread female involvement in the guerrilla struggle against Portuguese colonialism in Mozambique. In these and other cases, however, the expectations of female guerrillas—that the common male-female struggle for independence would translate into a common male-female struggle against gender inequality in their respective societies— were not borne out. "Time and time again, a pattern has emerged where

women play a significant role during the armed struggle," explains anthropologist Henrietta L. Moore, "but once the revolutionary government is installed, women's needs and interests fade from political agendas, and the political rhetoric fails to give rise to active programs for women's emancipation."

The evolution and aftermath of Eritrea's successful guerrilla struggle for independence from Ethiopia (1961–93) highlights evolving gender relations. The insurgency was led by the Eritrean People's Liberation Front (EPLF), which fully embraced the integration of women at all levels of the guerrilla struggle. Approximately 35 percent of the EPLF's active guerrilla fighters were women at the time of military victory in 1991. When the victorious guerrilla units marched into the capital on May 24, the female soldiers were reported to have been "treated with awe." "Teenage girls began to imitate their distinctive style," explained one account, "growing their neat-plaited corn-rows into a wilder Afro hairstyle, swapping traditional dresses for men's trousers and volunteering for military training."

The EPLF actively promoted gender equality during the civil war. The guerrilla organization sponsored the formation of the National Union of Eritrean Women (NUEW), a national organization designed to promote women's rights, and passed a series of gender-related laws. In all areas controlled by the TPLF, "bride prices" (dowries) were outlawed, the age of consent to marriage was raised to 18, and it became legal for women to own property. In 1977, the EPLF also began to permit marriages between guerrilla fighters in forward operational areas, leading to a dramatic increase in the number of "guerrilla marriages."

With the end of the guerrilla struggle, the government's decision to demobilize, especially the female guerrilla fighters, served as but one issue of a renewed national debate over the proper role of women in Eritrean society. Demobilized female guerrillas found themselves returning to a civilian world dominated by traditional images of women as inferior to men and primarily responsible for family and home. This clash of gender images resulted in a divorce rate of at least 50 percent for the guerrilla marriages that took place in the field. "Women fighters say many of their male colleagues have buckled under family pressure to divorce their soldier wives for younger—and preferably virgin—brides," explained one report. "The women face tremendous pressure to leave the army and stay at home with the children."

Amair Adhana, a former guerrilla fighter who joined the TPLF at age 14 and became a journalist after demobilization, is critical of government policies. "In the field, the men respected us—our brains, our strength—but in this society of ours, they now respect make-up, nice hair, being a proper housewife. . . . If we kneel down now to what they want, we'll end up back in the kitchen." It is precisely for this reason that several former female guerrillas founded the Eritrean Women War Veterans Association, which aids women in the process of achieving financial independence. "We need to change laws and ways of thinking," concludes Adhana. "This new fight is only beginning."

Quotations are from "Eritrea: Changing the Status of Women," *WIN News* 21, no. 2 (1995): 52, and "The Kitchen Calls: Eritrea," *The Economist* 331, no. 7869 (June 25, 1994). See also Meredeth Turshen and Clotilde Twagiramariya, eds., *What Women Do in Wartime: Gender and Conflict in Africa* (New York: St. Martin's, 1998).

biased recruitment patterns is that African militaries in actuality promote societal competition and conflict, in the extreme leading to the breakdown of central authority along ethnic or racial lines.

The military dictatorship established in Liberia in 1980 by Master Sergeant Doe is an example of how African militaries become the focal points of ethnic conflict and contribute to ethnic fragmentation. After leading a military coup against the popularly hated government of President William Tolbert, Doe ordered the purging of "distrustful" ethnic groups and their replacement with officers and recruits from his own Krahn ethnic group.[31] The ethnic tensions that resulted from the Krahn's newfound political status were aggravated in 1985 by further purges. In response to an attempted military coup primarily associated with the Mano and Gio ethnic groups, the Krahn-dominated military expelled their remaining numbers from the military and subsequently carried out "brutal assaults" against the Mano and Gio civilian populations.[32] The rising spiral of ethnic violence intensified in 1990, when the Doe regime was overthrown by the National Patriotic Front of Liberia (NPFL), a guerrilla army primarily composed of fighters from the Gio and Mano ethnic groups and led by Charles Taylor. An Interim Government of National Unity (IGNU) broke down amidst conflict between Taylor's NPFL and other ethnically dominated guerrilla armies, most notably the United Liberation Movement of Liberia (ULIMO), which drew its support from the Krahn and Mandingo ethnic groups. Seven years of civil war ended in July 1997, when the country's first democratic elections resulted in Charles Taylor and his New Patriotic Party (NPP) assuming the presidency.

Military Is Best Prepared to Promote Development

A final myth often promoted by military leaders is that the military is better qualified than its civilian leaders to promote economic development.[33] According to this argument, African militaries, unlike other national institutions, such as political parties, are the best trained in using modern technology and therefore are presumably the best prepared to harness this technology for the overall modernization of the national economy. The primary problem with this view is that an ability to use technology for destructive purposes does not automatically translate into an ability to use technology to promote economic development. Indeed, according to the logic promoted by military leaders, the reverse of their argument should also hold true: Civilian managers trained in advanced technology in the civilian economy should be well prepared to manage the use of such technology in combat situations. The obvious response of military leaders to such an argument, of course, is to note the "special" characteristics associated with being a military officer and leading troops into battle.

The debate over whether military or civilian governments have more successfully promoted development has been the subject of numerous statistical studies.[34] One conclusion of these studies is that military-dominated regimes tend to increase military budgets and the size and technological capabilities of their respective militaries. The statistics also demonstrate that military regimes at best fare no better, and usually slightly worse, than their civilian counterparts in ensuring expanding gross national products (GNPs), greater levels of domestic investment, and higher levels of exports. It is widely accepted that these two trends are not only related but mutually reinforcing: The military's tendency to divert scarce national resources to expanding military establishments constitutes at least one reason for the poor economic performance of military regimes. It is important to note, however, that 40 years of comparative evidence does not conclusively suggest the greater effectiveness of civilian regimes. As suggested by Robin Luckham, a specialist of the role of the military in African politics and society, perhaps only one general pattern exists: "So far, *neither* military nor civilian governments have been able to resolve the development crises facing African states."[35]

DEMILITARIZATION AND
TRANSITIONS TO CIVILIAN RULE

The common assumption of African public opinion is that civilian-dominated political systems constitute the proper norm of civil–military relations. Even military leaders intent on maintaining themselves in power are forced to offer, at minimum, rhetorical support for an eventual "return" to civilian rule, usually accompanied by some sort of specific timetable. The notion of **demilitarization,** sometimes called promoting the **civilianization** of military regimes, became increasingly important in the post-1989 era as African policymakers and pro-democracy movements sought to consolidate transitions to democracy (see Chapter 10).[36]

South Africa offers a splendid case for understanding the process of demilitarization, despite the fact that it was technically ruled by a civilian regime during the apartheid era. From its creation in 1948 to its ultimate demise in 1994, the apartheid system, based on separation of the races and a white minority's political domination of a black majority, maintained itself in power through the widespread militarization of South African society.[37] The South African Defense Force (SADF) doubled in size to 85,000 soldiers from 1975 to 1989 and could count on nearly 400,000 reserve forces that had received military training. The SADF also oversaw the military training of white children in a cadet program that expanded from 56,000 members in 1975 to 250,000 in 1987. Even the South African Police, which exceeded over 100,000 officers in 1994, received extensive military training and maintained a large arsenal of military equipment, including tanks and armored personnel carriers. The primary purpose of this militarized security apparatus was to prevent the emergence of a black majority-ruled regime led by the African National Congress (ANC) and its guerrilla allies.

The historic transition in 1994 to a multiracial democratic system headed by Nelson Mandela, the leader of the ANC who spent nearly three decades (1962–91) in apartheid prisons, represented the worst-case scenario for at least some of the senior white officers in the SADF and other security-related offices of the former apartheid state. As a result, numerous commentators publicly worried whether elements of the SADF and its allies would seek to derail the transition process by organizing a military coup against the last apartheid-era government of F. W. DeKlerk, who agreed to cede power after losing the elections of 1994. Although fears of a military coup proved unfounded, the Mandela administration confronted the difficult task of assuming control over a racist security apparatus that once was devoted to using all legal and illegal means to keep the ANC from assuming power. One of the Mandela administration's most delicate tasks has been to oversee a demilitarization process designed to restore civilian control over a security apparatus that had become too powerful in the formulation of South African domestic and foreign policies.[38]

The Mandela administration's initial success in demilitarizing highlights the prospects and dilemmas associated with similar programs throughout Africa. One conclusion revolves around the timing of negotiations.[39] Specifically, agreement over the military's future role in the domestic political system should be sought during the transition process. The logic behind this simple element of democratic transitions is that failure to reach agreement on a demilitarization process leaves in place "nonreformed and possibly disloyal" security forces that may seek to undermine the new political order.[40] It is imperative to seek agreement "when previous government officials who are committed to change have not been completely delegitimized and still have some influence and leverage over the state security apparatus."[41]

In South Africa, the military leaders of the apartheid regime and the ANC outlined the structure and missions of the new South African National Defence Force (SANDF) before the presidential elections of 1994.[42] A clandestine agreement was reached between the old SADF and Umkhonto we Sizwe, the military wing of the ANC, after negotiations at Simonstown, South Africa, in April 1993.[43] The negotiations and the agreement were critical to the success of the transition process, especially in terms of dispelling any doubts concerning the loyalty of the largely white SADF. "What is remarkable," explains William Gutteridge, a specialist of the South African military, "is that the military, in spite of their more direct antagonism [toward Mandela and the ANC government], had by the time the election took place in April 1994 gone further in preparing the future than any other department of the state."[44]

A second conclusion drawn from the South African case is the importance of clearly outlining the exact nature of civil-military relations in a popularly accepted constitutional document.[45] Democratic mechanisms for ensuring civilian oversight of the military must be created, including a civilian-managed ministry of defense, civilian control of the military budget, and ultimate approval of senior promotions and professional training.[46] The South African constitution even stipulates that the South African security forces, including the South African Defense Force, "must teach and require their members to act in accordance with the Constitution and the law, including customary international law and international agreements binding on the [South African] Republic" (Art. 5, Para. 6). It is important to recognize, however, that constitutions merely establish the guidelines of civil-military relations. The true test of the demilitarization process is the actual application of constitutional principles.

A third conclusion that can be drawn from the South African case is that the military must reflect the ethnic and racial diversity of the country's population. This commonsense approach was the hallmark of a series of regional conferences on civil-military relations held in Burundi (1993), Benin (1995), Mozambique (1996), and Sierra Leone (1997), that were jointly sponsored by the African-American Institute (AAI) and the U.S. Agency for International Development.[47] This lesson was particularly challenging in the South African context due to the necessity of integrating previously opposed military forces into a unified SANDF, including 85,000 SADF soldiers, 30,000 guerrilla fighters from Umkhonto we Sizwe, 6,000 guerrilla fighters from the Azanian People's Liberation Army (the military wing of the Pan-African Congress, PAC), and 7,000 soldiers from four black "homelands" created by the apartheid state.[48] Despite early tensions over salaries and ranks, particularly among the newly integrated Umkhonto we Sizwe forces, the SANDF serves as a model for integrating previously opposed military forces.[49]

A fourth conclusion, centering on the desire to trim oversized defense budgets and standing armies, applies particularly to countries attempting to consolidate democracy in the aftermath of civil conflict.[50] Although logic demands demobilization of both guerrilla fighters and the national army to focus scarce resources on promoting socioeconomic development, practical political concerns often call for the expansion of the national military. In the short term, it is more important to first establish a unified national army that includes former guerrillas and standing armies than to disenfranchise any given group. In the transition to an inclusive democracy, one is better off maintaining once-opposed troops in a newly unified command.

In South Africa, the competing goals of long-term socioeconomic development and short-term political-military stability were resolved in favor of the latter. Joe Modise, a former guerrilla commander of Umkhonto we Sizwe and Minister of Defense under the Mandela administration, underscored his intention to maintain an oversized SANDF of at least 70,000 soldiers. As succinctly noted by South African President Thabo Mbeki, "We could hardly take 30,000 combatants from the ANC and throw them on the streets."[51] Like their counterparts from other portions of the SANDF, these guerrilla fighters were "proud of their role" in the struggle to create a multiracial and democratic South Africa and understandably "wanted to keep their jobs in an economy where unemployment is high."[52]

The greatest threat of the demilitarization process, of course, is that previously powerful militaries return to their barracks but remain poised for reintervention. The evolving threat of military coups to African politics and society is clearly illustrated in Figure 9.2. In contrast to the 1960s, when the number of military coups reached its peak, the first 3 years (2000–02) of this century have witnessed a sharp decline in successful military coups. This trend may suggest

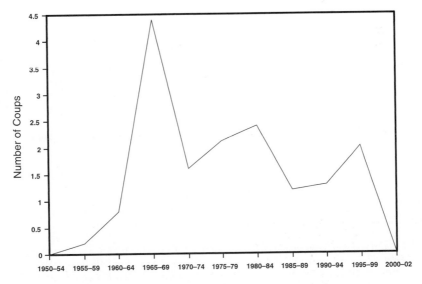

FIGURE 9.2 Incidence of Military Coups (Five-Year Averages, 1950–2002)

the declining importance of military intervention due to the growing strength of democratic transitions in the post–cold war era. Recall, however, that the transition to independent civilian governments during the 1950s ultimately stalled, only to be followed by an explosion of coups that made the 1960s the **decade of the military.** In this regard, the only permanent solution to the demilitarization dilemma will be the strengthening of democratic cultures where military elites are socialized into serving and protecting the supremacy of civilian democratic rule.

KEY TERMS

military coup d'état
men on horseback
leaders in khaki
military plots
coups of descending order
palace coup
contagion effect
spectrum of civil-military relations
civilian supremacy model

watchdog model
balance wheel model
direct rule model
social transformation model
revolution from above
bloodless coup
demilitarization
civilianization
decade of the military

FOR FURTHER READING

Assensoh, A. B., and Yvette Alex-Assensoh. *African Military History and Politics: Coups and Ideological Incursions, 1900–Present.* New York: Palgrave, 2001.

Bienen, Henry. *Armies and Parties in Africa.* New York: Africana, 1978.

Decalo, Samuel. *Coups and Army Rule in Africa: Motivations and Constraints* (2nd ed.). New Haven: Yale University Press, 1990.

Decalo, Samuel. *The Stable Minority: Civilian Rule in Africa, 1960–1990.* Gainesville: Florida Academic, 1998.

Edgerton, Robert B. *Africa's Armies: From Honor to Infamy.* Boulder: Westview, 2002.

Foltz, William J., and Henry S. Bienen, eds. *Arms and the African: Military Influences on Africa's International Relations.* New Haven: Yale University Press, 1985.

Frazer, Jendayi. "Conceptualizing Civil-Military Relations during Democratic Transition." *Africa Today* 42, no. 1–2 (1995): 39–48.

Harbeson, John B., ed. *The Military in African Politics.* New York: Praeger, 1987.

Hills, Alice. *Policing Africa: Internal Security and the Limits of Liberalization.* Boulder: Lynne Rienner, 2000.

Howe, Herbert M. *Ambiguous Order: Military Forces in African States.* Boulder: Lynne Rienner, 2001.

Khadiagala, Gilbert M. "The Military in Africa's Democratic Transitions: Regional Dimensions." *Africa Today* 42, no. 1–2 (1995): 61–74.

Liebenow, J. Gus. "The Military Factor in African Politics: A Twenty-Five-Year Perspective." In Gwendolen M. Carter and Patrick O'Meara, eds. *African Independence: The First Twenty-Five Years.*

Bloomington: Indiana University Press, 1985. pp. 126–59.

Luckham, Robin. "The Military, Militarization, and Democratization in Africa: A Survey of Literature and Issues." *African Studies Review* 37 (1994): 13–76.

McGowan, Pat, and Thomas H. Johnson. "African Military Coups d'État and Underdevelopment: A Quantitative Historical Analysis." *The Journal of Modern African Studies* 22, no. 4 (1984): 633–66.

McGowan, Pat, and Thomas H. Johnson. "Sixty Coups in Thirty Years: Further Evidence regarding African Military Coups d'État." *The Journal of Modern African Studies* 24, no. 3 (1986): 539–46.

Nyang'oro, Julius E. "National Security and Defense Expenditure in Africa: A Political and Economic Analysis." *Africa Development* 17, no. 4 (1992): 5–28.

Odetola, Olatunde. *Military Regimes and Development: A Comparative Analysis of African Societies.* London: George Allen and Unwin, 1982.

Onwumechili, Chuka. *African Democratization and Military Coups.* New York: Praeger, 1998.

Pateman, Roy. "Intelligence Agencies in Africa: A Preliminary Assessment." *The Journal of Modern African Studies* 30, no. 4 (1992): 569–86.

Turshen, Meredeth, and Clotilde Twagiramariya, eds. *What Women Do in Wartime: Gender and Conflict in Africa.* New York: St. Martin's, 1998.

NOTES

1. For a listing of personnel strengths and military equipment of African militaries during this period, see William G. Thom, "Sub-Saharan Africa's Changing Military Environment," *Armed Forces and Society* 11, no. 1 (1984): 34–38.

2. The countries were Benin, Congo, Sudan, Togo, and Zaire. See J. Gus Liebenow, "The Military Factor in African Politics: A Twenty-Five-Year Perspective," in Gwendolen M. Carter and Patrick O'Meara, eds., *African Independence: The First Twenty-Five Years* (Bloomington: Indiana University Press, 1985), p. 127.

3. See Patrick J. McGowan, "African Military *Coups d'État,* 1956–2001: Frequency, Trends and Distribution" unpublished paper which was provided by the author. See also Pat McGowan and Thomas H. Johnson, "African Military Coups d'État and Underdevelopment: A Quantitative Analysis," *The Journal of Modern African Studies* 22, no. 4 (1984): 634–35, and Pat McGowan and Thomas H. Johnson. "Sixty Coups in Thirty Years: Further Evidence regarding

African Military Coups d'État." *The Journal of Modern African Studies* 24, no. 3 (1986): 539–46.

4. For example, see Richard P. Y. Li and William R. Thompson, "The 'Coup Contagion' Hypothesis," *Journal of Conflict Resolution* 19, no. 1 (1975): 63–88.

5. J. Gus Liebenow, *African Politics: Crises and Challenges* (Bloomington: Indiana University Press, 1986), pp. 237–66.

6. Ibid., p. 251.

7. See James J. Zaffiro, "Foreign Policymaking in an African Democracy: Evolution of Structures and Processes," in Stephen John Stedman, ed., *Botswana: The Political Economy of Democratic Development* (Boulder: Lynne Rienner, 1993), pp. 154–55.

8. See Liebenow, *African Politics,* pp. 251–52.

9. See Michael Bratton and Nicolas van de Walle, *Democratic Experiments in Africa: Regime Transitions in Comparative Perspective* (Cambridge: Cambridge University Press, 1997), pp. 212–13.

10. See Liebenow, *African Politics,* p. 252.

11. See J. Gus Liebenow, *Liberia: The Quest for Democracy* (Bloomington: Indiana University Press, 1987), pp. 197–211.

12. Ibid.

13. Ibid.

14. Liebenow, *African Politics,* p. 252.

15. See Larry Diamond, "Nigeria: The Uncivic Society and the Descent into Praetorianism," in Larry Diamond, Juan J. Linz, and Seymour Martin Lipset, eds., *Politics in Developing Countries: Comparing Experiences with Democracy* (Boulder: Lynne Rienner, 1995), pp. 417–91.

16. Liebenow, *African Politics,* p. 252.

17. See Edmond J. Keller, *Revolutionary Ethiopia: From Empire to People's Republic* (Bloomington: Indiana University Press, 1988), and John W. Harbeson, *The Ethiopian Transformation: The Quest for the Postimperial State* (Boulder: Westview, 1988).

18. Liebenow, *African Politics,* pp. 255–64.

19. Ibid., pp. 255–56.

20. See I. M. Lewis, "The Politics of the 1969 Coup," *The Journal of Modern African Studies* 10, no. 3 (1972): 383–408.

21. Liebenow, *African Politics,* pp. 254–55.

22. Ibid., p. 255.

23. Diamond, "Nigeria: The Uncivic Society," pp. 442–64.

24. Ibid., p. 444.

25. Ibid., p. 449.

26. Ibid., pp. 449–50.

27. Ibid., p. 450.

28. Liebenow, *African Politics,* p. 257.

29. Edmond Keller, "Remaking the Ethiopian State," in I. William Zartman, ed., *Collapsed States: The Disintegration and Restoration of Legitimate Authority* (Boulder: Lynne Rienner, 1995), pp. 125–39. See also Edmond Keller, *Revolutionary Ethiopia: From Empire to People's Republic* (Bloomington: Indiana University Press, 1988).

30. Liebenow, *African Politics,* pp. 257–60.

31. See Martin Lowenkopf, "Liberia: Putting the State Back Together Again," in Zartman, *Collapsed States,* pp. 91–108.

32. Ibid., p. 92.

33. Liebenow, *African Politics,* pp. 261–64.

34. For an introduction, see John Ravenhill, "Comparing Regime Performance in Africa: Limitations of Cross-National Aggregate Analysis," *The Journal of Modern African Studies* 18, no. 1 (1980): 99–126, K. Gyimah-Brempong, "Defense Spending and Economic Growth in Sub-Saharan Africa: An Econometric Investigation," *Journal of Peace Research* 26, no. 1 (1989): 79–90.

35. Robin Luckham, "The Military, Militarization, and Democratization in Africa: A Survey of Literature and Issues," *African Studies Review* 37, no. 2 (1994): 52.

36. See William Gutteridge, "Undoing Military Coups in Africa," *Third World Quarterly* 7, no. 1 (1985): 78–89. See also Michael Chege, "The Military in the Transition to Democracy in Africa: Some Preliminary Observations," *CODESRIA Bulletin* 3 (1995): 13.

37. For an overview, see Neta C. Crawford, "South Africa's New Foreign and Military Policy: Opportunities and Constraints," *Africa Today* 42, no. 1–2 (1995): 88–121. See also Jacklyn Cock and Laurie Nathan, eds., *Society at War: The Militarization of South Africa* (New York: St. Martin's, 1989).

38. See Nelson Mandela, "South Africa's Future Foreign Policy," *Foreign Affairs* 72, no. 5 (1993): 86–97.

39. For discussion, see Jendayi Frazer, "Conceptualizing Civil-Military Relations during Democratic Transition," *Africa Today* 42, no. 1–2 (1995): 42–44.

40. Ibid., p. 43.

41. Ibid.

42. See Crawford, "South Africa's New Foreign and Military Policy," pp. 89, 101.

43. Norma Kriger and Patrick Bond, "Negotiations and the Military in South Africa," *Africa Today* 42, no. 1–2 (1995): 125.

44. Quoted in Kriger and Bond, "Negotiations and the Military," p. 129.

45. See William J. Foltz, "Officer Politicians," *Africa Report* 38, no. 3 (May–June 1993): 66.

46. See Bratton and van de Walle, *Democratic Experiments,* p. 245.

47. See in particular two early reports published by AAI: *The Bujumbura Conference. Democratization in Africa: The Role of the Military. Bujumbura, Burundi, February 1–4, 1993* (New York: AAI, 1993) and *Democratization in Africa: The Role of the Military. Report of the Second Regional Conference. The African-American Institute. Cotonou, Benin* (New York: AAI, 1995). Reports were not published for the latter two conferences.

48. Crawford, "South Africa's New Foreign and Military Policy," p. 90.

49. See Kriger and Bond, "Negotiations and the Military," pp. 128–32.

50. See Donald Rothchild, "On Implementing Africa's Peace Accords: From Defection to Cooperation," *Africa Today* 42, no. 1–2 (1995): 8–38, and Kimberly Mahling Clark, "The Demobilization and Reintegration of Soldiers: Perspectives from USAID," *Africa Today* 42, no. 1–2 (1995): 49–60.

51. Quoted in ibid., p. 101.

52. Ibid.

10

ᴧᴧᴧ

Democratic Experiments and Multiparty Politics

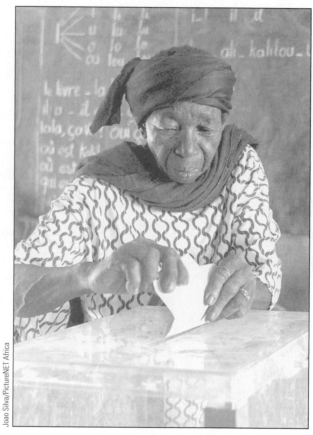

Joao Silva/PictureNET Africa

A woman voting in Mali's 2002 presidential elections.

OZENS OF COUNTRIES in Africa, Asia, Latin America, and Eastern and Southern Europe transitioned from authoritarian to democratic forms of governance during the last quarter of the twentieth century. This global trend has prompted proponents of democracy to speak of the **third wave of democratization** in world history (the first two waves began in the 1820s and the 1940s).[1] In the case of Africa, this third wave was sparked by the fall of the Berlin Wall in 1989. The collapse of single-party regimes throughout Eastern Europe and the former Soviet Union set powerful precedents for African pro-democracy activists who had already begun organizing against human rights abuses and political repression. Severe economic stagnation and decline in most African economies served as the internal spark for political discontent. The most notable outcome of this historic turning point, often called **Africa's second independence** or **Africa's second liberation,** was the discrediting of more than 30 years of experimentation with single-party political systems in favor of more democratic forms of governance based on multiparty politics and the protection of human rights. This chapter is devoted to exploring the evolution of the rich and varied forms of democratic experimentation that are presently unfolding throughout the African continent.[2]

ESTABLISHMENT OF SINGLE-PARTY POLITICAL SYSTEMS

The political frameworks bequeathed to the African continent at the beginning of the contemporary independence era embodied an **authoritarian-democratic paradox** in which African leaders, educated in authoritarianism during the colonial era, were expected to perform like seasoned experts in democracy. Despite their almost complete disregard for the promotion of democratic values during the colonial era, departing colonial administrators hastily constructed political arrangements that purported to embody Western democratic ideals, such as **systems of checks-and-balances,** in which offices of the president, legislatures, and judiciaries would balance each other's power and prevent the emergence of authoritarianism. The relatively decentralized **Westminster model** of parliamentary governance was grafted onto the authoritarian structures of colonial rule in the former British colonies, and the more centralized **Elysée model** was similarly introduced into France's former colonies.[3] For the most part, however, the so-called democracies left behind by the departing colonial powers represented largely untested and ill-suited political practices and procedures that in any case were not grounded in African traditions or political cultures.

Except in the unique case of Botswana, the first generation of African leadership resolved this paradox of independence by replacing the political systems left behind by the former colonial powers with more authoritarian forms of governance based on a centralization of power and personal rule.[4] Even the most principled of African leaders turned to a variety of authoritarian measures to enhance their political power and ensure political survival at the expense of competing political interests. Among those actions taken were the:

- Staffing of bureaucracies, militaries, and police forces with members of the leader's ethnic or clan groups, as well as with those of their principal ethnic or clan allies

- Rejection of "federalist" arrangements, such as constitutional amendments, that allowed for the political autonomy of groups or regions based on ethnic, linguistic, or religious claims

- Marginalization or even disbanding of independent parliaments and judiciaries that at best became "rubber stamp" organizations incapable of serving as a check on the powers of the executive

- Imprisonment or exile of vocal critics from civil society, including women's groups, labor unions, student organizations, and religious groups

- Outlawing of rival political parties (see Chapter 8)

The creation of **single-party political systems** constituted the most significant political act undertaken by African leaders during the contemporary independence era.[5] These parties ranged from Chama Cha Mapinduzi (CCM), a mass-mobilizing party created by Julius Nyerere, the former socialist leader of Tanzania, to the Workers Party of Ethiopia (WPE), a vanguard party created by Mengistu Haile Mariam, the former Marxist leader of Ethiopia, and the Kenya African National Union (KANU), the sole ruling party of capitalist-oriented Kenya that was created by former President Jomo Kenyatta and strengthened by his successor, Daniel arap Moi (see Chapter 6). In short, regardless of their political ideology, nearly all African leaders exhibited authoritarian tendencies that resulted in the creation of single-party political systems.[6]

African leaders offered numerous rationales to justify the establishment of political monopolies over their political systems.[7] The first justification was that single-party systems reflected traditional African political systems as they existed before the imposition of direct colonial rule.[8] According to this argument, the single-party system was not to be perceived as a "temporary aberration" from a universal norm of multiparty democracy but rather as a "modern adaptation of traditional African political behavior."[9] Unlike the divisive nature of Western multiparty systems in which one party emerges dominant and the others are marginalized, the concept of single-party democracy was heralded as conducive to promoting the traditional African norm of **consensus building** in which all participants have the right to voice their opinions and decisions are made only when agreed on by all present. It is for precisely this reason that Tanzanian President Nyerere chose ujamaa (the Kiswahili term for brotherhood) as the symbolic guiding principle of the CCM and his country's "return" to traditional African socialism.[10]

A second rationale for creating single-party systems was the imperative of responding to existing crises of development. African leaders argued against "wasting" scarce resources on competitive politics when their countries were confronted with crises of development ("How can we quickly develop our society?"), crises of administration ("How do we quickly educate the required leaders?"), and crises of governance ("How do we quickly satisfy rising popular demands for the fruits of independence?").[11] Just as unity was crucial to the attainment of independence, argued those who led the nationalist struggles during the 1950s, so too was unity important once that independence had been achieved. Equally important, African leaders feared that multiparty systems would foster the fragmentation of ethnically diverse African societies and therefore perceived the single-party system as one of the most important tools for transforming colonially inspired, artificial states into true nations.

A third rationale, offered especially by African leaders from the Marxist tradition, underscored the **vanguard role** that single parties were expected to play. Drawing on the Leninist concept that the "masses" of individual African societies needed to be led by an "enlightened elite," the single party was envisioned as serving to protect and promote Marxist revolutions on the African continent.[12] The single party was particularly oriented toward the future evolution of African societies, especially in terms of ensuring industrial development and the promotion of basic human needs, such as guaranteed access to adequate food, shelter, and health care.

The nearly 30-year experiment with single-party rule achieved few positive results.[13] Even in the most benevolent of examples, such as Nyerere's ujamaa experiment in Tanzania, the country made significant strides in promoting mass literacy and the provision of basic human needs only at the expense of a failed overall economy that witnessed an annual average decline of 7 percent in agricultural output. One of the primary reasons for this failure was that the initially voluntary villagization program, the centerpiece of the ujamaa development strategy in which peasants were grouped in new communal villages, ultimately became coercive. Many peasants were forced to move from their traditional lands to village projects that were either poorly conceived or simply inappropriate for farming practices. If the state inevitably became coercive and therefore counterproductive to the goal of development in the most benevolent of single-party systems, one has only to imagine its impact on the development of the most authoritarian single-party systems, such as the Marxist-inspired tyranny created in Mengistu's Ethiopia.

The most notable problem associated with the single-party experiment of Tanzania and its contemporaries was that it led to a stagnation of ideas. For example, although Tanzanian legislative candidates were allowed to run against each other under the unified banner of the CCM, they were not permitted to question the socialist ideology of the Nyerere regime. Candidates could debate how best to carry out party-approved policies but were unable to offer alternatives to misguided policies. In this and other cases, African leaders who felt they "knew best" restricted the range of political debate to such a degree that the single party ultimately became a means for maintaining control rather than a dynamic tool for promoting change and development.

The growing stagnation of single-party rule from the 1950s to the end of the 1980s was matched by the growing power and influence of African militaries and African military leaders (see Chapter 9). The sharp increase in military coups d'état led to the replacement of entrenched civilian leaders with their military counterparts and became one of the most important forms of regime change in African politics during the initial decades of the contemporary independence era. Most important, the emergence of military leaders as power brokers in African presidential mansions and parliaments did not usher in a new period of democracy and prosperity but instead led to new forms of military-led authoritarianism as bad as, if not worse than, their civilian counterparts.

POLITICAL TRANSITION
AND EXPERIMENTATION WITH
MULTIPARTY POLITICS

The downfall of single-party communist systems throughout Eastern Europe and the former Soviet Union beginning in 1989 sent shock waves throughout the African continent.[14] The rejection of single-party rule in its intellectual heartland ensured that African leaders could no longer justify the continuation of this model on the African continent. "If the owners of socialism have withdrawn from the one-party system," proclaimed Frederick Chiluba, the leader of the Zambian prodemocracy movement and future president of Zambia,

---

A Closer Look: NONPARTY SYSTEMS? UGANDA'S "MOVEMENT DEMOCRACY"

Uganda has successfully avoided the multiparty demands of the "third wave" of democratization in Africa by establishing and expanding a **nonparty system,** which its supporters call **movement democracy.** This unique brand of political system was inspired by the political thought of Yoweri Kaguta Museveni, whose guerrilla movement, the National Resistance Army (NRA), assumed power in 1986.

The defining characteristic of movement democracy is the suspension of any political party involvement in local and national elections. The political system is instead based on **mass participatory democracy** in which all citizens are members of the national movement and therefore eligible to vote; all forms of "sectarianism," including ethnically, religiously, and regionally based differences are eliminated, and human rights are supported. Although originally inspired by Marxist economic strategies, Museveni has emerged as one of Africa's most fervent supporters of free-market capitalism.

The administrative structure of movement democracy is a series of councils known as Local Committees that, at the individual village level, are composed of representatives directly elected by citizens of the village. Each successive, higher level of council, including the parish, the county, and finally the district, is composed of representatives elected by the previous level of governance. The political system therefore embodies a pyramidal structure, the top of which is dominated by Museveni. This system of governance was widely legitimized in presidential elections in 1996 and 2001, in which Museveni won 75 and 69 percent of the popular vote, respectively. In addition, a referendum held later in 2001 resulted in a 88 percent vote in favor of continuing the non-party system, although only 51 percent of the electorate turned out to vote.

The simple and understandable reason for these victories, according to J. Oloka-Onyango, a Ugandan scholar, is that Museveni delivered on his pledge of building a "lasting sense" of peace and security out of political and economic chaos. From 1962 to 1986, hundreds of thousands of Ugandans died under the dictatorial abuses of Apollo Milton Obote and Major General Idi Amin, the latter of whom embodies the dubious distinction of having led one of Africa's most tyrannical regimes. By the beginning of the 1980s, Uganda had become economically chaotic: Smuggling, magendo (black marketeering), and triple-digit inflation dominated a failing national economy. "In the event that some might have forgotten this, the NRM (National Resistance Movement) used the image of skulls . . . and the sound of gunshots in its electoral campaign advertising," explains Oloka-Onyango. "The message was simple: A vote

against Museveni was a vote for a reversion to the chaos of the past."

Despite Museveni's victory in the 1996 and 2001 presidential elections, his concept of movement democracy is being challenged on several fronts. First, as the pre-1986 era becomes increasingly distant in the collective memory of the Ugandan people, the demands of opposition politicians for the restoration of multiparty politics is gaining popularity. Like the concerns voiced by critics of the single-party systems that dominated the African landscape from the 1950s to the 1980s, opposition politicians claim that Museveni's movement democracy stifles debate and therefore runs the risk of ultimately becoming the means for maintaining control, rather than a dynamic tool for promoting change and development.

The most significant long-term challenge, however, is that the survival of movement democracy inherently depends on the continued vitality of Museveni himself. "The movement system has failed to institutionalize mechanisms of governance distinct from the personality of Museveni," explains Oloka-Onyango. "The success of the Ugandan experiment will be sealed only if it can extricate itself from reliance on a single individual." If history is any guide, personalized political systems such as Uganda's movement democracy rarely, if ever, survive the death of the political leader.

Quotations are from J. Oloka-Onyango, "Uganda's 'Benevolent' Dictatorship," *Current History* 96, no. 610 (1997) 212–16. See also Nelson Kasfir, "'No-Party Democracy' in Uganda," *Journal of Democracy* 9, no. 2 (1998): 49–63, and Yoweri Kaguta Museveni, *Sowing the Mustard Seed: The Struggle for Freedom and Democracy in Uganda* (London: Macmillan, 1997).

"who are the Africans to continue with it?"[15] Equally important, authoritarian leaders could no longer use cold war rhetoric as the means for ensuring super-power attention and therefore the financial and military support necessary to prevent opposition movements from taking power; the Soviet Union had ceased to exist and a new Russian regime preoccupied with domestic economic restructuring had largely withdrawn from the African continent, while the United States and its Western allies were increasingly prone to link African support for democratization and economic liberalization to future commitments of foreign assistance and preferential trade agreements (see Chapter 12).

The emergence of a Western consensus in favor of promoting democratic principles coincided with the rise of increasingly vocal and powerful African pro-democracy movements. Popular protests and demands for political reform often emerged as a response to the intensification of government-sponsored political repression and human rights abuses throughout the 1980s. This trend peaked in 1991, when a total of eighty-six popular protests were recorded in thirty African countries.[16] Protestors were emboldened by the adoption of continent-wide human rights norms, which was confirmed by the ratification of the African Charter of Human and Peoples' Rights by the majority of African countries at the beginning of the 1990s. Protesters were also driven by the severe deterioration of African economies that made it difficult for individual families, already perilously close to abject poverty, to acquire basic foodstuffs and other necessities of day-to-day living.[17]

The convergence of these domestic and international trends resulted in a period of democratic transition previously unknown in African history. Whereas many of these experiments resulted in the replacement of single-party systems with more inclusive forms of multiparty politics, several potential transitions to democracy have either stalled, are being co-opted, or have been completely derailed by authoritarian leaders intent upon maintaining power. Indeed, the range of political change that has occurred in Africa since 1989 is best characterized as a spectrum of political transition, ranging from the peaceful replacement of incumbent leaders via multiparty elections at one extreme to a complete breakdown in the transition process and the unfolding of civil war at the other. At least six types of political transition have unfolded on the African continent in the post-1989 era (see Figure 10.1).[18]

Change via Multiparty Elections

The impact on Africa of the third wave of democratization is demonstrated by the dramatic expansion of **multiparty competition** in African political systems from 1990 to 1994.[19] During the preceding 5-year period (1985–89), truly competitive elections were held in only five African countries: Botswana, Gambia, Mauritius, Senegal, and Zimbabwe. From 1990 to 1994, more than

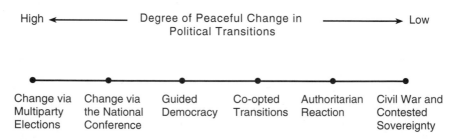

FIGURE 10.1   Spectrum of Political Transition

thirty-eight countries held competitive elections. Most important, twenty-nine of the multiparty contests of the 1990–94 era constituted **founding elections** in which "the office of the head of government is openly contested following a period during which multiparty political competition was denied."[20]

South Africa's founding election of April 26–29, 1994, serves as one of the most heralded examples of African democratic transition. For the first time, voters of all races cast ballots in free and fair elections that ushered in South Africa's first multiracial, multiethnic, and multiparty democracy. Nelson Mandela, who had spent nearly 28 years in prison under the previous apartheid system, was elected president, and the party he represents, the African National Congress (ANC), won 63 percent of the popular vote, 252 of 400 seats in the National Assembly, and a majority share of seats in seven of the nine provincial legislatures. F. W. de Klerk, the last president of the apartheid era, and his Afrikaner-based National Party (NP), which dominated South African politics from 1948 to 1994, won only 21 percent of the popular vote (82 National Assembly seats) but majority control of the legislature in the Western Cape province, which is predominantly inhabited by Afrikaners. The third most influential presidential candidate was Chief Mangosuthu Buthelezi, a prominent Zulu leader. His predominantly Zulu-based political party, the Inkatha Freedom Party (IFP), won 10 percent of the popular vote, ensuring forty seats in the National Assembly as well as a majority victory in the KwaZulu-Natal province, which is largely inhabited by the Zulu ethnic group. The fact that both the NP and the IFP won at least 10 percent each of the popular vote ensured their inclusion in a constitutionally mandated government of national unity. "From the moment the results were in and it was apparent that the ANC was to form the government, I saw my mission as one of preaching reconciliation, of binding the wounds of the country, of engendering trust and confidence," explains Nelson Mandela in his autobiography. "At every opportunity, I said all South Africans must now unite and join hands and say we are one country, one nation, one people, marching together into the future."[21]

Change via the National Conference

A second important vehicle of the transition process, which became particularly influential in francophone Africa, is the **national conference**.[22] In this scenario, a broad coalition of leaders from all sectors of society, including elders and the heads of women's organizations, ethnic and religious leaders, labor and student activists, and ruling and opposition political leaders, holds a national gathering that serves as the basis for debating the outlines of a new democratic political order. In its ideal form, such a conference builds on the traditional African concept of consensus building in which all participants have the right to voice their opinions and decisions are made only when agreed on by all members present (unlike the more widespread Western concept of majority rule).

The democratization process under the guidance of the national conference generally follows five major steps.[23] First, a broad coalition of leaders responds to a growing crisis of governance in the country by convening a national conference in the capital city. The guiding principle of this body is its self-appointed "sovereignty" (i.e., independence) from either the existing constitutional framework or any interference on the part of the ruling regime. Second, the national conference appoints a transitional government that initially seeks a dialogue with the ruling regime. Over time, however, a weakened president is either gradually robbed of his executive powers or is simply declared an illegitimate authority who no longer has the authority to lead. In either case, the president is usually reduced to a figurehead. Fourth, the national conference transforms itself into a transitional legislative body (often called the High Council) that, in turn, formally elects a prime minister who manages the transition process. Finally, the transitional government adopts a new constitution and holds legislative and presidential elections, subsequently dissolving itself on the inauguration of the newly elected democratic regime.

The strong appeal of the national conference model was primarily due to the dramatic success achieved in Benin.[24] More than 18 years of authoritarian rule under the Marxist dictatorship of Mathieu Kérékou were peacefully overcome by a 488-member national conference that lasted 10 days. During February 19–28, 1990, the national conference declared its sovereignty, provided Kérékou with political amnesty while at the same time stripping him of his official powers, and drafted a timetable that ultimately led to the successful holding of multiparty elections in 1991. The critical element that contributed to the success of this democratization process was Kérékou's peaceful acceptance of the national conference's self-declared right to take control of the political process. As observed by Jacques Mariel Nzouankeu, director of the Center for Study and Research on Plural Democracy in the Third World (CERDET), Kérékou still enjoyed the loyalty of the Beninois Armed Forces and presumably could have crushed the opposition with military force.[25] Moreover, the military elite itself constituted a potential threat to the national conference in that the transition to a civilian regime inevitably ensured a reduction in the political power of the military. Nonetheless, both Kérékou and his military officers eventually accepted the popular legitimacy of the national conference and embraced its timetable for the introduction of multiparty politics to Benin.[26]

Guided Democratization

The model of **guided democratization** is one in which an authoritarian (often military) regime that is nonetheless committed to democratization maintains tight control over the transition process. The hallmark of this model is a powerful and usually charismatic leader who, due to the lack of any major competing centers of power, can slowly institute **democratization from above** according to his own timetable and preferences.

The Ghanaian military regime of Flt. Lt. Jerry Rawlings provides a clear-cut example of the process of guided democratization.[27] Assuming power in a military coup d'état in June 1979, Rawlings led the Ghanaian Armed Forces back to the barracks in September 1979 after Dr. Hilla Limann was elected president in democratic elections. However, political corruption, economic stagnation, and popular discontent with the Limann regime prompted Rawlings to once again assume the leadership of Ghana in a coup in December 1981. Rather than returning to the barracks for a second time, Rawlings remained in power as the head of the Provisional National Defense Council (PNDC), a military-based revolutionary organ that outlawed opposition political parties and implemented its vision to economically restructure the country. The unchallenged status of the PNDC would only be altered in 1992—nearly 11 years after assuming power—when Rawlings decided that Ghana was ready for another attempt at multiparty democracy.

Rawlings oversaw a deliberately slow and measured liberalization of the Ghanaian political system that included the writing of a new constitution, the legalization of opposition political parties, the emergence of a private press, and the creation of independent national human rights organizations.[28] In multiparty presidential elections held in November 1992, a combination of popular support in the rural areas, careful planning, and strong control exerted by the ruling PNDC led to a Rawlings victory with 58.3 percent of the popular vote. Claiming that Rawlings and the PNDC had exerted "excessive control" over an inherently flawed election process, opposition leaders boycotted the legislative elections held 1 month later, thereby ensuring a sweep of the National Legislature by pro-Rawlings parties.[29] Despite the fact that electoral irregularities, most notably flawed voter registration lists reportedly favoring the incumbent government, marred the democratization process, Rawlings nonetheless emerged from the 1992 elections firmly in control of the Ghanaian political system. As was the case with other military leaders intent on promoting guided democracy from above, however, Rawlings's "toughest test" was that of "shedding the image of the radical military dictator and becoming a democratic constitutional ruler able to create a climate of tolerance."[30]

Co-Opted Transitions

A fourth scenario occurs when leaders are able to **co-opt the transition process** and maintain themselves in power despite the holding of relatively free and fair elections. The co-optation of the democratic process usually follows three major steps.[31] First, unlike the successful cases of transition by national conference, the president under this scenario is acutely aware of the precarious nature of his political rule and acts in a quick, albeit relatively peaceful, manner to preempt the democratization forces. The usual course of action is to quickly accede to opposition demands to dismantle the single-party system and to legalize all opposition parties in a new multiparty framework. Second, rather than giving the new opposition parties time to organize, and therefore present a viable and competitive alternative to the voters, "snap" elections (often to be held within months) are announced by the ruling party. In this case, the ruling party, which usually still commands a formidable organizational structure and supporters in every region of the country, advocates for the proliferation of numerous new parties so as to divide the opposition vote. Finally, during the period immediately preceding the elections, the ruling party uses its monopoly of the government-controlled print, radio, and television media to dominate the political debate. The net result is a "peaceful," albeit tainted, victory by the ruling president and party.

Multiparty elections held in Côte d'Ivoire in October 1990 offer a classic example of a ruling party's ability to peacefully co-opt the democratization process.[32] Considered by many analysts to be a "master tactician," President Félix Houphouët-Boigny "completely outmaneuvered" his country's pro-democracy movement by "promptly legalizing all political parties and acceding to their fullest demands—open presidential and legislative elections—rushing the democratic transformation before opposition leaders could expand or redefine their demands, sharpen their tactics, or properly organize for electoral contests."[33] "When some requested a delay (so they could get organized) this was rejected on the grounds of *their own* recent demonstrations for instant national elections," explains Samuel Decalo, a noted observer of the democratization process in Africa. "Election funds were allocated to all parties so they could not claim being at a disadvantage (some parties took the funds and withdrew from the elections!), and the outcome was never in doubt."[34] Deep divisions in an

---

A Closer Look: ASSESSING THE SPREAD OF DEMOCRACY IN AFRICA

A confidence in the inevitable spread of multiparty democracy is one of the bedrock principles of the liberal intellectual tradition (see Chapter 13). The expansion of African transitions to democracy in the aftermath of the end of the cold war has strengthened the liberal position and has fostered a series of efforts by foreign policy think tanks and research institutes to measure the strength of this democratization trend.

The Comparative Survey on Freedom annually published by Freedom House, a think tank in Washington, D.C., constitutes one of the most widely cited measurement projects. The survey uses a seven-point scale ("1" being the highest and "7" being the lowest) to assess two dimensions of freedom: **political rights,** such as the ability to form political organizations free from government intrusion, and **civil liberties,** such as freedom of speech and assembly. The two scores are combined to create a **freedom index,** ranging from the highest

combined positive rating of "2" to the highest combined negative rating of "14." Countries can then be grouped into three categories: (1) democratic: high degree of freedom (2–5 points); (2) partially democratic: medium degree of freedom (6–10 points); (3) undemocratic: low degree of freedom (11–14 points).

According to the Freedom House survey results for 2002, 21 percent (eleven countries) of Africa's political systems are democratic, whereas 41 percent (twenty-two countries) are partially democratic and 38 percent (twenty countries) are undemocratic (see Map 10.1). When compared to earlier surveys, that for 2002 clearly suggests that democracy has made significant strides in Africa since the fall of the Berlin Wall in 1989. In 1988, for example, only 4 percent (two countries) of Africa's political systems were democratic, whereas 31 percent (sixteen countries) were partially democratic and 65 percent (thirty-three countries) were undemocratic.

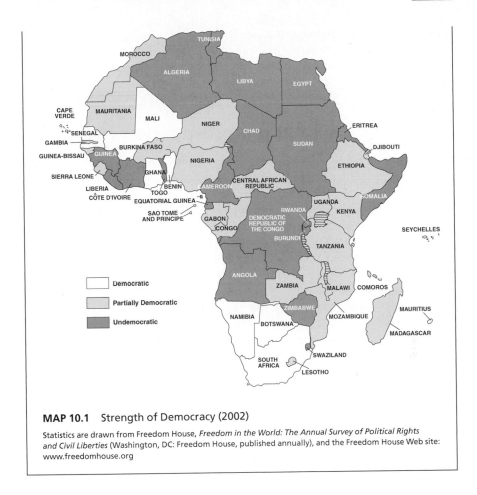

MAP 10.1   Strength of Democracy (2002)

Statistics are drawn from Freedom House, *Freedom in the World: The Annual Survey of Political Rights and Civil Liberties* (Washington, DC: Freedom House, published annually), and the Freedom House Web site: www.freedomhouse.org

unprepared opposition and government control of all the major media outlets not only ensured Houphouët-Boigny's victory in presidential elections, with approximately 81 percent of the popular vote, but his ruling party, the Parti Démocratique de la Côte d'Ivoire-Rassemblement Démocratique Africain (PDCI-RDA, Democratic Party of Côte d'Ivoire–African Democratic Assembly), won 163 out of a total of 175 seats in the National Assembly. In short, Houphouët-Boigny's foresight and ability to act quickly and decisively enabled him to peacefully co-opt the democratization process under the guise of free, but unfair, multiparty elections that left the opposition forces with little alternative but to accept the results and set their sights on future electoral contests.

Authoritarian Reaction

In contrast to the previous examples of democratization, **authoritarian reaction** entails the use of state-sponsored violence against proponents of democracy to preserve the status quo. In this case, the incumbent leader conducts elections that are neither free nor fair, with the intent of stealing votes. The promotion of ethnic fighting to divide the opposition and intimidate the general population is often one of the hallmarks of this model. After "winning" the election, the leader subsequently seeks to silence the opposition through such varied means as imprisonment, exile, and, in extreme cases, execution.

The example of Cameroon demonstrates the extent to which incumbent leaders are willing to maintain themselves in office through the use of authoritarian tactics.[35] In October 1992, President Paul Biya and his ruling Cameroon People's Democratic Movement (CPDM) declared victory in the country's first multiparty presidential elections with 40 percent of the popular vote. During the 2 years preceding the elections, human rights groups estimate that at least 400 people associated with the democratization movement were killed by the Biya regime, and the elections themselves were fraught with gross violations of human rights and electoral procedures. "Widespread irregularities during the election period, on election day, and in the tabulation of results seriously calls into question, for any fair observer, the validity of the outcome," explained a report of the U.S. National Democratic Institute for International Affairs (NDI), one of the foreign groups that monitored the elections. "It would not be an exaggeration to suggest that this election system was designed to fail."[36]

Biya's self-proclaimed victory in the elections was followed by a wave of repression and arrests directed against opposition elites. For example, John Fru Ndi, the leader of the Social Democratic Front (SDF) who took second place in the presidential elections with 36 percent of the popular vote, was placed under house arrest with 135 of his supporters. Another 200 opposition figures were also jailed, and a state of emergency was declared in the province of Western Cameroon. "The brutality of the forces of law and order, particularly during arrests, is very alarming," explained Solomon Nfor Gwei, the chairman of Cameroon's National Commission for Human Rights and Freedom. "Many detainees are continuously being subjected to psychological and physical torture, some of whom we saw in great pain, with swollen limbs and genitals, blisters and deep wounds, and cracks on skulls."[37] In this and other cases, the facade of victory actually encourages authoritarian leaders to unleash waves of repression designed to maintain the status quo at any cost.

Civil War and Contested Sovereignty

At worst, the authoritarian response of the incumbent leader can lead to civil war and the complete breakdown of the state. The result is a state of **contested sovereignty** in which no one group can assert its authority over the entire territory or construct a government considered to be legitimate, either domestically or internationally.

This extreme scenario was characteristic of the bloody clan warfare that erupted in Somalia after Somali dictator Mohammed Siad Barre was overthrown by a coalition of guerrilla forces in January 1991. Rather than abide by an October 2, 1990, accord in which the major guerrilla groups agreed to decide the shape of a post-Siad political system, the United Somali Congress

(USC), by virtue of its control of the capital, unilaterally named a Hawiye clan member, Ali Mahdi Mohammed, president of the country. This move heightened the already tense relations between the Isaak-dominated Somali National Movement (SNM), the Hawiye-dominated USC, and the Ogadeni-dominated Somali Patriotic Movement (SPM), as well as relations among scores of other, less-organized clan groupings.[38]

In an action based on a strongly held Isaak belief that the north would continue to be victimized by a southern-dominated government, the SNM announced on May 17, 1991, that the former British Somaliland territory was seceding from the 1960 union to become the Somaliland Republic. This event was followed by the intensification of clan conflict in the southern portion of the country between the USC and the SPM, which, in turn, was exacerbated by a regrouping of Siad's Darod clan groupings under the military banner of the Somali National Front (SNF). Moreover, a brutal intraclan power struggle erupted in Mogadishu between USC forces loyal to interim President Mahdi (a member of the Abgal subclan of the Hawiye) and those led by General Mohamed Farah Aidid (a member of the Habar Gedir subclan of the Hawiye). In short, once the common political enemy no longer existed, traditional clan differences, worsened by the dictatorial divide-and-rule practices of the Siad years, led to an intensification of clan conflict and famine throughout southern and central Somalia.

As it became increasingly clear that the United Nations Security Council was incapable of managing intensifying levels of clan conflict and famine, President George Bush announced in a live television address to the American public on December 4, 1992, that U.S. troops would be deployed in Somalia to "create a secure environment" for the distribution of famine-relief aid. Five days later the first contingent of U.S. troops, led by three teams of Navy SEALs (Sea-Air-Land Commandos), landed on the beaches of Mogadishu and secured the airport and the port. The U.S. military landing, designated "Operation Restore Hope," was carried out under the auspices of a UN Security Council resolution sanctioning foreign intervention. In the weeks that followed, 38,000 troops from twenty countries (including approximately 24,000 U.S. military personnel) occupied various cities and towns throughout central and southern Somalia and began the task of opening food supply routes, as well as creating distribution networks.[39]

Despite the withdrawal of U.S. troops in May 1994 and the withdrawal of all remaining UN troops in May 1995, a permanent political solution to the Somali crisis as of 2003 has yet to be found. Southern clans refuse to accept the self-proclaimed independence of the northern-based Somaliland Republic, which remains unrecognized by any other country in the world. In the south, a weak central government under the leadership of Abdikassim Salad Hassan was formed in 2000, but the extent of its political control is limited to the capital city of Mogadishu. As of 2003, territory outside the capital remained under the control of regional clan leaders. Although famine on the scale of that witnessed in 1991–92 has not recurred, thousands of Somalis have died in the periodic intensification of clan-based conflict. The primary problem remains the lack of a centralized Somali state capable of exerting authority over the entire Somali nation. Conflict is sure to continue as long as the Somali people remains divided among dozens of clan-dominated fiefdoms.

DEMOCRATIC CONSOLIDATION
OR DECAY?

The future prospect of the third wave of democratization on the African continent has fostered both optimism and pessimism. Optimism was initially generated by a host of early successes, most notably what numerous observers have called the South African "miracle": the emergence of Nelson Mandela as the first democratically elected leader of South Africa.[40] Pessimism has been increasingly generated by the simple reality that several transitions to democracy have resulted in **democratic decay,** often ending in military coups d'état and a return to authoritarianism.[41] In 1999 alone, for example, the military took power in four African countries, including Côte d'Ivoire, once thought by most observers to be relatively safe from the threat of military intervention (the other three countries in which the military took power were Comoros, Guinea-Bissau, and Niger).

Even in those cases marked by a successful transition to more democratic forms of governance, newly elected leaders confront the long-term challenge of ensuring the **consolidation** (institutionalization) of democratic practices in political systems still marked by democratic fragility.[42] "The frequency of democratic breakdowns in this century—and the difficulties of consolidating new democracies—must give serious pause to those who would argue . . . for the inevitability of global democracy," explains Larry Diamond, a senior research fellow at the Hoover Institution.[43] "As a result, those concerned about how countries can move 'beyond authoritarianism and totalitarianism' must also ponder the conditions that permit such movement to endure. . . . To rid a country of an authoritarian regime or dictator is not necessarily to move it fundamentally beyond authoritarianism."[44]

One means for assessing the consolidation of democracy is to examine the evolution of political rights enjoyed by African populations, including the ability to form political organizations free from government intrusion; the meaningful representation of ethnic, racial, religious, and other minority groups in the political process; and the right to choose national and local political leaders through free and fair competitive elections. Although individual countries will obviously vary, the African continent as a whole has benefited from the steadily rising protection of political rights since 1989 (see Figure 10.2). It is important to note, however, that the establishment of a multiparty political system, the political right most often cited by Western observers as the linchpin of democratic practice, can actually undermine the process of democratic consolidation, especially when electoral arrangements make it difficult, if not impossible, for the opposition party to emerge victorious in national elections.

FIGURE 10.2   Protection of Political Rights

Source: Statistics are drawn from Freedom House, *Freedom in the World: The Annual Survey of Political Rights and Civil Liberties* (Washington, DC: Freedom House, annual editions).

Botswana is often heralded as a model for more recently emerging democracies because it is Africa's oldest surviving multiparty democracy, in which free and fair elections have been held regularly since independence in 1966.[45] A close examination of legislative election results has nonetheless prompted some critics to characterize Botswana as a de facto single-party system (see Table 10.1).[46] Despite the proliferation of political parties, ranging from the labor-oriented Botswana Labour Party (BLP) to the socialist-inspired Botswana National Front (BNF), the ruling Botswana Democratic Party (BDP) consistently has won no less than 68 percent of all seats in eight legislative elections that were held between 1965 and 1999.[47] The BDP has been able to maintain its political monopoly in large part due to a political system that heavily favors the incumbent president and his ruling party.[48]

It is for precisely this reason that some proponents of democratization argue that the true test of Africa's newly established democratic systems is their ability to foster and survive the **alternation of power** between rival political parties. Benin serves as an excellent example of a multiparty democracy that has successfully weathered an alternation of power through the ballot box. The net political outcome of the 1990 national conference was the 1991 holding of "founding elections" in which a technocrat, Nicéphore Soglo, was elected president. Mathieu Kérékou, the former Marxist dictator, graciously accepted defeat and retired from the political system, only to return 5 years later as the leading opposition candidate in the 1996 presidential elections. With Soglo's reelection campaign severely hampered by the poor performance of the national economy and public perceptions of his disregard for the average citizen, Kérékou overcame the political odds and emerged victorious in the presidential elections. Dubbed the "chameleon" by friends and enemies alike, a reference to his changing political views, Kérékou's return to office served as a powerful example of the further consolidation of democratic practices on the African continent.

Table 10.1 Legislative Election Results in Botswana (Parties Winning at Least One Seat)

	1965	1969	1974	1979	1984	1989	1994	1999
BDP	28 (90)	24 (77)	27 (84)	29 (91)	29 (85)	31 (91)	27 (68)	33 (82.5)
BNF	— (—)	3 (10)	2 (6)	2 (6)	4 (12)	3 (9)	13 (32)	6 (15)
BPP	3 (10)	3 (10)	2 (6)	1 (3)	1 (3)	0 (0)	0 (0)	0 (0)
BIP	0 (0)	1 (3)	1 (3)	0 (0)	0 (0)	0 (0)	0 (0)	0 (0)
BCP	0 (0)	0 (0)	0 (0)	0 (0)	0 (0)	0 (0)	0 (0)	1 (2.5)
	31 (100)	31 (100)	32 (100)	32 (100)	34 (100)	34 (100)	40 (100)	40 (100)

BDP = Botswana Democratic Party
BNF = Botswana National Front
BPP = Botswana People's Party
BIP = Botswana Independent Party
BCP = Botswana Congress Party

Sources: Statistics are drawn from Botswana Government, *Report to Minister of Public Service and Information on the General Election* (various years, including 1979, 1984, 1989, and 1994), and James H. Polhemus, "Botswana Votes: Parties and Elections: An African Democracy," *The Journal of Modern African Studies* 21, no. 3 (1983): 397–430. See also Andreas Danevad, "Responsiveness in Botswana Politics: Do Elections Matter?" *The Journal of Modern African Studies* 33, no. 3 (1995): 381–402.

A second means for assessing the consolidation of democracy is to determine the nature and depth of civil liberties enjoyed by African populations, including the right to freedom of speech and assembly; access to vigorous, independent media; constitutional guarantees of due process by independent judiciaries; freedom of religion and worship; and the general protection of individual rights regardless of one's ethnicity, race, religious creed, or gender. Although individual cases vary, the African continent as a whole has enjoyed the steadily rising protection of civil liberties since 1989 (see Figure 10.3). It is

FIGURE 10.3 Protection of Civil Liberties

Source: Statistics are drawn from Freedom House, *Freedom in the World: The Annual Survey of Political Rights and Civil Liberties* (Washington, DC: Freedom House, annual editions).

for precisely this reason, argue optimists of Africa's democratic prospects, that one can speak of the gradual strengthening of a **democratic culture** that increasingly will become self-sustaining.

The caution one must nonetheless exercise when assessing the consolidation of newly formed democracies is clearly demonstrated by events in Zambia. In 1991, the country transitioned successfully from a single-party system, headed by President Kenneth Kaunda, to a multiparty political system under the leadership of President Frederick Chiluba and his Movement for Multiparty Democracy (MMD) party.[49] As a labor leader from civil society, Chiluba seemingly represented a new generation of political leaders intent on opening the political spaces in their political systems. Eighteen months after achieving victory, however, Chiluba reinstated a "state of emergency" that had existed throughout Kaunda's rule and arrested and detained without charges fourteen members of the official opposition, the United National Independence Party (UNIP). Critics of the government's actions drew parallels between Kaunda's use of states of emergency during the 1970s and the 1980s to silence political opponents and Chiluba's desire to curb rising criticism of his regime's inability to resolve Zambia's pressing economic problems. Most important, critics noted that the domination of Zambia's parliament by Chiluba's ruling MMD party (125 out of 150 seats) called into question the independence of the legislature from the executive, especially after Chiluba successfully acquired legislative approval for his harsh measures.[50]

An important aspect of Chiluba's political predicament was the *economic* dimension of the democratization process. Like leaders who took office beginning in the 1950s, Chiluba confronted unrealistic popular expectations that the fruits of democratization, especially higher wages and better living conditions, would be widely and quickly shared after multiparty elections. Indeed, a significant portion of the Zambian people believed a multiparty system would somehow serve as a panacea for the country's economic problems. However, the combination of the overall weakness of the Zambian state and the constraints imposed on executive action by even the minimal checks-and-balances of the democratic system led to little success in the economic realm, followed by growing public weariness and disenchantment with Chiluba's administration.

Chiluba's declining popularity presented the same authoritarian-democratic paradox confronted by the first generation of African leaders during the 1950s. Although largely socialized and trained in an authoritarian tradition, as were his predecessors, Chiluba was expected to abide by the "rules of the game" of Zambia's multiparty political system. Strict adherence to those rules, however, threatened to seal Chiluba's political fate in the 1996 presidential elections, especially after former president Kaunda accepted opposition backing and announced his entry into the race. As a result, Chiluba oversaw the ratification of two constitutional amendments that harkened back to the authoritarian excesses of his predecessor and threatened to undermine the very democratic political system he sought to create. The first required that the parents of any presidential candidate be Zambians by birth. The second limited any presidential candidate to two terms of office. Since Kaunda's parents were born in neighboring Malawi, and he had ruled Zambia for a total of 27 years (1964–1991), he was forced to withdraw from the race. Chiluba's political maneuvering removed the only serious challenge to his rule and ensured his reelection.[51]

Whether Africa's third wave of democratization will result in further democratic consolidation or democratic decay will depend largely on how the current generation of democratically elected elites responds to the authoritarian-democratic paradox. Will they graciously accept defeat and join the ranks of the **loyal opposition,** as was the case in Soglo's defeat in the 1996 Beninois presidential elections, or will they increasingly turn to a variety of authoritarian tactics to maintain themselves in power, as Chiluba's manipulation of the 1996 Zambian presidential elections illustrates? Indeed, the response of the first generation of African leaders to this authoritarian-democratic paradox in the 1950s ushered in nearly four decades of single-party rule. The ways in which Africa's newly elected democratic leaders continue to resolve these paradoxes potentially portend the creation of new forms of political rule, destined to last well throughout the first half of the twenty-first century.

KEY TERMS

third wave of democratization
Africa's second independence
Africa's second liberation
authoritarian-democratic paradox
systems of checks-and-balances
Westminster model
Elysée model
single-party political systems
consensus building
vanguard role
nonparty system
movement democracy
mass participatory democracy
multiparty competition
founding elections

national conference
guided democratization
democratization from above
co-optation of the transition process
political rights
civil liberties
freedom index
authoritarian reaction
contested sovereignty
democratic decay
consolidation
alternation of power
democratic culture
loyal opposition

FOR FURTHER READING

Ake, Claude. *Democracy and Development in Africa.* Washington, DC: Brookings Institution, 1996.

Bratton, Michael, and Nicolas van de Walle. *Democratic Transitions in Africa: Regime Transitions in Comparative Perspective.* Cambridge: Cambridge University Press, 1997.

Clark, John F., and David Gardinier, eds. *Political Reform in Francophone Africa.* Boulder: Westview, 1997.

Chole, Eshetu, and Jibrin Ibrahim, eds. *Democratization Processes in Africa: Problems and Prospects.* Dakar: CODESRIA, 1995.

Decalo, Samuel. *The Stable Minority: Civilian Rule in Africa*. Gainesville: Florida Academic, 1997.

Hyden, Goran, and Michael Bratton, eds. *Governance and Politics in Africa*. Boulder: Lynne Rienner, 1992.

Joseph, Richard, ed. *The Democratic Challenge in Africa*. Atlanta: The Carter Center, 1994.

Joseph, Richard, ed. *State, Conflict, and Democracy in Africa*. Boulder: Lynne Rienner, 1999.

Krieger, Winfried Jung Silke, ed. *Culture and Democracy in Africa South of the Sahara*. Mainz, Germany: V. Hase and Koehler Verlag, 1994.

Lumumba-Kasongo, Tukumbi. *The Rise of Multipartyism and Democracy in the Context of Global Change: The Case of Africa*. New York: Praeger, 1998.

Mamdani, Mahmood, and Ernest Wamba-dia-Wamba, eds. *African Studies in Social Movements and Democracy*. Dakar: CODESRIA, 1995.

Ndegwa, Stephen, ed. *A Decade of Democracy in Africa*. Leiden, The Netherlands: Brill, 2001.

Ottaway, Marina. *Africa's New Leaders: Democracy or State Reconstruction?* Washington, DC: Carnegie Endowment for International Peace, 1999.

Sandbrook, Richard. *The Politics of Africa's Economic Recovery*. Cambridge: Cambridge University Press, 1993.

Schaffer, Frederic C. *Democracy in Transition: Understanding Politics in an Unfamiliar Culture*. Ithaca: Cornell University Press, 1998.

Schraeder, Peter J., ed. *Exporting Democracy: Rhetoric vs. Reality*. Boulder: Lynne Rienner, 2002.

Sisk, Timothy D., and Andrew Reynolds, eds. *Elections and Conflict Management in Africa*. Washington: United States Institute of Peace, 1998.

Tripp, Aili Mari. *Women and Politics in Uganda*. Madison: University of Wisconsin Press, 2000.

Widner, Jennifer A. *Economic Change and Political Liberalization in Sub-Saharan Africa*. Baltimore: Johns Hopkins University Press, 1994.

Wiseman, John A., ed. *Democracy and Political Change in Sub-Saharan Africa*. New York: Routledge, 1995.

NOTES

1. See Samuel P. Huntington, *The Third Wave: Democratization in the Late Twentieth Century* (Norman: University of Oklahoma Press, 1991).

2. For an introduction to this vast literature, see Michael Bratton and Nicolas van de Walle, *Democratic Experiments in Africa: Regime Transitions in Comparative Perspective* (Cambridge: Cambridge University Press, 1997). See also Rob Buijtenhuijs and Céline Thiriot. *Democratization in Sub-Saharan Africa, 1992–1995: An Overview of the Literature* (Leiden: African Studies Centre, 1995).

3. For example, see Donald Rothchild, "On the Application of the Westminster Model to Ghana," *Centennial Review* 4, no. 4 (Fall 1960), and Barry Munslow, "Why Has the Westminster Model Failed in Africa?" *Parliamentary Affairs* 36 (1983): 218–28.

4. See Robert H. Jackson and Carl G. Rosberg, *Personal Rule in Black Africa* (Berkeley: University of California Press, 1982).

5. For a good overview, see Ruth Berins Collier, *Regimes in Tropical Africa: Changing Forms of Supremacy, 1945–75* (Berkeley: University of California Press, 1982).

6. For an early analysis, see Martin Kilson, "Authoritarian and Single-Party Tendencies in African Politics," *World Politics* 25, no. 2 (1963): 262–94. See also Lanciné Sylla, *Tribalisme et Parti Unique en Afrique Noire* (Paris: Presses de la Fondation Nationale des Sciences Politiques, 1977).

7. For a good overview, see J. Gus Liebenow, *African Politics: Crises and Challenges* (Bloomington: Indiana University Press, 1986), pp. 225–29.

8. For a critique, see John Lonsdale, "African Pasts in African Futures," *Canadian Journal of African Studies* 23, no. 1 (1989): 126–46.

9. Ibid., p. 226.

10. See Julius Nyerere, *Freedom and Socialism: Uhuru and Ujamaa* (Dar es Salaam: Oxford University Press, 1968).

11. Liebenow, *African Politics,* p. 225.

12. Ibid., pp. 228–29.

13. For example, compare the assessments provided by Peter Anyang' Nyong'o, "Africa: The Failure of One-Party Rule," *Journal of Democracy* 3, no. 1 (1992): 90–96, and Samuel Decalo, "The Process, Prospects, and Constraints of Democratization in Africa," *African Affairs* 91 (1992): 7–35.

14. For example, see Douglas Anglin, "Southern African Responses to Eastern European Developments," *The Journal of Modern African Studies* 28, no. 3 (1990): 431–55.

15. Quoted in Bratton and van de Walle, *Democratic Experiments in Africa,* pp. 105–6.

16. Ibid., p. 3.

17. Jennifer A. Widner, *Economic Change and Political Liberalization in Sub-Saharan Africa* (Baltimore: Johns Hopkins University Press, 1994). See also Nicolas van de Walle, *African Economies and the Politics of Permanent Crisis, 1979–1999* (Cambridge: Cambridge University Press, 2001).

18. This spectrum draws and expands on the work of Guy Martin, "Preface: Democratic Transition in Africa," *Issue: A Quarterly Journal of Opinion* 21, no. 1–2 (1993): 6–7.

19. For the most comprehensive analysis, see Bratton and van de Walle, *Democratic Experiments in Africa.*

20. Bratton and van de Walle, *Democratic Experiments in Africa,* p. 198.

21. See Nelson Mandela, *Long Walk to Freedom: The Autobiography of Nelson Mandela* (Boston: Little, Brown, 1995), pp. 619–20.

22. For an overview, see Pearl Robinson, "The National Conference Phenomenon in Francophone Africa," *Comparative Studies in Society and History* 36 (1994): 575–610. See also John F. Clark and David Gardinier, eds., *Political Reform in Francophone Africa* (Boulder: Westview, 1997).

23. See Martin, "Preface: Democratic Transition in Africa," p. 6.

24. For discussion, see Jacques Mariel Nzouankeu, "The Role of the National Conference in the Transition to Democracy in Africa: The Cases of Benin and Mali," *Issue* 21, no. 1–2 (1993): 44–50, and John R. Heilbrunn, "Social Origins of National Conferences in Benin and Togo," *The Journal of Modern African Studies* 31, no. 2 (1993): 277–99.

25. Nzouankeu, "The Role of the National Conference," p. 45.

26. Ibid.

27. See Naomi Chazan, "Planning Democracy in Africa: A Comparative Perspective on Nigeria and Ghana," *Policy Sciences* 22 (1989): 325–57.

28. See Ruby Ofori, "Ghana: The Elections Controversy," *Africa Report* 38, no. 4 (July–August 1993): 33–35.

29. Richard Joseph, "Ghana: A Winning Formula," *Africa Report* 38, no. 1 (January–February 1993): 45–46.

30. Ofori, "Ghana: The Elections Controversy," p. 35.

31. Ibid.

32. For a summary, see Jennifer A. Widner, "The 1990 Elections in Côte d'Ivoire," *Issue* 201 (1991): 31–40. See also Yves Fauré, "Democracy and Realism: Reflections on the Case of Côte d'Ivoire," *Africa: Journal of the International African Institute* 63, no. 3 (1993): 313–29.

33. Decalo, "The Process, Prospects, and Constraints," p. 27.

34. Ibid.

35. For discussion, see Mark Hubbard, "Cameroon: A Flawed Victory," *Africa Report* 38, no. 1 (January–February 1993): 41–44.

36. Quoted in ibid., p. 42.

37. Quoted in ibid.

38. For an overview of the origins and evolution of these guerrilla groups, see Daniel Compagnon, "The Somali Opposition Fronts: Some Comments and Questions," *Horn of Africa* 13, no. 1–2 (1990).

39. See Walter Clarke and Jeffrey Herbst, eds., *Learning from Somalia: The Lessons of Armed Humanitarian Intervention* (Boulder: Westview, 1997). See also John L. Hirsch and Robert B. Oakley, *Somalia and Operation Restore Hope: Reflections on Peacemaking and Peacekeeping* (Washington, DC: The United States Institute for Peace, 1995).

40. See Michael Bratton, "After Mandela's Miracle in South Africa," *Current History* 97, no. 619 (May 1998): 214–19. See also Richard Joseph, "Africa: The Rebirth of Political Freedom," *Journal of Democracy* 2 (1992): 11–25. For a more recent positive analysis, see E. Gyimah-Boadi, "The Rebirth of African Liberalism," *Journal of Democracy* 9, no. 2 (1998): 18–31.

41. For example, see René Lemarchand, "Africa's Troubled Transitions," *Journal of Democracy* 3, no. 4 (October 1992): 98–109. See also Richard Joseph, "Africa, 1990–1997: From *Abertura* to Closure," *Journal of Democracy* 9, no. 2 (1998): 3–17.

42. See Richard Sandbrook, "Transitions without Consolidation: Democratization in Six African Cases," *Third World Quarterly* 17, no. 1 (1996): 69–87.

43. Larry Diamond, "Beyond Authoritarianism and Totalitarianism: Strategies for Democratization," *The Washington Quarterly* (Winter 1989): 142.

44. Ibid.

45. See John A. Wiseman, "Multipartyism in Africa: The Case of Botswana," *African Affairs* 76, no. 302 (1977): 70–79. See also John Holm and Patrick Molutsi, eds., *Democracy in Botswana* (Gaborone: Macmillan Botswana, 1989).

46. See Roger Charlton, "The Politics of Elections in Botswana," *Africa: Journal of the International African Institute* 63, no. 3 (1993): 330–71.

47. Other parties include the Botswana Congress Party (BCP), the Botswana Independence Party (BIP), the Botswana People's Party (BPP), and the Botswana Progressive Union (BPU).

48. Other factors favoring the incumbent include a "weak" civil society and government domination of the media. See Patrick P. Molutsi and John D. Holm, "Developing Democracy When Civil Society Is Weak: The Case of Botswana," *African Affairs* 89, no. 356 (1990): 323–40, and James J. Zaffiro, "The Press and Political Opposition in an African Democracy: The Case of Botswana," *The Journal of Commonwealth and Comparative Politics* 27, no. 1 (1989): 51–73.

49. For an overview, see Eric Bjornlund, Michael Bratton, and Clark Gibson, "Observing Multiparty Elections in Africa: Lessons from Zambia," *African Affairs* 91 (1992): 405–31.

50. See Melinda Ham, "Zambia: History Repeats Itself," *Africa Report* 38, no. 3 (May–June 1993): 13–16.

51. Bratton and van de Walle, *Democratic Experiments in Africa,* pp. 233, 260.

11

♔

Foreign Policy Making and the Pursuit of Pan-Africanism

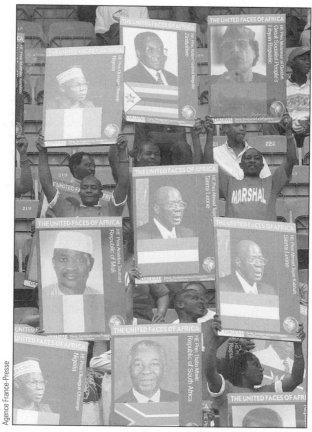

Agence France-Presse

Posters of African leaders being waved at the official launching of the African Union in 2002, in Durban, South Africa.

S ENEGALESE FOREIGN MINISTER Doudou Thiam wrote one of the first scholarly books on African foreign policy at the beginning of the contemporary independence era.[1] He called for policymakers of the newly independent African countries to rally around the foreign policy goals of pan-Africanism and African cultural consciousness while avoiding involvement in the "intense ideological conflict" between the United States and the Soviet Union.[2] Thiam's book was published in 1963, a noteworthy year in that it coincided with the launching of the Organization of African Unity (OAU), the first intergovernmental organization composed of all independent African states and designed to promote the **pan-African ideal** of African political cooperation. Later years have witnessed the emergence and rapid expansion of a wide range of experiments in regional economic integration, designed to promote the economic dimension of the pan-African ideal. In the aftermath of the cold war, renewed discussions over the viability of creating an African Defense Force signaled a new determination on the part of African leaders to promote the military dimension of pan-Africanism. In addition, in 2002, African leaders meeting in South Africa officially launched the African Union, the latest political manifestation of the pan-African ideal that replaced the OAU. After briefly setting out the foreign policy–making context, most of this chapter is devoted to exploring the nature and evolution of these experiments in pan-Africanism.

UNDERSTANDING THE FOREIGN POLICY–MAKING CONTEXT

A strong sense of the interconnectedness between domestic and foreign policies has always been a mark of great diplomats throughout the world. In the 1960s, Senegalese Foreign Minister Thiam eloquently argued that any attempt at disengaging foreign and domestic policies was simply a matter of "practical convenience," with each constituting "two scales in the same balance, two aspects of the same indivisible reality."[3] More than 25 years later, Ousmane Tanor Dieng, a senior political advisor to Senegalese President Abdou Diouf, cited the momentous changes occurring in the international system as a result of the cold war's end and reaffirmed the importance of understanding the interplay between domestic and international factors in foreign policy.[4] As a result, any understanding of African support for the cherished foreign policy goal of promoting the pan-African ideal must begin with an understanding of the variety of governmental and nongovernmental actors that contribute to the formulation and implementation of African foreign policy.[5] An in-depth analysis of the Senegalese foreign policy establishment clearly demonstrates the diversity of elements involved in the foreign policy decision-making process.[6]

President and Bureaucracies of the Executive Branch

Like many other African constitutions, the Senegalese constitution embodies the widely shared belief that foreign policy constitutes the domaine réservé (privileged realm) of the president. Specifically drawing on the highly centralized Elysée model of France's Fifth Republic, the president is granted a wide array of foreign policy prerogatives under the constitution: He is recognized as the commander in chief of the Armed Forces (Article 39); empowered to name Senegalese diplomats abroad and accredit those from foreign countries (Article 40); and authorized to negotiate, ratify, and approve international agreements (Article 75), except in certain specified realms, such as peace treaties and agreements with international organizations that require ratification by the National Assembly (Article 76).[7] As is the case with its counterparts throughout the African continent, any analysis of Senegalese foreign policy must therefore begin with the personal beliefs and idiosyncrasies of that country's presidents: Léopold Sédar Senghor (1960–80), Abdou Diouf (1981–2000), and Abdoulaye Wade (2000–present).

Each African head of state is usually complemented by an officially designated vice president or prime minister who occupies the second most influential position in the policy-making establishment. In the case of Senegal, the constitution stipulates that the president is to appoint a prime minister to manage the day-to-day functioning of the government. Unlike his counterparts in other African political systems, the Senegalese prime minister is not beholden to the National Assembly. However, the prime minister maintains a Diplomatic Cabinet under the guidance of a diplomatic advisor, and therefore plays an influential role in the foreign policy–making process. The current prime minister, Idrissa Seck, has long-standing professional and personal links with President Wade, and his office works closely with the Office of the President and the foreign affairs bureaucracies in the pursuit of Senegalese foreign policy goals.[8]

The Ministry of Foreign Affairs is usually the largest and most active of the foreign affairs bureaucracies in African policy-making establishments, taking responsibility for much of the day-to-day administration of foreign relations, including the management of the country's diplomatic network abroad.[9] As Map 11.1 demonstrates, the number of embassies maintained by individual African countries varies widely. One can distinguish between four tiers of diplomacy, with some countries, such as Botswana, maintaining fewer than fifteen embassies abroad, followed by moderate (sixteen to thirty embassies) and high (thirty-one to forty-five embassies) levels, represented by Namibia and Senegal, respectively. The diplomatic giants of the continent, however, each maintain at least forty-five embassies abroad. Not surprisingly, this group includes important regional powers, such as Egypt, Nigeria, and South Africa. A fascinating regional trend is that all the North African countries, including Tunisia and Morocco, can be counted among the diplomatic giants of the African continent, at least when measured in terms of the number of embassies maintained abroad.

As the titular head of the diplomatic network abroad, the Minister of Foreign Affairs is potentially a key player in the policy-making network. Direct

MAP 11.1 Diplomatic Representation (Number of Embassies Maintained Abroad in 2000)

Source: Data set compiled by the author.

access to the president, combined with links to the far-reaching foreign affairs bureaucracy, also provide the minister with important bureaucratic tools to set the foreign policy agenda.[10] In the case of Senegal, for example, former Minister of Foreign Affairs Ibrahima Fall was the driving force behind the Diouf administration's adoption of a more "progressive" stance toward regional African issues, such as the decision to recognize the Marxist regime of Angola, headed by José Eduardo dos Santos.[11] Cheikh Tidiane Gadio, serving as the current Minister of Foreign Affairs, carries these bureaucratic tools as well.

The Ministry of Defense is another foreign affairs bureaucracy that has played an influential role in African foreign policies. This bureaucracy has initiated military coups d'état, which in turn have led to the establishment of military-dominated regimes on the African continent (see Chapter 9). In several cases, however, the transition to a civilian democracy has been accompanied by policies designed to decrease both the size of the military establishment and its involvement in governmental affairs, including in the realm of foreign policy. In South Africa during the 1980s, for example, the military strongly argued in favor of the Afrikaner regime's decision to undertake destabilization policies against its immediate neighbors.[12] In the wake of the country's first democratic elections in 1994, therefore, the new government headed by Nelson Mandela pledged to restore greater government control over a military force that had become too dominant in both domestic and foreign policies.[13]

In the case of Senegal, strong adherence to the republican ideal of civilian control of the military has not prevented military leaders from playing important behind-the-scenes roles in shaping Senegal's political history.[14] During the 1963 constitutional crisis between President Senghor and Prime Minister Mamadou Dia, for example, pro-Senghor military forces prevailed over those preferring to depose the president. Indeed, the Senegalese Ministry of Defense is a powerful bureaucratic actor that increased its influence during the 1980s and the 1990s due to Senegal's recurring security problems.[15] Military officers have called for the strengthening of the armed forces (most notably the purchase of helicopters) to seek a military solution to the intermittent guerrilla war in the Casamance region of southern Senegal. They have also strongly argued in favor of "hot pursuit" operations against neighboring countries (e.g., Gambia and Guinea-Bissau), which have been accused of providing sanctuary to the guerrillas and inadequately controlling their national territories.[16] Overall, the military played an especially influential role in Senegalese foreign policy throughout the Diouf administration, ranging from Senegal's involvement in a number of peace-keeping operations, such as the Cease-Fire Monitoring Group (ECOMOG) in Liberia during the 1980s that was sponsored by the Economic Community of West African States (ECOWAS), to President Diouf's decision to use military force in 1981 to restore President Daouda Diawara to power in Gambia and in 1998 to maintain President João Bernardo Vieira in power in Guinea-Bissau.[17]

Role of National Legislatures in Foreign Policy

The legislative branch of government has also played an increasingly influential role in African foreign policies.[18] It has served as a vocal arena of national debate, particularly in countries such as Benin that significantly liberalized their political systems during the 1990s. The primary reason behind this newfound legislative role is the creation of democratic political systems that embody the concept of separation of powers between the various branches of government.[19] A question that requires further research is whether the newly empowered legislatures will largely restrict themselves to the national arena, calling to mind the old maxim that "politics stops at the water's edge," or if they will continue to have a growing voice in the realm of foreign affairs.

Beginning in the 1980s, the Senegalese National Assembly emerged as an increasingly vocal arena of national debate. Largely reduced to the role of a "rubber stamp" institution during the Senghor years (there was no opposition voice between 1964 and 1978), the National Assembly increasingly has questioned government policies since the lifting of multiparty restrictions in 1981, most notably in the aftermath of the 1993 legislative elections, in which candidates from five opposition parties won a total of thirty-six seats in the 120-seat

National Assembly. The most important foreign affairs components of the National Assembly include the Committee on Foreign Affairs and over twenty Friendship Groups that promote formal and informal contacts between Senegalese representatives and their counterparts in foreign countries.

The willingness of Senegalese representatives to challenge the Executive Branch's foreign policy remains relatively lukewarm, however, and when it does occur it is largely restricted to issues related to the Senegalese economy, such as the domestic costs and impacts of foreign-sponsored structural adjustment programs (SAPs). Furthermore, the National Assembly must cope with a weak constitutional role relative to that of the Executive Branch, as well as a historically negative public image as constituting nothing more than applaudisseurs (applauders of government policies). The National Assembly's role in foreign affairs is also seriously hampered by the lack of economic resources, most notably the lack of a sufficient budget that would allow committees and representatives to hire staffs and independently conduct research and fact-finding missions. "If we want the National Assembly to truly play its constitutionally mandated role," explains former Representative Sémou Pathé Guèye, "we must put an end to the disastrous conditions under which Representatives work."[20] As further lamented by Representative Iba Der Thiam, representatives do not even enjoy individual offices in which to work and privately receive members of their constituencies.[21]

Foreign Policy Impact of Nongovernmental Actors

The formulation and implementation of African foreign policies are also influenced by a wide variety of nongovernmental actors. The print and broadcast media, for example, have flourished in the liberal political environment associated with transitions to democracy during the 1990s.[22] In the case of Senegal, numerous private newspapers play an important agenda-setting role and, at the very least, offer a more critical perspective of day-to-day issues in foreign policy.[23] For example, the German government's March 1996 decision to place Senegal on the list of nondemocratic countries for which requests for political asylum would be routinely considered was picked up by the Senegalese press and turned into a public debate, prompting Minister of Communication Serigne Diop to hold a widely reported special meeting with the German Ambassador to Senegal.[24]

The growing communities of Africans living and working outside Africa also influence the foreign policies of their countries of origin. The seriousness with which the Senegalese government treats nearly 500,000 Senegalese living and working abroad (one of every sixteen citizens) is aptly demonstrated by the June 1993 decision to rename the Ministry of Foreign Affairs the Ministry of Foreign Affairs and of Senegalese Abroad.[25] When one examines the growing Senegalese inclination toward closer ties with the United States during the 1980s and the 1990s, one cannot help but wonder to what degree this has been influenced by the large numbers of Senegalese who sought their fortunes in the United States and can now mobilize financial resources for various business

A Closer Look: LEON H. SULLIVAN (AFRICAN/ AFRICAN-AMERICAN) SUMMIT

A crucial element of the pan-African ideal is the creation of global links between the African continent and peoples of African descent in other regions of the world diaspora. The **Leon H. Sullivan Summit,** formerly known as the **African/African-American Summit,** captures the essence of this global vision, by seeking to promote closer ties between the fifty-three countries of the African continent and the African-American community that composes approximately 12 percent of the U.S. population. Although the idea of fostering links between Africa and the African-American community enjoys a rich intellectual history, the idea for a summit came to fruition under the leadership of Reverend Leon Sullivan, who died of leukemia in 2001. Originally conceived by Sullivan as a vehicle for strengthening cultural links, the African/African-American Summit has burgeoned into a forum for enhancing international trade and investment.

The inaugural summit was held in Abidjan, Côte d'Ivoire (1991), followed by summits in Libreville, Gabon (1993), Dakar, Senegal (1995), Harare, Zimbabwe (1997), and Accra, Ghana (1999). The Abuja, Nigeria meeting, originally planned for 2001, was ultimately rescheduled for July 14–18, 2003, due to Sullivan's death

in 2001. One of the most noteworthy components of the Dakar meeting, which the author attended, was the organizing of an "American Day," a series of workshops and presentations held by numerous U.S. government officials who are responsible for promoting U.S.-African trade and investment. The primary theme of the presentations by U.S. government officials was "building bridges to commercial partnerships." A special emphasis was placed on explaining the "nuts and bolts" of promoting trade and investment, including the proper agencies and individuals to contact, the legal statutes and regulations governing economic partnerships, and sources of financial support and loan guarantees. The most popular U.S. government speaker was Secretary of Commerce Ronald H. Brown, who zealously promoted U.S. trade and investment in Africa before his tragic death in 1995.

The personal impact of these summits was best captured by Leonard Bennet, an African-American attorney who participated in 1997: "We go back [to the United States] with a very positive image of Africa and the fact that we have blacks running their own countries is truly reflective of what we as blacks can achieve. We go back a changed people."

Leon H. Sullivan (African/African-American) Summits

1st   Abidjan, Côte d'Ivoire (April 17–19, 1991)

2nd   Libreville, Gabon (May 24–28, 1993)

3rd   Dakar, Senegal (May 1–6, 1995)

4th   Harare, Zimbabwe (July 22–25, 1997)

5th   Accra, Ghana (May 17–21, 1999)

6th   Abuja, Nigeria (scheduled for July 14–18, 2003)

Discussion draws on the author's attendance at the third African/African-American Summit in Dakar, Senegal. See also the Summit Website: http://www.thesummit.org

undertakings in their country of birth. Indeed, in 1996 the Senegalese government helped create an investment consortium of Senegalese living in the United States, as a means for attracting greater investment into Senegal and promoting expanding trade links between the two countries.

Public opinion has also exerted an influential, albeit intermittent, influence in African foreign policies. As in other African countries, the strengthening of the democratization process portends greater popular input into the policy-making process, as the policies of a new generation of African leaders are held accountable to public opinion. In the case of Senegal, it has been argued that public opinion, inflamed by radio broadcasts by Radio France Internationale, was the primary factor leading to bloody clashes between Senegal and Mauritania in 1989.[26] Despite the fact that this conflict was neither desired nor promoted by President Diouf of Senegal or President Ould Taya of Mauritania, both these leaders, despite their best efforts to contain public passions, confronted violent clashes that spiraled out of control. In a sense, both leaders, as well as the foreign policies of their respective countries, became "prisoners" of public opinion.[27]

One must also consider the impact of religious groups and leaders on African foreign policies.[28] In the case of Senegal, religious leaders known as marabouts have historically been an integral part of the domestic political system and play both informal and formal roles in the making of foreign policy.[29] For example, the marabouts played a critical role in reducing tensions between Senegal and Mauritania in the aftermath of the 1989 border conflict by undertaking an unofficial form of shuttle diplomacy across the river that separates the two countries. The power of the marabouts is derivative of the population's belief in the spiritual powers of their personal religious guides. The marabouts enjoy almost complete financial autonomy from state control due to a complex system of alms collection by taalibe (disciples) who, depending on the charisma and power of individual marabouts, can channel enormous amounts of money into a designated cause. The marabouts therefore can mobilize potent protest to undesired foreign policies and supporting others with little fear of state retribution. A dramatic case in point occurred in the mid-1980s, when the Diouf administration was forced to withdraw an invitation to Pope John Paul II to visit the country due to the threats of leading marabouts to call upon their taalibe to occupy the runways at the international airport. Although the Pope was subsequently reinvited and visited Senegal several years later in 1991, to the wide acclaim of both Muslims and Christians, the marabouts had clearly served notice that sensitive issues had to be raised with them in advance if the president wished to avoid embarrassing public confrontations. In short, a complete understanding of the formulation and implementation of Senegal's foreign policy, as well as that of other African countries with sizeable Muslim populations, must account for the role of religion.

Finally, one must take into account the foreign policy impact of guerrilla groups that are opposed to the central authority of their countries and that create parallel diplomatic networks to promote their guerrilla causes. Such networks are typically limited to neighboring countries that provide economic and military support and that serve as the bases of military operations. In the case of Senegal, a secessionist guerrilla insurgency led by the Mouvement des Forces Démocratiques de Casamance (MFDC, Movement of the Democratic Forces of Casamance) has intermittently maintained diplomatic offices in neighboring Gambia and Guinea-Bissau. The most extensive diplomatic network maintained by an African guerrilla insurgency was that of the African National Congress (ANC). From 1960, the year that the ANC was banned by South Africa's apartheid regime, to 1994, the year that Nelson Mandela emerged victorious in South Africa's first multiracial, multiparty democratic elections, the ANC established forty-three diplomatic missions in Africa, Asia, Europe, and the Western Hemisphere, each of which was maintained during various lengths of time (see Table 11.1).

Table 11.1 ANC Diplomatic Missions Maintained Abroad during the Anti-Apartheid Struggle

AFRICA

Algeria (Algiers) 1962–93	Morocco (Rabat) 1962–?
Angola (Luanda) 1975–95	Mozambique (Maputo) 1975–95
Botswana (Gaborone) 1984–94	Namibia (Windhoek) 1990–94
Egypt (Cairo) 1964–94	Nigeria (Lagos) 1976–94
Ethiopia (Addis Ababa) 1980s-95	Senegal (Dakar) 1975–94
Ghana (Accra) 1985–89	Swaziland (Mbabane) 1976–94
Kenya (Nairobi) 1987–94	Tanzania (Dar-es-Salaam & Morogoro) 1962–95
Lesotho (Maseru) 1975–94	Uganda (Kampala) 1989–92
Libya (Tripoli) 1987–94	Zambia (Lusaka) 1964–93
Madagascar (Antananarivo) 1980s–94	Zimbabwe (Harare) 1980–94

ASIA

Australia (Sydney) 1984–93	Japan (Tokyo) 1988–94
India (New Delhi) 1967–94	Malaysia (Kuala Lumpur) 1991–95

EUROPE

Belgium (Brussels) 1981–94	Italy (Rome) 1972–94
Denmark (Copenhagen) 1985–94	Netherlands (Amsterdam) 1988–94
Finland (Helsinki) 1988–93	Norway (Oslo) 1970s-92
France (Paris) 1981–94	Romania (Bucharest) 1982–92
Germany, East (Berlin) 1978–90	Soviet Union/Russia (Moscow) 1987–94
Germany, West (Bonn) 1984–93	Spain (Madrid) 1987–94
Great Britain (London) 1960–95	Sweden (Stockholm) 1977–94
Hungary (Budapest) 1990–94	

WESTERN HEMISPHERE

Canada (Ottawa) 1969–94	United Nations (New York) 1974–94
Cuba (Havana) 1978–94	United States (Washington, DC) 1989–94

SOURCE: Adapted from data provided by Roger Pfister. See also Pfister, "Gateway to International Victory: The Diplomacy of the African National Congress in Africa, 1960–1994," *The Journal of Modern African Studies*. 41, 3 (2003): 51–73.

PAN-AFRICANISM AND THE
SEARCH FOR AFRICAN UNITY

Inspired by the anticolonial activities of peoples of African descent living in North America and the West Indies during the nineteenth and twentieth centuries, African nationalists sought to promote a unified African front against colonial rule. What subsequently became known as the pan-African ideal was most forcefully enunciated for the first time at the 1945 meeting of the Pan-African Congress held in Manchester, England. At the conference, participants adopted a Declaration to the Colonial Peoples that affirmed the "rights" of all colonized peoples to be "free from foreign imperialist control, whether political or economic," and "to elect their own governments, without restrictions from foreign powers."[30] In a separate Declaration to the Colonial Powers, participants underscored that if the colonial powers were "still determined to rule mankind by force, then Africans, as a last resort, may have to appeal to force in the effort to achieve freedom."[31]

The pan-African ideal gained momentum as a result of the first wave of independence during the 1950s. In an opening address to the first gathering of independent African nations on African soil, held in 1958 in Accra, Ghana, President Kwame Nkrumah proclaimed, "Never before has it been possible for so representative a gathering of African Freedom Fighters to assemble in a free independent African state for the purpose of planning for a final assault upon imperialism and colonialism."[32] According to Nkrumah, the realization of the pan-African ideal required a commitment between African leaders and their peoples to guide their countries through four stages: (1) "the attainment of freedom and independence," (2) "the consolidation of that independence and freedom," (3) "the creation of unity and community between the African states," and (4) "the economic and social reconstruction of Africa."[33]

Despite overwhelming agreement among African leaders that pan-Africanism constituted a worthy foreign policy goal, sharp disagreement existed over the proper path to ensure such unity. One group of primarily francophone countries known as the **Brazzaville Group** (named after the capital of Congo-Brazzaville) sought a minimalist approach: the coordination of national economic policies through standard diplomatic practices. Little consideration was given to the possibility of creating continent-wide institutions. In sharp contrast, Nkrumah and other leaders, who belonged to what became known as the **Casablanca Group** (named after the Moroccan city), argued instead that the success of pan-Africanism required a political union of all independent African countries, patterned after the federal model of the United States. In speech after speech, Nkrumah promoted two key themes that became the hallmark of this international vision: "Africa must unite!" and "Seek ye first the political kingdom!"[34]

A third group of African leaders, who belonged to what became known as the **Monrovia Group** (named after the capital of Liberia), rejected the idea of political union as both undesirable and unfeasible, primarily due to the assumption that African leaders would jealously guard their countries' new-found independence. They nonetheless sought a greater degree of cooperation than that espoused by the Brazzaville Group. Led by Alhaji Abubakar Tafawa Balewa, the Prime Minister of Nigeria, the Monrovia Group called for the creation of a looser organization of African states. According to this vision, African countries would guard their independence but promote growing cooperation and the harmonization of policies in a variety of functional areas, most notably economic, scientific, educational, and social development. An important component of the Monrovia Group approach was a desire to create continent-wide institutions that would oversee and strengthen policy harmonization.

On May 25, 1963, thirty-one African heads of state largely embraced the Monrovia vision by launching the **Organization of African Unity (OAU),** the first pan-African, intergovernmental organization of independent African countries based on African soil. Addis Ababa, Ethiopia, was chosen as the site for the OAU headquarters, and all major decisions and resolutions were formally discussed at the annual Assembly of Heads of State and Government (see the accompanying box). The **sovereign equality** of all member states was an important guiding principle of the organization, which differed significantly from the **Great Power domination** of the United Nations, given the special power conferred on the five permanent members (Britain, China, France, Russia, and the United States) of the UN Security Council.

Although the OAU's 39-year existence, which came to an end in 2002 with the launching of the African Union (discussed below), has been correctly described as a "victory for pan-Africanism,"[35] both critics and sympathetic observers questioned the organization's ability to play an effective role in African politics and international relations. In a special issue of the *Nigerian Journal of International Affairs,* which assessed the OAU's continued relevance on the "Silver Jubilee" (25-year) anniversary of the organization's creation, one Nigerian scholar expressed "sadness" over the fact that, despite the best of intentions, the OAU had failed to live up to the expectations of its original framers.[36] The OAU's effectiveness can be assessed by exploring several elements of the OAU Charter.

The most important theme of the OAU Charter was support for the inviolability of frontiers inherited from the colonial era. Due to the multiethnic nature of most African countries, African leaders were concerned that changing even one boundary would open a Pandora's box of ethnically based secessionist movements and lead to the further **Balkanization** of the African continent into ever smaller economic and political units. In the case of the Nigerian civil war (1967–70), for example, the OAU not only refused to sanction aid provision to Biafra, the secessionist southeastern portion of the country, but voted a series of resolutions that underscored official support for the Nigerian federal government.[37] This decision upset international human rights activists, as well as several African countries aiding the secessionist government, because the military-dominated Nigerian government was using starvation as a means to bring the Biafrans—government and general population alike—to their knees.[38]

As ethnic tensions and separatist movements intensified in the post–cold war era, African leaders remained firmly committed to maintaining borders inherited from the colonial era. Although the OAU recognized the sovereignty of Eritrea in 1993, after a UN-sponsored referendum in that country resulted in overwhelming popular support for independence, African leaders subsequently noted that this process did not question the hallowed concept of the inviolability of frontiers. Unlike most African countries, Eritrea was federated to Ethiopia after independence from colonial rule and therefore enjoyed the legal right to withdraw from that voluntary union. However, in similar cases of voluntary federation that have unraveled in the post–cold war era, such as northern Somalia's 1991 unilateral declaration of independence as the Somaliland Republic, as well as other cases where a disgruntled region, such as the southern Sudan, has affirmed the right of self-determination, the OAU continued to reaffirm the concept of territorial integrity.

A second guiding principle of the OAU Charter was noninterference in the internal affairs of member states. In the early years of the organization, African leaders debated whether to allow military leaders who had illegally deposed their civilian counterparts to maintain their OAU seats. This debate was resolved in favor of recognizing whatever group controlled the reins of power in a particular country.[39] More significant was the silence among African leaders concerning human rights abuses in OAU member states. "Increased repression, denial of political choice, restrictions on the freedom of association, and like events occurred, with rare murmurs of dissent," explains Claude Welch Jr., a specialist of human rights in Africa. "The OAU seemed to function as a club of presidents, engaged in a tacit policy of not inquiring into each other's practices."[40] During the 1970s, for example, Ugandan dictator Idi Amin was elected OAU chair despite his personal involvement in "politically sanctioned repression and murders" in Uganda.[41]

Although still highly reluctant to criticize their counterparts, African leaders began to accept a growing role for the OAU in addressing human rights abuses at the beginning of the 1980s. In 1981, the annual Assembly of Heads of State and Government held in Banjul, Gambia, adopted the **African Charter on Human and People's Rights** (popularly called the **Banjul Charter**). This human rights code officially went into effect in October 1986 and has served as the guiding principle for a variety of human rights groups that emerged during the 1980s.[42] In addition to encompassing **first generation rights** (civil and political liberties) usually associated with the Western world and **second generation rights** (economic and social rights) usually associated with the socialist world, the Banjul Charter has been described as "breaking some new ground" by adopting **third generation rights** intended to protect the rights of individual peoples or ethnic groups.[43]

Despite the ratification of the Banjul Charter, however, the OAU's response to events in Nigeria during 1995 demonstrated the difficulty of translating human rights rhetoric into policy action. In response to disturbances among the Ogoni ethnic group in southeastern Nigeria, which began in 1990 over control of that region's vast oil resources, Nigeria's military regime

A Closer Look: AFRICAN SUMMITRY

A hallmark of African international relations is the regular use of summit meetings between the senior leaders of the continent's 53 countries. The most noteworthy example of this phenomenon was the annual **Summit of Heads of State and Government** convened by the Organization of African Unity (OAU) from its founding summit in Addis Ababa, Ethiopia, in 1963, to its 38th and final summit in Durban, South Africa, in 2002, which also served as the founding summit of the African Union. The OAU summit served as a unique diplomatic meeting ground that gave African leaders an important regional forum for engaging in debate and promoting African views on a variety of international issues. Hosting the summit was a prestigious honor, most notably due to the international attention that resulted from the arrival of Africa's leading political leaders and their influential entourages. Great care was devoted to ensuring that the role of summit chairperson was shared widely (the leaders of 27 countries enjoyed this status), and that this honor was equitably divided among Africa's five major regions: West Africa (26 percent), East Africa (26 percent), North Africa (18 percent), Central Africa (15 percent), and Southern Africa (15 percent). South Africa's selection as the site for the final OAU summit and the founding summit of the African Union signaled the important roles played by former President Nelson Mandela as a symbol of Africa's emancipation and by President Thabo Mbeki as a leader of an African renaissance designed to strengthen Africa's political-military and socioeconomic presence within the world. Like its predecessor, the African Union will maintain the tradition of African summitry by holding an annual meeting of heads of state and government.

Host Countries Chairpeople of OAU (1963–2002) and African Union (2002–present) Summits

***   Founding OAU Summit: Addis Ababa, Ethiopia (1963)
          Emperor Haile Selassie (Ethiopia)
1st   Cairo, Egypt (July 21–24, 1964)
          Gamal Abdel Nasser (Egypt)
2nd   Accra, Ghana (October 21–25, 1965)
          Kwame Nkrumah (Ghana)
3rd   Addis Ababa, Ethiopia (November 5–9, 1966)
          Emperor Haile Selassie (Ethiopia)
4th   Kinshasa, Congo-Kinshasa (September 11–14, 1967)
          Mobutu Sese Seko (Congo-Kinshasa)
5th   Algiers, Algeria (September 13–16, 1968)
          Houari Boumedienne (Algeria)
6th   Addis Ababa, Ethiopia (September 6–10, 1969)
          Ahmadou Ahidjo (Cameroon)
7th   Addis Ababa, Ethiopia (September 1–5, 1970)
          Kenneth Kaunda (Zambia)
8th   Addis Ababa, Ethiopia (June 21–23, 1971)
          Moktar Ould Daddah (Mauritania)
9th   Rabat, Morocco (June 12–15, 1972)
          King Hassan II (Morocco)
10th   Addis Ababa, Ethiopia (May 23–25, 1973)
          Yakabu Gowan (Nigeria)
11th   Mogadishu, Somalia (June 12–15, 1975)
          Mohammed Siad Barre (Somalia)
12th   Kampala, Uganda (July 28–August 1, 1975)
          Idi Amin (Uganda)

13th   Port Louis, Mauritius (July 2–5, 1977)
        Seewoosagur Ramgoolam (Mauritius)
14th   Libreville, Gabon (July 2–5, 1977)
        Omar Bongo (Gabon)
15th   Khartoum, Sudan (July 18–21, 1978)
        Gaafar Mohammed Numeiri (Sudan)
16th   Monrovia, Liberia (July 17–21, 1979)
        William Tolbert (Liberia)
17th   Freetown, Sierra Leone (July 1–4, 1980)
        Siaka Stevens (Sierra Leone)
18th   Nairobi, Kenya (July 24–28, 1981)
        Daniel arap Moi (Kenya)
19th   Tripoli, Libya (1982)—cancelled due to boycott
19th   Addis Ababa, Ethiopia (June 8–11, 1983)
        Mengistu Haile Marian (Ethiopia)
20th   Addis Ababa, Ethiopia (November 12–15, 1984)
        Julius Nyerere (Tanzania)
21st   Addis Ababa, Ethiopia (July 18–20, 1985)
        Abdou Diouf (Senegal)
22nd   Addis Ababa, Ethiopia (July 28–30, 1986)
        Sassou Nguesso (Congo-Brazzaville)
23rd   Addis Ababa, Ethiopia (July 27–30, 1987)
        Kenneth Kaunda (Zambia)
24th   Addis Ababa, Ethiopia (May 24–28, 1988)
        Moussa Traoré (Mali)
25th   Addis Ababa, Ethiopia (July 24–26, 1989)
        Hosni Moubarak (Egypt)
26th   Addis Ababa, Ethiopia (July 9–11, 1990)
        Yoweri Museveni (Uganda)
27th   Abuja, Nigeria (June 3–5, 1991)
        Ibrahim Babangida (Nigeria)
28th   Dakar, Senegal (June 29–July 1, 1992)
        Abdou Diouf (Senegal)
29th   Cairo, Egypt (June 28–29, 1993)
        Hosni Mubarak (Egypt)
30th   Tunis, Tunisia (June 13–15, 1994)
        Zine El-Abidine Ben Ali (Tunisia)
31st   Addis Ababa, Ethiopia (June 26–28, 1995)
        Meles Zenawi (Ethiopia)
32nd   Yaounde, Cameroon (July 8–10, 1996)
        Paul Biya (Cameroon)
33rd   Harare, Zimbabwe (June 2–4, 1997)
        Robert Mugabe (Zimbabwe)
34th   Ouagadougou, Burkina Faso (June 8–10, 1998)
        Blaise Compaoré (Burkina Faso)
35th   Algiers, Algeria (July 12–14, 1999)
        Abdelaziz Bouteflika (Algeria)
36th   Lome, Togo (July 10–12, 2000)
        Gnassingbé Eyadéma (Togo)
37th   Lusaka, Zambia (July 9–11, 2001)
        Frederick Chiluba (Zambia)

***   Transitional Summit, Durban, South Africa (July 8–10, 2002)
        Final OAU Summit and Founding Summit of the African Union
        Thabo Mbeki (South Africa)

1st   Maputo, Mozambique (scheduled for July 2003)

unleashed a brutal campaign of suppression that included the November 1995 execution of Nobel Peace Prize candidate Ken Saro-Wiwa and eight other Ogoni activists on trumped-up murder charges.[44] Although OAU Secretary General Salim Ahmed Salim expressed "disappointment" over the fact that the Nigerian generals failed to "respond positively" to OAU appeals for clemency, the organization did not adopt concrete, comprehensive measures (e.g., imposition of economic sanctions) to punish or to internationally isolate the Nigerian regime.[45]

The peaceful settlement of all disputes via negotiation, mediation, conciliation, or arbitration constituted a third guiding principle of the OAU. Yet strict adherence to the first two principles—support for territorial integrity and non-interference in internal affairs—historically impeded the OAU's ability to mediate internal conflicts or conflicts between two or more member states. In the case of the 1967–70 Nigerian civil war, almost reflexive support for the territorial integrity of Nigeria seriously called into doubt, at least from the view of the secessionist Igbos, the OAU's ability to serve as an impartial negotiator. For this reason the OAU Commission of Mediation, Arbitration, and Conciliation was "stillborn"[46] and most African-initiated arbitration efforts were carried out ad hoc by African presidents. For example, Djiboutian President Hassan Gouled Aptidon used his country's stature as the headquarters for the Intergovernmental Authority on Development (IGAD) to mediate the conflict between Ethiopia and Somalia. According to I. William Zartman, a specialist of conflict resolution, such efforts led to success in only 33 percent of roughly twenty-four cases, and this success was often only temporary as warring parties returned to the battlefield.[47]

The ability to dispatch peace-keeping or peace-making forces once a conflict has broken out is a critical aspect of conflict resolution. The OAU Founding Fathers tried to prepare for this eventuality by planning the creation of an African High Command, a multinational military force composed of military contingents from OAU member states. The African High Command never made it beyond the planning stage, however, leading once again to a variety of ad hoc measures. In 1981, the OAU sponsored the creation of a short-term, all-African military force designed to resolve an expanding civil war in Chad.[48] Composed of approximately 4,800 troops from the Democratic Republic of the Congo (Congo-Kinshasa), Nigeria, and Senegal, the OAU force "failed to achieve any concrete solution" due to financial, logistical, and political difficulties and within a few months was "forced to withdraw."[49]

Two developments nonetheless underscored the OAU's desire to take a more proactive role in African conflicts in the post–cold war era. In 1993, the OAU Assembly of Heads of State and Government adopted a resolution creating the Mechanism for Conflict Prevention, Management and Resolution, a formal consultative process ideally designed to prevent the outbreak and further spread of conflicts on the African continent.[50] The inspiration for this consultative process was a forward-thinking document, "Toward a Conference on Security, Stability, Development, and Cooperation in Africa," popularly called the **Kampala Document,** which was the result of a 1991 conference convened by former Nigerian President Olusegun Obasanjo.

The most important development, however, revolved around the possibility of creating a multinational **African Defense Force,** able to respond militarily to African crises. In May 1997, African leaders agreed that such a force should be comprised of existing military units of contributing OAU member states and that these units would be equipped with the aid of foreign powers, most notably the United States and France. The African Defense Force would remain under the operational command of the OAU. Unresolved issues included which countries should be eligible to contribute forces (e.g., should involvement be limited to democratic countries?) and what type of decision-making body should be able to authorize when and where to intervene (e.g., should intervention be based on the consensus of all OAU member-states or should a smaller body of representative members be responsible?). Discussions concerning the African Defense Force nonetheless remained at an exploratory stage, and the Mechanism for Conflict Prevention, Management and Resolution remained largely untested.

A fourth guiding principle of the OAU Charter was the unswerving opposition to colonialism and white minority rule. Principally concerned with the past existence of minority white-ruled regimes in Zimbabwe, Namibia, South Africa, and the former Portuguese territories of Angola, Mozambique, Guinea-Bissau, and Sao Tome and Principe, the OAU established a Liberation Committee based in Dar es Salaam, Tanzania, to aid liberation movements with both economic and military assistance.[51] Although disagreements often arose over which tactics would best ensure transitions to majority-ruled governments (e.g., should one support dialogue with a white regime or fund a guerrilla insurgency?), every OAU member expressed public opposition to the continued existence of minority white-ruled regimes. The work of the Liberation Committee largely came to an end in 1994, when South Africa transitioned to a multiracial, multiparty democracy.

The OAU entered the history books July 8–10, 2002 as leaders from more than forty African countries met in Durban, South Africa, to launch the **African Union,** a pan-African organization designed to build on the successes of the OAU in the continuing search for African unity. Amara Essy, a distinguished statesman from Côte d'Ivoire, was chosen to serve as interim chairperson of the African Union's Commission and Thabo Mbeki, president of South Africa, hosted the summit. Like its OAU predecessor, the African Union will hold an annual summit of heads of state and government, adopt official positions on a wide array of diplomatic topics affecting the African continent, and create a number of offices and institutions designed to strengthen African cooperation.

Although as of this writing the exact final shape and structure of the African Union are being worked out in preparation for the planned July 2003 meeting of heads of state in Maputo, Mozambique, the broad structural outlines and guiding principles of the organization have become clear. As concerns structure, the African Union will be led by a ten-member executive body—the African Commission—that will be served by a president, vice president, and eight additional commissioners who will be responsible for the following eight broad portfolios:

- Political Affairs, such as democratic elections and human rights

- Peace and Security, most notably efforts devoted to conflict resolution

- Economic Affairs, inclusive of promoting regional integration

- Infrastructure and Energy, such as the development of the transportation and telecommunications sectors

- Social Affairs, ranging from sports and migration to health issues and anti-drug efforts

- Human Resources, Science and Technology, such as education and new information technologies

- Commerce and Industry, most notably efforts devoted to trade and investment

- Rural Economy and Agriculture, inclusive of food security and protection of the environment

The first members of the executive committee are expected to be elected at the July 2003 meeting in Maputo, Mozambique. The ten positions are to be divided equally among representatives from each of Africa's five major regions (in other words, two members from each region), as well as according to gender (five positions for women and five positions for men).

Several guiding principles of the organization clearly indicate a new path in African regional cooperation that builds on both the successes and failures of the OAU. In sharp contrast to the OAU, the African Union has not enshrined in its founding charter the concept of the inviolability of frontiers inherited from the colonial era. Despite its commitment to the territorial integrity of African countries, the African Union maintains a greater deal of flexibility in dealing with both ongoing and future conflicts by not including such a rigid and restrictive principle in its founding document. Especially noteworthy is the African Union's rejection of the OAU principle of noninterference in the domestic affairs of member countries. Member states have instead agreed that the African Union has the right to intervene in the domestic affairs of member states in cases of gross violations of human rights and genocide and war crimes. In addition, all member states commit themselves to strengthening democratic practices, most notably holding free and fair elections and ensuring freedom of expression. In the international realm, an important African Union–sponsored initiative is the New Partnership for Africa's Development (NEPAD), designed to strengthen Africa's position in the global economy and attract greater levels of foreign aid and investment (see Chapter 12). Together these principles have reignited a sense of African optimism in the pursuit of the cherished goal of pan-Africanism.

REGIONAL ECONOMIC COOPERATION AND INTEGRATION

Inspired by the success of the European Union and encouraged by the UN-sponsored **Economic Commission for Africa (ECA)** based in Addis Ababa, Ethiopia, African leaders have sought to create regional entities capable of promoting regional cooperation and integration. This vision of African international relations was best outlined by the OAU's publication in 1981 of a document, *Lagos Plan of Action for the Economic Development of Africa, 1980–2000,* which proposed the establishment of an **African Economic Community (AEC)** that would be based on an **African Common Market (ACM).**[52] The guiding logic of the *Lagos Plan of Action* is that the creation of intergovernmental economic organizations in each of Africa's five major regions—North, East, West, Southern, and Central Africa—is the best means for ensuring the ultimate creation of a continent-wide AEC. Treaty discussions were launched at the Twenty-Seventh Annual Meeting of the OAU Heads of State and Government, held in 1991 in Abuja, Nigeria, and a treaty was signed in 1994. The thirty-third OAU summit, held in 1997 in Harare, Zimbabwe, also served as the first summit of the AEC.

The flourishing of experiments in regional cooperation and integration throughout the contemporary independence era demonstrates the commitment of African leaders to the economic dimension of the pan-African ideal. By the end of the 1980s, it was estimated that at least 160 intergovernmental economic groupings existed on the African continent, with thirty-two such organizations in West Africa alone.[53] Among the most notable economic groupings in each of Africa's major regions (including dates of launching) are the Economic Community of West African States (ECOWAS, 1975), the Union of the Arab Maghreb (UAM in North Africa, 1989), the Southern African Development Community (SADC, 1980), the Economic Community of Central African States (ECCAS, 1983), and the Intergovernmental Authority on Development (IGAD) in Northeast Africa (1986) (see Map 11.2). These regional organizations are complemented by a few larger groupings, such as the Lomé Convention, which promotes preferential trade links between the European Union and dozens of countries from Africa, the Caribbean, and the Pacific.

African leaders offer several rationales for seeking regional cooperation and integration. The simplest reason is the firm belief that there is strength in numbers. To compete effectively in an increasingly competitive international economic system, dominated by economic superpowers (e.g., the United States and Japan) and powerful regional economic entities (e.g., the European Union), African countries must band together and pool their resources. Second, African leaders want to promote self-sustaining economic development and particularly the industrialization of the African continent. Struggling with the reality that many of their countries are economically impoverished and lack the tools to create advanced industries, African leaders believe they can build on the strengths of their neighbors to forge integrated and self-sustaining regional economies.

Most important, regional economic schemes are perceived as the best means of creating self-reliant development, thereby reducing and eventually ridding the African continent of the ties of dependency inherited from the colonial era.[54] For example, African leaders are rightfully concerned that national control over the evolution of their respective economies is constrained by Africa's trade dependency on Europe, at the expense of intraregional trade links with African countries. For this reason the primary objective of early regional economic schemes was to promote intraregional trade with neighbors who theoretically share a set of development objectives, either due to special geographic features, historical ties, or a shared religion, such as Islam in North Africa.[55] By strengthening these ties with like-minded neighbors, a stronger

MAP 11.2   Select Regional Economic Organizations

African economic entity is expected to emerge that will be able to reduce foreign influence and strengthen Africa's collective ability to bargain with non–African powers more equally.

Early optimism began to wane in the aftermath of the launching of several regional integration efforts, which included the creation of supranational authorities and formal economic unions designed to promote intraregional trade and investment. In the case of the East African Community (EAC), the 1967 decision of Kenya, Tanzania, and Uganda to create a common market with common services, coordinated by a supranational governing body, collapsed less than 10 years later and was followed in 1978–79 by Tanzania's military intervention in Uganda to overthrow the dictatorial regime of Idi Amin. As explained by Olatunde Ojo, a specialist of regional cooperation and integration in Africa, several factors that contributed to the EAC's decline clarify why other similar efforts, from the 1960s to the 1980s, either failed or demonstrated minimal progress.[56]

An initial problem was the polarization of national development and the perception of unequal gains.[57] As typically occurred in other cases in Africa where the creation of a common market served as the cornerstone of the regional grouping, the most industrialized country (Kenya) usually reaped the benefits of economic integration at the expense of its partners (Uganda and Tanzania). For example, Kenya's share of intracommunity trade increased from 63 percent in 1968 to 77 percent in 1974, whereas Uganda's share decreased from 26 to 6 percent during the same period. In addition, despite the fashioning of a common policy toward the establishment of new operations by multinational corporations (MNCs), most of these firms decided to locate their bases of operations in Kenya due to its more advanced economy and workforce, as well as its extensive infrastructural network of roads, railroads, ports, and airports.

The EAC also foundered due to the inadequacy of compensatory and corrective measures.[58] In every integration scheme, some countries inevitably benefit more than others. As a result, policymakers can implement measures, such as regional development banks or disproportionate customs revenue sharing, to correct the imbalance and compensate those countries expected to lose out in the short term. In the case of the EAC, a regional development bank was created to disburse funds to the three members as follows: Kenya (22 percent), Tanzania (38 percent), and Uganda (40 percent). However, in this and other cases of integration in Africa, even the richest members usually cannot subsidize bank operations. The actual finances provided to the most needy members therefore never even begin to approach true development needs or completely compensate for losses.

A third stumbling block to successful regional integration of the EAC was ideological differences and the rise of economic nationalism.[59] Simply put, ideological differences often ensure a radically different approach to development projects, which in turn can significantly hinder regional integration (see Chapter 6). In the case of Kenya, a pro-West capitalist regime was very open to private enterprise and foreign investment, particularly the opening of local offices of MNCs. The socialist-oriented regime of Tanzania, however, opted for a self-help strategy known as ujamaa (the Kiswahili word for brotherhood), which not only denounced private enterprise as exploitative but restricted the flow of foreign investment and strongly controlled the MNCs. When combined with the growing public perception of unequal gains between the two countries, these ideological differences led to often acrimonious public debate between President Jomo Kenyatta of Kenya and President Julius Nyerere of Tanzania and to the rise of economic nationalism in both countries.

A final element that contributed to the EAC's decline was the impact of foreign influences.[60] Whereas Kenya developed close relationships with the Western bloc nations (e.g., the United States and Great Britain), Tanzania pursued close links with the socialist bloc (particularly the People's Republic of China), and Uganda sought links with the former Soviet Union and the Arab world. These links ensured that the EAC became embroiled in the cold war rivalry of the 1960s and the 1970s and contributed to the creation of an externally directed "strategic image" that prompted EAC member states to look "outward" toward their foreign patrons rather than "inward" toward their natural regional partners.

Beginning in the 1980s, the failure and stagnation of classic integration schemes prompted African leaders to undertake looser forms of regional **economic cooperation** in a variety of functionally specific areas, such as transportation infrastructure (e.g., regional rail links), energy (e.g., hydroelectric projects on common rivers), and telecommunications.[61] The logic behind pursuing this form of regionalism is that it does not require the creation of supranational authorities, nor does it require policymakers to sacrifice national control over the sensitive areas of foreign trade and investment. This looser form of economic cooperation is gathering strength in the post–cold war era, particularly as democratically elected elites increasingly assume power and seek to promote cooperation with other democracies in their regions.

The 1992 transformation of the Southern African Development Coordination Conference (SADCC) into the Southern African Development Community (SADC) is a good example of this growing trend in African regional relations. Originally conceived as a vehicle for reducing the economic dependence of the Frontline States on South Africa during the apartheid era, the transformed SADC now counts South Africa among its members and is seeking to enhance traditional cooperation in a variety of functional realms, most notably transportation.[62] The new SADC stands poised at "the threshold of a new era," according to several reports published by the African Development Bank in conjunction with the World Bank and the Development Bank of South Africa.[63] "Although its effects and the inequities it has embedded will linger for a long time to come, the demise of apartheid opens up prospects unimaginable even a few years ago," explains one report. "New opportunities have emerged in every sector of economic activity for expanded trade and mutually beneficial exchanges of all kinds among the countries of southern Africa."[64]

Several factors are essential to understanding the optimism surrounding SADC's status as a potential model for economic cooperation in Africa, particularly in terms of reducing Southern Africa's dependence on foreign economic interests and creating the basis for self-sustaining development in the post–cold war era.[65] First, the inclusion of a highly industrialized South Africa provides SADC with an engine for economic growth that has reinvigorated the entire region. In this regard, South Africa is playing a leadership role similar to that enjoyed by Germany in the European Union, the United States in NAFTA, and Nigeria in ECOWAS. The vast majority of SADC members (seven out of ten) also share a British colonial heritage. Although a shared colonial past is not a precondition for effective regional cooperation, it facilitates such technical matters as which language should serve as the official language of communication (in the case of SADC, English).

A third facilitating factor is the decline in ideological differences between SADC member states that accompanied the end of the cold war. Whereas Angola, Mozambique, and Zimbabwe have discarded in varying degrees their adherence to Marxist principles of development, South Africa has officially renounced its apartheid system and Tanzania and Zambia have dismantled significant portions of their formerly socialist economies. In essence, there is a growing consensus among SADC member states that effective regional economic cooperation must be based on a shared commitment to some variant of the liberal capitalist model of development (see Chapter 6).

SADC's greatest strength is a regional commitment to conflict resolution and to the promotion of shared democratic values.[66] The cold war's end and the rise of democratization movements have led to the end of civil wars and the holding of democratic elections throughout the region, although authoritarian trends in both Swaziland and Zimbabwe during 2002 were part of a more negative trend. One of the most important lessons of regional integration theory, which draws on the success of the European Union, is that the existence of elites with a shared commitment to democracy is the foundation of long-term economic cooperation and development. For this reason the 1992 Windhoek Treaty (named after the capital of Namibia), which consecrated the launching of SADC, underscored the political dimension of regional relationships and its critical role in the continued expansion of economic cooperation.[67] The leaderships of SADC member states recognize that the fruits of pan–Africanism can only be achieved by the settlement of civil war and the promotion of democracy throughout the African continent. As a result, conflict resolution remains an important cornerstone of the pan–African ideal at the beginning of the twenty-first century.

KEY TERMS

pan–African ideal
Leon H. Sullivan Summit
Brazzaville Group
Casablanca Group
Monrovia Group
Organization of African Unity (OAU)
sovereign equality
Great Power domination
Balkanization
African Charter on Human and
　People's Rights
Banjul Charter
first generation rights

second generation rights
third generation rights
OAU Summit of Heads of State and
　Government
Kampala Document
African Defense Force
African Union
Economic Commission for Africa
　(ECA)
African Economic Community
　(AEC)
African Common Market (ACM)
economic cooperation

FOR FURTHER READING

Aluko, Olajide, ed. *The Foreign Policies of African States*. London: Hodder and Stoughton, 1977.

Aly, Ahmad A. H. M. *Economic Cooperation in Africa: In Search of Direction*. Boulder: Lynne Rienner, 1994.

Amate, C. O. C. *Inside the OAU: Pan-Africanism in Practice*. New York: St. Martin's, 1986.

Bach, Daniel C., ed. *Regionalisation in Africa: Integration and Disintegration*. Oxford: James Currey, 1999.

Beaseley, Ryan K., et al., eds. *Foreign Policy in Comparative Perspective: Domestic and International Influences on State Behavior*. Washington, DC: CQ Press, 2001.

El-Ayouty, Yassin, ed. *The Organization of African Unity after Thirty Years*. New York: Praeger, 1994.

Hook, Steven W., ed. *Comparative Foreign Policy: Adaptation Strategies of the Great and Emerging Powers*. Upper Saddle River: Prentice Hall, 2002.

Khadiagala, Gilbert M. *Allies in Adversity: The Frontline States in Southern African Security, 1975–1993*. Athens: Ohio University Press, 1994.

Khadiagala, Gilbert M., and Terrence Lyons, eds. *African Foreign Policies:*

Power and Process. Boulder: Lynne Rienner, 2001.

Lavergne, Real, ed. *Regional Integration and Cooperation in West Africa: A Multidimensional Perspective*. Trenton: Africa World, 1997.

McKay, Vernon, ed. *African Diplomacy: Studies in the Determinants of Foreign Policy*. New York: Praeger, 1966.

Ojo, Olatunde. "Regional Cooperation and Integration." In Olatunde Ojo, D. K. Orwa, and C. M. B. Utete, *African International Relations*. London: Longman, 1985 (pp. 142–83).

Olusanya, G. O. "Reflections on the First Twenty-Five Years of the Organization of African Unity." *Nigerian Journal of International Affairs* 14, no. 1 (1988): 67–72.

Onwuka, Ralph I, and Amadu Sesay, eds. *The Future of Regionalism in Africa*. New York: St. Martin's, 1985.

Oyejide, Ademola, and Ibrahim Elbadawi and Paul Collier, eds. *Regional Integration and Trade Liberalization in Sub-Saharan Africa*. New York: St. Martin's, 1997.

Shaw, Timothy M., and Olajide Aluko, eds. *The Political Economy of African*

Foreign Policy. New York: St. Martin's, 1984.

Shivji, Issa G. *The Concept of Human Rights in Africa*. Dakar: CODESRIA, 1989.

Thiam, Doudou. *The Foreign Policy of African States*. New York: Praeger, 1965.

Wright, Stephen., ed. *African Foreign Policies*. Boulder, CO: Westview, 1998.

Zartman, I. William., ed. *Traditional Cures for Modern Conflicts: African Conflict "Medicine."* Boulder: Lynne Rienner, 1999.

NOTES

1. Doudou Thiam, *La Politique Étrangère des États Africains: Ses Fondements Idéologiques, Sa Réalité Présênte, Sês Perspectives d'Avenir* (Paris: Presses Universitaires de France, 1963).

2. Ibid., pp. 2, 116.

3. Thiam, *La Politique Étrangère*, p. xi.

4. Ousmane Tanor Dieng, "Exposé sur la Politique Extérieure du Sénégal," speech delivered on September 15, 1989, to a meeting of members of the ruling Socialist Party (text provided by the Ministry of Foreign Affairs).

5. For a general introduction to the African foreign policy literature, see Stephen Wright, ed., *African Foreign Policies* (Boulder: Westview, 1998); Vernon McKay, ed., *African Diplomacy: Studies in the Determinants of Foreign Policy* (New York: Praeger, 1966); Kenneth Ingham, ed., *The Foreign Relations of African States* (London: Butterworth, 1974); Olajide Aluko, ed., *The Foreign Policies of African States* (London: Hodder and Stoughton, 1977); and Timothy M. Shaw and Olajide Aluko, eds., *The Political Economy of African Foreign Policy* (New York: St. Martin's, 1984).

6. For an introduction to this literature, see W. A. E. Skurnik, *The Foreign Policy of Senegal* (Evanston: Northwestern University Press, 1972). See also Momar-Coumba Diop, ed., *Le Sénégal et Ses Voisins* (Dakar: Sociétés-Espaces-Temps, 1994), and Peter J. Schraeder (with Nefertiti Gaye), "Senegal's Foreign Policy: Challenges of Democratization and Marginalization," *African Affairs* 96 (1997): 485–508.

7. See Cheikh Tidiane Thiam, *Droit Public du Sénégal* (vol. 1): *L'État et le Citoyen* (Dakar: Les Editions du CREDILA, 1993).

8. See Badara Diouf, "Le Nouveau Gouvernement: Un Nouveau Challenge pour Habib Thiam," *Le Soleil* (March 16, 1994): 8.

9. See Maurice A. East, "Foreign Policy Making in Small States: Some Theoretical Observations Based on a Study of the Uganda Ministry of Foreign Affairs," *Policy Sciences* 4, no. 4 (1973): 491–508. See also O. O. Fafowora, "The Role of the Ministry of External Affairs in the Formulation of Nigerian Foreign Policy: Personal Reminiscences," *Quarterly Journal of Administration* 18, no. 3–4 (1983–84): 92–110.

10. Elhadj Mbodj, "Senegal's Foreign Policy." Typed notes of a presentation made at the University of Wisconsin, Madison (no date).

11. Ibid.

12. See Kenneth W. Grundy, *The Militarization of South African Politics* (Bloomington: Indiana University Press, 1986).

13. See Nelson Mandela, "South Africa's Future Foreign Policy," *Foreign Affairs* 72, no. 5 (1993): 86–97. See also Neta Crawford, "South Africa's New Foreign and Military Policy: Opportunities and Constraints," *Africa Today* 43, no. 1–2 (1995): 88–121.

14. See Momar-Coumba Diop and Moussa Paye, "Armée et Pouvoir au Sénégal." Paper presented at a

CODESRIA-sponsored seminar on "Military and Militarism in Africa," Accra, Ghana, April 21–23, 1993, pp. 8–9.

15. Ibid. See also Abdoulaye Ndiaye, "Généraux Civils," *Jeune Afrique* no. 1934 (February 3–9, 1998), pp. 44–45.

16. Personal interviews at Senegal's Ministry of Defense, Spring 1996.

17. For an excellent overview, see Robert A. Mortimer, "Senegal's Role in Ecomog: The Francophone Dimension in the Liberian Crisis," *Journal of Modern African Studies* 34, no. 2 (1996): 293–306.

18. For a historical overview, see Victor T. Le Vine, "Parliaments in Francophone Africa: Some Lessons from the Decolonization Process," in Joel Smith and Lloyd D. Musolf, eds., *Legislatures in Development: Dynamics of Change in New and Old States* (Durham: Duke University Press, 1979), pp. 125–54.

19. For example, see Philip W. Alderfer, "Legislators' Attitudes in a New Democracy: The Zambian Experience." Paper presented at the thirty-eighth annual meeting of the African Studies Association, Orlando, Florida, November 3–6, 1995.

20. Quoted in Papa Mor Sylla, "Le Travail des Députés: Entre les Séances-Marathon et le Repos Prolongé," *Le Soleil* (July 27, 1995): 5.

21. Ibid.

22. See Louise M. Bourgaulf, *Mass Media in Sub-Saharan Africa* (Bloomington: Indiana University Press, 1995).

23. See Abdou Latif Coulibaly, "Rôle de la Presse dans la Sauvegarde et la Consolidation de la Démocratie au Sénégal," *Afrique Espoir* no. 12 (December 1994): 15–19.

24. See the series of articles and op-ed pieces in *Le Soleil, Le Sud,* and *Wal Fadjri* during the week of March 11–18, 1996.

25. Joel Millman, *The Other Americans: How Immigrants Renew Our Country, Our Economy, and Our Values* (New York: Viking, 1997), p. 198.

26. See Ron Parker, "The Senegal-Mauritania Conflict of 1989: A Fragile Equilibrium," *The Journal of Modern African Studies* 29, no. 1 (1991): 155–71, and Anthony G. Pazzanita, "Mauritania's Foreign Policy: The Search for Protection," *The Journal of Modern African Studies* 30, no. 2 (1992): 281–304.

27. It has also been argued that negative public reactions to the deaths of Senegalese peacekeepers taking part in ECOMOG operations in Liberia played a significant role in President Diouf's decision to withdraw these troops in 1993. Mortimer, "Senegal's Role in Ecomog," p. 300.

28. For example, see Sulayman Nyang, "The Islamic Factor in Libya's Africa Policy," *Africa and the World* 1, no. 2 (1988): 13–23.

29. See Leonardo A. Villalón, *Islamic Society and State Power in Senegal: Disciples and Citizens in Fatick* (Cambridge: Cambridge University Press, 1995).

30. Adekunle Ajala, "Background to the Establishment, Nature, and Structure of the Organization of African Unity," *Nigerian Journal of International Affairs* 14, no. 1 (1988): 36.

31. Ibid.

32. Quoted in ibid., p. 39.

33. Ibid., p. 30.

34. See David Rooney, *Kwame Nkrumah: The Political Kingdom in the Third World* (New York: St. Martin's, 1980).

35. G. O. Olusanya, "Reflections on the First Twenty-Five Years of the Organization of African Unity," *Nigerian Journal of International Affairs* 14, no. 1 (1988): 67.

36. Ibid., p. 80.

37. Bukar Bukarambe, "Regional Order and Local Disorder: The OAU and Civil Wars in Africa," *Nigerian Journal of International Relations* 14, no. 1 (1988): 98.

38. For example, see John J. Stremlau, *The International Politics of the Nigerian Civil War, 1967–1970* (Princeton: Princeton University Press, 1977).

39. R. A. Akindele, "The Organization of African Unity: Four Grand Debates among African Leaders Revisited,"

Nigerian Journal of International Affairs 14, no. 1 (1988): 82–85.

40. Claude E. Welch Jr., "The Organization of African Unity and the Promotion of Human Rights," *The Journal of Modern African Studies* 29, no. 4 (1991): 537.

41. Ibid., p. 538.

42. Ibid.

43. Ibid., pp. 538–39.

44. See Eghosa E. Osaghae, "The Ogoni Uprising: Oil Politics, Minority Agitation and the Future of the Nigerian State," *African Affairs* 94, no. 376 (1995): 325–44.

45. Quoted in Howard W. French, "Nigeria Comes on Too Strong." *New York Times* (November 19, 1995): E3.

46. I. William Zartman, "Inter-African Negotiation," in John W. Harbeson and Donald Rothchild, eds., *Africa in World Politics: Post–Cold War Challenges* (Boulder: Westview, 1995), pp. 209–33.

47. I. William Zartman, ed., *Collapsed States: The Disintegration and Restoration of Legitimate Authority* (Boulder: Lynne Rienner, 1995), p. 241.

48. See I. William Zartman and Samuel Amoo, "Mediation by Regional Organizations: The OAU in Chad," in Jacob Bercovitch and Jeffrey Rubin, eds., *Mediation in International Relations* (New York: St. Martin's, 1992).

49. Ibrahim A. Gambari, "The Role of Foreign Intervention in African Reconstruction," in I. William Zartman, ed. *Collapsed States: The Disintegration and Restoration of Legitimate Authority* (Boulder: Lynne Rienner, 1995), p. 229.

50. Zartman, *Collapsed States,* p. 243.

51. R. A. Akindele, "The Organization of African Unity and Conflict Situation in Southern Africa," *Nigerian Journal of International Affairs* 14, no. 1 (1988): 124–54.

52. Guy Martin, "African Regional Cooperation and Integration: Achievements, Problems and Prospects," in Ann Seidman and Frederick Anang, eds., *Twenty-First Century Africa: Toward A*

New Vision of Self-Sustainable Development (Trenton: Africa World, 1992), p. 70.

53. Ibid., p. 73.

54. See S. K. B. Asante (with David Chanaiwa), "Pan-Africanism and Regional Integration," in Ali A. Mazrui, ed. *General History of Africa* (vol. 8): *Africa since 1935* (Paris: UNESCO, 1993), pp. 724–43.

55. See Kenneth Grundy, "The Impact of Region on Contemporary African Politics," in Gwendolen M. Carter and Patrick O'Meara, eds., *African Independence: The First Twenty-Five Years* (Bloomington: Indiana University Press, 1985), pp. 97–125.

56. Olatunde Ojo, "Regional Cooperation and Integration," in Olatunde Ojo, D. K. Orwa, and C. M. B. Utete, *African International Relations* (London: Longman, 1985), pp. 142–83. See also Christian P. Potholm and Richard A. Fredland, eds., *Integration and Disintegration in East Africa* (Lanham: University Press of America, 1980), and Arthur Hazlewood, *Economic Integration: The East African Experience* (London: Heinemann, 1975).

57. Olatunde Ojo, "Regional Cooperation and Integration," pp. 159–61.

58. Ibid., pp. 161–66.

59. Ibid., pp. 166–69.

60. Ibid., pp. 169–71.

61. Ahmad A. H. M. Aly, *Economic Cooperation in Africa: In Search of Direction* (Boulder: Lynne Rienner, 1994).

62. These countries include Angola, Botswana, Lesotho, Malawi, Mozambique, Swaziland, Tanzania, Zambia, and Zimbabwe. For an analysis of their evolving interaction, see Gilbert M. Khadiagala, *Allies in Adversity: The Frontline States in Southern African Security, 1975–1993* (Athens: Ohio University Press, 1994).

63. Colleen Lowe Morna, "Southern Africa: New Era of Cooperation," *Africa Report* 40, no. 3 (1995): 65.

64. Ibid.

65. For example, see Jesmond Blumenfeld, *Economic Interdependence in Southern Africa:*

From Conflict to Cooperation? (New York: St. Martin's, 1992). For a more recent analysis, see Richard Gibb, "Southern African in Transition: Prospects and Problems Facing Regional Integration," *The Journal of Modern African Studies* 36, no. 2 (1998): 287–306.

66. Thomas Ohlson and Stephen John Stedman (with Robert Davies), *The New Is Not Yet Born: Conflict Resolution in Southern Africa* (Washington, DC: Brookings Institution, 1994).

67. The treaty states that Southern African leaders "must find a more abiding basis for continuing political solidarity and cooperation, in order to guarantee mutual peace and security in the region; and to free resources from military to productive development activities." Ibid.

12

▲▲▲

Africa in World Politics

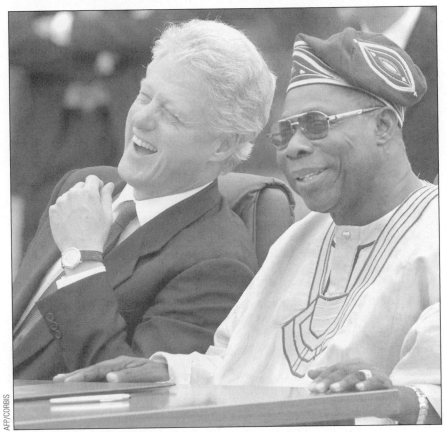

President Bill Clinton, with Nigerian President Olusegun Obasanjo, at a news conference in Abuja, Nigeria, in 2000.

S EVERAL INTERNATIONAL EVENTS have influenced the evolution of African politics and society during the contemporary independence era. The extended global conflict of World War II (1935–45) heralded the decline of Europe as the most powerful region of the world and the emergence of African nationalist movements intent on achieving independence from colonial rule. The outbreak and intensification of the **cold war** (1947–89) transformed the newly independent African countries into proxy battlefields between the United States and the former Soviet Union, the unparalleled superpowers of the post–World War II era. African conflicts often having little, if anything, to do with the ideological concerns of communism or capitalism threatened to become East-West flashpoints in the face of growing U.S.-Soviet involvement. A third watershed event, the fall of the Berlin Wall in 1989, signaled the end of the cold war but not the end of international rivalry in Africa. The ideologically based cold war between the United States and the former Soviet Union was replaced by a **cold peace,** in which the major northern industrialized democracies struggled for economic supremacy in the highly competitive economic environment of the 1990s.[1] The security dimension of this cold peace became evident in the aftermath of the September 11, 2001, terrorist attacks against the World Trade Center in New York and the Pentagon in Washington, D.C., as the United States sought to enlist its African allies in a global war on terrorism. This chapter is devoted to exploring the involvement of a host of international actors in African politics and society from the cold war to the cold peace.

ROLE OF FOREIGN POWERS

Many important policies affecting the future of African politics and society are decided in Paris, Washington, Berlin, and Tokyo, the capitals of the four **Great Powers** that remain heavily involved throughout Africa at the beginning of the twenty-first century.[2] France maintains extensive political-military and economic relationships with African countries, most notably in **francophone Africa,** those former French and Belgian colonies where, among a variety of factors, French serves as an "official language of administration and education."[3] The United States often became the most influential political-military actor in the nonfrancophone portions of the African continent during the cold war era and has increasingly sought to promote economic links in the post–cold war era.[4] Japan and Germany emerged during the 1980s as extremely involved economic actors and have achieved the status of the second or third most important sources of economic aid or trade for individual African countries (often behind the leading roles of France and the United States).[5]

Britain's official interest in maintaining privileged colonial ties, once rivaled only by that of France, dramatically waned during the cold war.[6] Economic decline forced British policymakers to make difficult decisions as to where limited economic resources would contribute most to British foreign policy interests, leading ultimately to the downgrading of British ties with most of its former colonies. In recent years, however, Britain, under the leadership of Prime Minister Tony Blair, has become more active in African international relations, as demonstrated by its leadership role in dispatching peacekeeping troops to Sierra Leone in West Africa. Britain's most noteworthy ongoing involvement with its former African colonies takes place in the context of the **Commonwealth of Nations,** a loose association of former British colonies that holds an annual summit meeting of heads of state.

Other, traditionally less powerful colonial powers, such as Spain, were never important diplomatic players due to the lack of extensive colonial holdings.[7] Weaker colonial powers demonstrated only sporadic interest in their former colonies during times of crisis, such as Belgium in Central Africa and Italy in the Horn of Africa.[8] Portugal, however, has exhibited a renewed interest in strengthening cultural ties with its former colonies and played an important role in promoting the resolution of civil wars in Angola and Mozambique during the 1990s.[9]

Despite extensive involvement during the cold war era, the former **communist bloc** countries have drastically reduced their political-military and economic presence on the African continent. The preoccupation of Russian leaders with the economic and political restructuring of the former Soviet Union has precluded any meaningful diplomatic role in Africa.[10] The one notable vestige of the previously active foreign policy of the People's Republic of China (PRC) is an ongoing diplomatic battle with Taiwan as to which capital, Beijing or Taipei, African governments recognize as the official seat of the Chinese government.[11] Other communist bloc countries that once enjoyed privileged relations with the African continent either completely disappeared (e.g., the former East Germany, which now constitutes part of a reunified Germany)[12] or became marginalized (e.g., Cuba) due to their pariah status in the international system and a drastic reduction in aid formerly provided by their socialist patrons.[13]

A variety of **middle powers** plays varying roles on the African continent. Canada and the Nordic countries, most notably Sweden, demonstrate a strong humanitarian interest, particularly concerning famine relief in the Horn of Africa and Southern Africa.[14] During the height of the Arab-Israeli conflict, Israel pursued an aggressive policy that exchanged Israeli technical aid for diplomatic recognition of the state of Israel.[15] Other Middle Eastern powers, such as Saudi Arabia, pursue religiously based policies regarding the predominantly Muslim states of North and Northeast Africa.[16] Iran in particular seeks to foster links with Islamist regimes and movements in the Sudan, Egypt, and Algeria. India and Brazil lead their regions in seeking to expand economic relations with the African continent.[17]

GREAT POWERS AND AFRICA DURING THE COLD WAR (1947–1989)

As the nationalist urges of independence movements swept the countries of Africa during the 1950s, two U.S. politicians of widely divergent political perspectives underscored the necessity of rethinking U.S. foreign policy toward Africa. "For too many years," Vice President Richard M. Nixon noted in 1957, after returning from a 22-day tour of the continent, "Africa in the minds of many Americans has been regarded as a remote and mysterious continent which was the special province of big game hunters, explorers, and motion picture makers."[18] Recognizing the importance of an emerging Africa in the international context of the East-West struggle, Nixon recommended that President Dwight D. Eisenhower authorize the creation of a separate Bureau of African Affairs in the State Department, an idea that reached fruition in 1958.

Also in 1957, Senator John F. Kennedy criticized what he perceived as Washington's inability to come to grips with the question of colonialism and the growing forces of nationalism in Africa.[19] He specifically criticized Washington's strong support for France's counterinsurgency war against Algerian nationalists seeking independence for the North African colony. Kennedy later warned that the "only real question is whether these new nations will look West or East—to Moscow or to Washington—for sympathy, help, and guidance in their effort to recapitulate, in a few decades, the entire history of modern Europe and America." To blunt what he perceived as the steady decline of U.S. prestige in Africa as a result of growing communist bloc influence, Kennedy concluded that the U.S. government "must embark on a bold and imaginative new program for the development of Africa."[20]

Despite their partisan rivalries, Nixon and Kennedy shared cold war beliefs that sought to enlist African leaders on the side of the United States in an emerging East-West rivalry with the communist bloc countries. The policymakers of Charles de Gaulle's France, Mao Zedong's China, and Nikita Khrushchev's Soviet Union shared Washington's perception of Africa's importance in the emerging cold war environment of the 1950s. As a result, they were equally fervent in the pursuit of African allies, contributing to Africa's emergence as an arena of Great Power competition. The nature of this competition during the cold war is nicely illustrated by the specific involvement of the United States and France in francophone Africa.

Complementary Interests among the Western Powers

American and French foreign policies were driven by different sets of motivating factors during the cold war. American policymakers were guided by the ideological interest of containing the former Soviet Union and its communist allies.[21] A variety of presidential doctrines, beginning with the Truman Doctrine in 1947 and culminating in the Reagan Doctrine of the 1980s, declared Washington's right to intervene against communist advances throughout the world, including in francophone Africa. As a result, pro–West administrations, such as Senegal under President Abdou Diouf, were treated as potential American allies deserving of foreign aid, whereas Marxist administrations, such as Madagascar under Didier Ratsiraka, were isolated. American policymakers also sought special relationships with strategically important regional actors, such as Morocco in North Africa, Ethiopia in the Horn of Africa, and South Africa in Southern Africa, that offered special military access rights or maintained important U.S. technical facilities (e.g., telecommunications stations) deemed critical to containment policies in Africa.[22]

French policymakers sought first and foremost to consolidate and promote the rayonnement (spread) of the most notable aspects of French culture, including the French language and intellectual traditions.[23] Also called the promotion of **la francophonie** (a greater French-speaking community), this policy is best represented by the Franco–African summit attended by the leaders of France and francophone Africa (see the accompanying box). Economic interests were perceived by French policymakers as both parallel and integral to the promotion of French culture, as witnessed by the organization of thirteen former French colonies and Equatorial Guinea in the **zone franc (the franc zone).** Created in 1947, the franc zone constitutes a supranational financial system in which France serves as the central bank, and a common currency, the Communauté Financière Africaine (CFA) franc, is tied to the French franc and guaranteed by the French treasury. By wedding its fiscal policy to the franc zone, France sought to preserve monetary stability and French influence throughout francophone Africa.[24]

As long as the United States and France were pursuing fundamentally different but complementary foreign policy interests, francophone Africa remained the beneficiary of a **complementary cold war order** in which U.S.-French relations tended to be balanced, cooperative, and predictable.[25] Regardless of whether France was led by the conservative partisans of Charles de Gaulle or the socialists of François Mitterrand, French policymakers predictably claimed that historical links and geographical proximity justified placing francophone Africa in France's sphere of influence. The implicit assumption of what serves as the French version of the Monroe Doctrine is that francophone Africa constituted France's **domaine réservé (natural preserve)** or **chasse gardée (private hunting ground)** and therefore remained "off limits" to other great powers, regardless of whether they were friends like the United States and the other northern industrialized democracies or enemies like the former Soviet Union and other "radical" powers.[26]

During the cold war, this conception of francophone Africa was wholeheartedly accepted and even encouraged by American policymakers. The White House in particular expected France and the other European allies to take the lead in their former colonial territories. As succinctly stated by George Ball, undersecretary of state in the Kennedy administration, the United States recognized Africa as a "special European responsibility," just as European nations were expected to recognize "our [U.S.] responsibility in Latin America."[27] According to American policymakers, France emerged as the only European power with both the long-term political will and the requisite military force

A Closer Look: FRANCO-AFRICAN SUMMITS IN THE PURSUIT OF LA FRANCOPHONIE

France's determination to preserve and strengthen la francophonie is best demonstrated by the biannual **Franco-African summit** attended by the presidents of France and franco-phone Africa. These summits, typically described as the centerpiece of franco-African cultural relations, are designed to strengthen already close personal relationships between the French president and his African counter-parts. The careful nurturing of close, high-level personal ties is the corner-stone of each gathering and is equally important as regards the day-to-day decision making related to French foreign policy toward Africa. Although the worldwide **Francophone sum-mit,** the ninth of which was held in Lebanon in 2002, also serves as a meeting ground of French and African heads of state, it does not serve as intimate a role as the Franco-African summit due to the attendance of powerful francophone states, most notably Canada and, to a lesser degree, Belgium, that are perceived by France as cultural rivals.

Franco-African Summits

1st	Paris, France (November 13, 1973)
2nd	Bangui, Central African Republic (March 5, 1975)
3rd	Paris, France (May 10–11, 1976)
4th	Dakar, Senegal (April 20–21, 1977)
5th	Paris, France (May 22–23, 1978)
6th	Kigali, Rwanda (May 21–22, 1979)
7th	Nice, France (May 8–10, 1980)
8th	Paris, France (November 3–4, 1981)
9th	Kinshasa, Democratic Republic of the Congo (October 8–9, 1982)
10th	Vittel, France (October 3–4, 1983)
11th	Bujumbura, Burundi (December 11–12, 1984)
12th	Paris, France (December 11–13, 1985)
13th	Lome, Togo (November 14–15, 1986)
14th	Antibes, France (December 10–12, 1987)
15th	Casablanca, Morocco (December 14–16, 1988)
16th	La Baule, France (June 19–21, 1990)
17th	Libreville, Gabon (October 5–7, 1992)
18th	Biarritz, France (November 7–9, 1994)
19th	Ouagadougou, Burkina Faso (December 4–6, 1996)
20th	Paris, France (November 27–28, 1998)
21st	Yaounde, Cameroon (January 17–19, 2001)
22nd	Paris, France (February 19–21, 2003)

capable of thwarting communist powers from exploiting instability, prompting some analysts to refer to France as Washington's de facto gendarme (policeman) in francophone Africa.[28]

Africa as a Proxy Battlefield for East-West Conflict

A second trend of the cold war era was the emergence of the African continent as a battlefield for proxy wars, as both the Western and communist blocs became militarily involved in regional conflicts.[29] In almost every case, regional conflict was exacerbated by one superpower's reaction to the other's involvement in a particular crisis situation. Soviet involvement, as well as its mere threat, was enough to capture the attention of Western, especially American, policymakers and often provoke an escalation of the conflict. Western intervention in the Democratic Republic of the Congo (Congo-Kinshasa) during 1978 is an illustrative case.

On May 13, 1978, the U.S. Assistant Secretary of State for African Affairs Richard Moose awoke to a phone call informing him that, on the night before, the Front de Libération Nationale du Congo (FLNC, Front for the National Liberation of the Congo) had mounted its second invasion of Congo-Kinshasa in little over a year. In just 4 days, the FLNC was able to capture the mining center of Kolwezi, the capital of Congo-Kinshasa's Shaba province, and the source of nearly 75 percent of the country's export earnings. With the safety of U.S. and European citizens at risk and the pro-West Mobutu Sese Seko facing a serious threat to his rule, the Carter administration received requests from the French and Belgian governments to take part in a joint military operation that would include military engagements with the FLNC. From the perspective of President Carter and his closest advisors, the Shaba conflict quickly evolved into an international East-West crisis due to its origins in Marxist-ruled Angola and the possibility that the insurgents were being accompanied by Cuban advisors and troops.

President Carter adopted the consensus opinion of his senior national security advisors to take part in a joint military operation. The U.S. role included the provision of transport and logistical support for French and Belgian paratroopers. In a total of thirty-eight flight missions, U.S. planes transported approximately 2,500 French and Belgian troops and accompanying munitions and transport vehicles to the staging area of Kamina for an eventual assault of 400 French paratroopers on the primary objective of Kolwezi. Although the French forces established control over Kolwezi and routed the remainder of FLNC forces in Shaba, 100 Europeans and thousands of Africans lost their lives.[30]

The cold war rhetoric of senior U.S. policymakers clearly underscored the East-West dimension of this crisis. In an opening statement at a press conference on May 25, 1978, Carter sternly remarked that the Cuban leader Fidel Castro bore a "heavy responsibility" for the "deadly attack" that was launched from Angolan territory.[31] This tough talk was reinforced by even stronger cold war rhetoric by National Security Advisor Zbigniew Brzezinski. In a May 28 television appearance on *Meet the Press,* Brzezinski claimed that the invasion had been launched with Moscow's blessing and charged the Soviets with a "shortsighted attempt to exploit global difficulties."[32] Moreover, the Shaba crisis was portrayed as constituting part of a larger pattern of Soviet-Cuban advances in Africa. Not only were more than 20,000 Cuban troops stationed in Angola but the Soviets and the Cubans had decisively intervened on the side of Marxist Ethiopia in that country's 1977–78 war with Somalia—leaving behind nearly 15,000 Cuban troops and Soviet advisors. Already under fire from conservative congressional critics for being "soft" on communism, the White House's response to the Shaba crisis was intended to show how "tough" and "decisive" the president could be when it came to communism.[33]

Contradictions in the Search for Allies

The importance the Great Powers attached to cultivating African allies during the cold war often resulted in contradictory policies when the normative goal of promoting democracy clashed with the pursuit of strategic interests. In the case of France, one can argue that French policymakers sought to spread French culture with the same ideological fervor with which American policymakers sought to prevent the spread of communism. Consequently, when francophone countries renounced their special relationship with France, as Guinea did in 1958 when it voted against the creation of a revised French community of states under the leadership of Paris, French retribution was swift: All aid to Guinea was abruptly cut off by an angry de Gaulle. But as long as these countries maintained strong support for la francophonie and close ties with France, even authoritarian leaders were unlikely to find themselves under heavy pressure from Paris to democratize. For example, when asked why France did not militarily intervene when David Dacko, the democratically elected president of the Central African Republic, was overthrown in a military coup d'état in 1966, Jacques Foccart, the architect of French foreign policy under de Gaulle, replied that the new leader, Jean-Bedel Bokassa, "after all was a very pro-French military man."[34]

Contradictions were also evident in Washington's policies toward Africa. Whenever the ideal of democracy clashed with the national security objective of containing communism, containment often prevailed at the expense of democracy. For this reason both Democratic and Republican administrations were willing to downplay the internal shortcomings of a variety of U.S. allies, such as Ethiopia's Haile Selassie, Somalia's Siad Barre, Congo-Kinshasa's Mobutu Sese Seko, and a host of Afrikaner regimes in South Africa, in favor of their strong support for U.S. anticommunist policies.[35] Even the Carter administration's human rights program, which questioned the wisdom of identifying the United States with inherently unstable dictatorships, was compromised by strategic exceptions. When the pursuit of human rights clashed with perceived national security interests, especially in countries of strategic importance, such as Iran, the Philippines, South Korea, and Congo-Kinshasa, national security interests prevailed.[36]

COLD WAR TO COLD PEACE
(1989–PRESENT)

The end of the cold war transformed the international order and set the stage for dramatic changes in Great Power involvement in Africa. The most notable immediate change was that one superpower, the Soviet Union, ceased to exist, and its successor state, the Russian Republic, was too preoccupied with the economic and political restructuring of its domestic system to play an extensive role on the African continent. Equally important, Germany and Japan had overcome the defeat of World War II to join the United States and France as the most influential Great Powers on the African continent. Overly optimistic expectations of Great Power cooperation in the pursuit of such normative goods as democracy promotion and socioeconomic development in the post–cold war era were nonetheless dampened by the emergence of a cold peace in which the northern industrialized democracies competed throughout the 1990s for markets and influence throughout the African continent. The security dimension of this cold peace emerged in the aftermath of the September 11, 2001, terrorist attacks against the World Trade Center in New York and the Pentagon in Washington, D.C., as the United States sought to enlist the African continent in a global war on terrorism. The specific themes of this cold peace are once again best demonstrated by principally focusing on American and French involvement in francophone Africa.

Evolving Foreign Policy Interests

The fall of the Berlin Wall marked the beginning of the end of the complementary cold war order between the United States and France in francophone Africa and its gradual replacement with a new competitive environment. In the case of France, policymakers were confronted by an intensifying economic crisis on the African continent that created rising pressures for change in the carefully crafted web of economic ties that bound the French economy to those of francophone Africa.[37] With many of their clients on the verge of financial bankruptcy, French policymakers initially decided to undertake an economic bailout that entailed massive increases in foreign aid. French aid to francophone Africa increased from the already substantial level of $3.7 billion in 1980–82 to $8.2 billion in 1990–92—a nearly 120 percent increase during a 10-year period. Once it became clear that the short-term bailouts were insufficient and that projected aid levels were beyond France's fiscal capabilities, French policymakers took the extraordinary step in January 1994 of devaluing the CFA franc by 50 percent. The decision sent shockwaves throughout the CFA franc zone, which had never before suffered a devaluation; it clearly signaled that France's commitment to the cultural imperative of la francophonie no longer took precedence over the pursuit of economic self-interest in an increasingly competitive, post–cold war world.

In the case of the United States, the end of the cold war initially fostered the decline of ideologically based policies in favor of the pursuit of trade and investment. In 1996, the Clinton administration unveiled America's first formal trade policy for aggressively pursuing new markets throughout Africa, including in francophone Africa.[38] The centerpiece of this economic strategy was congressional legislation, the **Africa Growth and Opportunity Act (AGOA)**, passed by both houses of Congress under the prodding of the Clinton White House during its second term in office and subsequently embraced by the Bush administration. Africa's enhanced economic standing in Washington was perhaps best captured by President Clinton's decision to make a 12-day presidential visit to Africa in 1998, which included stops in Botswana, Ghana, Rwanda, Senegal, South Africa, and Uganda. For the first time in U.S. history, a sitting U.S. president had led an extended diplomatic mission to Africa, intent on improving U.S.-Africa ties and promoting U.S. trade and investment on the African continent.

The Bush administration's response to the terrorist attacks of September 11, 2001, nonetheless demonstrated the durability of strategic interests in Great Power involvement in Africa. These attacks profoundly influenced U.S. foreign policy as the Bush administration announced a global war on terrorism, including pledges to aid countries threatened by terrorism, that harkened back to the initial stages of the cold war when the Truman administration underscored the need to aid countries threatened by communism. In the case of the African continent, the Bush administration has focused its efforts on North and East Africa. The microstate and former French colony of Djibouti, for example, emerged in 2003 as the site for the Defense Department's Combined Joint Task Force, the primary responsibility of which is to maintain surveillance over the movement of potential terrorist groups in neighboring Eritrea, Ethiopia, Kenya, Somalia, Sudan, and Yemen. Djibouti also agreed to station over 800 U.S. Special Forces on its territory, whose function is to carry out military operations against terrorist groups in the region. Djibouti is not unique but rather indicative of the strengthening of U.S. security ties with African countries deemed important to the war on terrorism.

Economic Competition among the Great Powers

U.S. economic policy toward Africa, beginning with the Clinton administration, has been accompanied by a series of highly publicized speeches rejecting Washington's past support for Europe's privileged economic role in its former colonies in favor of a more aggressive approach to promoting U.S. trade and investment. "The African market is open to everyone," explained former Assistant Secretary of State for African Affairs Herman Cohen in a 1995 speech in Libreville, Gabon. "We must accept free and fair competition, equality between all actors."[39] An outgrowth of this aggressive trade policy was the intensification of economic competition between the United States and the other northern industrialized democracies as they competed for economic influence and markets throughout Africa. This economic competition became especially pronounced in U.S.-French relations, most notably in the highly lucrative petroleum, telecommunications, and transport industries in francophone Africa. In the eyes of French policymakers, the penetration of American and other Western companies constituted "at best an intrusion" and "at worst an aggression" into France's chasse gardée. The seriousness with which this issue was treated at the highest levels of the French policy-making establishment was demonstrated by the public admission of Minister of Cooperation Michel Roussin that a series of meetings had been held on how best to "defend" French interests, including those in the economic realm, against those of the United States.[40]

Intense competition between the government of Congo-Brazzaville, Elf-Aquitaine (the French oil corporation), and Occidental Petroleum Corporation (Oxy), a U.S.-based oil company, is an excellent example of the potential future stakes involved in rising U.S.-French economic competition.[41] Desperately in need of nearly $200 million to pay government salaries before legislative elections, newly elected President Pascal Lissouba "naturally turned for help to Elf-Aquitaine (which controls 80 percent of the country's oil production)."[42] When its French manager refused to approve either a $300 million loan or "a request for a $300 million mortgage on the future production of three promising new offshore oil deposits," Lissouba initiated secret negotiations with the U.S.-based Oxy. An agreement was signed but renounced 8 months later by the Lissouba administration due to "intense French pressure."[43]

U.S.-French competition in the highly lucrative petroleum industry is not limited to Congo-Brazzaville. In Benin, for example, the alternation of power from President Nicéphore Soglo (1991–96) to Mathieu Kérékou (who was elected in 1996) coincided with rising U.S.-French competition over the right to explore for offshore oil reserves.[44] That President Kérékou emerged victorious in the 1996 elections with French assistance against the American-backed Soglo led some to assume that a French company (in this case, Elf-Aquitaine) would be favored over its primary American competitor (The Bettis Group from Dallas, Texas). The contract, however, was awarded to the American company. In Senegal, the administration of President Abdou Diouf in 1995 was able to withstand intense French pressures to maintain the preferential treatment awarded to French petroleum companies under his predecessor (President Léopold Sédar Senghor), subsequently signing a contract with a consortium of South African and American petroleum companies to exploit newly discovered oil fields off Senegal's southwestern coast.[45] The actions of both the Kérékou and Diouf administrations are not unique but rather indicate a more competitive foreign policy environment in which francophone African leaders are less reflexive to French foreign policy interests.[46]

An important aspect of burgeoning U.S.-French competition in francophone Africa is the willingness of local U.S. ambassadors to serve as advocates for business, in essence mirroring the activities of their local French counterparts and constituting a return to the pre–cold war era when U.S. diplomatic missions were more concerned with promoting economic linkages.[47] A new breed of diplomat has increasingly made the promotion of U.S. trade and investment an important component of U.S. embassy activities in the host country. Numerous examples stand out: Ambassador Mark Johnson facilitated the spread of U.S. Internet and related computer technology to Senegal, Ambassador William A. Dameron III successfully pushed for the further opening of Côte d'Ivoire to U.S. petroleum interests, and Ambassador Hume A. Horan aided the growing involvement of U.S. mining interests in Mali. "In the past, the U.S. government was not as willing to serve as an advocate for business, and as a result Americans were here in name only, at least as concerns trade and investment," explained one private businessperson whose words captured the essence of America's changing economic vision of the African continent. "This definitely changed under the Clinton administration, which most notably aided us by helping to keep the local playing field level from the often unfair economic practices of our competitors and working with and facilitating our access to key government officials interested in what we could bring."[48] This comment indicates a changing U.S. Foreign Service that has elevated the role of economics in the training and mandate given its ambassadors in all regions of the world, including francophone Africa.

Rhetoric versus Reality in Support for Democratization

The end of the cold war raised expectations that the Western democracies could make democracy and human rights the cornerstones of a new democratic international order that would be consistently applied to all regions of the world, including in francophone Africa. Scholars, activists, and policymakers in both the United States and France increasingly coalesced around the concept of making political democratization a precondition for the improvement of economic and political relations with Paris and Washington. Democracy promotion, however, has never served as the principal foreign policy interest of the northern industrialized democracies. At best it has played a secondary role behind more self-interested foreign policy pursuits. As a result, although democracy promotion has emerged as a more salient foreign policy issue during the post–cold war era, it nonetheless tends to be compromised when it conflicts with more central foreign policy interests of Paris and Washington.[49]

In the case of France, the administration of President François Mitterrand initially embraced African democratization movements in a much-quoted speech at the 1990 Franco-African summit held in La Baule, France, and warned his counterparts in francophone Africa that future French aid would be contingent on their willingness to promote true democratic change. What became known as the **la Baule Doctrine** suggested that the promotion of democracy would become the new hallmark of French foreign policy. The bold rhetoric of democratization was nonetheless contradicted by the reality of ongoing foreign aid programs designed to keep pro-French leaders in power.[50] In the case of Cameroon, French aid to the authoritarian regime of President Paul Biya expanded from $159 million in 1990 to $436 million in 1992, the year of the country's first multiparty presidential elections. The primary reason for the dramatic increase in French assistance was to aid Biya's victory, especially as the most popular opposition candidate was John Fru Ndi, an anglophone politician perceived as a threat to French interests in Cameroon. Any misconceptions generated by earlier French rhetoric were resolved at the 1992 Franco-African summit held in Libreville, Gabon. At this meeting, French Prime Minister Pierre Bérégovoy privately stated that when confronted with the potentially conflicting goals of promoting democracy, ensuring development, and maintaining security, the leaders of francophone Africa were expected to adopt the following order of priorities: above all, security, followed by development and, finally, democratization.[51]

The election of Jacques Chirac as president of France in May 1995 coincided with an increasingly turbulent period in French foreign policy.[52] The growing contradictions in French support for democratization policies were shown by the Chirac administration's response to a 1996 coup d'état in Niger, the first against a democratically elected government in France's former colonies since the beginning of the democratization process in 1990. Despite a 1995 commitment by Minister of Cooperation Jacques Godfrain that France would intervene to reinstate a democratically elected government if a defense treaty had been signed with that country, France refused to intervene in Niger and ultimately decided to work with the military regime headed by Colonel Ibrahim Maïnassara Baré.[53] Not surprisingly, the democratically elected francophone neighbors of Niger were worried by French inaction. In a throwback to an earlier era of authoritarian rule and highly questionable democratic practices, Colonel Baré announced that there would be multiparty elections in 1996, presented himself as the candidate of the ruling party, and subsequently won the election to the congratulatory toasts of local French diplomats.

Contradictions are also evident in U.S. support for democratization policies. At the very least, punitive measures designed to enforce prodemocracy rhetoric are at best unevenly applied depending on the perceived importance of the African country. The Clinton administration was quick to enforce comprehensive economic sanctions against the ministate of Gambia when that country's military took power in a coup d'état in 1994, but it refused to impose comprehensive economic sanctions against the military dictatorship of Nigeria that would have affected U.S. access to Nigerian oil, the mainstay of the Nigerian economy (although it did impose a variety of more limited sanctions, such as the suspension of military cooperation). In addition, in the aftermath of the terrorist attacks of September 11, 2001, against the World Trade Center and the Pentagon, the Bush White House had to weigh the benefits of democracy promotion when the pursuit of such a policy would potentially alienate important African allies in the war on terrorism. In the case of Djibouti, for example, a decision to make democracy promotion the principal U.S. foreign policy objective theoretically would have precluded the stationing on Djiboutian soil of the U.S. Defense Department's Combined Joint Task Force, including nearly 900 U.S. troops. Indeed, all three of Washington's North African allies in the war on terrorism (Egypt, Morocco, and Tunisia) lack democratic political systems. "In short," explained one member of the U.S. Embassy in Tunis, "foreign policy is about choosing, and in this case there is no question that the security interest of combating global terrorism with our allies in North Africa is more important than the degree to which the peoples of these countries enjoy democratic forms of governance."[54]

Regional variations nonetheless exist. U.S. diplomats have typically been more vocal than their French counterparts in their support for democracy movements in francophone West Africa. The unusually vocal stances of these diplomats is at least partially the result of a self-interested calculation that the United States has little to lose and everything to gain by excoriating pro-French elites who impede the transition to a new political order. The logic of diplomatic competition at the local level is based on perceptions of the democratization process as a zero-sum game—that is, one country's gain is another's loss. From the perspective of local U.S. ambassadors, for example, promoting multiparty democracy is a low-cost strategy with potentially high returns—namely, the replacement of pro-French elites with new leaders potentially more sensitive to U.S. interests. From the perspective of local French ambassadors, the reverse holds true, which explains why French policymakers often tend to emerge as protectors of the status quo.

A Closer Look: JAPANESE NEOMERCANTILISM IN AFRICA

Japan has traditionally pursued a **neomercantilist** foreign policy toward Africa that underscores the overriding importance of securing economic self-interest (kokueki) relative to other foreign policy goals. The hallmark of Japanese neomercantilism has been the vigorous use of a generous foreign aid budget to penetrate foreign economic markets and promote Japanese trade and investment. As a result, Japanese foreign aid has been overwhelmingly targeted toward four categories of countries: (1) important sources of raw materials vital to Japanese industry, such as copper in Zambia; (2) potential future sources of such raw materials, including chromium in Sudan; (3) major sources of highly valued Japanese foodstuffs, such as fish products from Senegal; or (4) major economic markets capable of absorbing Japanese exports, such as Nigeria.

A close partnership between government and big business (kanzai ittaishugi) is an essential ingredient of Japan's economic success in Africa. All Japanese government agencies, most notably the Ministry of Finance, the Ministry of Economy, Trade, and Industry (METI), and the Japanese International Cooperation Agency (JICA), operate from the assumption that big business and diplomacy are both complementary and mutually reinforcing. They therefore highlight the importance of working closely with the Japanese business community (zaikai) to promote Japanese trade and investment in Africa. Even in the Ministry of Foreign Affairs, the Japanese bureaucracy most inclined to argue the political ramifications of a given policy, career diplomats accept and promote the economic imperatives of international diplomacy.

The close partnership between government and big business is strengthened by a wide variety of ancillary groups and organizations. The Japan External Trade Organization (JETRO) maintains offices in the capitals of several strategically located countries—Côte d'Ivoire, Egypt, Kenya, Nigeria, South Africa, Tanzania, and Zimbabwe—that represent the most important economies on the African continent. The Japan Overseas Cooperation Volunteers (JOCV) program, the Japanese equivalent of the U.S. Peace Corps, sends abroad more than 1,000 Japanese volunteers annually, with approximately 25–30 percent sent to serve in African countries. Japanese policymakers and corporate leaders have also formed numerous "private" committees, such as the Africa Society of Japan and the Keidanren Committee on Sub-Saharan Africa, that guide official government policy. The Keidanren Committee has been especially effective in that it includes the leadership of dozens of the most influential Japanese corporations.

For further discussion, see Jun Morikawa, *Japan and Africa: Big Business and Diplomacy* (Trenton: Africa World, 1997).

In Benin, for example, President Nicéphore Soglo's victory in the first presidential elections to be held after his country's transition to democracy in 1991
led to the formation of an administration less dependent on France and more
interested in promoting closer foreign policy ties with the United States.[55] It is
precisely for this reason, argue critics of French policies in Africa, that local
French diplomats provided significant support to Soglo's authoritarian predecessor, Mathieu Kérékou, who emerged victorious in the 1996 presidential
elections. Although he ultimately accepted the 1996 election results, Soglo
remained sharply critical of the "northern countries" (read "France"), who he
at least partially blamed for his defeat at the hands of Benin's former dictator of
nineteen years. Regardless of France's ultimate role in the 1996 presidential
elections, however, Kérékou's reemergence did not signal a return to the same
Beninois-French relationship that existed prior to 1991. The strengthening of
several competing institutional actors, most notably a vibrant national assembly,
has contributed to growing pluralism in Beninois foreign policy.

INVOLVEMENT IN THE UNITED NATIONS

African leaders consider membership in the United Nations and its related
agencies to be one of the most important elements of African international
relations. In addition to serving as a concrete symbol of African independence,
UN membership has historically given African leaders an important international forum for promoting African views on a variety of international issues,
such as unequivocal support for complete decolonization, opposition to
apartheid in South Africa, the promotion of socioeconomic development, and
the need for disarmament and attention to regional security. Most important,
the UN provides a unique forum for diplomatic negotiations. Financially
unable to maintain embassies throughout the world, let alone throughout the
African continent, African diplomats take advantage of the fact that almost all
countries maintain a permanent mission in New York to carry out the day-to-
day business of diplomacy.[56]

UN agencies play substantial administrative and developmental roles in
many African countries. In several African capital cities, there are a variety of UN
offices whose budgets and staffs sometimes approach those of their counterparts in the host government. In Dakar, Senegal, offices represent a variety of
UN agencies, including the United Nations Development Programme (UNDP),
the United Nations International Children's Emergency Fund (UNICEF), the
United Nations High Commissioner for Refugees (UNHCR), the World
Health Organization (WHO), the International Labour Organization (ILO),
and the United Nations Educational, Scientific, and Cultural Organization
(UNESCO). Capturing the sentiment of African policymakers during the
1960s, a Senegalese diplomat noted that "these agencies were perceived as critical to the fulfillment of African development goals during the initial independence era and provided a source of hope, especially for those African

countries lacking both the resources and the expertise to implement the studies and programs pursued by each of these agencies."[57]

In the aftermath of the cold war, however, a vocal segment of African leaders and intellectuals is sometimes apt to associate the UN with foreign intervention and the imposition of Western values. This perception is due to the replacement of the classic international norms of sovereignty and nonintervention in the affairs of UN member-states with a new set of norms that focus on human rights protection and humanitarian intervention, particularly to save refugees and other peoples threatened by civil conflict and starvation.[58] As aptly noted by former UN Secretary General Boutros-Ghali, "the time of absolute and exclusive sovereignty . . . has passed; its theory was never matched by reality."[59] Indeed, as Table 12.1 demonstrates, the UN has undertaken twenty peace-keeping missions in Africa, sixteen launched in the post–cold war era.

The series of UN-sponsored military interventions in Somalia from 1992 to 1995 serves as one of the most notable examples of the UN's interventionist role in African politics and society. At its height, the UN military operation included over 38,000 troops from twenty countries and led to the effective occupation of southern and central Somalia. The intervention was launched in the absence of any official invitation from a legal Somali authority (which, in any case, did not exist) and in direct opposition to heavily armed militia groups who shared a historical mistrust of UN intentions and operations dating back to the colonial era.[60] From the perspective of the UN, the collapse of the Somali state and the intensification of a brutal civil war demanded UN intervention; the conflict was not only spilling over into the neighboring territories of Kenya, Ethiopia, and Djibouti but had contributed to the creation of a humanitarian crisis in which approximately 330,000 Somalis were at "imminent risk of death."[61] According to this logic, the UN could justify international intervention, even in the absence of an official invitation by a legally constituted authority, on the grounds of "abatement" of a threat to international peace.[62]

The Somali case is part of a growing international trend of prompting even internationally recognized governments to accept UN-sponsored humanitarian intervention.[63] In Sudan, for example, a combination of civil war and drought-induced famine, which led to the deaths of over 500,000 civilians since 1986, prompted the United Nations Office of Emergency Operations in Africa (OEOA) to undertake a humanitarian intervention in 1989 known as Operation Lifeline Sudan.[64] Constituting one of the largest peacetime humanitarian interventions undertaken in UN history, Operation Lifeline Sudan was made possible only by mounting international pressure on the Sudanese regime to recognize the scope of the problem and to accept UN-sponsored intervention. Ultimate acceptance, however, did not ensure ultimate happiness on the part of the Sudanese regime. "Even when the initial issues of involvement are resolved, relations between the donors and the recipient country or population are never entirely harmonious," explains a group of specialists on conflict resolution, led by Francis M. Deng, a Sudanese national who served as Special Representative of the United Nations Secretary General for Internally

Table 12.1 United Nations Peacekeeping Missions in Africa
(As of April 2003)

COUNTRY	MISSION NAME	DATES
Egypt	UNEF I—First United Nations Emergency Force	11/1956–6/1967
Democratic Republic of the Congo	ONUC—United Nations Operation in Congo	7/1960–6/1964
Egypt	UNEF II—Second United Nations Emergency Force	10/1973–7/1979
Angola	UNAVEM I—United Nations Angola Verification Mission I	12/1988–5/1991
Morocco (Western Sahara)	MINURSO—United Nations Mission for the Referendum in Western Sahara	4/1991–present
Angola	UNAVEM II—United Nations Angola Verification Mission II	5/1991–2/1995
Somalia	UNOSOM I—United Nations Operation in Somalia I	4/1992–3/1993
Mozambique	ONUMOZ—United Nations Operation in Mozambique	12/1992–12/1994
Somalia	UNOSOM II—United Nations Operation in Somalia II	3/1993–3/1995
Rwanda/Uganda	UNOMUR—United Nations Observer Mission Uganda-Rwanda	9/1993–9/1994
Liberia	UNOMIL—United Nations Observer Mission in Liberia	9/1993–9/1997
Rwanda	UNAMIR—United Nations Assistance Mission for Rwanda	10/1993–3/1996
Chad/Libya	UNASOG—United Nations Aouzou Strip Observer Group	5/1994–6/1994
Angola	UNAVEM III—United Nations Angola Verification Mission III	2/1995–6/1997
Angola	MONUA—United Nations Observer Mission in Angola	6/1997–2/1999
Central African Republic	MINURCA—United Nations Mission in the Central African Republic	4/1998–2/2000
Sierra Leone	UNOMSIL—United Nations Observer Mission in Sierra Leone	7/1998 10/1999
Sierra Leone	UNAMSIL—United Nations Mission in Sierra Leone	10/1999–present
Democratic Republic of the Congo	MONUC—United Nations Organization Mission of the Democratic Republic of the Congo	12/1999–present
Ethiopia & Eritrea	UNMEE—United Nations Mission in Ethiopia and Eritrea	7/2000–present

SOURCE: United Nations Home page: http://www.un.org/

Displaced Persons. "The dichotomy expressed between 'us' and 'them' becomes inevitable as the nationals feel their pride injured by their own failure and dependency, while the donors and relief workers resent the lack of gratitude and appreciation."[65]

INFLUENCE OF INTERNATIONAL
FINANCIAL INSTITUTIONS

African perceptions of eroding sovereignty have been reinforced by the rising influence of international financial institutions in African economies. By the beginning of the 1980s, African leaders were struggling to respond to the effects of a continent-wide economic crisis. A combination of internal economic decline and mounting international debt was compounded by the "crisis of the state": the existence of bloated, corrupt, and inefficient government bureaucracies increasingly incapable of responding to the day-to-day needs of their respective populations (see Chapter 8). To obtain necessary international capital, most African leaders had little choice but to turn to two international financial institutions: the International Monetary Fund (IMF), which issues short-term stabilization loans to ensure economic solvency, and the World Bank, which issues long-term loans to promote economic development. Unlike typical loans that simply require the recipient to make regularly scheduled payments over a specific period, those of the IMF and the World Bank have included a series of externally imposed demands, typically referred to as **conditionalities,** designed to restructure African economies and political systems in the image of the northern industrialized democracies.[66]

The emergence of **economic conditionalities** was signaled by the 1981 publication of a World Bank study, *Accelerated Development in Sub-Saharan Africa: An Agenda for Action.* The conclusion of this report was that misguided decisions of the first generation of African leaders were responsible for the mounting economic crisis of the 1980s. To resolve this crisis, the World Bank and the IMF proposed linking all future flows of Western financial capital to the willingness of African leaders to sign and implement **structural adjustment programs (SAPs):** economic blueprints designed to radically restructure African economies. Four sets of private sector reforms are characteristic of SAPs: (1) the termination of food subsidies that kept food prices artificially low, effectively discouraging farmers from planting food crops; (2) the devaluation of national currencies to stimulate exports and the domestic production of manufactured products; (3) the trimming of government bureaucracies; and (4) the privatization of parastatals (state-owned corporations). In short, the SAPs embodied the liberal economic consensus of the northern industrialized democracies that Africa's future economic success depended on the pursuit of an export-oriented strategy of economic growth that systematically dismantled all forms of governmental intervention in national economies.[67]

A second World Bank report published in 1989, *Sub-Saharan Africa: From Crisis to Sustainable Growth: A Long-Term Perspective Study,* heralded the emergence of **political conditionalities** in IMF and World Bank–sponsored SAPs. In addition to claiming that African countries following IMF and World Bank economic prescriptions were performing better than those that were not, the 1989 report went beyond previous studies by underscoring that the success of economic reforms depended on the promotion of **good governance,** the creation of transparent, accountable, and efficient political systems patterned after those of the northern industrialized democracies. Simply put, the 1989 report signaled an emerging consensus in favor of making all future flows of Western financial capital contingent on the willingness of African leaders to promote the liberalization of their respective political systems.

The economic and political conditionalities imposed by the IMF and the World Bank have been repeatedly challenged by African policymakers and academics. During the 1980s, the SAPs were criticized for their complete disregard for the political dilemmas African leaders confront.[68] IMF and World Bank economists failed to consider that cutting off government food subsidies, one of the previously cited four pillars of private sector reform always included in SAPs, could lead to often violent urban riots. In Sudan, for example, the launching of an SAP in 1985 sparked an urban insurrection that contributed to the overthrow of the regime of Gaafar Mohammed Nimeiri.[69] The implementation of the three remaining pillars of private sector reform also entailed serious political risks, due to their tendency to reinforce short-term economic hardships. The devaluation of the national currency meant an immediate decline in the already marginal buying power of the average citizen, and the trimming of government bureaucracies and the privatization of parastatals triggered significant increases in already high levels of national unemployment. In retrospect, the lack of political sensitivity was because the SAPs were usually formulated by international economists with little (if any) political training or firsthand knowledge of the individual African countries their programs were supposed to serve.

SAPs were also strongly challenged by African policymakers and academics during the 1990s despite the fact that both the IMF and the World Bank had undertaken serious efforts to assess and, when possible, incorporate, African sentiments into policy-planning documents. Africans were particularly critical of the consensus of IMF and World Bank economists that economic and political conditionalities were mutually reinforcing and therefore could be pursued simultaneously.[70] As demonstrated by Africa's experiments with democratization after the fall of the Berlin Wall in 1989, the creation of democratic political systems complete with institutional checks-and-balances has hindered the implementation of SAPs (see Chapter 10). Indeed, democratically elected African presidents and congressional representatives often hesitate to enact legislation that will place significant economic burdens on already impoverished populations and thereby potentially contribute to their political demise the next time elections are held.

One dimension of African critiques of SAPs involves the applicability of the so-called **Asian model of development:** rapid export-oriented growth that led to the economic success of the "Asian tigers" of Hong Kong, South Korea, Singapore, and Taiwan.[71] The example of South Korea is especially noteworthy. Success in this case was largely due to authoritarian policies that directly contradict the political conditionalities imposed on African leaders. In South Korea, a military leadership intent on ending corruption and promoting economic development illegally took power in a 1961 military coup d'état and significantly curtailed political pluralism and participation.[72] The implications of this "lesson" (i.e., that the successful implementation of unpopular SAPs requires an enlightened form of authoritarianism) were reinforced by Ghana's implementation of SAPs during the 1980s under the authoritarian leadership of Flt. Lt. Jerry Rawlings. Often cited by IMF and World Bank studies as a model for other African countries, the Rawlings regime was able to impose draconian initiatives due to its iron-fisted control over the political system. The authoritarian nature of the Rawlings regime enabled it to impose SAPs that discriminated against the urban population, particularly workers, while preventing the strikes and urban unrest that derailed similar programs in other African countries.[73]

African leaders have sought to curb the impact of economic and political conditionalities by formulating alternative frameworks for development. One of the earliest attempts was the adoption of the **Lagos Plan of Action (LPA)** at the 1980 OAU Assembly of Heads of State and Government held in Freetown, Sierra Leone. The LPA was not taken seriously in international financial circles due to its contradictory assumption that Western governments and financial institutions would finance the pursuit of self-reliant economic development designed to delink the African continent from the international economic system. In 1989, the Economic Commission for Africa (ECA) published a document, *African Alternative Framework to Structural Adjustment Programmes for Socioeconomic Recovery and Transformation (AAF-SAP),* that drew at least the grudging acceptance of IMF and World Bank economists. Acknowledging that African leaders were partially responsible for Africa's economic crisis and that some form of economic restructuring was necessary, the 1989 report nonetheless castigated the IMF and World Bank for ignoring the social and political impacts of SAPs. The report specifically called on international donor agencies to promote **structural adjustment with a human face:** to plan for and respond to the short-term negative social impacts (e.g., rising unemployment) that inevitably accompany the good-faith efforts on the part of African leaders to implement SAPs.

The most recent and far-reaching alternative framework for development advanced by African leaders is the **New Partnership for Africa's Development (NEPAD).** The essence of NEPAD is that African countries must undertake economic and political reforms if they wish to attract the foreign capital from the northern industrialized democracies that is deemed necessary to Africa's future development.[74] Specifically, African leaders are seeking increases in grant aid (as opposed to loans that must be paid back) and foreign investment and trade from the northern industrialized democracies. In return, they have agreed to establish a peer review mechanism in which African leaders will assess and critique the degree to which African countries are undertaking promised economic and political reforms. Although important hurdles remain (e.g., critics have questioned how Libya and other nondemocratic African countries can take part in the peer review committee), an important step in the NEPAD initiative was educating and seeking the agreement of key northern leaders. To this end, the four major African proponents of the NEPAD initiative—Presidents Abdulaziz Bouteflika of Algeria, Thabo Mbeki of South Africa, Olusegun Obasanjo of Nigeria, and Abdoulaye Wade of Senegal—attended the 2002 annual meeting of the Group of 8 (G-8), where they received endorsements for NEPAD and promises of increased aid from the leaders of the eight most powerful northern industrialized democracies: Canada, France, Germany, Italy, Japan, Russia, the United Kingdom, and the United States. Although the African Union and the United Nations have also endorsed NEPAD, only time will tell if rhetoric will be matched by increased flows of foreign capital from the northern industrialized democracies, as well as the strengthening of economic and political reforms on the part of African leaders.

EVOLVING EQUATION OF
MILITARY INTERVENTION

A variety of African security challenges, most notably the emergence of **collapsed states**[75] beset by ethnic, religious, and political rivalries, has fostered renewed debate over the desirability of foreign military intervention in African conflicts. According to one estimate, twenty-four of Africa's fifty-three countries experienced sustained civil strife during the 1990s.[76] The lack of an African consensus over how to respond to these conflicts has invariably fostered a variety of military interventions by at least four sets of actors: (1) the United Nations, as demonstrated by its approval of sixteen peace-keeping missions in Africa since 1989; (2) African regional organizations, such as the decision of the Economic Community of West African States (ECOWAS) to sponsor a series of Nigerian-led military operations in Liberia; (3) foreign powers, most notably France, the United States, and, to a lesser degree, the United Kingdom, as witnessed by its dispatch of British troops to Sierra Leone; and (4) African powers, as demonstrated by South Africa's military intervention in neighboring Lesotho. From the perspective of pan-Africanists, such ad hoc interventions, especially those undertaken by foreign powers without the consent of either the local or international communities, are ultimately undesirable; rather than representing an African consensus opinion, such interventions are theoretically driven by the self-interests of the intervening country.

An analysis of U.S. and French interventionist practices offers important insights into the evolving military equation in the post–cold war era. The military role of the United States, often deemed the "sole superpower" with a responsibility to act, was sharply influenced by a series of U.S.-led military operations in Somalia known as Operation Restore Hope, most notably after eighteen U.S. soldiers were killed and seventy-eight others wounded in October 1993 in a fierce battle in Mogadishu, Somalia.[77] The Somali "debacle," as it came to be known, served as the cornerstone of a policy directive, Presidential Decision Directive 25 (PDD-25), that announced an extremely cautious U.S.

approach to ethnically and religiously based conflicts in Africa. When confronted in 1994 with rising popular demands for U.S. intervention in Rwanda,
for example, the Clinton administration, fearful of being drawn into "another
Somalia," not only initially blocked the dispatch of 5,500 troops requested by
UN Secretary-General Boutros Boutros-Ghali, it instructed administration
spokespeople to avoid labeling the unfolding ethnic conflict "genocide" lest
such a label further inflame American public sympathy and demand American
intervention, as was the case in Somalia, or trigger American obligations under
international treaties dealing with genocide and its prevention.[78]

The experience in Somalia also significantly affected the Clinton administration's approach to conflict resolution, most notably by resolving a debate
between two currents of thought in the administration. The first emphasized
the classic belief that African issues unnecessarily distract the administration and
potentially plunge the White House into unwanted domestic political contro-
versies. According to this viewpoint, American involvement (even in terms
of conflict resolution) should be restricted to avoid entanglement in "future
Somalias."[79] A second, more activist approach also derived from the Somali
experience but underscored that the massive costs associated with Operation
Restore Hope could have been avoided by earlier, preventive action. "The
choice is not between intervening or not intervening," explained one policy-
maker at the beginning of the Clinton administration. "It is between getting
involved early and doing it at a cheaper cost, or being forced to intervene in a
massive, more costly way later."[80] As witnessed by the Clinton administration's
cautious approach to the initial stages of the Rwandan conflict, the events of
October 1993 in Somalia clearly strengthened the position of those warning
against getting too closely involved in "intractable" conflicts in Africa.

The Bush administration entered office in 2001 with a more "realist" vision
of international affairs that nonetheless shared its predecessor's maxim of avoiding undue U.S. involvement in African conflicts. This tendency was clearly
indicated during the presidential campaign, when Bush noted that the Clinton
administration had done "the right thing" in deciding not to intervene in the
unfolding genocide in Rwanda in 1994.[81] Bush administration policy was formalized by Secretary of State Colin Powell, who underscored during his confirmation hearings before the U.S. Senate the need for Africans to "do more for
themselves" in the realm of conflict resolution. "In Sierra Leone, Liberia,
Angola, the Congo [Kinshasa], and elsewhere, this means stopping the killing,
taking the weapons out of the hands of children, ending corruption, seeking
compromises, and beginning to work in peace and dialogue rather than war
and killing," explained Powell. "It means giving the profits from oil and diamonds and other precious resources to schools and hospitals and decent roads
instead of to bombs, bullets, and feuding warlords."[82] Indeed, according to
what could be labeled the "Powell doctrine" for Africa, African diplomats and
military forces, and not those of foreign powers (including the United States),
must take the lead in responding to African crises and conflicts.

France, arguably the most militarily active foreign power on the African
continent during the cold war, has also recast its military role in the post–cold

war era. The evolving nature of French military intervention was captured by the Chirac administration's response to a series of crises in the Great Lakes region, most notably the emergence and spread in 1997 of a guerrilla insurgency in Congo-Kinshasa that successfully sought to overthrow the authoritarian regime of Mobutu Sese Seko.[83] French policymakers perceived the Great Lakes crisis in francophone-anglophone terms: The guerrilla insurgency in eastern Congo-Kinshasa was led by Laurent-Désiré Kabila, who in turn was strongly supported by and allied with the Rwandan government of Paul Kagame and the Ugandan government of Yoweri Museveni. As a result, the French considered Kabila's guerrilla movement to be under Anglo-Saxon influence and therefore hostile to France. The worst-case scenario envisioned by French policymakers occurred when Kabila's guerrilla army overthrew the Mobutu regime in May 1997 and installed a new government (with Kabila as president) strongly allied with Rwanda and Uganda, which in turn were closely allied with the United States. According to this vision, Kabila's emergence as the president of Congo-Kinhasa not only constituted a clear victory for Anglo-Saxon influence at the expense of la francophonie, it raised the possibility that Congo-Kinshasa might serve as a potential springboard for the further spread of Anglo-Saxon influence throughout francophone Africa, a fear that was dampened after Kabila had a political falling out with his former Rwandan and Ugandan allies, who subsequently launched a second guerrilla insurgency in 1998 designed to militarily overthrow the Kabila regime.

The Chirac administration's attempts at playing a more proactive military role in the Great Lakes region were restrained by a variety of factors, including the lack of interest among the other Great Powers to authorize a UN-sponsored, multilateral military force; the publicly stated promise of the Rwandan government and Kabila's guerrilla forces to militarily engage with and inflict heavy casualties on French forces; and the French military's limited military capability to independently move and sustain the large numbers of troops and equipment that would have been necessary for a long-term engagement in such a vast military theater. France's long-term military role in Africa was most dramatically affected by the decision to restructure and downsize the French military that followed in the aftermath of Lionel Jospin's election as Prime Minister in 1997 and the emergence of a divided government under Chirac's conservative political forces (which controlled the presidency) and Jospin's Socialist Party and allies (which were responsible for forming a new government). As part of this general reorganization, a decision was made to both downsize the French military presence in Africa and, in some cases, such as the Central African Republic, to eliminate French military bases completely.

The restructuring of French-African military relations is tied to ongoing debates in the French foreign policymaking establishment between the so-called **anciens** (the "ancients"), who favor activist measures (including direct military intervention) to maintain pro-French clients in power, and the **modernes** (the "moderns"), who emphasize the need to move beyond France's interventionist past in its former colonies.[84] At least as far back as February 1994, when the CFA franc was devalued, moves have been afoot to isolate the old-line defenders of France's chasse gardée in Africa. No case demonstrated the rising influence of the moderns better than Chirac's rejection of the use of military force to return Henri Konan Bédié to power in Côte d'Ivoire, one of the linchpins of French foreign policy in francophone Africa, after his regime had been overthrown in a December 1999 military coup and replaced with a military regime led by General Gueï. Less than 3 years later, however, French military intervention in Côte d'Ivoire to prevent the government of President Laurent Gbagbo, who had succeeded Gueï in 2000, from being overturned by a guerrilla insurgency, clearly demonstrated the enduring legacy of the ancients in French foreign policy toward Africa.[85]

One post–cold war military strategy of the Great Powers has involved support for the **African Crisis Response Initiative (ACRI),** a military aid program designed to train African armies in the art of peace keeping and peace making so that African countries can take the lead in resolving African conflicts. An earlier version of this initiative, the U.S.-promoted African Crisis Response Force (ACRF), was denounced by France as a unilateral measure that did not take into account French desires, as well as those of African countries that presumably would contribute troops. ACRI, however, has been based on the comparatively harmonious planning between the American, British, and French military establishments. Training continues, and there has been a significant amount of cooperation in multinational military exercises. While not without friction, this cooperation is based on the recognition of common American, British, and French military interests and the unwillingness and/or inability of the Great Powers to commit major new public, especially military resources to Africa.

The African dimension of an evolving interventionist equation is best captured by two developments. First, a series of successful guerrilla insurgencies fostered the rise during the 1990s of what was often called a "new bloc" of African leaders that included Isaias Afwerki of Eritrea, Meles Zenawi of Ethiopia, Yoweri Museveni of Uganda, and Paul Kagame of Rwanda.[86] Successful in the pursuit of power primarily due to their control over strong, disciplined, and battle-tested guerrilla armies, this new generation of elites shared a commitment to create "responsive and accountable" but not necessarily democratic governments that significantly reordered the foreign policy relationships pursued by their predecessors. Equally important has been the greater willingness on the part of African regional powers, most notably Nigeria and South Africa, to flex their military muscle in their regions. Indeed, South Africa's self-anointed role as leader of the "African renaissance," the strengthening of democratic practices and economic liberalization throughout Africa since the fall of the Berlin Wall in 1989, is part of a conscious effort among South African policymakers to underscore their country's unique position as an intermediary between the African continent and leading foreign powers in all other regions of the world.[87]

An important outcome of these trends during the post–cold war era has been the rising tendency of African countries to militarily intervene in their neighbors. The most-cited example of this new trend was the expansion of civil conflict in Congo-Kinshasa into what foreign observers now commonly call Africa's "First World War." At its height in 2002, this conflict was marked by the introduction of massive numbers of ground troops by at least five Africa countries: Angola, Namibia, and Zimbabwe, which were fighting on the side of Congo-Kinshasa's government, and Rwanda and Uganda, which were seeking to topple that government. Although the individual stakes of African countries contributing troops to this conflict were extremely varied,[88] together they underscored an emerging reality of African international relations at the dawn of a new millennium: the rising importance of regional military balances of power and the political-military and economic interests of regional actors. Africa, having provided a battlefield for superpower interests during the cold war, provides another for rising African powers intent on dominating the international relations of their respective regions.

KEY TERMS

cold war
cold peace
Great Powers
francophone Africa
Commonwealth of Nations
communist bloc
middle powers
la francophonie
zone franc (franc zone)
complementary cold war order
domaine réservé (natural preserve)
chasse gardée (private hunting
  ground)
Franco-African summit
Francophone summit
Africa Growth and Opportunity Act
  (AGOA)
la Baule Doctrine

neomercantilist
conditionalities
economic conditionalities
structural adjustment programs
  (SAPs)
political conditionalities
good governance
Asian model of development
Lagos Plan of Action (LPA)
structural adjustment with a
  human face
New Partnership for Africa's
  Development (NEPAD)
collapsed states
anciens (ancients)
modernes (moderns)
African Crisis Response Initiative
  (ACRI)

FOR FURTHER READING

Akinrinade, Sola, and Amadu Sesay, eds. *Africa in the Post–Cold War International System*. London: Cassell Academic, 1998.

Anda, Michael O. *International Relations in Contemporary Africa*. Lanham: University Press of America, 2000.

Brune, Stepan, Joachim Betz, and Winrich Kuhne, eds. *Africa and Europe: Relations of Two Continents in Transition*. Munster and Hamburg: Lit Verlag, 1994.

Callaghy, Thomas, Ronald Kassimir, and Robert Latham, eds. *Intervention and*

Transnationalism in Africa: Global-Local Networks of Power. Cambridge: Cambridge University Press, 2001.

Callaghy, Thomas M., and John Ravenhill, eds. *Hemmed In: Responses to Africa's Economic Decline.* New York: Columbia University Press, 1993.

Clapham, Christopher. *Africa and the International System: The Politics of State Survival.* Cambridge: Cambridge University Press, 1996.

Decalo, Samuel. *Israel and Africa: Forty Years, 1956–1996.* Gainesville: Florida Academic, 1997.

DeLancey, Mark W., William Cyrus Reed, Rebecca Spyke, and Peter Steen. *African International Relations: An Annotated Bibliography* (2nd ed.). Boulder: Westview, 1997.

Deng, Francis M., Sadikiel Kimaro, Terrence Lyons, Donald Rothchild, and I. William Zartman. *Sovereignty as Responsibility: Conflict Management in Africa.* Washington, DC: Brookings Institution, 1996.

Dunn, Kevin C., and Timothy M. Shaw, eds. *Africa's Challenge to International Relations Theory.* New York: Palgrave, 2001.

Engel, Ulf, and Robert Kappel, eds. *Germany's Africa Policy Revisited: Interests, Images, and Incrementalism.* Munster: Lit Verlag, 2002.

Harbeson, John W., and Donald Rothchild, eds. *Africa in World Politics: The African State System in Flux* (3rd ed.). Boulder: Westview, 1995.

Laïdi, Zaki. *The Superpowers and Africa: The Constraints of a Rivalry 1960–1990.* Chicago: University of Chicago Press, 1990.

Mkandawire, Thandika, and Adebayo Olukoshi, eds. *Between Liberalization and Oppression: The Politics of Structural Adjustment in Africa.* Dakar: CODESRIA, 1995.

Morikawa, Jun. *Japan and Africa: Big Business and Diplomacy.* Trenton: Africa World, 1997.

Neuman, Stephanie G. *International Relations Theory and the Third World.* New York: St. Martin's Press, 1998.

Patman, Robert G. *The Soviet Union and the Horn of Africa: The Diplomacy of Intervention and Disengagement.* Cambridge: Cambridge University Press, 1990.

Prendergast, John. *Frontline Diplomacy: Humanitarian Aid and Conflict in Africa.* Boulder: Lynne Rienner, 1996.

Schraeder, Peter J. *United States Foreign Policy toward Africa: Incrementalism, Crisis, and Change.* Cambridge: Cambridge University Press, 1994.

Snow, Phillip. *The Star Raft: China's Encounter with Africa.* New York: Weidenfeld and Nicolson, 1988.

NOTES

1. See Jeffrey E. Garten, *A Cold Peace: America, Japan, Germany, and the Struggle for Supremacy* (New York: The Twentieth Century Fund, 1993).

2. See Waldemar Nielson, *The Great Powers and Africa* (New York: Praeger, 1969), and Olajide Aluko, ed., *Africa and the Great Powers in the 1980s* (Lanham: University Press of America, 1987).

3. See Guy Martin, "Francophone Africa in the Context of Franco-African Relations," in John W. Harbeson and Donald Rothchild, eds., *Africa in World Politics,* 2nd ed. (Boulder: Westview, 1995).

4. See Peter J. Schraeder, *Incrementalism, Crisis, and Change: United States Foreign Policy toward Africa* (Cambridge: Cambridge University Press, 1994).

5. For Germany, see Ulf Engel and Robert Kappel, eds., *Germany's Africa Policy Revisited: Interests, Images, and Incrementalism* (Munster: Lit Verlag, 2002). For Japan, see William R. Nester,

Japan and the Third World: Patterns, Power, Prospects (New York: St. Martin's, 1992).

6. See Yusuf Bangura, *Britain and Commonwealth Africa: The Politics of Economic Relations, 1951–75* (Manchester: Manchester University Press, 1983). See also David Styan, "Does Britain Have an Africa Policy?" *L'Afrique Politique* (1996): 261–86.

7. See Phillip C. Naylor, "Spain and France and the Decolonization of Western Sahara: Parity and Paradox, 1975–87," *Africa Today* 34, no. 3 (1987): 7–16. See also Aaron Segal, "Spain and Africa: The Continuing Problem of Ceuta and Melilla," in Colin Legum and Marion E. Doro, eds., *Africa Contemporary Record: Annual Survey and Documents 1987–88,* vol. 20 (New York: Africana, 1989), pp. A71–A77.

8. See Maria Cristina Ercolessi, "Italy's Policy in Sub-Saharan Africa," in Stefan Brune, Joachim Betz, and Winrich Kuhne, eds., *Africa and Europe: Relations of Two Continents in Transition* (Munster and Hamburg: Lit Verlag, 1994), pp. 87–108.

9. See Norman MacQueen, "Portugal and Africa: The Politics of Re-Engagement," *The Journal of Modern African Studies* 23, no. 1 (1985): 31–51.

10. See Robert G. Patman, *The Soviet Union and the Horn of Africa: The Diplomacy of Intervention and Disengagement* (Cambridge: Cambridge University Press, 1990).

11. See Bruce D. Larkin, *China and Africa, 1949–1970: The Foreign Policy of the People's Republic of China* (Berkeley: University of California Press, 1971), and Philip Snow, *The Star Raft: China's Encounter with Africa* (Ithaca: Cornell University Press, 1986). See also Yan Xuetong, "Sino-African Relations in the 1990s," *CSIS Africa Notes* 84 (1988): 1–5.

12. See Gareth M. Winrow, *The Foreign Policy of the GDR in Africa* (Cambridge: Cambridge University Press, 1990).

13. See Carmelo Mesa-Lago and June S. Beikin, eds., *Cuba in Africa* (Pittsburgh: University of Pittsburgh, 1982).

14. See Olav Stokke, ed., *Western Middle Powers and Global Poverty: The Determinants of the Aid Policies of Canada, Denmark, the Netherlands, Norway, and Sweden* (Uppsala: Scandinavian Institute of African Studies, 1989).

15. See Joel Peters, *Israel and Africa: The Problematic Friendship* (New York: St. Martin's, 1992). See also Samuel Decalo, *Israel and Africa: Forty Years, 1956–1996* (Gainesville: Florida Academic, 1997).

16. See John Creed and Ken Menkhaus, "The Rise of Saudi Regional Power and the Foreign Policies of Northeast African States," *Northeast African Studies* 8, no. 2 (1986): 1–22.

17. For Brazil, see P. D. Collins, "Brazil in Africa: Perspectives on Economic Cooperation among Developing Countries," *Development Policy Review* 3, no. 1 (1985): 21–48. For India, see Ajay K. Dubey, *Indo-African Relations in the Post-Nehru Era (1965–1985)* (Delhi: Kalinga, 1990).

18. Richard M. Nixon, "The Emergence of Africa, Report to President Eisenhower by Vice President Nixon," *Department of State Bulletin* 36, no. 930 (April 22, 1957): 640.

19. John F. Kennedy, "The Challenge of Imperialism: Algeria," in Theodore C. Sorensen, *"Let the Word Go Forth": The Speeches, Statements, and Writings of John F. Kennedy* (New York: Delacorte, 1988), pp. 331–37.

20. John F. Kennedy, "The New Nations of Africa," in Theodore C. Sorensen, *"Let the Word Go Forth,"* pp. 365, 368.

21. See Steven W. Hook and John Spanier, *American Foreign Policy since World War II,* 15th ed. (Washington, DC: Congressional Quarterly, 2002).

22. For example, see Jeffrey A. Lefebvre, *Arms for the Horn: U.S. Security Policy in Ethiopia and Somalia 1953–1991* (Pittsburgh: University of Pittsburgh Press, 1991).

23. Edward A. Kolodziej, *French Foreign Policy under DeGaulle and Pompidou: The Politics of Grandeur* (Ithaca: Cornell University Press, 1974).

24. Olivier Vallée, *Le Prix de l'Argent CFA: Heurs et Malheurs de la Zone Franc* (Paris: Karthala, 1989).

25. For discussions of the foreign aid regime of the cold war and its aftermath, see Steven W. Hook, *National Interest and Foreign Aid* (Boulder: Lynne Rienner, 1995).

26. Martin, "Continuity and Change," 1995.

27. George Ball, *The Disciples of Power* (Boston: Little, Brown, 1968).

28. See James O. Goldsborough, "Dateline Paris: Africa's Policeman," *Foreign Policy* 33 (Winter 1978–79): 174–90.

29. See Zaki Laïdi, *The Superpowers and Africa: The Constraints of a Rivalry 1960–1990* (Chicago: University of Chicago Press, 1990), and Arthur L. Gavshon, *Crisis in Africa: Battleground of East and West* (Boulder: Westview, 1984).

30. See U.S. House of Representatives, Committee on International Relations, Subcommittee on International Security and Scientific Affairs, *Congressional Oversight of War Powers Compliance: Zaire Airlift,* Hearing, August 10, 1978, 95th Congress, 2nd Session (Washington, DC: Government Printing Office, 1978).

31. See "News Conferences, May 4 and 25 (Excerpts)," *Department of State Bulletin* 78, no. 2016 (July 1978): 18.

32. See "Meet the Press," *Department of State Bulletin* 78, no. 2016 (July 1978): 26.

33. Personal interview with Moose, June 26, 1989.

34. Foccart, *Foccart Parle,* 1995, p. 287.

35. Michael Clough, *U.S. Policy toward Africa and the End of the Cold War* (New York: Council on Foreign Relations, 1994), pp. 76–100.

36. For an overview of U.S. containment policies, see F. Ugboaja Ohaegbulam, "Containment in Africa: From Truman to Reagan," *TransAfrica Forum* 6, no. 1 (Fall 1988): 7–34.

37. For a discussion of these trends, see Richard Sandbrook, *The Politics of Africa's Economic Recovery* (Cambridge: Cambridge University Press, 1993), and

Thomas M. Callaghy and John Ravenhill, eds., *Hemmed In: Responses to Africa's Economic Decline* (New York: Columbia University Press, 1993).

38. Department of Commerce, "A Comprehensive Trade and Development Policy for the Countries of Africa. A Report Submitted by the President of the United States to the Congress," February 1996.

39. Copy of speech provided by the U.S. Embassy in Libreville, Gabon.

40. Antoine Glaser and Stephen Smith, *L'Afrique sans Africains: Le Rêve Blanc du Continent Noir* (Paris: Editions Stock, 1994).

41. Martin, "Francophone Africa," 1995, pp. 180–81.

42. Ibid., p. 180.

43. Ibid., p. 181.

44. John R. Heilbrunn, "The Flea on Nigeria's Back: The Foreign Policy of Benin," in Stephen Wright, ed., *African Foreign Policies* (Boulder: Westview, 1999), pp. 43–65.

45. Peter J. Schraeder (with Nefertiti Gaye), "Senegal's Foreign Policy: Challenges of Democratization and Marginalization," *African Affairs* 96 (October 1997): 485–508.

46. Howard W. French, "West Africa's New Oil Barons: Equatorial Guinea Joins the Region's Bonanza," *New York Times* (March 7, 1998).

47. For a historical overview, see Peter Duignan and L. H. Gann, *The United States and Africa: A History* (Cambridge: Cambridge University Press, 1984).

48. Interview in 1996 in Gaborone, Botswana, with Michael A. Weaver, manager of plant operations for Owens-Corning in Botswana.

49. See Peter J. Schraeder, *Exporting Democracy: Rhetoric vs. Reality* (Boulder: Lynne Rienner, 2002).

50. See Agir Ici et Survie, *La France à Biarritz: Mise en Examen de la Politique Française* (Paris: Karthala, 1995). See also Jean-François Bayart, *La Politique Africaine de François Mitterrand* (Paris: Karthala, 1984).

51. Glaser and Smith, *L'Afrique sans Africains,* 1994, p. 102.

52. See Roland Marchal, "La France en Quête d'une Politique Africaine?" *Politique Étrangère* no. 4 (Winter 1995–96): 903–16.

53. See Howard W. French, "France's Army Keeps Grip in African Ex-Colonies," *New York Times* (May 22, 1996): A3.

54. Interview, January 24, U.S. Embassy, Tunis, Tunisia.

55. Emmanuel V. Adjovi, *Une Élection Libre en Afrique: La Présidentielle du Bénin (1996)* (Paris: Karthala, 1998).

56. K. Mathews, "The African Group at the UN as an Instrument of African Diplomacy," *Nigerian Journal of International Affairs* 14, no. 1 (1988): 226–58.

57. Personal interview, Dakar, Senegal, January 1995.

58. Francis M. Deng et al., *Sovereignty as Responsibility: Conflict Management in Africa* (Washington, DC: Brookings Institution, 1996), p. 5.

59. Boutros Boutros-Ghali, *An Agenda for Peace: Preventive Diplomacy, Peace-Making, and Peace-Keeping* (New York: United Nations, 1992), p. 9.

60. Somali distrust of the UN stems from the 1950 decision of that international body to support the reimposition of Italian colonial rule over what is currently known as the Republic of Somalia. See John L. Hirsch and Robert B. Oakley, *Somalia and Operation Restore Hope: Reflections on Peace-Making and Peace-Keeping* (Washington, DC: United States Institute for Peace, 1995).

61. Terrence Lyons and Ahmed I. Samatar, *Somalia: State Collapse, Multilateral Intervention, and Strategies for Political Reconstruction* (Washington, DC: Brookings Institution, 1995), p. 24.

62. Christopher C. Joyner, "International Law," in Peter J. Schraeder, ed., *Intervention into the 1990s: U.S. Foreign Policy in the Third World* (Boulder: Lynne Rienner, 1995), pp. 229–46.

63. Francis M. Deng, *Protecting the Dispossessed: A Challenge for the International Community* (Washington, DC: Brookings Institution, 1993).

64. Francis M. Deng and Larry Minear, *The Challenges of Famine Relief: Emergency Operations in the Sudan* (Washington, DC: Brookings Institution, 1992).

65. Deng et al., *Sovereignty as Responsibility,* p. 11.

66. For an excellent overview, see Thomas M. Callaghy and John Ravenhill, eds., *Hemmed In: Responses to Africa's Economic Decline* (New York: Columbia University Press, 1993).

67. Stephen K. Commins, ed., *Africa's Development Challenges and the World Bank: Hard Questions, Costly Choices* (Boulder: Lynne Rienner, 1988), and Bonnie K. Campbell and John Loxley, eds., *Structural Adjustment in Africa* (New York: St. Martin's, 1989).

68. See Jennifer A. Widner, ed., *Economic Change and Political Liberalization in Sub-Saharan Africa* (Baltimore: Johns Hopkins University Press, 1994).

69. See Ernest Harsch, "After Adjustment," *Africa Report* (May–June 1989): 48.

70. See Richard Sandbrook, *The Politics of Africa's Economic Recovery* (Cambridge: Cambridge University Press, 1993).

71. World Bank, *The East Asian Miracle: Economic Growth and Public Policy* (Washington, DC: World Bank, 1993).

72. See Thomas M. Callaghy and John Ravenhill, "If Korea Can Do It, Why Not Africa? Or: Limited Current Relevance But Possible Future Model," in Callaghy and Ravenhill, *Hemmed In,* p. 546.

73. See Jeffrey Herbst, *The Politics of Reform in Ghana, 1982–1991* (Berkeley: University of California Press, 1993).

74. For an overview, see Kempe Ronald Hope, Sr., "From Crisis to Renewal: Toward a Successful Implementation of the New Partnership for Africa's Development," *African Affairs* 101, no. 404 (July 2002): 387–402.

75. See I. William Zartman, ed., *Collapsed States: The Disintegration and*

Restoration of Legitimate Authority (Boulder: Lynne Rienner, 1995).

76. Crawford Young, "Order and Disorder in Postcolonial Africa," in John F. Clark, ed., *The African Stakes of the Congo War* (New York: Palgrave, 2002), p. 13.

77. See Walter Clarke and Jeffrey Herbst, eds., *Learning from Somalia: The Lessons of Armed Humanitarian Intervention* (Boulder: Westview, 1997).

78. Douglas Jehl, "Officials Told to Avoid Calling Rwanda Killings 'Genocide,'" *New York Times* (June 10, 1994): A8.

79. See Jim Cason and Bill Martin, "Clinton and Africa: Searching for a Post–Cold War Order," *Bulletin: Association of Concerned Africa Scholars.* Nos. 38–39 (Winter 1993): 2.

80. Ibid.

81. Quoted in Howard W. French, "In Congo, a Lesson in Where Easy Paths Lead," *New York Times* (January 21, 2001): A3.

82. "Statement of Secretary of State-Designate Colin L. Powell Prepared for the Confirmation Hearing of the U.S. Senate Committee on Foreign Relations Scheduled for 10:30 A.M., January 17, 2001." Accessed at http://www.senate.gov/%7Eforeign/testimony/wt_powell_011701.txt.

83. See Peter J. Schraeder, "Cold War to Cold Peace: Explaining U.S.-French Competition in Francophone Africa," *Political Science Quarterly* 115, no. 3 (2000): 415.

84. Agir Ici et Survie, *Les Dossiers Noirs de la Politique Africaine de la France: Jacques Chirac et la Françafrique* (L'Harmattan: Paris, 1995).

85. For a slightly contrarian view, see Tony Chafter, "Franco-African Relations: No Longer So Exceptional?" *African Affairs* 101, no. 404 (July 2002): 343–64.

86. See Don Connell and Frank Smyth, "Africa's New Bloc," *Foreign Affairs* 77 (March/April 1998): 80–94. See also Marina Ottaway, *Africa's New Leaders: Democracy or State Reconstruction?* (Washington, DC: Carnegie Endowment for International Peace, 1999).

87. See Ivan Crouzel, "La 'Renaissance Africaine': Un Discours Sud-Africain?" *Politique Africaine* no. 77 (March): 171–82.

88. John F. Clark, ed., *The African Stakes of the Congo War* (New York: Palgrave, 2002).

13

Study of Africa in the Liberal Tradition

M. Crawford Young, Professor Emeritus, Department of Political Science and African Studies Program, University of Wisconsin/Madison.

THE STUDY OF AFRICAN politics and society has been dominated by a **liberal tradition** that envisions the development of free-market democracies on the African continent similar to those found in the Western democracies of Canada, Europe, Japan, and the United States. In the 1950s, liberal scholars assumed that African countries, as well as developing countries in Asia, Latin America, and the Middle East, would advance along the same path of political and economic development already traveled by their Western counterparts. Subsequent decades clearly demonstrated, however, that political and economic development can proceed along many different paths, each strewn with different obstacles and dead ends. The dramatic changes associated with the end of the cold war, most notably the spread of pro-democracy movements throughout the African continent, have reinvigorated research in the liberal tradition, which continues to point to the Western democratic tradition as the model to be emulated by African leaders. This chapter highlights the general evolution of the major themes and scholarly concerns of the liberal tradition, from the 1950s to the present.

PREDOMINANCE OF MODERNIZATION THEORY (1950s–EARLY 1960s)

In 1955, David E. Apter captured the sentiments of an entire generation of Africanist scholars in the liberal tradition when he underscored the "tremendous sense of excitement" associated with carrying out field research in the soon-to-be-independent African country of Ghana.[1] For Apter and his contemporaries, the African continent represented an intellectual challenge which, similar to that faced by the Western explorers of the eighteenth and nineteenth centuries, offered the possibility of making discoveries that could ensure both fame and fortune in their given academic disciplines. Unlike the earlier explorers, however, the scholars of the 1950s carried with them an intellectual blueprint for understanding the development of Africa that became known as **modernization theory.**

Building on the disciplines of economics, psychology, sociology, and political science, modernization theory was promoted by Africanists as the key to Africa's development. The economic dimension of modernization theory draws on the theories of economists such as Walt W. Rostow. In his widely cited book, *The Stages of Economic Growth: A Noncommunist Manifesto* (1960), Rostow argues that all countries evolve through the same "stages of growth" as leaders seek to transform "backward" agriculturally based societies into modern industrial economies.[2] Drawing on the experience of the Western industrialized countries, modernization theorists argued that African countries were at the starting point of a process that would mechanize agriculture and industrialize major urban areas. According to these theorists, the growth rate of a country's gross national product (GNP) constitutes one of the best measures of the modernization process.

The social dimension of modernization theory draws on advances in the fields of psychology and sociology, by such noted scholars as Max Weber and Talcott Parsons. Of particular concern to researchers interested in the social aspect of the modernization equation is the process by which individuals replaced their "traditional" (often pejoratively described as "primitive") ways of thinking in favor of a more "modern" outlook on life. The modernization approach assumes that ethnic divisions in African countries (which were perceived as hindrances to development) would fade away as modernizing societies became "melting pots" similar to the perceived experiences of the United States and the other Western countries. Several factors were thought to contribute to the creation of a modern society: urbanization, where individuals moved from the rural areas to the towns and cities; exposure to various forms of mass media (especially newspapers and radio); formal education at the high school and university levels; and occupational experiences, such as working in "modern" factories.[3]

The political dimension of modernization theory draws on classic theories of democratic pluralism in the field of political science.[4] Scholars believed that the key to political development was a rapidly growing electorate both willing and able to participate in the political process. A growth in political participation was expected to foster the growth and specialization of government agencies, as African leaders responded to the legitimate demands of their respective populations. In short, the sum of the economic, social, and political components of modernization theory is the firm belief that the newly independent African countries were on a path leading to the creation of modern industrialized democracies.

One approach of modernization theory that became popular during the 1950s was **structural-functionalism.** As outlined in the landmark work, *Politics of the Developing Areas* (1960), edited by Gabriel A. Almond and James S. Coleman, the structural-functionalist approach assumes that all political systems perform similar "functions," despite the fact that these functions may be performed by different "structures." The function of "interest articulation," in which a political leader or official defines and acts on popular interests, for example, may be performed by an elected Senator in the U.S. political system or by the Ogaz, a hereditary prince, in the Somali political system.[5] Although the two systems in which the leaders operate differ significantly, both the Senator and the Ogaz perform the same political function.[6]

The structural-functionalist approach represented the desire of scholars within the liberal tradition to promote a **value-neutral** (bias-free) **scientific framework** for comparing any political system, regardless of its culture or history. As demonstrated by the Almond and Coleman volume, however, structural-functionalism and the modernization literature in general were based on several assumptions. For example, Almond and Coleman assume that ethnic attachments hinder development, and industrialization is regarded as the ideal end of a modern economy. In the political realm the assumptions of modernization theory are especially clear. Those familiar with the U.S. political system have noted that Almond and Coleman's neat division of governmental functions into three separate categories (rule making, rule application, and rule adjudication) bears a strong resemblance to the U.S. Constitution's classic separation of powers between the three major branches of government (congressional, executive, and judicial).[7] Indeed, the core assumption of the structural-functionalist approach is that all African political systems will eventually evolve into stable multiparty democracies, patterned after the United States and the other Western countries.

The optimistic belief that modernization theory could serve as a blueprint for African development during the 1950s and the 1960s directly resulted from a unique convergence of several historical trends. The extended global conflict of World War II heralded the success and desirability of liberal democracy. Not only had the United States led the Allies in defeating Nazi Germany and Imperial Japan, occupation by the Allied forces had contributed to the nurturing of democratic forms of government in both defeated countries. This optimism was reinforced by an equally firm belief in the scholarly community that technological advancements in the West would lead to the resolution of problems historically associated with industrial societies, such as poverty and unemployment. As a result, scholars began to focus on transferring their knowledge and technical expertise to the newly emerging independent countries of the developing South. The dramatic pace of decolonization that began in Africa during the 1950s made the African continent a region of particular interest to U.S. scholars in a variety of disciplines, most notably political science. The emergence of cold war conflict between the United States and the former Soviet Union added ideological urgency to the perceived necessity of promoting economic, social, and political modernization in Africa. In sharp contrast to their contemporaries, scholars during the 1950s and the 1960s were much more willing to accept the cold war rationales of the U.S. government and worked with its various agencies to ensure the defeat of communism on the African continent. Finally, a widely shared belief in American "exceptionalism," the view that the United States was uniquely qualified to lead the world, led U.S. scholars to conclude that their models of development would be both relevant and easily applied to an African context.[8]

RISE OF MODERNIZATION REVISIONISM
(LATE 1960s)

The first major critiques of the modernization approach to African politics emerged from within the liberal tradition during the late 1960s. Rather than seeking to completely discredit their predecessors in the discipline, critics sought to revise what they perceived as significant but rectifiable flaws within an otherwise sound approach. The body of scholarship produced by this generation of Africanists became known as **modernization revisionism.**[9]

The first major revisionist critique calls into question the tendency of earlier scholars to portray the modernization process as a "zero-sum" game, in which "advances" toward certain levels of modernity in an African political and social system are inevitably accompanied by an equal "decline" in that system's traditional culture. According to this logic, a 20 percent advance in modern institutions, for example, would be accompanied by a 20 percent decline in traditional institutions. Revisionist scholars argue instead that traditional institutions often adapt to, and coexist with, modern institutions. As a result, a society conceivably could assume many modern characteristics at the same time that it retained or even enhanced various aspects of its traditional culture.

In the case of northern Nigeria, C. S. Whitaker Jr., demonstrates in *The Politics of Tradition: Continuity and Change in Northern Nigeria 1946–1966* (1970) how the creation and expansion of modern political institutions, such as the national parliament, cabinet system, and political parties, was accompanied by the strengthening of the political roles played by traditional Muslim leaders known as emirs.[10] Political leaders associated with the Northern Peoples' Congress (NPC), a modern postindependence political institution that might have undermined the traditional leaders, instead sustained and cultivated the power and influence of the traditional emirs. "Far from modern institutions having simply driven out traditional ones," explains Whitaker, "elements of the institutions of each type or origin coalesced to form a workable system of power and authority."[11]

A second major revisionist critique disputes the assumption of earlier scholars that traditional attitudes and institutions are inherently irrational and therefore hinder the modernization process. Modernization revisionists instead underscored the importance of building on traditional cultures and values to promote development in the newly independent African countries. According to the modernization revisionists, disregarding the importance of such traditional characteristics as ethnic affiliations and beliefs constitutes a formula for disaster.

According to Whitaker's study of northern Nigeria, the importance of traditional values in the modernization process was clearly illustrated by the role of political parties in regional elections during the 1960s. "A principal function of any 'modern' political party operating under a system of representative government on a foundation of mass suffrage is to mobilize the mass electorate for the exercise of choice at the ballot box," explains Whitaker in a summary of the modernization imperative of creating a multiparty political system. "A cardinal aspect of this function is communication with the electorate: the formulation and articulation of issues and interests which will stimulate the attention, sympathy, and support of as many of that electorate as possible."[12] However, in sharp contrast to what the modernization theorists originally had predicted, the NPC party successfully performed the "mobilization" function of the political system by appealing to such traditional values as the "religious duty to obey and protect hereditary leaders."[13] In many cases, those politicians shortsighted enough to wholeheartedly embrace modernization theory and ignore the importance of appealing to traditional values were vanquished by their competitors.

A Closer Look: AFRICAN STUDIES ASSOCIATION

The **African Studies Association (ASA)** is the leading North American nonprofit organization that fosters the exchange of information and ideas among scholars and practitioners interested in the study of Africa. The organization was officially launched at a conference held in New York City, March 22–24, 1957, that was attended by thirty-five individuals and currently counts more than 3,000 individuals among its formal membership. Approximately 1,200 participants take part in its annual meeting devoted to Africa. The association publishes several scholarly journals, most notably *African Studies Review* and *African Issues.*

Despite the adoption of an interdisciplinary approach to the study of Africa, the ASA has not been without controversy. The first, and perhaps most significant, internal conflict occurred October 15–18, 1969, when the ASA's Black Caucus staged a series of protests at the twelfth annual meeting held in Montreal, Canada. At issue in this dispute were the demands of African-American scholars to have a larger say in the governance of the organization. The meetings were disrupted when the association refused to accede to the demand that 50 percent of the ASA's Board of Directors should be African-American scholars. The often heated and acerbic debates that followed created a rift that has yet to be completely healed. One result of African-American concerns over who controlled the collection and dissemination of Africana knowledge was the birth on June 29, 1969, of the **African Heritage Studies Association (AHSA),** a rival African studies association targeted primarily toward the African American scholarly community.

Subsequent debates in the ASA have also taken on an ideological tone. Some conservative Africanists claim they have been marginalized in the field of African studies. In a spirited debate, L. H. Gann critiqued what he perceived as a liberal bias in the study of Africa. Gann and other conservative Africanists were particularly critical of the 1993 decision of the ASA and other regional studies associations, most notably the Latin American Studies Association, to officially oppose the National Security Education Program (NSEP), a language studies program funded through the U.S. Defense Department, in which student grantees would sign a contract agreeing to work in some capacity for a national security agency of the U.S. government after completing their study and research abroad. One attempt to counterbalance the perceived liberal bias of the ASA was the creation of the **American African Affairs Association (AAAA),** a scholarly association of conservative Africanists.

These issues notwithstanding, the hallmark of current ASA policy is to be as inclusive as possible. Whereas ASA-sponsored organizations include the African Islamic Studies Association, Gays and Lesbians in African Studies, and the Women's Caucus, ASA-associate organizations include the Association of African Women Scholars and the Association of Concerned African Scholars. Finally, ASA-affiliate organizations include the Africa-America Institute and the African Association of Political Science.

See David Robinson, "The African Studies Association at Age 35," *African Studies Review* 37, no. 2 (1994): 1–12; Cyprian Lamar Rowe, "Crisis in African Studies: The Birth of the African Heritage Studies Association," *Black Academy Review* 1, no. 3 (1970): 3–10; and L. H. Gann, "The Struggle for African Area Studies: A View from Wisconsin—A Response," *Issue: A Journal of Opinion* 18, no. 1 (1989): 51–53, as well as the responses to Gann's article in the next issue. See also the ASA Web site: http://www.africanstudies.org/

A third major revisionist critique questions the assumption that modernization constitutes a **unilinear** (one-way) process in which traditional characteristics
such as ethnic affiliations ultimately would erode over time, replaced by more
modern forms of affiliation (e.g., professional or community-based organizations). Revisionist scholars argue instead that ethnicity and other forms of
ordering traditional societies (such as clan and caste) often are revitalized and
strengthened by the modernization process. In some instances, the modernization process even fostered the creation of an ethnic self-consciousness or group
identity where none before had existed. For example, at the beginning of the
twentieth century, the Igbo ethnic group constituted a "classical segmented
political system" in which approximately 200 separate Igbo villages and communities shared a common language, culture, and beliefs but lacked common
governance or any sense of nationhood (see Chapter 2).[14] By the late 1960s,
however, the growth of Igbo nationalism contributed to the secession of the
Igbo-inhabited southeastern province of Nigeria, an act that led to a civil war
(1967–70) from which the Nigerian federal government emerged victorious.

The creation of an ethnic group identity among the Igbo was especially relevant to the revisionist critique of modernization theory because the Igbos had
often been characterized by foreign observers as one of the most modern of
Nigeria's ethnic groups. The highly egalitarian nature of Igbo political culture,
which places great emphasis on seeking status through individual achievement
rather than personal connections, was seen to embody the positive elements of
a modern political culture. Indeed, the Igbo appeared to constitute a textbook
example of a modernizing people. Moving to the urban areas in search of
higher education and economic advancement, Igbos eventually began to dominate "white collar" positions in education, journalism, business, and politics.
They were also responsible for forming the National Council of Nigerian Citizens (NCNC), the first political party with a truly countrywide program.
Unlike the more parochial, ethnically based parties, the NCNC mobilized
popular support that transcended individual ethnic groups. In short, if one
would have asked a modernization theorist during the 1950s which of Nigeria's ethnic groups was most likely to secede based on the "parochial" principle
of ethnic identity, the Igbo ethnic group of southeastern Nigeria would not
have been at the top of the list.

Despite their willingness to criticize modernization theory, the modernization revisionists simply seek to revise the shortcomings of what is still considered
to be an otherwise sound approach for understanding political and socioeconomic change in Africa. In fact, both modernization theorists and their revisionist counterparts share many optimistic assumptions about the development
process. Among the most important of these assumptions are the desirability of
a rapidly expanding electorate willing and able to take part in the political
process, the mutually reinforcing nature of rising levels of participation and
the promotion of equality and stability in developing societies, a perception of
protests and violence as the "exceptions" rather than the norm of politics, and
the emergence of multiparty democratic political systems as the natural outcome of the modernization process.

CONCERN WITH STABILITY
AND THE POLITICS OF ORDER
(LATE 1960s–EARLY 1970s)

Several trends during the 1960s contributed to the rise of a more pessimistic genre of scholarship that for the first time called into question the optimistic assumptions held by modernization theorists and revisionists.[15] The most important of these trends was the dramatic rise in violence and instability in the newly independent nation-states of Africa. In addition to the spread of guerrilla insurgencies, secessionist movements, civil wars, and assassinations for political gain, African militaries increasingly were taking power away from civilian leaders in military coups d'état. Before 1963, there were only two successful military coups: the Sudan in 1956 and the Democratic Republic of the Congo (Congo-Kinshasa) in 1960. From this point forward, an explosion of military involvement in the policymaking process began. From 1965 to 1969, there were on average more than four successful coups each year. This violent trend was a far cry from the peaceful, democratic transfers of power expected by modernization theorists and their revisionist counterparts.

The changing demands of U.S. foreign policy in the 1960s also influenced the rise of pessimism toward the modernization process in Africa. The intensification of the cold war during this period led the administration of John F. Kennedy and its successors to formulate counterinsurgency doctrines, designed to defeat what were perceived as communist-inspired guerrilla insurgencies in the developing world. Counterinsurgency was a key justification of the growing U.S. military involvement in Vietnam and emphasized the containment of communism by means which often ran counter to the optimistic ideals of modernization theory. When the normative goal of modernization theory, the creation of democratic political systems, clashed with anticommunist national security interests, U.S. leaders often supported national security efforts even when it meant creating alliances with unsavory, undemocratic leaders in Africa and other portions of the developing world.[16] In short, anticommunist, authoritarian African leaders curried U.S. favor because they helped carry out containment policies that curtailed communist expansion.

The changes in U.S. domestic politics during the 1960s also contributed to the rise of a more pessimistic view of the modernization process in Africa. In addition to being concerned with instability abroad, U.S. policymakers were troubled by growing levels of protest and violence at home. Policymakers were especially troubled by the potential for violence associated with the civil rights movement and growing protests against U.S. military involvement in the Vietnam War. As a result, slogans of "law and order" became the focal points of presidential campaigns carried out by Barry Goldwater in 1964 and Richard M. Nixon in 1968. These slogans were reinforced—again, counter to the optimistic ideals of modernization theorists—by violent government responses to public demonstrations, ranging from the attacks on political protestors by riot police at the 1968 Democratic convention in Chicago, Illinois, to the killings by National Guardsmen of seven antiwar protestors at Kent State University in 1970.

The net result of these three trends was a shift in the modernization literature from the optimistic belief in **political development** to a more pessimistic expectation of **political decay** (conflict and chaos) in the newly independent African countries.[17] In a landmark work that captured this shift and altered the debate in academic and political circles, Samuel P. Huntington in *Political Order in Changing Societies* (1968) argues that rather than contributing to democracy and stability, the modernization process fosters political instability in the developing world, often with dire consequences for U.S. foreign policy.[18] According to Huntington and his contemporaries, democracy is neither a natural nor a direct end result of modernization. Rather, countries attempting to modernize are faced with six major **crises of development,** which, if not solved, could lead to the downfall of regimes and the spread of political decay:

- **Crisis of identity:** Creating a common nationalist outlook among ethnically, linguistically, and religiously diverse peoples

- **Crisis of legitimacy:** Building a national consensus on the legitimate exercise of authority

- **Crisis of participation:** Guiding rising public demands for inclusion in the political decision-making process

- **Crisis of penetration:** Creating an effective government presence throughout the territory

- **Crisis of distribution:** Balancing public demands for goods and services with the government's responsibility to provide public goods, such as economic growth

- **Crisis of integration:** Creating harmonious relationships among the society's many groups and interests competing for access to and control of the political decision-making process.[19]

According to Huntington, the solution to these crises is **institutionalization,** the creation of strong government structures able to ensure political stability and order throughout society. "The most important political distinction among countries," explains Huntington, "concerns not their *form* of government but their *degree* of government."[20] In sharp contrast to the optimistic impulse of modernization theorists and revisionists to favor rapidly expanding levels of popular political participation, Huntington and his contemporaries argue that the process of institutionalization had to be the top priority of African leaders. According to this interpretation of African politics and society, African leaders were to dramatically limit the levels of popular political participation in the name of ensuring stability and order.

The primary institutions that scholars of order focus on as crucial to maintaining stability include African militaries, bureaucracies inherited from colonial rule, and, most important, political parties. In fact, despite the fact that he remains strongly opposed to communism, Huntington especially admired the Leninist model of creating a "vanguard" single party, such as once existed in the former Soviet Union and the other communist countries of the Eastern bloc. "They may not provide liberty," explains Huntington, "but they do provide

---

A Closer Look: SHOULD RESEARCHERS WORK WITH THE U.S. GOVERNMENT?

A much-debated question in the field of African studies that has received renewed attention in the aftermath of the September 11, 2001, terrorist attacks against the World Trade Center and the Pentagon is the extent to which scholars should work with U.S. government agencies in the formulation and implementation of U.S. foreign policy toward Africa. The African Studies Center at Michigan State University addressed this question in 1990 by sending out a survey to 2,592 U.S. Africanists "with an ongoing interest in the study of Africa" (23 percent responded).

The results of this survey (see Table 13.1) offer two important insights. First, the type of government agency involved affects whether an Africanist will cooperate with the U.S. government. Africanists are wary of becoming involved with military and intelligence institutions, including the

Central Intelligence Agency (CIA), the Defense Intelligence Agency (DIA), and colleges and universities that fall under the umbrella of the U.S. Defense Department (e.g., The Defense University). Africanists are still wary of but increasingly likely to become associated with institutions that focus on the political or diplomatic aspects of national security, such as the Department of State. The greatest level of acceptance is accorded to government institutions that (1) promote scholarly research independent of direct government control (e.g., the National Science Foundation [NSF]), (2) primarily focus on the socioeconomic development of the African continent (e.g., the United States Agency for International Development [USAID]), and (3) freely and openly debate the outlines of policy with direct public input (e.g., the U.S. Congress).

Table 13.1 Should Researchers Work with the U.S. Government? (Percent of Scholars Who Responded "Yes" to Specific Institutions)*

	CONDUCT SPONSORED RESEARCH IN AFRICA	CONDUCT SPONSORED RESEARCH IN U.S.	DELIVER LECTURE OR TESTIFY	ATTEND WORKSHOP OR HEARING	OFFER INFORMAL ADVICE
CIA or DIA	8	10	27	34	31
The Defense University	12	13	38	42	38
Department of State	47	49	81	85	84
U.S. Congress	66	69	86	88	88
U.S. AID	71	67	84	89	87
National Science Foundation (NSF)	78	75	82	86	82

* Responses were to the following statement: "If invited in the future, I would participate in the following Africa policy activities listed below."

The nature of the task also affects whether an Africanist will cooperate with the U.S. government. Most Africanists would refuse to undertake research related to Africa that was directly sponsored by military or intelligence agencies. A higher number of Africanists nonetheless would be willing to deliver a lecture or offer informal advice to officials working in these agencies. Indeed, Africanists across the board are more willing to engage in occasional contacts than pursue extended research relationships with all government agencies.

The willingness to lecture and offer advice is further substantiated by the strong belief of 79 percent of Africanists that they have "an obligation" to use their regional knowledge "to participate actively in the formation of U.S. policy toward Africa." The question therefore is not so much one of whether Africanists should work with the U.S. government but with what institutions and in what capacity.

Discussion drawn from Michael Bratton, Reinhard Heinisch, and David S. Wiley, "How Africanists View U.S. Policy: Results of a Survey," *Issue: A Journal of Opinion* 19, no. 2 (1991): 14–31.

authority; they do create governments that govern."[21] The appeal of these single-party political systems thus lay not in their ideology (communism) but rather in their ability to set the agenda for development, to serve as vehicles for mobilizing scarce resources, and to control what are perceived as the "destabilizing" influences of growing popular political participation.

In *Creating Political Order: The Party-States of West Africa* (1966), Aristide R. Zolberg offers an early example of the political order approach in an African context.[22] As is evident from the title, Zolberg perceives the single-party system as providing the primary prerequisite—order—for the successful modernization of African societies. Although he cautions that such a political system is neither "genuinely democratic" nor able to ensure the "immediate and revolutionary change in the human condition," he argues that strong single parties "might help relieve the heavy burdens of imitation and self-doubt with which Africans have been saddled too long and might enable them to regain confidence in their ability to rule themselves."[23] "That, ultimately," he concludes in the last sentence of the book, "is the only soil in which democracy has been known to grow."[24] As we discuss in Chapter 10, the so-called **politics of order** was firmly embraced by the vast majority of African leaders who oversaw the creation and maintenance of single-party regimes from the 1950s to the 1980s.

DEMANDS FOR POLICY RELEVANCE AND PUBLIC POLICY RESEARCH (MID-1970s–1980s)

The liberal tradition of studying African politics and society experienced yet another transformation that began in the mid-1970s and continued throughout the 1980s. During this period, scholars sought to make their research agendas more **policy relevant** in response to critiques that their "grand theories" were so abstract as to be of little use for solving the day-to-day policy problems faced by African policymakers. For example, an African prime minister trained in the United States may have wondered about the relevance of modernization theory as he attempted to resolve a national labor strike. In short, scholars in the liberal tradition were being called on by policymakers to move beyond grand theorizing in favor of research focusing on the everyday management problems faced by African policymakers.

The demands for policy relevance resulted in the emergence of two broad streams of **public policy research** that draw on the disciplines of economics and political science.[25] The first stream of research, the **political-economy approach,** is based on the assumption that politics and economics are so inextricably intertwined that previous attempts at examining each discipline in isolation offered solutions that did not apply to "real-world" conditions. One aspect of this approach is the adoption of **rational-choice models** from the discipline of economics. These models assume that individuals are "rational" (logical) and make their decisions based on a "cost-benefit analysis" of the trade-offs between a variety of possible outcomes. The political component of this approach emphasizes the necessity of understanding the array of policy choices available to individual policymakers and groups in society as they bargain for an outcome that they (rationally) perceive as being in their best interests.

In *Markets and States in Tropical Africa: The Political Basis of Agricultural Policies* (1981), Robert H. Bates clearly falls within the political-economy tradition.[26] The primary purpose of the book is to explain why food production declined in Africa during the initial decades of the contemporary independence era, thereby contributing to recurring cycles of famine and starvation. The starting point of Bates's analysis is the assumption that individuals make choices based on a rational analysis of their self-interests. As a result, the answer to the question posed at the beginning of his book—"Why should reasonable men adopt public policies that have harmful consequences for the societies they govern?"—is found in the political calculations made by African policymakers.[27]

A second stream of public policy research focuses on **public policy analysis,** the assessment of the "outputs" (end results) of government policies and programs. Public policy analysis is devoted to exploring the strategies available to policymakers for solving the economic, social, and political problems associated with the development process. This "problem-solving approach" is very action oriented; it is used to analyze the choices available to policymakers and then determine which of those choices is most appropriate for development.

Donald Rothchild and Robert L. Curry Jr., in *Scarcity, Choice, and Public Policy in Middle Africa* (1979), clearly fall within the tradition of public policy analysis.[28] First, the mere fact that these two authors collaborated—Rothchild is a political scientist and Curry is an economist—underscores their commitment to a political-economy approach. Second, the authors assume that rational government policies are the result of cost-benefit considerations made by African policymakers. The most important aspect of the book is its emphasis on adopting a "problem-solving approach" to aid African policymakers in overcoming the "constraints" imposed by such factors as economic scarcity, environmental degradation, and inherited colonial institutions. In short, Rothchild and Curry argue that African leaders have the ability to make "choices" from a variety of "strategies," each of which entails different trade-offs depending on the nature of policy goals selected by that leadership.

The Rothchild and Curry book is also significant in that it addresses one of the major criticisms advanced by dependency theorists and other scholars associated with the "critical tradition" of African politics and society (see Chapter 14). As discussed in the following chapter, dependency theorists argue that the liberal tradition focuses too heavily on the internal (domestic) sources of development problems in Africa. They believe that an emphasis should be placed on the external (international) constraints faced by these countries. Rothchild and Curry respond to this critique by adding two new "crises of development" to the six crises outlined by the theorists of order:

- **Crisis of national survival:** Ensuring the survival of the territorial integrity of the country as originally constituted at independence
- **Crisis of foreign control:** Securing economic, social, and political freedom from external control

The recognition of the importance of international factors in Rothchild and Curry's book clearly demonstrates the rising influence of certain elements of the critical tradition within the thinking of liberal theorists during the 1970s and the 1980s, though both schools of thought remained strongly divided throughout this period.

An important element in the shift toward public policy research during the 1970s and the 1980s was a growing emphasis on the role of the "African state": the formal institutions of power in African political systems, including but not limited to the presidency, judiciary, government bureaucracies, national legislature, and military forces (see Chapter 8). More precisely, scholars increasingly focused on the relationship of the state to both domestic groups (such as African elites and ethnic groups) and international groups (such as foreign elites and international organizations). An excellent example of this trend is a jointly edited volume by Donald Rothchild and Victor A. Olorunsola, *State versus Ethnic Claims: African Policy Dilemmas* (1983), which explores the evolving relationship between weak African states and increasingly vocal ethnic groups who feel disenfranchised from the political process.[29] By the end of the 1980s, the state had become the focal point of liberal Africanists seeking to understand the successes and failures of over three decades of African independence from colonial rule.

NEW DIRECTIONS (1990s–PRESENT)

The end of the cold war marked the emergence of a new era in liberal scholarship devoted to the African continent. An important aspect of this new era is that the ideological guiding principles of the cold war—anticommunism and containment of the Soviet Union—no longer influence scholarship as they did during the modernization era of the 1950s and the 1960s. Equally important, the end of the cold war reinforced the historical tendency of foreign scholars and academic institutions to neglect the African continent in favor of other regions of perceived greater interest, most notably Europe, Asia, and the Middle East. This trend is aptly demonstrated by the U.S. federal government's declining commitment of financial resources to African studies programs and basic research devoted to Africa, as well as the decision of several foundations, such as the Social Science Research Council (SSRC), to end their specialized programs devoted to Africa.[30] Although as of this writing it is still too early to judge, it is likely that the terrorist attacks of September 11, 2001, against the World Trade Center and the Pentagon will lead to the restoration of some of these research funds, albeit in a direction that principally focuses on the largely Muslim-inhabited regions of North and East Africa due to their perceived strategic importance to the widening U.S. war on global terrorism.

The liberal tradition nonetheless has produced an impressive amount of scholarship that points the reader in at least seven broad research directions. First and foremost is renewed scholarly interest in the emergence and consolidation of multiparty democracy in Africa (see Chapter 10). Reminiscent of the optimism expressed by modernization theorists during the 1950s and the 1960s, the liberal tradition at the end of the 1980s was reinvigorated by the emergence of pro-democracy movements that fostered dozens of experiments in multiparty democracy throughout the African continent. An initial euphoria surrounded what some scholars optimistically called Africa's "second independence," making transitions to democracy the most studied topic in the field of African studies during the 1990s. The seminal book of this vast scholarly enterprise is Michael Bratton and Nicolas van de Walle, *Democratic Experiments in Africa: Regime Transition in Comparative Perspective* (1997), which offers an impressive statistical analysis of all democratic transitions that took place between 1989 and 1994.[31] This book, which has become the yardstick by which all later studies of democratization will be judged, emphasizes the importance of domestic factors in African transitions, with a particular focus on the impact of political protests and the specific nature of a country's political and electoral institutions. Although contemporary scholars from the liberal tradition, unlike their predecessors of the 1950s and the 1960s, no longer assume that the consolidation of African democracies will be either easy or automatically assured, they nonetheless point to the Western democratic tradition as the model to be emulated by African leaders.

A second research direction in the liberal tradition that is strongly tied to the democratization literature involves the study of civil society, the vast array of voluntary associations throughout society, such as political parties, labor unions, women's organizations, and religious groups, that seeks access to state power (see Chapter 8). Whereas African leaders consistently co-opted and repressed these groups, effectively silencing people's demands on the state from the 1950s to the 1980s, the end of the cold war coincided with the resurgence of vibrant and vocal civil societies intent on opening up the political space in their respective countries. The debates over the nature and future implications of this trend are nicely captured in *Civil Society and the State in Africa* (1994), edited jointly by John W. Harbeson, Donald Rothchild, and Naomi Chazan.[32] According to these scholars, civil society constitutes the "missing key" to sustained political reform throughout the African continent.[33] Subsequent scholars have nonetheless cautioned that one should not assume, as is often the case in the civil society literature, that these groups are inherently democratic due to their critical roles in pressuring authoritarian leaders to liberalize their political systems. Indeed, field research by a new generation of scholars, such as that conducted by Amy S. Patterson in rural Senegal, clearly demonstrates that groups in civil society are sometimes far from democratic despite the fact that they have contributed to the opening up of the "political space" in their respective countries.[34]

A third research direction is due to a renewed interest in the concept of ethnicity as crucial to an informed understanding of African politics and society (see Chapter 5). One view, derivative of modernization theory, optimistically argues that Africa's multiplying ethnic conflicts in the post–cold war era can be resolved by creative solutions, such as the decentralization of authority away from central governments in favor of greater power to local state governments, that recognize the importance of ethnic diversity but maintain the territorial boundaries of the nation-state. As explained by Donald Rothchild in *Managing Ethnic Conflict in Africa: Pressures and Incentives for Cooperation* (1997), "third-party" mediators particularly can be highly effective in facilitating the resolution of ethnic conflicts, which are not inevitable in the post–cold war world.[35] Another view, which stems from the "politics of order" branch of the liberal tradition, perceives the growth of ethnic and other wider cultural tensions as inevitable now that international relations are no longer dominated by the two superpowers. This scholarly tradition is best captured in the widely debated book by Samuel P. Huntington, *The Clash of Civilizations and the Remaking of World Order* (1996), which essentially argues that cultural clashes between Western civilization and those of other regions of the world will serve as the defining characteristic of the twenty-first century.[36] Although Huntington dismisses the importance of African culture in his book, he and other scholars representative of this tradition are inclined to focus on the need for stability and order to ensure the continued territorial integrity of African countries in the face of ethnic conflict.

A fourth research direction that has rapidly expanded in recent years argues that gender, not ethnicity, is the social dimension in need of greater research attention in the liberal tradition. Specifically, proponents of a gender-based approach emphasize that our understanding of the classic themes of African politics and society can only be enriched by focusing on those individuals—African women—who compose roughly 50 percent of all African societies. In the case of the literature devoted to democratization, for example, Aili Mari Tripp, author of *Women and Politics in Uganda* (2000), offers a compelling example of why a focus on gender is so important.[37] Tripp demonstrates that extensive female involvement in Ugandan politics, which as of 1994 included the inauguration of Wandera Specioza Kazibwe as that country's first female vice president, was part of a more general trend of rising female involvement in African politics throughout the 1990s. Indeed, as of 2003, women composed on average 13 percent of all representatives in African legislatures. "In the past 10 years, African women have made unprecedented political progress," concludes Tripp. "Although daunting obstacles to their advancement remain, if the 1990s are any indication, the decade ahead is certain to see even greater political involvement on the part of women."[38] According to Tripp and her contemporaries, such as Sylvia Tamale, *When Hens Begin to Crow: Gender and Parliamentary Politics in Uganda* (1999), the necessity of incorporating gender into any analysis of the Ugandan political system represents but the tip of the iceberg of what is needed in terms of gender-based research in all of the topical subfields of African politics and society.[39]

A fifth research direction involves the degree to which the African state has facilitated or hindered Africa's socioeconomic and political-military development. The most noteworthy example of this trend is Jeffrey Herbst, *States and Power in Africa: Comparative Lessons in Authority and Control* (2000).[40] Herbst adopts a political-geography approach that underscores that African state-builders have confronted a challenge inherently different than that experienced by their European counterparts. "The fundamental problem facing state-builders in Africa—be they colonial kings, colonial governors, or presidents in the independence era—has been to project authority over inhospitable territories that contain relatively low densities of people," explains Herbst.[41] "Relatively low population densities in Africa have automatically meant that it always has been more expensive for states to exert control over a given number of people compared to Europe and other densely settled areas."[42] This conclusion has generated a great deal of debate in both the liberal and especially the critical traditions (see Chapter 14) in that it boldly questions the conventional wisdom concerning the enduring impact of colonial rule. According to Herbst, the true problem facing African leaders—sparsely inhabited geographical expanses—existed before the arrival of the colonial powers and was in reality little changed by their often brutal but relatively brief occupation of the African continent. The essence of this book, therefore, is the essential continuity between how precolonial and postcolonial African leaders have responded to the same political geography. This book, and the arguments it makes, will clearly serve as a benchmark for all future studies devoted to understanding the contemporary manifestations of the precolonial independence era and the long-term impacts of colonialism.

A sixth research direction focuses on the actions and decisions of African elites as the key to unlocking Africa's socioeconomic and political-military dilemmas. As captured in the title of a book, *The Criminalization of the State in Africa* (1998), written by Jean-François Bayart, Stephen Ellis, and Béatrice Hibou, African elites have manipulated the African state in the pursuit of illicit activities designed to ensure their personal enrichment).[43] In its most extreme form, this research direction suggests that the sowing of political disorder by African elites is part of the natural landscape of African politics and society and that these elites will even knowingly pursue a strategy of state collapse in the pursuit of political advantage. This is the view of Patrick Chabal and Jean-Pascal Daloz, authors of *Africa Works: Disorder as Political Instrument* (1999), who essentially conclude that African societies embody "an inbuilt bias in favor of greater disorder."[44] A more guardedly optimistic portrayal is provided by Nicolas van de Walle, author of *African Economies and the Politics of Permanent Crisis, 1979–1999* (2001), who nonetheless provides a sobering analysis of how the wrong-headed decisions of African elites have contributed to a period of sustained economic crisis.[45] The primary dilemma, according to van de Walle, is the continued importance throughout Africa of neopatrimonial forms of governance in which power is ultimately vested in an individual leader as opposed to legally based institutions. "Outwardly the state has all the trappings of a Weberian rational-legal system, with written laws and a constitutional order," explains van de Walle. "However, this official order is constantly subverted by a patrimonial logic in which office-holders almost systematically appropriate public resources for their own uses and political authority is largely based on clientilist practices, including patronage."[46] This neopatrimonial order, which van de Walle judges to be incompatible with economic growth and development, is neither static nor permanent as suggested by Chabal and Daloz but rather potentially (and positively) subject to global forces of change, including the process of democratization.[47]

A final research direction explores the ability of nonstate actors to form illicit networks at the intersection of the domestic and the international systems that are beyond the control of the state. The most noted scholar in this research direction is William Reno, whose early work on one case study, *Corruption and State Politics in Sierra Leone* (1995),[48] was followed by a more comparative analysis, *Warlord Politics and African States* (1998).[49] The cornerstone of Reno's analysis is that warlords are able to use their control over valuable local resources, such as diamonds in the case of Sierra Leone, as a source of income to fund numerous illicit activities, most notably the mounting of guerrilla insurgencies against centralized state control. History has clearly demonstrated, argues Reno, that foreign actors, most notably multinational corporations, are more than willing to enter into financial arrangements with local warlords as long as those warlords control access to the valued resource or territory in question. Critics have noted, however, that one must be wary of attempts to generalize from Reno's "worst-scenario" case studies (i.e., the most extreme cases of state collapse) to the broader universe of all fifty-three African countries. Indeed, as van de Walle aptly notes, for every extreme case of state collapse, with Liberia being noted as one of the "paradigmatic" cases, there exist other cases of effective conflict resolution and state-building such as Mozambique.[50]

Together these seven research directions demonstrate the continued vitality of the liberal tradition of African politics and society at the beginning of the twenty-first century. Far from achieving agreement on the specifics of which liberal theories are most relevant to the socioeconomic and political-military challenges confronting African policymakers, the liberal tradition embodies a rich diversity of competing ideas, theories, and policy prescriptions. Vigorous intellectual debate and disagreement will surely continue over the prospects of democratization, the strength and importance of civil society, the inevitability of ethnic cooperation and conflict, the role of the state, the actions and decisions of African elites, and the importance of nonstate networks. These differences notwithstanding, proponents of the liberal tradition remain bound together by their common belief in the Western democratic tradition as the model to be emulated by African leaders.

KEY TERMS

liberal tradition
modernization theory
structural-functionalism
value-neutral scientific framework
modernization revisionism
African Studies Association
    (ASA)
African Heritage Studies Association
    (AHSA)
American African Affairs Association
    (AAAA)
unilinear
political development
political decay
crises of development

crisis of identity
crisis of legitimacy
crisis of participation
crisis of penetration
crisis of distribution
crisis of integration
institutionalization
politics of order
policy relevant research
public policy research
political-economy approach
rational-choice models
public policy analysis
crisis of national survival
crisis of foreign control

FOR FURTHER READING

Almond, Gabriel A., and James S. Coleman, eds. *Politics of the Developing Areas*. Princeton: Princeton University Press, 1960.

Apter, David E., and Carl G. Rosberg, eds. *Political Development and the New Realism in Sub-Saharan Africa*. Charlottesville: University Press of Virginia, 1994.

Bayart, Jean-François, Stephen Ellis, and Béatrice Hibou. *The Criminalization of the State in Africa*. Oxford: James Currey, 1998.

Bratton, Michael, and Nicolas van de Walle. *Democratic Experiments in Africa: Regime Transition in Comparative Perspective*. Cambridge: Cambridge University Press, 1997.

Chabal, Patrick, and Jean-Pascal Daloz. *Africa Works: Disorder as Political Instrument*. Oxford: James Currey, 1999.

Coleman, James S. (edited by Richard L. Sklar). *Nationalism and Development in Africa: Selected Essays*. Berkeley: University of California Press, 1994.

Coleman, James S., and C. R. D. Halisi. "American Political Science and Tropical Africa: Universalism vs. Relativism." *African Studies Review* 26, nos. 3–4 (1983): 25–62.

Harbeson, John W., Donald Rothchild, and Naomi Chazan, eds. *Civil Society and the State in Africa*. Boulder: Lynne Rienner, 1994.

Herbst, Jeffrey. *States and Power in Africa: Comparative Lessons in Authority and*

Control. Princeton: Princeton University Press, 2000.

Khadiagala, Gilbert M. "Reflections on Development Theory and Political Practice in Africa." *A Current Bibliography on African Affairs* 22, no. 4 (1990): 343–70.

Kilson, Martin. "African Political Change and the Modernization Process." *Journal of Modern African Studies* 1, no. 14 (1963): 425–44.

Menkhaus, Kenneth J. "Political and Social Change." In Mark W. DeLancey, ed., *Handbook of Political Science Research on Sub-Saharan Africa: Trends from the 1960s to the 1990s*. Westport: Greenwood, 1992 (pp. 9–40).

O'Brien, Donal Cruise. "Modernization, Order, and the Erosion of a Democratic Ideal: American Political Science 1960–70." *Journal of Development Studies* 8, no. 2 (1972): 351–78.

Packenham, Robert. *Liberal America and the Third World: Political Development Ideas in Foreign Aid and Social Science*. Princeton: Princeton University Press, 1973.

Reno, William. *Warlord Politics and African States*. Boulder: Lynne Rienner, 1998.

Rothchild, Donald. *Managing Ethnic Conflict in Africa: Pressures and Incentives for Cooperation*. Washington, DC: Brookings Institution, 1997.

Staniland, Martin. *American Intellectuals and African Nationalists, 1955–1970*. New Haven: Yale University Press, 1991.

Tripp, Aili Mari. *Women and Politics in Uganda*. Madison: University of Wisconsin Press, 2000.

van de Walle, Nicolas. *African Economies and the Politics of Permanent Crisis, 1979–1999*. Cambridge: Cambridge University Press, 2001.

Wunsch, James S. "Development Administration in Africa: 1960–1990." In Mark W. DeLancey, ed., *Handbook of Political Science Research on Sub-Saharan Africa: Trends from the 1960s to the 1990s*. Westport: Greenwood, 1992 (pp. 41–72).

NOTES

1. See David E. Apter, *The Gold Coast in Transition* (Princeton: Princeton University Press, 1955). After Ghana's independence in 1957, the title was changed to *Ghana in Transition*. The quotation is taken from the second revised edition (Princeton: Princeton University Press, 1972), p. xxiii.

2. Walt W. Rostow, *The Stages of Economic Growth: A Noncommunist Manifesto* (Cambridge: Cambridge University Press, 1960).

3. See, for example, Daniel Lerner, *The Passing of Traditional Society: Modernizing the Middle East* (New York: The Free Press, 1958), and Alex Inkeles and David H. Smith, *Becoming Modern: Individual Change in Six Developing Countries* (Cambridge: Cambridge University Press, 1974).

4. For example, see A. F. K. Organski, *The Stages of Political Development* (New York: Knopf, 1965).

5. Gabriel A. Almond and James S. Coleman, eds., *Politics of the Developing Areas* (Princeton: Princeton University Press, 1960). For a more extensive analysis of structural functionalism, see Gabriel A. Almond and G. Bingham Powell Jr., *System, Process, and Policy: Comparative Politics* (Boston: Little, Brown, 1978).

6. Among the other political functions said to be performed by all political systems are political socialization and recruitment, interest aggregation, and political communication.

7. See, for example, Vicky Randall and Robin Theobold, *Political Change and Underdevelopment: A Critical Introduction to Third World Politics,* 2nd ed. (Durham: Duke University Press, 1998), p. 28.

8. See Robert A. Packenham, *Liberal America and the Third World: Political Development Ideas in Foreign Aid and Social Science* (Princeton: Princeton University Press, 1973). See also Irene L. Grendzier, *Managing Political Change: Social Scientists and the Third World* (Boulder: Westview, 1985).

9. This term was originally coined by Samuel P. Huntington, "The Change to Change," *Comparative Politics* 3, no. 3 (1971): 283–332. For general overviews of this theme, see Joseph Gusfield, "Tradition and Modernity: Misplaced Polarities in the Study of Social Change," *American Journal of Sociology* 72 (1967): 351–62, and Reinhard Bendix, "Tradition and Modernity Reconsidered," *Studies in Comparative Society and History* 9, no. 3 (1967): 292–346, and Randall and Theobold, *Political Change and Underdevelopment,* Ch. 2.

10. C. S. Whitaker Jr., *The Politics of Tradition: Continuity and Change in Northern Nigeria 1946–1966* (Princeton: Princeton University Press, 1970).

11. Ibid., p. 460 (emphasis added).

12. Ibid., p. 464.

13. Ibid.

14. See Paul Anber, "Modernization and Political Disintegration: Nigeria and the Igbos," *Journal of Modern African Studies* 5, no. 2 (1967): 163–79.

15. For the analysis that formed the basis of this discussion, see Donal Cruise O'Brien, "Modernization, Order, and the Erosion of a Democratic Ideal: American Political Science 1960–70," *Journal of Development Studies* 8, no. 2 (1972): 351–78. See also Mark Kesselman, "Order or Movement? The Literature of Political Development as Ideology," *World Politics* 26, no. 1 (1973): 139–54.

16. For a discussion of these and other themes related to U.S. intervention in the Third World, see Peter J. Schraeder, ed., *Intervention into the 1990s: U.S. Foreign Policy in the Third World* (Boulder: Lynne Rienner, 1992).

17. See Samuel P. Huntington, "Political Order and Political Decay," *World Politics* 17, no. 3 (1965): 386–430.

18. Samuel P. Huntington, *Political Order in Changing Societies* (New Haven: Yale University Press, 1968).

19. See Leonard Binder et al., *Crises and Sequences in Political Development* (Princeton: Princeton University Press, 1971).

20. Huntington, *Political Order in Changing Societies,* p. 7 (emphasis added).

21. Ibid., p. 8.

22. Aristide R. Zolberg, *Creating Political Order: The Party-States of West Africa* (Chicago: Rand McNally). See also his earlier study, *One-Party Government in the Ivory Coast* (Princeton: Princeton University Press, 1964, rev. ed., 1969).

23. Zolberg, *Creating Political Order,* p. 161.

24. Ibid.

25. For a discussion of this trend, see Richard A. Higgott, *Political Development Theory: The Contemporary Debate* (London: Croom Helm, 1983), pp. 21–42.

26. Robert H. Bates, *Markets and States in Tropical Africa: The Political Basis of Agricultural Policies* (Berkeley: University of California Press, 1981). See also his earlier work, *Rural Responses to Industrialization: A Study of Village Zambia* (New Haven: Yale University Press, 1976).

27. Ibid., p. 132.

28. Donald Rothchild and Robert L. Curry Jr., *Scarcity, Choice, and Public Policy in Middle Africa* (Berkeley: University of California Press, 1979).

29. Donald Rothchild and Victor A. Olorunsola, eds., *State versus Ethnic Claims: African Policy Dilemmas* (Boulder: Westview, 1983). See also Donald Rothchild and Naomi Chazan, eds., *The Precarious Balance: State and Society in Africa* (Boulder: Westview, 1988).

30. Jane I. Guyer, *African Studies in the United States: A Perspective* (Atlanta: African Studies Association, 1996).

31. Michael Bratton and Nicolas van de Walle, *Democratic Experiments in Africa: Regime Transition in Comparative Perspective* (Cambridge: Cambridge University Press, 1997).

32. John W. Harbeson, Donald Rothchild, and Naomi Chazan, eds., *Civil Society and the State in Africa* (Boulder: Lynne Rienner, 1994).

33. Ibid., p. 1.

34. Amy S. Patterson, "Participation and Democracy at the Grassroots: A Study of Development Projects in Rural Senegal," doctoral dissertation, Indiana University, 1996.

35. Donald Rothchild, *Managing Ethnic Conflict in Africa: Pressures and Incentives for Cooperation* (Washington, DC: Brookings Institution, 1997). See also Harvey Glickman, ed., *Ethnic Conflict and Democratization in Africa* (Atlanta: African Studies Association, 1995).

36. Samuel P. Huntington, *The Clash of Civilizations and the Remaking of World Order* (New York: Simon & Schuster, 1996).

37. Aili Mari Tripp, *Women and Politics in Uganda* (Madison: University of Wisconsin Press, 2000).

38. Aili Mari Tripp, "The New Political Activism in Africa," *Journal of Democracy* 12, no. 3 (2001): 154.

39. Sylvia Tamale, *When Hens Begin to Crow: Gender and Parliamentary Politics in Uganda* (Boulder: Westview, 1999).

40. Jeffrey Herbst, *States and Power in Africa: Comparative Lessons in Authority and Control* (Princeton: Princeton University Press, 2000).

41. Ibid., p. 11.

42. Ibid.

43. Jean-François Bayart, Stephen Ellis, and Béatrice Hibou, *The Criminalization of the State in Africa* (Oxford: James Currey, 1998).

44. Patrick Chabal and Jean-Pascal Daloz, *Africa Works: Disorder as Political Instrument* (Oxford: James Currey, 1998), p. 162.

45. Nicolas van de Walle, *African Economies and the Politics of Permanent Crisis, 1979–1999* (Cambridge: Cambridge University Press, 2001).

46. Ibid., pp. 51–52.

47. Ibid., p. 273.

48. William Reno, *Corruption and State Politics in Sierra Leone* (Cambridge: Cambridge University Press, 1995).

49. William Reno, *Warlord Politics and African States* (Boulder: Lynne Rienner, 1998).

50. van de Walle, *African Economies,* pp. 184–87.

14

W

Study of Africa in the Critical Tradition

Richard L. Sklar

Richard L. Sklar, Professor Emeritus, Department of
Political Science and James S. Coleman African Studies
Center, University of California, Los Angeles (UCLA).

THE STUDY OF AFRICAN politics and society has been enriched by a **critical tradition** that questions the prevailing liberal model of political and socioeconomic development. In its most extreme form, this scholarly tradition emphasizes that the achievement of true development will occur only in the aftermath of revolutionary struggles and the creation of populist regimes throughout the African continent. Unlike proponents of the liberal tradition, who sought to emulate the political and economic systems of the northern industrialized democracies of Canada, Europe, Japan, and the United States, critical scholars instead sought inspiration from a variety of socialist countries, including Cuba, the People's Republic of China (PRC), the Soviet Union, and Eastern Germany. The fall of the Berlin Wall, the decline of single-party Marxist regimes, and the fragmentation of the former Soviet Union into several independent and noncommunist countries triggered an intellectual crisis in the critical tradition. Although the vast majority of scholars associated with this tradition continue to embrace some variant of the socialist ideal, the declining popularity of socialist and especially Marxist ideals among a new generation of African policymakers has prompted a significant reexamination of critical thought. This chapter highlights the general evolution of the major themes and scholarly concerns of the critical tradition, from the 1960s to the present.

DEPENDENCY THEORY AND THE DEVELOPMENT OF UNDERDEVELOPMENT (LATE 1960s–EARLY 1970s)

A body of literature known as **dependency theory** became the first critical perspective to gain acceptance in the African scholarly community during the contemporary independence era. Emerging as a major alternative to liberal theories of development during the late 1960s and the early 1970s, dependency theory originated among Latin American specialists such as André Gunder Frank,[1] who criticized liberal theorists for being too "Western centric" in their analyses.

Dependency theorists were particularly concerned with understanding why, despite the optimistic projections of modernization theory, the regions of the southern hemisphere were suffering from economic stagnation, dictatorial leaders, and political instability and unrest. Whereas liberal theorists had argued that *internal* shortcomings, such as misguided economic policies and poor leadership, were at the center of these problems, dependency theorists argued that *external* constraints, most notably the domination of the developing countries by the industrialized powers of Western Europe and North America, were responsible for most economic and political misery in the southern hemisphere.

Dependency theorists argue that international relations between capitalist countries and underdeveloped areas are inherently exploitative and that the international capitalist system is the primary cause of this exploitation. In *How*

Europe Underdeveloped Africa (1972), Walter Rodney argues that, before the spread of international capitalism by the end of the sixteenth century, Africa was developing both politically and economically, as were most regions of the non-European world.[2] Yet, as foreign encroachment by Europe, culminating in direct colonial rule, increasingly led to Africa's inclusion in the global capitalist system, all forms of independent development on the continent were extinguished. Instead, European domination led to the **development of underdevelopment:** the gradual impoverishment of the African continent as previous African development was "blunted, halted, and turned back."[3]

The "development of underdevelopment" thesis categorizes all countries as either **metropoles** (the centers of economic and political power) or **satellites** (those areas controlled and exploited by the metropoles). In the case of the French empire, France served as the metropole and its colonies (e.g., Senegal and Côte d'Ivoire in West Africa) constituted the satellites. According to the dependency theorists, the maintenance of this highly unequal international structure was made possible by African **compradors** (political and economic elites) who knowingly or not served as the cultural, economic, military, or political agents of the European colonialists. Most important, this relationship did not change once African countries achieved independence from European colonial rule beginning in the 1950s but rather was reinforced by **neocolonial** leaders who remained more interested in maintaining ties with foreign powers than contributing to the true development of their own countries.

For dependency theorists, the development of the northern industrialized countries and the underdevelopment of countries in the southern hemisphere are inextricably linked. Indeed, the early dependency theorists concluded that the exploitation of Africa was critical to the development of advanced industrial capitalism in Europe. "It would be extremely simpleminded to say that colonialism in Africa or anywhere else *caused* Europe to develop its science and technology," explains Rodney. "However, it would be entirely accurate to say that the colonization of Africa and other parts of the world formed an indispensable link in a chain of events which made possible the technological transformation of the base of European capitalism."[4]

Dependency theorists argue that the **extraction of surplus** is the basic process that led to the development of the European metropoles and the underdevelopment of the African satellites during both the colonial and independence eras. In the case of European investment in Africa, for example, dependency theorists argue that the net result, especially during the colonial era, was an outflow of capital that benefited Europe at the expense of Africa. As discussed in Chapter 3, European administration of the colonial territories ensured that substandard wages could be paid to African workers and that little, if any, profits were reinvested in the colonies in the form of social services designed to benefit Africans. Most profits were instead repatriated back to the European metropoles where they contributed to the material well-being of Europeans. "In this sense," concludes Rodney, "the colonies were the generators of the capital rather than the countries into which foreign capital was plowed."[5] In short, Rodney accepts the basic argument of traditional dependency theorists that colonialism led to the stagnation and underdevelopment of the African continent.

CIRCULATIONIST REVISIONS OF DEPENDENCY THEORY (1970s)

During the 1970s, a group of scholars called **circulationists** revised dependency theory and offered a more sophisticated analysis of the development of underdevelopment thesis.[6] Drawing on the writings of Arghiri Emmanuel, *Unequal Exchange: A Study of the Imperialism of Trade* (1972), these scholars focus on the exploitative nature of international trade relationships that benefit the northern industrialized countries at the expense of the various regions of the southern hemisphere.[7]

Immanuel Wallerstein, founder of the Fernand Braudel Center for the Study of the World System at the State University of New York, Binghamton, has contributed greatly to the sophistication of dependency theory and is recognized as the leading scholar in the circulationist tradition. In *The Capitalist World-Economy* (1979),[8] and a massive three-volume work, *The Modern World System* (1974, 1980, 1989),[9] Wallerstein contributed to the sophistication of dependency theory by historically analyzing the rise of what he calls the **capitalist world economy,** an exploitative worldwide capitalist system controlled by the major industrial powers. This system is marked by alternating periods of economic expansion and contraction (i.e., economic decline) of the world economy in which **core countries** (metropoles) emerge and **peripheral countries** (satellites) grow more impoverished. According to this view, the creation of European empires in Africa at the end of the nineteenth century (the "scramble for Africa" described in Chapter 3) was the direct result of a contraction in the capitalist world economy from 1873 to 1897.[10]

Wallerstein's second contribution to dependency theory is a more concise analysis of the possibility for development and social change in the regions of the southern hemisphere. In keeping with the development of underdevelopment thesis, Wallerstein argues that true social change can only occur when the entire capitalist world economy has been overthrown. Any attempt at social change by one country in the current confines of the capitalist world economy, according to this analysis, is ultimately destined to fail. In the case of the Soviet Union, a country once admired by many critical theorists as capable of leading revolutionary change in Africa, the circulationists argue that the socialist ideals of the Russian revolution of 1917 were doomed from the start, due to its isolation in an extremely hostile capitalist world economy dominated by the United States. The eventual overthrow of communism and the fragmentation of the Soviet Union in 1991 confirmed this view. According to Wallerstein, meaningful development for Africa will only occur once the capitalist world economy

---

A Closer Look: ASSOCIATION OF CONCERNED AFRICA SCHOLARS

The Association of Concerned Africa Scholars (ACAS) was founded in 1977 by a group of Africanists who believe that academics should be effective political activists in addition to excellent teachers and researchers. The primary purposes of this group are threefold:

- Formulate alternative analyses of Africa and U.S. government policy
- Develop communication and action networks between the peoples and scholars of Africa and the United States
- Mobilize support in the United States on critical, current issues related to Africa

Eight sets of principles have historically guided ACAS activities:

- Opposition to apartheid, racial and class domination, and minority rule
- Support for efforts by African states to end their economic dependency
- Recognition of the right of African nations to political autonomy and

to their own forms of social and economic organization

- Support for democratic governments, genuine popular participation, and the right to form political parties
- Commitment to the protection of human rights
- Support for colleagues in Africa who face political repression
- Greater equity in North/South economic relations
- Economic and technical support for African peoples to help them deal with the pressing needs and crises of the continent

The ACAS Executive Committee and Board of Directors are composed of distinguished Africanists who pursue the ACAS political agenda through the funding of a Political Action Committee, a lobbying office in Washington, D.C., and the publication of a trimestrial newsletter, the *ACAS Bulletin*. For further information, visit the ACAS home page at http://www.prairienet.org/acas/

---

has been overthrown by worldwide revolution and replaced by a world economy based on socialist principles.

Wallerstein's most important contribution to dependency theory is a more sophisticated understanding of the metropolis-satellite (core–periphery) model of the world economy originally proposed by André Gunder Frank. Disagreeing with what he perceived as an overly simplistic view of a world in which countries are either extremely powerful (the core) or in the process of being marginalized (the periphery), Wallerstein pointed out the existence of a third tier of **semiperipheral countries** that are neither very powerful nor completely impoverished.[11] These countries constitute rising regional powers that are economically and politically powerful in their immediate regions and aspire to someday join the core in its control of the capitalist world system. The semiperipheral countries are further distinguished in that they are both exploited by the core and exploiters of the periphery. For example, whereas the semiperipheral power of Nigeria is perceived as being exploited by the core country of

Great Britain (the former colonial power), it nonetheless exploits peripheral powers in the West African region, such as Benin, with which it has strong political and economic ties. Other African powers that have been called potentially influential semiperipheral countries include Côte d'Ivoire and Senegal in West Africa; Algeria, Libya, and Egypt in North Africa; Ethiopia and Kenya in East Africa; the Democratic Republic of the Congo (Congo-Kinshasa) in Central Africa; and South Africa in Southern Africa.[12]

Wallerstein argues that the existence of the semiperiphery is the primary reason the capitalist world economy has not yet been overthrown in favor of a socialist world economy. For revolution to occur, the world system must become polarized between the few richest countries and the vast majority burdened by high levels of urban poverty, mass unemployment, and rising social unrest. This process, according to Wallerstein, began during the worldwide expansion of the capitalist world economy at the beginning of the fifteenth century and continues to unfold as Africa becomes increasingly marginalized at the beginning of the twenty-first century. The semiperiphery delays the process of polarization by undermining the creation of a unified front against the core. These countries instead perceive themselves as economically and politically better off than the peripheral countries and thus either intentionally or unintentionally serve as the agents of the core by seeking to strengthen their standing in an otherwise exploitative system. It is important to remember, however, that the semiperiphery is only perceived as a temporary palliative to an aging, increasingly dysfunctional capitalist world economy that will eventually polarize and result in world revolution.

MARXISM'S IMPACT ON THE DEVELOPMENT OF CRITICAL THOUGHT (EARLY 1970s)

Karl Marx (1818–1883) was a German scholar whose writings served as the inspiration for more than a century of scholarship highly critical of the liberal tradition, as well as the ideological basis for seven decades of communist rule in the former Soviet Union.[13] Writing during the nineteenth century, Marx was surrounded by a variety of social ills that accompanied the expansion of free market capitalism known as the **industrial revolution,** the process whereby the countries of Europe were transformed from agriculturally based rural societies into industrially based urban societies. The absence of strict child labor laws and other forms of government regulation of the workplace meant that it was not uncommon to find children 6 years old working in unsafe factory conditions, and people of all ages working 14-hour days with no health-care benefits or sick leave. In short, Marx lived during an era in which the spread of free market capitalism appeared to foster new forms of human exploitation.

Three elements of Marxist theory are important to understanding the evolution of the critical tradition. First, Marx argues that all societies can be divided into classes, which are bound together in a relationship of exploitation (see Chapter 5).[14] In capitalist society, a dominant bourgeoisie (property-owning) class exploits the work of the proletariat (working) class. Marx was particularly concerned with the ability of a rising bourgeoisie to expropriate the property of the petty bourgeoisie in capitalist societies.[15] This process results in a growing class of propertyless workers (the proletariat) who are forced to either accept poor jobs and unsafe working conditions or starve. Most important, once propertyless, workers are caught in a vicious cycle in which their labor serves to create more property and wealth for the bourgeoisie. In essence, workers become trapped in a miserable existence akin to slavery, but this condition is not permanent, Marx claims, for it can be overcome through proletarian revolution.

Second, Marx argues that a revolutionary situation emerges when advances in technological, scientific, and other forms of material development (the **forces of production**) outgrow an outmoded system of ownership of property among classes (the **relations of production**) such that the dominant class finds it increasingly difficult to maintain control over the rest of society through its traditional means.[16] Because no "civilized" society ever forfeits its material level of development, the net result of the growing contradiction between the forces of production and the relations of production is a heightened class struggle in which the ruling class is eventually overthrown. According to Marx, such revolutionary events are part of a general historical trend in which all societies are moving along the same path of development.[17] In the *Manifesto of the Communist Party* (1848), for example, Marx suggests that all societies have to pass through ancient, feudal, and capitalist **modes of production** (the combination of the forces and the relations of production) on the path to achieving what he perceives as the inevitable and desirable final stage of revolutionary development: a socialist (communist) society in which the proletariat reigns supreme.

It is important to note, however, that Marx held a highly negative view of what he called "Asiatic" (non-Western) societies.[18] Similar to the viewpoint adhered to by the modernization theorists described in Chapter 13, Marx suggests that non-Western societies, including those in Africa, were stagnant, backward, and led by barbarians and despots. This negative perception was reinforced by a firm belief that these same societies, unlike those of Europe, lacked the ability to move *independently* through the various stages of historical revolutionary development on the path to socialism.[19] As a result, Marx concluded that the spread of colonialism was a "brutal but necessary" stage[20] in their historical development; brutal in the sense that the colonial powers often adopted barbaric methods to defeat peoples unwilling to submit themselves to foreign rule, and "necessary" in the sense that colonial rule facilitated the introduction of capitalism—the preliminary stage to socialism—into "backward" areas around the globe. Marx was particularly impressed by the ability of the European powers to transplant "modern" (capitalist) types of industry, such as factories and transportation networks, to the southern hemisphere, thereby providing a spark that would ignite the modernization process. In India, for example, Marx describes the construction of British-designed railroads as critical to the colony's future development: "The railway system will therefore become, in India, truly the forerunner of modern industry."[21] Unlike the expectations of modernization theorists, however, Marx argues that colonialism and the implementation of capitalism are *developmental* in that they constitute a necessary stage in the advancement toward socialist revolution in the southern hemisphere. Despite the fact that Marx recognized the terrible costs associated with the spread of capitalism under the guise of colonialism, he argued that they were costs worth paying if the result was the creation of a socialist society.[22]

A group of scholars best called neo-Marxists drew on classical Marxism to criticize the dependency approach of the 1970s, contributing to a rising debate that also questioned several aspects of the world systems approach of the circulationists. Like the evolution of scholarship in the liberal tradition during this same period, these scholars criticized their predecessors for promoting grand theories that were so abstract as to be of little use to African **political activists,** who were interested in promoting socioeconomic change in their respective countries. Dependency and world systems theories were of little use to African leaders who sought practical solutions to guide their countries toward socialist alternatives. A Marxist union leader might similarly wonder how abstract theories of class relations in African societies could be applied to seek changes in labor laws and the working conditions of factory workers. The **neo-Marxist school** addressed these practical problems and dominated the critical tradition of African politics and society from the late 1970s to the late 1980s.[23]

The work of Samir Amin, an Egyptian scholar, is recognized as serving as an intellectual bridge between the dependency/circulationist and neo-Marxist traditions.[24] In one of his most-cited works, *Neo-Colonialism in West Africa* (1973), Amin demonstrates his intellectual attachment to the dependency and circulationist approaches by arguing that the development of West Africa has been "blocked" by the region's incorporation into an inherently unequal capitalist world economy and that this state of affairs has been reinforced by neo-colonial West African leaders during the contemporary independence era.[25] Amin documents how Senegal's economy was structured around the production of virtually nothing but groundnuts (peanuts) during nearly a century of French colonial rule. As discussed in Chapter 3, this agricultural specialization provided the French with inexpensive heating oil, which is derivative of groundnuts, and hampered the economic development of Senegal. The largely groundnut-oriented economy was maintained even after independence due to the shared interests of French investors and political elites who sought to maintain privileged ties with the country, as well as Senegalese leaders who depended on profits from this sector to maintain power. The net result of this "outwardly directed" development strategy, according to Amin, has been a permanent crisis of public finances, tight dependence on foreign technical assistance, and an increasing balance of payment deficits. Rather than generating an "internal dynamism" geared toward the domestic needs of the Senegalese population, this path has resulted in the Senegalese economy being highly dependent on foreign interests and investment.[26] Amin thus declares that the "groundnut economy, far from contributing to Senegal's development, is making possible the plunder of its economy and its continuation in a state of underdevelopment."[27]

However, Amin sets the tone for a series of neo-Marxist critiques by "parting company" with the dependency and circulationist approaches in two major areas.[28] In the case of dependency theory, Amin suggests that one cannot assume that the "extraction of surplus" from the peripheral areas of the southern hemisphere was necessary for the development of the northern industrialized countries, because, he argues, development of individual countries and/or regions can occur independently. Although colonial exploitation of African colonies aided development in the northern industrialized countries, the wealth of northern countries was not contingent on exploitation. As Amin argues in one of his later books, *Delinking: Towards a Polycentric World* (1990), African countries can pursue **autocentric (self-reliant) development** by attempting to withdraw in various degrees from the capitalist world economy.[29] Simply put, Amin rejects the development of underdevelopment thesis in favor of a more nuanced view that accounts for a variety of developmental processes and outcomes.

Amin also departs from the circulationist tradition by rejecting the notion that only one mode of production, the capitalist world economy, exclusively exists in the international system.[30] The broad differences both between and within African economies suggests that it is far too simplistic to try and include them all in the broad category of the capitalist mode of production. The international system is instead composed of both capitalist and noncapitalist economies that coexist in geographical regions (e.g., West Africa), individual countries (e.g., Senegal), and even subnational regions of individual countries (e.g., the southern Casamance region of Senegal).

MARXISM AND THE EMERGENCE OF A NEO-MARXIST SCHOOL OF THOUGHT (LATE 1970s–1980s)

Building on the scholarship of Amin and others, a neo-Marxist school of thought that emerged at the end of the 1970s contributed to the reformulation of critical thought in at least four areas. First, neo-Marxist scholars reject the development of underdevelopment thesis. Although certainly in agreement with their dependency/circulationist colleagues that capitalism is inherently exploitative, neo-Marxist scholars nonetheless disagree that the worldwide expansion of capitalism has had a permanent negative effect on Africa. Similar to its portrayal in classical Marxism, the spread of capitalism to Africa is instead viewed as one developmental stage in an overall movement toward socialism.

A Closer Look: WESTERN SOCIAL SCIENCE AS IMPERIALISM?

Professor Claude Ake, whose life was tragically cut short in a plane crash in Nigeria on November 7, 1996, remains one of the most noted Nigerian scholars from the critical tradition. Born in Nigeria, Ake received a Ph.D. in political science from Columbia University in New York and served as the president of the Nigerian Political Science Association and as the executive director of the Council for the Development of Social Science Research in Africa (CODESRIA). In 1992, he founded and became the director of the Centre for Advanced Social Science (CASS) in Port Harcourt, Nigeria. A steadfast critic of Nigeria's military dictatorships, Ake was also at the forefront of academic debates concerning the proper place of Western scholarship in Nigerian institutions of higher learning.

One of Ake's most provocative books, *Social Science as Imperialism: The Theory of Political Development* (1982), assesses the impact of Western social science on its related disciplines in Africa. Ake severely criticizes what he labels the academic imperialism of Western social scientists who have dominated international debates over the proper path of development for African countries. Ake's critique of Western social science is threefold:

- "It foists, or at any rate attempts to foist on the developing countries, capitalist values, capitalist institutions, and capitalist development."

- "It focuses social science analysis on the question of how to make the developing countries more like the West."

- "It propagates mystifications, and modes of thought and action which serve the interests of capitalism and imperialism." (p. xiii)

To overcome this intellectual imperialism, Ake underscores the necessity of promoting a more Africa-centric and socialist-oriented academic tradition that builds on African heritages and serves African interests. Ake argues that African social scientists should commit themselves to research that will facilitate the radical transformation of African governments from the essentially Western-oriented, elite-based model originally handed down from the departing colonial powers, to one that fosters "mass" interests and development needs, particularly in the neglected rural areas of most African countries.

For further discussion see Ufot B. Inamete, "The Profile and Development of Political Science in Nigeria," *International Studies Notes* 15, no. 3 (1990): 85–90, and Yolamu Borongo, ed., *Political Science in Africa: A Critical Review* (London: Zed, 1983).

Neo–Marxist scholars also recognize that individual African countries can achieve **dependent development** in the capitalist world system. Semiperipheral countries have experienced rising levels of industrial output, mechanization of agriculture, and urbanization. It is the combination of these factors that, according to classical Marxism, promotes the emergence of an urban proletariat capable of leading class struggle and revolution in the pursuit of socialism.

The third contribution of neo–Marxist scholars to the evolution of the critical tradition is the application of class analysis to explain the historical evolution of African politics and society. Neo–Marxist scholars have underscored the necessity of moving beyond unwieldy notions of core, semiperipheral, and peripheral countries in favor of analyzing cooperation and conflict among the variety of class groupings that compose individual African countries. This approach is most notable in the analysis of the evolution and impact of African ruling classes. As already noted, both the dependency theorists and the circulationists tend to dismiss the importance of African elites as independent actors, suggesting instead that they are always wittingly or unwittingly serving the interests of foreign powers. This results in a mechanistic understanding of political change that completely disregards the power actually wielded by African ruling classes.

The neo-Marxist scholars have sought to correct this shortcoming not only by classifying and analyzing various types of African ruling classes, ranging from the so-called bureaucratic bourgeoisie (civil service and government employees) to the commercial bourgeoisie (top executives of major business enterprises), but also by examining the goals and impacts of other classes within African societies, such as the petty bourgeoisie (individuals involved in smaller trading activities), the proletariat (urban-based, wage-earning, working class), and the rural peasantry (see Chapter 5). One of the most noted works in this genre is Irving Leonard Markovitz, *Power and Class in Africa: An Introduction to Change and Conflict in African Politics* (1977), which adopts the concept of class to analyze the historical evolution of African politics and society, including an extremely detailed discussion of the impact of colonialism on traditional African class structures.[31] Markovitz is particularly concerned with the impact of the bureaucratic bourgeoisie, which he defines as the "combined ruling group consisting of the top political leaders and bureaucrats, the traditional rulers and their descendants, the leading members of the liberal professions, the rising business bourgeoisie, and top members of the military and police forces."[32]

A final contribution of the neo-Marxist tradition was a growing emphasis on the role of the "state," particularly in terms of its relationship to powerful international and domestic classes (see Chapter 8). According to the dependency theorists, the state serves the same function as a hinge on a door: Just as the hinge allows for the door to open so that individuals may enter into a room, the state facilitates the penetration and control of African societies by external powers.[33] It is for precisely this reason that the dependency theorists often dismiss African elites as neocolonial leaders who knowingly or unknowingly open the door to foreign interests to the detriment of their respective societies. The neo-Marxist scholars disagree sharply with the "hinge" conceptualization of the state. They argue instead that the ruling class of the state can cooperate with the dominant economic classes of society to pursue capitalist development that runs counter to the interests of foreign powers. For example, despite the fact that one of the most noted early works by Colin Leys, *Underdevelopment in Kenya: The Political Economy of Colonialism* (1974), clearly falls in the dependency tradition, his later analysis incorporated several of the critiques of the neo-Marxist tradition.[34] Specifically, Leys argues in his later works that Kenya's ruling classes and dominant economic classes combined forces to achieve a form of capitalist development that favors the Kenyan bourgeoisie at the expense of external economic interests.

An important debate in the neo-Marxist tradition during this period involved whether the African state merely reflects the interests of the dominant socioeconomic class of a particular African country (the orthodox Marxist interpretation) or whether the ruling class of the state itself can be independent of, and carry out policies counter to, that powerful domestic economic class. One of the most notable contributions to this debate was offered in 1978 by Richard L. Sklar, who argued that "class relations, at bottom, are determined by relations of power, not production."[35] This brief quote highlights Sklar's belief that the ruling classes of the African state must not be perceived as mere reflections of that society's economic system, nor as mere puppets of its dominant economic class. Rather, it is important to focus on the *political* basis of competition between classes in African societies and recognize that a wide range of possibilities exists, in terms of class domination and control. Whereas in one case the dominant economic class of a society may control the actions of the ruling class of the state, the reverse may also be true depending on the power relationship between the two classes. In short, Sklar argues that one cannot automatically assume that one class or coalition of class groupings will always dominate other internal or even international class groupings. One must instead examine the potentially different political realities of class relationships in individual case studies.

NEW DIRECTIONS (1990s–PRESENT)

The end of the cold war signified the beginning of a new era for critical scholarship devoted to understanding African politics and society. The decline of communism in Eastern Europe and the former Soviet Union removed an ideological beacon of hope for African Marxists seeking socioeconomic development independent of the capitalist path. Ideological allies on the African continent, such as Marxist regimes in Ethiopia and Angola, suddenly found themselves cut adrift by new leaders in Eastern Europe and Russia who were seeking to cultivate cooperative relationships with the West. Even African students were not immune. After the reunification of East and West Germany, thousands of African students from a variety of socialist and Marxist countries studying in East Germany were informed that their scholarships and visas had been terminated and were told to return to their countries of origin. As poignantly stated by Timothy M. Shaw, one of the most prolific scholars in the critical tradition, these events ushered in a "profound period of revisionism" at the beginning of the 1990s as the "revolutionary, nationalist scenario" anticipated by African radicals at the end of World War II gave way to an extreme "pessimism."[36]

The revisionism undertaken by critical scholars has produced an impressive array of scholarship that points the reader in at least six broad research directions. First and foremost is a resurgence of debate over preferred forms of political governance. The downfall of communist regimes in Eastern Europe and the former Soviet Union, the intellectual heartland of single-party rule, reinforced the growing tendency of critical scholars to question the viability of single-party political systems in Africa. Critical scholars nonetheless typically perceive the so-called "third wave" of democratization and the role of foreign powers in promoting multiparty democracy as a form of neocolonialism that is contributing to the **recolonization** of the African continent. According to Claude Ake, the adoption of multiparty political systems in many cases has fostered the **democratization of disempowerment,** a process whereby multiparty elections allow for the rotation of self-interested elites of different parties while the vast majority of the population remains disempowered from the political system.[37] As Ake poignantly argues in *Democracy and Development in Africa* (1996), true democracy is not based on multiparty elections but the assurance of "popular" (mass) participation in African political systems.[38] The solution, according to Richard L. Sklar, is the nurturing of **developmental democracy,** a polity in which group, as opposed to individual, self-interests are paramount.[39] According to Sklar, the specific norms of this polity—interaction of group leaders who are accountable to their members, the pursuit of social justice, and economic and political freedoms—are ideally suited to the African environment. Indeed, Sklar concludes that developmental democracy offers the best alternative to "the cruel choice between laissez-faire liberalism without social justice, on the one hand, and dictatorial forms of state-centred economic development, on the other."[40]

A second research direction focuses on the role of social movements in the struggle for more inclusive forms of governance. An excellent example of this research focus is *African Studies in Social Movements and Democracy* (1995), edited by Mahmood Mamdani and Ernest Wamba-dia-Wamba.[41] This volume is the result of an extended research project, including workshops held in Algiers, Algeria, and Harare, Zimbabwe, that brought together specialists from throughout the African continent. The contributors adopted a broad perspective of social movements that includes any group activity autonomous (independent) of the state. As a result, individual chapters explore such varied topics as national liberation movements, ethnically based nationality movements, and religiously based revivalist movements. The thread linking these and other movements, according to Mamdani and Wamba-dia-Wamba, is a shared experience of past oppression and the constant struggle initially for survival and later for the creation of more inclusive forms of governance.

A third research direction that has especially expanded in recent years involves the imperative of "engendering" the social sciences. Specifically, proponents of such an approach argue in favor of making gender an integral element of our approach to various concepts and themes in African politics and society. This is precisely the theme of *Women and the State in Africa* (1989), edited by Jane L. Parpart and Kathleen A. Staudt, which captured the tone of gender-based scholarship at the beginning of the post–cold war era by arguing in favor of making gender integral to any understanding of the African state.[42] "Gender, as we see it, is central to any and all efforts to conceptualize the 'modern' state, whether it be its historical origins, current composition, or management of the extraction and distribution of resources," explain Parpart and Staudt. "We have been struck by the absence of attention to women and the state in several bodies of knowledge."[43] The critical conclusion of this and other books is the need for African women to be in the forefront of reforming inherently unequal and exploitative gender relationships in their respective societies. An excellent example of this theme is April A. Gordon, *Transforming Capitalism and Patriarchy: Gender and Development in Africa* (1996), whose book explores the evolving relationship between patriarchy (indigenous male dominance) and capitalism and its subsequent impact on the role of women in African development.[44] Gordon's book embodies two core arguments: (1) that the interests of patriarchy and capitalism, which once collaborated in the exploitation and control of African women, no longer coincide in contemporary Africa, and (2) that existing patriarchal structures and capitalist development can be reformed by creative new strategies and alliances among African women to improve their status and opportunities in African societies.

A fourth research direction explores the growing power and influence wielded by international financial institutions, most notably the International Monetary Fund (IMF) and the World Bank. Although critical scholars, such as Fantu Cheru in *The Silent Revolution in Africa: Debt, Development, and Democracy* (1989), focused on the imperialist influence wielded by these organizations during the 1980s, this attention intensified in the 1990s when the former Soviet Union—the only significant alternative source of development assistance outside the Western world—ceased to exist.[45] In essence, the decline and fragmentation of the Soviet Union strengthened the international financial monopoly of the Western powers that control institutions such as the IMF and the World Bank. This left African leaders with little bargaining leverage when Western offers of foreign assistance and loans were accompanied by increasingly strident demands for the restructuring of their domestic economies (see Chapter 12). As aptly argued by Thandika Mkandawire and Adebayo Olukoshi in *Between Liberalization and Oppression: The Politics of Structural Adjustment in Africa* (1995), the foreign imposition of what are commonly called "structural adjustment programs" (SAPs) often runs counter to the legitimate needs of social forces and therefore corrupts true efforts at creating responsive democracy in most African countries.[46] This theme was returned to in a subsequent book, *Our Continent, Our Future: African Perspectives on Structural Adjustment* (1999), that Mkandawire wrote with Charles C. Soludo.[47] Drawing on the conclusions of thirty commissioned studies that were written by Africans from throughout the continent, the book underscores the need for Africans to retake the initiative in the structural adjustment debate and provides specific policy recommendations that are said to constitute part of an emerging African consensus on the topic.

A fifth research agenda focuses on the impact of **imperialism**—the domination of one country by another—on Africa's evolving relationships with foreign powers during the post–cold war era. One view, which draws on the dependency tradition, can be characterized as **neoimperialism.** According to this perspective, the granting of legal independence to African countries that began in the 1950s did little to alter the constraining web of economic, political, military, and cultural ties that perpetuate the continued exploitation of the African continent by the northern industrialized capitalist countries and their respective multinational corporations. This is the position of Tukumbi Lumumba-Kasongo, author of *The Dynamics of Economic and Political Relations between Africa and Foreign*

Powers: A Study in International Relations (1999) who argues that Africa's exploitation has actually increased in the post–cold war environment.[48] An alternative view, which can be called **postimperialism,** is advanced in a book, *Postimperialism and World Politics* (1999), edited by Richard L. Sklar and David G. Becker,[49] as well as in a series of articles written by Sklar.[50] According to this perspective, multinational corporations can play both positive and negative roles, depending on the nature of the relationship between the international wing of the corporation's managerial bourgeoisie, which is typically headquartered in a northern capitalist country, and the local indigenous African wing of that managerial bourgeoisie. "It would be innocent and illusory to suppose that partnership agreements with transnational corporations are ideological neutral," explains Sklar, who agrees that they ultimately transmit the capitalist values of the northern industrialized democracies to the African countries within which they operate. "However, the transmission of ideas and attitudes between the partners of a dominant class alliance is not a one-way process," concludes Sklar. "Members of the corporate international bourgeoisie are just as likely to be sensitized to the developmental values of their host country partners as the other way around."[51]

Finally, the end of the cold war solidified the thinking of an **African nationalist school of thought** in the critical tradition.[52] This school of thought, also called the **Dar school,** originally grew out of a core group of African scholars based at the University of Dar es Salaam in Tanzania that founded the African Association of Political Science (AAPS) in 1973. These scholars argue that the critical tradition's classic focus on the negative impacts of the international economic system and domestic economic classes must be complemented by a growing recognition of the substantial political power and autonomy enjoyed by the African state. Specifically, scholarship must reflect the indigenous power of African political institutions and actors in their relationships with domestic and international economic actors. An important practical element of this school of thought is the conscious attempt to promote Africa-focused scholarship that builds on African research networks and the interests of African scholars. The present-day embodiment of the Dar school is the Council for the Development of Social Science Research in Africa (CODESRIA), the leading pan-African social science research institute that is based in Dakar, Senegal.[53] CODESRIA sponsors a wide array of research activities, including the creation of research networks in individual African countries, the sponsorship of workshops at CODESRIA headquarters that are attended by a new generation of scholars from throughout the African continent, and a publishing house that provides one of the most important outlets for critical scholarship written by African scholars.

CODESRIA and other like-minded African research institutes have emerged as the leaders of efforts to reinvigorate the critical tradition at the beginning of the twenty-first century. The declining popularity of socialist and especially Marxist ideals among a new generation of African policy makers has prompted a significant reexamination of critical thought. As is the case with their liberal counterparts (see Chapter 13), critical scholars are far from achieving agreement as to which of their theories are most relevant for the socioeconomic and political–military challenges confronting African policymakers. They nonetheless remain bound together by their common belief in the need to confront the often disastrous social and economic costs associated with liberal models of development. They are particularly united in their opposition to rising foreign involvement in African economies and political systems, most notably the West's attempt to impose SAPs and multiparty political systems.

KEY TERMS

critical tradition
dependency theory
development of underdevelopment
metropoles
satellites
compradors
neocolonial
extraction of surplus
circulationists
capitalist world economy
core countries
peripheral countries
semiperipheral countries
industrial revolution
forces of production

relations of production
modes of production
political activists
neo-Marxist school
autocentric (self-reliant)
    development
dependent development
recolonization
democratization of disempowerment
developmental democracy
imperialism
neoimperialism
postimperialism
African nationalist school of thought
Dar school

FOR FURTHER READING

Ake, Claude. *Democracy and Development in Africa.* Washington, DC: Brookings Institution, 1996.

Ake, Claude. *Social Science as Imperialism: The Theory of Political Development.* Ibadan: Ibadan University Press, 1982.

Amin, Samir. *Delinking: Toward a Polycentric World.* London: Zed, 1990.

Avineri, Shlomo. *Karl Marx on Colonialism and Modernization: His Dispatches and Other Writings on China, India, Mexico, the Middle East, and North Africa.* Garden City: Doubleday, 1968.

Barongo, Yolamu, ed. *Political Science in Africa: A Critical Review.* London: Zed, 1983.

Cheru, Fantu. *The Silent Revolution in Africa: Debt, Development, and Democracy.* London: Zed, 1989.

Falola, Toyin, ed. *African Politics in Postimperial Times: The Essays of Richard L. Sklar.* Trenton, NJ: Africa World Press, 2002.

Fatton, Jr., Robert. *Predatory Rule: State and Civil Society in Africa.* Boulder: Lynne Rienner, 1992.

Gordon, April A. *Transforming Capitalism and Patriarchy: Gender and Development in Africa.* Boulder: Lynne Rienner, 1996.

Mamdani, Mahmood, and Ernest Wamba-dia-Wamba, eds. *African Studies in Social Movements and Democracy.* Dakar: CODESRIA, 1995.

Markovitz, Irving Leonard. *Power and Class in Africa: An Introduction to Change and Conflict in African Politics.* Englewood Cliffs: Prentice-Hall, 1977.

Mkandawire, Thandika. "The Social Sciences in Africa: Breaking Local Barriers and Negotiating International Presence. The Bashorun M. K. O. Abiola Distinguished Lecture Presented to the 1996 African Studies Association Annual Meeting," *African Studies Review* 40, no. 2 (1997): 15–36.

Mkandawire, Thandika, and Charles C. Souldo. *Our Continent, Our Future: African Perspectives on Structural Adjustment.* Trenton, NJ: Africa World Press, 1999.

Nzongola-Ntalaja. *Revolution and Counterrevolution in Africa: Essays in Contemporary Politics.* London: Zed, 1989.

Packenham, Robert A. *The Dependency Movement: Scholarship and Politics in Development Studies.* Cambridge: Harvard University Press, 1992.

Parpart, Jane L., and Kathleen A. Staudt, eds. *Women and the State in Africa.* Boulder: Lynne Rienner, 1990.

Rodney, Walter. *How Europe Underdeveloped Africa.* Washington, DC: Howard University Press, 1982, rev. ed.

Shaw, Timothy M. "Reformism, Revisionism, and Radicalism in African Political Economy during the 1990s." *The Journal of Modern African Studies* 29, no. 2 (1991): 191–212.

Shaw, Timothy M. *Toward a Political Economy for Africa: The Dialectics of Dependence.* New York: St. Martin's, 1985.

Sklar, Richard L., and David G. Becker, eds. *Postimperialism and World Politics.* Westport: Praeger, 1999.

NOTES

1. See, for example, Frank's *Capitalism and Underdevelopment in Latin America: Historical Studies of Chile and Brazil* (New York: Monthly Review, 1967).

2. Walter Rodney, *How Europe Underdeveloped Africa* (Washington, DC: Howard University Press, 1982)(rev. ed., with a postscript by A. M. Babu).

3. Ibid., p. 224.

4. Ibid., p. 174.

5. Ibid., p. 212.

6. See Richard A. Higgott, *Political Development Theory: The Contemporary Debate* (London: Croom Helm, 1983), pp. 58–62.

7. Arghiri Emmanuel, *Unequal Exchange: A Study of the Imperialism of Trade* (London: New Left, 1976). See also Christopher Chase-Dunn, *Global Formation: Structures of the World Economy* (Oxford: Basil Blackwell, 1989), and Michael Barratt-Brown, *Fair Trade: Reform and Realities in the International Trading System* (London: Zed, 1993).

8. Immanuel Wallerstein, *The Capitalist World-Economy* (Cambridge: Cambridge University Press, 1979)

9. The subtitles of each of these volumes (published by Academic Press, New York) are (vol. 1) *Capitalist Agriculture and the Origins of the European World-Economy in the Sixteenth Century*; (vol. 2) *Mercantilism and the Consolidation of the European World-Economy, 1600–1750* (1980); and (vol. 3) *The Second Era of Great Expansion of the Capitalist World-Economy, 1730–1840s* (1989).

10. See Immanuel Wallerstein, "The Three Stages of African Involvement in the World Economy," in Peter C. W. Gutkind and Immanuel Wallerstein, eds., *The Political Economy of Contemporary Africa* (Thousand Oaks: Sage, 1976), p. 39.

11. For discussion, see Immanuel Wallerstein, "Dependence in an Interdependent World: The Limited Possibilities of Transformation within the Capitalist-World Economy,"

African Studies Review 17, no. 1 (1974): 1–26.

12. See, for example, Karen A. Mingst, "The Ivory Coast at the Semiperiphery of the World-Economy," *International Studies Quarterly* 32 (1988): 259–74.

13. For an overview, see Ronald H. Chilcote, *Theories of Comparative Politics: The Search for a Paradigm* (Boulder: Westview, 1981), pp. 81–135.

14. For discussion, see Karl Marx, *Manifesto of the Communist Party* (1848), as reproduced in Robert C. Tucker, ed., *The Marx-Engels Reader* (New York: W. W. Norton, 1978), pp. 469–500.

15. See Karl Marx, *Capital,* vol. 1 (1867), Chs. 26–32, as reproduced in ibid., pp. 431–38.

16. For a discussion of the various versions of Marx's theory of revolution, see Claudio Katz, *From Feudalism to Capitalism: Marxian Theories of Class Struggle and Social Change* (New York: Greenwood, 1989).

17. For an analysis of how Marx himself began to question the universal nature of his theory, see Teodor Shanin, ed., *Late Marx and the Russian Road* (New York: Monthly Review, 1983).

18. For an overview of his writings devoted to the Third World, see Shlomo Avineri, *Karl Marx on Colonialism and Modernization: His Dispatches and Other Writings on China, India, Mexico, the Middle East, and North Africa* (New York: Doubleday, 1968).

19. Ibid., p. 11.

20. Ibid., p. 12.

21. Ibid., p. 129.

22. For a summary of the debates over this issue, see Stephen Katz, "The Problems of Europocentrism and Evolutionism in Marx's Writings on Colonialism," *Political Studies* 38 (1990): 672–86.

23. For a critique of this literature, see Otwin Marenin, "Resolving Epistemological Contradictions in Marxist African Studies," *The Journal of Modern African Studies* 27, no. 4 (1989): 641–69.

24. See Higgott, *Political Development Theory,* pp. 60–61.

25. Samir Amin, *Neocolonialism in West Africa* (New York: Monthly Review, 1973). Translated from the French by Francis McDonagh. Originally published as *L'Afrique de l'Ouest est Bloquée* (Paris: Les Éditions de Minuit, 1971).

26. Ibid., p. 270.

27. Ibid., p. 11.

28. Higgott, *Political Development Theory,* p. 61.

29. Samir Amin, *Delinking: Toward a Polycentric World* (London: Zed, 1990). Translated from the French by Michael Wolfers. Originally published as *La Déconnexion* (Paris: Éditions La Découverte, 1985).

30. See Samir Amin, *Unequal Development: An Essay on the Social Formations of Peripheral Capitalism* (New York: Monthly Review, 1976), pp. 293–386. Translated from the French by Brian Pearce. Originally appeared as *Le Développement Inégal* (Paris: Les Éditions de Minuit, 1973).

31. Irving Leonard Markovitz, *Power and Class in Africa: An Introduction to Change and Conflict in African Politics* (Englewood Cliffs: Prentice-Hall, 1977).

32. Irving Leonard Markovitz, ed., *Studies in Power and Class in Africa* (New York: Oxford University Press, 1987), p. 8.

33. See, for example, Hamza Alavi, "The State in Postcolonial Societies: Pakistan and Bangladesh," *New Left Review* 74 (1972): 59–81. The metaphor is taken from Higgott, *Political Development Theory,* p. 67.

34. Colin Leys, *Underdevelopment in Kenya: The Political Economy of Colonialism* (London: Heinemann, 1974). For examples of his later work, see "The 'Overdeveloped' Postcolonial State: A Re-Evaluation," *Review of African Political Economy* 5 (1976): 39–48, and "Underdevelopment and Dependency: Critical Notes," *Journal of Contemporary Asia* 7, no. 1 (1977): 92–107.

35. Richard L. Sklar, "The Nature of Class Domination in Africa," *The Journal of Modern African Studies* 17, no. 4 (1978): 536.

36. Timothy M. Shaw, "Reformism, Revisionism, and Radicalism in African Political Economy during the 1990s," *The Journal of Modern African Studies* 29, no. 2 (1991): 192.

37. Claude Ake, "The Democratization of Disempowerment." Paper presented at a conference on democratization sponsored by the Transnational Institute, Cologne, Germany, November 13, 1993.

38. Claude Ake, *Democracy and Development in Africa* (Washington, DC: Brookings Institution, 1996).

39. Richard L. Sklar, "Toward a Theory of Developmental Democracy," in Toyin Falola, ed., *African Politics in Postimperial Times: The Essays of Richard L. Sklar* (Trenton, NJ: Africa World Press, 2002), pp. 87–106.

40. Ibid., p. 103.

41. Mahmood Mamdani and and Ernest Wamba-dia-Wamba, eds., *African Studies in Social Movements and Democracy* (Dakar: CODESRIA, 1995).

42. Jane L. Parpart and Kathleen A. Staudt, eds., *Women and the State in Africa* (Boulder: Lynne Rienner, 1990).

43. Ibid., p. 1.

44. April A. Gordon, *Transforming Capitalism and Patriarchy: Gender and Development in Africa* (Boulder: Lynne Rienner, 1996).

45. Fantu Cheru, *The Silent Revolution in Africa: Debt, Development, and Democracy* (London: Zed, 1989).

46. Thandika Mkandawire and Adebayo Olukoshi, eds., *Between Liberalization and Oppression: The Politics of Structural Adjustment in Africa* (Dakar: CODESRIA, 1995).

47. Thandika Mkandawire and Charles C. Souldo, *Our Continent, Our Future: African Perspectives on Structural Adjustment* (Trenton, NJ: Africa World Press, 1999).

48. Tukumbi Lumumba-Kasongo, *The Dynamics of Economic and Political Relations between Africa and Foreign Powers: A Study in International Relations* (Westport: Praeger, 1999).

49. Richard L. Sklar and David G. Becker, eds., *Postimperialism in World Politics* (Westport: Praeger, 1999).

50. See the following essays by Sklar as reprinted in Falola, "Postimperialism: A Class Analysis of Corporate Expansion," *African Politics in Postimperial Times*: (pp. 651–72); "Postimperialism Revisited" (pp. 673–78); and "The Concept of Postimperialism and Its Implications" (pp. 701–28).

51. Sklar, "The Concept of Postimperialism and Its Implications," p. 678.

52. See Naomi Chazan et al., *Politics and Society in Contemporary Africa* (Boulder: Lynne Rienner, 1992), p. 20. Chazan et al. perceive this school of thought as a synthesis of the liberal and critical traditions, whereas this essay emphasizes their influence in the critical tradition.

53. For an examination of this theme by a former director of CODESRIA, see Thandika Mkandawire, "The Social Sciences in Africa: Breaking Local Barriers and Negotiating International Presence. The Bashorun M. K. O. Abiola Distinguished Lecture Presented to the 1996 African Studies Association Annual Meeting," *African Studies Review* 40, no. 2 (1997): 15–36.

Appendix 1

LIST OF ACRONYMS

Acronym	Definition
AAAA	American African Affairs Association (U.S.)
AAF-SAP	African Alternative Framework to Structural Adjustment Programmes for Socioeconomic Recovery and Transformation
AAI	African-American Institute (U.S.)
AAPS	African Association of Political Science
ACAS	Association of Concerned Africa Scholars (U.S.)
ACM	African Common Market
ACRF	African Crisis Response Force
ACRI	African Crisis Response Initiative
AEC	African Economic Community
AEF	Afrique Equatoriale Française (French Equatorial Africa)
AFDL	Alliance des Forces Démocratiques pour la Libération (Alliance of Democratic Forces for Liberation) (Democratic Republic of the Congo)
AGOA	Africa Growth and Opportunity Act
AHD	African Historical Dictionaries series (U.S.)
AHSA	African Heritage Studies Association (U.S.)
AOF	Afrique Occidentale Française (French West Africa)
ANC	African National Congress (South Africa)
ANC	Armée Nationale Congolaise (Congolese National Army) (Democratic Republic of the Congo)
ASA	African Studies Association (U.S.)
BCP	Botswana Congress Party
BDF	Botswana Defence Force
BDF	Botswana Democratic Front
BDP	Botswana Democratic Party
BHN	Basic Human Needs
BIP	Botswana Independent Party
BLP	Botswana Labour Party
BNF	Botswana National Front

BPP	Botswana People's Party
BPU	Botswana Progressive Union
CASS	Centre for Advanced Social Science (Nigeria)
CCM	Chama Cha Mapinduzi (Revolutionary Party) (Tanzania)
CELZA	Cultures et Elevages du Zaire (Farms and Ranches of Zaire) (Democratic Republic of the Congo)
CERDET	Center for Study and Research on Democracy in the Third World (Senegal)
CFA	Communauté Financière Africaine (African Financial Community)
CIA	Central Intelligence Agency (U.S.)
CIES	Council for International Exchange of Scholars (U.S.)
CITES	Convention on International Trade in Endangered Species
CODESRIA	Council for the Development of Social Science Research in Africa (Senegal)
COSATU	Confederation of South African Trade Unions
CPDM	Cameroon People's Democratic Movement
CND	Centre National de Documentation (National Documentation Center) (Democratic Republic of the Congo)
CNN	Cable News Network (U.S.)
DIA	Defense Intelligence Agency (U.S.)
DOM-TOM	Départements d'Outre Mer-Territoires d'Outre-Mer (Overseas Departments and Territories) (France)
DSP	Division Spéciale Présidentielle (Special Presidential Division) (Democratic Republic of the Congo)
EAC	East African Community
ECA	Economic Commission for Africa
ECCAS	Economic Community of Central African States
ECOMOG	ECOWAS Monitoring Group (Liberia)
ECOWAS	Economic Community of West African States
ELF	Eritrean Liberation Front
EPLF	Eritrean People's Liberation Front
EPRDF	Ethiopian People's Revolutionary Democratic Front
FAZ	Forces Armées Zairoises (Zairian Armed Forces) (Democratic Republic of the Congo)
FDLD	Front Démocratique pour la Libération de Djibouti (Democratic Front for the Liberation of Djibouti)
FEPACI	Fédération Panafricaine des Cinéastes (Pan-African Filmmakers Federation) (Burkina Faso)
FESPACO	Festival Panafricain du Cinéma et de la Télévision de Ouagadougou (Pan-African Film and Television Festival of Ouagadougou) (Burkina Faso)
FLNC	Front de Libération Nationale du Congo (National Front for the Liberation of the Congo) (Democratic Republic of the Congo)
FNLA	Frente Nacional de Libertação de Angola (Front for the National Liberation of Angola)
FPR	Front Patriotique Rwandais (Rwandan Patriotic Front)

FRELIMO	Frente de Libertação de Moçambique (Front for the Liberation of Mozambique)
FRUD	Front pour la Restauration de la Démocratie (Front for the Restoration of Democracy) (Djibouti)
G-8	Group of Eight
GDP	gross domestic product
GEAR	Growth, Employment, and Redistribution (South Africa)
GNP	gross national product
IFP	Inkatha Freedom Party (South Africa)
IGAD	Intergovernmental Authority on Development
IGNU	Interim Government of National Unity (Liberia)
ILO	International Labour Organisation
IMF	International Monetary Fund
ISA	International Studies Association
JCC	Journées Cinématographiques de Carthage (Film Days of Carthage) (Tunisia)
JETRO	Japan External Trade Organization
JICA	Japanese International Cooperation Agency
JMPR	Jeunesse du Mouvement Populaire de la Revolution (Youth of the Popular Movement of the Revolution) (Democratic Republic of the Congo)
JOCV	Japan Overseas Cooperation Volunteers
KANU	Kenya African National Union
LPA	Lagos Plan of Action
LPAI	Ligue Populaire Africaine pour l'Indépendance (African Popular League for Independence) (Djibouti)
METI	Ministry of Economy, Trade, and Industry (Japan)
MFDC	Mouvement des Forces Démocratiques de Casamance (Movement of the Democratic Forces of Casamance) (Senegal)
MINURCA	United Nations Mission in the Central African Republic
MINURSO	United Nations Mission for the Referendum in Western Sahara (Morocco)
MMD	Movement for Multiparty Democracy (Zambia)
MNCs	multinational corporations
MONUA	United Nations Observer Mission in Angola
MONUC	United Nations Organization Mission of the Democratic Republic of the Congo
MPL	Mouvement Populaire de Libération (Popular Movement of Liberation) (Djibouti)
MPLA	Movimento Popular de Libertação de Angola (Popular Movement for the Liberation of Angola)
MPR	Mouvement Populaire de la Révolution (Popular Movement of the Revolution) (Democratic Republic of the Congo)
MTTs	mobile training teams (U.S.)
NAFTA	North American Free Trade Agreement
NCA	Nations of Contemporary Africa series (U.S.)
NCNC	National Council of Nigeria and the Cameroons
NCNC	National Council of Nigerian Citizens

NDI	National Democratic Institute for International Affairs (U.S.)
NEPAD	New Partnership for Africa's Development
NMW	Nations of the Modern World series (U.S.)
NP	National Party (South Africa)
NPC	Northern Peoples' Congress (Nigeria)
NPFL	National Patriotic Front of Liberia
NPP	New Patriotic Party (Liberia)
NRA	National Resistance Army (Uganda)
NRM	National Resistance Movement (Uganda)
NSC	National Security Council (U.S.)
NSEP	National Security Education Program (U.S.)
NSF	National Science Foundation (U.S.)
NUEW	National Union of Eritrean Women
OAU	Organization of African Unity
OEOA	United Nations Office of Emergency Operations in Africa
OLF	Oromo Liberation Front (Ethiopia)
ONUC	United Nations Operation in Congo (Democratic Republic of the Congo)
ONUMOZ	United Nations Operation in Mozambique
OPEC	Organization of Petroleum Exporting Countries
PAC	Pan African Congress (South Africa)
PAIGC	Partido Africano da Indepêndencia da Guiné e Cabo Verde (Independence African Party of Guinea and Cape Verde)
PDCI-RDA	Parti Démocratique de la Côte d'Ivoire–Rassemblement Démocratique pour l'Assemblée (Democratic Party of Côte d'Ivoire–African Democratic Assembly)
PDD-25	Presidential Decision Directive 25 (U.S.)
PIT	Parti de l'Indépendance et du Travail (Independence and Workers Party) Senegal
PMAC	Provisional Military Administrative Council (Ethiopia)
PNDC	Provisional National Defense Council (Ghana)
POW	Prisoner of War
PPD	Parti Populaire Djiboutien (Djiboutian Popular Party)
PRC	People's Redemption Council (Liberia)
PRC	People's Republic of China
RAINBOW	Research, Action, and Information Network for Bodily Integrity of Women
RPF	Rwandan Patriotic Front
RPP	Rassemblement Populaire pour le Progrès (Popular Assembly for Progress) (Djibouti)
SACP	South African Communist Party
SADC	Southern African Development Community
SADCC	Southern African Development Coordination Conference
SADF	South African Defense Force
SADR	Saharan Arab Democratic Republic
SALT	Strategic Arms Limitation Talks
SANDF	South African National Defence Force

SAPs	structural adjustment programs
SDF	Social Democratic Front (Cameroon)
SEALs	Sea-Air-Land Commandos (U.S.)
SNF	Somali National Front
SNM	Somali National Movement
SOZACOM	Société Zairoise pour la Commercialisation des Minéraux (Zairian Company for the Commercialization of Minerals) (Democratic Republic of the Congo)
SPM	Somali Patriotic Movement
SRC	Supreme Revolutionary Council (Somalia)
SSRC	Social Science Research Council (U.S.)
SWAPO	South West Africa People's Organization (Namibia)
TANZAM	Tanzanian-Zambian Railroad
TPLF	Tigrean People's Liberation Front (Ethiopia)
UAM	Union of the Arab Maghreb
UDI	Unilateral Declaration of Independence (Zimbabwe)
UDPS	Union pour la Démocratie et le Progrès Social (Union for Democracy and Social Progress) (Democratic Republic of the Congo)
UGEC	Union Générale des Etudiants Congolais (General Union of Congolese Students) (Democratic Republic of the Congo)
ULIMO	United Liberation Movement of Liberia
UN	United Nations
UNAMIR	United Nations Assistance Mission for Rwanda
UNAMSIL	United Nations Mission in Sierra Leone
UNASOG	United Nations Aouzou Strip Observer Group
UNAVEM I	United Nations Angola Verification Mission I
UNAVEM II	United Nations Angola Verification Mission II
UNAVEM III	United Nations Angola Verification Mission III
UNAZA	Université Nationale du Zaire (National University of Zaire) (Democratic Republic of the Congo)
UNDP	United Nations Development Programme
UNEF I	First United Nations Emergency Force (Egypt)
UNEF II	Second United Nations Emergency Force (Egypt)
UNESCO	United Nations Educational, Scientific, and Cultural Organization
UNI	Union Nationale de l'Indépendance (National Union for Independence) (Djibouti)
UNICEF	United Nations International Children's Emergency Fund
UNIP	United National Independence Party (Zambia)
UNITA	União Nacional para a Independência Total de Angola (National Union for the Total Independence of Angola)
UNMEE	United Nations Mission in Eritrea and Ethiopia
UNHCR	United Nations High Commissioner for Refugees
UNOMIL	United Nations Observer Mission in Liberia
UNOMSIL	United Nations Observer Mission in Sierra Leone
UNOMUR	United Nations Observer Mission Uganda-Rwanda
UNOSOM I	United Nations Operation in Somalia I
UNOSOM II	United Nations Operation in Somalia II

UNTC	Union Nationale des Travailleurs Congolais (National Union of Congolese Workers) (Democratic Republic of the Congo)
UPC	Union des Populations du Cameroun (Union of the Populations of Cameroon)
UPEZA	Union Progressiste des Etudiants Zairois (Progressive Union of Zairian Students) (Democratic Republic of the Congo)
USAID	United States Agency for International Development
USC	United Somali Congress
USIA	United States Information Agency
USOR	Union Sacrée de l'Opposition Radicale (Sacred Union of Radical Opposition) (Democratic Republic of the Congo)
WBS	World Bibliographical Series
WHO	World Health Organization
WIGMO	Western International Ground Maintenance Organization
WPE	Workers Party of Ethiopia
WSLF	Western Somali Liberation Front
ZANU	Zimbabwe African Nationalist Union
ZAPU	Zimbabwe African People's Union

Appendix 2

COUNTRY NAME CHANGES
IN AFRICA DURING
THE CONTEMPORARY
INDEPENDENCE ERA

Original Name	Current Name/Disposition
Basutoland	Lesotho
Bechuanaland	Botswana
Belgian Congo	Democratic Republic of the Congo (often called Congo-Kinshasa)
Biafra	Secessionist portion of southeastern Nigeria that declared independence in 1967. A 3-year civil war (1967–70) ended in defeat and reincorporation into Nigeria.
British Somaliland	Former British colony that 5 days after independence in 1960 voluntarily federated with Italian Somaliland to form the Republic of Somalia.
British Togoland	Ghana
Central African Empire	Central African Republic
Dahomey	Benin
French Congo	Congo (often called Congo-Brazzaville)
French Equatorial Africa (AEF)	French colonial unit that included Cameroon, Central African Republic, Chad, Congo (Brazzaville), and Gabon.
French Somali Coast	Djibouti
French Somaliland	Djibouti
French Soudan	Mali
French Territory of Afars and Issas	Djibouti
French West Africa (AOF)	French colonial unit that included Benin, Burkina Faso, Côte d'Ivoire, Guinea, Mali, Mauritania, Niger, and Senegal.
German East Africa	Tanzania
Gold Coast	Ghana

Italian Somaliland	Former Italian colony that after independence in 1960 voluntarily federated with British Somaliland to form the Republic of Somalia.
Ivory Coast	Côte d'Ivoire
Kamerun	Cameroon
Katanga	Secessionist province of southeastern Democratic Republic of the Congo that declared its independence in 1960. Secession was ultimately rejected after a Katangese leader, Moise Tshombe, was named prime minister of the Democratic Republic of the Congo. Also known as Shaba province.
Malagasy Republic	Madagascar
Mali Federation	Short-lived (3-month) federation of two former French colonies that subsequently declared independence in 1961 as the countries of Senegal and Mali.
Northern Cameroons	Northern portion of a British trusteeship territory that opted through a United Nations–sponsored plebiscite in 1961 to federate with Nigeria.
Northern Rhodesia	Zambia
Nyasaland	Malawi
Oubangui Chari	Central African Republic
Portuguese Guinea	Guinea-Bissau
Rhodesia	Zimbabwe
Ruanda-Urundi	Former Belgian trusteeship territory that achieved independence in 1961 as two separate countries: Burundi and Rwanda.
Saharan Arab Democratic Republic (SADR)	Former Spanish territory annexed by Morocco and Mauritania that has declared its independence. Mauritania renounced any claims to its portion, which was annexed by Morocco.
Senegambia	Unsuccessful federation (1981–89) of two independent countries (Senegal and Gambia) that reverted back to their separate, independent status in 1989.
Shaba	See Katanga
Somaliland Republic	Former British Somaliland territory that seceded from the Republic of Somaliland in 1991. As of 2003, no country has recognized Somaliland's independence.
South West Africa	Namibia
Southern Cameroons	Southern portion of a British trusteeship territory that opted through a United Nations–sponsored plebiscite in 1961 to federate with Cameroon.
Southern Rhodesia	Zimbabwe
Spanish Guinea	Equatorial Guinea
Spanish Sahara	See Saharan Arab Democratic Republic (SADR)
Tanganyika	Tanzania
Togoland	Togo
United Arab Republic	Unsuccessful federation of Egypt and Syria (1958–61).
Upper Volta	Burkina Faso
Western Sahara	See Saharan Arab Democratic Republic (SADR)
Zaire	Democratic Republic of the Congo
Zanzibar	Former British colony that federated with Tanzania in 1964.

Appendix 3

POLITICAL LEADERSHIP IN AFRICA DURING THE CONTEMPORARY INDEPENDENCE ERA

Country	Political Leadership	
ALGERIA	1962–65	Ahmed Ben Bella
(Algiers)	1965–78	Col. Houari Boumedienne
	1978–79	Rabah Bitat
	1979–92	Col. Benjedid Chadli Benjedid
	1992	Mohammed Boudiaf
	1992–94	Ali Kafi
	1994–99	Gen. Liamine Zeroual
	1999–	Abdelaziz Bouteflika
ANGOLA	1975–79	Antonio Agostinho Neto
(Luanda)	1979–	José Eduardo dos Santos
BENIN	1960–63	Hubert Coutoucou Maga
(Porto-Novo)	1963–64	Lt. Col. Christophe Soglo
	1964–65	Sourou-Migan Apithy
	1965	Tahirou Congacou
	1965–67	Gen. Christophe Soglo
	1967–68	Lt. Col. Alphonse Amadou Alley
	1968–69	Émile-Derlin Zinsou
	1969–70	Lt. Col. Paul Émile de Souza
	1970–72	Hubert C. Maga
	1972	Justin Ahomadegbé
	1972–91	Col. Mathieu Kérékou
	1991–96	Nicéphore Soglo
	1996–	Mathieu Kérékou

BOTSWANA	1966–80	Sir Seretse Khama
(Gaborone)	1980–98	Quett Ketumile J. Masire
	1998–	Festus Mogae
BURKINA FASO	1960–66	Maurice Yaméogo
(Ouagadougou)	1966–80	Lt. Col. Sangoulé Lamizana
	1980–82	Col. Sayé Zerbo
	1982–83	Maj. Jean Baptiste Ouedraogo
	1983–87	Capt. Thomas Sankara
	1987–	Capt. Blaise Compaoré
BURUNDI	1962–66	King Mwami Mwambutsa IV
(Bujumbura)	1966	King Mwami Ntare V
	1966–76	Capt. Michel Micombero
	1976–87	Col. Jean-Baptiste Bagaza
	1987–93	Maj. Pierre Buyoya
	1993	Melchior Ndadaye
	1993–94	Sylvie Kinigi
	1994	Cyprien Ntaryamira
	1994–96	Sylvestre Ntibantunganya
	1996–	Maj. Pierre Buyoya
CAMEROON	1960–82	Ahmadou Ahidjo
(Yaounde)	1982–	Paul Biya
CAPE VERDE	1975–81	Aristides Pereira
(Praia)	1991–02	Antònio Mascarenhas Monteiro
	2002–	Pedro Pires
CENTRAL	1960–66	David Dacko
AFRICAN	1966–79	Col. Jean-Bédel Bokassa
REPUBLIC	1979–81	David Dacko
(Bangui)	1981–93	Gen. André Kolingba
	1993–03	Ange-Félix Patassé
	2003–	François Bozizé
CHAD	1962–75	Ngarta (François) Tombalbaye
(Ndjamena)	1975–79	Gen. Félix Malloum
	1979	Lol Mahamat Chaoua
	1979–82	Goukouni Oueddei
	1982–90	Hissène Habré
	1990–	Lt. Gen. Idriss Déby
COMOROS	1975	Ahmed Abdullah Abderemane
(Moroni)	1975–76	Prince Said Mohammed Jaffar
	1975–78	Ali Soilih
	1978–89	Ahmed Abdallah Abderemane
	1989	Bob Denard
	1989–96	Said Mohamed Djohar
	1996–98	Mohamad Taki Abdulkarim
	1998–1999	Tadjiddine Ben Said Massonde
	1999–	Col. Azzali Assoumani

CONGO	1960–63	Abbé Fulbert Youlou
(Brazzaville)	1963–68	Alphonse Massamba-Débat
	1968–77	Capt. Marien Ngouabi
	1977–79	Col. Joachim Yhombi-Opango
	1979–91	Col. Dénis Sassou-Nguesso
	1991–92	André Milongo
	1992–97	Pascal Lissouba
	1997–	Gen. Dénis Sassou-Nguesso
CÔTE D'IVOIRE	1960–93	Félix Houphouët-Boigny
(Abidjan)	1993–99	Henri Konan Bédié
	1999–00	Gen. Robert Gueï
	2000–	Laurent Gbagbo
DEMOCRATIC	1960	Patrice Lumumba
REPUBLIC OF	1960–61	Col. Mobutu Sese Seko (formerly
THE CONGO		Joseph Désiré Mobutu)
(Kinshasa)	1961	Joseph Ileo
	1961–64	Cyrille Adoula
	1964–65	Moise Tshombe
	(from 1960–65, Joseph Kasavubu served as president)	
	1965–97	Gen. Mobutu Sese Seko
	1997–01	Laurent-Désiré Kabila
	2001–	Joseph Kabila
DJIBOUTI	1977–99	Hassan Gouled Aptidon
(Djibouti City)	1999	Ismael Omar Guelleh
EGYPT	1922–52	King Farouk
(Cairo)	1952–54	Gen. Muhammad Neguib
	1954–70	Col. Gamal Abdel Nasser
	1970–81	Col. Anwar Sadat
	1981–	Lt. Gen. Hosni Mubarak
EQUATORIAL	1968–79	Francisco Macías Nguema
GUINEA	1979–	Brig. Gen. Teodoro Obiango Nguema Mbasogo
(Malabo)		
ERITREA	1993–	Isaias Afwerki
(Asmara)		
ETHIOPIA	1270–85	Yekuno Amlak
(Addis Ababa)	1285–94	Saloman I
	1294–99	Bahr Asgad; Senfa Asgad; Hezba Ared; Kedma Asgad; Zhin Asgad
	1299–1314	Wedem Ared
	1314–44	Amda Seyon I
	1344–72	Newaya Krestos
	1372–82	Newaya Maryam
	1382–1413	Dauti (David) I
	1413–14	Tewodos (Theodore) I
	1414–29	Yeskaq

ETHIOPIA	1429–34	Endreyas; Takla Maryam; Sarwa Iyasus; Amda Iyasus
(Addis Ababa)	1434–68	Zara Yakob
(continued)	1468–78	Baeda Maryam
	1478–94	Eskender
	1494	Amda Seyon II
	1494–1508	Naod
	1508–40	Lebna Dengel (Dauti II)
	1540–59	Galawdewos (Claudius)
	1559–63	Minas
	1563–97	Sarsa Dengel
	1597–1603	Yaqob (I)
	1603–4	Za Dengel
	1604–7	Yaqob (II)
	1607–32	Susneyos
	1632–67	Fasiladas
	1667–82	Yohannes I
	1682–1706	Isayu I
	1706–8	Takla Haymanot
	1708–11	Tewoflos
	711–16	Yostos
	1716–21	Dauti III
	1721–30	Bakaffa (Asma Giorgis)
	1730–55	Iyasu II (with Menetewab as regentess)
	1755–69	Iyoas I
	1769–1855	"Era of the princes" in which at least eighteen men held the title of emperor in as many as thirty different periods.[1]
	1855–68	Tewodros (Theodore) II
	1868–72	Takla Giorgis II
	1872–89	Yohannes (John) IV
	1889–1913	Menelik II
	1914–16	Iyasu V (Lij Iyasu)
	1916–30	Zauditu (Empress)
	930–74	Emperor Haile Selassie
	1974	Lt. Gen. Aman Andom
	1974–77	Brig. Gen. Teferi Banti
	1977–91	Maj. Mengistu Haile Mariam
	1991–95	Meles Zenawi
	1995–01	Ngasso Gidada
	2001–	Girma Wolde-Giyorgis Lucha
GABON	1961–67	Léon M'Ba
(Libreville)	1967–	Omar Bongo
GAMBIA	1965–94	Dawda Kairaba Jawara
(Banjul)	1994–	Capt. Yahya A. J. J. Jammeh
GHANA	1957–66	Kwame Nkrumah
(Accra)	1966–69	Lt. Gen. Joseph A. Ankrah

GHANA	1969	Brig. Gen. Akwasi O. Afrifa
(Accra)	1969–72	Kofi A. Busia
(continued)	1972–78	Lt. Col. Ignatius K. Acheampong
	1978–79	Lt. Gen. Frederick Akuffo
	1979	Flt. Lt. Jerry Rawlings
	1979–81	Dr. Hilla Limann
	1981–01	Flt. Lt. Jerry Rawlings
	2001–	John Agyekum Kufuor
GUINEA	1958–84	Ahmed Sékou Touré
(Conakry)	1984–	Col. Lansana Conté
GUINEA-BISSAU	1974–80	Luíz De Almeida Cabral
Bissau)	1980–99	Gen. João Bernardo Vieira
	1999–00	Malam Bacai Sanha
	2000–	Koumba Yala
KENYA	1963–78	Jomo Kenyatta
(Nairobi)	1978–02	Daniel arap Moi
	2002–	Mwai Kibaki
LESOTHO	1966–70	King Motlotlehi Moshoeshoe II
(Maseru)	1970–86	Chief Leabua Jonathan
	1986–91	Maj. Gen. Justin Lekhanya
	1991–93	Col. Elias P. Ramaema
	1993–95	Ntsu Mokhehle
	1995–96	King Moshoeshoe II
	1996–	King Letsie III
LIBERIA	1848–56	Joseph J. Roberts I
(Monrovia)	1856–64	Stephen A. Benson
	1864–68	Daniel B. Warner
	1868–70	James S. Payne I
	1870–71	Edward J. Roye
	1871–72	James S. Smith
	1872–76	Joseph J. Roberts II
	1876–78	James S. Payne II
	1878–83	Anthony W. Gardiner
	1883–84	Alfred F. Russell
	1884–92	Hilary R. W. Johnson
	1892–96	Joseph J. Cheeseman
	1896–00	William D. Coleman
	1900–04	Garretson W. Gibson
	1904–12	Arthur Barclay
	1912–20	Daniel E. Howard
	1920–30	Charles D. B. King
	1930–44	Edwin J. Barclay
	1944–71	William V. S. Tubman
	1971–80	William R. Tolbert
	1980–90	Samuel K. Doe

LIBERIA	1990–94	Amos Sawyer
(Monrovia)	1994–95	David D. Kpormakor
(continued)	1995–96	Wilton Sankawulo
	1996–97	Ruth Sando Perry
	1997–	Charles Taylor
LIBYA	1951–69	King Idris
(Tripoli)	1969–	Col. Muammar Mohammed Qaddafi
MADAGASCAR	1960–72	Philibert Tsiranana
(Antananarivo)	1972–75	Gen. Gabriel Ramanantstoa
	1975	Col. Richard Ratsimandrava
	1975	Gen. Gilles Andriamahazo
	1975–93	Lt. Comdr. Didier Ratsiraka
	1993–96	Albert Zafy
	1996–97	Norbert Ratsirahonana
	1997	Albert Zafy
	1997–02	Didier Ratsiraka
	2002–	Marc Ravalomanana
MALAWI	1964–94	Hastings Kamuzu Banda
(Lilongwe)	1994–	Bakili Muluzi
MALI	1960–68	Modibo Keita
(Bamako)	1968–91	Lt. Moussa Traoré
	1991–92	Lt. Col. Amadou Toumani Touré
	1992–02	Alpha Oumar Konaré
	2002–	Amadou Toumani Touré
MAURITANIA	1960–78	Moktar Ould Daddah
(Nouakchott)	1978–79	Lt. Col. Mustapha Ould Mohammed Salek
	1979	Lt. Col. Ahmed Ould Bouceif
	1979	Lt. Col. Mohammed Khouna Haidalla
	1979–80	Lt. Col. Mohammed Mahmoud Ould Louly
	1980–84	Lt. Col. Mohammed Khouna Haidalla
	1984–	Col. Maaouya Ould Sidi Ahmed Taya
MAURITIUS	1968–82	Seewoosagur Ramgoolam
(Port Louis)	1982–95	Aneerood Jugnauth
	1995–02	Navin Ramgoolam
	2002–	Karl Offman
MOROCCO	1956–61	King Mohammed V
(Rabat)	1961–99	King Hassan II
	1999–	King Mohamed VI
MOZAMBIQUE	1975–86	Samora Moisés Machel
(Maputo)	1986–	Joaquim Alberto Chissano
NAMIBIA	1990–	Sam Shafiishuna Nujoma
(Windhoek)		

NIGER	1960–74	Hamani Diori
(Niamey)	1974–87	Lt. Col. Seyni Kountché
	1987–91	Col. Ali Saïbou
	1991–93	Amadou Cheiffou
	1993–96	Mahamane Ousmane
	1996–99	Col. Ibrahim Mainassara Baré
	1999	Commander Daouda Malam Wanke
	1999–	Mamadou Tandja
NIGERIA	1960–66	Alhaji Abubakar Tafawa Belewa
(Abuja)	1966	Gen. Johnson Aguiyi-Ironsi
	1966–75	Lt. Col. Yakabu Gowon
	1975–76	Brig. Gen. Murtala Mohammed
	1976–79	Lt. Gen. Olusegun Obasanjo
	1979–83	Alhaji Shehu Shagari
	1983–85	Maj. Gen. Mohammed Buhari
	1985–93	Maj. Gen. Ibrahim Babangida
	1993	Chief Ernest Adegunle Shonekan
	1993–98	Gen. Sani Abacha
	1998–99	Gen. Abdulsalami Abubakar
	1999–	Olusegun Obasanjo
RWANDA	1962–73	Grégoire Kayibanda
(Kigali)	1973–94	Maj. Gen. Juvénal Habyarimana
	1994	Dr. Théodore Sindikugbabo
	1994–00	Pasteur Bizimungu
	2000–	Maj. Gen. Paul Kagame
SAO TOME	1975–91	Manuel Pinto da Costa
& PRINCIPE	1991–01	Miguel Trovoada
(Sao Tome)	2001–	Fradique de Menezes
SENEGAL	1960–80	Léopold Sédar Senghor
(Dakar)	1981–00	Abdou Diouf
	2000–	Abdoulaye Wade
SEYCHELLES	1976–77	James R. Mancham
(Victoria)	1977–	France Albert René
SIERRA LEONE	1961–64	Milton Margai
(Freetown)	1964–67	Albert Margai
	1967–68	Lt. Col. Andrew Juxon-Smith
	1968–85	Siaka Stevens
	1985–92	Maj. Gen. Joseph Saidu Momoh
	1992–96	Capt. Valentine E. M. Strasser
	1996	Brig. Gen. Julius Maada Bio
	1996–97	Ahmad Tejan Kabbah
	1997–98	Lt. Col. Johnny Paul Koromah
	1998–	Ahmed Tejan Kabbah

SOMALIA	1960–67	Aden Abdullah Osman Daar
(Mogadishu)	1967–69	Abdirashid Ali Sharmarke
	1969–91	Maj. Gen. Mohamed Siad Barre
	1991–00	No central government (state collapse).
	2000–	Abdikassim Salad Hassan (weak central government; territories outside capital controlled by individual clan leaders).
SOUTH AFRICA	1994–99	Nelson M. Mandela
(Pretoria)	1999–	Thabo Mbeki
SUDAN	1956	Ismail al-Azhari
(Khartoum)	1956–58	Abdullah Khalil
	1958–64	Lt. Gen. Ibrahim Abboud
	1964–65	Sir el-Khatim el-Khalifah
	1965–66	Muhammed Ahmad Mahgoub
	1966–67	Sayed Sadiq el-Mahdi
	1967–69	Muhammed Ahmad Mahgoub
	1969	Abubakr Awadallah
	1969–85	Col. Gaafar Mohammed Nimeiri
	1985–86	Lt. Gen. Abdel Rahman Swar al Dahab
	1986–89	Ahmed Ali el-Mirghani
	1989–	Lt. Gen. Omar Hassan Ahmad al-Bashir
SWAZILAND	1968–82	King Sobhuza II
(Mbabane)	1982–83	Dzeliwe Shongwe
	1983–86	Ntombi Thawala
	1986–	King Mswati III
TANZANIA	1961–85	Julius Nyerere
(Dodoma)	1985–95	Ali Hassan Mwinyi
	1995–	Benjamin Mkapa
TOGO	1960–63	Sylvanus Olympio
(Lome)	1963–67	Nicholas Grunitzky
	1967	Col. Kleber Dadjo
	1967–	Gen. Gnassingbé Eyadéma
TUNISIA	1956–87	Habib Bourguiba
(Tunis)	1987–	Zine El-Abidine Ben Ali
UGANDA	1962–71	Apollo Milton Obote
(Kampala)	1971–79	Maj. Gen. Idi Amin
	1979	Yusuf Lule
	1979–80	Godfrey Binaisa
	1980	Paulo Mwanga
	1980–85	Apollo Milton Obote
	1985–86	Lt. Gen. Tito Okello
	1986–	Yoweri Museveni

ZAMBIA	1964–91	Kenneth D. Kaunda
(Lusaka)	1991–01	Frederick Chiluba
	2001–	Levy Mwanawasa
ZIMBABWE	1980–	Robert Mugabe
(Harare)		

Sources: See Harvey Glickman, ed., *Political Leaders of Contemporary Africa South of the Sahara: A Biographical Dictionary* (Westport: Greenwood, 1992); April A. Gordon and Donald L. Gordon, eds., *Understanding Contemporary Africa,* 3rd ed. (Boulder: Lynne Rienner, 2001); Robert H. Jackson and Carl G. Rosberg, *Personal Rule in Black Africa: Prince, Autocrat, Prophet, Tyrant* (Berkeley: University of California Press, 1982); Mark R. Lipschutz and R. Kent Rasmussen, *Dictionary of African Historical Biography,* 2nd ed. (Berkeley: University of California Press, 1987); and Alan Rake, *Who's Who in Africa: Leaders for the 1990s* (Lanham: Scarecrow, 1992).

NOTE

1. Mark R. Lipschutz and R. Kent Rasmussen, *Dictionary of African Historical Biography,* 2nd ed. (Berkeley: University of California Press, 1987), p. 65.

Index

A

AAF-SAP *See* African Alternative Framework to Structural Adjustment Programmes for Socioeconomic Recovery and Transformation (AAF-SAP)

AAI *See* African-American Institute (AAI)

Abdalla, Raqiya Haji Dualeh, 119

Abidjan, 86

Abomey kingdom, 40–41, 43

Abrahams, Peter, 159–160

Abyssinia *See* Ethiopia

ACAS *See* Association of Concerned Africa Scholars (ACAS)

Achebe, Chinua, 157, 159

Acronyms, list of, 341–346

Adhana, Amair, 213

Administrative centers, creation of, 86

AEF *see* Afrique Equatoriale Française (AEF); French Equatorial Africa (AEF)

Afar clan, 106–107

Africa Growth and Opportunity Act (AGOA), 279

Africa Proconsularis, 50

Africa's second independence, 223

Africa's second liberation, 223

Africa Works: Disorder as Political Instrument (Chabal & Daloz), 317

African/African-American Summits, 250

African Alternative Framework to Structural Adjustment Programmes for Socioeconomic Recovery and Transformation (AAF-SAP), 290

African-American Institute (AAI), 216

African Apprenticeship: An Autobiographical Journey in Southern Africa (Perham), 57

African Association of Political Science (AAPS), 336

African bourgeoisie, 114–115

African Charter on Human and Peoples' Rights, 228, 255

African Common Market (ACM), 261

African Crisis Response Force (ACRF), 294

African Crisis Response Initiative (ACRI), 294

African Defense Force, 245, 259

African Economic Community (AEC), 261

African Economies and the Politics of Permanent Crisis, 1979-1999 (van de Walle), 317

African Financial Community (CFA) *See* Communauté Financière Africaine (CFA)

African Heritage Studies Association (AHSA), 306

African Historical Dictionaries (AHD), 15

African National Congress (ANC), 84, 85, 133–134, 150, 194, 195, 196, 215, 216, 229, 252

African nationalist school of thought, 336

African peasantry, 115–116

African proletariat, 115

African renaissance, 6, 7

African Socialism and Its Application to Kenya, 135

African Studies Association (ASA), 306

African Studies in Social Movements and Democracy (Mamdani & Wamba-dia-Wamba), 334

African summitry, 256–257

African Union, 2, 245, 254, 256, 260–261, 291

Africanization of state institutions, 178–179

Afrikaners, 84

Afrique Equatoriale Française (AEF), 59

Afrique Occidentale Française (AOF), 59

Afro-optimism, 14

Afro-pessimism, 14

Afwerki, Isaias, 193, 294

Age-grade systems, 28, 43

Age of exploration, 51

Age-sets, 28, 32, 102

Agriculture
    during precolonial independence era, 34
    food production, decline in, 71–72, 115, 187
    mono-crop economies, 70–72
    national development and, 137–140

Agro-pastoralism, 34

Ahidjo, Ahmadou, 157

Aidid, Mohamed Farah, 235

Aidoo, Ama Ata, 162

AIDS, 138–139, 150

Ake, Claude, 7, 74, 89, 117, 331, 334

Alafin (sacred leader), of Oyo empire, 31, 40–42, 111

Algeria, 15, 50, 59, 83, 92, 132, 212, 273, 274, 327

Alliance of Democratic Forces for Liberation (AFDL), 192

Almond, Gabriel A., 303

Alpers, Edward A., 144

Alternation of power, 237

Amazons, 45

American African Affairs Association (AAAA), 306

American Colonization Society, 68

Americo-Liberian elite, 68–69

Amin, Samir, 329–330

Amina, Queen, 44

Anany, Jérôme, 182

ANC *See* African National Congress (ANC)

Anciens, 293

Angola, 15, 112, 133, 146, 207, 247, 259, 265, 273, 295, 333

Anti-West populism, 132

AOF *See* Afrique Occidentale Française (AOF); French West Africa (AOF)

Apartheid, 84, 85, 215

Apter, David E., 302

Aptidon, Hassan Gouled, 258

Arab slave trade, 8

Arab world, early contacts with, 50–57

Armah, Ayi Kwei, 162

Asante kingdom, 39, 44, 58–59

Asantewa, Yaa, Queen Mother, 45, 59

Asia, decolonization of, 91–92

Asian model of development, 289–290

Assimilados, 61

Assimilation policy, 61

Association of Concerned Africa Scholars (ACAS), 326

Association of Évolués of Stanleyville, 89

Associational groups, 31–32

Associational monarchy, 31–32

Atlantic Charter, 93

Atlantic slave trade, 8, 52–54

Authenticity policy, 178
Authoritarian–democratic paradox, 223
Authoritarian legacy of colonialism
    economic legacy, 74–75
    political legacy, 67–69
Authoritarian reaction, 233–234
Autocentric (self-reliant) development, 330
Autonomous village system, 29
A Wreath for Udomo (Abrahams), 159–160
Azikiwe, Nnamdi, 89

B
Bâ, Mariama, 162–163
Babangida, Ibrahim, 210–211
Baker, Florence, 57
Baker, Samuel, 57
Balance wheel model, 206–208
Balewa, Tafawa, 121, 202, 254
Balkanization, 96, 254
Ball, George, 275
Bamba, Amadou, 108, 109
Banda, Emmanuel, 182
Band organizations, 24–25
Bandung Conference (1955), 92
Banjul Charter, 228, 255
Baré, Maïnassara Ibrahim, 283
*Barrel of a Pen: Resistance to
    Repression in Neocolonial Kenya*
    (Ngugi), 156
Basic human needs (BHN), 145
Bates, Robert H., 312
Bayart, Jean-François, 316
BCP *See* Botswana Congress Party
BDF *See* Botswana Defence Force
    (BDF)
BDP *See* Botswana Democratic Party
    (BDP)
Beautyful Ones Are Not Yet Born, The
    (Armah), 162
Becker, David G., 336
Bédié, Henri Konan, 294
Belgium, 50, 59, 61, 183, 273, 277

Bella, Ben, 92
Benin, 14, 15, 43–44, 133, 203, 248, 281, 285, 327
    democracy in, 237
    national conference in, 230
Bennet, Leonard, 250
Bérégovoy, Pierre, 282
Berlin Conference (1884-1885), 5, 50, 51, 81
Berlin Wall, fall of, 223, 272, 279
Bete political system, 43
*Between Liberalization and Oppression:
    The Politics of Structural Adjustment
    in Africa* (Mkandawire &
    Olukoshi), 335
Biafra, 66, 94, 120, 122, 123, 254
Biko, Steven, 164, 195
BIP *See* Botswana Independent Party
    (BIP)
Bismarck, Otto von, 50, 58
Biya, Paul, 234, 282
Biyidi, Alexandre, 157, 158
Black Consciousness Movement, 164, 195
Blair, Tony, 273
Blood in the Sun trilogy (Farah), 171
Bloodless coup, 210
BLP *See* Botswana Labour Party (BLP)
BNF *See* Botswana National Front
    (BNF)
Bokassa, Jean-Bedel, 278
Botswana, 6, 14, 15, 25, 33, 102, 138, 203, 228, 246
    civilian supremacy model in, 205
    democracy in, 237
    ivory trade in, 144
Botswana Congress Party (BCP), 238
Botswana Defence Force (BDF), 205
Botswana Democratic Party (BDP), 102, 237, 238
Botswana Independent Party (BIP), 238
Botswana Labour Party (BLP), 237
Botswana National Front (BNF), 237, 238

Botswana People's Party (BPP), 238
Botswana Progressive Union (BPU),
     243
Bourgeoisie
   African, 114–115
   foreign, 112–114
   Marxist view of, 328
Bouseif, Ibrahim Salam, 36
Bouteflika, Abdulaziz, 291
Boutros-Ghali, Boutros, 286, 292
Boye, Mame Madior, 246
Boyle, Patrick M., 124
Boy! (Oyono), 159
BPP See Botswana People's Party
     (BPP)
BPU See Botswana Progressive Union
     (BPU)
Bratton, Michael, 150, 314
Brazil, 273
Brazzaville Group, 253
Bridewealth, 42
British Somaliland, 63, 64
Brown, Ronald H., 250
Brzezinski, Zbigniew, 277
Bula Matari, 67, 178
Bureaucratic bourgeoisie, 114
Burkina Faso, 15, 203, 204
Burma, 92
Burton, Richard Francis, 57
Burundi, 15, 83, 202
Bush, George H. W., 9, 235
Bush, George W., 279, 280, 283, 292
Buthelezi, Mangosuthu, 229

C
Caesar, Julius, 50
Callaghy, Thomas, 189
Cambodia, 92
Cameroon, 15–16, 58, 157, 234,
     282
Cameroon People's Democratic
     Movement (CPDM), 234
Canada, 273, 291
Cape Verde, 16, 59, 112, 133, 203
Capitalism, 2, 131, 149
   capitalist-socialist hybrid, 149–150

development and, 131–132, 133,
     134, 135, 136, 137, 140, 141,
     143, 145, 147, 148
Capitalist model of development, 131.
     See also Kenya
Capitalist movement, 149
Capitalist-socialist hybrid, 149–150
Capitalist world economy, 325
Capitalist World Economy, The
     (Wallerstein), 325
Carter, Jimmy, 277, 278
Carthage, 50
Carthaginian Empire, 50
Casablanca Group, 253
CASS See Centre for Advanced Social
     Science (CASS)
Castro, Fidel, 277
CELZA See Cultures et Elevages du
     Zaire (CELZA)
Censorship, 157, 163
Center for Study and Research on
     Democracy in the Third World
     (CERDET), 230
Central African Republic, 16
Central Intelligence Agency (CIA),
     183
Centralized monarchy, 32
Centralized political systems,
     29–32
   associational monarchy, 31–32
   centralized monarchy, 32
   pyramidal monarchy, 30–31
Centre for Advanced Social Science
     (CASS), 331
Centre National de Documentation
     (CND), 183
CERDET See Center for Study and
     Research on Democracy in the
     Third World (CERDET)
Ceuta, 8, 60, 84
Ceylon, 92
CFA See Communauté Financière
     Africaine (CFA)
Chabal, Patrick, 317
Chad, 16, 258
Chaka (Mofolo), 158

Chama Cha Mapinduzi (CCM), 224, 225
Chartered companies, 70
Chasse gardée (private hunting ground), 5, 275
Chazan, Naomi, 315
Checks-and-balances, 31, 66, 180–181, 223
Cheru, Fantu, 335
Chiluba, Frederick, 117, 226–227, 239
China, People's Republic of (PRC), 112, 139, 141, 144, 254, 264, 273, 274
Chirac, Jacques, 282–283, 293
Chissano, Joaquim Alberto, 207
CIES See Council for International Exchange of Scholars (CIES)
Cinema, 160–161
Circulationists, 325–327
City-states, 29
Civil disobedience, 92
Civil liberties, 146–147, 232, 238–239
Civil society, 177, 181, 189–191. See also State-society relationship
liberal tradition and, 314–315
Civil Society and the State in Africa (Harbeson, Rothchild & Chazan, eds.), 315
Civil War, United States, 55, 68
Civilianization, 215
Civilian supremacy model, 205
Clans, 26, 28, 101, 102. See also specific clans
Clark, John F., 188
Clash of Civilizations and the Remaking of World Order, The (Huntington), 315
Class, 101, 110–119, 122–124
cooperation and conflict, 116–119
divisions within African Society, 112–116
in Nigerian civil war, 120, 122–123
Marxist analysis of, 111–112, 116, 328

neo-Marxist analysis of, 332
political and societal ramifications of, 110–112
Class factions, 112–116
African bourgeoisie, 114–115
African peasantry, 115–116
African proletariat, 115
foreign bourgeoisie, 112–114
Classical segmented system, 26
Clinton, Bill, 9, 279, 280, 283, 292
Clitoridectomy, 119
Close Sesame (Farah), 170–171
Closed economic systems, 69–70
CND See Centre National de Documentation (CND)
Coercive apparatus, 182–183
Coffee, 189
Cohen, Herman, 280
Cold peace, 272
economic competition among Great Powers, 280–282
evolving foreign policy interests, 279–280
support for democratization, 282–285
Cold war, 111–112, 123–124, 133, 264, 272, 274–278, 304, 308
Africa as proxy battlefield for East-West conflict, 8–9, 276–278
complementary interests among western powers, 274–276
contradictory policies in search for allies, 278
end of, 245, 265, 313–314, 333
nationalism and, 93–94
Coleman, James S., 303
Collapsed states, 291
Collectivization, 139–140
Colonial Era (1884-1951), 4, 5, 49–75
dependency-decolonization debate on, 5–6
direct colonial rule, imposition of, 57–61
early contacts with Europe and Arab world, 50–57

Colonial Era (1884-1951) (*continued*)
  infrastructure development in, 72–73
  novels on, 159
  political-military impacts of, 62–69, 316–317
  socioeconomic impacts of, 69–75, 316–317
Commanding heights of the economy, 137, 142
Commercial bourgeoisie, 114
Commonwealth of Nations, 273
Communauté Financière Africaine (CFA), 115, 275, 279, 293
Communist bloc countries, 273
Comoros, 16, 84, 236
Compaoré, Blaise, 204
Complementary cold war order, 275
Compradors, 324
Concentration of state power, 177–185
  Africanization of state institutions, 178–179
  bureaucratic expansion and growth of parastatals, 179–180
  checks-and-balances, dismantling of, 180–181
  coercive apparatus, expansion of, 182–183
  co-optation and silencing of civil society, 181–182
  personal rule networks, creation of, 183–185
Condé, Laqui, 91
Conditionalities, 288
Confederation of South African Trade Unions (COSATU), 150
Conference of Berlin (1884-1885) *See* Berlin Conference (1884-1885)
Conference on the Enabling Environment for Private Sector Contributions to Development, 149
Congo-Brazzaville, 16, 133, 146, 281

Congo-Kinshasa *See* Democratic Republic of the Congo (Congo-Kinshasa)
Consensus building, 224
Consolidation of democratic practices, 236–240
Contagion effect, 204
Contemporary Independence Era (1951-present), 4, 5, 80–96
  country name changes during, 347–348
  nationalism and, 89–94
  political leadership during, 349–357
  self-determination and rise of secessionist movements, 94–96
Contested sovereignty, 234–236
Convention on International Trade in Endangered Species (CITES), 144
Convention on the Prohibition of the Use, Stockpiling, Production and Transfer of Antipersonnel Mines and on Their Destruction, 207
Co-opted transition process, 231–233
Copper, 186–187
Coquery-Vidrovitch, Catherine, 43, 44, 59, 74
Core countries, 325, 326–327
Corruption
  of Babangida regime in Nigeria, 210–211
  of Mobutu regime in Congo-Kinshasa, 187–188, 189
  petty, 187
Corruption and State Politics in Sierra Leone (Reno), 317
COSATU *See* Confederation of South African Trade Unions (COSATU)
Côte d'Ivoire, 16, 86, 87, 236, 281, 294, 327
  capitalism in, 131
  elections in, 232–233
Council for International Exchange of Scholars (CIES), xii

Council for the Development of Social Science Research in Africa (CODESRIA), 336

Coups d'état *See* Military coups d'état

Coups of descending order, 204, 210

CPDM *See* Cameroon People's Democratic Movement (CPDM)

Cradle of humankind, 24

Creating Political Order: The Party-States of West Africa (Zolberg), 311

Criminalization of the State in Africa, The (Bayart, Ellis & Hibou), 316

Crisis of development, 309

Crisis of distribution, 309

Crisis of foreign control, 313

Crisis of identity, 309

Crisis of integration, 309

Crisis of legitimacy, 309

Crisis of national survival, 313

Crisis of participation, 309

Crisis of penetration, 309

Crisis of the African state, 177, 186–192, 288
    domestic violence and conflict, 191–192
    economic crisis, 186–188, 288
    resurgence of civil societies and, 189–191
    social goods, inability of state to provide, 188–189

Critical tradition, 322–337

Cuba, 64, 146, 273, 277

Cult of personality, 185

Cultures et Elevages du Zaire (CELZA), 180

Curry, Robert L., Jr., 312–313

D

Daarood clan, 26

Dacko, David, 278

Dahomey kingdom, 43–44, 45

Dakar-Bamako railway line, 72, 73, 111

Daloz, Jean-Pascal, 317

Dameron, William A., III, 281

Dar school, 336

Decade of the military, 218

Decalo, Samuel, 232

Declaration to the Colonial Peoples, 90, 253

Declaration to the Colonial Powers, 90, 253

Decolonising the Mind: The Politics of Language (Ngugi), 156

Decolonization process, 81, 82–84

Decolonization school of thought, 5–6

Defense Intelligence Agency (DIA), 310

de Gama, Vasco, 51

de Gaulle, Charles, 112, 274, 275, 278

de Klerk, F. W., 215, 229

Delinking: Towards a Polycentric World (Amin), 330

Demilitarization, 215–218

Democracy and democratization, 2, 6–7, 117
    assessing spread of, 232–233
    consolidation of democratic practices, 236–240
    elections, spread of, 6
    in post-cold war era, 282–285
    in South Africa, 84–85, 94, 229, 236
    liberal tradition and, 314
    movement democracy, 226–227
    patronage-style, 105
    third wave of, 223
    transition to, 226–236

Democracy and Development in Africa (Ake), 334

Democratic culture, 239

Democratic decay, 236

Democratic Experiments in Africa: Regime Transition in Comparative Perspective (Bratton & van de Walle), 314

Democratic Republic of the Congo (Congo-Kinshasa), 16, 58, 278, 327
  authenticity policy, 178
  concentration of state power in, 178–185
  domestic violence and conflict, 191–192
  economic crisis in, 186–188
  First World War of Africa in, 294–295
  French intervention in, 117, 277–278, 293
  independence of, 83
  resurgence of civil societies in, 190–191
  social services decline in, 188–189
  transnational class cooperation in, 117
  U.S. foreign policy and, 9, 183
Democratization from above, 230
Democratization of disempowerment, 6, 117, 334
Deng, Francis M., 286
Départements d'Outre Mer-Territores d'Outre-Mer (DOM-TOM), 59
Dependency-decolonization debate, 5–6
Dependency school of thought, 5
Dependency theory, 313, 323–325
Dependent development, 331
Dergue, 118, 136, 139–140, 140, 142, 209
Desert oases, 38
d'Estaing, Giscard, 117
Development, ideologies of *See* Ideologies
Development choices and ideology, 135–142
  agriculture, role of, 137–140
  foreign powers and investment, role of, 141–142
  HIV/AIDS and development, 138–139, 150

  primary engine of development, 136–137
  purpose of development, 135–136
  rural peasantry, perception of, 140
Development of underdevelopment, 324, 325
Development performance and ideology, 143–148
  autonomy from foreign control, 145–146
  economic growth, 143–148
  human dignity, 146–147
  political participation, 147–148
  socioeconomic equality, 145
Developmental democracy, 334
de Villiers, Marq, 36
Devil on the Cross (Ngugi), 156–157
DIA *See* Defense Intelligence Agency (DIA)
Dia, Mamadou, 248
Diagne, Blaise, 109
Diamond, Larry, 121, 210–211, 236
Dias, Dinis, 56
Diawara, Daouda, 248
Dictatorships, 6
Dien Bien Phu, 92
Dieng, Ousmane Tanor, 245
Digil clan, 26
Dineson, Isak, 57
Dingane, 32
Dini, Ahmed, 106, 107
Diop, Serigne, 249
Diouf, Abdou, 109, 245, 246, 247, 248, 251, 275, 281
Diplomacy, in Precolonial Independence Era, 39–42
Diplomatic immunity, 39
Dir clan, 26
Direct colonial rule, 57–61
Direct rule, as basis of French colonialism, 61
Direct rule model, 208
Discovery, ownership based on, 58

Diversity visa program lottery, 185
Divide and conquer policy, 59
Divide-and-rule, 67–69
Division Spéciale Présidentielle (DSP), 183
Djibouti, 2, 16, 63, 64, 119
  ethnic politics in, 105–107
  independence of, 84
  role in U.S. war on terrorism, 280, 283
Documentary realism, 172
Doe, Samuel K., 69, 206, 213
Domaine réservé (natural preserve), 275
DOM-TOM *See* Départements d'Outre Mer-Territoires d'Outre-Mer (DOM-TOM); Overseas Departments and Territories (DOM-TOM)
Dowry, 42
DSP *See* Division Spéciale Présidentielle (DSP)
Dual economies, 73
Dynamics of Economic and Political Relations between Africa and Foreign Powers: A Study in International Relations (Lumumba-Kasongo), 335–336

E

East African Community (EAC), 263–264
ECOMOG *See* ECOWAS Monitoring Group (ECOMOG)
Economic Commission for Africa (ECA), 261, 290
Economic Community of Cental African States (ECCAS), 261
Economic Community of West African States (ECOWAS), 261, 265, 291
Economic conditionalities, 288, 289, 290
Economic cooperation, 264
Economic crisis, 186–188, 288
Economic growth, 143

Economics
  crisis of the African state and, 186–188, 288
  in colonial independence era, 69–75
  in precolonial independence era, 33–38, 43
  international financial institutions and, 288–291, 335
  regional economic cooperation and integration, 261–265
  under military governance, 214
Economy of affection, 115
ECOWAS Monitoring Group (ECOMOG), 248
Edgerton, Robert B., 45
Edo people, 44, 67
Education, 87–88, 188
Effective occupation, 58
Efuru (Nwapa), 162
Egypt, 16, 52, 59, 82, 92, 132, 246, 273, 283, 327
Eisenhower, Dwight D., 274
El Jem, 50
Elections, 6, 7, 229
Elf-Aquitaine, 281
Ellis, Stephen, 316
Elysée model, 223
Emancipation Proclamation, 55, 68
Emecheta, Buchi, 162
Emigration, 184–185
Emmanuel, Arghiri, 325
Encyclopedia of Africa South of the Sahara, 101
England *See* Great Britain
Engulu, Baanga, 185
Equatorial Guinea, 17
Eritrea, 17, 60, 110, 119, 193, 203, 255, 280
  independence of, 84, 94, 194–195, 212–213, 255
  OAU recognition of, 255
Eritrean Liberation Front (ELF), 94
Eritrean People's Liberation Front (EPLF), 94, 211, 212–213

Essy, Amara, 259

Ethiopia, 14, 17, 44, 50, 59, 62–63,
64, 68, 84, 92, 193, 224, 225,
275, 278, 280, 327, 333
Eritrean independence and, 84, 94,
194–195, 212–213, 255
Italy's invasion and occupation of, 8,
82, 90
Marxist model of development in,
131, 133, 134–136, 137,
139–140, 142, 143, 145–146,
147, 148
military in political governance of,
211–212
Ogaden war (Ethiopia-Somalia),
64, 145–146, 168, 171–172,
277
overthrow of Mengistu regime by
EPRDF, 194–196, 211–212
revolution in, 118–119, 135–136
social transformation model in,
208–209
Ethiopian People's Revolutionary
Democratic Front (EPRDF),
194–196, 211–212
Ethnic balance, 105
Ethnic compacts
breakdown of, 106–110
creation of, 103–106
Ethnic intermediaries, 103–104
Ethnic voluntary associations, 88
Ethnicity, 101–110, 120–122,
123–124. *See also* Age-sets; Clans;
specific ethnic groups
defined, 101
ethnic compacts, 103–110
ethnic intermediaries, 103–104
ethnic violence, 106–110
in Nigerian civil war, 120–122
liberal tradition and, 315
modernization process and, 307
political and societal ramifications
of, 101–103
voluntary associations based on, 88
European slave trade *See* Atlantic slave
trade

European Union (EU), 69–70, 262,
265
Evans-Pritchard, E. E., 29
Évolués, 61, 110–111
Ewe people, 43, 67
Excision, 119
Extraction of surplus, 324–325

F

Fall, Aminta Sow, 162
Fall, Ibrahima, 247
Family reunification program, 184
Farah, Nuruddin, 165–172
Farms and Ranches of Zaire
(CELZA), 180
FAZ *See* Forces Armées Zairoises
(FAZ)
FDLD *See* Front Démocratique pour
la Libération de Djibouti (FDLD)
Federation of Nigerian Literary
Societies, 89
Fédération Panafricaine des Cinéastes
(FEPACI), 160
Female circumcision, 118–119
Female genital mutilation, 118–119
FEPACI *See* Fédération Panafricaine
des Cinéastes (FEPACI)
Fifth wave of independence, 94
Film industry, 160–161
Financial institutions, 288–291, 335
Finn, F. K., 58
First generation rights, 255
First United Nations Emergency
Force (UNEF I), 287
First wave of independence, 83
First World War of Africa, 294–295
Foccart, Jacques, 112–114, 278
Food production
decline of, from 1950s to 1980s,
71–72, 115, 187
mono-crop economies and, 71–72
Forced labor, 74
Forces Armées Zairoises (FAZ), 183
Forces of production, 328
Foreign aid, 141, 142, 145–146, 279,
282

Foreign bourgeoisie, 112–114

Foreign investment, 141–142

Foreign policy making, 245–252. *See also* Pan-Africanism

  executive branch bureaucracies and president, role of, 246–248

  guerrilla groups impacting, 251–252

  national legislatures, role of, 248–249

  nongovernmental actors impact on, 249–252

  public opinion and, 251

  religion and, 251

Foreign relations

  during cold war, 274–278

  foreign powers, role of, 272–273

  international financial institutions, influence of, 288–291, 335

  involvement in United Nations, 285–287

  military intervention, 291–295

  pan-Africanism *See* Pan-Africanism

  policy making, 245–252

  post-cold war, 278–285

  regional economic cooperation and integration, 261–265

Founding elections, 6, 229

Fourth wave of independence, 84

France, 5, 45, 50, 90–91, 92, 115, 141, 158, 183, 254, 274, 291

  cold war foreign policy, 274, 275–276

  colonialism and, 45, 57, 59, 61, 62–63, 67, 71, 74, 110–111, 112–114

  Democratic Republic of the Congo and, 117, 277–278, 293

  in post-cold war era, 272, 279, 280–285

  military interventions by, 117, 277–278, 291, 292–294

Franco-African summits, 276

Francophone Africa, 272

Francophonie, la, 275, 276

Franc zone, 275

Frank, André Gunder, 323, 326

Freedom House, 146–148, 232–233

Freedom index, 232

French Equatorial Africa (AEF), 59

French West Africa (AOF), 59

From a Crooked Rib (Farah), 165–166

Front Démocratique pour la Libération de Djibouti (FDLD), 107

Front for the Liberation of Mozambique (FRELIMO), 83, 212

Front for the National Liberation of the Congo (FLNC), 117, 277

Front pour la Restauration de la Démocratie (FRUD), 107

FRUD *See* Front pour la Restauration de la Démocratie (FRUD)

Functional voluntary associations, 88–89

G

G-8 *See* Group of Eight (G-8)

Gabon, 17

Gadaboursi clan, 106

Gadio, Cheikh Tidiane, 247

Gambia, 6, 17, 228, 248, 283

Gandhi, Mohandas K., 92

Gann, L. H., 306

Gatling gun, 59

Gbagbo, Laurent, 294

GDP *See* Gross domestic product (GDP)

Gellar, Sheldon, 71, 73

Gender. *See also* Women

  critical tradition and, 334–335

  female circumcision, debate over, 118–119

  in colonial era, 73–74

  in precolonial independence era, 42–45

  liberal tradition and, 315–316

  novels promoting equality, 164–165

  role of, in politics, 7–8

Génération sacrifiée (sacrificed generation), 188

Genocide, 110
  in Rwanda, 110, 292
  in Somalia, 95, 109
German East Africa Company, 70
Germany, 50, 59–60, 70, 141, 249,
    265, 272, 273, 279, 291, 304
Ghadames, 38
Ghana, 17, 39, 43, 92, 204
  colonialism in, 59, 67, 74
  ethnic groups and intermediaries in,
    104
  guided democratization in,
    230–231
  independence of, 83
  interclass cooperation in, 116–117
  structural adjustment programs
    (SAPs) in, 290
Ghat, 38
Gifts (Farah), 171
Gikuyu ethnic group, 119
Gio ethnic group, 213–214
GNP *See* Gross national product
    (GNP)
Godfrain, Jacques, 283
God's Bits of Wood (Ousmane), 111,
    164–165
Gods Must Be Crazy, The (movie), 25
Gold, 38
Gold Coast *See* Ghana
Goldwater, Barry, 308
Good governance, 288–289
Gordon, April, 42, 44, 74, 184, 335
Gorée Island, 55, 56
Gould, David J., 187
Gouled Aptidon, Hassan, 106, 107
Gowon, Yakabu, 66, 208
Graybill, Lyn S., 195
Great Britain, 5, 50, 51, 92, 141, 254,
    264, 291, 327
  colonialism and, 57, 58–59, 60–61,
    62–63, 64, 66, 67, 74, 75, 82, 87,
    120, 122
  in post-cold war era, 272–273
  slave trade and, 54–55
Great expectations-minimal
    capabilities paradox, 177

Great Power domination, 254
Great Powers
  during cold war era, 274–278
  in post-cold war era, 272–273,
    278–285, 294
Great Zimbabwe, 35
Gross domestic product (GDP), 145
Gross national product (GNP), 2, 135,
    143, 182, 214, 302
Group of Eight (G-8), 291
Growth, Employment, and
    Redistribution (GEAR), 150
Gruenbaum, Ellen, 119
Gruhn, Isebill V., 207
Gueï, General, 294
Guelleh, Ismael Omar, 107
Guerrilla insurgencies, 83–84, 133,
    193, 294, 308
  in Algeria, 92
  in Angola, 83–84
  in Democratic Republic of the
    Congo (Congo-Kinshasa), 117,
    183
  in Djibouti, 107
  in Ethiopia, 94, 135, 211–212
  in Kenya, 83
  in Mozambique, 83
  in Namibia, 84
  in Rwanda, 110
  in Senegal, 248, 251–252
  in Somalia, 210
  in Somaliland Republic, 108–110
  in South Africa, 84
  in Zimbabwe, 84
  types of, 192
  women in, 212–213
Guéye, Sémou Pathé, 249
Guided democratization, 230–231
Guinea, 17, 278
  independence of, 83
  populist socialism in, 132
Guinea-Bissau, 17, 59, 112, 132, 236,
    248, 259
Gunboat diplomacy, 68
Gutteridge, William, 216
Gwei, Solomon Nfor, 234

H

Habyarimana, Juvenal, 110
Harbeson, John W., 315
Hassan, Abdikassim Salad, 235
Hausa/Fulani ethnic group, 64,
    65–66, 87, 120–121
Hawiye clan, 26, 109–110, 235
Head, Bessie, 162
Heavy Hand on Cameroon: Autopsy of
    Decolonization (Biyidi), 158
Hegemonic powers, 51
Henry the Navigator, Prince, 51
Herbst, Jeffrey, 188, 316
Hibou, Béatrice, 316
Hierarchical political system, 32
Hirtle, Sheila, 36
HIV/AIDS, 138–139, 150
Hong Kong, 289
Horan, Hume A., 281
Houphouët-Boigny, Félix, 87, 131,
    232, 233
House of Slaves, Gorée Island, 56
How Europe Underdeveloped Africa
    (Rodney), 323–324
Human dignity, 146–147
Humanist socialism, 132
Human rights, 146–147, 228,
    255–256
Hunter-gatherer groups, 24–25, 33
Huntington, Samuel P., 309–311, 315
Hutu ethnic group, 110

I

Ideologies, 2. *See also* Capitalism;
    Marxism; Socialism
    development choice and, 134–142
    development performance and,
        143–148
    evolution of African, 131–134
Ideology and Development in Africa
    (Young), 134, 143
Idi Amin, 227, 255, 263
Igbo ethnic group, 64, 65–66, 87, 94,
    120–122, 123, 307
IGNU *See* Interim Government of
    National Unity (IGNU)

Ilboudo, Patrick, 160
Ile Ife, 31, 40
ILO *See* International Labour
    Organisation (ILO)
Imperialism, 335
Imperial mindset, 57
Independence, 4, 5, 6, 81, 82–84, 94
    novels on, 159–160
    second independence of Africa,
        223
    waves of, 83–84, 94
Independence African Party of
    Guinea and Cape Verde
    (PAIGC), 83
India, 92, 144, 273, 329
Indirect rule, 61
Indonesia, 92
Industrial revolution, 55, 327
Infibulation, 119
Informal economies, 189
Informal empire, 55
Infrastructure development in colonial
    era, 72–73
Inkatha Freedom Party (IFP), 229
Institutionalization, 309
Interclass conflict, 118–119
Interclass cooperation, 116–117
Intergovernmental Authority on
    Development (IGAD), 261
Interim Government of National
    Unity (IGNU), 214
International Campaign to Ban
    Landmines, 207
International Labour Organisation
    (ILO), 285
International Monetary Fund (IMF),
    116, 133, 189, 288–289, 335
International Studies Association
    (ISA), xxv
International system
    African foreign relations and *See*
        Foreign relations
    impact of, 8–11
    shifting structure of, post World
        War II, 93–94
Internet resources, 10–11

In the Fog of the Season's End
(La Guma), 164
Intraclass conflict, 117–118
Investment, 141–142
Iran, 273, 278
Ironsi, J. T. U. Aguiyi, 121, 123
Irredentism, 63–64
ISA *See* International Studies
Association (ISA)
Isaak clan, 26, 106, 108–110, 235
Islam, 3, 37, 42, 52
Islamic brotherhoods, 108–109
Islamic revivalism, 2, 81
Islamic slave trade, 52, 54
Israel, 273
Issa clan, 26–27, 105, 106, 107
Issa xeer, 26–27
Italian Somaliland, 60, 63, 64
Italy, 8, 29, 50, 60, 62–63, 82, 90,
273, 291
Ivory trade, 144
Iwofa status, 40
Iye, Ali Moussa, 26

J
Japan, 141, 144, 261, 272, 279, 284,
291, 304
Japanese International Cooperation
Agency (JICA), 284
Japan External Trade Organization
(JETRO), 284
Japan Overseas Cooperation
Volunteers (JOCV), 284
JCC *See* Journées Cinématogra-
phiques de Carthage (JCC)
JETRO *See* Japan External Trade
Organization (JETRO)
Jeunesse du Mouvement Populaire de
la Révolution (JMPR), 182
JICA *See* Japanese International
Cooperation Agency (JICA)
Jihads, 52
Jirreh, Ahmed, 95
JMPR *See* Jeunesse du Mouvement
Populaire de la Revolution
(JMPR)

JOCV *See* Japan Overseas Coopera-
tion Volunteers (JOCV)
John Paul II, Pope, 251
Johnson, Mark, 281
Johnson, Thomas H., 202
Jospin, Lionel, 293
Journals, researching Africa in, 12–13
Journées Cinématographiques de
Carthage (JCC), 160

K
Kabila, Laurent-Désiré, 9, 192, 193,
293
Kaboré, Gaston, 160
Kagame, Paul, 192, 193, 293, 294
Kalamazoo Spice Extraction
Company, 142
Kamanda, Kamanda wa, 182
Kampala Document, 259
Kasinga, Fauziya, 118, 119
Kasson, John A., 50
Kaunda, Kenneth, 132, 239
Kazibwe, Wandera Specioza, 315–316
Kebeles, 137
Keenadiid, Cismaan Yuusuf, 169
Keller, Edmond J., 118
Kennedy, John F., 93–94, 274, 308
Kenya, 17, 28, 64, 102, 224, 263–264,
280, 327, 332
African bourgeoisie in, 114–115
capitalist model of development,
131, 134, 135, 136, 137, 140,
141, 143, 145, 147, 148
ivory trade in, 144
Mau Mau guerrilla insurgency, 83
Kenya African National Union
(KANU), 148, 224
Kenyatta, Jomo, 114, 131, 134, 137,
140, 141, 143, 147, 148, 224,
264
Kérékou, Mathieu, 230, 237,
281, 285
Khrushchev, Nikita, 274
Kibaki, Mwai, 134
Kimba, Evariste, 182
Kleptocracy, 187

Kola nuts
use in diplomatic negotiations, 39–40
women's role in trade of, 43
Konaré, Oumar, 206
Krahn ethnic group, 213–214
Kulaks, 115, 140

L
La Baule Doctrine, 282
Lagos Plan of Action for the Economic Development of Africa, 1980-2000, 261
Lagos Plan of Action (LPA), 290
La Guma, Alex, 164
Lame Leviathans, 186
Lamizana, Sangoulé, 204
Landmines, 207
Laos, 92
Leaders in khaki, 202
League of Nations, 59–60, 68
Leon H. Sullivan (African/African-American) Summits, 250
Leopold II, King, 58
Leslie, Winsome, 191
Lesotho, 17, 138
Lewis, I. M., 33
Leys, Colin, 332
Liberal tradition, 301–318
Liberation Committee, 259
Liberation insurgencies, 192
Liberia, 18, 50, 59, 92, 291, 317
balance-wheel model in, 206–208
military in political governance of, 206–208, 213–214
U.S. government and, 68–69, 82
Libya, 2, 5, 18, 50, 60, 81, 83, 133, 148, 290, 327
Liebenow, J. Gus, 68, 205, 206–208, 209
Ligue Populaire Africaine pour l'Indépendance (LPAI), 106
Limann, Hilla, Dr., 230–231
Lincoln, Abraham, 55, 68
Lissouba, Pascal, 281
Little, Kenneth, 86

Local expatriate class, 114
London Missionary Society, 57
Loyal opposition, 240
LPAI *See* Ligue Populaire Africaine pour l'Indépendance (LPAI)
Luckham, Robin, 214
Lugard, Lord, 61
Lumpenproletariat, 115
Lumumba, Patrice, 9
Lumumba-Kasongo, Tukumbi, 335–336
Luxury goods, 38

M
Maasai ethnic group, 28, 43, 102, 119
Madagascar, 18, 133, 275
Mahamba, Alexander, 182
Mahdi Mohammed, Ali, 235
Malawi, 18
Mali, 18, 73, 119, 206, 281
Mamdani, Mahmood, 334
Managing Ethnic Conflict in Africa: Pressures and Incentives for Cooperation (Rothchild), 315
Mandate territory, 60
Mandela, Nelson, 6, 14, 81, 84–85, 133–134, 149, 150, 215, 229, 236, 248, 252, 256
Manifesto of the Communist Party (Marx), 328
Mano ethnic group, 213–214
Mao Zedong, 180, 274
Maps (Farah), 171–172
Marabouts, 108–109, 251
Marketing boards, 74–75, 115, 180, 187
Market-oriented trade, 34–36
Markets and States in Tropical Africa: The Political Basis of Agricultural Policies (Bates), 312
Markovitz, Irving Leonard, 332
Marx, Karl, 111, 133, 327–329
Marxism, 2, 111–112, 131, 149, 327–329
class analysis of, 111–112, 116, 328

Marxism (*continued*)
  development and, 133–136, 137,
    139–140, 141–142, 143,
    145–146, 147, 148
Marxist model of development, 133.
  See also Ethiopia
Mass participatory democracy, 226
Matrilineal society, 43, 66, 67
Matrilocal, 43
Mau Mau guerrilla insurgency, 83
Mauritania, 18, 251
Mauritania Caesarensis, 50
Mauritania Tingitana, 50
Mauritius, 6, 18, 203, 228
Mayotte, 59
Mazrui, Ali A., 90
Mbande, Nzinga, Queen, 44
Mbeki, Thabo, 14, 150, 217, 256,
  259, 291
Mbodj, Bathie, 133
McGowan, Patrick J., 202
Mecca, 52
Medina, 52
Melilla, 8, 60, 84
Melting pots, 81, 86
Mende people, 32, 43, 44
Menetewab, 44
Mengistu Haile Mariam, 94, 118–119,
  131, 134–135, 136, 137, 142,
  143, 145–146, 147, 148, 149,
  194, 209, 224, 225
Men on horseback, 202
METI *See* Ministry of Economy,
  Trade, and Industry (METI)
Metropoles, 324, 325, 326–327
Metropolitan bourgeoisie, 112–114
MFDC *See* Mouvement des Forces
  Démocratiques de Casamance
  (MFDC)
Middle powers, 273
Military aid, 145–146
Military coups d'état, 69, 226, 308
  evolving threat of, 217–218
  in Burkina Faso, 204
  in Congo-Brazzaville, 133
  in Congo-Kinshasa, 178

  in Ethiopia, 118, 134
  in Ghana, 230, 231
  in Liberia, 206, 213
  in Mali, 206
  in Niger, 283
  in Nigeria, 120, 121, 123, 208, 283
  in Portugal, 83, 133
  in Somalia, 95, 108, 165, 166, 167,
    209–210
  trends in, 202–204
Military governance
  economic development under,
    214
  effectiveness of, 209–214
  efficiency of, 210–211
  legitimacy of, 209–210
  political governance and, 205–209
  stability provided by, 211–212
  transitions to civilian rule, 215–218
  unifying structure provided by,
    212–214
Military interventions, 291–295
  OAU and, 258–259
Military plots, 202–203
Ministry of Economy, Trade, and
    Industry (METI), 284
MINURCA *See* United Nations
    Mission in the Central African
    Republic (MINURCA)
MINURSO *See* United Nations
    Mission for the Referendum in
    Western Sahara (MINURSO)
Missionary societies, 57
Mission civilisatrice, 57–58
Mitterrand, François, 275, 282
Mkandawire, Thandika, 335
MMD *See* Movement for Multiparty
    Democracy (MMD)
Mobile training teams (MTTs), 183
Mobutu, Joseph Désiré *See* Mobutu
    Sese Seko
Mobutu Sese Seko, 9, 117, 178, 179,
    180, 181–182, 183, 185,
    187–188, 189, 190, 192, 193,
    277, 278, 293
MOD alliance, 109

Modern World System, The (Wallerstein), 325
Modernes, 293
Modernization revisionism, 304–307
Modernization theory, 102, 302–304
Modes of production, 328
Modise, Joe, 217
Mofolo, Thomas, 158
Mohammed, Murtala, 208
Moi, Daniel arap, 134, 224
Mono-crop economies, 70–72
Mono-mineral economies, 70–72
Monroe, James, 68
Monrovia Group, 253–254
MONUA *See* United Nations Observer Mission in Angola (MONUA)
MONUC *See* United Nations Organization Mission of the Democratic Republic of the Congo (MONUC)
Moore, Henrietta, 212
Moose, Richard, 277
Morocco, 8, 18, 50, 59, 83, 84, 246, 275, 283
Mother-in-chief, 43
Mouvement des Forces Démocratiques de Casamance (MFDC), 252
Mouvement Populaire de Libération (MPL), 107
Movement democracy, 226–227
Movement for Multiparty Democracy (MMD), 239
Moyo, Ambrose, 52
Mozambique, 2, 8, 14, 18, 112, 133, 207, 212, 259, 265, 273, 317
MPL *See* Mouvement Populaire de Libération (MPL)
MTTs *See* Mobile training teams (MTTs)
Muhammad, 52
Multinational corporations (MNCs), 141, 263, 264
Multiparty competition, 228
Multiparty elections, 6, 7, 228–229

Multiparty politics, 226–236
Museveni, Yoweri, 138, 192, 193, 194, 226, 227, 293, 294
Mutual aid society, 88
Mwinyi, Ali Hassan, 116

N
Naked Needle, A (Farah), 166–167
Namibia, 18, 25, 33, 58, 84, 144, 203, 246, 259, 295
Napoleonic Code, 74
Nasser, Gamal Abdel, 132
National conference, 229–230
National Council of Nigeria and the Cameroons (NCNC), 89
National Council of Nigerian Citizens (NCNC), 307
National Democratic Institute for International Affairs (NDI), 234
National Documentation Center (CND), 183
National Front for the Liberation of Angola (FNLA), 83
National Geographic image of Africa, 14
Nationalism, 4
   anticolonial character of, 82
   Asian decolonization and, 91–92
   defined, 81
   domestic influences on rise of, 86–89
   education and, 87–88
   international influences on rise of, 89–94
   novels on, 159–160
   Pan-Africanism and, 89–90
   trends in, 81–85
   urbanization and, 86
   voluntary associations and, 88–89
   World Wars I and II and, 90–91
Nationalization, 137, 142, 179–180
National Party (NP), 229
National Patriotic Front of Liberia (NPFL), 214
National Resistance Army (NRA), 226

National Resistance Movement (NRM), 227

National Science Foundation (NSF), 310

National Security Education Program (NSEP), 306

National self-determination, 81

National Union for the Total Independence of Angola (UNITA), 83

National Union of Etrirean Women (NUEW), 213

Nations of Contemporary Africa (NCA), 15

Nations of the Modern World (NMW), 15

Nation-states, 30, 62, 81

Nation-state system, imposition of European, 62

Natural preserve, 275

NDI *See* National Democratic Institute for International Affairs (NDI)

Ndi, John Fru, 234, 282

N'Diaye, Joseph, 56

Neocolonialism, 5, 324

Neo-Colonialism in West Africa (Amin), 329

Neoimperialism, 335

Neo-Marxist school, 329–333

Neomercantilism, 284

Neopatrimonialism, 183–185

Netherlands, 51

New bloc of African leaders, 193, 294

New Partnership for Africa's Development (NEPAD), 260, 290–291

New Patriotic Party (NPP), 214

New York Times, The, 14

Ngaahika Ndeenda (Ngugi), 164

Ngouabi, Marien, 133

Ngugi wa Thiong'o, 156–157, 163–164

Niger, 18, 236, 283

Nigeria, 2, 19, 31, 44, 87, 94, 203, 246, 255–258, 265, 283, 294, 305

  as semiperipheral country, 326–327

  civil war (1967–1970), 66, 120–123, 254, 258, 307

  colonialism in, 59, 64–66, 75

  direct rule model in, 208

  military coups d'état in, 120, 121, 123, 208, 283

  military in political governance of, 208, 210–211

  nationalist brand of capitalism in, 131–132

  voluntary associations in, 89

Nigerian Union of Students, 89

Nimeiri, Gaafar Mohammed, 289

Nixon, Richard M., 274, 308

Nkrumah, Kwame, 90, 159, 160, 253

No Bride Price (Rubadiri), 161–162

Nonalignment, 93

Nonparty system, 226–227

North Africa, 3, 4, 50. *See also* Saharan Africa

North American Free Trade Association (NAFTA), 69–70, 265

Northern coastal cities, 38

Northern Peoples' Congress (NPC), 305

Northern terminals, 38

Novels and novelists, 155–172. *See also* specific novelists

  political dilemmas faced by, 156–158

  politically committed novelists, 163–172

  political themes, 158–163

NP *See* National Party (NP)

NPC *See* Northern Peoples' Congress (NPC)

NPFL *See* National Patriotic Front of Liberia (NPFL)

NPP *See* New Patriotic Party (NPP)

NRA *See* National Resistance Army (NRA)

NRM *See* National Resistance Movement (NRM)

NSEP *See* National Security Education Program (NSEP)

NSF *See* National Science Foundation (NSF)

Ntare V, King, 202

NUEW *See* National Union of Eritrean Women (NUEW)

Nurture capitalism, 136

Nwapa, Flora, 162

Nyerere, Julius, 116, 131, 134, 135, 140, 141, 143, 145, 147, 148, 149, 224, 225, 264

Nzimiro, Ikenna, 122, 123

Nzouankeu, Jacques Mariel, 230

O

Obasanjo, Olusegun, 259, 291

Obote, Apollo Milton, 227

Occidental Petroleum Corporation, 281

OEOA *See* United Nations Office of Emergency Operations in Africa (OEOA)

Official censorship, 157, 163

Ogaden war (Ethiopia-Somalia), 64, 145–146, 168, 171–172, 277

Ogoni ethnic group, 255–258

Ojo, Olatunde, 263

Ojukwu, Chukwuemeka, 122, 123

Oloka-Onyango, J., 227

Olorunsola, Victor A., 313

Olukoshi, Adebayo, 335

Omar, Dullah, 195

ONUC *See* United Nations Operation in Congo (ONUC)

ONUMOZ *See* United Nations Operation in Mozambique (ONUMOZ)

Order, and stability, 308–311

Organization of African Unity (OAU), 245, 254–261

Organization of Petroleum Exporting Countries (OPEC), 187

Oromo Liberation Front (OLF), 211

Osman, Aden Abdulla, 165

Ouedraogo, Jean Baptiste, 204

Our Continent, Our Future: African Perspectives on Structural Adjustment (Mkandawire & Soludo), 335

Ousmane, Sembène, 72, 111, 164–165

Out of Africa (Dineson), 57

Overseas Departments and Territories (DOM-TOM), 59

Oyo empire, 31, 34, 40–42, 111

Oyo Mesi (royal council), 31, 41–42

Oyono, Ferdinand, 159

P

Pakistan, 92

Palace coups, 204

Pan-African Congress (PAC), 84, 90, 253

Pan-African Film and Television Festival (FESPACO), 160

Pan-African ideal, 90, 245, 253

Pan-Africanism, 245, 253–261
economic dimension of, 261–265
nationalism and, 89–90
Organization of African Unity (OAU) and, 245, 254–261
summits, 256–257

Pan-Arabism, 133

Parastatals, 75, 179, 180, 187

Parpart, Jane L., 44, 66–67, 334

Parsons, Talcott, 303

Parti Démocratique de la Côte d'Ivoire-Rassemblement Démocratique pour l'Assemblée (PDCI-RDA), 233

Parti Populaire Djiboutien (PPD), 107

Pass laws, 85

Pastoral nomadism, 33
Pasyina, Monsengwo, 190
Patriarchal governance, 66–67
Patrilineal society, 43
Patrilocal, 43
Patronage-style democracy, 105
Patron–client relationships, 183–185
Patterson, Amy S., 315
PDCI-RDA *See* Parti Démocratique
    de la Côte d'Ivoire-Rassemble-
    ment Démocratique pour
    l'Assemblée (PDCI-RDA)
PDD-25 *See* Presidential Decision
    Directive 25
Peanut production, in Senegal, 71,
    329–330
Peasantry, 115–116, 140
People's Redemption Council (PRC),
    206
Perham, Margary, 57
Peripheral countries, 325, 326–327
Personal rule networks, 183–185
Petals of Blood (Ngugi), 164
Peters, Carl, 70
Petty bourgeoisie, 114
Petty corruption, 187
Philippines, 278
Piot, Peter, Dr., 138
*Plan to Intensify the Development of
    African Agriculture in Kenya, A,*
    137
Poaching, 144
Policy relevance of research,
    311–313
Political activists, 329
Political bourgeoisie, 114
Political conditionalities, 288, 289,
    290
Political decay, 309
Political development, 309
Political-economy approach to
    research, 312
Politically committed novelists,
    163–172
  Farah, and Somalia, 165–172
  gender equality, 164–165

neglected popular elements of
    society, 163–164
societal divisions, destructive nature
    of, 164
Political-military impacts of
    colonialism, 62–69
  authoritarian legacy, 67–69
  checks-and-balances, destruction
    of, 66
  division of African ethnic groups
    among several states, 62–64
  European nation-state system,
    imposition of, 62
  incorporation of several African
    nations into one state, 64–66
  liberal tradition and, 316–317
  patriarchal forms of governance,
    reinforcement of, 66–67
Political-military transformations, 6–8
Political Order in Changing Societies
    (Huntington), 309
Political participation, 147–148
Political parties
  ethnicity and, 102
  in Congo-Kinshasa, 181, 190–191
  in Djibouti, 106, 107
  Leninist model of, 310–311
  multiparty politics and, 226–236
  single-party systems and, 223–226,
    310–311
Political rights, 232
Political systems
  centralized, 29–32
  class and, 110–112
  development and participation in,
    147–148
  ethnicity and, 101–103
  military governance *See* Military
    governance
  multiparty systems, 226–236
  nonparty system, 226–227
  segmented, 24–29
  single-party, 223–226, 310–311
Politics of conservation, 144
Politics of language choice, 156–157
Politics of order, 311

Politics of the Developing Areas (Almond & Coleman, eds.), 303
Politics of Tradition: Continuity and Change in Northern Nigeria 1946-1966 (Whitaker), 305
Polyandry, 42
Polygamy, 42
Polygyny, 42, 43, 52
Pompidou, Georges, 88, 112
Popular Movement for the Liberation of Angola (MPLA), 83
Popular Movement of the Revolution (MPR), 181
Populist socialism, 132, 133
Poro society, 32
Portugal, 50, 51, 59, 61, 81, 83, 112, 133, 273
Post-cold war era *See* Cold peace
Postimperialism, 336
Postimperialism and World Politics (Sklar & Becker, eds.), 336
Potholm, Christian P., 24, 30
POW *See* Prisoner of War (POW)
Powell, Colin, 292
Powell doctrine, 292
Power and Class in Africa: An Introduction to Change and Conflict in African Politics (Markovitz), 332
PPD *See* Parti Populaire Djiboutien (PPD)
Precolonial Independence Era (prior to 1884), 4, 5, 23–45
  centralized political systems, 29–32
  diplomacy and warfare, 39–42
  economic systems and trade, 33–38, 43
  segmented political systems, 24–29
  women and gender, 42–45
Predatory states, 186
Prempeh I, 59
Presidential Decision Directive (PDD), 25, 291
Prisoner of War (POW), 91
Private hunting ground, 275

Private land ownership, 74
Pro-democracy movements, 2, 9, 133, 228
Progressive farmer, 140
Proletariat, 115, 328
Proportionality principle, 105
Provisional Military Administrative Council (PMAC), 118, 136, 208–209
Provisional National Defense Council (PNDC), 231
Public policy analysis, 312–313
Public policy research, 312–313
Publishing outlets, for novelists, 158
Pyramidal monarchy, 30–31

Q
Qaddafi, Muammar, 133

R
Rahanweyn clan, 26
Railroad systems, 72–73
Rassemblement Populaire pour le Progrès (RPP), 106, 107
Rational-choice models, 312
Ratsiraka, Didier, 275
Rawlings, Jerry, 116, 117, 204, 230, 231, 290
Reagan doctrine, 274
Recolonization, 334
Red Sea slave trade, 52
Reer, 26
Reform insurgencies, 192
Regicide, 32
Regional economic cooperation, 261–265
Relations of production, 328
Religious intermediaries, 108–109
Reno, William, 317
Research
  books, 15–20
  in critical tradition, 322–337
  in liberal tradition, 301–318
  Internet resources, 10–11
  policy relevance in, 311–313
  public policy research, 312–313

Research (*continued*)
relationship with U.S. government agencies, 310–311
scholarly journals, 12–13
Reth (divine king) of Shilluk people, 28–29
Réunion, 59
Revolution from above, 134, 209
Rhodesia *See* Zimbabwe
Ritually stratified segmented system, 28–29
Rodney, Walter, 323–324, 325
Roman Empire, 50
Romero, Patricia W., 57
Roosevelt, Franklin D., 93
Rostow, Walt W., 302
Rothchild, Donald, 105, 312–313, 315
Rousseau, Jean-Jacques, 26
Roussin, Michel, 280
RPP *See* Rassemblement Populaire pour le Progrès (RPP)
Rubadiri, David, 161–162
Russia *See* Soviet Union
Rwanda, 14, 19, 192, 193, 291–292, 293, 295
genocide in, 110, 292
independence of, 83
Rwandan Patriotic Front (FPR), 110

S
SACP *See* South African Communist Party (SACP)
Sacrificed Generation, The (film), 115
SADF *See* South African Defense Force (SADF)
Saharan Africa, 3–4. *See also* North Africa
Salazar, Antonio de Oliveira, 61
Salim, Salim Ahmed, 258
SALT *See* Strategic Arms Limitation Talks (SALT)
Sande society, 32
Sankara, Thomas, 204
San people, 25, 33
Santos, José Eduardo dos, 247

Sao Tome and Principe, 19, 59, 112, 133, 259
Sardines (Farah), 170
Saro-Wiwa, Ken, 258
Satellites, 324, 325, 326–327
Satyagraha, 92
Saudi Arabia, 52, 64, 273
Scandinavia, 141
Scarcity, Choice, and Public Policy in Middle Africa (Rothchild & Curry, Jr.), 312–313
Scientific colonialism, 61
Scientific socialism, 133
Scramble for Africa, 50, 52, 58, 59, 68
SDF *See* Social Democratic Front (SDF)
Sea-Air-Land Commandos (SEALs), 235
SEALs *See* Sea-Air-Land Commandos (SEALs)
Secessionist movements, 94–96, 107–110
Second generation rights, 255
Second tier empires, 59
Second United Nations Emergency Force (UNEF II), 287
Second wave of independence, 83
Secrets (Farah), 171
Secret societies, 32, 43
Segmented political systems, 24–29
autonomous village system, 29
band organizations, 24–25
classical segmented system, 26
ritually stratified segmented system, 28–29
universalistic segmented system, 28
Selassie, Haile, 90, 94, 118, 136, 194, 208, 278
Self-determination of peoples, 94
Semiperipheral countries, 326–327
Senegal, 6, 19, 61, 87, 88, 112, 132, 228, 275, 281, 327
colonialism and, 55, 56, 71, 73
foreign policy-making in, 246, 247, 248–252
Islamic brotherhoods in, 108–109

lumpenproletariat in, 115
peanut production in, 71, 329–330
Senghor, Léopold Sédar, 61, 88, 109, 132, 246, 248, 281
Separatist insurgencies, 192
Separatist movements *See* Secessionist movements
Seychelles, 2, 19, 84
Shadow states, 186
Shaka Zulu, 32
Sharpeville massacre, 85
Shaw, Timothy M., 333
Shermarke, Abdirashid Ali, 165
Shilluk people, 28–29
Shona empire, 35
Siad Barre, Mohammed, 95, 108–109, 165, 166, 167, 168, 169, 170, 171, 209–210, 234, 278
Sierra Leone, 19, 32, 44, 273, 291, 317
Silent Revolution in Africa: Debt, Development, and Democracy (Cheru), 335
Singapore, 289
Single-party political systems, 223–226, 310–311
Sisters in Affliction: Circumcision and Infibulation of Women in Africa (Abdalla), 119
Sklar, Richard L., 116, 120, 149, 333, 334, 336
Slash-and-burn technique, 34
Slavery and slave trade, 8, 38, 52–55, 56
Smith, Ian, 84
Smuggling, 189
SNF *See* Somali National Front (SNF)
Social Democratic Front (SDF), 234
Social goods, 188–189
Socialism, 2, 112, 131, 149
capitalist-socialist hybrid, 149–150
development and, 132, 133, 135, 136–139, 140, 141, 143, 145, 147, 148
Socialist model of development, 132. *See also* Tanzania

Social movements, 334
Social science, 331
Social Science as Imperialism: The Theory of Political Development (Ake), 331
Social Science Research Council (SSRC), 314
Social transformation model, 208–209
Société Zairoise pour la Commercialisation des Minéraux (SOZACOM), 180
Socioeconomic equality, 145
Socioeconomic impacts of colonialism, 69–75
authoritarian legacy of state, 74–75
closed economic systems, creation of, 69–70
gender bias in national development, 73–74
liberal tradition and, 316–317
mono-crop or mono-mineral economies, creation of, 70–72
Socioeconomic transformations, 6–8
Soglo, Nicéphore, 237, 240, 281, 285
So Long a Letter (Bâ), 162–163
Soludo, Charles C., 335
Somalia, 14, 19, 29, 119, 133, 255, 278, 280
alphabet of, 168–169
civil war in, 234–236
Farah and novels on, 165–172
independence of, 83
irredentist movement in, 63–64
military coups d'état, 165, 166–167
Ogaden war (Ethiopia-Somalia), 64, 145–146, 168, 171–172, 277
secessionist movement, 95, 108–110
United Nations intervention in, 235, 286
U.S. intervention in, 235, 291–292

Somali ethnic group, 26–27, 33,
     62–63, 101, 105–106,
     108–110
Somali National Front (SNF), 235
Somali National Movement (SNM),
     109, 235
Somali Patriotic Movement (SPM),
     235
Somaliland Republic, 95, 108–110,
     235, 255
South Africa, 6, 19, 59, 81, 84–85,
     203, 246, 247–248, 259, 264,
     275, 291, 294, 327
  demilitarization in, 215–217
  democracy in, 84–85, 94, 229, 236
  development in, 149–150
  Mandela and, 6, 14, 81, 84–85,
     133–134, 149, 150, 215, 229,
     236, 248, 252, 256
  novels on, 164
  Truth and Reconciliation
     Commission, 194–195, 196
South African Communist Party
     (SACP), 150
South African Defense Force (SADF),
     215, 216
South African National Defense Force
     (SANDF), 216–217
Southern African Development
     Community (SADC), 69–70,
     261, 264–265
Southern terminals, 38
South Korea, 278, 289–290
South-West Africa People's
     Organization (SWAPO), 84
Sovereign equality, 254
Soviet Union, 8, 9, 64, 93–94, 112,
     133, 139, 141, 146, 226, 254,
     264, 273, 291. See also Cold war
  fragmentation of, 94, 227, 278–279,
     325, 335
  single-party system in, 310–311
SOZACOM See Société Zairoise pour
     la Commercialisation des
     Minéraux (SOZACOM)
Spain, 5, 8, 50, 60, 273

Spectrum of civil-military relations,
     205
Stability, and order, 308–311
Stages of Economic Growth: A
     Noncommunist Manifesto, The
     (Rostow), 302
Stanley, Henry, 67
State, 177, 313, 332. See also State-
     society relationship
State necessities, 38
States and Power in Africa: Comparative
     Lessons in Authority and Control
     (Herbst), 316
State-society relationship, 177
  balance in, 193–196
  concentration of state power at
     expense of civil society, 177–185
  crisis of state and resurgence of civil
     society, 186–192
State versus Ethnic Claims: African Policy
     Dilemmas (Rothchild &
     Olorunsola, eds.), 313
Staudt, Kathleen A., 334
Stockton, Robert F., 68
Stone Virgins (Vera), 164
Structural adjustment programs
     (SAPs), 133, 189, 288,
     289–290
Structural adjustment with a human
     face, 290
Structural-functionalism, 303–304
Sub-Saharan Africa, 3–4
Subsistence-oriented trade, 34
Sudan, 2, 19, 28–29, 92, 119, 255,
     273, 280, 289
  independence of, 83
  United Nations humanitarian
     intervention in, 286–287
Sullivan, Leon H., 250
Summit of Heads of State of
     Government (OAU), 256
Summits
  African/African-American
     Summits, 250
  African summitry, 256–257
  Franco-African, 276

Supreme Revolutionary Council (SRC), 209
Suzerain kingdoms, 40
Swahili city-states, 29
Swahili coast slave trade, 52
Swahili culture, 29
Swarns, Rachel L., 150
Swaziland, 19, 138, 265
Sweden, 141, 273
Sweet and Sour Milk (Farah), 168–169
Systems of checks-and-balances
    See Checks-and-balances

T
Taiwan, 273, 289
Tamale, Sylvia, 316
Tanganyika, 70
Tanzania, 20, 28, 29, 224, 225, 263–264, 265
    African peasantry in, 116
    single-party political system in, 225
    socialist model of development in, 131, 134, 135, 136–139, 140, 141, 143, 145, 147, 148
    villagization program, 136–137, 138–139, 140, 225
Taya, Ould, 251
Taylor, Charles, 69, 214
Thiam, Doudou, 245
Thiam, Iba Der, 249
Things Fall Apart (Achebe), 159
Third generation rights, 255
Third wave of democratization, 223
Third wave of independence, 83–84
Thirty Years' War, 62
Tigrean People's Liberation Front (TPLF), 135, 196, 211
Timbuktu, 38, 70
Tirailleurs Sénégalais, Les, 67, 90, 91
Togo, 20, 58, 118
Togoland, 70
Tolbert, William, 213
Tonga people, 34, 44
Touré, Ahmed Sékou, 132

Touré, Amadou Toumani, 206
Trade
    closed economic systems and, 69–70
    in precolonial independence era, 33–38, 43
    slave trade, 8, 38, 52–55, 56
    trans-Saharan trade network, 4, 35–36, 37–38, 52, 70
    U.S.-French competition in post-cold war era, 280–282
    women and, 43
Transforming Capitalism and Patriarchy: Gender and Development in Africa (Gordon), 335
Transhumance patterns, 29
Transnational class cooperation, 117
Trans-Saharan slave trade, 38, 52
Trans-Saharan trade network, 4, 35–36, 37–38, 52, 70
Traoré, Moussa, 206
Treaties, effective occupation through, 58
Treaty of Westphalia (1648), 62
Triangular trade, 54
Tribute, 40–41
Tripoli, 38
Tripp, Aili Mari, 315–316
Truman, Harry, 280
Truman doctrine, 274
Trusteeship, 60
Truth and Reconciliation Commission, 194–195, 196
Tshisekedi, Etienne, 190–191, 193
Tswana ethnic group, 25, 102
Tunisia, 20, 50, 59, 246, 283
    independence of, 83
    U.S. war on terrorism and, 9–11
Tutsi ethnic group, 110
Tutu, Desmond, 194

U
UDI *See* Unilateral Declaration of Independence (UDI)
UDPS *See* Union pour la Démocratie et le Progrès Social (UDPS)

Uganda, 8, 20, 138, 192, 193, 194, 226–227, 255, 263–264, 293, 295

UGEC *See* Union Générale des Etudiants Congolais (UGEC)

Ujamaa: Essays on Socialism (Nyerere), 135

Ujamaa socialism, 116, 134, 135, 136–137, 138–139, 140, 141, 145, 149, 224, 225, 264

Ujamaa vijijini (village socialism), 136–137, 138–139

ULIMO *See* United Liberation Movement of Liberia (ULIMO)

Umkhonto we Sizwe, 216–217

UN *See* United Nations

UNAMIR *See* United Nations Assistance Mission for Rwanda (UNAMIR)

UNAMSIL *See* United Nations Mission in Sierra Leone (UNAMSIL)

UNASOG *See* United Nations Aouzou Strip Observer Group (UNASOG)

UNAVEM *See* United Nations Angola Verification Mission (UNAVEM)

UNAZA *See* Université Nationale du Zaire (UNAZA)

Underdevelopment in Kenya: The Political Economy of Colonialism (Leys), 332

UNDP *See* United Nations Development Programme (UNDP)

UNEF I *See* First United Nations Emergency Force (UNEF I)

UNEF II *See* Second United Nations Emergency Force (UNEF II)

Unequal Exchange: A Study of the Imperialism of Trade (Emmanuel), 325

UNESCO *See* United Nations Educational, Scientific, and Cultural Organization (UNESCO)

UNHCR *See* United Nations High Commissioner for Refugees (UNHCR)

UNI *See* Union Nationale de l'Indepéndance (UNI)

UNICEF *See* United Nations International Children's Emergency Fund (UNICEF)

Unilateral Declaration of Independence (UDI), 84

Unilinear process, 307

Union des Populations du Cameroun (UPC), 157

Union Générale des Etudiants Congolais (UGEC), 182

Union Nationale de l'Indepéndance (UNI), 107

Union Nationale des Travailleurs Congolais (UNTC), 182

Union of the Arab Maghreb (UAM), 261

Union pour la Démocratie et le Progrès Social (UDPS), 190

Union Progressiste des Etudiants Zairois (UPEZA), 190

Union Sacrée de l'Opposition Radicale (USOR), 190

UNIP *See* United National Independence Party (UNIP)

United Liberation Movement of Liberia (ULIMO), 214

United National Independence Party (UNIP), 239

United Nations, 68, 291
  Great Power domination of, 254
  HIV/AIDS program, 138
  involvement of African nations in, 285–287
  peacekeeping and humanitarian intervention by, 286–287, 291

United Nations Angola Verification Mission I (UNAVEM I), 287

United Nations Angola Verification Mission II (UNAVEM II), 287

United Nations Angola Verification
Mission III (UNAVEM III), 287
United Nations Aouzou Strip Observer
Group (UNASOG), 287
United Nations Assistance Mission for
Rwanda (UNAMIR), 287
United Nations Development
Programme (UNDP), 285
United Nations Educational,
Scientific, and Cultural
Organization (UNESCO), 56,
285
United Nations High Commissioner
for Refugees (UNHCR), 285
United Nations International
Children's Emergency Fund
(UNICEF), 285
United Nations Mission for the
Referendum in Western Sahara
(MINURSO), 287
United Nations Mission in Eritrea and
Ethiopia (UNMEE), 287
United Nations Mission in Sierra
Leone (UNAMSIL), 287
United Nations Mission in the Central
African Republic (MINURCA),
287
United Nations Observer Mission in
Angola (MONUA), 287
United Nations Observer Mission in
Liberia (UNOMIL), 287
United Nations Observer Mission in
Sierra Leone (UNOMSIL), 287
United Nations Observer Mission in
Uganda-Rwanda (UNOMUR),
287
United Nations Office of Emergency
Operations in Africa (OEOA),
286
United Nations Operation in Congo
(ONUC), 287
United Nations Operation in
Mozambique (ONUMOZ),
287
United Nations Operations on
Somalia (UNOSOM), 287

United Nations Organization
Mission of the Democratic
Republic of the Congo
(MONUC), 287
United Somali Congress (USC),
109–110, 234–235
United States, 8, 9, 51, 64, 93–94,
141, 254, 261, 264, 265, 291,
304, 308–309, 314. *See also*
Cold war
and Liberia, 68–69, 82
as melting pot, 81
Congo-Kinshasa and, 9, 183
democratization and, 227–228
emigration to, 184–185
federal form of government
of, 31
in post-cold war era, 279–282,
283–284, 285
in Somalia, 235, 291–292
Senegalese in, 249–251
slave trade and, 52–53, 54–55
war on terrorism, 9–11, 272, 280,
283, 314
United States Agency for
International Development
(USAID), 310
Universalistic segmented
system, 28
Université Nationale du Zaire
(UNAZA), 182
UNMEE *See* United Nations Mission
in Eritrea and Ethiopia
(UNMEE)
UNOMIL *See* United Nations
Observer Mission in Liberia
(UNOMIL)
UNOMSIL *See* United Nations
Observer Mission in Sierra
Leone (UNOMSIL)
UNOMUR *See* United Nations
Observer Mission in Uganda-
Rwanda (UNOMUR)
UNOSOM *See* United Nations
Operations on Somalia
(UNOSOM)

UNTC *See* Union Nationale des Trevailleurs Congolais (UNTC)
UPC *See* Union des Populations du Cameroun (UPC)
UPEZA *See* Union Progressiste des Etudiants Zairois (UPEZA)
Urbanization, 86, 115
USAID *See* United States Agency for International Development (USAID)
USOR *See* Union Sacrée de l'Opposition Radicale (USOR)

V

Value-neutral scientific framework, 303
van de Walle, Nicolas, 314, 317
Vanguard role, 225
Variations on the Theme of an African Dictatorship trilogy (Farah), 167
Vera, Yvonne, 164
Vieira, João Bernardo, 248
Vietnam, 92
Vietnam War, 112, 308
Villagization program, 136–137, 138–139, 140, 225
Voluntary associations, 88–89
von Blixen, Karen *See* Dineson, Isak

W

Wade, Abdoulaye, 114, 246, 291
Wallerstein, Immanuel, 325–327
Wamba-dia-Wamba, Ernest, 334
Warfare, in precolonial Independence era, 39–42
Warlord insurgencies, 192
Warlord Politics and African States (Reno), 317
Warlord states, 186
War of 1812, 55
War on terrorism, U.S., 9–11, 272, 280, 283, 314
Warrior Women: The Amazons of Dahomey and the Nature of War (Edgerton), 45

Watchdog model, 206
Waves of independence, 83–84, 94
Weber, Max, 303
Welch, Claude, Jr., 255
West African Student Union, 89
Western International Ground Maintenance Organization (WIGMO), 183
Western Somali Liberation Front (WSLF), 171
Westminster model, 223
When Hens Begin to Crow: Gender and Parliamentary Politics in Uganda (Tamale), 316
Whitaker, C. S., Jr., 120, 305
White man's burden, 57–58
WHO *See* World Health Organization (WHO)
WIGMO *See* Western International Ground Maintenance Organization (WIGMO)
Williams, Jody, 207
Windhoek Treaty, 265
Winternitz, Helen, 191
Women. *See also* Gender
   European women explorers, in colonial era, 57
   in colonial era, 57, 66–67, 73–74
   in guerrilla insurgencies, 212–213
   in precolonial independence era, 42–45
   novels on status of, 162–163
   role in politics, 7–8
Women and Politics in Uganda (Tripp), 315
Women and the State in Africa (Parpart & Staudt), 334
Women's Voices on Africa: A Century of Travel Writings (Romero, ed.), 57
Workers Party of Ethiopia (WPE), 224
World Bank, 116, 133, 189, 288–289, 335

World Bibliographical Series (WBS), 15
World Health Organization (WHO), 285
World War I, 50, 59, 90
World War II, 8, 60, 90–91, 93, 272, 304
WSLF *See* Western Somali Liberation Front (WSLF)

X

Xaashi, Ibraahiim, 169
Xala (Ousmane), 164

Y

Yaméogo, Maurice, 204
Yemen, 280
Yoruba people, 31, 34, 40, 64, 65, 87, 120
Young, Crawford, 67, 102, 103, 121, 123, 134, 136, 143

Z

Zaire *See* Democratic Republic of the Congo (Congo-Kinshasa)
Zambia, 20, 34, 44, 132, 138, 265
African proletariat in, 115
authoritarian tactics in, 239–240
intraclass conflict in, 117–118
Zartman, I. William, 6, 258
Zenawi, Meles, 193, 294
Zerbo, Sayé, 204
Zimbabwe, 6, 20, 35, 60–61, 84, 138, 144, 228, 259, 265, 294
Zimbabwe African Nationalist Union (ZANU), 84
Zimbabwe African People's Union (ZAPU), 84
Zolberg, Aristide R., 311
Zone franc (franc zone), 275
Zulu empire, 32